BEGINNING C# AND .NET

Continues

BEGINNING

C# and .NET

BEGINNING
C# and .NET
2021 EDITION

Benjamin Perkins

Jon D. Reid

wrox™

A Wiley Brand

ABOUT THE AUTHORS

Benjamin Perkins is currently employed at Microsoft in Munich, Germany, as a Senior Escalation Engineer for IIS, ASP.NET, and Azure App Services. He has been working professionally in the IT industry for over two decades. He started computer programming with QBasic at the age of 11 on an Atari 1200XL desktop computer. He takes pleasure in the challenges that troubleshooting technical issues have to offer and savors in the rewards of a well-written program. After completing high school, he joined the United States Army. After successfully completing his military service, he attended Texas A&M University in College Station, Texas, where he received a Bachelor of Business Administration in Management Information Systems. He also received a Master of Business Administration from the European University.

His roles in the IT industry have spanned the entire spectrum including programmer, system architect, technical support engineer, team leader, and mid-level management. While employed at Hewlett-Packard, he received numerous awards, degrees, and certifications. He has a passion for technology and customer service and looks forward to troubleshooting and writing more world-class technical solutions. "My approach is to write code with support in mind, and to write it once correctly and completely so we do not have to come back to it again, except to enhance it."

Benjamin has written numerous magazine articles and training courses and is an active blogger. His catalog of books covers C# Programming, IIS, NHibernate, Open Source, and Microsoft Azure.

➤ Connect with Benjamin on LinkedIn: www.linkedin.com/in/csharpguitar

➤ Follow Benjamin on Twitter @csharpguitar: twitter.com/csharpguitar

➤ Read Benjamin's blog: www.thebestcsharpprogrammerintheworld.com

➤ Visit Benjamin on GitHub: github.com/benperk

Benjamin is married to Andrea and has two wonderful children, Lea and Noa.

Jon D. Reid is a Program Manager in Research and Development for IFS AB (www.ifs.com) focusing on Field Service Management. He has coauthored many books on Microsoft technologies, including *Beginning C# 7 Programming with Visual Studio 2017*, *Fast Track C#*, *Pro Visual Studio .NET*, and many others.

ABOUT THE TECHNICAL EDITOR

Rod Stephens is a long-time developer and author who has written more than 250 magazine articles and 35 books that have been translated into different languages around the world. During his career, Rod has worked on an eclectic assortment of applications in such fields as telephone switching, billing, repair dispatching, tax processing, wastewater treatment, concert ticket sales, cartography, and training for professional football teams.

Rod's popular C# Helper website (`www.csharphelper.com`) receives millions of hits per year and contains tips, tricks, and example programs for C# programmers. His VB Helper website (`www.vb-helper.com`) contains similar material for Visual Basic programmers.

You can contact Rod at: `RodStephens@csharphelper.com` or `RodStephens@vb-helper.com`.

ABOUT THE TECHNICAL EDITOR

ACKNOWLEDGMENTS

It takes a lot of work to get content into a presentable format for students and IT professionals to read and get value from. The authors indeed have technical knowledge and experiences to share, but without the technical writers, technical reviewers, developers, editors, publishers, graphic designers, the list goes on, providing their valuable input, a book of high quality could not be written. The rate of change occurs too quickly for an individual to perform all these tasks and still publish a book that is valid before the technology becomes stale. This is why authors worked together with great teams to get all the components of the book together quickly. It was done to ensure that the most up-to-date information gets to the reader while the features are still fresh and current. I would like to thank Rod Stephens for his technical review and suggestions throughout the process. Lastly, I would like to thank all the numerous people behind the scenes who helped get this book together.

CONTENTS

INTRODUCTION

THE C# LANGUAGE WAS UNVEILED TO THE WORLD when Microsoft announced the first version of its .NET Framework in 2002. Since then, its popularity has rocketed, and it has arguably become the language of choice for desktop, web, cloud, and cross-platform developers who use .NET. Part of the appeal of C# comes from its clear syntax, which derives from C/C++ but simplifies some things that have previously discouraged some programmers. Despite this simplification, C# has retained the power of C++, and there is no reason now not to move into C#. The language is not difficult, and it is a great one with which to learn elementary programming techniques. This ease of learning combined with the capabilities of the .NET Framework make C# an excellent way to start your programming career.

The latest release of C# is C# 9 (included with.NET 5.0 and .NET Framework 4.8), which builds on the existing successes and adds even more attractive features. The latest releases of both Visual Studio and Visual Studio Code line of development tools also bring many tweaks and improvements to make your life easier and to dramatically increase your productivity.

This book is intended to teach you about all aspects of C# programming, including the language itself, desktop, cloud, and cross-platform programming, making use of data sources, and some new and advanced techniques. You will also learn about the capabilities of Visual Studio and all the ways that this product can aid your application development.

The book is written in a friendly, mentor-style fashion, with each chapter building on previous ones, and every effort is made to ease you into advanced techniques painlessly. At no point will technical terms appear from nowhere to discourage you from continuing; every concept is introduced and discussed as required. Technical jargon is kept to a minimum, but where it is necessary, it, too, is properly defined and laid out in context.

The authors of this book are both experts in their field and are enthusiastic in their passion for the C# language and .NET. Nowhere will you find two people better qualified to take you under their collective wing and nurture your understanding of C# from first principles to advanced techniques. Along with the fundamental knowledge it provides, this book is packed full of helpful hints, tips, exercises, and full-fledged example code (available for download on this book's web page at www .wiley.com and at github.com/benperk/BeginningCSharpAndDotNET) that you will find yourself returning to repeatedly as your career progresses.

We pass this knowledge on without begrudging it and hope that you will be able to use it to become the best programmer you can be. Good luck, and all the best!

WHO THIS BOOK IS FOR

This book is for everyone who wants to learn how to program in C# using .NET. It is for absolute beginners who want to give programming a try by learning a clean, modern, elegant programming language. But it is also for people familiar with other programming languages who want to explore the .NET platform, as well as for existing .NET developers who want to give Microsoft's .NET flagship language a try.

WHAT THIS BOOK COVERS

The early chapters cover the language itself, assuming no prior programming experience. If you have programmed in other languages before, much of the material in these chapters will be familiar. Many aspects of C# syntax are shared by other languages, and many structures are common to practically all programming languages (such as looping and branching structures). However, even if you are an experienced programmer, you will benefit from looking through these chapters to learn the specifics of how these techniques apply to C#.

If you are new to programming, you should start from the beginning, where you will learn basic programming concepts and become acquainted with both C# and the .NET platform that underpins it. If you are new to .NET but know how to program, you should read Chapter 1 and then skim through the next few chapters before continuing with the application of the C# language. If you know how to program but have not encountered an object-oriented programming language before, you should read the chapters from Chapter 8 onward.

Alternatively, if you already know the C# language, you might want to concentrate on the chapters dealing with the most recent .NET and C# language developments, specifically the chapters on collections, generics, and C# language enhancements (Chapters 11 and 12).

The chapters in this book have been written with a dual purpose in mind: They can be read sequentially to provide a complete tutorial in the C# language, and they can be dipped into as required for reference material.

In addition to the core material, starting with Chapter 3 most chapters also include a selection of exercises at the end, which you can work through to ensure that you have understood the material. The exercises range from simple multiple choice or true/false questions to more complex exercises that require you to modify or build applications. The answers to all the exercises are provided in the Appendix. You can also find these exercises as part of the wiley.com code downloads on this book's page at www.wiley.com.

Every chapter receives an overhaul with every new release of C# and .NET, the less relevant material is removed, and new material added. All the code has been tested against the latest version of the development tools used, and all the screenshots have been retaken in the most current version of the Windows OS to provide the most current windows and dialog boxes. New highlights of this edition include the following:

➤ Additional and improved code examples for you to try out

➤ Examples of programming ASP.NET Core for running cross-platform

➤ Examples of programming cloud applications, using Azure SDK to create and access cloud resources

HOW THIS BOOK IS STRUCTURED

This book is divided into four sections:

➤ **Introduction**—Purpose and general outline of the book's contents

➤ **The C# Language**—Covers all aspects of the C# language, from the fundamentals to object-oriented techniques

➤ **Data Access**—How to use data in your applications, including data stored in files on your hard disk, data stored in XML format, and data in databases

➤ **Additional Techniques**—An examination of some extra ways to use C# and .NET, including cloud and cross-platform development, ASP.NET Web API, Windows Presentation Foundation (WPF), Windows Communication Foundation (WCF), and Universal Windows Applications

The following sections describe the chapters in the three major parts of this book.

The C# Language (Chapters 1–13)

Chapter 1 introduces you to C# and how it fits into the .NET landscape. You will learn the fundamentals of programming in this environment and how Visual Studio (VS) fits in.

Chapter 2 starts you off with writing C# applications. You will look at the syntax of C# and put the language to use with sample command-line and Windows applications. These examples demonstrate just how quick and easy it can be to get up and running, and along the way you will be introduced to the Visual Studio development environment and the basic windows and tools that you'll be using throughout the book.

Next, you will learn more about the basics of the C# language. You will learn what variables are and how to manipulate them in Chapter 3. You will enhance the structure of your applications with flow control (looping and branching) in Chapter 4, and you will see some more advanced variable types such as arrays in Chapter 5. In Chapter 6 you will start to encapsulate your code in the form of functions, which makes it much easier to perform repetitive operations and makes your code much more readable.

By the beginning of Chapter 7 you will have a handle on the fundamentals of the C# language, and you will focus on debugging your applications. This involves looking at outputting trace information as your applications are executed, and at how Visual Studio can be used to trap errors and lead you to solutions for them with its powerful debugging environment.

From Chapter 8 onward you will learn about object-oriented programming (OOP), starting with a look at what this term means and an answer to the eternal question, "What is an object?" OOP can seem quite difficult at first. The whole of Chapter 8 is devoted to demystifying OOP and explaining what makes it so great, and you will not actually deal with much C# code until the very end of the chapter.

Everything changes in Chapter 9, when you put theory into practice and start using OOP in your C# applications. This is where the true power of C# lies. You will start by looking at how to define classes and interfaces, and then move on to class members (including fields, properties, and methods) in Chapter 10. At the end of that chapter, you will start to assemble a card game application, which is developed over several chapters and will help to illustrate OOP.

Once you have learned how OOP works in C#, Chapter 11 moves on to look at common OOP scenarios, including dealing with collections of objects, and comparing and converting objects. Chapter 12 looks at a useful feature of C# that was introduced in .NET 2.0: generics, which enable you to create very flexible classes. Next, Chapter 13 continues the discussion of the C# language and OOP with some additional techniques, notably events, which become important in, for example, Windows programming. Chapter 13 wraps up the fundamentals by focusing on C# language features that were introduced in some of the more recent versions of C#.

Data Access (Chapters 14–17)

Chapter 14 looks at how your applications can save and retrieve data to disk, both as simple text files and as more complex representations of data. You will also learn how to compress data and how to monitor and act on file system changes.

In Chapter 15 you will learn about the de facto standard for data exchange—namely XML—and a rapidly emerging format called JSON. By this point in the book, you will have touched on XML several times in preceding chapters, but this chapter lays out the ground rules and shows you what all the excitement is about.

The remainder of this part looks at LINQ, which is a query language built into .NET. You start in Chapter 16 with a general introduction to LINQ, and then you will use LINQ to access a database and other data in Chapter 17.

Additional Techniques (Chapters 18–21)

Chapter 18 introduces .NET Standard and .NET Core, which are tools used for targeting any application type—for example, Windows Presentation Foundation (WPF), Windows, and ASP.NET. An emerging application is one that can run cross-platform such as on Linux or macOS. The chapter provides instructions for installing .NET and creating and implementing a .NET Standard library. Additionally, descriptions of ASP.NET and its many different types (e.g., ASP.NET Webforms, ASP.NET MVC, and ASP.NET Core) are covered.

Chapter 19 starts by describing what cloud programming is and discusses the cloud-optimized stack. The cloud environment is not identical to the way programs have been traditionally coded, so a few cloud programming patterns are discussed and defined. To complete this chapter, you require an Azure trail account, which is free to create and comes with some credits so that you can create and test out an App Service Web App. Then, using the Azure SDK with C#, you create and access a storage account from an ASP.NET web application.

In Chapter 20, you learn how to create an ASP.NET Web API and consume it using a Blazor WebAssembly App. Then this chapter provides an introduction to Windows Communication Foundation (WCF), which provides you with the tools you need for enterprise-level programmatic access to information and capabilities across local networks and the internet. You will see how you can use WCF to expose complex data and functionality to web and desktop applications in a platform-independent way.

Chapter 21 starts by introducing you to what is meant by Windows programming and looks at how this is achieved in Visual Studio. It focuses on WPF (Windows Presentation Foundation) as a tool that enables you to build desktop applications in a graphical way and assemble advanced applications with a minimum of effort and time. You will start with the basics of WPF programming and build up your knowledge to more advanced concepts.

WHAT YOU NEED TO USE THIS BOOK

The code and descriptions of C# and .NET in this book apply to C# 9 and .NET 4.8. You do not need anything other than .NET to understand this aspect of the book, but many of the examples require a development tool. This book uses the most current version of Visual Studio Community 2019 as its primary development tool. Use Visual Studio Community 2019 to create Windows, cloud, and cross-platform applications as well as SQL Server Express for applications that access databases.

The source code for the samples is available for download from this book's page on www.wiley.com and at github.com/benperk/BeginningCSharpAndDotNET.

CONVENTIONS

To help you get the most from the text and keep track of what is happening, we've used a number of conventions throughout the book.

TRY IT OUT

The *Try It Out* is an exercise you should work through, following the text in the book.

1. These exercises usually consist of a set of steps.
2. Each step has a number.
3. Follow the steps through to the end.

How It Works

After each *Try It Out*, the code you've typed will be explained in detail.

> **WARNING** *Warnings hold important, not-to-be-forgotten information that is directly relevant to the surrounding text.*

> **NOTE** *Shaded boxes like this hold notes, tips, hints, tricks, or asides to the current discussion.*

As for styles in the text:

➤ We *italicize* new terms and important words when we introduce them.

➤ We show keyboard strokes like this: Ctrl+A.

➤ We show filenames, URLs, and code within the text like so:

`persistence.properties`

We present code in two different ways:

```
We use a monofont type with no highlighting for most code examples.
We use bold to emphasize code that is particularly important in the present
context or to show changes from a previous code snippet.
```

SOURCE CODE

As you work through the examples in this book, you may choose either to type in all the code manually or to use the source code files that accompany the book. All the source code used in this book is available for download on this book's page at `www.wiley.com` and at `github.com/benperk/BeginningCSharpAndDotNET`.

Most of the code on `www.wiley.com` is compressed in a .ZIP, .RAR archive, or similar archive format appropriate to the platform. Once you download the code, just decompress it with an appropriate compression tool.

> **NOTE** *Because many books have similar titles, you may find it easiest to search by ISBN; this book's ISBN is 978-1-119-79578-0.*

ERRATA

We make every effort to ensure that there are no errors in the text or in the code. However, no one is perfect, and mistakes do occur. If you find an error in one of our books, like a spelling mistake or faulty piece of code, we would be very grateful for your feedback. By sending in errata, you may save another reader hours of frustration, and at the same time, you will be helping us provide even higher quality information.

To find the errata page for this book, go to this book's page at `www.wiley.com` and click the Errata link. On this page you can view all errata that have been submitted for this book.

PART I
The C# Language

PART II

The C# Language

1

Introducing C#

WHAT YOU WILL LEARN IN THIS CHAPTER

➤ What .NET is

➤ What C# is

➤ Explore Visual Studio

Welcome to the first chapter of the first part of this book. Part I provides you with the basic knowledge you need to get up and running with C#. Specifically, this chapter provides an overview of .NET and C#, including what these technologies are, the motivation for using them, and how they relate to each other.

This chapter begins with a general discussion of .NET, which contains many concepts that are tricky to come to grips with initially. This means that the discussion, of necessity, covers many concepts in a short amount of space. However, a quick look at the basics is essential to understand how to program in C#. Later in the book, you revisit many of the topics covered here, exploring them in more detail.

After this general .NET introduction, the chapter provides a basic description of C# itself, including its origins and similarities to C++. Finally, you look at the primary tool used throughout this book: Visual Studio (VS). Visual Studio is an Integrated Development Environment (IDE) that Microsoft has produced since the late 1990s and gets updated regularly with new features. Visual Studio includes all sorts of capabilities including full support for desktop, cloud, web, mobile, database, machine learning, AI, and cross-platform programming that you will learn about throughout this book.

WHAT IS .NET?

.NET is a revolutionary software framework created by Microsoft for developing computer programs. To begin with, note that .NET provides more than the means for creating programs that target the Windows operating system. .NET is fully open source and fully supports running cross platform. *Cross platform* means that the code you write using .NET will run on Linux and MacOS operating systems as well. The source code for .NET is open source and you can find it at `github.com/dotnet/core`.

The .NET software framework is made of prewritten computer code, which provides simple access to basic computing resources like the hard drive and computer memory. One aspect of this framework is referred to as the *Base Class Library* (BCL), which contains the `System` class. You will become very familiar with it as you progress through this book. Taking a deeper look into the source code inside the `System` class, you will find that it includes the definitions of data *types* like `strings`, `integers`, `Boolean`, and `characters`. If you need one of these data types in your program to store information, you can use the already written .NET code to achieve that. If such code did not already exist, you would need to use low-level programming languages like assembly or machine code to allocate and manage the required memory yourself. The basic types found in the `System` class also facilitate interoperability between .NET programming languages, a concept referred to as the *Common Type System* (CTS). Interoperability means that a `string` in C# has the same attributes and behaviors as a `string` in Visual Basic or F#. Besides supplying this source code library, .NET also includes the *Common Language Runtime* (CLR), which is responsible for the execution of all applications developed using the .NET library; more on that later.

In addition to the `System` class, .NET contains many, many other classes, often called modules. Some would say it is a gigantic library of object-oriented programming (OOP) code categorized into different modules—you use portions of it depending on the results you want to achieve. For example, `System.IO` and `System.Text` are the classes you would use to read and write to files located on a computer hard drive. A programmer can manipulate the contents of a file simply by using the code that already exists in the `System.IO` class without needing to manage handles or load the file from the hard drive into memory. There exist many classes in .NET that help programmers write programs at a fast pace, because all of the low-level code required to achieve their tasks has already been written. The programmer only needs the knowledge of which classes they require to achieve the program objectives.

Not only does .NET speed up application development, but it also can be utilized by numerous other programming languages, not just C# (which is the subject of this book). Programs written in C++, F#, Visual Basic, and even older languages such as COBOL can use the classes that exist in .NET. These languages have access to the code in the .NET library, but the code written in one programming language can communicate with code from another. For example, a program written in C# can make use of code written in Visual Basic or F# and vice versa. All of these examples are what makes .NET such an attractive prospect for building customized software.

.NET Framework, .NET Standard, and .NET Core

When the .NET Framework was originally created, it targeted the Windows operating system platform. Through the years, the .NET Framework code was forked to support numerous other platforms like IoT devices, desktops, mobile devices, and other operating systems. You may recognize some of the branches going by the names of .NET Compact Framework, .NET Portable, or .NET Micro Framework. Each of these forks contained its own, slightly modified BCL. Take note that a BCL is more than just `strings`, `Booleans`, and `integers`. It includes capabilities like file access, string manipulation, managing streams, storing data in collections, security attributes, and many others.

Having even a slightly different BCL required a programmer to learn, develop, and manage the subtle difference between the BCLs for each .NET fork. Each fork of the .NET Framework that targeted desktops, the Internet, or mobile platforms could have significant implementation differences, even though each program used .NET. It was (and still is) very common for a company to have desktop, website, and phone applications that ran the same program logic but did so on those different platforms. In that scenario, using .NET required a version of the company's application for each platform. That was not efficient. This is the problem that the .NET Standard solved. The .NET Standard provided a place for programmers to create application logic that could be used across any of the .NET Framework forks. The .NET Standard made the different platforms, like desktop, mobile, and web, BCL agnostic by decoupling a company's program logic from platform-specific dependencies.

.NET Core was the open source, cross-platform version of the .NET library. This fork of the code could be used to create programs that targeted numerous different platforms and operating systems like Linux, MacOS, and of course Windows. It was also the fork that would eventually become the one and only maintained branch of the .NET source code library. As of 2020, knowing about the .NET Framework, .NET Standard, and .NET Core is no longer as relevant as it once was. These three branches of .NET must be mentioned here because you will still likely see them, read about them, and be confronted with them for some years to come. It is important that you know what they are and their purpose, in case you need to work on a project that implements them. As of 2020, there is a new version of .NET simply named ".NET." .NET is fully open source, is fully cross platform, and can be used on many platforms without having to support multiple versions, forks, and branches of your program.

Writing Programs Using .NET

Creating a computer program with .NET means writing code that uses existing code found within the .NET library. In this book you use Visual Studio for developing your programs. Visual Studio is a powerful, integrated development environment that supports C# (as well as C++, Visual Basic, F#, and some others). The advantage of this environment is the ease with which .NET features can be integrated into your code. The code that you create will be entirely C# but use .NET throughout, and also some additional tools in Visual Studio, where necessary. For C# code to execute, it must be converted into a language that the target operating system understands, known as *native code*. This conversion is called *compiling*, an act that is performed by a *compiler*, which is a two-stage process.

CIL and JIT

When you compile code that uses .NET, you don't immediately create operating system–specific native code. Instead, you compile your code into *Common Intermediate Language* (CIL) code. This code isn't specific to any operating system (OS) and isn't specific to C#. Other .NET languages—Visual Basic .NET or F#, for example—also compile to this language as a first stage. This compilation step is carried out by Visual Studio when you develop C# applications.

Obviously, more work is necessary to execute an application. That is the job of a *just-in-time* (JIT) compiler, which compiles CIL into native code that is specific to the OS and machine architecture being targeted. Only at this point can the OS execute the application. The *just-in-time* part of the name reflects the fact that CIL code is compiled only when it is needed. This compilation can happen on the fly while your application is running, although luckily this isn't something that you normally need to worry about as a developer. Unless you are writing extremely advanced code where performance is critical, it's enough to know that this compilation process will churn along merrily in the background, without interfering.

In the past, it was often necessary to compile your code into several applications, each of which targeted a specific operating system and CPU architecture. Typically, this was a form of optimization (to get code to run faster on an AMD chipset, for example), but at times, it was critical (for applications to work in both Win9x and WinNT/2000 environments, for example). This is now unnecessary because JIT compilers (as their name suggests) use CIL code, which is independent of the machine, operating system, and CPU. Several JIT compilers exist, each targeting a different architecture, and the CLR uses the appropriate one to create the native code required.

The beauty of all this is that it requires a lot less work on your part—in fact, you can forget about system-dependent details and concentrate on the more interesting functionality of your code.

> **NOTE** As you learn about .NET, you might come across references to Microsoft Intermediate Language (MSIL). MSIL was the original name for CIL, and many developers still use this terminology today. See en.wikipedia.org/wiki/Common_Intermediate_Language for more information about CIL (also known as Intermediate Language [IL]).

Assemblies

When you compile an application, the CIL code is stored in an *assembly*. Assemblies include both executable application files that you can run directly from Windows without the need for any other programs (these have an .exe file extension) and libraries (which have a .dll extension) for use by other applications.

In addition to containing CIL, assemblies also include *meta* information (that is, information about the information contained in the assembly, also known as *metadata*) and optional *resources* (additional data used by the CIL, such as sound files and pictures). The meta information enables assemblies to be fully self-descriptive. You need no other information to use an assembly, meaning you avoid situations such as failing to add required data to the system registry and so on, which was often a problem when developing with other platforms.

This means that deploying applications is often as simple as copying the files into a directory on a remote computer. Because no additional information is required on the target systems, you can just run an executable file from this directory and, assuming the CLR is installed for .NET targeted applications, you're good to go. Depending on the deployment scenario, the modules required to run the program are included in the deployment package which means no additional configurations.

From a .NET perspective, you won't necessarily want to include everything required to run an application in a single directory. You might write some code that performs tasks required by multiple applications. In situations like these, it is often useful to place the reusable code in a place accessible to all applications. In .NET, this place is the *global assembly cache* (GAC). Placing code in the GAC is simple—you just place the assembly containing the code in the directory containing this cache.

Managed Code

The role of the CLR doesn't end after you have compiled your code to CIL and a JIT compiler has compiled that to native code. Code written using .NET is *managed* when it is executed (a stage usually referred to as *runtime*). This means that the CLR looks after your applications by managing memory, handling security, allowing cross-language debugging, and so on. By contrast, applications that do not run under the control of the CLR are said to be *unmanaged*, and certain languages such as C++ can be used to write such applications, which, for example, access low-level functions of the operating system. However, in C#, you can write only code that runs in a managed environment. You will make use of the managed features of the CLR and allow .NET itself to handle any interaction with the operating system.

Garbage Collection

One of the most important features of managed code is the concept of *garbage collection*. This is the .NET method of making sure that the memory used by an application is freed up completely when the application is no longer using it. Prior to .NET, this was mostly the responsibility of programmers, and a few simple errors in code could result in large blocks of memory mysteriously disappearing as a result of being allocated to the wrong place in memory. That usually meant a progressive slowdown of your computer, followed by a system crash.

.NET garbage collection works by periodically inspecting the memory of your computer and removing anything from it that is no longer needed. There is no set time frame for this; it might happen thousands of times a second, once every few seconds, or whenever, but you can rest assured that it will happen.

There are some implications for programmers here. Because this work is done for you at an unpredictable time, applications have to be designed with this in mind. Code that requires a lot of memory to run should tidy itself up, rather than wait for garbage collection to happen, but that isn't as tricky as it sounds.

Fitting It Together

Before moving on, let's summarize the steps required to create a .NET application as discussed previously:

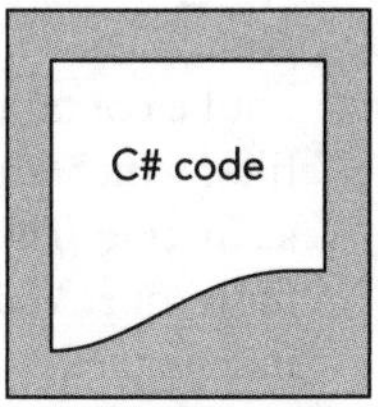

1. Application code is written using a .NET-compatible language such as C# (see Figure 1-1).

2. That code is compiled into CIL, which is stored in an assembly (see Figure 1-2).

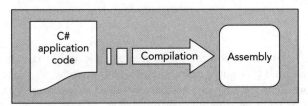

FIGURE 1-1

FIGURE 1-2

3. When this code is executed (either in its own right if it is an executable or when it is used from other code), it must first be compiled into native code using a JIT compiler (see Figure 1-3).

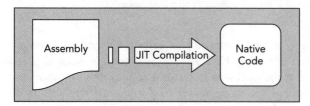

FIGURE 1-3

4. The native code is executed in the context of the managed CLR, along with any other running applications or processes, as shown in Figure 1-4.

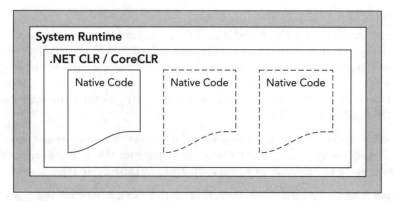

FIGURE 1-4

Linking

Note one additional point concerning this process. The C# code that compiles into CIL in step 2 need not be contained in a single file. It is possible to split application code across multiple source-code files, which are then compiled together into a single assembly. This extremely useful process is known as *linking*. This is required because it is far easier to work with several smaller files than one enormous one. You can separate logically related code into an individual file so that it can be worked on independently and then practically forgotten about when completed. This also makes it easy to locate specific pieces of code when you need them and enables teams of developers to divide the programming burden into manageable chunks. This allows individuals to "check out" pieces of code to work on without risking damage to otherwise satisfactory sections or sections other people are working on.

WHAT IS C#?

C#, as mentioned earlier, is one of the languages you can use to create applications that will run in the .NET CLR. It is an evolution of the C and C++ languages and has been created by Microsoft specifically to work with the .NET platform. The C# language has been designed to incorporate many of the best features from other languages while clearing up their problems.

Developing applications using C# is simpler than using C++ because the language syntax is simpler. Still, C# is a powerful language, and there is little you might want to do in C++ that you can't do in C#. Having said that, those features of C# that parallel the more advanced features of C++, such as directly accessing and manipulating system memory, can be carried out only by using code marked as *unsafe*. This advanced programmatic technique is potentially dangerous (hence its name) because it is possible to overwrite system-critical blocks of memory with potentially catastrophic results. For this reason, and others, this book does not cover that topic.

At times, C# code is slightly more verbose than C++. This is a consequence of C# being a *typesafe* language (unlike C++). In layperson's terms, this means that once some data has been assigned to a type, it cannot subsequently transform itself into another unrelated type. Consequently, strict rules must be adhered to when converting between types, which means you will often need to write more code to carry out the same task in C# than you might write in C++. However, there are benefits to this—the code is more robust, debugging is simpler, and .NET can always track the type of a piece of data at any time. In C#, you therefore might not be able to do things such as "take the region of memory 4 bytes into this data and 10 bytes long and interpret it as X," but that's not necessarily a bad thing.

C# is just one of the languages available for .NET development, but it is certainly the best. It has the advantage of being the only language designed from the ground up for .NET and is the principal language used in versions of .NET that are ported to other operating systems. To keep languages such as the .NET version of Visual Basic as similar as possible to their predecessors yet compliant with the CLR, certain features of the .NET code library are not fully supported, or at least require unusual syntax.

By contrast, C# can make use of every feature the .NET code library has to offer. Also, each new version of .NET has included additions to the C# language, partly in response to requests from developers, making it even more powerful.

Applications You Can Write with C#

.NET has no restrictions on the types of applications that are possible. C# uses the framework and therefore has no restrictions on possible applications. However, here are a few of the more common application types:

➤ **Desktop applications**—Applications, such as Microsoft Office, that have a familiar Windows look and feel about them. This is made simple by using the Windows Presentation Foundation (WPF) module of .NET, which is a library of *controls* (such as buttons, toolbars, menus, and so on) that you can use to build a Windows user interface (UI).

➤ **Cloud/web applications**—.NET includes a powerful system named ASP.NET Core, for generating web content dynamically, enabling personalization, security, and much more. Additionally, these applications can be hosted and accessed in the cloud, for example on the Microsoft Azure platform.

➤ **Mobile applications**—Using both C# and Xamarin mobile UI framework you can target mobile applications that target the Android operating system.

➤ **Web APIs**—An ideal framework for building RESTful HTTP services that support a broad variety of clients, including mobile devices and browsers. These are also referred to as REST APIs.

➤ **WCF services**—A way to create versatile distributed applications. With WCF, you can exchange virtually any data over local networks or the Internet, using the same simple syntax regardless of the language used to create a service or the system on which it resides. This is an older technology that would require an older version of the .NET Framework to create.

Any of these types of applications might also require some form of database access, which can be achieved using the ADO.NET (Active Data Objects .NET) feature set of .NET, through the Entity Framework, or through the LINQ (Language Integrated Query) capabilities of C#. Many other resource assemblies can be utilized that are helpful with creating networking components, outputting graphics, performing complex mathematical tasks, and so on.

C# in This Book

Part I of this book deals with the syntax and usage of the C# language without too much emphasis on .NET. This is necessary because you cannot use .NET at all without a firm grounding in C# programming. You will start off even simpler, in fact, and leave the more involved topic of OOP until you have covered the basics. These are taught from first principles, assuming no programming knowledge at all.

After that, you will be ready to move on to developing more complex (but more useful) applications. Part II examines data access (for ORM database concepts, filesystem, and XML data) and LINQ. Part III explores additional techniques like REST API, the cloud, and Windows Desktop.

VISUAL STUDIO

In this book, you use the most recent version of the Visual Studio development tool for all of your C# programming, from simple command-line applications to more complex project types. A development tool, or Integrated Development Environment (IDE), such as Visual Studio is not essential for developing C# applications, but it makes things much easier. You can (if you want to) manipulate C# source code files in a basic text editor, such as the ubiquitous Notepad application, and compile code into assemblies using the command-line compiler that is part of .NET. However, why do this when you have the power of an IDE to help you?

Visual Studio Products

Microsoft supplies several versions of Visual Studio. For example:

➤ Visual Studio Community

➤ Visual Studio Professional

➤ Visual Studio Enterprise

➤ Visual Studio Code

➤ Visual Studio for Mac

Visual Studio Code, Mac, and Community are freely available at `visualstudio.microsoft.com/downloads`. The Professional and Enterprise versions have additional capabilities, which carry a cost.

The various Visual Studio products enable you to create almost any C# application you might need. Visual Studio Code is a simple yet robust code editor that runs on Windows, Linux, and iOS. Visual Studio Community, unlike Visual Studio Code, retains the same look and feel as Visual Studio Professional and Enterprise. Microsoft offers many of the same features in Visual Studio Community as exist in the Professional and Enterprise versions; however, some notable features are absent, like deep debugging capabilities and code optimization tools. However, not so many features are absent that you cannot use Community to work through the chapters of this book. Visual Studio Community is the version of the IDE used to work the examples in this book.

Solutions

When you use Visual Studio to develop applications, you do so by creating *solutions*. A solution, in Visual Studio terms, is more than just an application. Solutions contain *projects,* which might be Console Applications, WPF projects, Cloud/Web Application projects, ASP.NET Core projects, and so on. Because solutions can contain multiple projects, you can group together related code in one place, even if it will eventually compile to multiple assemblies in various places on your hard disk.

This is especially useful because it enables you to work on shared code (which might be placed in the GAC) at the same time as applications that use this code. Debugging code is a lot easier when only one development environment is used because you can step through instructions in multiple code modules.

▶ WHAT YOU LEARNED IN THIS CHAPTER

TOPIC	KEY CONCEPTS
.NET fundamentals	.NET is Microsoft's code development library. It includes a Common Type System (CTS) and Common Language Runtime (CLR). .NET applications are written using object-oriented programming (OOP) methodology, and usually contain managed code. Memory management of managed code is handled by the .NET runtime; this includes garbage collection.
.NET applications	Applications written using .NET are first compiled into CIL. When an application is executed, the CLR uses a JIT to compile this CIL into native code as required. Applications are compiled, and different parts are linked together into assemblies that contain the CIL.
.NET Core	.NET Core works similarly to the .NET Framework; however, instead of using the CLR it uses CoreCLR. .NET Core is a branch of the original .NET Framework, which can be run cross platform.
.NET Standard	.NET Standard provides a unified class library that can be targeted from multiple .NET platforms like the .NET Micro Framework, .NET Core, and Xamarin.
C# basics	C# is one of the languages included in .NET. It is an evolution of previous languages such as C++ and can be used to write any number of applications, including web, cross-platform, and desktop applications.
Integrated Development Environments (IDEs)	You can use Visual Studio to write any type of .NET application using C#. You can also use the free, but powerful, Community product to create .NET applications in C#. This IDE works with solutions, which can consist of multiple projects.

2

Writing a C# Program

WHAT YOU WILL LEARN IN THIS CHAPTER

➤ Understanding Visual Studio basics

➤ Writing a simple console application

➤ Writing a simple desktop application

CODE DOWNLOADS FOR THIS CHAPTER

The code downloads for this chapter are found on the book page at www.wiley.com. Click the Downloads link. The code can also be found at github.com/benperk/BeginningCSharpAnd-DotNET. The code is in the Chapter02 folder and individually named according to the names throughout the chapter.

Now that you have spent some time learning what C# is and how it fits into .NET, it's time to get your hands dirty and write some code. You use Visual Studio Community (VS) throughout this book, so the first thing to do is have a look at some of the basics of this development environment.

Visual Studio is an enormous and complicated product, and it can be daunting to first-time users, but using it to create basic applications can be surprisingly simple. As you start to use Visual Studio in this chapter, you will see that you do not need to know a huge amount about it to begin playing with C# code. Later in the book you will see some of the more complicated operations that Visual Studio can perform, but for now a basic working knowledge is all that is required.

After you have looked at the IDE, you put together two simple applications. You do not need to worry too much about the code in these applications for now; you just want to prove that things work. By working through the application-creation procedures in these early examples, they will become second nature before too long.

You will learn how to create two basic types of applications in this chapter: a *console application* and a *desktop application*.

The first application you create is a simple *console application*. Console applications do not use the graphical windows environment, so you will not have to worry about buttons, menus, interaction with the mouse pointer, and so on. Instead, you run the application in a command prompt window and interact with it in a much simpler way.

The second application is a *desktop application*, which you create using Windows Presentation Foundation (WPF). The look and feel of a desktop application is very familiar to Windows users, and (surprisingly) the application doesn't require much more effort to create. However, the syntax of the code required is more complicated, even though in many cases you do not have to worry about details.

You use both types of applications in Part II and Part III of the book, with more emphasis on console applications at the beginning. The additional flexibility of desktop applications isn't necessary when you are learning the C# language, while the simplicity of console applications enables you to concentrate on learning the syntax without worrying about the look and feel of the application.

THE VISUAL STUDIO DEVELOPMENT ENVIRONMENT

When you begin the installation of Visual Studio Community you are prompted with a window similar to Figure 2-1. It provides a list of workloads, individual components, and language packs to install along with the core editor.

Check the following Workloads and click the Install button:

➤ **Desktop & Mobile**—.NET desktop development

　　➤ .NET Framework 4.8 development tools

➤ **Web & Cloud**—ASP.NET and web development

➤ **Web & Cloud**—Azure development

➤ **Other Toolsets**—.NET Core cross-platform development

After installation is complete, when Visual Studio is first loaded, it immediately presents you with the option to Sign in to Visual Studio using your Microsoft Account. By doing this, your Visual Studio settings are synced between devices so that you do not have to configure the IDE when using it on multiple workstations. If you do not have a Microsoft Account, follow the process for the creation of one and then use it to sign in. If you do not want to sign in, click the "Not now, maybe later" link, and continue the initial configuration of Visual Studio. It is recommended that at some point you sign in and get a developer license.

If this is the first time you've run Visual Studio, you will be presented with a list of preferences intended for users who have experience with previous releases of this development environment. The choices you make here affect a number of things, such as the layout of windows, the way that console windows run, and so on. Therefore, choose Visual C# from the drop-down; otherwise, you might find that things don't quite work as described in this book. Note that the options available vary depending on the options you chose when installing Visual Studio, but as long as you chose to install C# this option will be available.

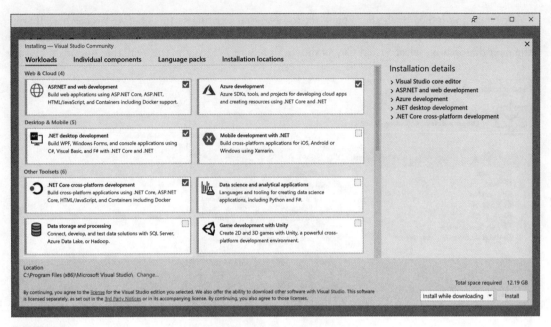

FIGURE 2-1

If this isn't the first time that you've run Visual Studio, and you chose a different option the first time, don't panic. To reset the settings to Visual C#, you simply have to import them. To do this, select Tools ➪ Import and Export Settings, and choose the Reset All Settings option, shown in Figure 2-2.

FIGURE 2-2

Click Next, and indicate whether you want to save your existing settings before proceeding. If you have customized things, you might want to do this; otherwise, select No and click Next again. From the next dialog box, select Visual C#, as shown in Figure 2-3. Again, the available options may vary.

FIGURE 2-3

Finally, click Finish, then Close to apply the settings.

The Visual Studio environment layout is completely customizable, but the default is fine here. With C# Developer Settings selected, it is arranged as shown in Figure 2-4.

The main window is where all your code is displayed and will be different depending on which kind of solution you are creating. The one illustrated in Figure 2-4 is an ASP.NET Core Web Application; the startup page provides some links and additional information relevant to that application type. This window can contain many documents, each indicated by a tab, so you can easily switch between several files by clicking their filenames. It also has other functions: It can display GUIs that you are designing for your projects, plain-text files, HTML, and various tools that are built into Visual Studio. You will come across all of these in the course of this book.

Above the main window are toolbars and the Visual Studio menu. Several different toolbars can be placed here, with functionality ranging from saving and loading files to building and running projects to debugging controls. Again, you are introduced to these as you need to use them.

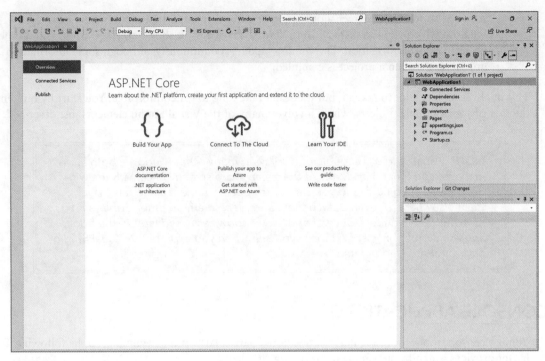

FIGURE 2-4

Here are brief descriptions of each of the main features that you will use the most:

➤ The Toolbox window pops up when you click its tab. It provides access to, among other things, the user interface building blocks for desktop applications. Another tab, Server Explorer, can also appear here (selectable via the View ➪ Server Explorer menu option) and includes various additional capabilities, such as Azure subscription details, providing access to data sources, server settings, services, and more.

➤ The Solution Explorer window displays information about the currently loaded *solution*. A solution, as you learned in the previous chapter, is Visual Studio terminology for one or more projects along with their configurations. The Solution Explorer window displays various views of the projects in a solution, such as what files they contain and what is contained in those files.

➤ The Git Changes window displays information about the current Git Repository connection. This allows you access to source control, bug tracking, build automation, and other functionality. However, this is an advanced subject and is not covered in this book.

➤ Just below the Solution Explorer window, you can display a Properties window, shown in Figure 2-4; it appears only when you are working on a project (you can also toggle its display using View ➪ Properties Window). This window provides a more detailed view of the project's contents, enabling you to perform additional configuration of individual elements. For example, you can use this window to change the appearance of a button in a desktop application.

➤   Also not shown in the screenshot is another extremely important window: the Error List window, which you can display using View ➪ Error List. It shows errors, warnings, and other project-related information. The window updates continuously, although some information appears only when a project is compiled.

This might seem like a lot to take in, but it doesn't take long to get comfortable. You start by building the first of your example projects, which involves many of the Visual Studio elements just described.

> **NOTE** *Visual Studio is capable of displaying many other windows, both informational and functional. Many of these can share screen space with the windows mentioned here, and you can switch between them using tabs, dock them elsewhere, or even detach them and place them on other displays if you have multiple monitors. Several of these windows are used later in the book, and you'll probably discover more yourself when you explore the Visual Studio environment in more detail.*

CONSOLE APPLICATIONS

You use console applications regularly in this book, particularly at the beginning, so the following Try It Out provides a step-by-step guide to creating a simple one.

TRY IT OUT Creating a Simple Console Application: ConsoleApp1\Program.cs

1.   Create a new Console Application project by selecting File ➪ New ➪ Project, as shown in Figure 2-5.

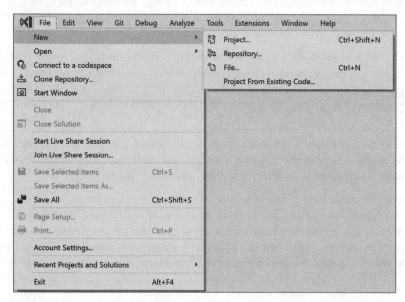

FIGURE 2-5

2. Ensure that C# is selected from the All Languages drop-down and choose the Console Application project (see Figure 2-6). Click the Next button and Change the Location text box to C:\BeginningCSharpAndDotNET\Chapter02 (this directory is created automatically if it does not already exist). Leave the default text in the Name text box (ConsoleApp1) and the other settings as they are.

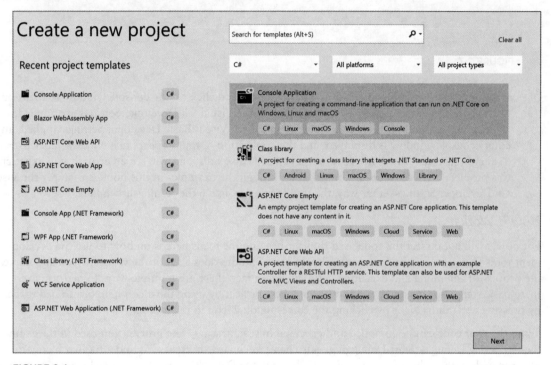

FIGURE 2-6

3. Select .NET 5.0 from the Target Framework dropdown then click the Create button.

4. Once the project is initialized, add the following lines of code to the Program.cs file displayed in the main window:

```
namespace ConsoleApp1
{
    class Program
    {
        static void Main(string[] args)
        {
            // Output text to the screen.
            Console.WriteLine("The first app in Beginning C# and .NET!");
            Console.ReadKey();
        }
    }
}
```

5. Select the Debug ⇨ Start Debugging menu item. After a few moments, you should see the window shown in Figure 2-7.

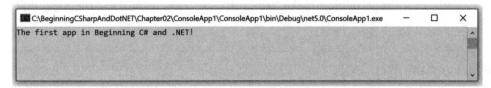

FIGURE 2-7

6. Press any key to exit the application (you might need to click on the console window to focus on it first). The display in Figure 2-7 appears only if the Visual C# Developer Settings are applied, as described earlier in this chapter. For example, with Visual Basic Developer Settings applied, an empty console window is displayed, and the application output appears in a window labeled `Imme-diate`. In this case, the `Console.ReadKey()` code also fails, and you see an error. If you experience this problem, the best solution for working through the examples in this book is to apply the Visual C# Developer Settings—that way, the results you see match the results shown here.

How It Works

For now, I will not dissect the code used thus far because the focus here is on how to use the development tools to get code up and running. Clearly, Visual Studio does a lot of the work for you and makes the process of compiling and executing code simple. In fact, there are multiple ways to perform even these basic steps—for instance, you can create a new project by using the menu item mentioned earlier, by pressing Ctrl+Shift+N, or by clicking the corresponding icon in the toolbar.

Similarly, your code can be compiled and executed in several ways. The process you used in the example—selecting Debug ⇨ Start Debugging—also has a keyboard shortcut (F5) and a toolbar icon. You can also run code without being in debugging mode using the Debug ⇨ Start Without Debugging menu item (or by pressing Ctrl+F5), or compile your project without running it (with debugging on or off) using Build ⇨ Build Solution or pressing F6. Note that you can execute a project without debugging or build a project using toolbar icons, although these icons do not appear on the toolbar by default. After you have compiled your code, you can also execute it simply by running the .exe file produced in Windows Explorer, or from the command prompt. To do this, open a command prompt window, change the directory to `C:\BeginningCSharpAndDotNET\Chapter02\ConsoleApp1\ConsoleApp1\bin\Debug\net5.0`, type **ConsoleApp1**, and press Enter.

NOTE *In future examples, when you see the instructions "create a new console project" or "execute the code," you can choose whichever method you want to perform these steps. Unless otherwise stated, all code should be run with debugging enabled. In addition, the terms "start," "execute," and "run" are used interchangeably in this book, and the discussions following the examples always assume that you have exited the application in the example.*

Console applications terminate as soon as they finish execution, which can mean that you do not get a chance to see the results if you run them directly through the IDE. To get around this in the preceding example, the code is told to wait for a key press before terminating, using the following line:

```
Console.ReadKey();
```

You will see this technique used many times in later examples. Now that you've created a project, you can take a more detailed look at some of the regions of the development environment.

The Solution Explorer

By default, the Solution Explorer window is docked in the top-right corner of the screen. As with other windows, you can move it wherever you like, or you can set it to auto-hide by clicking the pin icon. The Solution Explorer window shares space with another useful window called Class View, which you can display using View ⇨ Class View. Figure 2-8 shows both of these windows with all nodes expanded (you can toggle between them by clicking the tabs at the bottom of the window when the window is docked).

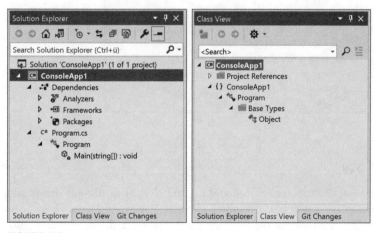

FIGURE 2-8

This Solution Explorer view shows the files that make up the `ConsoleApp1` project. The file to which you added code, `Program.cs`, is shown along with the project Dependencies.

> **NOTE** *All C# code files have a* `.cs` *file extension.*

You can use this window to change what code is displayed in the main window by double-clicking `.cs` files; right-clicking them and selecting View Code; or selecting them and clicking the toolbar button that appears at the top of the window. You can also perform other operations on files here, such as renaming them or deleting them from your project. Other file types can also appear here, such as project resources (resources are files used by the project that might not be C# files, such as bitmap images and sound files). Again, you can manipulate them through the same interface.

You can also expand code items such as `Program.cs` to see what is contained. This overview of your code structure can be a very useful tool; it also enables you to navigate directly to specific parts of your code file, instead of opening the code file and scrolling to the part you want.

The Dependencies entry contains a list of the .NET libraries you are using in your project. You will look at this later; the standard references are fine for now. Class View presents an alternative view of your project by showing the structure of the code you created. You'll come back to this later in the book; for now, the Solution Explorer display is appropriate. As you click files or other icons in these windows, notice that the contents of the Properties window (shown in Figure 2-9) changes.

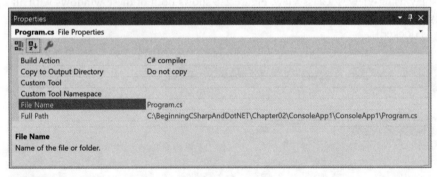

FIGURE 2-9

The Properties Window

The Properties window (select View ⇨ Properties Window if it is not already displayed) shows additional information about whatever you select in the window above it. For example, the view shown in Figure 2-9 is displayed when the `Program.cs` file from the project is selected. This window also displays information about other selected items, such as user interface components (as shown in the "Desktop Applications" section of this chapter).

Often, changes you make to entries in the Properties window affect your code directly, adding lines of code or changing what you have in your files. With some projects, you spend as much time manipulating things through this window as making manual code changes.

The Error List Window

Currently, the Error List window (View ➪ Error List) isn't showing anything interesting because there is nothing wrong with the application. However, this is a particularly useful window indeed. As a test, remove the semicolon from one of the lines of code you added in the previous section. After a moment, you should see a display like the one shown in Figure 2-10.

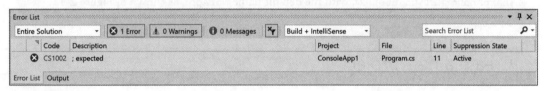

FIGURE 2-10

In addition, the project will no longer compile.

> **NOTE** In Chapter 3, when you start looking at C# syntax, you will learn that semicolons are expected throughout your code—at the end of most lines, in fact.

This window helps you eradicate bugs in your code because it keeps track of what you must do to compile projects. If you double-click the error shown here, the cursor jumps to the position of the error in your source code (the source file containing the error will be opened if it isn't already open), so you can fix it quickly. Red wavy lines appear at the positions of errors in the code, so you can quickly scan the source code to see where problems lie.

The error location is specified as a line number. By default, line numbers are not displayed in the Visual Studio text editor, but that is something well worth turning on. To do so, tick the Line Numbers check box in the Options dialog box (selected via the Tools ➪ Options menu item). It appears in the Text Editor ➪ All Languages ➪ General category.

You can also change this setting on a per-language basis through the language-specific settings pages in the dialog box. Many other useful options can be found through this dialog box, and you will use several of them later in this book.

DESKTOP APPLICATIONS

It is often easier to demonstrate code by running it as part of a desktop application than through a console window or via a command prompt. You can do this using user interface building blocks to piece together a user interface.

The following Try It Out shows just the basics of doing this, and you will see how to get a desktop application up and running without a lot of details about what the application is doing. You will use WPF here, which is Microsoft's recommended technology for creating desktop applications. Later, you will take a detailed look at desktop applications and learn much more about what WPF is and what it is capable of.

TRY IT OUT Creating a Simple Windows Application: WpfApp1\MainWindow. xaml and WpfApp1\MainWindow.xaml.cs

1. Create a new project of type WPF Application in the same location as before (`C:\BeginningC-SharpAndDotNET\Chapter02`), with the default name `WpfApp1` as shown in Figure 2-11.

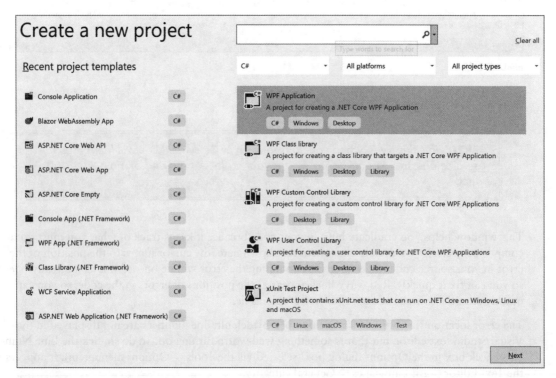

FIGURE 2-11

2. Click Next, select .NET 5.0 from the Target Framework dropdown, then press the Create button. You should see a new tab that is split into two panes. The top pane shows an empty window called MainWindow, and the bottom pane shows some text. This text is the code that is used to generate the window, and you'll see it change as you modify the UI.

3. Click the Toolbox tab on the top left of the screen, then double-click the Button entry in the Common WPF Controls section to add a button to the window.

4. Double-click the button that has been added to the window.

5. The C# code in MainWindow.xaml.cs should now be displayed. Modify it as follows (only part of the code in the file is shown here for brevity):

```csharp
private void button_Click(object sender, RoutedEvetnArgs e)
{
    MessageBox.Show("The first desktop app in the book!");
}
```

6. Run the application.

7. Click the button presented to open a message dialog box, as shown in Figure 2-12.

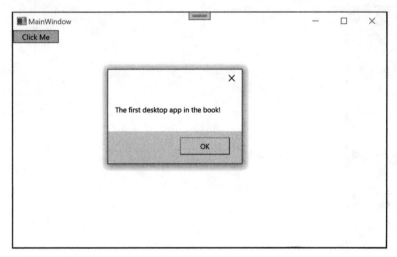

FIGURE 2-12

8. Click OK, and then exit the application by clicking the X in the top-right corner, as is standard for desktop applications.

How It Works

Again, the IDE has done a lot of work for you and made it simple to create a functional desktop application with little effort. The application you created behaves just like other windows—you can move it around, resize it, minimize it, and so on. You do not have to write the code to do that—it just works. The same is true for the button you added. Simply by double-clicking it, the IDE knew that you wanted to write code to execute when a user clicked the button in the running application. All you had to do was provide that code, getting full button-clicking functionality for free.

Of course, desktop applications are not limited to plain windows with buttons. Look at the Toolbox window where you found the Button option and you will see a whole host of user interface building blocks (known as *controls*), some of which might be familiar. You will use most of these at some point in the book, and you will find that they are all easy to use and save you a lot of time and effort.

The code for your application, in `MainWindow.xaml.cs`, does not look much more complicated than the code in the previous section, and the same is true for the code in the other files in the Solution Explorer window. The code in `MainWindow.xaml` (the split-pane view where you added the button) also looks straightforward.

This code is written in XAML, which is the language used to define user interfaces in WPF applications.

Now take a closer look at the button you added to the window. In the top pane of `MainWindow.xaml`, click once on the button to select it. When you do so, the Properties window in the bottom-right corner of the screen shows the properties of the button control (controls have properties much like the files shown in the previous example). Ensure that the application is not currently running, scroll down to the `Content` property, which is currently set to `Button`, and change the value to `Click Me`, as shown in Figure 2-13.

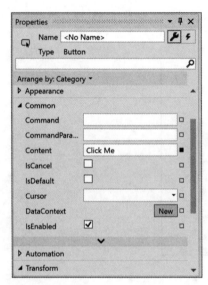

FIGURE 2-13

The text written on the button in the designer should also reflect this change, as should the XAML code, as shown in Figure 2-14.

FIGURE 2-14

There are many properties for this button, ranging from simple formatting of the color and size to more obscure settings such as data binding, which enables you to establish links to data. As briefly mentioned in the previous example, changing properties often results in direct changes to code, and this is no exception, as you saw with the XAML code change. However, if you switch back to the code view of Main-Window.xaml.cs, you won't see any changes there. This is because WPF applications are capable of keeping the design aspects of your applications (such as the text on a button) separate from the functionality aspects (such as what happens when you click a button).

> **NOTE** It is also possible to use Windows Forms to create desktop applications. WPF is a newer technology that is intended to replace Windows Forms and provides a far more flexible and powerful way to create desktop applications, which is why this book does not cover Windows Forms.

▶ **WHAT YOU LEARNED IN THIS CHAPTER**

TOPIC	KEY CONCEPTS
Visual Studio settings	This book requires the C# Development Settings option, which you choose when you first run Visual Studio or by resetting the settings.
Console App	Console applications are simple command-line applications, used in much of this book to illustrate techniques. Create a new console application with the Console Application template that you see when you create a new project in Visual Studio. To run a project in debug mode, use the Debug ⇨ Start Debugging menu item, or press F5.
IDE windows	The project contents are shown in the Solution Explorer window. The properties of the selected item are shown in the Properties window. Errors are shown in the Error List window.
Desktop applications	Desktop applications are applications that have the look and feel of standard Windows applications, including the familiar icons to maximize, minimize, and close an application. They are created with the WPF App (.NET) template in the New Project dialog box.

3

Variables and Expressions

WHAT YOU WILL LEARN IN THIS CHAPTER

➤   Understanding basic C# syntax

➤   Using variables

➤   Using expressions

CODE DOWNLOADS FOR THIS CHAPTER

The code downloads for this chapter are found on the book page at www.wiley.com. Click the Downloads link. The code can also be found at github.com/benperk/BeginningCSharpAnd-DotNET. The code is in the Chapter03 folder and individually named according to the names throughout the chapter.

To use C# effectively, it is important to understand what you're actually doing when you create a computer program. Perhaps the most basic description of a computer program is that it is a series of operations that manipulate data. This is true even of the most complicated examples, including vast, multi-featured Windows applications (such as the Microsoft Office Suite). Although this is often completely hidden from users of applications, it is always going on behind the scenes.

To illustrate this further, consider the display unit of your computer. What you see onscreen is often so familiar that it is difficult to imagine it as anything other than a "moving picture." In fact, what you see is only a representation of some data, which in its raw form is merely a stream of 0s and 1s stashed away somewhere in the computer's memory. Any onscreen action—moving a mouse pointer, clicking an icon, typing text into a word processor—results in the shunting around of data in memory.

Of course, simpler situations show this just as well. When using a calculator application, you are supplying data as numbers and performing operations on the numbers in much the same way as you would with paper and pencil—but a lot quicker and with no chance of mistakes!

If computer programs are fundamentally performing operations on data, this implies that you need a way to store that data and some methods to manipulate it. These two functions are provided by *variables* and *expressions*, respectively, and this chapter explores what that means, both in general and specific terms.

First, though, you will take a look at the basic syntax involved in C# programming, because you need a context in which you can learn about and use variables and expressions in the C# language.

BASIC C# SYNTAX

The look and feel of C# code is like that of C++ and Java. This syntax can look quite confusing at first and it is a lot less like written English than some other languages. However, as you immerse yourself in the world of C# programming, you will find that the style used is a sensible one, and it is possible to write very readable code without much effort.

Unlike the compilers of some other languages such as Python, C# compilers ignore additional spacing in code, whether it results from spaces, carriage returns, or tab characters (collectively known as *whitespace characters*). This means you have a lot of freedom in the way that you format your code, although conforming to certain rules can help make your code easier to read.

C# code is made up of a series of *statements*, each of which is terminated with a semicolon. Because whitespace is ignored, multiple statements can appear on one line, although for readability it is usual to add carriage returns after semicolons, to avoid multiple statements on one line. It is perfectly acceptable (and quite normal), however, to use statements that span several lines of code.

C# is a *block-structured language*, meaning statements are part of a block of code. These blocks, which are delimited with curly brackets ({ and }), may contain any number of statements, or none at all. Note that the curly bracket characters do not need accompanying semicolons.

For example, a simple block of C# code could take the following form:

```
{
    <code line 1, statement 1>;
    <code line 2, statement 2>
        <code line 3, statement 2>;
}
```

Here the `<code line x, statement y>` sections are not actual pieces of C# code; this text is used as a placeholder where C# statements would go. In this case, the second and third lines of code are part of the same statement, because there is no semicolon after the second line. Indenting the third line of code makes it easier to recognize that it is actually a continuation of the second line.

The following simple example uses *indentation* to clarify the C# itself. This is standard practice, and in fact, Visual Studio automatically does this for you by default. In general, each block of code has its own level of indentation, meaning how far to the right it is. Blocks of code may be nested inside each other (that is, blocks may contain other blocks), in which case nested blocks will be indented further:

```
{
    <code line 1>;
    {
        <code line 2>;
        <code line 3>;
    }
    <code line 4>;
}
```

In addition, lines of code that are continuations of previous lines are usually indented further as well, as in the third line of code in the first code example.

> **NOTE** Look in the Visual Studio Options dialog box (select Tools ➪ Options) to see the rules that Visual Studio uses for formatting your code. There are many of these, in subcategories of the Text Editor ➪ C# ➪ Code Style ➪ Formatting node. Most of the settings here reflect parts of C# that have not been covered yet, but you might want to return to these settings later if you want to tweak them to suit your personal style better. For clarity, this book shows all code snippets as they would be formatted by the default settings.

Of course, this style is by no means mandatory. If you do not use it, however, you will quickly find that things can get very confusing as you move through this book!

Comments are something else you often see in C# code. A comment is not, strictly speaking, C# code at all, but it happily cohabits with it. Comments are self-explanatory: They enable you to add descriptive text to your code—in plain English (or French, German, Mongolian, and so on)—that is ignored by the compiler. When you start dealing with lengthy code sections, it's useful to add reminders about exactly what you are doing, such as "this line of code asks the user for a number" or "this code section was written by Benjamin."

C# provides two ways of doing this. You can either place markers at the beginning and end of a comment, or you can use a marker that means "everything on the rest of this line is a comment." The latter method is an exception to the rule mentioned previously about C# compilers ignoring carriage returns, but it is a special case.

To indicate comments using the first method, you use /* characters at the start of the comment and */ characters at the end. These may occur on a single line, or on different lines, in which case all lines in between are part of the comment. The only thing you cannot type in the body of a comment is */, because that is interpreted as the end marker. For example, the following are okay:

```
/* This is a comment */
/* And so. . .
            . . . is this! */
```

The following, however, causes problems:

```
/* Comments often end with "*/" characters */
```

Here, the end of the comment (the characters after `"*/`) will be interpreted as C# code, and errors will occur.

The other commenting approach involves starting a comment with `//`. After that, you can write whatever you like—as long as you keep to one line! The following is okay:

```
// This is a different sort of comment.
```

The following fails, however, because the second line is interpreted as C# code:

```
// So is this,
   but this bit isn't.
```

This sort of commenting is useful to document statements because both can be placed on a single line:

```
<A statement>;        // Explanation of statement
```

It was stated earlier that there are two ways of commenting C# code, but there is a third type of comment in C#—although strictly speaking this is an extension of the `//` syntax. You can use single-line comments that start with three `/` symbols instead of two, like this:

```
/// A special comment
```

Under normal circumstances, they are ignored by the compiler—just like other comments—but you can configure Visual Studio to extract the text after these comments and create a specially formatted text file when a project is compiled. You can then use it to create documentation. In order for this documentation to be created, the comments must follow the rules of XML documentation as described at `docs.microsoft.com/en-us/dotnet/csharp/programming-guide/xmldoc`—a subject not covered in this book but one that is well worth learning about if you have some spare time.

A *very* important point about C# code is that it is *case sensitive*. Unlike some other languages, you must enter code using exactly the right case, because using an uppercase letter instead of a lowercase one will prevent a project from compiling. For example, consider the following line of code, taken from Chapter 2:

```
Console.WriteLine("The first app in Beginning C# Programming!");
```

This code is understood by the C# compiler, as the case of the `Console.WriteLine()` command is correct. However, none of the following lines of code work:

```
console.WriteLine("The first app in Beginning C# and .NET!");
CONSOLE.WRITELINE("The first app in Beginning C# and .NET!");
Console.Writeline("The first app in Beginning C# and .NET!");
```

Here, the case used is wrong, so the C# compiler will not know what you want. Luckily, as you will soon discover, Visual Studio is very helpful when it comes to entering code, and most of the time it knows (as much as a program can know) what you are trying to do. As you type, it suggests commands that you might like to use, and it tries to correct case problems.

BASIC C# CONSOLE APPLICATION STRUCTURE

Here, you'll take a closer look at the console application example from Chapter 2 (`ConsoleApp1`) and break down the structure a bit. Here's the code:

```csharp
using System;
namespace ConsoleApp1
{
    class Program
    {
        static void Main(string[] args)
        {
            // Output text to the screen.
            Console.WriteLine("The first app in Beginning C# and .NET!");
            Console.ReadKey();
        }
    }
}
```

You can immediately see that all the syntactic elements discussed in the previous section are present here—semicolons, curly braces, and comments—along with appropriate indentation.

The most important section of code now is the following:

```csharp
static void Main(string[] args)
{
    // Output text to the screen.
    Console.WriteLine("The first app in Beginning C# and .NET!");
    Console.ReadKey();
}
```

This is the code that is executed when you run your console application. Well, to be more precise, the code block enclosed in curly braces is executed. The comment line does not do anything, as mentioned earlier; it is just there for clarity. The other two code lines output some text to the console window and wait for a response, respectively, although the exact mechanisms of this do not need to concern you for now.

The code outlining functionality for a Windows application is such a useful feature. You can use that functionality with the `#region` and `#endregion` keywords, which define the start and end of a region of code that can be expanded and collapsed. For example, you could modify the generated code for `ConsoleApp1` as follows:

```csharp
#region Using directives
using System;
#endregion
```

This enables you to collapse this code into a single line and expand it again later should you want to look at the details. The `using` statements contained here, and the `namespace` statement just underneath, are explained at the end of this chapter.

> **NOTE** *Any keyword that starts with a # is a preprocessor directive and not, strictly speaking, a C# keyword. Other than the two described here,* #region *and* #endregion, *these can be quite complicated, and they have very specialized uses. This is one subject you might like to investigate yourself after you have worked through this book. Read more about them here:* docs.microsoft.com/en-us/dotnet/csharp/language-reference/preprocessor-directives.

For now, don't worry about the other code in the example, because the purpose of these first few chapters is to explain basic C# syntax, so the exact method of how the application execution gets to the point where Console.WriteLine() is called is of no concern. Later, the significance of this additional code will be made clear.

VARIABLES

As mentioned earlier, variables are concerned with the storage of data. Essentially, you can think of variables in computer memory as boxes sitting on a shelf. You can put things in boxes and take them out again, or you can just look inside a box to see if anything is there. The same goes for variables; you place data in them and can take it out or look at it, as required.

Although all data in a computer is effectively the same thing (a series of 0s and 1s), variables come in different flavors, known as *types*. Using the box analogy again, boxes come in different shapes and sizes, so some items fit only in certain boxes. The reasoning behind this type system is that different types of data may require different methods of manipulation, and by restricting variables to individual types, you can avoid mixing them up. For example, it would not make much sense to treat the series of 0s and 1s that make up a digital picture as an audio file.

To use variables, you must *declare* them. This means that you must assign them a *name* and a *type*. After you have declared variables, you can use them as storage units for the type of data that you declared them to hold.

C# syntax for declaring variables merely specifies the type and variable name:

```
<type> <name>;
```

If you try to use a variable that hasn't been declared, your code won't compile, but in this case, the compiler tells you exactly what the problem is, so this isn't really a disastrous error. Trying to use a variable without assigning it a value also causes an error, but, again, the compiler detects this.

Simple Types

Simple types include types such as numbers and Boolean (true or false) values that make up the fundamental building blocks for your applications. Unlike complex types, simple types cannot have children or attributes. Most of the simple types available are numeric, which at first glance seems a bit strange—surely, you only need one type to store a number, don't you?

The reason for the plethora of numeric types is because of the mechanics of storing numbers as a series of 0s and 1s in the memory of a computer. For integer values, you simply take several *bits* (individual digits that can be 0 or 1) and represent your number in binary format. A variable storing N bits enables you to represent any number between 0 and (2^N – 1). Any numbers above this value are too big to fit into this variable.

For example, suppose you have a variable that can store two bits. The mapping between integers and the bits representing those integers is therefore as follows:

```
0 = 00
1 = 01
2 = 10
3 = 11
```

To store more numbers, you need more bits (three bits enable you to store the numbers from 0 to 7, for example).

The inevitable result of this system is that you would need an infinite number of bits to be able to store every imaginable number, which is not going to fit in your trusty PC. Even if there were a quantity of bits you could use for every number, it surely wouldn't be efficient to use all these bits for a variable that, for example, was required to store only the numbers between 0 and 10 (because storage would be wasted). Four bits would do the job fine here, enabling you to store many more values in this range in the same space of memory.

Instead, several different integer types can be used to store various ranges of numbers, which take up differing amounts of memory (up to 64 bits). These types are shown in Table 3-1.

> **NOTE** *Each of these types uses one of the standard types defined in .NET. As discussed in Chapter 1, this use of standard types is what enables language interoperability. The names you use for these types in C# are aliases for the types defined in the library. Table 3-1 lists the names of these types as they are referred to in the .NET library.*

TABLE 3-1: Integer Types

TYPE	ALIAS FOR	ALLOWED VALUES
sbyte	System.SByte	Integer between −128 and 127
byte	System.Byte	Integer between 0 and 255
short	System.Int16	Integer between −32768 and 32767
ushort	System.UInt16	Integer between 0 and 65535
int	System.Int32	Integer between −2147483648 and 2147483647
uint	System.UInt32	Integer between 0 and 4294967295
long	System.Int64	Integer between −9223372036854775808 and 9223372036854775807
ulong	System.UInt64	Integer between 0 and 18446744073709551615

The u character before some variable names is shorthand for *unsigned*, meaning that you cannot store negative numbers in variables of those types, as shown in the Allowed Values column of Table 3-1.

Of course, you also need to store *floating-point* values, those that are not whole numbers. You can use three floating-point variable types: float, double, and decimal. The first two store floating points in the form 6m × 2^e, where the allowed values for m and e differ for each type. decimal uses the alternative form 6m × 10^e. These three types are shown in Table 3-2, along with their allowed values of m and e, and the limits in real numeric terms shown in the last two columns of the table.

TABLE 3-2: Floating-Point Types

TYPE	ALIAS FOR	MIN M	MAX M	MIN E	MAX E	APPROX MIN VALUE	APPROX MAX VALUE
float	System.Single	0	2^{24}	−149	104	1.5×10^{-45}	3.4×10^{38}
double	System.Double	0	2^{53}	−1075	970	5.0×10^{-324}	1.7×10^{308}
decimal	System.Decimal	0	2^{96}	−28	0	1.0×10^{-28}	7.9×10^{28}

In addition to numeric types, three other simple types are available (see Table 3-3).

TABLE 3-3: Text and Boolean Types

TYPE	ALIAS FOR	ALLOWED VALUES
char	System.Char	Single Unicode character, stored as an integer between 0 and 65535
bool	System.Boolean	Boolean value, true or false
string	System.String	A sequence of characters

Note that there is technically no upper limit on the number of characters making up a string, because it can use varying amounts of memory.

The Boolean type bool is one of the most used variable types in C#, and indeed similar types are equally prolific in code in other languages. Having a variable that can be either true or false has important ramifications when it comes to the flow of logic in an application. As a simple example, consider how many questions can be answered with true or false (or yes and no). Performing comparisons between variable values or validating input are just two of the programmatic uses of Boolean variables that you will examine very soon.

Now that you have seen these types, consider a short example that declares and uses them. In the following Try It Out, you use some simple code that declares two variables, assigns them values, and then outputs these values.

TRY IT OUT Using Simple Type Variables: Ch03Ex01\Program.cs

1. Create a new Console Application called Ch03Ex01 and save it in the directory C:\BeginningC-SharAndDotNET\Chapter03.

2. Add the following code to Program.cs:

```
static void Main(string[] args)
{
    int myInteger;
    string myString;
    myInteger = 17;
    myString = "\"myInteger\" is";
    Console.WriteLine($"{myString} {myInteger}");
    Console.ReadKey();
}
```

3. Execute the code. The result is shown in Figure 3-1.

```
C:\BeginningCSharpAndDotNET\Chapter03\Ch03Ex01\Ch03Ex01\bin\Debug\net5.0\Ch03Ex01.exe      —      □      ×
"myInteger" is 17
```

FIGURE 3-1

How It Works

The added code performs three tasks:

➤ It declares two variables.
➤ It assigns values to those two variables.
➤ It outputs the values of the two variables to the console.

Variable declaration occurs in the following code:

```
int myInteger;
string myString;
```

The first line declares a variable of type int with a name of myInteger, and the second line declares a variable of type string called myString.

> **NOTE** Variable naming is restricted; you cannot use just any sequence of characters. You learn about this in the section titled "Variable Naming."

The next two lines of code assign values:

```
myInteger = 17;
myString = "\"myInteger\" is";
```

Here, you assign two fixed values (known as literal values in code) to your variables using the = assignment operator (the "Expressions" section of this chapter has more details about operators). You assigned the integer value 17 to myInteger, *and you assigned the following string (including the quotes) to* myString:

```
"myInteger" is
```

When you assign string literal values in this way, double quotation marks are required to enclose the string. Therefore, certain characters might cause problems if they are included in the string itself, such as the double quotation characters, and you must escape some characters by substituting a sequence of other characters (an escape sequence) that represents the characters you want to use. In this example, you use the sequence \" *to escape a double quotation mark:*

```
myString = "\"myInteger\" is";
```

If you did not use these escape sequences and tried coding this as follows, you would get a compiler error:

```
myString = ""myInteger" is";
```

Note that assigning string literals is another situation in which you must be careful with line breaks—the C# compiler rejects string literals that span more than one line. If you want to add a line break, then use the escape sequence for a newline character in your string, which is \n. *For example, consider the following assignment:*

```
myString = "This string has a\nline break.";
```

This string would be displayed on two lines in the console view as follows:

```
This string has a
line break.
```

All escape sequences consist of the backslash symbol followed by one of a small set of characters (you will see the full set later). Because this symbol is used for this purpose, there is also an escape sequence for the backslash symbol itself, which is simply two consecutive backslashes (\\).

Getting back to the code, there is one more new line to look at:

```
Console.WriteLine($"{myString} {myInteger}");
```

The $ sign in front of the double quote is the symbol used to implement a feature known as String Interpolation and looks similar to the simple method of writing text to the console that you saw in the first example, but now you are

> specifying your variables. It's too soon to dive into the details of this line of code, but suffice it to say that it is the technique you will be using in the first part of this book to output text to the console window.
>
> This method of outputting text to the console is what you use to display output from your code in the examples that follow. Finally, the code includes the line shown in the earlier example for waiting for user input before terminating:
>
> ```
> Console.ReadKey();
> ```
>
> Again, the code is not dissected now, but you will see it frequently in later examples. For now, understand that it pauses code execution until you press a key.

Variable Naming

As mentioned in the previous section, you cannot just choose any sequence of characters as a variable name. This is not as worrying as it might sound, however, because you're still left with a very flexible naming system.

The basic variable naming rules are as follows:

➤ The first character of a variable name must be a letter, an underscore character (_), or the *at* symbol (@).

➤ Subsequent characters may be letters, underscore characters, or numbers.

There are also certain keywords that have a specialized meaning to the C# compiler, such as the `using` and `namespace` keywords shown earlier. If you use one of these by mistake, the compiler complains, however, so do not worry about it.

For example, the following variable names are fine:

```
myBigVar
VAR1
_test
```

These are not, however:

```
99BottlesOfBeer
namespace
It's-All-Over
```

Literal Values

The previous Try It Out showed two examples of literal values: an integer (`17`) and a string (`"\"myInteger\" is"`). The other variable types also have associated literal values, as shown in Table 3-4. Many of these involve *suffixes*, whereby you add a sequence of characters to the end of the literal value to specify the type desired. Some literals have multiple types, determined at compile time by the compiler based on their context (also shown in Table 3-4).

TABLE 3-4: Literal Values

TYPE(S)	CATEGORY	SUFFIX	EXAMPLE/ALLOWED VALUES
`Bool`	Boolean	None	`true` or `false`
`int, uint, long, ulong`	Integer	None	`100`
`uint, ulong`	Integer	u or U	`100U`
`long, ulong`	Integer	l or L	`100L`
`Ulong`	Integer	ul, uL, Ul, UL, lu, lU, Lu, or LU	`100UL`
`Float`	Real	f or F	`1.5F`
`double`	Real	None, d, or D	`1.5`
`decimal`	Real	m or M	`1.5M`
`char`	Character	None	`'a'`, or escape sequence
`string`	String	None	`"a. . .a"`, may include escape sequences

Binary Literals and Digit Separators

No matter how sophisticated or complex programming syntax becomes, computers function in only two states, 0 and 1, also known as binary (base 2). If you wanted, you could code all your programs as a sequence of 0s and 1s and then run that program. Although that is neither feasible nor recommended, by doing so you alleviate the burden from the interpreters of converting the program from, for example, C#, decimal (base 10), octal (base 8), or hexadecimal (base 16). There is not a lot of value to gain from doing that, so using binary is reserved for very specific scenarios that require it. For example, you might need to pass values to a third-party code package in binary, hexadecimal, or ASCII form. For the most part, unless those literals are required, you should code using a programming language like C#.

Deep technical knowledge and historical understandings of nibbles, bits, bytes, characters, words, bin, hex, octal, and so on are required to deeply understand when, where, how, and why to use these literals. Instead of going deeper into the historical question of "why" and professional-level discussions of "how," it's enough for now to know that, for example, you can use binary literals as an elegant way to store values as constants for pattern matching and comparison, as well as for implementing bit masks. As shown with the binary versus hex example in the following code lines, you can see that the binary numbers are rotated by a single bit from right to left. The hex values have no pattern, which makes it more difficult to quickly determine what the intent of the code might be.

```
int[] binaryPhases = { 0b00110001, 0b01100010, 0b11000100, 0b10001001 };
int[] hexPhases    = { 0x31, 0x62, 0xC4, 0x89 };
```

Now you have some context, and instead of going too deep too fast into pattern matching and bit masks, the remainder of this section specifically focuses on C# *binary literals* and *digital separators*.

You can read more about binary pattern matching and bit masks on your own to increase your knowledge after reading this book and gaining more coding experience.

To better understand the C# binary literal feature, take, for example, the following code:

```
int[] numbers = {1, 2, 4, 8, 16 };
```

In C#, the values added to the numbers array can be written directly in binary, as shown here.

```
int[] numbers = { 0b0001, 0b0010, 0b00100, 0b0001000, 0b00010000 };
```

As with hexadecimals where the prefix is 0x, the compiler will recognize any value beginning with 0b as a binary value and process it as such. As you can imagine, binary values for larger numbers get long and it is easy to make mistakes when you type them in manually. Take the number 128, for example, which has a binary value of 10000000—that is, a 1 followed by 7 zeros. This is where digit separators can help. Take the following code as an example:

```
int[] numbers = { 32, 64, 128 };
int[] numbers = { 0b0010_0000, 0b0100_0000, 0b1000_0000 };
```

Knowing that you can separate the binary literal into groups of digits helps the readability and management of the code. Digit separators are not limited only to binary values: They can be used with int, decimal, float, and double as well. The following line of code represents the value of Pi using a separator after every third digit. The primary reason for digit separators is to make the code easier to read.

```
const double Pi  = 3.141_592_653_589_793_238_462_643_383_279_502;
```

String Literals

Earlier in the chapter, you saw a few of the escape sequences you can use in string literals. Table 3-5 lists these for reference purposes.

TABLE 3-5: Escape Sequences for String Literals

ESCAPE SEQUENCE	CHARACTER PRODUCED	UNICODE (HEX) VALUE OF CHARACTER
\'	Single quotation mark	0x0027
\"	Double quotation mark	0x0022
\\	Backslash	0x005C
\0	Null	0x0000
\a	Alert (causes a beep)	0x0007
\b	Backspace	0x0008
\f	Form feed	0x000C
\n	New line	0x000A
\r	Carriage return	0x000D
\t	Horizontal tab	0x0009
\v	Vertical tab	0x000B

The Unicode Value of Character column of Table 3-5 shows the hexadecimal values of the characters as they are found in the Unicode character set. As well as the previously described escape sequences, you can specify any Unicode character using a Unicode escape sequence. These consist of the standard \ character followed by a u and a four-digit hexadecimal value (for example, the four digits after the x in Table 3-5).

This means that the following strings are equivalent:

```
"Benjamin\'s string."
"Benjamin\u0027s string."
```

Obviously, you have more versatility using Unicode escape sequences.

You can also specify strings *verbatim*. This means that all characters contained between two double quotation marks are included in the string, including end-of-line characters and characters that would otherwise need escaping. The only exception to this is the escape sequence for the double quotation mark character, which must be specified to avoid ending the string. To do this, place the @ character before the string:

```
@"Verbatim string literal."
```

This string could just as easily be specified in the normal way, but the following requires the @ character:

```
@"A short list:
item 1
item 2"
```

Verbatim strings are particularly useful in filenames, as these use plenty of backslash characters. Using normal strings, you would have to use double backslashes all the way along the string:

```
"C:\\Temp\\MyDir\\MyFile.doc"
```

With verbatim string literals, you can make this more readable. The following verbatim string is equivalent to the preceding one:

```
@"C:\Temp\MyDir\MyFile.doc"
```

> **NOTE** As shown later in the book, strings are reference types. This contrasts with the other types you have seen in this chapter, which are value types. One consequence of this is that strings can also be assigned the value null, which means that the string variable does not reference a string (or anything else, for that matter).

EXPRESSIONS

C# contains several *operators* for the purpose of performing operations on values. By combining operators with variables and literal values (together referred to as *operands* when used with operators), you can create *expressions*, which are the basic building blocks of computation.

The operators available range from the simple to the complex, some of which you might never encounter outside of mathematical applications. The simple ones include all the basic mathematical operations, such as the + operator to add two operands; the complex ones include manipulations of variable content via the binary representation of this content. There are also logical operators specifically for dealing with Boolean values, and assignment operators such as =.

This chapter focuses on the mathematical and assignment operators, leaving the logical ones for the next chapter, where you will examine Boolean logic in the context of controlling program flow.

Operators can be roughly classified into three categories:

➤ **Unary**—Act on single operands

➤ **Binary**—Act on two operands

➤ **Ternary**—Act on three operands

Most operators fall into the binary category, with a few unary ones and a single ternary one called the *conditional operator* (the conditional operator is a logical one and is discussed in Chapter 4). Let us start by looking at the mathematical operators, which span both the unary and binary categories.

Mathematical Operators

There are five simple mathematical operators, two of which (+ and -) have both binary and unary forms. Table 3-6 lists each of these operators, a short example of its use, and the result when it is used with simple numeric types (integer and floating point).

TABLE 3-6: Simple Mathematical Operators

OPERATOR	CATEGORY	EXAMPLE EXPRESSION	RESULT
+	Binary	`var1 = var2 + var3;`	var1 is assigned the value that is the sum of var2 and var3.
-	Binary	`var1 = var2 - var3;`	var1 is assigned the value that is the value of var3 subtracted from the value of var2.
*	Binary	`var1 = var2 * var3;`	var1 is assigned the value that is the product of var2 and var3.
/	Binary	`var1 = var2 / var3;`	var1 is assigned the value that is the result of dividing var2 by var3.
%	Binary	`var1 = var2 % var3;`	var1 is assigned the value that is the remainder when var2 is divided by var3.
+	Unary	`var1 = +var2;`	var1 is assigned the value of var2.
-	Unary	`var1 = -var2;`	var1 is assigned the value of var2 multiplied by -1.

> **NOTE** *The + (unary) operator is slightly odd, as it has no effect on the result. It does not force values to be positive, as you might assume—if var2 is -1, then +var2 is also -1. However, it is a universally recognized operator and as such is included. The most useful fact about this operator is shown later in this book when you look at operator overloading.*

The examples use simple numeric types because the result can be unclear when using the other simple types. What would you expect if you added two Boolean values, for example? In this case, nothing, because the compiler complains if you try to use + (or any of the other mathematical operators) with `bool` variables. Adding `char` variables is also slightly confusing. Remember that `char` variables are stored as numbers, so adding two `char` variables also results in a number (of type `int`, to be precise). This is an example of *implicit conversion*, which you will learn a lot more about shortly (along with explicit conversion), because it also applies to cases where `var1`, `var2`, and `var3` are of mixed types.

The binary + operator *does* make sense when used with string type variables. In this case, the table entry should read as shown in Table 3-7.

TABLE 3-7: The String Concatenation Operator

OPERATOR	CATEGORY	EXAMPLE EXPRESSION	RESULT
+	Binary	`var1 = var2 + var3;`	`var1` is assigned the value that is the concatenation of the two strings stored in `var2` and `var3`.

None of the other mathematical operators, however, work with strings.

The other two operators you should look at here are the increment and decrement operators, both of which are unary operators that can be used in two ways: either immediately before or immediately after the operand. The results obtained in simple expressions are shown in Table 3-8.

TABLE 3-8: Increment and Decrement Operators

OPERATOR	CATEGORY	EXAMPLE EXPRESSION	RESULT
++	Unary	`var1 = ++var2;`	`var1` is assigned the value of `var2 + 1`. `var2` is incremented by 1.
--	Unary	`var1 = --var2;`	`var1` is assigned the value of `var2 - 1`. `var2` is decremented by 1.
++	Unary	`var1 = var2++;`	`var1` is assigned the value of `var2`. `var2` is incremented by 1.
--	Unary	`var1 = var2--;`	`var1` is assigned the value of `var2`. `var2` is decremented by 1.

These operators always result in a change to the value stored in their operand:

➤ ++ always results in its operand being incremented by one.

➤ -- always results in its operand being decremented by one.

The differences between the results stored in var1 are a consequence of the fact that the placement of the operator determines when it takes effect. Placing one of these operators before its operand means that the operand is affected before any other computation takes place. Placing it after the operand means that the operand is affected after all other computation of the expression is completed.

This merits another example! Consider this code:

```
int var1, var2 = 5, var3 = 6;
var1 = var2++ * --var3;
```

What value will be assigned to var1? Before the expression is evaluated, the -- operator preceding var3 takes effect, changing its value from 6 to 5. You can ignore the ++ operator that follows var2, as it will not take effect until after the calculation is completed, so var1 will be the product of 5 and 5, or 25.

These simple unary operators come in very handy in a surprising number of situations. They are really just shorthand for expressions such as this:

```
var1 = var1 + 1;
```

This sort of expression has many uses, particularly where *looping* is concerned, as shown in the next chapter. The following Try It Out provides an example demonstrating how to use the mathematical operators, and it introduces a couple of other useful concepts as well. The code prompts you to type in a string and two numbers and then demonstrates the results of performing some calculations.

TRY IT OUT Manipulating Variables with Mathematical Operators: Ch03Ex02\ Program.cs

1. Create a new Console Application called Ch03Ex02 and save it to the directory C:\BeginningC-SharpAndDotNET\Chapter03.

2. Add the following code to Program.cs:

```csharp
static void Main(string[] args)
{
    double firstNumber, secondNumber;
    string userName;
    Console.WriteLine("Enter your name:");
    userName = Console.ReadLine();
    Console.WriteLine($"Welcome {userName}!");
    Console.WriteLine("Now give me a number:");
    firstNumber = Convert.ToDouble(Console.ReadLine());
    Console.WriteLine("Now give me another number:");
    secondNumber = Convert.ToDouble(Console.ReadLine());
    Console.WriteLine($"The sum of {firstNumber} and {secondNumber} is " +
                    $"{firstNumber + secondNumber}.");
    Console.WriteLine($"The result of subtracting {secondNumber} from " +
                    $"{firstNumber} is {firstNumber - secondNumber}.");
```

```
            Console.WriteLine($"The product of {firstNumber} and {secondNumber} " +
                        $"is {firstNumber * secondNumber}.");
            Console.WriteLine($"The result of dividing {firstNumber} by " +
                        $"{secondNumber} is {firstNumber / secondNumber}.");
            Console.WriteLine($"The remainder after dividing {firstNumber} by " +
                        $"{secondNumber} is {firstNumber % secondNumber}.");
            Console.ReadKey();
        }
```

3. Execute the code. The display shown in Figure 3-2 appears.

FIGURE 3-2

4. Enter your name and press Enter. Figure 3-3 shows the display.

FIGURE 3-3

5. Enter a number, press Enter, enter another number, and then press Enter again. Figure 3-4 shows an example result.

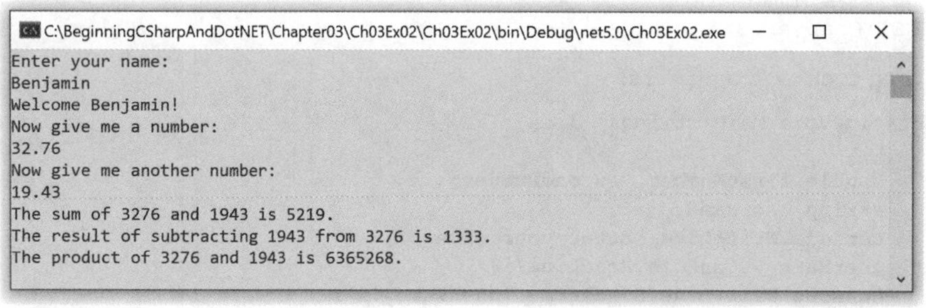

FIGURE 3-4

How It Works

As well as demonstrating the mathematical operators, this code introduces two important concepts that you will often come across:

➤ User input
➤ Type conversion

User input uses a syntax like the `Console.WriteLine()` command you've already seen—you use `Console.ReadLine()`. This command prompts the user for input, which is stored in a `string` variable:

```
string userName;
Console.WriteLine("Enter your name:");
userName = Console.ReadLine();
Console.WriteLine($"Welcome {userName}!");
```

This code writes the contents of the assigned variable, `userName`, straight to the screen.

You also read in two numbers in this example. This is slightly more involved, because the `Console.ReadLine()` command generates a string, but you want a number. This introduces the topic of *type conversion*, which is covered in more detail in Chapter 5, but let us have a look at the code used in this example.

First, you declare the variables in which you want to store the number input:

```
double firstNumber, secondNumber;
```

Next, you supply a prompt and use the command `Convert.ToDouble()` on a string obtained by `Console.ReadLine()` to convert the string into a `double` type. You assign this number to the `firstNumber` variable you have declared:

```
Console.WriteLine("Now give me a number:");
firstNumber = Convert.ToDouble(Console.ReadLine());
```

This syntax is remarkably simple, and many other conversions can be performed in a similar way.

The remainder of the code obtains a second number in the same way:

```
Console.WriteLine("Now give me another number:");
secondNumber = Convert.ToDouble(Console.ReadLine());
```

Next, you output the results of adding, subtracting, multiplying, and dividing the two numbers, in addition to displaying the remainder after division, using the remainder (%) operator:

```
Console.WriteLine($"The sum of {firstNumber} and {secondNumber} is " +
        $"{firstNumber + secondNumber}.");
Console.WriteLine($"The result of subtracting {secondNumber} from " +
        $"{firstNumber} is {firstNumber - secondNumber}.");
Console.WriteLine($"The product of {firstNumber} and {secondNumber} " +
        $"is {firstNumber * secondNumber}.");
Console.WriteLine($"The result of dividing {firstNumber} by " +
        $"{secondNumber} is {firstNumber / secondNumber}.");
Console.WriteLine($"The remainder after dividing {firstNumber} by " +
        $"{secondNumber} is {firstNumber % secondNumber}.");
```

Note that you are supplying the expressions, `firstNumber + secondNumber` and so on, as a parameter to the `Console.WriteLine()` statement, without using an intermediate variable:

```
Console.WriteLine($"The sum of {firstNumber} and {secondNumber} is " +
                  $"{firstNumber + secondNumber}.");
```

This kind of syntax can make your code very readable and reduce the number of lines of code you need to write.

Assignment Operators

So far, you have been using the simple = assignment operator, and it may come as a surprise that any other assignment operators exist at all. There are more, however, and they are quite useful! All the assignment operators other than = work in a similar way. Like =, they all result in a value being assigned to the variable on their left side based on the operands and operators on their right side.

Table 3-9 describes the operators.

TABLE 3-9: Assignment Operators

OPERATOR	CATEGORY	EXAMPLE EXPRESSION	RESULT
=	Binary	`var1 = var2;`	`var1` is assigned the value of `var2`.
+=	Binary	`var1 += var2;`	`var1` is assigned the value that is the sum of `var1` and `var2`.
-=	Binary	`var1 -= var2;`	`var1` is assigned the value that is the value of `var2` subtracted from the value of `var1`.
*=	Binary	`var1 *= var2;`	`var1` is assigned the value that is the product of `var1` and `var2`.
/=	Binary	`var1 /= var2;`	`var1` is assigned the value that is the result of dividing `var1` by `var2`.
%=	Binary	`var1 %= var2;`	`var1` is assigned the value that is the remainder when `var1` is divided by `var2`.

As you can see, the additional operators result in `var1` being included in the calculation, so code like

```
var1 += var2;
```

has the same result as

```
var1 = var1 + var2;
```

> **NOTE** *The += operator can also be used with strings, just like +.*

Using these operators, especially when employing long variable names, can make code much easier to read.

Operator Precedence

When an expression is evaluated, each operator is processed in sequence, but this does not necessarily mean evaluating these operators from left to right. As a trivial example, consider the following:

```
var1 = var2 + var3;
```

Here, the + operator acts before the = operator. There are other situations where operator precedence is not so obvious, as shown here:

```
var1 = var2 + var3 * var4;
```

In the preceding example, the * operator acts first, followed by the + operator, and finally the = operator. This is standard mathematical order, and it provides the same result as you would expect from working out the equivalent algebraic calculation on paper.

Similarly, you can gain control over operator precedence by using parentheses, as shown in this example:

```
var1 = (var2 + var3) * var4;
```

Here, the content of the parentheses is evaluated first, meaning that the + operator acts before the * operator.

Table 3-10 shows the order of precedence for the operators you have encountered so far. Operators of equal precedence (such as * and /) are evaluated from left to right.

TABLE 3-10: Operator Precedence

PRECEDENCE	OPERATORS
Highest	++, -- (used as prefixes); +, - (unary)
	*, /, %
	+, -
	=, *=, /=, %=, +=, -=
Lowest	++, -- (used as postfixes)

> **NOTE** *You can use parentheses to override this precedence order, as described previously. In addition, note that ++ and --, when used as postfixes, only have lowest priority in conceptual terms, as described in Table 3-10. They do not operate on the result of, say, an assignment expression, so you can consider them to have a higher priority than all other operators. However, because they change the value of their operand after expression evaluation, it is easier to think of their precedence as shown in Table 3-10.*

Namespaces

Before moving on, it is worthwhile to consider one more important subject—*namespaces*. These are the .NET way of providing containers for application code, such that code and its contents may be uniquely identified. Namespaces are also used as a means of categorizing items in .NET. Most of these items are type definitions, such as the simple types in this chapter (System.Int32 and so on).

C# code, by default, is contained in the *global namespace*. This means that items contained in this code are accessible from other code in the global namespace simply by referring to them by name. You can use the namespace keyword, however, to explicitly define the namespace for a block of code enclosed in curly brackets. Names in such a namespace must be *qualified* if they are used from code outside of this namespace.

A qualified name is one that contains all of its hierarchical information, which basically means that if you have code in one namespace that needs to use a name defined in a different namespace, you must include a reference to this namespace:

```
namespace LevelOne
{
    // code in LevelOne namespace
    // name "NameOne" defined
}
// code in global namespace
```

This code defines one namespace, LevelOne, and a name in this namespace, NameOne (no actual code is shown here to keep the discussion general; instead, a comment appears where the definition would go). Code written inside the LevelOne namespace can simply refer to this name using NameOne—no classification is necessary. Code in the global namespace, however, must refer to this name using the classified name LevelOne.NameOne.

Note one more important point here: The using statement does not in itself give you access to names in another namespace. Unless the code in a namespace is in some way linked to your project, by being defined in a source file in the project or being defined in some other code linked to the project, you won't have access to the names contained. In addition, if code containing a namespace is linked to your project, then you have access to the names contained in that code, regardless of whether you use using. The using statement simply makes it easier for you to access these names, and it can shorten otherwise lengthy code to make it more readable.

Going back to the code in `ConsoleApp1` shown at the beginning of this chapter, the following lines that apply to namespaces appear:

```
using System;
namespace ConsoleApp1
{
    ...
}
```

Some other common namespaces are shown here, for example:

```
using System.Collections.Generic;
using System.Linq;
using System.Text;
using System.Threading.Tasks;
```

The lines that start with the `using` keyword are used to declare that the `System`, `System.Collections.Generic`, `System.Linq`, `System.Text`, and `System.Threading.Tasks` namespaces will be used in this C# code and should be accessible from all namespaces in this file without classification. The `System` namespace is the root namespace for .NET applications and contains all the basic functionality you need for console applications. The other four namespaces are very often used in console applications, so they are there just in case. Additionally, notice that a namespace is declared for the application code itself, `ConsoleApp1`.

C# includes keywords called `using static`. These keywords allow the inclusion of static members directly into the scope of a C# program. For example, both Try It Out code walkthroughs in this chapter have used the `System.Console.WriteLine()` method, which is part of the `System.Console` static class. Notice that in these examples it is required to include the `Console` class combined with the `WriteLine()` method. When the `using static System.Console` namespace is added to the list of included namespaces, accessing the `WriteLine()` method no longer requires the preceding static class name.

EXERCISES

3.1 In the following code, how would you refer to the name `great` from code in the namespace `fabulous`?

```
namespace fabulous
{
    // code in fabulous namespace
}
namespace super
{
    namespace smashing
    {
        // great name defined
    }
}
```

3.2 Which of the following is not a legal variable name?

➤ `myVariableIsGood`

➤ `99Flake`

➤ `_floor`

➤ `time2GetJiggyWidIt`

➤ `wrox.com`

3.3 Is the string `"supercalifragilisticexpialidocious"` **too big to fit in a** `string` **variable? If so, why?**

3.4 By considering operator precedence, list the steps involved in the computation of the following expression:

```
resultVar += var1 * var2 + var3 % var4 / var5;
```

3.5 Write a console application that obtains four `int` values from the user and displays the product. Hint: You may recall that the `Convert.ToDouble()` command was used to convert the input from the console to a `double`; the equivalent command to convert from a `string` to an `int` is `Convert.ToInt32()`.

Answers to the exercises can be found in the Appendix.

▶ **WHAT YOU LEARNED IN THIS CHAPTER**

TOPIC	KEY CONCEPTS
Basic C# syntax	C# is a case-sensitive language, and each line of code is terminated with a semicolon. Lines can be indented for ease of reading if they get too long, or to identify nested blocks. You can include noncompiled comments with // or /* . . . */ syntax. Blocks of code can be collapsed into regions, also to ease readability.
Variables	Variables are chunks of data that have a name and a type. .NET defines plenty of simple types, such as numeric and string (text) types, for you to use. Variables must be declared and initialized for you to use them. You can assign literal values to variables to initialize them.
Expressions	Expressions are built from operators and operands, where operators perform operations on operands. There are three types of operators—unary, binary, and ternary—that operate on 1, 2, and 3 operands, respectively. Mathematical operators perform operations on numeric values, and assignment operators place the result of an expression into a variable. Operators have a fixed precedence that determines the order in which they are processed in an expression.
Namespaces	All names defined in a .NET application, including variable names, are contained in a namespace. Namespaces are hierarchical, and you often must qualify names according to the namespace that contains them in order to access them.

Flow Control

CODE DOWNLOADS FOR THIS CHAPTER

The code downloads for this chapter are found on the book page at www.wiley.com. Click the Downloads link. The code can also be found at github.com/benperk/ BeginningCSharpAndDotNET. The code is in the Chapter04 folder and individually named according to the names throughout the chapter.

All the C# code you have seen so far has had one thing in common. In each case, program execution has proceeded from one line to the next in top-to-bottom order, missing nothing. If all applications worked like this, then you would be extremely limited in what you could do. This chapter describes two methods for controlling program flow—that is, the order of execution of lines of C# code—*branching* and *looping*. Branching executes code conditionally, depending on the outcome of an evaluation, such as "Execute this code only if the variable myVal is less than 10." Looping repeatedly executes the same statements, either a certain number of times or until a test condition has been reached.

Both techniques involve the use of *Boolean logic*. In the previous chapter, you saw the bool type, but did not actually do much with it. In this chapter, you will use it a lot, so the chapter begins by discussing what is meant by Boolean logic, and then goes on to cover how you can use it in flow control scenarios.

BOOLEAN LOGIC

The `bool` type introduced in the previous chapter can hold one of only two values: `true` or `false`. This type is often used to record the result of some operation, so that you can act on this result. In particular, `bool` types are used to store the result of a *comparison*.

> **NOTE** As a historical aside, it is the work of the mid-nineteenth-century English mathematician George Boole that forms the basis of Boolean logic.

For instance, consider the situation (mentioned at the beginning of the chapter) in which you want to execute code based on whether a variable, `myVal`, is less than 10. To do this, you need some indication of whether the statement "`myVal` is less than 10" is `true` or `false`—that is, you need to know the Boolean result of a comparison.

Boolean comparisons require the use of Boolean *comparison operators* (also known as *relational operators*), which are shown in Table 4-1.

TABLE 4-1: Boolean Comparison Operators

OPERATOR	CATEGORY	EXAMPLE EXPRESSION	RESULT
==	Binary	`var1 = var2 == var3;`	`var1` is assigned the value `true` if `var2` is equal to `var3`, or `false` otherwise.
!=	Binary	`var1 = var2 != var3;`	`var1` is assigned the value `true` if `var2` is not equal to `var3`, or `false` otherwise.
<	Binary	`var1 = var2 < var3;`	`var1` is assigned the value `true` if `var2` is less than `var3`, or `false` otherwise.
>	Binary	`var1 = var2 > var3;`	`var1` is assigned the value `true` if `var2` is greater than `var3`, or `false` otherwise.
<=	Binary	`var1 = var2 <= var3;`	`var1` is assigned the value `true` if `var2` is less than or equal to `var3`, or `false` otherwise.
>=	Binary	`var1 = var2 >= var3;`	`var1` is assigned the value `true` if `var2` is greater than or equal to `var3`, or `false` otherwise.

In all cases in Table 4-1, `var1` is a `bool` type variable, whereas the types of `var2` and `var3` may vary.

You might use operators such as these on numeric values in code:

```
bool isLessThan10;
isLessThan10 = myVal < 10;
```

The preceding code results in `isLessThan10` being assigned the value `true` if `myVal` stores a value less than 10, or `false` otherwise.

You can also use these comparison operators on other types, such as strings:

```
bool isBenjamin;
isBenjamin = myString == "Benjamin";
```

Here, `isBenjamin` is `true` only if `myString` stores the string `"Benjamin"`.

You can also compare variables with Boolean values:

```
bool isTrue;
isTrue = myBool == true;
```

Here, however, you are limited to the use of the `==` and `!=` operators.

> **NOTE** *A common code error occurs if you unintentionally assume that because* `val1 < val2` *is* `false`, `val1 > val2` *is* `true`. *If* `val1 == val2`, *both these statements are* `false`.

The `&&` and `||` operators are known as *conditional Boolean operators* and are described in Table 4-2.

TABLE 4-2: Conditional Boolean Operators

OPERATOR	CATEGORY	EXAMPLE EXPRESSION	RESULT
`&&`	Binary	`var1 = var2 && var3;`	`var1` is assigned the value `true` if `var2` and `var3` are both `true`, or `false` otherwise. (Logical AND)
`||`	Binary	`var1 = var2 || var3;`	`var1` is assigned the value `true` if either `var2` or `var3` (or both) is `true`, or `false` otherwise. (Logical OR)

The result of these operators, `&&` and `||`, is exactly the same as for `&` and `|`, but there is an important difference in the way this result is obtained, which can even accomplish better performance. Both of these look at the value of their first operands (`var2` in Table 4-2) and, based on the value of this operand, may not need to process the second operands (`var3` in Table 4-2) at all.

If the value of the first operand of the `&&` operator is `false`, then there is no need to consider the value of the second operand, because the result will be `false` regardless. Similarly, the `||` operator returns `true` if its first operand is `true`, regardless of the value of the second operand.

Boolean Bitwise and Assignment Operators

Boolean comparisons can be combined with assignments by combining Boolean bitwise and assignment operators. These work in the same way as the mathematical assignment operators that were introduced in the preceding chapter (+=, *=, and so on). The Boolean versions are shown in Table 4-3. When expressions use both the assignment (=) and bitwise operators (&, |, and ^), the binary representation of the compared quantities is used to compute the outcome, instead of the integer, string, or similar values.

TABLE 4-3: Boolean Assignment Operators

OPERATOR	CATEGORY	EXAMPLE EXPRESSION	RESULT
&=	Binary	var1 &= var2;	var1 is assigned the value that is the result of var1 & var2.
|=	Binary	var1 |= var2;	var1 is assigned the value that is the result of var1 | var2.
^=	Binary	var1 ^= var2;	var1 is assigned the value that is the result of var1 ^ var2.

For example, the equation var1 ^= var2 is like var1 = var1 ^ var2 where var1 = true and var2 = false. When comparing the binary representation of false, which is 0000, to true, which is typically anything other than 0000 (usually 0001), var1 is set to true.

> **NOTE** The &= and |= assignment operators do not make use of the && and || conditional Boolean operators; that is, all operands are processed regardless of the value to the left of the assignment operator.

TRY IT OUT Using Boolean Operators: Ch04Ex01\Program.cs

1. Create a new Console Application called Ch04Ex01 and save it in the directory
   C:\BeginningCSharpAndDotNET\Chapter04.

2. Add the following code to Program.cs:

```
static void Main(string[] args)
{
    Console.WriteLine("Enter an integer:");
    int myInt = Convert.ToInt32(Console.ReadLine());
    bool isLessThan10 = myInt < 10;
    bool isBetween0And5 = (0 <= myInt) && (myInt <= 5);
    Console.WriteLine($"Integer less than 10? {isLessThan10}");
    Console.WriteLine($"Integer between 0 and 5? {isBetween0And5}");
    Console.WriteLine($"Exactly one of the above is true? " +
                    $"{isLessThan10 ^ isBetween0And5}");
    Console.ReadKey();
}
```

3. Execute the application and enter an integer when prompted. The result is shown in Figure 4-1.

```
C:\BeginningCSharpAndDotNET\Chapter04\Ch04Ex01\Ch04Ex01\bin\Debug\net5.0\Ch04Ex01.exe     —     □     ×
Enter an integer:
7
Integer less than 10? True
Integer between 0 and 5? False
Exactly one of the above is true? True
```

FIGURE 4-1

How It Works

The first two lines of code prompt for and accept an integer value using techniques you have already seen:

```
Console.WriteLine("Enter an integer:");
int myInt = Convert.ToInt32(Console.ReadLine());
```

You use `Convert.ToInt32()` to obtain an integer from the string input, which is simply another conversion command in the same family as the `Convert.ToDouble()` command used previously. Note that there is no check to make certain the user has entered an `integer`. If a value other than an `integer` is provided, for example a `string`, an exception would occur when trying to perform the conversion. You can handle this using a `try{}...catch{}` block or by checking if the entered value is an `integer` before performing the conversion using the `GetType()` method. Both approaches are discussed in later chapters.

Next, two Boolean variables, `isLessThan10` and `isBetween0And5`, are declared and assigned values with logic that matches the description in their names:

```
bool isLessThan10 = myInt < 10;
bool isBetween0And5 = (0 <= myInt) && (myInt <= 5);
```

These variables are used in the next three lines of code, the first two of which output their values, whereas the third performs an operation on them and outputs the result. You work through this code assuming that the user enters 7, as shown in the screenshot.

The first output is the result of the operation `myInt < 10`. If `myInt` is 6, which is less than 10, the result is `true`, which is what you see displayed. Values of `myInt` of 10 or higher result in `false`.

The second output is a more involved calculation: `(0 <= myInt) && (myInt <= 5)`. It uses two comparison operations to determine whether `myInt` is greater than or equal to 0 and less than or equal to 5, and a Boolean AND operation on the results obtained. With a value of 6, `(0 <= myInt)` returns `true`, and `(myInt <= 5)` returns `false`. The result is then `(true) && (false)`, which is `false`, as you can see from the display.

Finally, you perform a logical exclusive OR on the two Boolean variables `isLessThan10` and `isBetween0And5`. This will return `true` if one of the values is `true` and the other `false`; that is, it returns `true` only if `myInt` is 6, 7, 8, or 9. With a value of 6, as in the example, the result is `true`.

Operator Precedence Updated

Now that you have a few more operators to consider, Table 3-10, "Operator Precedence," from the previous chapter should be updated to include them. The new order is shown in Table 4-4.

TABLE 4-4: Operator Precedence (Updated)

PRECEDENCE	OPERATORS
Highest	++, -- (used as prefixes); (), +, - (unary), !, ~
	*, /, %
	+, -
	<<, >>
	<, >, <=, >=
	==, !=
	&
	^
	|
	&&
	||
	=, *=, /=, %=, +=, -=, <<=, >>=, &=, ^=, |=
Lowest	++, -- (used as suffixes)

This adds quite a few more levels but explicitly defines how expressions such as the following will be evaluated, where the `&&` operator is processed after the `<=` and `>=` operators (in this code `var2` is an int value):

```
var1 = var2 <= 4 && var2 >= 2;
```

It does not hurt to add parentheses to make expressions such as this one clearer. The compiler knows what order to process operators in, but we humans are prone to forget such things (and you might want to change the order). Writing the previous expression as

```
var1 = (var2 <= 4) && (var2 >= 2);
```

solves this problem by explicitly ordering the computation.

BRANCHING

Branching is the act of controlling which line of code should be executed next. The line to jump to is controlled by some kind of conditional statement. This conditional statement is based on a comparison between a test value and one or more possible values using Boolean logic.

This section describes three branching techniques available in C#:

➤ The ternary operator

➤ The `if` statement

➤ The `switch` statement

The Ternary Operator

The simplest way to perform a comparison is to use the ternary (or *conditional*) operator mentioned in the previous chapter. You have already seen unary operators that work on one operand, and binary operators that work on two operands, so it won't come as a surprise that this operator works on three operands. The syntax is as follows:

```
<test> ? <resultIfTrue>: <resultIfFalse>;
```

Here, `<test>` is evaluated to obtain a Boolean value, and the result of the operator is either `<resultIfTrue>` or `<resultIfFalse>` based on this value.

You might use this as follows to test the value of an `int` variable called `myInteger`:

```
string resultString = (myInteger < 10) ? "Less than 10"
                                        : "Greater than or equal to 10";
```

The result of the ternary operator is one of two strings, both of which may be assigned to `resultString`. The choice of which string to assign is made by comparing the value of `myInteger` to 10. In this case, a value of less than 10 results in the first string being assigned, and a value of greater than or equal to 10 results in the second string being assigned. For example, if `myInteger` is 4, then `resultString` will be assigned the string `Less than 10`.

The if Statement

The `if` statement is a far more versatile and useful way to make decisions. Unlike `?:` statements, `if` statements don't have a result (so you can't use them in assignments); instead, you use the statement to conditionally execute other statements.

The simplest use of an `if` statement is as follows, where `<test>` is evaluated (it must evaluate to a Boolean value for the code to compile) and the line of code that follows the statement is executed if `<test>` evaluates to `true`:

```
if (<test>)
    <code executed if <test> is true>;
```

After this code is executed, or if it is not executed due to `<test>` evaluating to `false`, program execution resumes at the next line of code.

You can also specify additional code using the `else` statement in combination with an `if` statement. This statement is executed if `<test>` evaluates to `false`:

```
if (<test>)
    <code executed if <test> is true>;
else
    <code executed if <test> is false>;
```

Both sections of code can span multiple lines using blocks in braces:

```
if (<test>)
{
    <code executed if <test> is true>;
}
else
{
    <code executed if <test> is false>;
}
```

As a quick example, you could rewrite the code from the previous section that used the ternary operator:

```
string resultString = (myInteger < 10) ? "Less than 10"
                                        : "Greater than or equal to 10";
```

Because the result of the `if` statement cannot be assigned to a variable, you must assign a value to the variable in a separate step:

```
string resultString;
if (myInteger < 10)
    resultString = "Less than 10";
else
    resultString = "Greater than or equal to 10";
```

Code such as this, although more verbose, is far easier to read and understand than the equivalent ternary form and enables far more flexibility.

The following Try It Out illustrates the use of the `if` statement.

TRY IT OUT   Using the if Statement: Ch04Ex02\Program.cs

1. Create a new Console Application called Ch04Ex02 and save it in the directory `C:\BeginningCSharpAndDotNET\Chapter04`.

2. Add the following code to `Program.cs`:

```
static void Main(string[] args)
{
    string comparison;
    Console.WriteLine("Enter a number:");
    double var1 = Convert.ToDouble(Console.ReadLine());
    Console.WriteLine("Enter another number:");
    double var2 = Convert.ToDouble(Console.ReadLine());
    if (var1 < var2)
        comparison = "less than";
    else
    {
        if (var1 == var2)
            comparison = "equal to";
        else
            comparison = "greater than";
    }
```

```
Console.WriteLine($"The first number is {comparison} " +
        $"the second number.");
Console.ReadKey();
    }
```

3. Execute the code and enter two numbers at the prompts (see Figure 4-2).

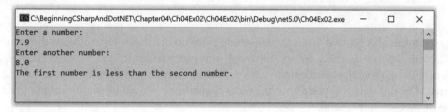

```
C:\BeginningCSharpAndDotNET\Chapter04\Ch04Ex02\Ch04Ex02\bin\Debug\net5.0\Ch04Ex02.exe      —      ☐      ✕
Enter a number:
7.9
Enter another number:
8.0
The first number is less than the second number.
```

FIGURE 4-2

How It Works

The first section of code is very familiar. It simply obtains two `double` values from user input:

```
string comparison;
Console.WriteLine("Enter a number:");
double var1 = Convert.ToDouble(Console.ReadLine());
Console.WriteLine("Enter another number:");
double var2 = Convert.ToDouble(Console.ReadLine());
```

Next, you assign a string to the `string` variable `comparison` based on the values obtained for `var1` and `var2`. First, you check whether `var1` is less than `var2`:

```
if (var1 < var2)
    comparison = "less than";
```

If this is not the case, then `var1` is either greater than or equal to `var2`. In the `else` section of the first comparison, you need to nest a second comparison:

```
else
{
    if (var1 == var2)
        comparison = "equal to";
```

The `else` section of this second comparison is reached only if `var1` is greater than `var2`:

```
else
        comparison = "greater than";
}
```

Finally, you write the value of `comparison` to the console:

```
Console.WriteLine($"The first number is {comparison} " +
        $the second number."
```

The nesting used here is just one method of performing these comparisons. You could equally have written this:

```
if (var1 < var2)
    comparison = "less than";
if (var1 == var2)
    comparison = "equal to";
if (var1 > var2)
    comparison = "greater than";
```

The disadvantage to this method is that you are performing three comparisons regardless of the values of var1 and var2. With the first method, you perform only one comparison if var1 < var2 is true, and two comparisons otherwise (you also perform the var1 == var2 comparison), resulting in fewer lines of code being executed. The difference in performance here is slight, but it would be significant in applications where speed of execution is crucial.

Checking More Conditions Using if Statements

In the preceding example, you checked for three conditions involving the value of var1. This covered all possible values for this variable. Sometimes, you might want to check for specific values—for example, if var1 is equal to 1, 2, 3, or 4, and so on. Using code such as the preceding example can result in annoyingly nested code:

```
if (var1 == 1)
{
    // Do something.
}
else
{
    if (var1 == 2)
    {
        // Do something else.
    }
    else
    {
        if (var1 == 3 || var1 == 4)
        {
            // Do something else.
        }
        else
        {
            // Do something else.
        }
    }
}
```

> **WARNING** It is a common mistake to write conditions such as if (var1 == 3 || var1 == 4) as if (var1 == 3 || 4). Here, owing to operator precedence, the == operator is processed first, leaving the || operator to operate on a Boolean and a numeric operand, which causes an error.

In these situations, consider using a slightly different indentation scheme and contracting the section of code for the `else` blocks (that is, using a single line of code after the `else` blocks, rather than a block of code). That way, you end up with a structure involving `else` `if` statements:

```
if (var1 == 1)
{
    // Do something.
}
else if (var1 == 2)
{
    // Do something else.
}
else if (var1 == 3 || var1 == 4)
{
    // Do something else.
}
else
{
    // Do something else.
}
```

These `else` `if` statements are really two separate statements, and the code is functionally identical to the previous code, but much easier to read. When making multiple comparisons such as this, consider using the `switch` statement as an alternative branching structure.

The switch Statement

The `switch` statement is like the `if` statement in that it executes code conditionally based on the value of a test. However, `switch` enables you to test for multiple values of a test variable in one go, rather than just a single condition. This test is limited to discrete values, rather than clauses such as "greater than X," so its use is slightly different; however, it can be a powerful technique.

The basic structure of a `switch` statement is as follows:

```
switch (<testVar>)
{
    case <comparisonVal1>:
        <code to execute if <testVar> == <comparisonVal1> >
        break;
    case <comparisonVal2>:
        <code to execute if <testVar> == <comparisonVal2> >
        break;
    ...
    case <comparisonValN>:
        <code to execute if <testVar> == <comparisonValN> >
        break;
    default:
        <code to execute if <testVar> != comparisonVals>
        break;
}
```

The value in `<testVar>` is compared to each of the `<comparisonValX>` values (specified with `case` statements). If there is a match, then the code supplied for this match is executed. If there is no match, then the code in the `default` section is executed if this block exists.

On completion of the code in each section, you have an additional command, `break`. It is illegal for the flow of execution to reach a second `case` statement after processing one `case` block.

> **NOTE** *The behavior in which execution is forbidden from flowing from one case block to the next is an area where C# differs from C++. In C++, the processing of case statements is allowed to run from one to another.*

The `break` statement here simply terminates the `switch` statement, and processing continues on the statement following the structure.

There are alternative methods for preventing flow from one `case` statement to the next in C# code. You can use the `return` statement, which results in termination of the current function, rather than just the `switch` structure (see Chapter 6 for more details about this), or a `goto` statement. `goto` statements work here because `case` statements actually define labels in C# code. Here is an example:

```
switch (<testVar>)
{
   case <comparisonVal1>:
      <code to execute if <testVar> == <comparisonVal1> >
      goto case <comparisonVal2>;
   case <comparisonVal2>:
      <code to execute if <testVar> == <comparisonVal2> >
      break;
   ...
```

Here's one exception to the rule that the processing of one `case` statement can't run freely into the next: If you place multiple `case` statements together (*stack* them) before a single block of code, then you are in effect checking for multiple conditions at once. If any of these conditions is met, then the code is executed. Here is an example:

```
switch (<testVar>)
{
   case <comparisonVal1>:
   case <comparisonVal2>:
      <code to execute if <testVar> == <comparisonVal1> or
                          <testVar> == <comparisonVal2> >
      break;
   ...
```

These conditions also apply to the `default` statement. There is no rule stipulating that this statement must be the last in the list of comparisons, and you can stack it with `case` statements if you want. Adding a breaking point with `break`, or `return`, ensures that a valid execution path exists through the structure in all cases.

The following Try It Out uses a `switch` statement to write different strings to the console, depending on the value you enter for a test string.

TRY IT OUT   Using the switch Statement: Ch04Ex03\Program.cs

1. Create a new Console Application called Ch04Ex03 and save it to the directory
    `C:\BeginningCSharpAndDotNET\Chapter04`.

2. Add the following code to `Program.cs`:

```
static void Main(string[] args)
{
    const string myName = "benjamin";
    const string niceName = "andrea";
    const string sillyName = "ploppy";
    string name;
    Console.WriteLine("What is your name?");
    name = Console.ReadLine();
    switch (name.ToLower())
    {
        case myName:
            Console.WriteLine("You have the same name as me!");
            break;
        case niceName:
            Console.WriteLine("My, what a nice name you have!");
            break;
        case sillyName:
            Console.WriteLine("That's a very silly name.");
            break;
    }
    Console.WriteLine($"Hello {name}!");
    Console.ReadKey();
}
```

3. Execute the code and enter a name. The result is shown in Figure 4-3.

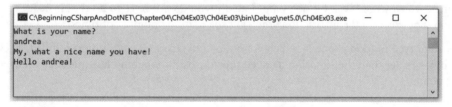

FIGURE 4-3

How It Works

The code sets up three constant strings, accepts a string from the user, and then writes out text to the console based on the string entered. Here, the strings are names.

When you compare the name entered (in the variable `name`) to your constant values, you first force it into lowercase with `name.ToLower()`. This is a standard command that works with all string variables, and it comes in handy when you are not sure what the user entered. Using this technique, the strings `Benjamin`, `benJamin`, `benjamin`, and so on all match the test string `benjamin`.

The switch statement itself attempts to match the string entered with the constant values you have defined, and, if successful, writes out a personalized message to greet the user. If no match is made, you offer a generic greeting.

LOOPING

Looping refers to the repeated execution of statements. This technique comes in very handy because it means that you can repeat operations as many times as you want (thousands or even millions of times) without having to write the same code each time.

As a simple example, consider the following code for calculating the amount of money in a bank account after 10 years, assuming that interest is paid each year and no other money flows into or out of the account:

```
double balance = 1000;
double interestRate = 1.05; // 5% interest/year
balance *= interestRate;
balance *= interestRate;
balance *= interestRate;
balance *= interestRate;
balance *= interestRate;
balance *= interestRate;
balance *= interestRate;
balance *= interestRate;
balance *= interestRate;
balance *= interestRate;
```

Writing the same code 10 times seems a bit wasteful, and what if you wanted to change the duration from 10 years to some other value? You would have to manually copy the line of code the required amount of times, which would be a bit of a pain! Luckily, you do not have to do this. Instead, you can have a loop that executes the instruction you want the required number of times.

Another important type of loop is one in which you loop until a certain condition is fulfilled. These loops are slightly simpler than the situation detailed previously (although no less useful), so they are a good starting point.

do Loops

do loops operate as follows: The code you have marked out for looping is executed, a Boolean test is performed, and the code executes again if this test evaluates to true, and so on. When the test evaluates to false, the loop exits.

The structure of a do loop is as follows, where <Test> evaluates to a Boolean value:

```
do
{
    <code to be looped>
} while (<Test>);
```

> **NOTE** *The semicolon after the* `while` *statement is required.*

For example, you could use the following to write the numbers from 1 to 10 in a column:

```
int i = 1;
do
{
    Console.WriteLine($"{i++}");
} while (i <= 10);
```

Here, you use the suffix version of the `++` operator to increment the value of `i` after it is written to the screen, so you need to check for `i <= 10` to include 10 in the numbers written to the console.

The following Try It Out uses this for a slightly modified version of the code shown earlier, where you calculated the balance in an account after 10 years. Here, you use a loop to calculate how many years it will take to get a specified amount of money in the account, based on a starting amount and a fixed interest rate.

TRY IT OUT   Using do Loops: Ch04Ex04\Program.cs

1. Create a new Console Application called Ch04Ex04 and save it to the directory
   `C:\BeginningCSharpAndDotNET\Chapter04`.

2. Add the following code to `Program.cs`:

```
static void Main(string[] args)
{
    double balance, interestRate, targetBalance;
    Console.WriteLine("What is your current balance?");
    balance = Convert.ToDouble(Console.ReadLine());
    Console.WriteLine("What is your current annual interest rate (in %)?");
    interestRate = 1 + Convert.ToDouble(Console.ReadLine()) / 100.0;
    Console.WriteLine("What balance would you like to have?");
    targetBalance = Convert.ToDouble(Console.ReadLine());
    int totalYears = 0;
    do
    {
        balance *= interestRate;
        ++totalYears;
    }
    while (balance < targetBalance);
    Console.WriteLine($"In {totalYears} year{(totalYears == 1 ? "": "s")} " +
            $"you'll have a balance of {balance}.");
    Console.ReadKey();
}
```

3. Execute the code and enter some values. A sample result is shown in Figure 4-4.

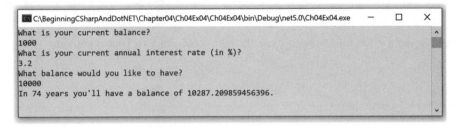

```
C:\BeginningCSharpAndDotNET\Chapter04\Ch04Ex04\Ch04Ex04\bin\Debug\net5.0\Ch04Ex04.exe        −     □     ✕
What is your current balance?
1000
What is your current annual interest rate (in %)?
3.2
What balance would you like to have?
10000
In 74 years you'll have a balance of 10287.209859456396.
```

FIGURE 4-4

How It Works

This code simply repeats the simple annual calculation of the balance with a fixed interest rate as many times as is necessary for the balance to satisfy the terminating condition. You keep a count of how many years have been accounted for by incrementing a counter variable with each loop cycle:

```
int totalYears = 0;
do
{
    balance *= interestRate;
    ++totalYears;
}
while (balance < targetBalance);
```

You can then use this counter variable as part of the result output:

```
Console.WriteLine($"In {totalYears} year{(totalYears == 1 ? "" : "s")} +
    $"you'll have a balance of {balance}.");
```

> **NOTE** Perhaps the most common usage of the ?: (ternary) operator is to conditionally format text with the minimum of code. Here, you output an "s" after "year" if totalYears is not equal to 1.

Unfortunately, this code is not perfect. Consider what happens when the target balance is less than the current balance. The output will be like what is shown in Figure 4-5.

```
C:\BeginningCSharpAndDotNET\Chapter04\Ch04Ex04\Ch04Ex04\bin\Debug\net5.0\Ch04Ex04.exe        −     □     ✕
What is your current balance?
10000
What is your current annual interest rate (in %)?
3.2
What balance would you like to have?
1000
In 1 year you'll have a balance of 10320.
```

FIGURE 4-5

do loops always execute at least once. Sometimes, as in this situation, this is not ideal. Of course, you could add an `if` statement:

```
int totalYears = 0;
if (balance < targetBalance)
{
    do
    {
        balance *= interestRate;
        ++totalYears;
    }
    while (balance < targetBalance);
}
Console.WriteLine($"In {totalYears} year{(totalYears == 1 ? "": "s")} " +
            $"you'll have a balance of {balance}.");
```

This approach can result in unnecessary complexity. A far better solution is to use a `while` loop.

while Loops

`while` loops are very similar to `do` loops, but they have one important difference: The Boolean test in a `while` loop takes place at the start of the loop cycle, not at the end. If the test evaluates to `false`, then the loop cycle is never executed. Instead, program execution jumps straight to the code following the loop.

Here's how `while` loops are specified:

```
while (<Test>)
{
    <code to be looped>
}
```

They can be used in almost the same way as `do` loops:

```
int i = 1;
while (i <= 10)
{
    Console.WriteLine($"{i++}");
}
```

This code has the same result as the `do` loop shown earlier; it outputs the numbers 1 to 10 in a column. The following Try It Out demonstrates how you can modify the last example to use a `while` loop.

TRY IT OUT | Using while Loops: Ch04Ex05\Program.cs

1. Create a new Console Application called Ch04Ex05 and save it to the directory `C:\BeginningCSharpAndDotNET\Chapter04`.

2. Modify the code as follows (use the code from Ch04Ex04 as a starting point, and remember to delete the `while` statement at the end of the original do loop):

```
static void Main(string[] args)
{
```

```
double balance, interestRate, targetBalance;
Console.WriteLine("What is your current balance?");
balance = Convert.ToDouble(Console.ReadLine());
Console.WriteLine("What is your current annual interest rate (in %)?");
interestRate = 1 + Convert.ToDouble(Console.ReadLine()) / 100.0;
Console.WriteLine("What balance would you like to have?");
targetBalance = Convert.ToDouble(Console.ReadLine());
int totalYears = 0;
while (balance < targetBalance)
{
    balance *= interestRate;
    ++totalYears;
}
Console.WriteLine($"In {totalYears} year{(totalYears == 1 ? "": "s")} " +
        $"you'll have a balance of {balance}.");
    if (totalYears == 0)
        Console.WriteLine(
            "To be honest, you really didn't need to use this calculator.");
Console.ReadKey();
}
```

3. Execute the code again, but this time use a target balance that is less than the starting balance, as shown in Figure 4-6.

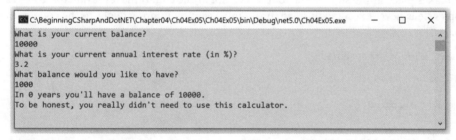

```
C:\BeginningCSharpAndDotNET\Chapter04\Ch04Ex05\Ch04Ex05\bin\Debug\net5.0\Ch04Ex05.exe    —    □    X
What is your current balance?
10000
What is your current annual interest rate (in %)?
3.2
What balance would you like to have?
1000
In 0 years you'll have a balance of 10000.
To be honest, you really didn't need to use this calculator.
```

FIGURE 4-6

How It Works

This simple change from a do loop to a while loop has solved the problem in the previous example. By moving the Boolean test to the beginning, you provide for a circumstance in which no looping is required, and you can jump straight to the result.

Of course, other alternatives are possible in this situation. For example, you could check the user input to ensure that the target balance is greater than the starting balance. In that case, you can place the user input section in a loop as follows:

```
Console.WriteLine("What balance would you like to have?");
do
{
    targetBalance = Convert.ToDouble(Console.ReadLine());
    if (targetBalance <= balance)
        Console.WriteLine("You must enter an amount greater than " +
```

```
                                  "your current balance!\nPlease enter another
   value.");
                   }
                   while (targetBalance <= balance);
```

This rejects values that do not make sense, so the output looks like Figure 4-7.

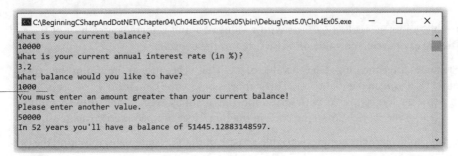

```
C:\BeginningCSharpAndDotNET\Chapter04\Ch04Ex05\Ch04Ex05\bin\Debug\net5.0\Ch04Ex05.exe      —    □    ×
What is your current balance?
10000
What is your current annual interest rate (in %)?
3.2
What balance would you like to have?
1000
You must enter an amount greater than your current balance!
Please enter another value.
50000
In 52 years you'll have a balance of 51445.12883148597.
```

FIGURE 4-7

This *validation* of user input is an important topic when it comes to application design. It is sometimes referred to as a *range check*, and many examples of it appear throughout this book.

for Loops

The last type of loop to look at in this chapter is the `for` loop. This type of loop executes a set number of times and maintains its own counter. To define a `for` loop, you need the following information:

➤ A starting value to initialize the counter variable

➤ A condition for continuing the loop, involving the counter variable

➤ An operation to perform on the counter variable at the end of each loop cycle

For example, if you want a loop with a counter that increments from 1 to 10 in steps of one, then the starting value is 1; the condition is that the counter is less than or equal to 10; and the operation to perform at the end of each cycle is to add 1 to the counter.

This information must be placed into the structure of a `for` loop as follows:

```
for (<initialization>; <condition>; <operation>)
{
   <code to loop>
}
```

This works exactly the same way as the following `while` loop:

```
<initialization>
while (<condition>)
{
   <code to loop>
   <operation>
}
```

Earlier, you used do and while loops to write out the numbers from 1 to 10. The code that follows shows what is required to do this using a for loop:

```
int i;
for (i = 1; i <= 10; ++i)
{
    Console.WriteLine($"{i}");
}
```

The counter variable, an integer called i, starts with a value of 1 and is incremented by 1 at the end of each cycle. During each cycle, the value of i is written to the console.

When the code resumes after the loop, i has a value of 11. That is because at the end of the cycle where i is equal to 10, i is incremented to 11. This happens before the condition i <= 10 is processed, at which point the loop ends. As with while loops, for loops execute only if the condition evaluates to true before the first cycle, so the code in the loop does not necessarily run at all.

As a final note, you can declare the counter variable as part of the for statement, rewriting the preceding code as follows:

```
for (int i = 1; i <= 10; ++i)
{
    Console.WriteLine($"{i}");
}
```

If you do this, though, the variable i will not be accessible from code outside this loop (see the "Variable Scope" section in Chapter 6).

Interrupting Loops

Sometimes you want finer-grained control over the processing of looping code. C# provides commands to help you here:

➤ break—Causes the loop to end immediately

➤ continue—Causes the current loop cycle to end immediately (execution continues with the next loop cycle)

➤ return—Jumps out of the loop and its containing function (see Chapter 6)

The break command simply exits the loop, and execution continues at the first line of code after the loop, as shown in the following example:

```
int i = 1;
while (i <= 10)
{
    if (i == 6)
        break;
    Console.WriteLine($"{i++}");
}
```

This code writes out the numbers from 1 to 5 because the break command causes the loop to exit when i reaches 6.

continue only stops the current cycle, not the whole loop, as shown here:

```
int i;
for (i = 1; i <= 10; i++)
{
    if ((i % 2) == 0)
        continue;
    Console.WriteLine(i);
}
```

In the preceding example, whenever the remainder of i divided by 2 is zero, the continue statement stops the execution of the current cycle, so only the numbers 1, 3, 5, 7, and 9 are displayed.

Infinite Loops

It is possible, through both coding errors and design, to define loops that never end, so-called *infinite loops*. As a very simple example, consider the following:

```
while (true)
{
    // code in loop
}
```

This can be useful, and you can always exit such loops using code such as break statements or manually by using the Windows Task Manager. However, when this occurs by accident, it can be annoying. Consider the following loop, which is like the for loop in the previous section:

```
int i = 1;
while (i <= 10)
{
    if ((i % 2) == 0)
        continue;
    Console.WriteLine($"{i++}");
}
```

Here, i is not incremented until the last line of code in the loop, which occurs after the continue statement. If this continue statement is reached (which it will be when i is 2), the next loop cycle will be using the same value of i, continuing the loop, testing the same value of i, continuing the loop, and so on. This will cause the application to freeze. Note that it is still possible to quit the frozen application in the normal way, so you won't have to reboot if this happens.

EXERCISES

4.1 If you have two integers stored in variables var1 and var2, what Boolean test can you perform to determine whether one or the other (but not both) is greater than 10?

4.2 Write an application that includes the logic from Exercise 1, obtains two numbers from the user, and displays them, but rejects any input where both numbers are greater than 10 and asks for two new numbers.

4.3 What is wrong with the following code?

```
int i;
for (i = 1; i <= 10; i++)
{
    if ((i % 2) = 0)
        continue;
    Console.WriteLine(i);
}
```

Answers to the exercises can be found in the Appendix.

▶ **WHAT YOU LEARNED IN THIS CHAPTER**

TOPIC	KEY CONCEPTS
Boolean logic	Boolean logic involves using Boolean (`true` or `false`) values to evaluate conditions. Boolean operators are used to perform comparisons between values and return Boolean results. Some Boolean operators are also used to perform bitwise operations on the underlying bit structure of values, and there are some specialized bitwise operators, too.
Branching	You can use Boolean logic to control program flow. The result of an expression that evaluates to a Boolean value can be used to determine whether a block of code is executed. You do this with `if` statements or the `?:` (ternary) operator for simple branching, or the `switch` statement to check multiple conditions simultaneously.
Looping	Looping allows you to execute blocks of code a number of times according to conditions you specify. You can use `do` and `while` loops to execute code while a Boolean expression evaluates to `true`, and `for` loops to include a counter in your looping code. Loops can be interrupted at their current cycle (with `continue`) or completely (with `break`). Some loops end only if you interrupt them; these are called infinite loops.

5

More about Variables

WHAT YOU WILL LEARN IN THIS CHAPTER

➤ Performing implicit and explicit conversions between types

➤ Creating and using enum types

➤ Creating and using struct types

➤ Creating and using arrays

➤ Manipulating string values

CODE DOWNLOADS FOR THIS CHAPTER

The code downloads for this chapter are found on the book page at www.wiley.com.
Click the Downloads link. The code can also be found at github.com/benperk/
BeginningCSharpAndDotNET. The code is in the Chapter05 folder and individually named
according to the names throughout the chapter.

Now that you have seen a bit more of the C# language, you can go back and tackle some of the
more involved topics concerning variables.

The first subject you look at in this chapter is *type conversion*, whereby you convert values
from one type into another. You have already seen a bit of this, but you look at it formally here.
A grasp of this topic gives you a greater understanding of what happens when you mix types in
expressions (intentionally or unintentionally), as well as a tighter control over the way that data
is manipulated. This helps you streamline your code and avoid nasty surprises.

Then you will look at a few more types of variables that you can use:

➤ **Enumerations**—Variable types that have a user-defined discrete set of possible values that can be used in a human-readable way.

➤ **Structs**—Composite variable types made up of a user-defined set of other variable types.

➤ **Arrays**—Types that hold multiple values of one type, allowing index access to the individual value.

These are slightly more complex than the simple types you have been using up to now, but they can make your life much easier. Finally, you will explore another useful subject concerning strings: basic string manipulation.

TYPE CONVERSION

Earlier in this book, you saw that all data, regardless of type, is simply a sequence of bits—that is, a sequence of zeros and ones. The meaning of the variable is determined by the way in which this data is interpreted. The simplest example of this is the char type. This type represents a character in the Unicode character set using a number. In fact, the number is stored in exactly the same way as a ushort—both of them store a number between 0 and 65535.

However, in general, the different types of variables use varying schemes to represent data. This implies that even if it were possible to place the sequence of bits from one variable into a variable of a different type (perhaps they use the same amount of storage, or perhaps the target type has enough storage space to include all the source bits), the results might not be what you expect.

Instead of this one-to-one mapping of bits from one variable into another, you need to use *type conversion* on the data. Type conversion takes two forms:

➤ **Implicit conversion**—Conversion from type A to type B is possible in all circumstances, and the rules for performing the conversion are simple enough for you to trust in the compiler.

➤ **Explicit conversion**—Conversion from type A to type B is possible only in certain circumstances or when the rules for conversion are complicated enough to merit additional processing of some kind.

Implicit Conversions

Implicit conversion requires no work on your part and no additional code. Consider the code shown here:

```
var1 = var2;
```

This assignment may involve an implicit conversion if the type of var2 can be implicitly converted into the type of var1; however, it could just as easily involve two variables with the same type, in which case no implicit conversion is necessary. For example, the values of ushort and char are effectively interchangeable, because both store a number between 0 and 65535. You can convert values between these types implicitly, as demonstrated by the following code:

```
ushort destinationVar;
char sourceVar = 'a';
```

```
destinationVar = sourceVar;
Console.WriteLine($"sourceVar val: {sourceVar}");
Console.WriteLine($"destinationVar val: {destinationVar}");
```

Here, the value stored in `sourceVar` is placed in `destinationVar`. When you output the variables with the two `Console.WriteLine()` commands, you get the following output:

```
sourceVar val: a
destinationVar val: 97
```

Even though the two variables store the same information, they are interpreted in different ways using their type.

There are many implicit conversions of simple types; `bool` and `string` have no implicit conversions, but the numeric types have a few. For reference, Table 5-1 shows the numeric conversions that the compiler can perform implicitly (remember that `char`s are stored as numbers, so `char` counts as a numeric type).

TABLE 5-1: Implicit Numeric Conversions

TYPE	CAN SAFELY BE CONVERTED TO
byte	short, ushort, int, uint, long, ulong, float, double, decimal
sbyte	short, int, long, float, double, decimal
short	int, long, float, double, decimal
ushort	int, uint, long, ulong, float, double, decimal
int	long, float, double, decimal
uint	long, ulong, float, double, decimal
long	float, double, decimal
ulong	float, double, decimal
float	Double
char	ushort, int, uint, long, ulong, float, double, decimal

Do not worry—you do not need to learn this table by heart because it's actually quite easy to work out which conversions the compiler can do implicitly. Back in Chapter 3, Tables 3-1, 3-2, and 3-3 showed the range of possible values for every simple numeric type. The implicit conversion rule for these types is this: Any type A whose range of possible values completely fits inside the range of possible values of type B can be implicitly converted into that type.

The reasoning for this is simple. If you try to fit a value into a variable but that value is outside the range of values the variable can take, then there will be a problem. For example, a `short` type variable is capable of storing values up to 32767, and the maximum value allowed into a `byte` is 255, so there could be problems if you try to convert a `short` value into a `byte` value. If the `short` holds a value between 256 and 32767, then it simply will not fit into a `byte`.

If you know that the value in your short type variable is less than 255, then you should be able to convert the value, right? The simple answer is that, of course, you can. The slightly more complex answer is that, of course, you can, but you must use an *explicit* conversion. Performing an explicit conversion is a bit like saying, "Okay, I know you've warned me about doing this, but I'll take responsibility for what happens."

Explicit Conversions

As the name suggests, an explicit conversion occurs when you explicitly ask the compiler to convert a value from one data type to another. These conversions require extra code, and the format of this code may vary, depending on the exact conversion method. Before you look at any of this explicit conversion code, look at what happens if you *do not* add any.

For example, the following modification to the code from the preceding section attempts to convert a short value into a byte:

```
byte destinationVar;
short sourceVar = 7;
destinationVar = sourceVar;
Console.WriteLine($"sourceVar val: {sourceVar}");
Console.WriteLine($"destinationVar val: {destinationVar}");
```

If you attempt to compile the preceding code, you will receive the following error:

```
Cannot implicitly convert type 'short' to 'byte'. An explicit conversion exists
(are you missing a cast?)
```

To get this code to compile, you need to add the code to perform an explicit conversion. The easiest way to do that in this context is to *cast* the short variable into a byte (as suggested by the preceding error string). Casting basically means forcing data from one type into another, and it uses the following simple syntax:

```
(<destinationType>)<sourceVar>
```

This will convert the value in *<sourceVar>* into *<destinationType>*.

> **NOTE** Casting is only possible in some situations. Types that bear little or no relation to each other are likely not to have casting conversions defined. For example, you cannot cast a numeric value into a string.

You can, therefore, modify your example using this syntax to force the conversion from a short to a byte:

```
byte destinationVar;
short sourceVar = 7;
destinationVar = (byte)sourceVar;
Console.WriteLine($"sourceVar val: {sourceVar}");
Console.WriteLine($"destinationVar val: {destinationVar}");
```

This results in the following output:

```
sourceVar val: 7
destinationVar val: 7
```

What happens when you try to force a value into an incompatible variable type? For example, you cannot fit a large integer into a numeric type that's too small. Modifying your code as follows illustrates this:

```
byte destinationVar;
short sourceVar = 281;
destinationVar = (byte)sourceVar;
Console.WriteLine($"sourceVar val: {sourceVar}");
Console.WriteLine($"destinationVar val: {destinationVar}");
```

This results in the following:

```
sourceVar val: 281
destinationVar val: 25
```

What happened? Well, look at the binary representations of these two numbers, along with the maximum value that can be stored in a byte, which is 255:

```
281 = 100011001
 25 = 000011001
255 = 011111111
```

You can see that the leftmost bit of the source data has been lost. This immediately raises a question: How can you tell when this happens? Obviously, there will be times when you will need to explicitly cast one type into another, and it would be nice to know if any data has been lost along the way. Not detecting this could cause serious errors—for example, in an accounting application or an application determining the trajectory of a rocket to the moon.

One way to do this is simply to check the value of the source variable and compare it with the known limits of the destination variable. Another technique is to force the system to pay special attention to the conversion at runtime. Attempting to fit a value into a variable when that value is too big for the type of that variable results in an *overflow*, and this is the situation you want to check for.

Two keywords exist for setting what is called the *overflow checking context* for an expression: checked and unchecked. You use these in the following way:

```
checked(<expression>)
unchecked(<expression>)
```

You can force overflow checking in the previous example:

```
byte destinationVar;
short sourceVar = 281;
destinationVar = checked((byte)sourceVar);
Console.WriteLine($"sourceVar val: {sourceVar}");
Console.WriteLine($"destinationVar val: {destinationVar}");
```

When this code is executed, it will crash with the error message shown in Figure 5-1 (this was compiled in a project called OverflowCheck).

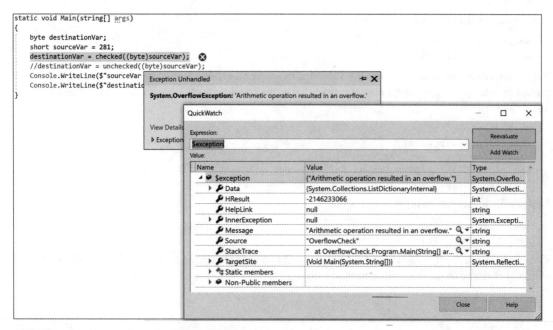

```
static void Main(string[] args)
{
    byte destinationVar;
    short sourceVar = 281;
    destinationVar = checked((byte)sourceVar);   ⊗
    //destinationVar = unchecked((byte)sourceVar);
    Console.WriteLine($"sourceVar
    Console.WriteLine($"destinatio
}
```

FIGURE 5-1

However, if you replace `checked` with `unchecked` in this code, you get the result shown earlier, and no error occurs. That is identical to the default behavior, also shown earlier.

You also can configure your application to behave as if every expression of this type includes the `checked` keyword unless that expression explicitly uses the `unchecked` keyword (in other words, you can change the default setting for overflow checking). To do this, you modify the properties for your project by right-clicking it in the Solution Explorer window and selecting the Properties option. Click Build on the left side of the window to bring up the Build settings.

The property you want to change is one of the Advanced settings, so click the Advanced button. In the dialog box that appears, enable the Check for Arithmetic Overflow/Underflow box, as shown in Figure 5-2. By default, this setting is disabled; enabling it provides the `checked` behavior detailed previously. This feature can have some impact on the execution speed of the program; therefore, disable it when it is no longer needed.

Explicit Conversions Using the Convert Commands

The type of explicit conversion you have been using in many of the Try It Out examples in this book is a bit different from those you have seen so far in this chapter. You have been converting string values into numbers using commands such as `Convert.ToDouble()`, which is obviously something that will not work for every possible string.

If, for example, you try to convert a string like `Number` into a double value using `Convert .ToDouble()`, you will see the dialog box shown in Figure 5-3 when you execute the code.

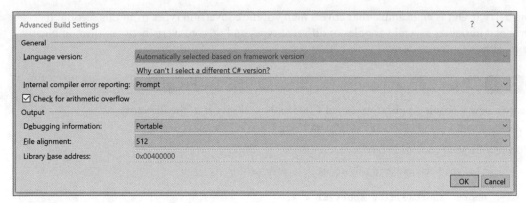

FIGURE 5-2

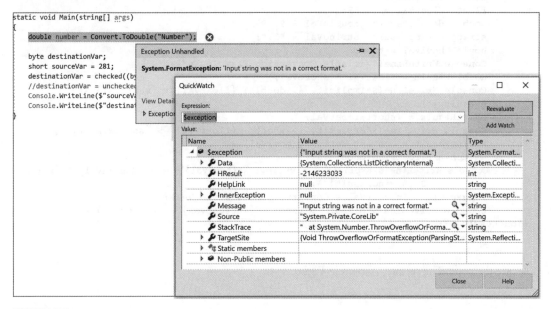

FIGURE 5-3

As you can see, the operation fails. For this type of conversion to work, the string supplied *must* be a valid representation of a number, and that number must be one that will not cause an overflow. A valid representation of a number is one that contains an optional sign (that is, plus or minus), zero or more digits, an optional period followed by one or more digits, and an optional "e" or "E" followed by an optional sign, one or more digits, and nothing else except spaces (before or after this sequence). Using all of these optional extras, you can recognize strings as complex as -1.2451e-24 as being a number.

The important thing to note about these conversions is that they are *always* overflow-checked, and the `checked` and `unchecked` keywords and project property settings have no effect.

The next Try It Out is an example that covers many of the conversion types from this section. It declares and initializes several variables of different types and then converts between them implicitly and explicitly.

TRY IT OUT   Type Conversions in Practice: Ch05Ex01\Program.cs

1. Create a new Console Application called Ch05Ex01 and save it in the directory `C:\BeginningCSharpAndDotNET\Chapter05`.

2. Add the following code to `Program.cs`:

```
static void Main(string[] args)
{
    short   shortResult, shortVal = 4;
    int     integerVal = 67;
    long    longResult;
    float   floatVal = 10.5F;
    double doubleResult, doubleVal = 99.999;
    string stringResult, stringVal = "17";
    bool   boolVal = true;
    Console.WriteLine("Variable Conversion Examples\n");
    doubleResult = floatVal * shortVal;
    Console.WriteLine($"Implicit, -> double: {floatVal} * {shortVal} ->
{ doubleResult }");
    shortResult = (short)floatVal;
    Console.WriteLine($"Explicit, -> short:  {floatVal} -> {shortResult}");
    stringResult = Convert.ToString(boolVal) +
        Convert.ToString(doubleVal);
    Console.WriteLine($"Explicit, -> string: \"{boolVal}\" + \"{doubleVal}\" -> " +
              $"{stringResult}");
    longResult = integerVal + Convert.ToInt64(stringVal);
    Console.WriteLine($"Mixed, -> long:   {integerVal} + {stringVal} ->
{longResult}");
    Console.ReadKey();
}
```

3. Execute the code. The result is shown in Figure 5-4.

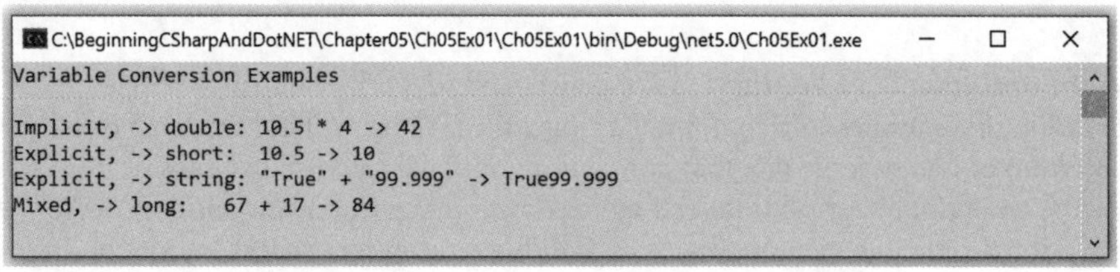

FIGURE 5-4

How It Works

This example contains all the conversion types you've seen so far—both in simple assignments, as in the short code examples in the preceding discussion, and in expressions. You need to consider both cases because the processing of *every* non-unary operator may result in type conversions, not just assignment operators. For example, the following multiplies a `short` value by a `float` value:

```
shortVal * floatVal
```

In situations such as this, where no explicit conversion is specified, implicit conversion will be used if possible. In this example, the only implicit conversion that makes sense is to convert the `short` into a `float` (as converting a `float` into a `short` requires explicit conversion), so this is the one that will be used.

However, you can override this behavior should you want, as shown here:

```
shortVal * (short)floatVal
```

> **NOTE** Interestingly, multiplying two `short` values together does not return a `short` value. Because the result of this operation is quite likely to exceed 32767 (the maximum value a `short` can hold), it actually returns an `int`.
>
> The conversion process can seem complex at first glance, but as long as you break expressions down into parts by taking the operator precedence order into account, you should be able to work things out.

COMPLEX VARIABLE TYPES

In addition to all the simple variable types, C# also offers three slightly more complex (but very useful) sorts of variables: enumerations (often referred to as enums), structs (occasionally referred to as structures), and arrays.

Enumerations

Each of the types you have seen so far (with the exception of `string`) has a clearly defined set of allowed values. Admittedly, this set is so large in types such as `double` that it can practically be considered a continuum, but it is a fixed set, nevertheless. The simplest example of this is the `bool` type, which can take only one of two values: `true` or `false`.

There are many other circumstances in which you might want to have a variable that can take one of a fixed set of results. For example, you might want to have an `orientation` type that can store one of the values `north`, `south`, `east`, or `west`.

In situations like this, *enumerations* can be very useful. Enumerations do exactly what you want in this `orientation` type: They allow the definition of a type that can take one of a finite set of values that you supply. What you need to do, then, is create your own enumeration type called `orientation` that can take one of the four possible values.

Note that there is an additional step involved here—you don't just declare a variable of a given type; you declare and detail a user-defined type and then declare a variable of this new type.

Defining Enumerations

You can use the `enum` keyword to define enumerations as follows:

```
enum <typeName>
{
    <value1>,
    <value2>,
    <value3>,
    ...
    <valueN>
}
```

Next, you can declare variables of this new type as follows:

```
<typeName> <varName>;
```

You can assign values using the following:

```
<varName> = <typeName>.<value>;
```

Enumerations have an *underlying type* used for storage. Each of the values that an enumeration type can take is stored as a value of this underlying type, which by default is `int`. You can specify a different underlying type by adding the type to the enumeration declaration:

```
enum <typeName> : <underlyingType>
{
    <value1>,
    <value2>,
    <value3>,
    ...
    <valueN>
}
```

Enumerations can have underlying types of `byte`, `sbyte`, `short`, `ushort`, `int`, `uint`, `long`, and `ulong`.

By default, each value is assigned a corresponding underlying type value automatically according to the order in which it is defined, starting from zero. This means that `<value1>` gets the value 0, `<value2>` gets 1, `<value3>` gets 2, and so on. You can override this assignment by using the `=` operator and specifying actual values for each enumeration value:

```
enum <typeName> : <underlyingType>
{
    <value1> = <actualVal1>,
    <value2> = <actualVal2>,
    <value3> = <actualVal3>,
    ...
    <valueN> = <actualValN>
}
```

In addition, you can specify identical values for multiple enumeration values by using one value as the underlying value of another:

```
enum <typeName> : <underlyingType>
{
    <value1> = <actualVal1>,
    <value2> = <value1>,
    <value3>,
    ...
    <valueN> = <actualValN>
}
```

Any values left unassigned are given an underlying value automatically, whereby the values used are in a sequence starting from 1 greater than the last explicitly declared one. In the preceding code, for example, *<value3>* will get the value *<value1>* + 1.

Note that this can cause problems, with values specified after a definition such as *<value2>* = *<value1>* being identical to other values. For example, in the following code, *<value4>* will have the same value as *<value2>*:

```
enum <typeName> : <underlyingType>
{
    <value1> = <actualVal1>,
    <value2>,
    <value3> = <value1>,
    <value4>,
    ...
    <valueN> = <actualValN>
}
```

Of course, if this is the behavior you want, then this code is fine. Note also that assigning values in a circular fashion will cause an error:

```
enum <typeName> : <underlyingType>
{
    <value1> = <value2>,
    <value2> = <value1>
}
```

The following Try It Out shows an example of all of this. The code defines and then uses an enumeration called orientation.

TRY IT OUT   Using an Enumeration: Ch05Ex02\Program.cs

1. Create a new Console Application called Ch05Ex02 and save it in the directory
   `C:\BeginningCSharpAndDotNET\Chapter05`.

2. Add the following code to `Program.cs`:

```
namespace Ch05Ex02
{
    enum orientation : byte
    {
        north = 1,
        south = 2,
```

```
            east  = 3,
            west  = 4
        }
        class Program
        {
            static void Main(string[] args)
            {
                orientation myDirection = orientation.north;
                Console.WriteLine($"myDirection = {myDirection}");
                Console.ReadKey();
            }
        }
    }
```

3. Execute the application. You should see the output shown in Figure 5-5.

FIGURE 5-5

4. Quit the application and modify the code in the Main() method as follows:

```
            byte directionByte;
            string directionString;
            orientation myDirection = orientation.north;
            Console.WriteLine($"myDirection = {myDirection}");
            directionByte = (byte)myDirection;
            directionString = Convert.ToString(myDirection);
            Console.WriteLine($"byte equivalent = {directionByte}");
            Console.WriteLine($"string equivalent = {directionString}");
            Console.ReadKey();
```

5. Execute the application again. The output is shown in Figure 5-6.

FIGURE 5-6

How It Works

This code defines and uses an enumeration type called `orientation`. The first thing to notice is that the type definition code is placed in your namespace, `Ch05Ex02`, but not in the same place as the rest of your code. That is because definitions are not executed; that is, at runtime you do not step through the code in a definition as you do the lines of code in your application. Application execution starts in the place you are used to and has access to your new type because it belongs to the same namespace.

The first iteration of the example demonstrates the basic method of creating a variable of your new type, assigning it a value, and outputting it to the screen. Next, you modify the code to show the conversion of enumeration values into other types. Note that you must use explicit conversions here. Even though the underlying type of `orientation` is `byte`, you still have to use the `(byte)` cast to convert the value of `myDirection` into a `byte` type:

```
directionByte = (byte)myDirection;
```

The same explicit casting is necessary in the other direction, too, if you want to convert a `byte` into an `orientation`. For example, you could use the following code to convert a `byte` variable called `myByte` into an `orientation` and assign this value to `myDirection`:

```
myDirection = (orientation)myByte;
```

Of course, you must be careful here because not all permissible values of `byte` type variables map to defined `orientation` values. The `orientation` type can store other `byte` values, so you won't get an error straight away, but this may break logic later in the application.

To get the string value of an enumeration value, you can use `Convert.ToString()`:

```
directionString = Convert.ToString(myDirection);
```

Using a `(string)` cast will not work because the processing required is more complicated than just placing the data stored in the enumeration variable into a `string` variable. Alternatively, you can use the `ToString()` command of the variable itself. The following code gives you the same result as using `Convert.ToString()`:

```
directionString = myDirection.ToString();
```

Converting a `string` to an enumeration value is also possible, except that here the syntax required is slightly more complex. A special command exists for this sort of conversion, `Enum.Parse()`, which is used in the following way:

```
(enumerationType)Enum.Parse(typeof(enumerationType), enumerationValue-
String);
```

This uses another operator, `typeof`, which obtains the type of its operand. You could use this for your `orientation` type as follows:

```
string myString = "north";
orientation myDirection = (orientation)Enum.Parse(typeof(orientation),
                                                  myString);
```

Of course, not all string values will map to an `orientation` value! If you pass in a value that does not map to one of your enumeration values, you will get an error. Like everything else in C#, these values are case sensitive, so you still get an error if your string agrees with everything in a value except its case (for example, if `myString` is set to `North` rather than `north`).

Structs

The *struct* (short for structure) is just that. That is, structs are data structures composed of several pieces of data, possibly of different types. They enable you to define your own types of variables based on this structure. For example, suppose that you want to store the route to a location from a starting point, where the route consists of a direction and a distance in miles. For simplicity, you can assume that the direction is one of the compass points (such that it can be represented using the `orientation` enumeration from the previous section), and that distance in miles can be represented as a `double` type.

You could use two separate variables for this with code you've seen already:

```
orientation myDirection;
double      myDistance;
```

There is nothing wrong with using two variables like this, but it is far simpler (especially where multiple routes are required) to store this information in one place.

Defining Structs

Structs are defined using the `struct` keyword as follows:

```
struct <typeName>
{
    <memberDeclarations>
}
```

The `<memberDeclarations>` section contains declarations of variables (called *data members* of the struct) in almost the same format as usual. Each member declaration takes the following form:

```
<accessibility> <type> <name>;
```

To allow the code that calls the struct to access the struct's data members, you use the keyword `public` for `<accessibility>`. For example:

```
struct route
{
    public orientation direction;
    public double      distance;
}
```

Once you have a struct type defined, you use it by defining variables of the new type:

```
route myRoute;
```

In addition, you have access to the data members of this composite variable via the period character:

```
myRoute.direction = orientation.north;
myRoute.distance  = 2.5;
```

This is demonstrated in the following Try It Out, where the `orientation` enumeration from the previous Try It Out is used with the `route` struct shown earlier. This struct is then manipulated in code to give you a feel for how structs work.

TRY IT OUT   Using a Struct: Ch05Ex03\Program.cs

1. Create a new Console Application called Ch05Ex03 and save it in the directory
    `C:\BeginningCSharpAndDotNET\Chapter05`.

2. Add the following code to `Program.cs`:

    ```
    namespace Ch05Ex03
    {
    ```

```
enum orientation: byte
{
    north = 1,
    south = 2,
    east  = 3,
    west  = 4
}
struct route
{
    public orientation direction;
    public double      distance;
}
class Program
{
    static void Main(string[] args)
    {
        route myRoute;
        int myDirection = -1;
        double myDistance;
        Console.WriteLine("1) North\n2) South\n3) East\n4) West");
        do
        {
            Console.WriteLine("Select a direction:");
            myDirection = Convert.ToInt32(Console.ReadLine());
        }
        while ((myDirection < 1) || (myDirection > 4));
        Console.WriteLine("Input a distance:");
        myDistance = Convert.ToDouble(Console.ReadLine());
        myRoute.direction = (orientation)myDirection;
        myRoute.distance = myDistance;
        Console.WriteLine($"myRoute specifies a direction of {myRoute
.direction} " +
                $"and a distance of {myRoute.distance}");
        Console.ReadKey();
    }
}
```

3. Execute the code, select a direction by entering a number between 1 and 4, and then enter a distance. The result is shown in Figure 5-7.

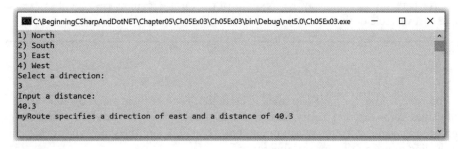

FIGURE 5-7

How It Works

Structs, like enumerations, are declared outside of the main body of the code. You declare your `route` struct just inside the namespace declaration, along with the `orientation` enumeration that it uses:

```
enum orientation: byte
{
    north = 1,
    south = 2,
    east  = 3,
    west  = 4
}
struct route
{
    public orientation direction;
    public double      distance;
}
```

The main body of the code follows a structure similar to some of the example code you've already seen, requesting input from the user and displaying it. You perform some simple validation of user input by placing the direction selection in a `do` loop, rejecting any input that isn't an integer between 1 and 4 (with values chosen such that they map onto the enumeration members for easy assignment).

> **NOTE** Input that cannot be interpreted as an integer will result in an error. You will see why this happens, and what to do about it, later in the book.

The interesting point to note is that when you refer to members of *route* they are treated exactly the same way that variables of the same type as the members. The assignment is as follows:

```
myRoute.direction = (orientation)myDirection;
myRoute.distance = myDistance;
```

You could simply take the input value directly into `myRoute.distance` with no ill effects as follows:

```
myRoute.distance = Convert.ToDouble(ReadLine());
```

The extra step allows for more validation, although none is performed in this code. Any access to members of a structure is treated in the same way. Expressions of the form `<structVar>.<memberVar>` can be said to evaluate to a variable of the type of `<memberVar>`.

Arrays

All the types you have seen so far have one thing in common: Each of them stores a single value (or a single set of values in the case of structs). Sometimes, in situations where you want to store a lot of data, this isn't very convenient. You may want to store several values of the same type at the same time, without having to use a different variable for each value.

For example, suppose you want to perform some processing that involves the names of all your friends. You could use simple string variables as follows:

```
string friendName1 = "Todd Anthony";
string friendName2 = "Kevin Holton";
string friendName3 = "Shane Laigle";
```

But this looks like it will require a lot of effort, especially because you need to write different code to process each variable. You could not, for example, iterate through this list of strings in a loop.

The alternative is to use an *array*. Arrays are indexed lists of variables stored in a single array type variable. For example, you might have an array called `friendNames` that stores the three names shown in the preceding string variables. You can access individual members of the array by specifying their index in square brackets, as shown here:

```
friendNames[<index>]
```

The index is simply an integer, starting with 0 for the first entry, using 1 for the second, and so on. This means that you can go through the entries using a loop:

```
int i;
for (i = 0; i < 3; i++)
{
    Console.WriteLine($"Name with index of {i}: {friendNames[i]}");
}
```

Arrays have a single *base type*—that is, individual entries in an array are all of the same type. This `friendNames` array has a base type of `string` because it is intended for storing `string` variables. Array entries are often referred to as *elements*.

Declaring Arrays

Arrays are declared in the following way:

```
<baseType>[] <name>;
```

Here, `<baseType>` may be any variable type, including the enumeration and struct types you've seen in this chapter. Arrays must be initialized before you have access to them. You can't just access or assign values to the array elements like this:

```
int[] myIntArray;
myIntArray[10] = 5;
```

Arrays can be initialized in two ways. You can either specify the complete contents of the array in a literal form or specify the size of the array and use the `new` keyword to initialize all array elements.

Specifying an array using literal values simply involves providing a comma-separated list of element values enclosed in curly braces:

```
int[] myIntArray = { 5, 9, 10, 2, 99 };
```

Here, `myIntArray` has five elements, each with an assigned integer value.

The other method requires the following syntax:

```
int[] myIntArray = new int[5];
```

Here, you use the `new` keyword to explicitly initialize the array, and a constant value to define the size. This method results in all the array members being assigned a default value, which is 0 for numeric types. You can also use nonconstant variables for this initialization:

```
int[] myIntArray = new int[arraySize];
```

In addition, you can combine these two methods of initialization if you want:

```
int[] myIntArray = new int[5] { 5, 9, 10, 2, 99 };
```

With this method, the sizes *must* match. You can't, for example, write the following:

```
int[] myIntArray = new int[10] { 5, 9, 10, 2, 99 };
```

Here, the array is defined as having 10 members, but only five are defined, so compilation will fail. A side effect of this is that if you define the size using a variable, then that variable must be a constant:

```
const int arraySize = 5;
int[] myIntArray = new int[arraySize] { 5, 9, 10, 2, 99 };
```

If you omit the `const` keyword, this code will fail.

As with other variable types, there is no need to initialize an array on the same line that you declare it. The following is perfectly legal:

```
int[] myIntArray;
myIntArray = new int[5];
```

In the following Try It Out you create and use an array of strings, using the example from the introduction to this section.

TRY IT OUT   Using an Array: Ch05Ex04\Program.cs

1. Create a new Console Application called Ch05Ex04 and save it in the directory
    `C:\BeginningCSharpAndDotNET\Chapter05`.

2. Add the following code to `Program.cs`:

```
static void Main(string[] args)
{
    string[] friendNames = { "Todd Anthony", "Mary Chris",
                             "Autry Rual" };
    int i;
    Console.WriteLine($"Here are {friendNames.Length} of my friends:");
    for (i = 0; i < friendNames.Length; i++)
    {
        Console.WriteLine(friendNames[i]);
    }
    Console.ReadKey();
}
```

3. Execute the code. The result is shown in Figure 5-8.

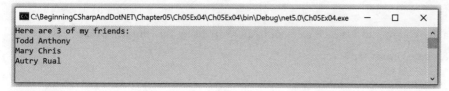

FIGURE 5-8

How It Works

This code sets up a `string` array with three values and lists them in the console in a `for` loop. Note that you have access to the number of elements in the array using `friendNames.Length`:

```
Console.WriteLine($"Here are {friendNames.Length} of my friends:");
```

This is a handy way to get the size of an array. Outputting values in a `for` loop is easy to get wrong. For example, try changing `<` to `<=` as follows:

```
for (i = 0; i <= friendNames.Length; i++)
{
    Console.WriteLine(friendNames[i]);
}
```

Compiling and executing the preceding code results in the dialog box shown in Figure 5-9.

Here, the code attempted to access `friendNames[3]`. Remember that array indices start from 0, so the last element is `friendNames[2]`. If you attempt to access elements outside of the array size, the code will fail. It just so happens that there is a more resilient method of accessing all the members of an array: using `foreach` loops.

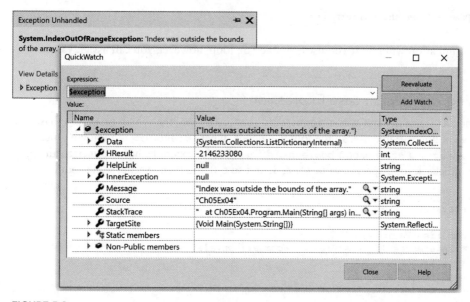

FIGURE 5-9

foreach Loops

A `foreach` loop enables you to address each element in an array using this simple syntax:

```
foreach (<baseType> <name> in <array>)
{
    // can use <name> for each element
}
```

This loop will cycle through each element, placing it in the variable `<name>` in turn, without danger of accessing illegal elements. You do not have to worry about how many elements are in the array, and you can be sure that you'll get to use each one in the loop. Using this approach, you can modify the code in the previous example as follows:

```
static void Main(string[] args)
{
    string[] friendNames = { "Todd Anthony", "Mary Chris",
                             "Autry Rual" };
    Console.WriteLine($"Here are {friendNames.Length} of my friends:");
    foreach (string friendName in friendNames)
    {
        Console.WriteLine(friendName);
    }
    Console.ReadKey();
}
```

The output of this code will be exactly the same as that of the previous Try It Out. The main difference between using this method and a standard `for` loop is that `foreach` gives you *read-only* access to the array contents, so you cannot change the values of any of the elements. You could not, for example, do the following:

```
foreach (string friendName in friendNames)
{
    friendName = "Lea the unicorn";
}
```

If you try this, compilation will fail. If you use a simple `for` loop, however, you can assign values to array elements.

Pattern Matching with switch case Expression

In Chapter 4, the `switch` statement was introduced. In that discussion, the switch cases were based on the value of a specific variable. Recall the following code, where `<testVar>` is a known type, for example an *integer*, a *string*, or a *boolean*. An *integer*, for example, has a numeric value, and the case would check for a specific value (1, 2, 3, and so on) and then execute some code when matched.

```
switch (<testVar>)
{
    case <comparisonVal1>:
        <code to execute if <testVar> == <comparisonVal1> >
        break;
    case <comparisonVal2>:
        <code to execute if <testVar> == <comparisonVal2> >
        break;
    ...
```

```
        case <comparisonValN>:
          <code to execute if <testVar> == <comparisonValN> >
          break;
        default:
          <code to execute if <testVar> != comparisonVals>
          break;
    }
```

It is also possible to match patterns in a switch case based on the type of variable, for example a *string* or *integer* array. Once you know the type, you can access methods and properties exposed by that type. Take the following switch structure:

```
    switch (<testVar>)
    {
        case int value:
          <code to execute if <testVar> is an int >
          break;
        case string s when s.Length == 0:
          <code to execute if <testVar> is a string with a length = 0 >
          break;
        ...
        case null:
          <code to execute if <testVar> == null >
          break;
        default:
          <code to execute if <testVar> != comparisonVals>
          break;
    }
```

Directly after the case keyword is the variable type you want to check for (*string*, *int*, and so on). The value of that type when there is a case match, is placed into the declared variable. For example, if <testVar> is an *integer* the value of the *integer* is stored in the variable called value. Next, notice the when keyword modifier—which is often referred to as an *filter expression* (discussed further in Chapter 7)—has been applied to the *switch case* expressions. The when keyword modifier lets you expand out or add additional conditions required to execute the code found within the case statement.

The following Try It Out covers what was just explained in more detail, plus a few additional concepts.

TRY IT OUT Using an Array: Ch05Ex05\Program.cs

1. Create a new Console Application called Ch05Ex05 and save it in the directory
    C:\BeginningCSharpAndDotNET\Chapter05.

2. Add the following code to Program.cs:

```
    static void Main(string[] args)
    {
      string[] friendNames = { "Todd Anthony", "Mary Chris",
                               "Autry Rual", null, "" };
      foreach (var friendName in friendNames)
      {
```

```
switch (friendName)
{
  case string t when t.StartsWith("T"):
    Console.WriteLine("This friends name starts with a 'T': " +
      $"{friendName} and is {t.Length - 1} letters long ");
    break;
  case string e when e.Length == 0:
    Console.WriteLine("There is a string in the array with no value");
    break;
  case null:
    Console.WriteLine("There was a 'null' value in the array");
    break;
  case var x:
    Console.WriteLine("This is the var pattern of type: " +
            $"{x.GetType().Name}");
    break;
  default:
    break;
  }
}

int sum = 0, total = 0, counter = 0, intValue = 0;
int?[] myIntArray = new int?[7] { 5, intValue, 9, 10, null, 2, 99 };
foreach (var integer in myIntArray)
{
 switch (integer)
 {
   case 0:
    Console.WriteLine($"Integer number '{ counter }' has a default value of 0");
     counter++;
     break;
   case int value:
     sum += value;
     Console.WriteLine($"Integer number '{ counter }' has a value of {value}");
     counter++;
     break;
   case null:
     Console.WriteLine($"Integer number '{ counter }' is null");
     counter++;
     break;
   default:
     break;
  }
 }
 Console.WriteLine($"The sum of all {counter} integers is {sum}");
 Console.ReadLine();
}
```

3. Execute the code. The result is shown in Figure 5-10.

```
C:\BeginningCSharpAndDotNET\Chapter05\Ch05Ex05\Ch05Ex05\bin\Debug\net5.0\Ch05Ex05.exe          —    □    ×
This friends name starts with a 'T': Todd Anthony and is 11 letters long
This is the var pattern of type: String
This is the var pattern of type: String
There was a 'null' value in the array
There is a string in the array with no value
Integer number '0' has a value of 5
Integer number '1' has a default value of 0
Integer number '2' has a value of 9
Integer number '3' has a value of 10
Integer number '4' is null
Integer number '5' has a value of 2
Integer number '6' has a value of 99
The sum of all 7 is 125
```

FIGURE 5-10

How It Works

In this Try It Out there are two `foreach` loops: one iterates through a `string[]` array and the other through an `int[]` array. The `foreach` loop that processes the `string[]` array purposely contains a `null` and an entry with no value for describing the concept of pattern patching in more detail:

```
string[] friendNames = { "Todd Anthony", "Mary Chris",
                         "Autry Rual", null, "" };
```

Within the `switch` expression there are four cases being checked:

```
case string t when t.StartsWith("T")
```

The most obvious difference you see, when comparing non–pattern patching `switch` statements with this example, is that instead of switching on a specific value, like 1, 2, or "Beginning C# Rocks," a type declaration of a `string` named t is provided directly after `case`. Once declared, t can be used to access the value stored in `friendName` and the methods and properties available from the `string` type. Notice that the method `StartsWith()` exposed via the `System.String` class is utilized after the `when` expression filter. The `StartsWith()` method accepts one parameter and if the string value contained in `friendName` begins with that parameter, in this example `"T"`, then the `case` is matched and the code for the case is executed.

The next `switch case` expression checks for an empty `string`:

```
case string e when e.Length == 0
```

Again, the `string` declaration named e references the `Length` property of the `System.String` class. If the length is equal to 0, then the code for that case is executed. The following code snippet is a `case` expression checking if the value in `friendName` is `null`:

```
case null
```

Finally, the following code snippet is an example of using the `var` declaration of x to capture any other variable type. We know all the elements in this array are strings, but in some other implementation this could be an array of unknown objects. Then, using the GetType() method of the System.Object class via x, we can see what type it is.

```
case var x
```

This expression raises a key point for the pattern matching feature in that the order of case expressions now matters. Had you placed the case var x expression at the top of the switch, it would catch all of the string or everything in the string[]. But do not worry, if you do this the compiler will complain and notify you that "the switch case has already been handled by a previous case." Keep in mind that now that you have this pattern matching capability, the expression filters need to be as precise as possible and should be unique within the switch statement.

The int[] array has a few points to drill down into as well:

```
int?[] myIntArray = new int?[7] { 5, intValue, 9, 10, null, 2, 99 };
```

First, notice that there is a question mark (?) directly after the int declaration. The question mark lets the compiler know that this int[] array can contain null objects; without it, a compile exception is displayed. Next, it is common to set an int with a default value of 0 when it is initialized. If you write a *switch case* expression where you expect integers, it should contain a check for that case specifically and handle that scenario appropriately:

```
case 0
```

If the check for 0 does not exist, then it would fall into the next case:

```
case int value:
    sum += value;
```

Adding a value of 0 to the sum does not result in a change in the value, which is what the code would do without the case 0 expression. Review the code and you see that only integers with a value other than 0 and null are added to the sum and counter. All iterations result in total being incremented by 1. You would not know, without coding for it, whether 0 is the actual value or if it was simply a default initialization added to the array. The case 0 gives you the opportunity to execute code to verify that.

The following code snippet illustrates a case expression checking if the value in value is null:

```
case null
```

In addition to the switch case expression pattern, pattern matching can be implemented using the is keyword. This keyword is not introduced until Chapter 11, which is where you learn how to implement pattern matching using is.

Multidimensional Arrays

A multidimensional array is simply one that uses multiple indices to access its elements. For example, suppose you want to plot the height of a hill against the position measured. You might specify a position using two coordinates, x and y. You want to use these two coordinates as indices, such that an array called hillHeight would store the height at each pair of coordinates. This involves using multidimensional arrays.

A two-dimensional array such as this is declared as follows:

```
<baseType>[,] <name>;
```

Arrays of more dimensions simply require more commas:

```
<baseType>[,,,] <name>;
```

This would declare a four-dimensional array. Assigning values also uses a similar syntax, with commas separating sizes. Declaring and initializing the two-dimensional array `hillHeight`, with a base type of `double`, an x size of 3, and a y size of 4 requires the following:

```
double[,] hillHeight = new double[3,4];
```

Alternatively, you can use literal values for initial assignment. Here, you use nested blocks of curly braces, separated by commas:

```
double[,] hillHeight = { { 1, 2, 3, 4 }, { 2, 3, 4, 5 }, { 3, 4, 5, 6 } };
```

This array has the same dimensions as the previous one—that is, three rows and four columns. By providing literal values, these dimensions are defined implicitly.

To access individual elements of a multidimensional array, you simply specify the indices separated by commas:

```
hillHeight[2,1]
```

You can then manipulate this element just as you can other elements. This expression will access the second element of the third nested array as defined previously (the value will be 4). Remember that you start counting from 0 and that the first number is the nested array. In other words, the first number specifies the pair of curly braces, and the second number specifies the element within that pair of braces. You can represent this array visually, as shown in Figure 5-11.

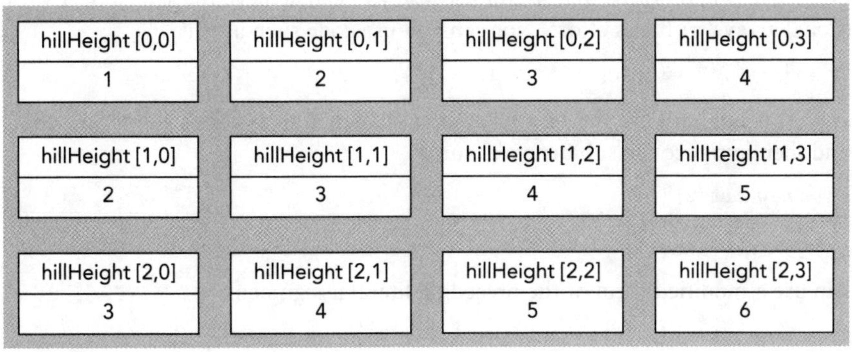

hillHeight [0,0]	hillHeight [0,1]	hillHeight [0,2]	hillHeight [0,3]
1	2	3	4

hillHeight [1,0]	hillHeight [1,1]	hillHeight [1,2]	hillHeight [1,3]
2	3	4	5

hillHeight [2,0]	hillHeight [2,1]	hillHeight [2,2]	hillHeight [2,3]
3	4	5	6

FIGURE 5-11

The `foreach` loop gives you access to all elements in a multidimensional way, just as with single-dimensional arrays:

```
double[,] hillHeight = { { 1, 2, 3, 4 }, { 2, 3, 4, 5 }, { 3, 4, 5, 6 } };
foreach (double height in hillHeight)
{
    Console.WriteLine($"{height}");
}
```

The order in which the elements are output is the same as the order used to assign literal values. This sequence is as follows (the element identifiers are shown here rather than the actual values):

```
hillHeight[0,0]
hillHeight[0,1]
hillHeight[0,2]
hillHeight[0,3]
hillHeight[1,0]
hillHeight[1,1]
hillHeight[1,2]
...
```

Arrays of Arrays

Multidimensional arrays, as discussed in the preceding section, are said to be *rectangular* because each "row" is the same size. Using the previous example, you can have a y coordinate of 0 to 3 for any of the possible x coordinates.

It is also possible to have *jagged* arrays, whereby "rows" may be varied sizes. For this, you need an array in which each element is another array. You could also have arrays of arrays of arrays, or even more complex situations. However, all this is possible only if the arrays have the same base type.

The syntax for declaring arrays of arrays involves specifying multiple sets of square brackets in the declaration of the array, as shown here:

```
int[][] jaggedIntArray;
```

Unfortunately, initializing arrays such as this isn't as simple as initializing multidimensional arrays. You cannot, for example, follow the preceding declaration with this:

```
jaggedIntArray = new int[3][4];
```

Even if you could do this, it would not be that useful because you can achieve the same effect with simple multidimensional arrays with less effort. Nor can you use code such as this:

```
jaggedIntArray = { { 1, 2, 3 }, { 1 }, { 1, 2 } };
```

You have two options. You can initialize the array that contains other arrays (let's call these sub-arrays for clarity) and then initialize the sub-arrays in turn:

```
jaggedIntArray = new int[2][];
jaggedIntArray[0] = new int[3];
jaggedIntArray[1] = new int[4];
```

Alternatively, you can use a modified form of the preceding literal assignment:

```
jaggedIntArray = new int[3][] { new int[] { 1, 2, 3 }, new int[] { 1 },
                                new int[] { 1, 2 } };
```

This can be simplified if the array is initialized on the same line as it is declared, as follows:

```
int[][] jaggedIntArray = { new int[] { 1, 2, 3 }, new int[] { 1 },
                           new int[] { 1, 2 } };
```

You can use `foreach` loops with jagged arrays, but you often need to nest these to get to the actual data. For example, suppose you have the following jagged array that contains 10 arrays, each of which contains an array of integers that are divisors of an integer between 1 and 10:

```
int[][] divisors1To10 = { new int[] { 1 },
                          new int[] { 1, 2 },
                          new int[] { 1, 3 },
                          new int[] { 1, 2, 4 },
                          new int[] { 1, 5 },
                          new int[] { 1, 2, 3, 6 },
                          new int[] { 1, 7 },
                          new int[] { 1, 2, 4, 8 },
                          new int[] { 1, 3, 9 },
                          new int[] { 1, 2, 5, 10 } };
```

The following code will fail:

```
foreach (int divisor in divisors1To10)
{
    Console.WriteLine(divisor);
}
```

The failure occurs because the array `divisors1To10` contains `int[]` elements, not `int` elements. Instead, you must loop through every sub-array, as well as through the array itself:

```
foreach (int[] divisorsOfInt in divisors1To10)
{
    foreach(int divisor in divisorsOfInt)
    {
        Console.WriteLine(divisor);
    }
}
```

As you can see, the syntax for using jagged arrays can quickly become complex! In most cases, it is easier to use rectangular arrays or a simpler storage method. Nonetheless, there may well be situations in which you are forced to use this method, and a working knowledge cannot hurt. An example of this happens when working with XML documents where some elements have sub-children and other do not.

STRING MANIPULATION

Your use of strings so far has consisted of writing strings to the console, reading strings from the console, and concatenating strings using the + operator. While programming more interesting applications, you will discover that manipulating strings is something that you end up doing *a lot*. Therefore, it is worth spending a few pages looking at some of the more common string-manipulation techniques available in C#.

To start with, a `string` type variable can be treated as a read-only array of `char` variables. This means that you can access individual characters using syntax like the following:

```
string myString = "A string";
char myChar = myString[1];
```

However, you can't assign individual characters this way. To get a `char` array that you can write to, you can use the following code. This uses the `ToCharArray()` command of the array variable:

```
string myString = "A string";
char[] myChars = myString.ToCharArray();
```

Then you can manipulate the `char` array the standard way. You can also use strings in `foreach` loops, as shown here:

```
foreach (char character in myString)
{
    Console.WriteLine($"{character}");
}
```

As with arrays, you can also get the number of elements using `myString.Length`. This gives you the number of characters in the string:

```
string myString = Console.ReadLine();
Console.WriteLine($"You typed {myString.Length} characters.");
```

Other basic string-manipulation techniques use commands with a format similar to this *<string>* `.ToCharArray()` command. Two simple, but useful, ones are *<string>*`.ToLower()` and *<string>* `.ToUpper()`. These enable strings to be converted into lowercase and uppercase, respectively. To see why this is useful, consider the situation in which you want to check for a specific response from a user—for example, the string `yes`. If you convert the string entered by the user into lowercase, then you can also check for the strings `YES`, `Yes`, `yeS`, and so on—you saw an example of this in the previous chapter:

```
string userResponse = Console.ReadLine();
if (userResponse.ToLower() == "yes")
{
    // Act on response.
}
```

This command, like the others in this section, does not actually change the string to which it is applied. Instead, combining this command with a string results in the creation of a new string, which you can compare to another string (as shown here) or assign to another variable. The other variable may be the same one that is being operated on:

```
userResponse = userResponse.ToLower();
```

This is an important point to remember, because just writing

```
userResponse.ToLower();
```

does not actually achieve very much!

There are other things you can do to ease the interpretation of user input. What if the user accidentally puts an extra space at the beginning or end of the input? In this case, the preceding code will not work. You need to trim the string entered, which you can do using the *<string>*`.Trim()` command:

```
string userResponse = Console.ReadLine();
userResponse = userResponse.Trim();
if (userResponse.ToLower() == "yes")
{
    // Act on response.
}
```

The preceding code is also able to detect strings like this:

```
" YES"
"Yes "
```

You can also use these commands to remove any other characters, by specifying them in a char array, for example:

```
char[] trimChars = {' ', 'e', 's'};
string userResponse = Console.ReadLine();
userResponse = userResponse.ToLower();
userResponse = userResponse.Trim(trimChars);
if (userResponse == "y")
{
    // Act on response.
}
```

This eliminates any occurrences of spaces, as well as the letters "e" and "s", from the beginning or end of your string. Provided there are not any other characters in the string, this will result in the detection of strings such as

```
"Yeeeees"
" y"
```

and so on.

You can also use the `<string>.TrimStart()` and `<string>.TrimEnd()` commands, which will trim spaces from the beginning and end of a string, respectively. These can also have char arrays specified.

You can use two other string commands to manipulate the spacing of strings: `<string>.PadLeft()` and `<string>.PadRight()`. They enable you to add spaces to the left or right of a string to force it to the desired length. You use them as follows:

```
<string>.PadX(<desiredLength>);
```

Here is an example:

```
myString = "Aligned";
myString = myString.PadLeft(10);
```

This would result in three spaces being added to the left of the word `Aligned` in `myString`. These methods can be helpful when aligning strings in columns, which is particularly useful for positioning strings containing numbers.

As with the trimming commands, you can also use these commands in a second way, by supplying the character to pad the string with. This involves a single char, not an array of chars as with trimming:

```
myString = "Aligned";
myString = myString.PadLeft(10, '-');
```

This would add three dashes to the start of `myString`.

There are many more of these string-manipulation commands, many of which are only useful in very specific situations. These are discussed as you use them in the forthcoming chapters. Before moving on, though, it is worth looking at one of the features contained in Visual Studio 2017 that you may have noticed over the course of the last few chapters, and especially this one. In the following Try It Out, you examine auto-completion, whereby the IDE tries to help you out by suggesting what code you might like to insert.

TRY IT OUT   Statement Auto-Completion in Visual Studio: Ch05Ex06\Program.cs

1. Create a new Console Application called Ch05Ex06 and save it in the directory
   `C:\BeginningCSharpAndDotNET\Chapter05`.

2. Type the following code into `Program.cs`, exactly as written, noting windows that pop up as
   you do so:

```
static void Main(string[] args)
{
    string myString = "This is a test.";
    char[] separator = {' '};
    string[] myWords;
    myWords = myString.
}
```

3. As you type the final period, the window shown in Figure 5-12 appears.

FIGURE 5-12

4. Notice the star next to the `Split` member in Figure 5-12. The member pop-up list uses artificial
   intelligence (AI) to guess the most likely option to be used in this scenario, in this case `Split`. When
   this feature is not present, an alphabetical list is presented, which would then require you to manually find the required member from the list. The pop-up window changes, and the Tooltip shown in
   Figure 5-13 appears.

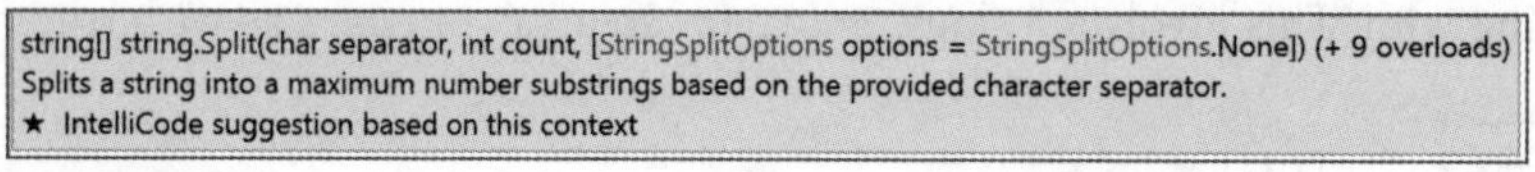

string[] string.Split(char separator, int count, [StringSplitOptions options = StringSplitOptions.None]) (+ 9 overloads)
Splits a string into a maximum number substrings based on the provided character separator.
★ IntelliCode suggestion based on this context

FIGURE 5-13

5. Type the following characters: **(se.** Another pop-up window and Tooltip appears, as shown in
   Figure 5-14.

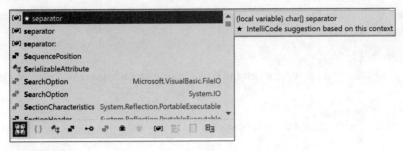

FIGURE 5-14

6. Then, type these two characters:) ;. The code should look as follows, and the pop-up windows should disappear:

```
static void Main(string[] args)
{
    string myString = "This is a test.";
    char[] separator = {' '};
    string[] myWords;
    myWords = myString.Split(separator);
}
```

7. Add the following code, noting the windows as they pop up:

```
static void Main(string[] args)
{
    string myString = "This is a test.";
    char[] separator = {' '};
    string[] myWords;
    myWords = myString.Split(separator);
    foreach (string word in myWords)
    {
        Console.WriteLine($"{word}");
    }
    Console.ReadKey();
}
```

8. Execute the code. The result is shown in Figure 5-15.

FIGURE 5-15

How It Works

Two main aspects of this code are the new string command used and the use of the auto-completion functionality. The command, `<string>.Split()`, converts a `string` into a `string` array by splitting it at the points specified. These points take the form of a `char` array, which in this case is simply populated by a single element, the space character:

```
char[] separator = {' '};
```

The following code obtains the substrings you get when the string is split at each space—that is, you get an array of individual words:

```
string[] myWords;
myWords = myString.Split(separator);
```

Next, you loop through the words in this array using `foreach` and write each one to the console:

```
foreach (string word in myWords)
{
    Console.WriteLine($"{word}");
}
```

> **NOTE** Each word obtained has no spaces, either embedded in the word or at either end. The separators are removed when you use `Split()`.

EXERCISES

5.1 Which of the following conversions can't be performed implicitly?

    a. `int` to `short`

    b. `short` to `int`

    c. `bool` to `string`

    d. `byte` to `float`

5.2 Show the code for a `color` enumeration based on the `short` type containing the colors of the rainbow plus black and white. Can this enumeration be based on the `byte` type?

5.3 Will the following code compile? Why or why not?

```
string[] blab = new string[5]
blab[5] = 5th string.
```

5.4 Write a console application that accepts a string from the user and outputs a string with the characters in reverse order.

5.5 Write a console application that accepts a string and replaces all occurrences of the string no with yes.

5.6 Write a console application that places double quotes around each word in a string.

Answers to the exercises can be found in the Appendix.

► **WHAT YOU LEARNED IN THIS CHAPTER**

TOPIC	KEY CONCEPT
Type conversion	You can convert values from one type into another, but there are rules that apply when you do so. Implicit conversion happens automatically, but only when all possible values of the source value type are available in the target value type. Explicit conversion is also possible, but you run the risk of values not being assigned as expected, or even causing errors.
Enumerations	Enums, or enumerations, are types that have a discrete set of values, each of which has a name. Enums are defined with the `enum` keyword. This makes them easy to understand in code because they are very readable. Enums have an underlying numeric type (`int` by default), and you can use this property of enum values to convert between enum values and numeric values.
Structs	Structs, or structures, are types that contain several different values at the same time. Structs are defined with the `struct` keyword. The values contained in a struct each have a name and a type; there is no requirement that every value stored in a struct is the same type.
Arrays	An array is a collection of values of the same type. Arrays have a fixed size, or length, which determines how many values they can contain. You can define multidimensional or jagged arrays to hold different amounts and shapes of data. You can also iterate through the values in an array with a `foreach` loop.

Functions

WHAT YOU WILL LEARN IN THIS CHAPTER

➤ Defining and using simple functions that don't accept or return any data

➤ Transferring data to and from functions

➤ Working with variable scope

➤ Using command-line arguments with the `Main()` function

➤ Supplying functions as members of struct types

➤ Using function overloading

➤ Using delegates

CODE DOWNLOADS FOR THIS CHAPTER

The code downloads for this chapter are found on the book page at www.wiley.com. Click the Downloads link. The code can also be found at github.com/benperk/BeginningCSharp-AndDotNET. The code is in the Chapter06 folder and individually named according to the names throughout the chapter.

All the code you have seen so far has taken the form of a single block, perhaps with some looping to repeat lines of code, and branching to execute statements conditionally. Performing an operation on your data has meant placing the code required right where you want it to work.

This kind of code structure is limited. Often, some tasks—such as finding the highest value in an array, for example—might need to be performed at several points in a program. You can place identical (or nearly identical) sections of code in your application whenever necessary, but this has its own problems. Changing even one minor detail concerning a common task (to correct a code error, for example) can require changes to multiple sections of code, which can be spread throughout the application. Missing one of these can have dramatic consequences and cause the whole application to fail. In addition, the application can get very lengthy.

The solution to this problem is to use *functions*. Functions in C# are a means of providing blocks of code that can be executed at any point in an application.

> **NOTE** *Functions of the specific type examined in this chapter are known as methods, but this term has a very specific meaning in .NET programming that will only become clear later in this book. Therefore, for now, the term "method" will not be used.*

For example, you could have a function that calculates the maximum value in an array. You can use the function from any point in your code, and use the same lines of code in each case. Because you need to supply this code only once, any changes you make to it will affect this calculation wherever it is used. The function can be thought of as containing *reusable* code.

Functions also have the advantage of making your code more readable, as you can use them to group related code together. This way, your application body can be very short, as the inner workings of the code are separated out. This is similar to the way in which you can collapse regions of code together in Visual Studio by expanding and contracting the objects in the Solution Explorer window. Doing so gives your application a more logical structure.

Functions can also be used to create multipurpose code, enabling them to perform the same operations on varying data. You can supply a function with information to work within the form of arguments, and you can obtain results from functions in the form of return values. In the preceding example, you could supply an array to search as an argument and obtain the maximum value in the array as a return value. This means that you can use the same function to work with a different array each time. A function definition consists of a name, a return type, and a list of parameters that specify the number and type of arguments that the function requires. The name and parameters of a function (but not its return type) collectively define the *signature* of a function.

DEFINING AND USING FUNCTIONS

This section describes how you can add functions to your applications and then use (call) them from your code. Starting with the basics, you will look at simple functions that do not exchange any data with code that calls them, and then look at more advanced function usage. The following Try It Out gets things moving.

TRY IT OUT   Defining and Using a Basic Function: Ch06Ex01\Program.cs

1.   Create a new Console Application called Ch06Ex01 and save it in the directory
     `C:\BeginningCSharpAndDotNET\Chapter06`.

2.   Add the following code to `Program.cs`:

```
class Program
{
    static void Write()
    {
        Console.WriteLine("Text output from function.");
    }
    static void Main(string[] args)
    {
        Write();
        Console.ReadKey();
    }
}
```

3.   Execute the code. The result is shown in Figure 6-1.

C:\BeginningCSharpAndDotNET\Chapter06\Ch06Ex01\Ch06Ex01\bin\Debug\net5.0\Ch06Ex01.exe — □ ×

Text output from function.

FIGURE 6-1

How It Works

The following four lines of your code define a function called `Write()`:

```
static void Write()
{
    Console.WriteLine("Text output from function.");
}
```

The code contained here simply outputs some text to the console window, but this behavior is not that important at the moment because the focus here is on the mechanisms behind function definition and use.

The function definition consists of the following:

➤   Two keywords: `static` and `void`
➤   A function name followed by parentheses: `Write()`
➤   A block of code to execute, enclosed in curly braces

NOTE *Function names are usually written in PascalCase, where you join words together capitalizing the first letter in each word.*

The code that defines the `Write()` *function looks very similar to some of the other code in your application:*

```
static void Main(string[] args)
{
    ...
}
```

That is because all the code you have written so far (apart from type definitions) has been part of a function. This function, `Main()`, *is the entry point function for a console application. When a C# application is executed, the entry point function it contains is called; and when that function is completed, the application terminates. All C# executable applications must have an entry point.*

The only difference between the `Main()` *function and your* `Write()` *function (apart from the lines of code they contain) is that there is some code inside the parentheses after the function name* `Main`. *This is how you specify parameters, which you will see in more detail shortly.*

Both `Main()` *and* `Write()` *are defined using the* `static` *and* `void` *keywords. The* `static` *keyword relates to object-oriented concepts, which you will come back to later in the book. For now, you only need to remember that all the functions you use in your applications in this section of the book must use this keyword.*

By contrast, `void` *is much simpler to explain. It is used to indicate that the function does not return a value. Later in this chapter, you will see the code that you need to use when a function has a return value.*

Moving on, the code that calls your function is as follows:

```
Write();
```

You simply type the name of the function followed by empty parentheses. When program execution reaches this point, the code in the `Write()` *function runs.*

NOTE *The parentheses used both in the function definition and where the function is called are mandatory. Try removing them if you like—the code won't compile.*

Return Values

The simplest way to exchange data with a function is to use a return value. Functions that have return values *evaluate* to that value exactly the same way that variables evaluate to the values they contain when you use them in expressions. Just like variables, return values have a type.

For example, you might have a function called GetString() whose return value is a string. You could use this in code, such as the following:

```
string myString;
myString = GetString();
```

Alternatively, you might have a function called GetVal() that returns a double value, which you could use in a mathematical expression:

```
double myVal;
double multiplier = 5.3;
myVal = GetVal() * multiplier;
```

When a function returns a value, you must modify your function in two ways:

➤ Specify the type of the return value in the function declaration instead of using the void keyword.

➤ Use the return keyword to end the function execution and transfer the return value to the calling code.

In code terms, this looks like the following in a console application function of the type you have been looking at:

```
static <returnType> <FunctionName>()
{
    ...
    return <returnValue>;
}
```

The only limitation here is that <returnValue> must be a value that either is of type <returnType> or can be implicitly converted to that type. However, <returnType> can be any type you want, including the more complicated types you've seen. This might be as simple as the following:

```
static double GetVal()
{
    return 3.2;
}
```

However, return values are usually the result of some processing carried out by the function; the preceding could be achieved just as easily using a const variable.

When the return statement is reached, program execution returns to the calling code immediately. No lines of code after this statement are executed, although this does not mean that return statements can only be placed on the last line of a function body. You can use return earlier in the code, perhaps after performing some branching logic. Placing `return` in a `for` loop, an `if` block, or any other structure causes the structure to terminate immediately and the function to terminate:

```
static double GetVal()
{
    double checkVal;
    // checkVal assigned a value through some logic (not shown here).
    if (checkVal < 5)
        return 4.7;
    return 3.2;
}
```

Here, one of two values is returned, depending on the value of `checkVal`. The only restriction in this case is that a `return` statement must be processed before reaching the closing } of the function. The following is illegal:

```
static double GetVal()
{
    double checkVal;
    // checkVal assigned a value through some logic.
    if (checkVal < 5)
        return 4.7;
}
```

If `checkVal` is `>= 5`, then no `return` statement is met, which is not allowed. All processing paths must reach a `return` statement. In most cases, the compiler detects this and gives you the error "not all code paths return a value."

Functions that execute a single line of code can use a feature called expression-bodied methods. The following function pattern uses a `=>` (lambda arrow) to implement this feature:

```
static <returnType> <FunctionName>() => <myVal1 * myVal2>;
```

For example, consider a `Multiply()` function, which can be written in either format:

```
static double Multiply(double myVal1, double myVal2)
{
    return myVal1 * myVal2;
}
```

It can also be written using the `=>` (lambda arrow). The result of the code written here expresses the intent of the function in a much simpler and consolidated way:

```
static double Multiply(double myVal1, double myVal2) => mVal1 * MyVal2;
```

Parameters

When a function needs to accept parameters, you must specify the following:

➤ A list of the parameters accepted by the function in its definition, along with the types of those parameters

➤ A matching list of arguments in each function call

> **NOTE** *Careful reading of the C# specification shows a subtle distinction between parameters and arguments. Parameters are defined as part of a function definition, whereas arguments are passed to a function by calling code. However, these terms are often used interchangeably, and nobody seems to get too upset about that.*

This involves the following code, where you can have any number of parameters, each with a type and a name:

```
static <returnType> <FunctionName>(<paramType> <paramName>, ...)
{
    ...
    return <returnValue>;
}
```

The parameters are separated using commas, and each of these parameters is accessible from code within the function as a variable. For example, a simple function might take two `double` parameters and return their product:

```
static double Product(double param1, double param2)
{
    ...
    return param1 * param2;
}
```

or

```
static double Product(double param1, double param2) => param1 * param2;
```

The following Try It Out provides a more complex example.

TRY IT OUT   Exchanging Data with a Function (Part 1): Ch06Ex02\Program.cs

1. Create a new Console Application called Ch06Ex02 and save it in the directory `C:\BeginningCSharpAndDotNET\Chapter06`.

2. Add the following code to `Program.cs`:

```
class Program
{
    static int MaxValue(int[] intArray)
    {
        int maxVal = intArray[0];
        for (int i = 1; i < intArray.Length; i++)
        {
            if (intArray[i] > maxVal)
                maxVal = intArray[i];
        }
        return maxVal;
    }
```

```
static void Main(string[] args)
{
    int[] myArray = { 1, 8, 3, 6, 2, 5, 9, 3, 0, 2 };
    int maxVal = MaxValue(myArray);
    Console.WriteLine($"The maximum value in myArray is {maxVal}");
    Console.ReadKey();
}
}
```

3. Execute the code. The result is shown in Figure 6-2.

FIGURE 6-2

How It Works

This code contains a function that does what the example function at the beginning of this chapter hoped to do. It accepts an array of integers as a parameter and returns the highest number in the array. The function definition is as follows:

```
static int MaxValue(int[] intArray)
{
    int maxVal = intArray[0];
    for (int i = 1; i < intArray.Length; i++)
    {
        if (intArray[i] > maxVal)
            maxVal = intArray[i];
    }
    return maxVal;
}
```

The function, MaxValue(), has a single parameter defined, which is an int array called intArray. It also has a return type of int. The calculation of the maximum value is simple. A local integer variable called maxVal is initialized to the first value in the array, and then this value is compared with each of the subsequent elements in the array. If an element contains a higher value than maxVal, then this value replaces the current value of maxVal. When the loop finishes, maxVal contains the highest value in the array and is returned using the return statement.

The code in Main() declares and initializes a simple integer array to use with the MaxValue() function:

```
int[] myArray = { 1, 8, 3, 6, 2, 5, 9, 3, 0, 2 };
```

The call to MaxValue() is used to assign a value to the int variable maxVal:

```
int maxVal = MaxValue(myArray);
```

Next, you write that value to the screen using WriteLine():

```
Console.WriteLine($"The maximum value in myArray is {maxVal}");
```

Parameter Matching

When you call a function, you must supply arguments that match the parameters as specified in the function definition. This means matching the parameter types, the number of parameters, and the order of the parameters. For example, the function

```
static void MyFunction(string myString, double myDouble)
{
   ...
}
```

cannot be called using the following:

```
MyFunction(2.6, "Hello");
```

Here, you are attempting to pass a double value as the first argument and a string value as the second argument, which is not the order in which the parameters are defined in the function definition. The code will not compile because the parameter type is wrong. In the "Overloading Functions" section later in this chapter, you will learn a useful technique for getting around this problem.

Parameter Arrays

C# enables you to specify one (and only one) special parameter for a function. This parameter, which must be the last parameter in the function definition, is known as a *parameter array*. Parameter arrays enable you to call functions using a variable number of parameters, and they are defined using the params keyword.

Parameter arrays can be a useful way to simplify your code because you do not have to pass arrays from your calling code. Instead, you pass several arguments of the same type, which are placed in an array you can use from within your function.

The following code is required to define a function that uses a parameter array:

```
static <returnType> <FunctionName>(<p1Type> <p1Name>, ...,
                                   params <type>[] <name>)
{
   ...
   return <returnValue>;
}
```

You can call this function using code like the following:

```
<FunctionName>(<p1>, ..., <val1>, <val2>, ...)
```

<val1>, <val2>, and so on are values of type <type>, which are used to initialize the <name> array. The number of arguments that you can specify here is almost limitless; the only restriction is that they must all be of type <type>. You can even specify no arguments at all.

The following Try It Out defines and uses a function with a params type parameter.

Exchanging Data with a Function (Part 2): Ch06Ex03\Program.cs

1. Create a new Console Application called Ch06Ex03 and save it in the directory
    `C:\\BeginningCSharpAndDotNET\Chapter06`.

2. Add the following code to `Program.cs`:

    ```
    class Program
    {
        static int SumVals(params int[] vals)
        {
            int sum = 0;
            foreach (int val in vals)
            {
                sum += val;
            }
            return sum;
        }
        static void Main(string[] args)
        {
            int sum = SumVals(1, 5, 2, 9, 8);
            Console.WriteLine($"Summed Values = {sum}");
            Console.ReadKey();
        }
    }
    ```

3. Execute the code. The result is shown in Figure 6-3.

```
C:\BeginningCSharpAndDotNET\Chapter06\Ch06Ex03\Ch06Ex03\bin\Debug\net5.0\Ch06Ex03.exe    —    ☐    ✕
Summed Values = 25
```

FIGURE 6-3

How It Works

The function `SumVals()` is defined using the `params` keyword to accept any number of `int` arguments
(and no others):

```
static int SumVals(params int[] vals)
{
    ...
}
```

The code in this function simply iterates through the values in the `vals` array and adds the values
together, returning the result.

In `Main()`, you call `SumVals()` with five integer arguments:

```
int sum = SumVals(1, 5, 2, 9, 8);
```

You could just as easily call this function with none, one, two, or 100 integer arguments—there is no limit to the number you can specify.

> **NOTE** *C# includes alternative ways to specify function parameters, including a far more readable way to include optional parameters. You will learn about these methods in Chapter 13, which looks at the C# language.*

Reference and Value Parameters

All the functions defined so far in this chapter have had value parameters. That is, when you have used parameters, you have passed a value into a variable used by the function. Any changes made to this variable in the function have no effect on the argument specified in the function call. For example, consider a function that doubles and displays the value of a passed parameter:

```
static void ShowDouble(int val)
{
    val *= 2;
    Console.WriteLine($"val doubled = {val}");
}
```

Here, the parameter, `val`, is doubled in this function. If you call it like this,

```
int myNumber = 5;
Console.WriteLine($"myNumber = {myNumber}");
ShowDouble(myNumber);
Console.WriteLine($"myNumber = {myNumber}");
```

then the text output to the console is as follows:

```
myNumber = 5
val doubled = 10
myNumber = 5
```

Calling `ShowDouble()` with `myNumber` as an argument does not affect the value of `myNumber` in `Main()`, even though the parameter it is assigned to, `val`, is doubled.

That is all very well, but if you *want* the value of `myNumber` to change, you have a problem. You could use a function that returns a new value for `myNumber`, like this:

```
static int DoubleNum(int val)
{
    val *= 2;
    return val;
}
```

You could call this function using the following:

```
int myNumber = 5;
Console.WriteLine($"myNumber = {myNumber}");
myNumber = DoubleNum(myNumber);
Console.WriteLine($"myNumber = {myNumber}");
```

However, this code is hardly intuitive and will not cope with changing the values of multiple variables used as arguments (as functions have only one return value).

Instead, you want to pass the parameter by *reference*, which means that the function will work with exactly the same variable as the one used in the function call, not just a variable that has the same value. Any changes made to this variable will, therefore, be reflected in the value of the variable used as an argument. To do this, you simply use the `ref` keyword to specify the parameter:

```
static void ShowDouble(ref int val)
{
    val *= 2;
    Console.WriteLine($"val doubled = {val}");
}
```

Then, specify it again in the function call (this is mandatory):

```
int myNumber = 5;
Console.WriteLine($"myNumber = {myNumber}");
ShowDouble(ref myNumber);
Console.WriteLine($"myNumber = {myNumber}");
```

The text output to the console is now as follows:

```
myNumber = 5
val doubled = 10
myNumber = 10
```

Note two limitations on the variable used as a `ref` parameter. First, the function might result in a change to the value of a reference parameter, so you must use a *nonconstant* variable in the function call. The following is therefore illegal:

```
const int myNumber = 5;
Console.WriteLine($"myNumber = {myNumber}");
ShowDouble(ref myNumber);
Console.WriteLine($"myNumber = {myNumber}");
```

Second, you must use an initialized variable. C# does not allow you to assume that a `ref` parameter will be initialized in the function that uses it. The following code is also illegal:

```
int myNumber;
ShowDouble(ref myNumber);
Console.WriteLine("myNumber = {myNumber}");
```

Up to now you have seen the `ref` keyword only applied to function parameters, but it is also possible to apply it to both local variables and returns. Here, `myNumberRef` references my `myNumber`, and changing my `myNumberRef` results in a change to `myNumber`. If the value of both `myNumber` and `myNumberRef` were displayed, the value would be 6 for both variables:

```
int myNumber = 5;
ref int myNumberRef = ref myNumber;
myNumberRef = 6;
```

It is also possible to use the `ref` keyword as a return type. Notice in the following code the `ref` keyword identifies the return type as `ref int` and is also in the code body, which instructs the function to return `ref val`:

```
static ref int ShowDouble(int val)
{
  val *= 2;
  return ref val;
}
```

If you attempted to compile the preceding function, you would receive an error. The reason is that you cannot pass a variable type as a function parameter by reference without prefixing the `ref` keyword to the variable declaration. See the following code snippet where the `ref` keyword is added—that function would compile and run as expected:

```
static ref int ShowDouble(ref int val)
{
  val *= 2;
  return ref val;
}
```

Variables like `strings` and `arrays` are reference types, and `arrays` can be returned with the `ref` keyword without a parameter declaration:

```
static ref int ReturnByRef()
{
  int[] array = { 2 };
  return ref array[0];
}
```

> **NOTE** Although `strings` are reference types, they are a special case because they are immutable. That means you cannot change them because a modification results in a new `string`; the old `string` is deallocated. The C# compiler will complain if you attempt to return a `string` by `ref`.

Out Parameters

In addition to passing values by reference, you can specify that a given parameter is an *out parameter* by using the `out` keyword, which is used in the same way as the `ref` keyword (as a modifier to the parameter in the function definition and in the function call). In effect, this gives you almost the same behavior as a reference parameter, in that the value of the parameter at the end of the function execution is returned to the variable used in the function call. However, there are important differences:

➤ Whereas it is illegal to use an unassigned variable as a `ref` parameter, you can use an unassigned variable as an `out` parameter.

➤ An out parameter must be treated as an unassigned value by the function that uses it.

This means that while it is permissible in calling code to use an assigned variable as an `out` parameter, the value stored in this variable is lost when the function executes.

As an example, consider an extension to the `MaxValue()` function shown earlier, which returns the maximum value of an array. Modify the function slightly so that you obtain the index of the element with the maximum value within the array. To keep things simple, obtain just the index of the first occurrence of this value when there are multiple elements with the maximum value. To do this, you add an `out` parameter by modifying the function as follows:

```
static int MaxValue(int[] intArray, out int maxIndex)
{
    int maxVal = intArray[0];
    maxIndex = 0;
    for (int i = 1; i < intArray.Length; i++)
    {
        if (intArray[i] > maxVal)
        {
            maxVal = intArray[i];
            maxIndex = i;
        }
    }
    return maxVal;
}
```

You might use the function like this:

```
int[] myArray = { 1, 8, 3, 6, 2, 5, 9, 3, 0, 2 };
Console.WriteLine("The maximum value in myArray is " +
                $"{MaxValue(myArray, out int maxIndex)}");
Console.WriteLine("The first occurrence of this value is " +
                $"at element {maxIndex + 1}");
```

That results in the following:

```
The maximum value in myArray is 9
The first occurrence of this value is at element 7
```

You must use the `out` keyword in the function call, just as with the `ref` keyword. Another useful situation for the `out` keyword is when parsing data in collaboration with the `TryParse()` method, which, in this case, checks if the input is an integer:

```
if (!int.TryParse(input, out int result))
{
  return null;
}
return result;
```

This code checks whether the value stored in the `input` variable is an `int`. If it is not of type `int`, then the code snippet returns `null`. If it is of type `int`, then it returns the integer value via the `out` variable declared as `result` to the calling function.

Tuples

There are numerous techniques for returning multiple values from a function. For example, you could use the `out` keyword, structs, or an array, or via a class discussed later in this chapter. Using the `out` keyword would achieve the goal of returning multiple values from a function; however, doing so uses that feature in a way it is not specifically designed to be used. Remember that the `out` keyword is intended for passing a parameter by reference without needing to initialize it first. Structs, arrays, and classes are all valid options but require extra code to create, initialize, reference, and read. A `tuple`, on the other hand, is a very elegant approach for achieving this objective with little overhead.

Because the `tuple` provides a very convenient and direct approach to return more than a single value from a function, it's most useful when a program does not need a struct or more complicated implementations. Take this simple example of a `tuple`:

```
var numbers = (1, 2, 3, 4, 5);
```

That code creates a `tuple` named `numbers` containing members `Item1`, `Item2`, `Item3`, `Item4`, and `Item5`, which are accessible using, for example:

```
var number = numbers.Item1;
```

Or, to give the members a specific name, you can specifically identify them:

```
(int one, int two, int three, int four, int five) nums = (1, 2, 3, 4, 5);
int first = nums.one;
```

A function declaration would look something like the following, which uses the `IEnumerable` interface. Interfaces are introduced later in Chapter 8, but for now, know that an `Enumerable` object means it exposes methods that allow the querying of the values contained within it.

```
private static (int max, int min, double average)
    GetMaxMin(IEnumerable<int> numbers)
    {
      return (Enumerable.Max(numbers),
              Enumerable.Min(numbers),
              Enumerable.Average(numbers));
    }
```

Then running the code from a simple console application using this code:

```
static void Main(string[] args)
{
  IEnumerable<int> numbers = new int[] { 1, 2, 3, 4, 5, 6 };
  var result = GetMaxMin(numbers);
  Console.WriteLine($"Max number is {result.max}, " +
                    $"Min number is {result.min}, " +
                    $"Average is {result.average}");
  Console.ReadLine();
}
```

results in the output shown in Figure 6-4. You can find the code discussed in the chapter download in `Tuple\Program.cs`.

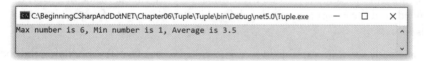

C:\BeginningCSharpAndDotNET\Chapter06\Tuple\Tuple\bin\Debug\net5.0\Tuple.exe — □ ×
Max number is 6, Min number is 1, Average is 3.5

FIGURE 6-4

> **NOTE** In Chapter 10, where creating classes and members is introduced, you will find an example of the deconstruction of a `tuple`. Understanding some basic class principles is required to grasp that concept completely, so read on and make note of the continuation of tuples in that chapter.

VARIABLE SCOPE

Throughout the preceding section, you might have been wondering why exchanging data with functions is necessary. The reason is that variables in C# are accessible only from localized regions of code. A given variable is said to have a *scope* from which it is accessible.

Variable scope is an important subject and one best introduced with an example. The following Try It Out illustrates a situation in which a variable is defined in one scope, and an attempt to use it is made in a different scope.

TRY IT OUT   Variable Scope: Using the Ch06Ex01\Program.cs

1.   Make the following changes to Ch06Ex01 in `Program.cs` created previously:

```
class Program
{
    static void Write()
    {
        Console.WriteLine($"myString = {myString}");
    }
    static void Main(string[] args)
    {
        string myString = "String defined in Main()";
        Write();
        Console.ReadKey();
    }
}
```

2.   Compile the code and note the error and warning that appear in the error list:

```
The name 'myString' does not exist in the current context
The variable 'myString' is assigned but its value is never used
```

How It Works

What went wrong? Well, the variable `myString` defined in the main body of your application (the `Main()` function) is not accessible from the `Write()` function.

The reason for this inaccessibility is that variables have a scope within which they are valid. This scope encompasses the code block that they are defined in and any directly nested code blocks. The blocks of code in functions are separate from the blocks of code from which they are called. Inside `Write()`, the name `myString` is undefined, and the `myString` variable defined in `Main()` is *out of scope*—it can be used only from within `Main()`.

In fact, you can have a completely separate variable in `Write()` called `myString`. Try modifying the code as follows:

```
class Program
{
    static void Write()
    {
        string myString = "String defined in Write()";
        Console.WriteLine("Now in Write()");
        Console.WriteLine($"myString = {myString}");
    }
}
```

```
        static void Main(string[] args)
        {
            string myString = "String defined in Main()";
            Write();
            Console.WriteLine("\nNow in Main()");
            Console.WriteLine($"myString = {myString}");
            Console.ReadKey();
        }
    }
```

This code does compile, resulting in the output shown in Figure 6-5.

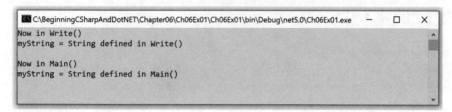

FIGURE 6-5

The operations performed by this code are as follows:

➤ `Main()` defines and initializes a string variable called `myString`.
➤ `Main()` transfers control to `Write()`.
➤ `Write()` defines and initializes a string variable called `myString`, which is a different variable from the `myString` defined in `Main()`.
➤ `Write()` outputs `Now in Write()` to the console.
➤ `Write()` outputs a string to the console containing the value of `myString` as defined in `Write()`.
➤ `Write()` transfers control back to `Main()`.
➤ `Main()` outputs `Now in Main()` to the console.
➤ `Main()` outputs a string to the console containing the value of `myString` as defined in `Main()`.

Variables whose scopes cover a single function in this way are known as *local variables*. It is also possible to have *global variables*, whose scopes cover multiple functions. Modify the code as follows:

```
    class Program
    {
        static string myString;
        static void Write()
        {
            string myString = "String defined in Write()";
            Console.WriteLine("Now in Write()");
            Console.WriteLine($"Local myString = {myString}");
            Console.WriteLine($"Global myString = {Program.myString}");
        }
        static void Main(string[] args)
        {
            string myString = "String defined in Main()";
            Program.myString = "Global string";
```

```
        Write();
        Console.WriteLine("\nNow in Main()");
        Console.WriteLine($"Local myString = {myString}");
        Console.WriteLine($"Global myString = {Program.myString}");
        Console.ReadKey();
    }
}
```

The result is now as shown in Figure 6-6.

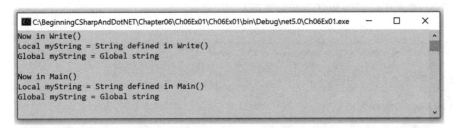

```
C:\BeginningCSharpAndDotNET\Chapter06\Ch06Ex01\Ch06Ex01\bin\Debug\net5.0\Ch06Ex01.exe      —    □    ×
Now in Write()
Local myString = String defined in Write()
Global myString = Global string

Now in Main()
Local myString = String defined in Main()
Global myString = Global string
```

FIGURE 6-6

Here, you have added another variable called `myString`, this time further up the hierarchy of names in the code. The variable is defined as follows:

```
static string myString;
```

Again, the `static` keyword is required. Without going into too much detail, understand that in this type of console application, you must use either the `static` or the `const` keyword for global variables of this form. If you want to modify the value of the global variable, you need to use `static` because `const` prohibits the value of the variable from changing.

To differentiate between this variable and the local variables in `Main()` and `Write()` with the same names, you must classify the variable name using a fully qualified name, as described in Chapter 3. Here, you refer to the global version as `Program.myString`. This is necessary only when you have global and local variables with the same name; if there were no local `myString` variables, you could simply use `myString` to refer to the global variable, rather than `Program.myString`. When you have a local variable with the same name as a global variable, the global variable is said to be *hidden*.

The value of the global variable is set in `Main()` with

```
Program.myString = "Global string";
```

and accessed in `Write()` with

```
Console.WriteLine($"Global myString = {Program.myString}");
```

You might be wondering why you should not just use this technique to exchange data with functions, rather than the parameter passing shown earlier. There are indeed situations where this is an acceptable way to exchange data, for example if you are writing a single object to be used as a plugin or a short script for use in a larger project. However, there are many scenarios where it is not a good idea. The most common issue with using global variables has to do with the management of concurrency. For example, a global variable can be written to and read from numerous methods within a class or from different threads. Can you be certain that the value in the global variable contains valid data if numerous threads and methods can write to it? Without some extra synchronization code, the answer is probably not. Additionally, over time it is possible the actual intent of the global variable is forgotten and used later for some other reason. Therefore, the choice of whether to use global variables depends on the intended use of the function in question.

The problem with using global variables is that they are generally unsuitable for "general-purpose" functions, which can work with whatever data you supply, not just data in a specific global variable. You will look at this in more depth a little later.

Variable Scope in Other Structures

One of the points made in the preceding section has consequences above and beyond variable scope between functions: that the scopes of variables encompass the code blocks in which they are defined and any directly nested code blocks. You can find the code discussed next in the chapter download in `VariableScopeInLoops\Program.cs`. This also applies to other code blocks, such as those in branching and looping structures. Consider the following code:

```
int i;
for (i = 0; i < 10; i++)
{
    string text = $"Line {Convert.ToString(i)}";
    Console.WriteLine($"{text}");
}
Console.WriteLine($"Last text output in loop: {text}");
```

Here, the string variable `text` is local to the `for` loop. This code won't compile because the call to `WriteLine()` that occurs outside of this loop attempts to use the variable `text`, which is out of scope outside of the loop. Try modifying the code as follows:

```
int i;
string text;
for (i = 0; i < 10; i++)
{
    text = $"Line {Convert.ToString(i)}";
    Console.WriteLine($"{text}");
}
Console.WriteLine($"Last text output in loop: {text}");
```

This code will also fail because variables must be declared and initialized before use, and `text` is only initialized in the `for` loop. The value assigned to `text` is lost when the loop block is exited as it isn't initialized outside the block. However, you can make the following change:

```
int i;
string text = "";
for (i = 0; i < 10; i++)
{
    text = $"Line {Convert.ToString(i)}";
    Console.WriteLine($"{text}");
}
Console.WriteLine($"Last text output in loop: {text}");
```

This time, `text` is initialized outside of the loop, and you have access to its value. The result of this simple code is shown in Figure 6-7.

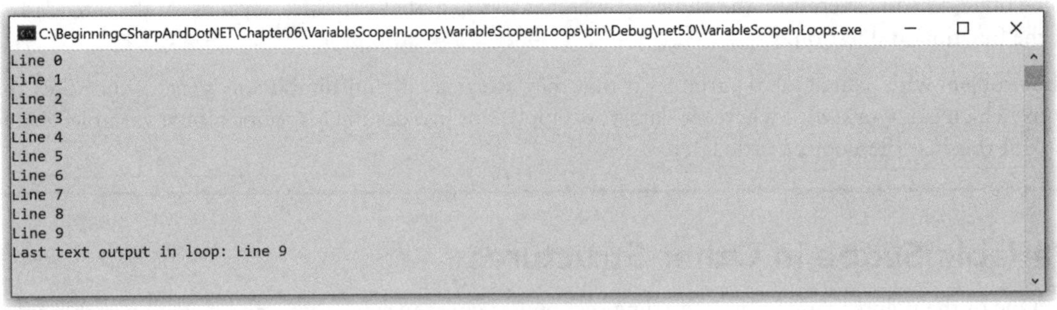

```
C:\BeginningCSharpAndDotNET\Chapter06\VariableScopeInLoops\VariableScopeInLoops\bin\Debug\net5.0\VariableScopeInLoops.exe
Line 0
Line 1
Line 2
Line 3
Line 4
Line 5
Line 6
Line 7
Line 8
Line 9
Last text output in loop: Line 9
```

FIGURE 6-7

The last value assigned to `text` in the loop is accessible from outside the loop. As you can see, this topic requires a bit of effort to come to grips with. It is not immediately obvious, considering the earlier example, `text` does not retain the empty string it is assigned before the loop in the code after the loop.

The explanation for this behavior is related to memory allocation for the `text` variable, and indeed any variable. Merely declaring a simple variable type does not result in very much happening. It is only when values are assigned to the variables that values are allocated a place in memory to be stored. When this allocation takes place inside a loop, the value is essentially defined as a local value and goes out of scope outside of the loop.

Even though the variable itself is not localized to the loop, the value it contains is. However, assigning a value outside of the loop ensures that the value is local to the main code, and is still in scope inside the loop. This means that the variable does not go out of scope before the main code block is exited, so you have access to its value outside of the loop.

Luckily for you, the C# compiler detects variable scope problems, and responding to the error messages it generates certainly helps you to understand the topic of variable scope.

Parameters and Return Values versus Global Data

Let us take a closer look at exchanging data with functions via global data and via parameters and return values. To recap, consider the following code:

```csharp
class Program
{
    static void ShowDouble(ref int val)
    {
        val *= 2;
        Console.WriteLine($"val doubled = {val}");
    }
    static void Main(string[] args)
    {
```

```
        int val = 5;
        Console.WriteLine($"val = {val}");
        ShowDouble(ref val);
        Console.WriteLine($"val = {val}");
        Console.ReadLine();
    }
}
```

> **NOTE** This code is slightly different from the code shown earlier in this chapter when you used the variable name `myNumber` in `Main()`. This illustrates the fact that local variables can have identical names and yet not interfere with each other.

Now compare it with this code:

```
class Program
{
    static int val;
    static void ShowDouble()
    {
        val *= 2;
        Console.WriteLine($"val doubled = {val}");
    }
    static void Main(string[] args)
    {
        val = 5;
        Console.WriteLine($"val = {val}");
        ShowDouble();
        Console.WriteLine($"val = {val}");
        Console.ReadLine();
    }
}
```

The results of these `ShowDouble()` functions are identical.

There are no hard-and-fast rules for using one technique rather than another, and both techniques are perfectly valid, but you might want to consider the following guidelines.

To start with, as mentioned when this topic was first introduced, the `ShowDouble()` version that uses the global value only uses the global variable `val`. To use this version, you must use this global variable. This limits the versatility of the function slightly and means that you must continuously copy the global variable value into other variables if you intend to store the results. In addition, global data might be modified by code elsewhere in your application, which could cause unpredictable results (values might change without you realizing it until it is too late). Finally, using a global variable named VAL would mean that no one else can use that name anyplace else in the project's code; if it does happen, then there would exist confusion as to which one is meant when referenced. Use global variables carefully.

Of course, it could also be argued that this simplicity makes your code more difficult to understand. Explicitly specifying parameters enables you to see at a glance what is changing. If you see a call that reads `FunctionName(val1, out val2)`, you instantly know that `val1` and `val2` are the important variables to consider and that `val2` will be assigned a new value when the function is completed. Conversely, if this function took no parameters, then you would be unable to make any assumptions about what data it manipulated.

Feel free to use either technique to exchange data. In general, use parameters rather than global data; however, there are certainly cases where global data might be more suitable, and it certainly is not an error to use that technique.

Local Functions

As mentioned at the beginning of this chapter where the concept of a function was introduced, the point was made that the reason for taking code out of the `Main(string[] args)` function is so that it can be reused instead of recoded multiple times within the same program. You should abide by that way of thinking when you design and create your programs in most situations.

Keep in mind that over time, the complexity of a program can significantly increase via an expansion of what it is expected to do. As the capabilities of the program increase, it is likely that many more functions will be added to enable them. The more functions a program has, the more difficult it is for other programmers to make changes such as fixing bugs or adding new features. Making changes becomes harder not only due to the number of functions, but also because the original intent of the functions can get lost. Such functions then could be used for reasons other than those the original author intended, which can cause serious problems when the wrong changes get made to them.

If you ever find yourself needing to modify functions you did not write, consider a *local function* instead. Local functions allow you to declare a function within the context of another function. Doing this can help readability and speed interpretation of the program's purpose.

Take this code, for example:

```
class Program
{
  static void Main(string[] args)
  {
    int myNumber = 5;
    Console.WriteLine($"Main Function = {myNumber}");
    DoubleIt(myNumber);
    Console.ReadLine();

    void DoubleIt(int val)
    {
      val *= 2;
      Console.WriteLine($"Local Function - val = {val}");
    }
  }
}
```

Notice that the function `DoubleIt()` exists within the `Main(string[] args)` function. It cannot be called from other functions contained in the `Program` class. The result of this simple code is shown in Figure 6-8.

FIGURE 6-8

You can find the code discussed in the chapter download in `LocalFunctions\Program.cs`.

THE MAIN() FUNCTION

Now that you have covered most of the simple techniques used in the creation and use of functions, it's time to take a closer look at the `Main()` function.

Earlier, you saw that `Main()` is the entry point for a C# application and that execution of this function encompasses the execution of the application. That is, when execution is initiated, the `Main()` function executes, and when the `Main()` function finishes, execution ends.

The `Main()` function can return either `void` or `int`, and can optionally include a `string[] args` parameter, so you can use any of the following versions:

```
static void Main()
static void Main(string[] args)
static int Main()
static int Main(string[] args)
```

The third and fourth versions return an `int` value, which can be used to signify how the application terminates, and often is used as an indication of an error (although this is by no means mandatory). In general, returning a value of 0 reflects normal termination (that is, the application has completed and can terminate safely).

The optional `args` parameter of `Main()` provides you with a way to obtain information from outside the application, specified at runtime. This information takes the form of *command-line parameters.*

When a console application is executed, any specified command-line parameters are placed in this `args` array. You can then use these parameters in your application. The following Try It Out shows this in action. You can specify any number of command-line arguments, each of which will be output to the console.

TRY IT OUT Command-Line Arguments: Ch06Ex04\Program.cs

1. Create a new Console Application called Ch06Ex04 and save it in the directory `C:\BeginningCSharpAndDotNET\Chapter06`.

2. Add the following code to `Program.cs`:

```
class Program
{
    static void Main(string[] args)
    {
        Console.WriteLine($"{args.Length} command line arguments were specified:");
        foreach (string arg in args)
```

```
            Console.WriteLine(arg);
        Console.ReadKey();
    }
}
```

3. Open the property pages for the project (right-click the Ch06Ex04 project name in the Solution Explorer window and select Properties).

4. Select the Debug page and add any command-line arguments you want to the Application arguments setting. Figure 6-9 shows an example.

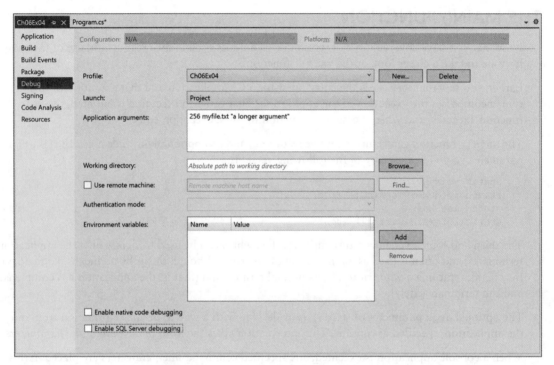

FIGURE 6-9

5. Run the application. Figure 6-10 shows the output.

```
C:\BeginningCSharpAndDotNET\Chapter06\Ch06Ex04\Ch06Ex04\bin\Debug\net5.0\Ch06Ex04.exe    —    □    ×
3 command line arguments were specified:
256
myfile.txt
a longer argument
```

FIGURE 6-10

How It Works

The code used here is quite simple:

```
Console.WriteLine($"{args.Length} command line arguments were specified:");
foreach (string arg in args)
    Console.WriteLine(arg);
```

You are just using the `args` parameter as you would any other string array. You are not doing anything fancy with the arguments; you're just writing whatever is specified to the screen. You supplied the arguments via the project properties in the IDE. This is a handy way to use the same command-line arguments whenever you run the application from the IDE, rather than type them at a command-line prompt every time. The same result can be obtained by opening a command prompt window in the same directory as the project output (`C:\BeginningCSharpAndDotNET\Chapter06\Ch06Ex04\Ch06Ex04\bin\Debug\net5.0`) and typing this:

```
Ch06Ex04 256 myFile.txt "a longer argument"
```

Each argument is separated from the next by spaces. To supply an argument that includes spaces, you can enclose it in double quotation marks, which prevents it from being interpreted as multiple arguments.

STRUCT FUNCTIONS

The previous chapter covered structure types for storing multiple data elements in one place. Structs are capable of a lot more than this. For example, they can contain functions as well as data. That might seem a little strange at first, but it is, in fact, especially useful. As a simple example, consider the following struct:

```
struct CustomerName
{
    public string firstName, lastName;
}
```

If you have variables of type `CustomerName` and you want to output a full name to the console, you are forced to build the name from its component parts. You might use the following syntax for a `CustomerName` variable called `myCustomer`, for example:

```
CustomerName myCustomer;
myCustomer.firstName = "Rual";
myCustomer.lastName = "Perkins";
Console.WriteLine($"{myCustomer.firstName} {myCustomer.lastName}");
```

By adding functions to structs, you can simplify this by centralizing the processing of common tasks. For example, you can add a suitable function to the struct type as follows:

```
struct CustomerName
{
    public string firstName, lastName;
    public string Name() => firstName + " " + lastName;
}
```

This looks much like any other function you have seen in this chapter, except that you haven't used the `static` modifier. The reasons for this will become clear later in the book; for now, it is enough to know that this keyword is not required for struct functions. You can use this function as follows:

```
CustomerName myCustomer;
myCustomer.firstName = "Rual";
myCustomer.lastName = "Perkins";
Console.WriteLine(myCustomer.Name());
```

This syntax is much simpler, and much easier to understand, than the previous syntax. The `Name()` function has direct access to the `firstName` and `lastName` struct members. Within the `CustomerName` struct, they can be thought of as global.

OVERLOADING FUNCTIONS

Earlier in this chapter, you saw how you must match the signature of a function when you call it. This implies that you need to have separate functions to operate on different types of variables. *Function overloading* provides you with the capability to create multiple functions with the same name, but each working with different parameter types. For example, earlier you used the following code, which contains a function called `MaxValue()`:

```
class Program
{
    static int MaxValue(int[] intArray)
    {
        int maxVal = intArray[0];
        for (int i = 1; i < intArray.Length; i++)
        {
            if (intArray[i] > maxVal)
                maxVal = intArray[i];
        }
        return maxVal;
    }
    static void Main(string[] args)
    {
        int[] myArray = { 1, 8, 3, 6, 2, 5, 9, 3, 0, 2 };
        int maxVal = MaxValue(myArray);
        Console.WriteLine($"The maximum value in myArray is {maxVal}");
        Console.ReadKey();
    }
}
```

This function can be used only with arrays of `int` values. You could provide differently named functions for different parameter types, perhaps renaming the preceding function as `IntArray-MaxValue()` and adding functions such as `DoubleArrayMaxValue()` to work with other types. Alternatively, you could just add the following function to your code:

```
static double MaxValue(double[] doubleArray)
{
    double maxVal = doubleArray[0];
    for (int i = 1; i < doubleArray.Length; i++)
    {
```

```
        if (doubleArray[i] > maxVal)
            maxVal = doubleArray[i];
    }
    return maxVal;
}
```

The difference here is that you are using `double` values. The function name, `MaxValue()`, is the same, but (crucially) its *signature* is different. That is because the signature of a function, as shown earlier, includes both the name of the function and its parameters. It would be an error to define two functions with the same signature, but because these two functions have different signatures, this is fine.

> **NOTE** *The return type of a function is not part of its signature, so you can't define two functions that differ only in return type; they would have identical signatures.*

After adding the preceding code, you have two versions of `MaxValue()`, which accept `int` and `double` arrays, returning an `int` or `double` maximum, respectively.

The beauty of this type of code is that you do not have to explicitly specify which of these two functions you want to use. You simply provide an array parameter, and the correct function is executed depending on the type of parameter used.

Note another aspect of the IntelliSense feature in Visual Studio: When you have the two functions shown previously in an application and then proceed to type the name of the function, for example, `MaxValue`, the IDE shows you the available overloads for that function. For example, if you type

```
double result = MaxValue
```

the IDE gives you information about both versions of `MaxValue()`, which you can scroll between using the Up and Down arrow keys, as shown in Figure 6-11.

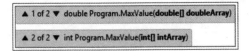

FIGURE 6-11

All aspects of the function signature are included when overloading functions. You might, for example, have two different functions that take parameters by value and by reference, respectively:

```
static void ShowDouble(ref int val)
{
    . . .
}
static void ShowDouble(int val)
{
    . . .
}
```

Deciding which version to use is based purely on whether the function call contains the `ref` keyword. The following would call the reference version:

```
ShowDouble(ref val);
```

This would call the value version:

```
ShowDouble(val);
```

Alternatively, you could have functions that differ in the number of parameters they require, and so on.

USING DELEGATES

A *delegate* is a type that enables you to store references to functions. Although this sounds quite involved, the mechanism is surprisingly simple. The most important purpose of delegates will become clear later in the book when you will look at events and event handling, but it is useful to briefly consider them here. Delegates are declared much like functions, but with no function body and using the `delegate` keyword. The delegate declaration specifies a return type and parameter list.

After defining a delegate, you can declare a variable with the type of that delegate. You can then initialize the variable as a reference to any function that has the same return type and parameter list as that delegate. Once you have done this, you can call that function by using the delegate variable as if it were a function.

When you have a variable that refers to a function, you can also perform other operations that would be otherwise impossible. For example, you can pass a delegate variable to a function as a parameter, and then that function can use the delegate to call whatever function it refers to, without knowing which function will be called until runtime. The following Try It Out demonstrates using a delegate to access one of two functions.

TRY IT OUT   Using a Delegate to Call a Function: Ch06Ex05\Program.cs

1. Create a new Console Application called Ch06Ex05 and save it in the directory
   `C:\BeginningCSharpAndDotNET\Chapter06`.

2. Add the following code to `Program.cs`:

```
class Program
{
    delegate double ProcessDelegate(double param1, double param2);
    static double Multiply(double param1, double param2) => param1 * param2;
    static double Divide(double param1, double param2) => param1 / param2;

    static void Main(string[] args)
    {
        ProcessDelegate process;
        Console.WriteLine("Enter 2 numbers separated with a comma:");
        string input = Console.ReadLine();
        int commaPos = input.IndexOf(',');
        double param1 = Convert.ToDouble(input.Substring(0, commaPos));
```

```
                double param2 = Convert.ToDouble(input.Substring(commaPos + 1,
                                                 input.Length - commaPos - 1));
                Console.WriteLine("Enter M to multiply or D to divide:");
                input = Console.ReadLine();
                if (input == "M")
                    process = new ProcessDelegate(Multiply);
                else
                    process = new ProcessDelegate(Divide);
                Console.WriteLine($"Result: {process(param1, param2)}");
                Console.ReadKey();
            }
        }
```

3. Execute the code and enter the values when prompted. Figure 6-12 shows the result.

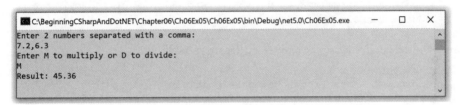

FIGURE 6-12

How It Works

This code defines a delegate (`ProcessDelegate`) whose return type and parameters match those of the two functions (`Multiply()` and `Divide()`). Notice that the `Multiply()` and `Divide()` functions use the => (lambda arrow / expression-bodied methods).

```
        static double Multiply(double param1, double param2) => param1 * param2;
```

The delegate definition is as follows:

```
        delegate double ProcessDelegate(double param1, double param2);
```

The `delegate` keyword specifies that the definition is for a delegate, rather than a function (the definition appears in the same place that a function definition might). Next, the definition specifies a `double` return value and two `double` parameters. The actual names used are arbitrary; you can call the delegate type and parameter names whatever you like. This example uses a delegate called `ProcessDelegate` and `double` parameters called `param1` and `param2`.

The code in `Main()` starts by declaring a variable using the new delegate type:

```
        static void Main(string[] args)
        {
            ProcessDelegate process;
```

Next, you have some standard C# code that requests two numbers separated by a comma, and then places these numbers in two `double` variables:

```
        Console.WriteLine("Enter 2 numbers separated with a comma:");
        string input = Console.ReadLine();
```

```
int commaPos = input.IndexOf(',');
double param1 = Convert.ToDouble(input.Substring(0, commaPos));
double param2 = Convert.ToDouble(input.Substring(commaPos + 1,
                                 input.Length - commaPos - 1));
```

> **NOTE** *For demonstration purposes, no user input validation is included here. If this were "real" code, you would spend much more time ensuring that you had valid values in the local* param1 *and* param2 *variables.*

Next, you ask the user to multiply or divide these numbers:

```
Console.WriteLine("Enter M to multiply or D to divide:");
input = Console.ReadLine();
```

Based on the user's choice, you initialize the process delegate variable:

```
if (input == "M")
    process = new ProcessDelegate(Multiply);
else
    process = new ProcessDelegate(Divide);
```

To assign a function reference to a delegate variable, you use slightly odd-looking syntax. Much like assigning array values, you can use the new keyword to create a new delegate. After this keyword, you specify the delegate type and supply an argument referring to the function you want to use—namely, the Multiply() or Divide() function. This argument does not match the parameters of the delegate type or the target function; it is a syntax unique to delegate assignment. The argument is simply the name of the function to use, without any parentheses.

In fact, you can use slightly simpler syntax here, if you want:

```
if (input == "M")
    process = Multiply;
else
    process = Divide;
```

The compiler recognizes that the delegate type of the process variable matches the signature of the two functions and automatically initializes a delegate for you. Which syntax you use is up to you, although some people prefer to use the longhand version, as it is easier to see at a glance what is happening.

Finally, call the chosen function using the delegate. The same syntax works, regardless of which function the delegate refers to:

```
Console.WriteLine($"Result: {process(param1, param2)}");
Console.ReadKey();
}
```

Here, you treat the delegate variable as if it were a function name. Unlike a function, though, you can also perform additional operations on this variable, such as passing it to a function via a parameter, as shown in this simple example:

```
static void ExecuteFunction(ProcessDelegate process)
    => process(2.2, 3.3);
```

This means that you can control the behavior of functions by passing them function delegates, much like choosing a "snap-in" to use. For example, you might have a function that sorts a string array alphabetically. You can use several techniques to sort lists, with varying performance depending on the characteristics of the list being sorted. By using delegates, you can specify the function to use by passing a sorting algorithm function delegate to a sorting function.

There are many such uses for delegates, but, as mentioned earlier, their most prolific use is in event handling, covered in Chapter 13.

EXERCISES

6.1 The following two functions have errors. What are they?

```
static bool Write()
{
    Console.WriteLine("Text output from function.");
}
static void MyFunction(string label, params int[] args, bool showLabel)
{
    if (showLabel)
        Console.WriteLine(label);
    foreach (int i in args)
        Console.WriteLine($"{i}");
}
```

6.2 Write an application that uses two command-line arguments to place values into a string and an integer variable, respectively. Then display those values.

6.3 Create a delegate and use it to impersonate the `Console.ReadLine()` function when asking for user input.

6.4 Modify the following struct to include a function that returns the total price of an order:

```
struct Order
{
    public string itemName;
    public int    unitCount;
    public double unitCost;
}
```

6.5 Add another function to the `Order` struct that returns a formatted string as follows (as a single line of text, where italic entries enclosed in angle brackets are replaced by appropriate values):

```
Order Information: <unit count> <item name> items at $<unit cost> each,
total cost $<total cost>
```

Answers to the exercises can be found in the Appendix.

▶ WHAT YOU LEARNED IN THIS CHAPTER

TOPIC	KEY CONCEPTS
Defining functions	Functions are defined with a name, zero or more parameters, and a return type. The name and parameters of a function collectively define the signature of the function. It is possible to define multiple functions whose signatures are different even though their names are the same—this is called *function overloading*. Functions can also be defined within struct types.
Return values and parameters	The return type of a function can be any type, or `void` if the function does not return a value. Parameters can also be of any type and consist of a comma-separated list of type and name pairs. A variable number of parameters of a specified type can be specified through a parameter array, which must come last in the parameter list. Parameters can be specified as `ref` or `out` parameters in order to return values to the caller. When calling a function, any arguments specified must match the parameters in the definition both in type and in order and must include matching `ref` and `out` keywords if these are used in the parameter definition.
Variable scope	Variables are scoped according to the block of code where they are defined. Blocks of code include functions as well as other structures, such as the body of a loop. It is possible to define multiple, separate variables with the same name at different scope levels.
Command-line parameters	The `Main()` function in a console application can receive command-line parameters that are passed to the application when it is executed. When executing the application, these parameters are specified by arguments separated by spaces, and longer arguments can be passed in quotes.
Delegates	As well as calling functions directly, it is possible to call them through delegates. Delegates are variables that are defined with a return type and parameter list. A given delegate type can match any function whose return type and parameters match the delegate definition.

7

Debugging and Error Handling

WHAT YOU WILL LEARN IN THIS CHAPTER

➤ Debugging methods available in the IDE

➤ Error-handling techniques available in C#

CODE DOWNLOADS FOR THIS CHAPTER

The code downloads for this chapter are found on the book page at www.wiley.com. Click the Downloads link. The code can also be found at github.com/benperk/BeginningCSharp-AndDotNET. The code is in the Chapter07 folder and individually named according to the names throughout the chapter.

So far, this book has covered all the basics of simple programming in C#. Before you move on to object-oriented programming in the next part, you need to look at debugging and error handling in C# code.

Errors in code are something that will always be with you. No matter how good a programmer is, problems will always slip through, and part of being a good programmer is realizing this and being prepared to deal with it. Of course, some problems are minor and don't affect the execution of an application, such as a spelling mistake on a button, but glaring errors are also possible, including those that cause applications to fail completely (usually known as *fatal errors*). Fatal errors include simple errors in code that prevent compilation (syntax errors), or more serious problems that occur only at runtime. Some errors are subtle. Perhaps your application fails to add a record to a database because a requested field is missing or adds a record with the wrong data in other restricted circumstances. Errors such as these, where application logic is in some way flawed, are known as *semantic errors* or *logic errors*.

Often, you will not know about these subtle errors until a user complains that something isn't working properly. This leaves you with the task of tracing through your code to find out what is happening and fixing it so that it does what it was intended to do. In these situations, the debugging capabilities of Visual Studio are a fantastic help. The first part of this chapter looks at some of the techniques available and applies them to some common problems.

Then, you will learn the error-handling techniques available in C#. These enable you to take precautions in cases where errors are likely, and to write code that is resilient enough to cope with errors that might otherwise be fatal. The techniques are part of the C# language, rather than a debugging feature, but the IDE provides some tools to help you here, too.

DEBUGGING IN VISUAL STUDIO

Earlier, you learned that you could execute applications in two ways: with debugging enabled or without debugging enabled. By default, when you execute an application from Visual Studio (VS), it executes with debugging enabled. This happens, for example, when you press F5 or click the green Start arrow in the toolbar. To execute an application without debugging enabled, choose Debug ⇨ Start Without Debugging, or press Ctrl+F5.

Visual Studio allows you to build applications in numerous configurations, including debug (the default) and release. You can switch between these configurations using the Solution Configurations drop-down menu in the Standard toolbar. It is possible to also change the configuration by selecting the Build menu item and then Connection Manager.

When you build an application in debug configuration and execute it in debug mode, more is going on than the execution of your code. Debug builds maintain *symbolic information* about your application, so that the IDE knows exactly what is happening as each line of code is executed. Symbolic information means keeping track of, for example, the names of variables used in uncompiled code, so they can be matched to the values in the compiled machine code application, which will not contain such human-readable information. This information is contained in .pdb files, which you may have seen in your computer's Debug directories.

In the release configuration, application code is optimized, and you cannot perform these operations. However, release builds also run faster; when you have finished developing an application, you will typically supply users with release builds because they will not require the symbolic information that debug builds include.

This section describes debugging techniques you can use to identify and fix areas of code that do not work as expected, a process known as *debugging*. The techniques are grouped into two sections according to how they are used. In general, debugging is performed either by interrupting program execution or by making notes for later analysis. In Visual Studio terms, an application is either running or in break mode—that is, normal execution is halted. You will look at the nonbreak mode (runtime or normal) techniques first.

Debugging in Nonbreak (Normal) Mode

One of the commands you have been using throughout this book is the `Console.WriteLine()` function, which outputs text to the console. As you are developing applications, this function comes in handy for getting extra feedback about operations:

```
Console.WriteLine("MyFunc() Function is about to be called.");
MyFunc("Do something.");
Console.WriteLine("MyFunc() Function execution completed.");
```

This code snippet shows how you can get extra information concerning a function called `MyFunc()`. This is all very well, but it can make your console output a bit cluttered; and when you develop other types of applications, such as desktop applications, you won't have a console to output information to. As an alternative, you can output text to a separate location—the Output window in the IDE.

Chapter 2, which describes the Error List window, mentions that other windows can also be displayed in the same place. One of these, the Output window, can be particularly useful for debugging. To display this window, select View ⇨ Output. This window provides information related to compilation and execution of code, including errors encountered during compilation. You can also use this window, shown in Figure 7-1, to display custom diagnostic information by writing to it directly.

> **NOTE** The Output window contains a drop-down menu from which different modes can be selected, including Build, Build Order, and Debug. These modes display compilation and runtime information, respectively. When you read "writing to the Output window" in this section, it actually means "writing to the debug mode view of the Output window."

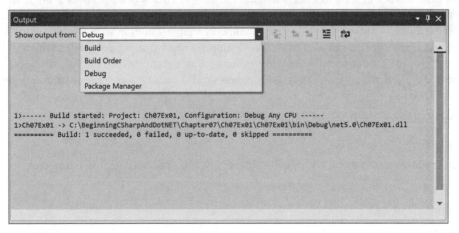

FIGURE 7-1

Alternatively, you might want to create a logging file, which has information appended to it when your application is executed. The techniques for doing this are much the same as those for writing text to the Output window, although the process requires an understanding of how to access the filesystem from C# applications. For now, leave that functionality on the back burner because there is plenty you can do without getting bogged down by file-access techniques.

Outputting Debugging Information

Writing text to the Output window at runtime is easy. You simply replace calls to `Console.Write-Line()` with the required call to write text where you want it. There are two commands you can use to do this:

➤   `Debug.WriteLine()`

➤   `Trace.WriteLine()`

These commands function in almost the same way, with one key difference—the first command works in debug builds only; the second works for release builds as well. In fact, the `Debug.Write-Line()` command will not even be compiled into a release build; it just disappears, which certainly has its advantages (the compiled code will be smaller, for one thing).

> **NOTE** *Both* `Debug.WriteLine()` *and* `Trace.WriteLine()` *methods are contained within the* `System.Diagnostics` *namespace, so you should include the statement* using `System.Diagnostics` *at the top of the code.*

These functions do not work exactly like `Console.WriteLine()`. They work with only a single string parameter for the message to output, rather than letting you insert variable values using `{X}` syntax. This means you must use an alternative technique to embed variable values in strings—for example, the + concatenation operator. You can also (optionally) supply a second string parameter, which displays a category for the output text. This enables you to see at a glance which output messages are displayed in the Output window, which is useful when similar messages are output from different places in the application.

The general output of these functions is as follows:

```
<category>: <message>
```

For example, the following statement, which has `"MyFunc"` as the optional category parameter,

```
Debug.WriteLine("Added 1 to i", "MyFunc");
```

would result in the following:

```
MyFunc: Added 1 to i
```

The next Try It Out demonstrates outputting debugging information in this way.

Writing Text to the Output Window: Ch07Ex01\Program.cs

1. Create a new Console Application called Ch07Ex01 and save it in the directory
   C:\BeginningCSharpAndDotNET\Chapter07.

2. Modify the code as follows:

```csharp
using System;
using System.Diagnostics;
namespace Ch07Ex01
{
    class Program
    {
        static void Main(string[] args)
        {
            int[] testArray = {4, 7, 4, 2, 7, 3, 7, 8, 3, 9, 1, 9};
            int maxVal = Maxima(testArray, out int[] maxValIndices);
            Console.WriteLine($"Maximum value {maxVal} found at element indices:");
            foreach (int index in maxValIndices)
            {
                Console.WriteLine(index);
            }
            Console.ReadKey();
        }
        static int Maxima(int[] integers, out int[] indices)
        {
            Debug.WriteLine("Maximum value search started.");
            indices = new int[1];
            int maxVal = integers[0];
            indices[0] = 0;
            int count = 1;
            Debug.WriteLine(string.Format(
                $"Maximum value initialized to {maxVal}, at element index 0."));
            for (int i = 1; i < integers.Length; i++)
            {
                Debug.WriteLine(string.Format(
                    $"Now looking at element at index {i}."));
                if (integers[i] > maxVal)
                {
                    maxVal = integers[i];
                    count = 1;
                    indices = new int[1];
                    indices[0] = i;
                    Debug.WriteLine(string.Format(
                        $"New maximum found. New value is {maxVal}, at " +
                        $"element index {i}."));
                }
                else
                {
                    if (integers[i] == maxVal)
                    {
```

```
                            count++;
                            int[] oldIndices = indices;
                            indices = new int[count];
                            oldIndices.CopyTo(indices, 0);
                            indices[count - 1] = i;
                            Debug.WriteLine(string.Format(
                                $"Duplicate maximum found at element index {i}."));
                        }
                    }
                }
                Trace.WriteLine(string.Format(
                    $"Maximum value {maxVal} found, with {count} occurrences."));
                Debug.WriteLine("Maximum value search completed.");
                return maxVal;
            }
        }
    }
```

3. Execute the code in debug mode. The result is shown in Figure 7-2.

FIGURE 7-2

4. Terminate the application and check the contents of the Output window (in debug mode). A truncated version of the output is shown here:

```
    ...
Maximum value search started.
Maximum value initialized to 4, at element index 0.
Now looking at element at index 1.
New maximum found. New value is 7, at element index 1.
Now looking at element at index 2.
Now looking at element at index 3.
Now looking at element at index 4.
Duplicate maximum found at element index 4.
Now looking at element at index 5.
Now looking at element at index 6.
Duplicate maximum found at element index 6.
Now looking at element at index 7.
New maximum found. New value is 8, at element index 7.
Now looking at element at index 8.
Now looking at element at index 9.
New maximum found. New value is 9, at element index 9.
Now looking at element at index 10.
Now looking at element at index 11.
Duplicate maximum found at element index 11.
Maximum value 9 found, with 2 occurrences.
Maximum value search completed.
The thread #### has exited with code 0 (0x0).
```

5. Change to Release mode using the drop-down menu on the Standard toolbar, as shown in Figure 7-3.

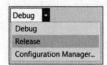

Debug
Debug
Release
Configuration Manager...

FIGURE 7-3

6. Run the program again, this time in release mode, and recheck the Output window when execution terminates. The output (again truncated) is as follows:

```
...
Maximum value 9 found, with 2 occurrences.
The thread #### has exited with code 0 (0x0).
```

How It Works

This application is an expanded version of one shown in Chapter 6, using a function to calculate the maximum value in an integer array. This version also returns an array of the indices where maximum values are found in an array, so that the calling code can manipulate these elements.

First, an additional `using` directive appears at the beginning of the code:

```
using System.Diagnostics;
```

This simplifies access to the functions discussed earlier because they are contained in the `System .Diagnostics` namespace. Without this `using` directive, code such as

```
Debug.WriteLine("Beginning C# and .NET");
```

would need further qualification, and would have to be rewritten as:

```
System.Diagnostics.Debug.WriteLine("Beginning C# and .NET");
```

The code in `Main()` simply initializes a test array of integers called `testArray`; it also declares another integer array called `maxValIndices` to store the index output of `Maxima()` (the function that performs the calculation), and then calls this function. Once the function returns, the code simply outputs the results.

`Maxima()` is slightly more complicated, but it does not use much code that you haven't already seen. The search through the array is performed in a similar way to the `MaxVal()` function in Chapter 6, but a record is kept of the indices of maximum values.

Note the function used to keep track of the indices (other than the lines that output debugging information). Rather than return an array that would be large enough to store every index in the source array (needing the same dimensions as the source array), `Maxima()` returns an array just large enough to hold the indices found. It does this by continually re-creating arrays of different sizes as the search progresses. This is necessary because arrays cannot be resized once they are created.

The search is initialized by assuming that the first element in the source array (called `integers` locally) is the maximum value and that there is only one maximum value in the array. Values can therefore be set for `maxVal` (the return value of the function and the maximum value found) and `indices`, the out parameter array that stores the indices of the maximum values found. `maxVal` is assigned the value of the first element in `integers`, and `indices` is assigned a single value, simply `0`, which is the index of the array's first element. You also store the number of maximum values found in a variable called `count`, which enables you to keep track of the `indices` array.

The main body of the function is a loop that cycles through the values in the `integers` array, omitting the first one because it has already been processed. Each value is compared to the current value of `maxVal` and ignored if `maxVal` is greater. If the currently inspected array value is greater than `maxVal`, then `maxVal` and `indices` are changed to reflect this. If the value is equal to `maxVal`, then `count` is incremented, and a new array is substituted for `indices`. This new array is one element bigger than the old `indices` array, containing the new index.

The code for this last piece of functionality is as follows:

```
if (integers[i] == maxVal)
{
    count++;
    int[] oldIndices = indices;
    indices = new int[count];
    oldIndices.CopyTo(indices, 0);
    indices[count - 1] = i;
    Debug.WriteLine(string.Format(
        $"Duplicate maximum found at element index {i}."));
}
```

This works by backing up the old `indices` array into `oldIndices`, an integer array local to this `if` code block. Note that the values in `oldIndices` are copied into the new `indices` array using the `<array>.CopyTo()` function. This function simply takes a target array and an index to use for the first element to copy to and pastes all values into the target array.

Throughout the code, various pieces of text are output using the `Debug.WriteLine()` and `Trace.WriteLine()` functions. These functions use the `string.Format()` function to embed variable values in strings in the same way as `Console.WriteLine()`. This is slightly more efficient than using the `+` concatenation operator.

When you run the application in debug mode, you see a complete record of the steps taken in the loop that give you the result. In release mode, you see just the result of the calculation, because no calls to `Debug.WriteLine()` are made in release builds.

Tracepoints

An alternative to writing information to the Output window is to use *tracepoints*. These are a feature of Visual Studio, rather than C#, but they serve the same function as using `Debug.WriteLine()`. Essentially, they enable you to output debugging information without modifying your code.

To demonstrate tracepoints, you can use them to replace the debugging commands in the previous example. (See the `Ch07Ex01TracePoints` file in the downloadable code for this chapter.) The process for adding a tracepoint is as follows:

1. Position the cursor at the line where you want the tracepoint to be inserted, for example line 31. The tracepoint will be processed *before* this line of code is executed.

2. To the left of the line number, click the side bar and a red circle appears. Hover your mouse pointer over the red circle placed next to the line of code and select the Settings menu item.

3. Check the Actions checkbox and type the string to be output in the Message text box in the Log a Message section. If you want to output variable values, enclose the variable name in curly braces.

4. Click OK. The red circle changes into a red diamond to the left of the line of code containing a tracepoint, and the highlighting of the line of code itself changes from red to white.

As implied by the title of the dialog box for adding tracepoints and the menu selections required for them, tracepoints are a form of breakpoint (and can cause application execution to pause, just like a breakpoint, if desired). You will look at breakpoints, which typically serve a more advanced debugging purpose, a little later in the chapter.

Figure 7-4 shows the tracepoint required for line 31 of `Ch07Ex01TracePoints`, where line numbering applies to the code after the existing `Debug.WriteLine()` statements have been removed.

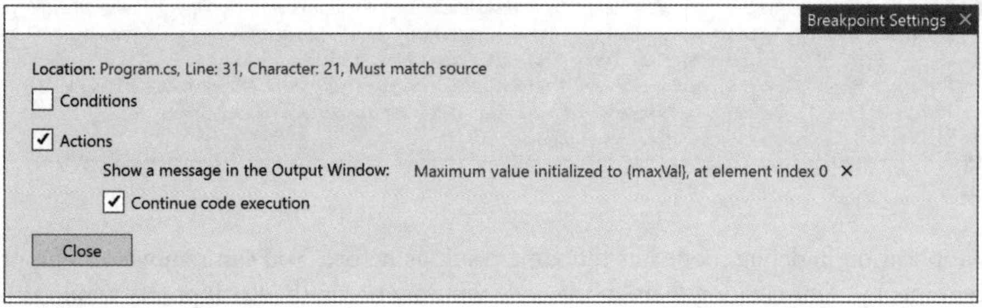

FIGURE 7-4

There is another window that you can use to quickly see the tracepoints in an application. To display this window, select Debug ⇨ Windows ⇨ Breakpoints from the Visual Studio menu. This is a general window for displaying breakpoints (tracepoints, as noted earlier, are a form of breakpoint). You can customize the display to show more tracepoint-specific information by adding the When Hit column from the Columns drop-down in this window. Figure 7-5 shows the display with this column configured and all the tracepoints added to `Ch07Ex01TracePoints`.

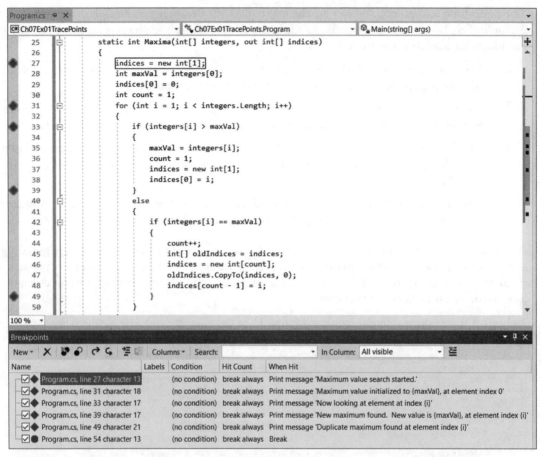

FIGURE 7-5

Executing this application in debug mode has the same result as before. You can remove or temporarily disable tracepoints by right-clicking them in the code window or via the Breakpoints window. In the Breakpoints window, the check box to the left of the tracepoint indicates whether the tracepoint is enabled; disabled tracepoints are unchecked and displayed in the code window as diamond outlines, rather than solid diamonds.

Diagnostics Output versus Tracepoints

Now that you have seen two methods of outputting essentially the same information, consider the pros and cons of each. First, tracepoints have no equivalent to the `Trace` commands; that is, there is no way to output information in a release build using tracepoints. This is because tracepoints are not included in your application. Tracepoints are handled by Visual Studio and, as such, do not exist in the compiled version of your application. You will see tracepoints doing something only when your application is running in the Visual Studio debugger.

The chief disadvantage of tracepoints is also their major advantage, which is that they are stored in Visual Studio. This makes them quick and easy to add to your applications as you need them, but also makes them all too easy to delete. Deleting a tracepoint is as simple as clicking the red diamond indicating its position, which can be annoying if you are outputting a complicated string of information.

One bonus of tracepoints, though, is the additional information that can be easily added, such as $FUNCTION, which adds the current function name to the output message. Although this information is available to code written using Debug and Trace commands, it is trickier to obtain. In summary, use these two methods of outputting debug information as follows:

➤ **Diagnostics output**—Use when debug output is something you always want to output from an application, particularly when the string you want to output is complex, involving several variables or a lot of information. In addition, Trace commands are often the only option should you want output during execution of an application built in release mode.

➤ **Tracepoints**—Use these when debugging an application to quickly output important information that may help you resolve semantic errors.

Debugging in Break Mode

The rest of the debugging techniques described in this chapter work in break mode. This mode can be entered in several ways, all of which result in the program pausing in some way.

Entering Break Mode

The simplest way to enter break mode is to click the Pause button in the IDE while an application is running. This Pause button is found on the Debug toolbar, which you should add to the toolbars that appear by default in Visual Studio. To do this, right-click in the toolbar area and select Debug. Figure 7-6 shows the Debug toolbar that appears.

FIGURE 7-6

The first three buttons on the toolbar allow manual control of breaking. In Figure 7-6, these are grayed out because they do not work with a program that isn't currently executing. The following sections describe the rest of the buttons as needed.

When an application is running, the toolbar changes to look like Figure 7-7.

FIGURE 7-7

The three buttons that were grayed out now enable you to do the following:

➤ Pause the application and enter break mode.

➤ Stop the application completely (this does not enter break mode; it just quits).

➤ Restart the application.

Pausing the application is perhaps the simplest way to enter break mode, but it doesn't give you fine-grained control over exactly where to stop. You are likely to stop in a natural pause in the application, perhaps where you request user input. You might also be able to enter break mode during a lengthy operation, or a long loop, but the exact stop point is likely to be random. In general, it is far better to use breakpoints.

Breakpoints

A *breakpoint* is a marker in your source code that triggers automatic entry into break mode. Break-points can be configured to do the following:

➤ Enter break mode immediately when the breakpoint is reached.

➤ Enter break mode when the breakpoint is reached if a Boolean expression evaluates to true.

➤ Enter break mode once the breakpoint is reached a set number of times.

➤ Enter break mode once the breakpoint is reached and a variable value has changed since the last time the breakpoint was reached.

These features are available only in debug builds. If you compile a release build, all breakpoints are ignored.

There are several ways to add breakpoints. To add simple breakpoints that break when a line is reached, just left-click the far left of the line of code. Alternatively, you can select the menu item Debug ⇨ Toggle Breakpoint from the menu or press F9 and the breakpoint is placed on the line of code that has focus.

A breakpoint appears as a red circle next to the line of code, which is highlighted, as shown in Figure 7-8.

You can also see information about a file's breakpoints using the Breakpoints window (you saw how to enable this window earlier). You can use the Breakpoints window to disable breakpoints, to delete breakpoints, and to edit the properties of breakpoints. You can also add labels to breakpoints, which is a handy way to group selected breakpoints. Notice that by removing the tick to the left of a description, a disabled breakpoint shows up as an unfilled red circle. You can see labels in the Labels column and filter the items shown in this window by label.

```csharp
static void Main(string[] args)
{
    int[] testArray = { 4, 7, 4, 2, 7, 3, 7, 8, 3, 9, 1, 9 };
    int maxVal = Maxima(testArray, out int[] maxValIndices);
    Console.WriteLine($"Maximum value {maxVal} found at element indices:");
    foreach (int index in maxValIndices)
    {
        Console.WriteLine(index);
    }
    Console.ReadKey();
}

static int Maxima(int[] integers, out int[] indices)
```

FIGURE 7-8

The other columns shown in the Breakpoints window, Condition and Hit Count, are only two of the available ones, but they are the most useful. You can edit these by right-clicking a breakpoint and selecting Conditions. Expanding the Conditions drop-down box displays the following options:

➤ Conditional Expression

➤ Hit Count

➤ Filter

Selecting Conditions opens a dialog box in which you can type any Boolean expression, which may involve any variables in scope at the breakpoint. For example, you could configure a breakpoint that triggers when it is reached and the value of maxVal is greater than 4 by entering the expression "maxVal > 4" and selecting the Is true option. You can also check whether the value of this expression has changed and only trigger the breakpoint then (you might trigger it if maxVal changed from 2 to 6 between breakpoint encounters, for example).

Selecting Hit Count from the drop-down list opens a dialog box in which you can specify how many times a breakpoint needs to be hit before it is triggered. A drop-down list offers the following options:

➤ Break always (default value)

➤ Break when the hit count is equal to

➤ Break when the hit count is a multiple of

➤ Break when the hit count is greater than or equal to

The option you choose, combined with the value entered in the text box next to the options, determines the behavior of the breakpoint. The hit count is useful in long loops, when you might want to break after, say, the first 5,000 cycles. It would be a pain to break and restart 5,000 times if you couldn't do this!

Other Ways to Enter Break Mode

There are two more ways to get into break mode. One is to enter it when an unhandled exception is thrown. This subject is covered later in this chapter when you will look at error handling. The other way is to break when an assertion is generated.

Assertions are instructions that can interrupt application execution with a user-defined message. They are often used during application development to test whether things are going smoothly. For example, at some point in your application you might require a given variable to have a value less than 10. You can use an assertion to confirm that this is true, interrupting the program if it is not. When the assertion occurs, you have the option to Abort, which terminates the application; Retry, which causes break mode to be entered; or Ignore, which causes the application to continue as normal.

As with the debug output functions shown earlier, there are two versions of the assertion function:

➤ Debug.Assert()

➤ Trace.Assert()

The Debug class is only compiled into debug builds, while Trace exists in release builds.

These functions take three parameters. The first is a Boolean value, whereby a value of `false` causes the assertion to trigger. The second and third are string parameters to write information both to a pop-up dialog box and the Output window. The preceding example would need a function call such as the following:

```
Debug.Assert(myVar < 10, "myVar is 10 or greater.",
             "Assertion occurred in Main().");
```

Assertions are often useful in the initial stages of user adoption of an application. You can distribute release builds of your application containing `Trace.Assert()` functions to keep tabs on things. Should an assertion be triggered, the user will be informed, and this information can be passed on to you. You can then determine what has gone wrong even if you do not know how it went wrong.

You might, for example, provide a brief description of the error in the first string, with instructions as to what to do next as the second string:

```
Trace.Assert(myVar < 10, "Variable out of bounds.",
             "Please contact vendor with the error code KCW001.");
```

Should this assertion occur, the user will see the dialog box shown in Figure 7-9.

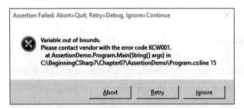

FIGURE 7-9

Admittedly, this isn't the most user-friendly dialog box in the world, as it contains a lot of information that could confuse users, but if they send you a screenshot of the error, you could quickly track down the problem.

Now it is time to look at what you can actually do after application execution is halted and you are in break mode. In general, you enter break mode to find an error in your code (or to reassure yourself that things are working properly). Once you are in break mode, you can use various techniques, all of which enable you to analyze your code and the exact state of the application at the point in its execution where it is paused.

Monitoring Variable Content

Monitoring variable content is just one example of how Visual Studio helps you a great deal by simplifying things. The easiest way to check the value of a variable is to hover the mouse over its name in the source code while in break mode. A Tooltip showing information about the variable appears, including the variable's current value.

You can also highlight entire expressions to get information about their results in the same way. For more complex values, such as arrays, you can even expand values in the Tooltip to see individual element entries.

It is possible to pin these Tooltip windows to the code view, which can be useful if there is a variable you are particularly interested in. Pinned Tooltips persist, so they are available even if you stop and restart debugging. You can also add comments to pinned Tooltips, move them around, and see the value of the last variable value, even when the application isn't running.

You may have noticed that when you run an application, the layout of the various windows in the IDE changes. By default, the following changes are likely to occur at runtime (this behavior may vary slightly depending on your installation):

➤ The Properties window disappears, along with some other windows, probably including the Solution Explorer window.

➤ A diagnostic Tools window opens that displays a Summary, Events, Memory Usage, and CPU Usage.

➤ The Error List window is replaced with two new windows across the bottom of the IDE window.

➤ Several new tabs appear in the new windows.

The new screen layout is shown in Figure 7-10. This may not match your display exactly, and some of the tabs and windows may not look exactly the same, but the functionality of these windows as described later will be the same, and this display is customizable via the View and Debug ⇨ Windows menus (during break mode), as well as by dragging windows around the screen to reposition them.

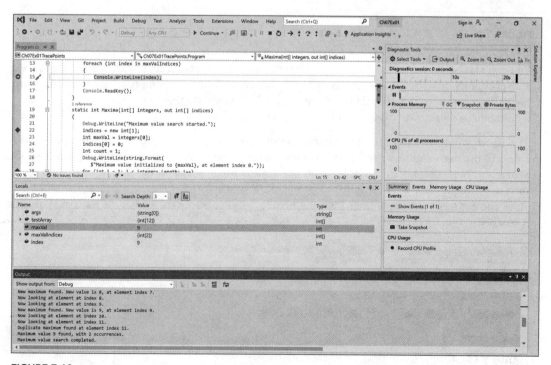

FIGURE 7-10

The new window that appears in the bottom-left corner is particularly useful for debugging. It enables you to keep tabs on the values of variables in your application when in break mode:

➤ **Autos**—Variables in use in the current and previous statements (Ctrl+D, A)

➤ **Locals**—All variables in scope (Ctrl+D, L)

➤ **Watch** *N*—Customizable variable and expression display (where N is 1 to 4, found on Debug ⇨ Windows ⇨ Watch)

All these tabs work in more or less the same way, with various additional features depending on their specific function. In general, each tab contains a list of variables, with information on each variable's name, value, and type. More complex variables, such as arrays, may be further examined using the expansion/contraction symbols to the left of their names, enabling a tree view of their content. For example, Figure 7-11 shows the Locals tab obtained by placing a breakpoint in the example code. It shows the expanded view for one of the array variables, `maxValIndices`.

Locals		
Name	Value	Type
args	{string[0]}	string[]
▷ testArray	{int[12]}	int[]
◢ maxValIndices	{int[2]}	int[]
[0]	9	int
[1]	11	int
maxVal	9	int
index	9	int

FIGURE 7-11

You can also edit the content of variables from this view. This effectively bypasses any other variable assignment that might have happened in earlier code. To do this, simply type a new value into the Value column for the variable you want to edit. You might do this to try out some scenarios that would otherwise require code changes, for example.

The Watch window enables you to monitor specific variables, or expressions involving specific variables. To use this window, type the name of a variable or expression into the Name column and view the results. Note that not all variables in an application are in scope all the time, and are labeled as such in a Watch window. For example, Figure 7-12 shows a Watch window with a few sample variables and expressions in it, obtained when a breakpoint just before the end of the `Maxima()` function is reached.

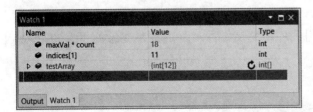

Watch 1		
Name	Value	Type
maxVal * count	18	int
indices[1]	11	int
▷ testArray	{int[12]}	↻ int[]

Output Watch 1

FIGURE 7-12

The `testArray` array is local to `Main()`, so you don't see a value here and it is grayed out.

Stepping through Code

So far, you've learned how to discover what is going on in your applications at the point where break mode is entered. Now it is time to see how you can use the IDE to step through code while remaining in break mode, which enables you to see the exact results of the code being executed. This is an extremely valuable technique for those of us who can't think as fast as computers can.

When Visual Studio enters break mode, a yellow arrow cursor appears to the left of the code view (which may initially appear inside the red circle of a breakpoint if a breakpoint was used to enter break mode) next to the line of code that is about to be executed, as shown in Figure 7-13.

```
Program.cs  ⊣ ×
C# Ch07Ex01TracePoints          ⌄  ⁺⚛Ch07Ex01TracePoints.Program          ⌄  ⚙ₐMaxima(int[] integers, out int[] indices)  ⌄  ⊹
                        0 references
     8      ⊟      static void Main(string[] args)
     9             {
 ⦿  10 ✒            int[] testArray = { 4, 7, 4, 2, 7, 3, 7, 8, 3, 9, 1, 9 };
     11             int maxVal = Maxima(testArray, out int[] maxValIndices);
     12             Console.WriteLine($"Maximum value {maxVal} found at element indices:");
     13     ⊟      foreach (int index in maxValIndices)
     14             {
     15                 Console.WriteLine(index);
     16             }
     17             Console.ReadKey();
     18             }
100 %  ⌄    ⊘ No issues found        ◈ ⌄   ◂ ▓▓▓▓▓▓▓▓▓▓▓▓▓▓▓▓▓▓▓▓▓          ▸    Ln: 10   Ch: 13   SPC   CRLF
```

FIGURE 7-13

This shows you what point execution has reached when break mode is entered. At this point, you can execute the program on a line-by-line basis. To do so, you use some of the Debug toolbar buttons shown in Figure 7-14.

FIGURE 7-14

The sixth, seventh, and eighth icons control program flow in break mode. In order, they are as follows:

➤ **Step Into**—Execute and move to the next statement to execute.

➤ **Step Over**—Similar to Step Into, but won't enter nested blocks of code, including functions.

➤ **Step Out**—Run to the end of the code block and resume break mode at the statement that follows.

To look at every single operation carried out by the application, you can use Step Into to follow the instructions sequentially. This includes moving inside functions, such as Maxima() in the preceding example. Clicking this icon when the cursor reaches line 16, which is the call to Maxima(), results in the cursor moving to the first line inside the Maxima() function. Alternatively, clicking Step Over when you reach line 16 moves the cursor straight to line 17, without going through the code in Maxima() (although this code is still executed). If you do step into a function that you aren't interested in, you can click Step Out to return to the code that called the function. As you step through code, the values of variables are likely to change. If you keep an eye on the monitoring windows just discussed, you can clearly see this happening.

You can also change which line of code will be executed next by right-clicking a line of code and selecting Set Next Statement, or by dragging the yellow arrow to a different line of code. This doesn't always work, such as when skipping variable initialization. However, it can be very useful for skipping problematic lines of code to see what will happen, or for repeating the execution of code by moving the arrow backward.

In code that has semantic errors, these techniques may be the most useful ones at your disposal. You can step through code right up to the point where you expect problems to occur, and the errors will be generated as if you were running the program normally. Or you can cause statements to be executed more than once by changing the executing code. Along the way, you can watch the data to see just what is going wrong. Later in this chapter, you'll step through some code to find out what is happening in an example application.

Immediate and Command Windows

The Command and Immediate windows (found on the Debug Windows menu) enable you to execute commands while an application is running. The Command window enables you to perform Visual Studio operations manually (such as menu and toolbar operations), and the Immediate window enables you to execute additional code besides the source code lines being executed, and to evaluate expressions.

These windows are intrinsically linked. You can even switch between them by entering commands— immed to move from the Command window to the Immediate window and cmd to move back.

This section concentrates on the Immediate window because the Command window is only really useful for complex operations. The simplest use of the Immediate window is to evaluate expressions, a bit like a one-shot use of the Watch windows. To do this, type an expression and press Return. The information requested will then be displayed. An example is shown in Figure 7-15.

FIGURE 7-15

You can also change variable content here, as demonstrated in Figure 7-16.

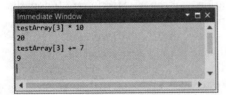

FIGURE 7-16

In most cases, you can get the effects you want more easily using the variable monitoring windows shown earlier, but this technique is still handy for tweaking values, and it's good for testing expressions.

The Call Stack Window

The final window to look at is the Call Stack window, which shows you the way in which the program reached the current location. In simple terms, this means showing the current function along with the function that called it, the function that called that, and so on (that is, a list of nested function calls). The exact points where calls are made are also recorded.

In the earlier example, entering break mode when in `Maxima()`, or moving into this function using code stepping, reveals the information shown in Figure 7-17.

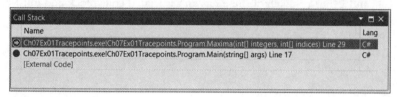

FIGURE 7-17

If you double-click an entry, you are taken to the appropriate location, enabling you to track the way code execution has reached the current point. This window is particularly useful when errors are first detected because you can see what happened immediately before the error. Where errors occur in commonly used functions, this helps you determine the source of the error.

ERROR HANDLING

The first part of this chapter explained how to find and correct errors during application development so that they don't occur in release-level code. Sometimes, however, you know that errors are likely to occur and there is no way to be 100 percent sure that they won't. In those situations, it may be preferable to anticipate problems and write code that is robust enough to deal with these errors gracefully, without interrupting execution.

Error handling is the term for all techniques of this nature, and this section looks at exceptions and how you can deal with them. An exception is an error generated either in your code or in a function called by your code that occurs at runtime. The definition of error here is vaguer than it has been up until now, because exceptions may be generated manually, in functions and so on. For example, you might generate an exception in a function if one of its string parameters doesn't start with the letter "a." Strictly speaking, this isn't an error outside of the context of the function, although the code that calls the function treats it as an error.

You've seen exceptions a few times already in this book. Perhaps the simplest example is attempting to address an array element that is out of range:

```
int[] myArray = { 1, 2, 3, 4 };
int myElem = myArray[4];
```

This outputs the following exception message and then terminates the application:

```
Index was outside the bounds of the array.
```

Exceptions are defined in namespaces, and most have names that make their purpose clear. In this example, the exception generated is called `System.IndexOutOfRangeException`, which makes sense because you have supplied an index that is not in the range of indices permissible in `myArray`. This message appears, and the application terminates, only when the exception is unhandled. In the next section, you'll see exactly what you must do to handle an exception.

try. . .catch. . .finally

The C# language includes syntax for *structured exception handling* (SEH). Three keywords mark code as being able to handle exceptions, along with instructions specifying what to do when an exception occurs: `try`, `catch`, and `finally`. Each of these has an associated code block and must be used in consecutive lines of code. The basic structure is as follows:

```
try
{
    ...
}
catch (<exceptionType> e) when (<filterIsTrue>)
{
    await <methodName(e);>
    ...
}
finally
{
    await <methodName;>
    ...
}
```

The `await` keyword is used to support advanced asynchronous programming techniques that avoid bottlenecks and can improve the overall performance and responsiveness of an application. Asynchronous programming, utilizing the `async` and `await` keywords, is not discussed in this book; nevertheless, as those keywords do simplify the implementation of this programming technique, it is highly recommended to learn about them.

It is also possible, however, to have a `try` block and a `finally` block with no `catch` block, or a `try` block with multiple `catch` blocks. If one or more `catch` blocks exist, then the `finally` block is optional; otherwise, it is mandatory. The usage of the blocks is as follows:

➤ `try`—Contains code that might throw exceptions ("throw" is the C# way of saying "generate" or "cause" when talking about exceptions).

➤ `catch`—Contains code to execute when exceptions are thrown. `catch` blocks can respond only to specific exception types (such as `System.IndexOutOfRangeException`) using `<exceptionType>`, hence the ability to provide multiple `catch` blocks. It is also possible to omit this parameter entirely, to get a general `catch` block that responds to all exceptions. C# 6 introduced a concept called *exception filtering* that is implemented by adding the when keyword after the exception type expressions. If that exception type occurs and the filter expression is true, only then will the code in the `catch` block execute.

➤ `finally`—Contains code that is always executed, either after the `try` block if no exception occurs, after a `catch` block if an exception is handled, or just before an unhandled exception moves "up the call stack." This phrase means that SEH allows you to nest `try...catch... finally` blocks inside one another, either directly or because of a call to a function within a `try` block. For example, if an exception is not handled by any `catch` blocks in the called function, it might be handled by a `catch` block in the calling code. Eventually, if no `catch` blocks are matched, then the application will terminate. The fact that the `finally` block is processed before this happens is the reason for its existence; otherwise, you might just as well place code outside of the `try...catch...finally` structure.

Here is the sequence of events that occurs after an exception occurs in code in a `try` block, also illustrated by Figure 7-18:

➤ The `try` block terminates at the point where the exception occurred.

➤ If a `catch` block exists, then a check is made to determine whether the block matches the type of exception that was thrown. If no `catch` block exists, then the `finally` block (which must be present if there are no `catch` blocks) executes.

➤ If a `catch` block exists but there is no match, then a check is made for other `catch` blocks.

➤ If a `catch` block matches the exception type and there is an exception filter that results in `true`, the code within it executes and then the `finally` block is executed (if it is present).

➤ If a `catch` block matches the exception type and there is no exception filter, the code it contains executes, and then the `finally` block executes if it is present.

➤ If no `catch` blocks match the exception type, then the `finally` block of code executes if it is present.

> **NOTE** If two `catch` blocks exist that handle the same exception type, only the code within the `catch` block with an exception filter resulting in `true` is executed. If a `catch` block also exists that handles the same exception type with no exception filter or an exception filter resulting in `false`, it is disregarded. Only one `catch` block code is executed.

The following Try It Out demonstrates handling exceptions. It shows throwing and handling them in several ways, so you can see how things work.

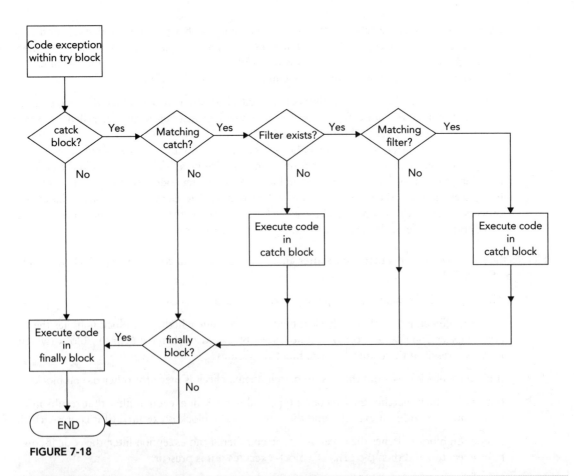

FIGURE 7-18

TRY IT OUT   Exception Handling: Ch07Ex02\Program.cs

1. Create a new Console Application called Ch07Ex02 and save it in the directory
   `C:\BeginningCSharpAndDotNET\Chapter07`.

2. Modify the code as follows (the line number comments shown here will help you match up your
   code to the discussion afterward; they are duplicated in the downloadable code for this chapter for
   your convenience):

```
class Program
{
    static string[] eTypes = { "none", "simple", "index",
                               "nested index", "filter" };

    static void Main(string[] args)
    {
        foreach (string eType in eTypes)
        {
```

```
    try
    {
        Console.WriteLine("Main() try block reached.");          // Line 15
        Console.WriteLine($"ThrowException(\"{eType}\") called.");
        ThrowException(eType);
        Console.WriteLine("Main() try block continues.");        // Line 18
    }
    catch (System.IndexOutOfRangeException e) when (eType == "filter")
    {
        Console.BackgroundColor = ConsoleColor.Red;
        Console.WriteLine("Main() FILTERED System.IndexOutOfRangeException" +
                        $"catch block reached. Message:\n\"{e.Message}\"");
        Console.ResetColor();

    }
    catch (System.IndexOutOfRangeException e)                    // Line 27
    {
        Console.WriteLine("Main() System.IndexOutOfRangeException catch " +
                        $"block reached. Message:\n\"{e.Message}\"");
    }
    catch                                                        // Line 32
    {
        Console.WriteLine("Main() general catch block reached.");
    }
    finally
    {
        Console.WriteLine("Main() finally block reached.");
    }
    Console.WriteLine();
    }
    Console.ReadKey();
}
static void ThrowException(string exceptionType)
{
    Console.WriteLine($"ThrowException(\"{exceptionType}\") reached.");
    switch (exceptionType)
    {
    case "none":
        Console.WriteLine("Not throwing an exception.");
        break;                                                   // Line 51
    case "simple":
        Console.WriteLine("Throwing System.Exception.");
        throw new System.Exception();                            // Line 54
    case "index":
        Console.WriteLine("Throwing System.IndexOutOfRangeException.");
        eTypes[5] = "error";                                     // Line 57
        break;
    case "nested index":
        try                                                      // Line 60
        {
            Console.WriteLine("ThrowException(\"nested index\") " +
                            "try block reached.");
            Console.WriteLine("ThrowException(\"index\") called.");
```

```
                    ThrowException("index");                        // Line 65
                }
                catch                                               // Line 67
                {
                    Console.WriteLine("ThrowException(\"nested index\") general"
                                    + " catch block reached.");
                    throw;
                }
                finally
                {
                    Console.WriteLine("ThrowException(\"nested index\") finally"
                                    + " block reached.");
                }
                break;
            case "filter":
                try                                                 // Line 86
                {
                    Console.WriteLine("ThrowException(\"filter\") " +
                                    "try block reached.");
                    Console.WriteLine("ThrowException(\"index\") called.");
                    ThrowException("index");                        // Line 91
                }
                catch                                               // Line 93
                {
                    Console.WriteLine("ThrowException(\"filter\") general"
                                    + " catch block reached.");
                    throw;
                }
                break;

        }
    }
}
```

> **NOTE** *Try commenting out the* `throw` *statements on lines 76 and 96 to get a better illustration of the exception filter functionality that was introduced with C# 6.*

3. Run the application. The result is shown in Figure 7-19.

```
C:\BeginningCSharpAndDotNET\Chapter07\Ch07Ex02\Ch07Ex02\bin\Debug\net5.0\Ch07Ex02.exe        —    □    ×
Main() try block reached.
ThrowException("nested index") called.
ThrowException("nested index") reached.
ThrowException("nested index") try block reached.
ThrowException("index") called.
ThrowException("index") reached.
Throwing System.IndexOutOfRangeException.
ThrowException("nested index") general catch block reached.
ThrowException("nested index") finally block reached.
Main() System.IndexOutOfRangeException catch block reached. Message:
"Index was outside the bounds of the array."
Main() finally block reached.

Main() try block reached.
ThrowException("filter") called.
ThrowException("filter") reached.
ThrowException("filter") try block reached.
ThrowException("index") called.
ThrowException("index") reached.
Throwing System.IndexOutOfRangeException.
ThrowException("filter") general catch block reached.
Main() FILTERED System.IndexOutOfRangeExceptioncatch block reached. Message:
"Index was outside the bounds of the array."
Main() finally block reached.
```

FIGURE 7-19

How It Works

This application has a `try` block in `Main()` that calls a function called `ThrowException()`. This function may throw exceptions, depending on the parameter it is called with:

➤ `ThrowException("none")`—Doesn't throw an exception

➤ `ThrowException("simple")`—Generates a general exception

➤ `ThrowException("index")`—Generates a `System.IndexOutOfRangeException` exception

➤ `ThrowException("nested index")`—Contains its own `try` block, which contains code that calls `ThrowException("index")` to generate a `System.IndexOutOfRangeException` exception

➤ `ThrowException("filter")`—Contains its own `try` block, which contains code that calls `ThrowException("index")` to generate a `System.IndexOutOfRangeException` exception where the exception filter results in `true`

Each of these `string` parameters is held in the global `eTypes` array, which is iterated through in the `Main()` function to call `ThrowException()` once with each possible parameter. During this iteration, various messages are written to the console to indicate what is happening. This code gives you an excellent opportunity to use the code-stepping techniques shown earlier in the chapter. By working your way through the code one line at a time, you can see exactly how code execution progresses.

Add a new breakpoint (with the default properties) to line 15 of the code, which reads as follows:

```
Console.WriteLine("Main() try block reached.");
```

NOTE *Code is referred to by line numbers as they appear in the download-able version of this code. If you have line numbers turned off, remember that you can turn them back on (select Tools ⇨ Options and then change the Line Numbers setting in the Text Editor ⇨ C# ⇨ General options section). Comments are included in the preceding code so that you can follow the text without having the file open in front of you.*

Run the application in debug mode. Almost immediately, the program will enter break mode, with the cursor on line 15. If you select the Locals tab in the variable monitoring window, you should see that eType *is currently* "none"*. Use the Step Into button to process lines 15 and 16 and confirm that the first lines of text have been written to the console. Next, use the Step Into button to step into the* ThrowException() *function on line 17.*

Once in the ThrowException() *function, the Locals window changes.* eType *and* args *are no longer in scope (they are local to* Main()*); instead, you see the local* exceptionType *argument, which is, of course,* "none"*. Keep clicking Step Into and you'll reach the* switch *statement that checks the value of* exceptionType *and executes the code that writes out the string* Not throwing an exception *to the screen. When you execute the* break *statement (on line 51), you exit the function and resume processing in* Main() *at line 18. Because no exception was thrown, the* try *block continues.*

Next, processing continues with the finally *block. Click Step Into a few more times to complete the* finally *block and the first cycle of the* foreach *loop. The next time you reach line 17,* ThrowException() *is called using a different parameter,* "simple"*.*

Continue using Step Into through ThrowException()*, and you'll eventually reach line 60:*

```
throw new System.Exception();
```

You use the C# throw *keyword to generate an exception. This keyword simply needs to be provided with a* new*-initialized exception as a parameter, and it will throw that exception. Here, you are using another exception from the* System *namespace,* System.Exception*.*

NOTE *When you use* throw *in a* case *block, no* break; *statement is necessary.* throw *is enough to end execution of the block.*

When you process this statement with Step Into, you find yourself at the general catch *block starting on line 32. There was no match with the earlier* catch *block starting on line 27, so this one is processed instead. Stepping through this code takes you through this block, through the* finally *block, and back into another loop cycle that calls* ThrowException() *with a new parameter on line 17. This time the parameter is* "index".

Now ThrowException() *generates an exception on line 57:*

```
eTypes[5] = "error";
```

The eTypes *array is global, so you have access to it here. However, here you are attempting to access the sixth element in the array (remember that counting starts at 0), which generates a* System.IndexOutOfRangeException *exception.*

This time there are multiple matched catch *blocks in* Main()*. One has a filter expression of* (eType == "filter") *on line 20, and the other, on line 27, has no filter expression. The value stored in* eType *is currently* "index" *and therefore the filter expression results in* false*, which skips this* catch *code block.*

Stepping into the code takes you to the next catch *block, starting at line 27. The* WriteLine() *call in this block writes out the message stored in the exception using* e.Message *(you have access to the exception through the parameter of the* catch *block). Again, stepping through takes you through the* finally *block (but not the second* catch *block, as the exception is already handled) and back into the loop cycle, again calling* ThrowException() *on line 17.*

When you reach the switch *structure in* ThrowException()*, this time you enter a new* try *block, starting on line 61. When you reach line 65, you perform a nested call to* ThrowException()*, this time with the parameter* "index"*. You can use the Step Over button to skip the lines of code that are executed here because you've been through them already. As before, this call generates a* System.IndexOutOfRangeException *exception, but this time it's handled in the nested* try...catch...finally *structure, the one in* ThrowException()*. This structure has no explicit match for this type of exception, so the general* catch *block (starting on line 67) deals with it.*

Continue stepping through the code and when you reach the switch *structure in the* ThrowException() *this time, you enter a new* try *block starting at line 86. When you reach line 91, you perform a nested call to* ThrowException() *same as before. However, this time when the* catch *block that handles the* System.IndexOutOfRangeException *in the* Main() *checks the filter expression*

continues

continued

of (eType == "filter"), *the result is* true *and that* catch *block is executed instead of the* catch *block handling the* System.IndexOutOfRangeException *without the exception filter.*

As with the earlier exception handling, you now step through this catch *block and the associated* finally *block, and reach the end of the function call, but with one crucial difference. Although an exception was thrown, it was also handled—by the code in* ThrowException(). *This means there is no exception left to handle in* Main(), *so you go straight to the* finally *block, at which point the application terminates.*

Throw Expressions

In the previous Try It Out, throw is used only within code statements where programmed actions take place. It is also possible to use throw in an expression as seen here:

```
friend ?? throw new ArgumentNullException(paraName: nameof(friend), message: "null")
```

This code snippet uses double questions marks (??) called the *null-coalescing operator* to check whether the value being assigned is null. If it is null then the ArgumentNullException function is thrown. If the value is not null, then the value is assigned to the variable.

Listing and Configuring Exceptions

The .NET Framework contains a host of exception types, and you are free to throw and handle any of these in your own code. The IDE supplies a dialog box for examining and editing the available exceptions, which can be called up with the Debug ⇨ Windows ⇨ Exception Settings menu item (or by pressing Ctrl+Alt+E). Figure 7-20 shows the Exception Settings dialog box.

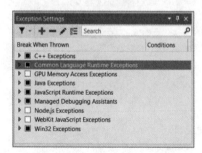

FIGURE 7-20

Exceptions are listed by category and .NET library namespace. You can see the exceptions in the System namespace by expanding the Common Language Runtime Exceptions arrowhead sign. The list includes the System.IndexOutOfRangeException exception you used earlier.

Each exception may be configured using the check boxes next to the exception type. When checked, the debugger will break when `Thrown`, causing a break into the debugger even for exceptions that are handled.

EXERCISES

7.1 "Using `Trace.WriteLine()` is preferable to using `Debug.WriteLine()`, as the `Debug` version works only in debug builds." Do you agree with this statement? If so, why?

7.2 Provide code for a simple application containing a loop that generates an error after 5,000 cycles. Use a breakpoint to enter break mode just before the error is caused on the 5,000th cycle. (Note: A simple way to generate an error is to attempt to access a nonexistent array element, such as `myArray[1000]` in an array with 100 elements.)

7.3 "`finally` code blocks execute only if a `catch` block isn't executed." True or false?

7.4 Given the enumeration data type `orientation` defined in the following code, write an application that uses structured exception handling (SEH) to cast a `byte`-type variable into an `orientation`-type variable in a safe way. (Note: You can force exceptions to be thrown using the `checked` keyword, an example of which is shown here. This code should be used in your application.)

```
enum Orientation : byte
{
    North = 1,
    South = 2,
    East  = 3,
    West  = 4
}
myDirection = checked((Orientation)myByte);
```

Answers to these exercises can be found in the Appendix.

▶ **WHAT YOU LEARNED IN THIS CHAPTER**

TOPIC	KEY CONCEPTS
Error types	Fatal errors cause your application to fail completely, either at compile time (syntax errors) or at runtime. Semantic, or logic, errors are more insidious and may cause your application to function incorrectly or unpredictably.
Outputting debugging information	You can write code that outputs helpful information to the Output window to aid debugging in the IDE. You do this with the `Debug` and `Trace` family of functions, where `Debug` functions are ignored in release builds. For production applications, you may want to write debugging output to a log file instead. You can also use tracepoints to output debugging information.
Break mode	You can enter break mode (essentially a state where the application is paused) manually, through breakpoints, through assertions, or when unhandled exceptions occur. You can add breakpoints anywhere in your code and you can configure breakpoints to break execution only under specific conditions. When in break mode, you can inspect the content of variables (with the help of various debug information windows) and step through code a line at a time to assist you in determining where the errors are.
Exceptions	Exceptions are errors that occur at runtime and that you can trap and process programmatically to prevent your application from terminating. There are many types of exceptions that can occur when you call functions or manipulate variables. You can also generate exceptions with the `throw` keyword.
Exception handling	Exceptions that are not handled in your code will cause the application to terminate. You handle exceptions with `try`, `catch`, and `finally` code blocks. `try` blocks mark out a section of code for which exception handling is enabled. `catch` blocks consist of code that is executed only if an exception occurs, and can match specific types of exceptions. You can include multiple `catch` blocks. `finally` blocks specify code that is executed after exception handling has occurred, or after the `try` block finishes if no exception occurs. You can include only a single `finally` block, and if you include any `catch` blocks, then the `finally` block is optional.

Introduction to Object-Oriented Programming

At this point in the book, you've covered all the basics of C# syntax and programming and have learned how to debug your applications. Already, you can assemble usable console applications. However, to access the real power of the C# language and .NET, you need to make use of *object-oriented programming* (OOP) techniques. In fact, as you will soon see, you have been using these techniques already, although to keep things simple we haven't focused on this.

This chapter steers away from code temporarily and focuses instead on the principles behind OOP. This leads you back into the C# language because it has a symbiotic relationship with OOP. All the concepts introduced in this chapter are revisited in later chapters, with illustrative code—so do not panic if you don't grasp everything in the first read-through of this material.

To start with, you will look at the basics of OOP, which include answering that most fundamental of questions, "What is an *object*?" You will quickly find that a lot of terminology related to

OOP can be confusing at first, but plenty of explanations are provided. You will also see that using OOP requires you to look at programming in a different way.

As well as discussing the general principles of OOP, this chapter looks at an area requiring a thorough understanding of OOP: desktop applications. This type of application relies on the Windows environment, with features such as menus, buttons, and so on. As such, it provides plenty of scope for description, and you will be able to observe OOP points effectively in the Windows environment.

WHAT IS OBJECT-ORIENTED PROGRAMMING?

Object-oriented programming seeks to address many of the problems with traditional programming techniques. The type of programming you have seen so far is known as *procedural programming*, which often results in so-called monolithic applications, meaning all functionality is contained in a few modules of code (often just one). With OOP techniques, you often use many more modules of code, with each offering specific functionality. Also, each module can be isolated or even completely independent of the others. This modular method of programming gives you much more versatility and provides more opportunity for code reuse.

To illustrate this further, imagine that a high-performance application on your computer is a top-of-the-range race car. Written with traditional programming techniques, this sports car is basically a single unit. If you want to improve this car, then you have to replace the whole unit by sending it back to the manufacturer and getting their expert mechanics to upgrade it, or by buying a new one. If OOP techniques are used, however, you can simply buy a new engine from the manufacturer and follow their instructions to replace it yourself, rather than taking a hacksaw to the bodywork.

In a more traditional application, the flow of execution is often simple and linear. Applications are loaded into memory, begin executing at point A, end at point B, and are then unloaded from memory. Along the way various other entities might be used, such as files on storage media, or the capabilities of a video card, but the main body of the processing occurs in one place. The code along the way is generally concerned with manipulating data through various mathematical and logical means. The methods of manipulation are usually quite simple, using basic types such as integers and Boolean values to build more complex representations of data.

With OOP, things are rarely so linear. Although the same results are achieved, the way of getting there is often quite different. OOP techniques are firmly rooted in the structure and meaning of data, and the interaction between that data and other data. This usually means putting more effort into the design stages of a project, but it has the benefit of extensibility. After an agreement is made as to the representation of a specific type of data, that agreement can be worked into later versions of an application, and even entirely new applications. The fact that such an agreement exists can reduce development time dramatically. This explains how the race car example works. The agreement here is how the code for the "engine" is structured, such that new code (for a new engine) can be substituted with ease, rather than requiring a trip back to the manufacturer. It also means that the engine, once created, can be used for other purposes. You could put it in a different car, or use it to power a submarine, for example.

OOP often simplifies things by providing an agreement about both the approach to data representation and the structure and usage of more abstract entities. For example, an agreement can be made not just on the format of data that should be used to send output to a device such as a printer, but also on the methods of data exchange with that device, including what instructions it understands, and so on. In the race car analogy, the agreement would include how the engine connects to the fuel tank, how it passes drive power to the wheels, and so on.

As the name of the technology suggests, this is achieved by using objects.

What Is an Object?

An *object* is a building block of an OOP application. This building block encapsulates part of the application, which can be a process, a chunk of data, or a more abstract entity.

In the simplest sense, an object can be similar to a struct type such as those shown earlier in the book, containing members of variable and function types. The variables contained make up the data stored in the object, and the functions contained allow access to the object's functionality. Slightly more complex objects might not maintain any data; instead, they can represent a process by containing only functions. For example, an object representing a printer might be used, which would have functions enabling control over a printer (so you can print a document, a test page, and so on).

Objects in C# are created from types, just like the variables you have seen already. The type of an object is known by a special name in OOP, its *class*. You can use class definitions to *instantiate* objects, which means creating a real, named *instance* of a class. The phrases *instance of a class* and *object* mean the same thing here; but *class* and *object* mean fundamentally different things.

> **NOTE** *The terms class and object are often confused, and it is important to understand the distinction. It might help to visualize these terms using the earlier race car analogy. Think of a class as the template for the car, or perhaps the plans used to build the car. The car itself is an instance of those plans, so it could be referred to as an object.*

In this chapter, you work with classes and objects using *Unified Modeling Language* (UML) syntax. UML is designed for modeling applications, from the objects that build them to the operations they perform to the use cases that are expected. Here, you use only the basics of this language, which are explained as you go along. UML is a specialized subject to which entire books are devoted, so its more complex aspects are not covered here.

Figure 8-1 shows a UML representation of your printer class, called `Printer`. The class name is shown in the top section of this box (you learn about the bottom two sections a little later).

Printer

FIGURE 8-1

Figure 8-2 shows a UML representation of an instance of this `Printer` class called `myPrinter`.

FIGURE 8-2

Here, the instance name is shown first in the top section, followed by the name of its class. The two names are separated by a colon.

Properties and Fields

Properties and fields provide access to the data contained in an object. This object data differentiates separate objects because it is possible for different objects of the same class to have different values stored in properties and fields.

The various pieces of data contained in an object together make up the *state* of that object. Imagine an object class that represents a cup of coffee, called CupOfCoffee. When you instantiate this class (that is, create an object of this class), you must provide it with a state for it to be meaningful. In this case, you might use properties and fields to enable the code that uses this object to set the type of coffee used, whether the coffee contains milk and/or sugar, whether the coffee is instant, and so on. A given coffee cup object would then have a given state, such as "Colombian filter coffee with milk and two sugars."

Both fields and properties are typed, so you can store information in them as string values, as int values, and so on. However, properties differ from fields in that they don't provide direct access to data. Objects can shield users from the nitty-gritty details of their data, which need not be represented on a one-to-one basis in the properties that exist. If you used a field for the number of sugars in a CupOfCoffee instance, then users could place whatever values they liked in the field, restricted only by the limits of the type used to store this information. If, for example, you used an int to store this data, then users could use any value between –2147483648 and 2147483647, as shown in Chapter 3. Obviously, not all values make sense, particularly the negative ones, and some of the large positive amounts might require an inordinately large cup. If you use a property for this information, you could limit this value to, say, a number between 0 and 2.

In general, it is better to provide properties rather than fields for state access because you have more control over various behaviors. This choice does not affect code that uses object instances because the syntax for using properties and fields is the same.

Read/write access to properties can also be clearly defined by an object. Certain properties can be read-only, allowing you to see what they are but not change them. This is often a useful technique for reading several pieces of state simultaneously. You might have a read-only property of the CupOfCoffee class called Description, returning a string representing the state of an instance of this class (such as the string given earlier) when requested. You might be able to assemble the same data by interrogating several properties, but a property such as this one might save you time and effort. You might also have write-only properties that operate in a similar way.

As well as this read/write access for properties, you can also specify a different sort of access permission for both fields and properties, known as *accessibility*. Accessibility determines which code can access these members—that is, whether they are available to all code (public), only to code within the class (private), or should use a more complex scheme (covered in more detail later in the chapter, when it becomes pertinent). One common practice is to make fields private and provide access to them via public properties. This means that code within the class has direct access to data stored in the field while the public property shields external users from this data and prevents them from placing invalid content there. Public members are said to be *exposed* by the class.

One way to visualize this is to equate it with variable scope. Private fields and properties, for example, can be thought of as local to the object that possesses them, whereas the scope of public fields and properties also encompasses code external to the object.

In the UML representation of a class, you use the second section to display properties and fields, as shown in Figure 8-3.

This is a representation of the CupOfCoffee class, with five members (properties or fields, because no distinction is made in UML) defined as discussed earlier. Each of the entries contains the following information:

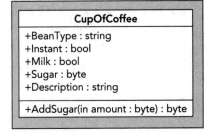

FIGURE 8-3

> ➤ Accessibility—A + symbol is used for a public member, a – symbol is used for a private member. In general, though, private members are not shown in the diagrams in this chapter because this information is internal to the class. No information is provided as to read/write access.

> ➤ The member name.

> ➤ The type of the member.

A colon is used to separate the member names and types.

Methods

Method is the term used to refer to functions exposed by objects. These can be called in the same way as any other function and can use return values and parameters in the same way—you looked at functions in detail in Chapter 6.

Methods are used to provide access to the object's functionality. Like fields and properties, they can be public or private, restricting access to external code, as necessary. They often make use of an object's state to affect their operations, and have access to private members, such as private fields, if required. For example, the CupOfCoffee class might define a method called AddSugar(), which would provide a more readable syntax for incrementing the amount of sugar than setting the corresponding Sugar property.

CupOfCoffee
+BeanType : string
+Instant : bool
+Milk : bool
+Sugar : byte
+Description : string
+AddSugar(in amount : byte) : byte

FIGURE 8-4

In UML, class boxes show methods in the third section, as shown in Figure 8-4.

The syntax here is like that for fields and properties, except that the type shown at the end is the return type, and method parameters are shown. Each parameter is displayed in UML with one of the following identifiers: return, in, out, or inout. These are used to signify the direction of data flow, where out and inout roughly correspond to the use of the C# keywords out and ref described in Chapter 6. in roughly corresponds to the default C# behavior, where neither the out nor ref keyword is used, and return signifies that a value is passed back to the calling method.

Everything's an Object

At this point, it is time to come clean: You have been using objects, properties, and methods throughout this book. In fact, everything in C# and .NET is an object! The `Main()` function in a console application is a method of a class. Every variable type you have looked at is a class. Every command you have used has been a property or a method, such as `<String>.Length`, `<String>.ToUpper()`, and so on. (The period character here separates the object instance's name from the property or method name, and methods are shown with `()` at the end to differentiate them from properties.)

Objects really are everywhere, and the syntax to use them is often quite simple. It has certainly been simple enough for you to concentrate on some of the more fundamental aspects of C# up until now. From this point on, you will begin to look at objects in detail. Bear in mind that the concepts introduced here have far-reaching consequences—applying even to that simple little `int` variable you have been happily playing around with.

The Life Cycle of an Object

Every object has a clearly defined life cycle. Apart from the normal state of "being in use," this life cycle includes two important stages:

➤ **Construction**—When an object is first instantiated it needs to be initialized. This initialization is known as *construction* and is carried out by a constructor function, often referred to simply as a *constructor* for convenience.

➤ **Destruction**—When an object is destroyed, there are often some clean-up tasks to perform, such as freeing memory. This is the job of a destructor function, also known as a *destructor*.

Constructors

Basic initialization of an object is automatic. For example, you do not have to worry about finding the memory to fit a new object into. However, at times you will want to perform additional tasks during an object's initialization stage, such as initializing the data stored by an object. A constructor is what you use to do this.

Class definitions typically contain at least one constructor. These constructors can include a *default constructor*, which is a parameter-less method with the same name as the class itself. A class definition might also include several constructor methods with parameters, known as *nondefault constructors*. These enable code that instantiates an object to do so in many ways, perhaps providing initial values for data stored in the object.

In C#, constructors are called using the `new` keyword. For example, you could instantiate a `CupOf-Coffee` object using its default constructor in the following way:

```
CupOfCoffee myCup = new CupOfCoffee();
```

Objects can also be instantiated using nondefault constructors. For example, the `CupOfCoffee` class might have a nondefault constructor that uses a parameter to set the bean type at instantiation:

```
CupOfCoffee myCup = new CupOfCoffee("Blue Mountain");
```

Constructors, like fields, properties, and methods, can be public or private. Code external to a class cannot instantiate an object using a private constructor; it must use a public constructor. In this way, you can, for example, force users of your classes to use a nondefault constructor.

Some classes have no public constructors, meaning it is impossible for external code to instantiate them (they are said to be *noncreatable*). However, that does not make them completely useless, as you will see shortly.

Destructors

Destructors are used by .NET to clean up after objects. In general, you do not have to provide code for a destructor method; instead, the default operation does the work for you. However, you can provide specific instructions if anything important needs to be done before the object instance is deleted.

For example, when a variable goes out of scope, it may not be accessible from your code; however, it might still exist somewhere in your computer's memory. Only when the .NET runtime performs its garbage collection clean-up is the instance completely destroyed.

Static and Instance Class Members

As well as having members such as properties, methods, and fields that are specific to object instances, it is also possible to have *static* (also known as *shared*, particularly to our Visual Basic brethren) members, which can be methods, properties, or fields. Static members are shared between instances of a class, so they can be thought of as global for objects of a given class. Static properties and fields enable you to access data that is independent of any object instances, and static methods enable you to execute commands related to the class type but not specific to object instances. When using static members, in fact, you do not even need to instantiate an object.

For example, the `Console.WriteLine()` and `Convert.ToString()` methods you have been using are static. At no point do you need to instantiate the `Console` or `Convert` classes (indeed, if you try, you'll find that you can't, as the constructors of these classes aren't publicly accessible, as discussed earlier). If you include the `using static System.Console;` declaration at the beginning of your program, `Console.` is not required and you can call `WriteLine()` directly.

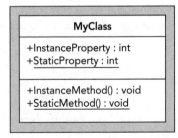

There are many situations such as these where static properties and methods can be used to good effect. For example, you might use a static property to keep track of how many instances of a class have been created. In UML syntax, static members of classes appear with underlining, as shown in Figure 8-5.

FIGURE 8-5

Static Constructors

When using static members in a class, you might want to initialize these members beforehand. You can supply a static member with an initial value as part of its declaration, but sometimes you might want to perform a more complex initialization, or perhaps perform some operations before assigning values or allowing static methods to execute.

You can use a static constructor to perform initialization tasks of this type. A class can have a single static constructor, which must have no access modifiers and cannot have any parameters. A static constructor can never be called directly; instead, it is executed when one of the following occurs:

➤ An instance of the class containing the static constructor is created.

➤ A static member of the class containing the static constructor is accessed.

In both cases, the static constructor is called first, before the class is instantiated or static members accessed. No matter how many instances of a class are created, its static constructor will be called only once. To differentiate between static constructors and the constructors described earlier in this chapter, all nonstatic constructors are also known as *instance constructors*.

Static Classes

Often, you will want to use classes that contain only static members and cannot be used to instantiate objects (such as `Console`). A shorthand way to do this, rather than make the constructors of the class private, is to use a *static class*. A static class can contain only static members and cannot have instance constructors, since by implication it can never be instantiated. Static classes can, however, have a static constructor, as described in the preceding section.

> **NOTE** If you are completely new to OOP, you might like to take a break before embarking on the remainder of this chapter. It is important to fully grasp the fundamentals before learning about the more complicated aspects of this methodology.

OOP TECHNIQUES

Now that you know the basics, and what objects are and how they work, you can spend some time looking at some of the other features of objects. This section covers all of the following:

➤ Interfaces

➤ Inheritance

➤ Polymorphism

➤ Relationships between objects

➤ Operator overloading

➤ Events

➤ Reference versus value types

Interfaces

An *interface* is a collection of public instance (that is, nonstatic) methods and properties that are grouped together to encapsulate specific functionality. After an interface has been defined, you can implement it in a class. This means that the class will then support all the properties and members specified by the interface.

Interfaces cannot exist on their own. You cannot "instantiate an interface" as you can a class. In addition, interfaces cannot contain any code that implements its members; it just defines the members. The implementation must come from classes that implement the interface.

In the earlier coffee example, you might group together many of the more general-purpose properties and methods into an interface, such as AddSugar(), Milk, Sugar, and Instant. You could call this interface something like IHotDrink (interface names are normally prefixed with a capital I). You could use this interface on other objects, perhaps those of a CupOfTea class. You could therefore treat these objects in a similar way, and they can still have their own individual properties (BeanType for CupOfCoffee and LeafType for CupOfTea, for example).

Interfaces implemented on objects in UML are shown using *lollipop* syntax (the line connected to the circle). In Figure 8-6, members of IHotDrink are split into a separate box using class-like syntax.

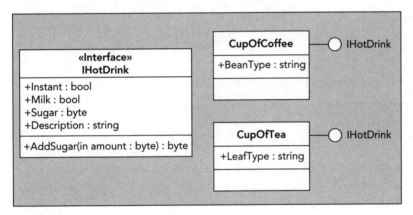

FIGURE 8-6

A class can support multiple interfaces, and multiple classes can support the same interface. The concept of an interface, therefore, makes life easier for users and other developers. For example, you might have some code that uses an object with a certain interface. Provided that you don't use other properties and methods of this object, it is possible to replace one object with another (code using the IHotDrink interface shown earlier could work with both CupOfCoffee and CupOfTea instances, for example). In addition, the developer of the object itself could supply you with an updated version of an object, and as long as it supports an interface already in use, it would be easy to use this new version in your code.

Once an interface is published—that is, it has been made available to other developers or end users—it is good practice not to change it. One way of thinking about this is to imagine the interface as a contract between class creators and class consumers. You are effectively saying, "Every class that supports interface X will support these methods and properties." If the interface changes later, perhaps due to an upgrade of the underlying code, this could cause consumers of that interface to run it incorrectly, or even fail. Instead, you should create a new interface that extends the old one, perhaps including a version number, such as X2. This has become the standard way of doing things, and you are likely to come across numbered interfaces frequently.

Disposable Objects

One interface of particular interest is IDisposable. An object that supports the IDisposable interface must implement the Dispose() method—that is, it must provide code for this method. This method can be called when an object is no longer needed (just before it goes out of scope, for example) and should be used to free up any critical resources that might otherwise linger until the destructor method is called during garbage collection. This gives you more control over the resources used by your objects.

C# enables you to use a structure that makes excellent use of this method. The using keyword enables you to initialize an object that uses critical resources in a code block, where Dispose() is automatically called at the end of the code block:

```
<ClassName> <VariableName> = new <ClassName>();
...
using (<VariableName>)
{
    ...
}
```

Alternatively, you can instantiate the object <VariableName> as part of the using statement:

```
using (<ClassName> <VariableName> = new <ClassName>())
{
    ...
}
```

In both cases, the variable <VariableName> will be usable within the using code block and will be disposed of automatically at the end (that is, Dispose() is called when the code block finishes executing).

Inheritance

Inheritance is one of the most important features of OOP. Any class may *inherit* from another, which means that it will have all the members of the class from which it inherits. In OOP terminology, the class being inherited from (*derived* from) is the *parent* class (also known as the *base* class). Classes in C# can derive only from a single base class directly, although of course that base class can have a base class of its own, and so on.

Inheritance enables you to extend or create more specific classes from a single, more generic base class. For example, consider a class that represents a farm animal (as used by ace octogenarian developer Old MacDonald in his livestock application). This class might be called Animal and possess methods such as EatFood() or Breed(). You could create a derived class called Cow, which would support all of these methods but might also supply its own, such as Moo() and SupplyMilk(). You could also create another derived class, Chicken, with Cluck() and LayEgg() methods.

In UML, you indicate inheritance using arrows, as shown in Figure 8-7.

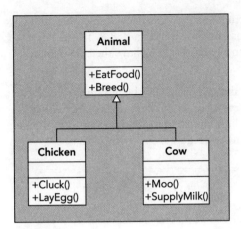

FIGURE 8-7

> **NOTE** In Figure 8-7, the member return types are omitted for clarity.

When using inheritance from a base class, the question of member accessibility becomes an important one. Private members of the base class are not accessible from a derived class, but public members are. However, public members are accessible to both the derived class and external code. Therefore, if you could use only these two levels of accessibility, you could not have a member that is accessible by both the base class and the derived class but is not accessible by external code.

To get around this, there is a third type of accessibility, *protected*, in which only the base class and derived classes have access to a member. As far as external code is aware, this is identical to a private member—it does not have access in either case.

As well as defining the protection level of a member, you can also define an inheritance behavior for it. Members of a base class can be *virtual*, which means that the member can be overridden by the class that inherits it. Therefore, the derived class can provide an alternative implementation for the member. This alternative implementation does not delete the original code, which is still accessible from within the class, but it does shield it from external code. If no alternative is supplied, then any external code that uses the member through the derived class automatically uses the base class implementation of the member.

> **NOTE** In UML, public members are denoted by a +. Other values are – (private), # (protected), italics (virtual).

> **NOTE** Virtual members cannot be private because that would cause a paradox—it is impossible to say that a member can be overridden by a derived class at the same time you say that it is inaccessible from the derived class.

In the animals example, you could make EatFood() virtual and provide a new implementation for it on any derived class—for example, just on the Cow class, as shown in Figure 8-8. This displays the EatFood() method on the Animal and Cow classes to signify that they have their own implementations.

Base classes may also be defined as *abstract* classes. An abstract class can't be instantiated directly; to use it you need to inherit from it. Abstract classes can have abstract members, which have no implementation in the base class, so an implementation must be supplied in the derived class. If Animal were an abstract class, then the UML would look as shown in Figure 8-9.

> **NOTE** *Abstract class names are shown in italics (or with a dashed line for their boxes). A class that is not abstract is called concrete.*

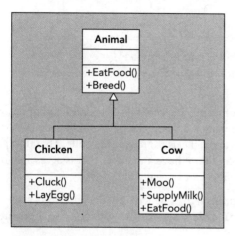

FIGURE 8-8

In Figure 8-9, both EatFood() and Breed() are shown in the derived classes Chicken and Cow, implying that these methods are either abstract (and, therefore, must be overridden in derived classes) or virtual (and, in this case, have been overridden in Chicken and Cow). Of course, abstract base classes can provide implementation of members, which is quite common. The fact that you cannot instantiate an abstract class doesn't mean you can't encapsulate functionality in it.

Finally, a class may be *sealed*. A sealed class cannot be used as a base class, so no derived classes are possible.

C# provides a common base class for all objects called object (which is an alias for the System. Object class in the .NET Framework). If a class is not derived from any other class, then it implicitly derives from object. You take a closer look at this class in Chapter 9.

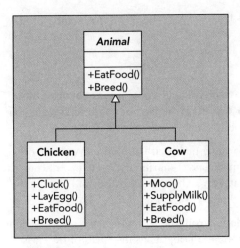

FIGURE 8-9

> **NOTE** *Interfaces, described earlier in this chapter, can also inherit from other interfaces. Unlike classes, interfaces can inherit from multiple base interfaces (in the same way that classes can support multiple interfaces).*

Polymorphism

One consequence of inheritance is that classes deriving from a base class have an overlap in the methods and properties that they expose. Because of this, it is often possible to treat objects instantiated from classes with a base type in common using identical syntax. For example, if a base class called `Animal` has a method called `EatFood()`, then the syntax for calling this method from the derived classes `Cow` and `Chicken` will be similar:

```
Cow myCow = new Cow();
Chicken myChicken = new Chicken();
myCow.EatFood();
myChicken.EatFood();
```

Polymorphism takes this a step further. You can assign an object that is of a derived type to a variable of one of the base types, as shown here:

```
Animal myAnimal = myCow;
```

No casting is required for this. You can then call methods of the base class through this variable:

```
myAnimal.EatFood();
```

This results in the implementation of `EatFood()` in the derived class being called. Note that you cannot call methods defined on the derived class in the same way. The following code will not work:

```
myAnimal.Moo();
```

However, you can cast a base type variable into a derived class variable and call the method of the derived class that way:

```
Cow myNewCow = (Cow)myAnimal;
myNewCow.Moo();
```

This casting causes an exception to be raised if the type of the original variable was anything other than Cow or a class derived from Cow. There are ways to determine the type of an object, which you will learn in the next chapter.

Polymorphism is an extremely useful technique for performing tasks with a minimum of code on different objects descending from a single class. It is not just classes sharing the same parent class that can make use of polymorphism. It is also possible to treat, say, a child and a grandchild class in the same way, if there is a common class in their inheritance hierarchy.

As a further note here, remember that in C# all classes derive from the base class object at the root of their inheritance hierarchies. It is therefore possible to treat all objects as instances of the class object. This is how WriteLine() can process an almost infinite number of parameter combinations when building strings. Every parameter after the first is treated as an object instance, allowing output from any object to be written to the screen. To do this, the method ToString() (a member of object) is called. You can override this method to provide an implementation suitable for your class, or simply use the default, which returns the class name (qualified according to any namespaces it is in).

Interface Polymorphism

Although you cannot instantiate interfaces in the same way as objects, you can have a variable of an interface type. You can then use the variable to access methods and properties exposed by this interface on objects that support it.

For example, suppose that instead of an Animal base class being used to supply the EatFood() method, you place this EatFood() method on an interface called IConsume. The Cow and Chicken classes could both support this interface, the only difference being that they are forced to provide an implementation for EatFood() because interfaces contain no implementation. You can then access this method using code such as the following:

```
Cow myCow = new Cow();
Chicken myChicken = new Chicken();
IConsume consumeInterface;
consumeInterface = myCow;
consumeInterface.EatFood();
consumeInterface = myChicken;
consumeInterface.EatFood();
```

This provides a simple way for multiple objects to be called in the same manner, and it does not rely on a common base class. For example, this interface could be implemented by a class called Venus-FlyTrap that derives from Vegetable instead of Animal:

```
VenusFlyTrap myVenusFlyTrap = new VenusFlyTrap();
IConsume consumeInterface;
consumeInterface = myVenusFlyTrap;
consumeInterface.EatFood();
```

In the preceding code snippets, calling `consumeInterface.EatFood()` results in the `EatFood()` method of the `Cow`, `Chicken`, or `VenusFlyTrap` class being called, depending on which instance has been assigned to the interface type variable.

Note here that derived classes inherit the interfaces supported by their base classes. In the first of the preceding examples, it might be that either `Animal` supports `IConsume` or that both `Cow` and `Chicken` support `IConsume`. Remember that classes with a base class in common do not necessarily have interfaces in common, and vice versa.

Relationships between Objects

Inheritance is a simple relationship between objects that results in a base class being completely exposed by a derived class, where the derived class can also have some access to the inner workings of its base class (through protected members). There are other situations in which relationships between objects become important.

This section takes a brief look at the following:

> **Containment**—One class contains another. This is like inheritance but allows the containing class to control access to members of the contained class and even perform additional processing before using members of a contained class.

> **Collections**—One class acts as a container for multiple instances of another class. This is like having arrays of objects, but collections have additional functionality, including indexing, sorting, resizing, and more.

Containment

Containment is simple to achieve by using a member field to hold an object instance. This member field might be public, in which case users of the container object have access to its exposed methods and properties, much like with inheritance. However, you will not have access to the internals of the class via the derived class, as you would with inheritance.

Alternatively, you can make the contained member object a private member. If you do this, then none of its members will be accessible directly by users, even if they are public. Instead, you can provide access to these members using members of the containing class. This means that you have complete control over which members of the contained class to expose, if any, and you can perform additional processing in the containing class members before accessing the contained class members.

For example, a `Cow` class might contain an `Udder` object with the public method `Milk()`. The `Cow` object could call this method as required, perhaps as part of its `SupplyMilk()` method, but these details will not be apparent (or important) to users of the `Cow` object.

Contained classes can be visualized in UML using an association line. For simple containment, you label the ends of the lines with 1s, showing a one-to-one relationship (one `Cow` instance will contain one `Udder` instance). You can also show the contained `Udder` class instance as a private field of the `Cow` class for clarity (see Figure 8-10).

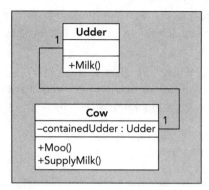

FIGURE 8-10

Collections

Chapter 5 described how you can use arrays to store multiple variables of the same type. This also works for objects (remember, the variable types you have been using are really objects, so this is no real surprise). Here is an example:

```
Animal[] animals = new Animal[5];
```

A *collection* is basically an array with bells and whistles. Collections are implemented as classes in much the same way as other objects. They are often named in the plural form of the objects they store—for example, a class called `Animals` might contain a collection of `Animal` objects.

The main difference from arrays is that collections usually implement additional functionality, such as `Add()` and `Remove()` methods to add and remove items to and from the collection. There is also usually an `Item` property that returns an object based on its index. More often than not this property is implemented in such a way as to allow more sophisticated access. For example, it would be possible to design `Animals` so that a given `Animal` object could be accessed by its name.

In UML you can visualize this as shown in Figure 8-11. Members are not included in Figure 8-11 because it is the relationship that is being illustrated. The numbers on the ends of the connecting lines show that one `Animals` object will contain zero or more `Animal` objects. You will take a more detailed look at collections in Chapter 11.

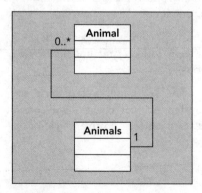

FIGURE 8-11

Operator Overloading

Earlier in the book, you saw how operators can be used to manipulate simple variable types. There are times when it is logical to use operators with objects instantiated from your own classes. This is possible because classes can contain instructions regarding how operators should be treated.

For example, you might add a new property to the `Animal` class called `Weight`. You could then compare animal weights using the following:

```
if (cowA.Weight > cowB.Weight)
{
    ...
}
```

Using operator overloading, you can provide logic that uses the `Weight` property implicitly in your code, so that you can write code such as the following:

```
if (cowA > cowB)
{
    ...
}
```

Here, the greater-than operator (`>`) has been *overloaded*. An overloaded operator is one for which you have written the code to perform the operation involved—this code is added to the class definition of one of the classes that it operates on. In the preceding example, you are using two `Cow` objects, so the operator overload definition is contained in the `Cow` class. You can also overload operators to work with different classes in the same way, where one (or both) of the class definitions contains the code to achieve this.

You can only overload existing C# operators in this way; you cannot create new ones. However, you can provide implementations for both unary (single operand) and binary (two operands) usages of operators such as + or >. You see how to do this in C# in Chapter 13.

Events

Objects can raise (and consume) *events* as part of their processing. Events are important occurrences that you can act on in other parts of code, like (but more powerful than) exceptions. You might, for example, want some specific code to execute when an `Animal` object is added to an `Animals` collection, where that code isn't part of either the `Animals` class or the code that calls the `Add()` method. To do this, you need to add an *event handler* to your code, which is a special kind of function that is called when the event occurs. You also need to configure this handler to listen for the event you are interested in.

You can create *event-driven applications*, which are far more prolific than you might think. For example, bear in mind that Windows-based applications are entirely dependent on events. Every button click or scroll bar drag you perform is achieved through event handling, as the events are triggered by the mouse or keyboard.

Later in this chapter you will see how this works in Windows applications, and there is a more in-depth discussion of events in Chapter 13.

Reference Types versus Value Types

Data in C# is stored in a variable in one of two ways, depending on the type of the variable. This type will fall into one of two categories: reference or value. The difference is as follows:

➤ Value types store themselves and their content in one place in memory (called the *stack*).

➤ Reference types hold a reference to somewhere else in memory (called the *heap*) where content is stored.

In fact, you do not have to worry about this too much when using C#. So far, you have used `string` variables (which are reference types) and other simple variables (most of which are value types, such as `int`) in pretty much the same way.

One key difference between value types and reference types is that value types always contain a value, whereas reference types can be `null`, reflecting the fact that they contain no value. It is, however, possible to create a value type that behaves like a reference type in this respect (that is, it can be `null`) by using *nullable types*. These are described in Chapter 12 when you look at the advanced technique of *generic types* (which include nullable types).

The only simple types that are reference types are `string` and `object`, although arrays are implicitly *reference types as well. Every class you create will be a reference type*, which is why this is stressed here.

OOP IN DESKTOP APPLICATIONS

In Chapter 2, you created a simple desktop application in C# using Windows Presentation Foundation (WPF). WPF desktop applications are heavily dependent on OOP techniques, and this section takes a look at this to illustrate some of the points made in this chapter. The following Try It Out enables you to work through a simple example.

TRY IT OUT   Objects in Action: Ch08Ex01

1. Create a new WPF Application called Ch08Ex01 and save it in the directory `C:\Beginning-CSharpAndDotNET\Chapter08`.

2. Add a new `Button` control using the Toolbox, and position it somewhere in the middle of `MainWindow`, as shown in Figure 8-12.

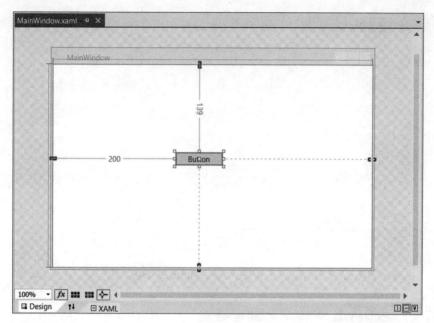

FIGURE 8-12

3. Double-click the button to add code for a mouse click. Modify the code that appears as follows:

```
private void Button_Click(object sender, RoutedEventArgs e)
{
    ((Button)sender).Content = "Clicked!";
    Button newButton = new Button();
    newButton.Width = 100;
    newButton.Height = 50;
    newButton.VerticalAlignment = VerticalAlignment.Top;
    newButton.Content = "New Button! ";
    newButton.Margin = new Thickness(10, 10, 200, 200);
    newButton.Click += newButton_Click;
    ((Grid)((Button)sender).Parent).Children.Add(newButton);
}
private void newButton_Click(object sender, RoutedEventArgs e)
{
    ((Button)sender).Content = "Clicked!!";
}
```

4. Run the application. The window is shown in Figure 8-13.

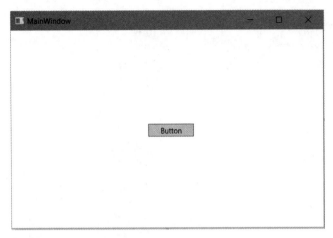

FIGURE 8-13

5. Click the button marked Button. The display changes (see Figure 8-14).

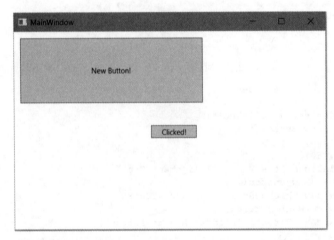

FIGURE 8-14

6. Click the button marked New Button! The display changes (see Figure 8-15).

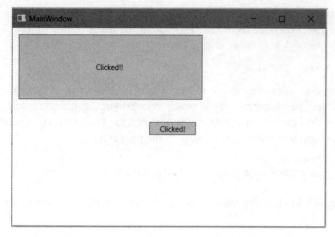

FIGURE 8-15

How It Works

By adding just a few lines of code, you've created a desktop application that does something, while at the same time illustrating some OOP techniques in C#. The phrase "everything's an object" is even more true when it comes to desktop applications. From the window that runs to the controls on the window, you need to use OOP techniques all the time. This example highlights some of the concepts you looked at earlier in this chapter to show how everything fits together.

The first thing you do in this application is add a new button to the MainWindow window. The button is an object; it's an instance of a class called Button, and the window is an instance of a class called Main-Window, which is derived from a class called Window. Next, by double-clicking the button, you add an event handler to listen for the Click event that the Button class exposes. The event handler is added to the code for the MainWindow object that encapsulates your application, as a private method:

```
private void Button_Click(object sender, RoutedEventArgs e)
{
}
```

The code uses the C# keyword private as a qualifier. Don't worry too much about that for now; the next chapter explains the C# code required for the OOP techniques covered in this chapter.

The first line of code you add changes the text on the button that is clicked. This makes use of polymorphism, described earlier in the chapter. The Button object representing the button that you click is sent to the event handler as an object parameter, which you cast into a Button type (this is possible because the Button object inherits from System.Object, which is the .NET class that object is an alias for). You then change the Content property of the object to change the text displayed:

```
((Button)sender).Content = "Clicked!";
```

Next, you create a new `Button` object with the `new` keyword (note that namespaces are set up in this project to enable this simple syntax; otherwise, you need to use the fully qualified name of this object, `System.Windows.Controls.Button`):

```
Button newButton = new Button();
```

You set the location of the button by using the `Width`, `Height`, and `VerticalAlignment` properties of the button. You also set the `Content` and `Margin` properties of the newly created `Button` object to suitable values for displaying the button. Note that the `Margin` property is of type `Thickness`, so you create a `Thickness` object using a nondefault constructor before assigning it to the property:

```
newButton.Content = "New Button!";
newButton.Margin = new Thickness(10, 10, 200, 200);
```

Elsewhere in the code a new event handler is added, which you use to respond to the `Click` event generated by the new button:

```
private void newButton_Click(object sender, RoutedEventArgs e)
{
    ((Button)sender).Content = "Clicked!!";
}
```

You register the event handler as a listener for the `Click` event, using overloaded operator syntax:

```
newButton.Click += newButton_Click;
```

Finally, you add the new button to the window. To do this, you find the parent of the existing button (using its `Parent` property), cast it to the correct type (which is `Grid`), and use the `Add()` method of the `Grid.Children` property to add the button, passing the button as a method parameter:

```
((Grid)((Button)sender).Parent).Children.Add(newButton);
```

This code looks more complicated than it actually is. Once you get the hang of the way that WPF represents the content of a window through a hierarchy of controls (including buttons and containers), this sort of thing will become second nature.

This short example used almost all of the techniques introduced in this chapter. As you can see, OOP programming needn't be complicated—it just requires a different point of view to get right.

EXERCISES

8.1   Which of the following are real levels of accessibility in OOP?

   a.   Friend

   b.   Public

   c.   Secure

   d.   Private

   e.   Protected

   f.   Loose

   g.   Wildcard

8.2 "You must call the destructor of an object manually or it will waste memory."
True or false?

8.3 Do you need to create an object to call a static method of its class?

8.4 Draw a UML diagram like the ones shown in this chapter for the following classes and interface:

- An abstract class called `HotDrink` that has the methods `Drink`, `AddMilk`, and `AddSugar`, and the properties `Milk` and `Sugar`

- An interface called `ICup` that has the methods `Refill` and `Wash`, and the properties `Color` and `Volume`

- A class called `CupOfCoffee` that derives from `HotDrink`, supports the `ICup` interface, and has the additional property `BeanType`

- A class called `CupOfTea` that derives from `HotDrink`, supports the `ICup` interface, and has the additional property `LeafType`

8.5 Write some code for a function that will accept either of the two cup objects in the preceding example as a parameter. The function should call the `AddMilk`, `Drink`, and `Wash` methods for any cup object it is passed.

Answers to the exercises can be found in the Appendix.

▶ WHAT YOU LEARNED IN THIS CHAPTER

TOPIC	KEY CONCEPTS
Objects and classes	Objects are the building blocks of OOP applications. Classes are type definitions that are used to instantiate objects. Objects can contain data and/or expose operations that other code can use. Data can be made available to external code through properties, and operations can be made available to external code through methods. Both properties and methods are class members. Properties can allow read access, write access, or both. Class members can be public (available to all code), or private (available only to code inside the class definition). In .NET, everything is an object.
Object life cycle	An object is instantiated by calling one of its constructors. When an object is no longer needed, it is destroyed by executing its destructor. To clean up after an object, it is often necessary to manually dispose of it. Disposal of the object happens when the `using` block is applied or if `IDispose` is implemented.
Static and instance members	Instance members are available only on object instances of a class. Static members are available only through the class definition directly and are not associated with an instance.
Interfaces	Interfaces are a collection of public properties and methods that can be implemented on a class. An instance-typed variable can be assigned a value of any object whose class definition implements that interface. Only the interface-defined members are then available through the variable.
Inheritance	Inheritance is the mechanism through which one class definition can derive from another. A class inherits members from its parent, of which it can have only one. Child classes cannot access private members in its parent, but it is possible to define protected members that are available only within a class or classes that derive from that class. Child classes can override members that are defined as virtual in a parent class. All classes have an inheritance chain that ends in `System.Object`, which has the alias `object` in C#.
Polymorphism	All objects instantiated from a derived class can be treated as if they were instances of an ancestor class.
Object relationships and features	Objects can contain other objects and can also represent collections of other objects. To manipulate objects in expressions, you often need to define how operators work with objects, through operator overloading. Objects can expose events that are triggered due to some internal process, and client code can respond to events by providing event handlers.

Defining Classes

WHAT YOU WILL LEARN IN THIS CHAPTER

➤ Defining classes and interfaces in C#

➤ Using the keywords that control accessibility and inheritance

➤ Discovering the `System.Object` class and its role in class definitions

➤ Using some helpful tools provided by Visual Studio (VS)

➤ Defining class libraries

➤ Knowing the differences and similarities between interfaces and abstract classes

➤ Exploring struct types

➤ Understanding important object copying considerations

CODE DOWNLOADS FOR THIS CHAPTER

The code downloads for this chapter are found on the book page at `www.wiley.com`. Click the Downloads link. The code can also be found at `github.com/benperk/BeginningCSharp-AndDotNET`. The code is in the Chapter09 folder and individually named according to the names throughout the chapter.

In Chapter 8, you looked at the features of object-oriented programming (OOP). In this chapter, you will put theory into practice and define classes in C#. You will not go so far as to define class members in this chapter, but you will concentrate on the class definitions themselves.

To begin, you explore the basic class definition syntax, the keywords you can use to determine class accessibility and more, and the way in which you can specify inheritance. You also look at interface definitions because they are like class definitions in many ways.

The rest of the chapter covers various related topics that apply when defining classes in C#.

CLASS DEFINITIONS IN C#

C# uses the `class` keyword to define classes:

```
class MyClass
{
   // Class members.
}
```

This code defines a class called `MyClass`. Once you have defined a class, you are free to instantiate it anywhere else in your project that has access to the definition. By default, classes are declared as *internal*, meaning that only code in the current project will have access to them. You can specify this explicitly using the `internal` access modifier keyword as follows (although you do not have to):

```
internal class MyClass
{
   // Class members.
}
```

Alternatively, you can specify that the class is public and should also be accessible to code in other projects. To do so, you use the `public` keyword:

```
public class MyClass
{
   // Class members.
}
```

In addition to these two access modifier keywords, you can also specify that the class is either *abstract* (cannot be instantiated, only inherited, and can have abstract members) or *sealed* (cannot be inherited). To do this, you use one of the two mutually exclusive keywords, `abstract` or `sealed`. An abstract class is declared as follows:

```
public abstract class MyClass
{
   // Class members, may be abstract.
}
```

Here, `MyClass` is a public abstract class, while internal abstract classes are also possible.

Sealed classes are declared as follows:

```
public sealed class MyClass
{
   // Class members.
}
```

As with abstract classes, sealed classes can be public or internal.

Inheritance can also be specified in the class definition. You simply put a colon after the class name, followed by the base class name:

```
public class MyClass : MyBase
{
   // Class members.
}
```

Only one base class is permitted in C# class definitions; and if you inherit from an abstract class, you must implement all the abstract members inherited (unless the derived class is also abstract).

The compiler does not allow a derived class to be more accessible than its base class. This means that an internal class can inherit from a public base, but a public class cannot inherit from an internal base. This code is legal:

```
public class MyBase
{
    // Class members.
}
internal class MyClass : MyBase
{
    // Class members.
}
```

The following code will not compile:

```
internal class MyBase
{
    // Class members.
}
public class MyClass : MyBase
{
    // Class members.
}
```

If no base class is used, the class inherits only from the base class System.Object (which has the alias object in C#). Ultimately, all classes have System.Object at the root of their inheritance hierarchy. You will take a closer look at this fundamental class a little later.

In addition to specifying base classes in this way, you can also specify interfaces supported after the colon character. If a base class is specified, it must be the first thing after the colon, with interfaces specified afterward. If no base class is specified, you specify the interfaces immediately after the colon. Commas must be used to separate the base class name (if there is one) and the interface names from one another.

For example, you could add an interface to MyClass as follows:

```
public class MyClass : IMyInterface
{
    // Class members.
}
```

All interface members must be implemented in any class that supports the interface, although you can provide an "empty" implementation (with no functional code) if you don't want to do anything with a given interface member, and you can implement interface members as abstract in abstract classes.

The following declaration is invalid because the base class MyBase isn't the first entry in the inheritance list:

```
public class MyClass : IMyInterface, MyBase
{
    // Class members.
}
```

The correct way to specify a base class and an interface is as follows:

```
public class MyClass : MyBase, IMyInterface
{
    // Class members.
}
```

Remember that multiple interfaces are possible, so the following is also valid:

```
public class MyClass : MyBase, IMyInterface, IMySecondInterface
{
    // Class members.
}
```

Table 9-1 shows the allowed access modifier combinations for class definitions.

TABLE 9-1: Access Modifiers for Class Definitions

MODIFIER	DESCRIPTION
none or internal	Class is accessible only from within the current project.
Public	Class is accessible from anywhere.
abstract or internal abstract	Class is accessible only from within the current project, and cannot be instantiated, only derived from.
public abstract	Class is accessible from anywhere, and cannot be instantiated, only derived from.
sealed or internal sealed	Class is accessible only from within the current project, and cannot be derived from, only instantiated.
public sealed	Class is accessible from anywhere, and cannot be derived from, only instantiated.
private	Class contents are accessible only from within the same class.
protected	Class contents are accessible from within the same class or a derived class.

Interface Definitions

Interfaces are declared in a similar way to classes, but using the `interface` keyword, rather than `class`:

```
interface IMyInterface
{
    // Interface members.
}
```

The access modifier keywords `public` and `internal` are used in the same way; and as with classes, interfaces are defined as internal by default. To make an interface publicly accessible, you must use the `public` keyword:

```
public interface IMyInterface
{
    // Interface members.
}
```

The keywords `abstract` and `sealed` are not allowed because neither modifier makes sense in the context of interfaces (they contain no implementation, so they cannot be instantiated directly, and they must be inheritable to be useful).

Interface inheritance is also specified in a similar way to class inheritance. The main difference here is that multiple base interfaces can be used, as shown here:

```
public interface IMyInterface : IMyBaseInterface, IMyBaseInterface2
{
    // Interface members.
}
```

Interfaces are not classes, and thus do not inherit from `System.Object`. However, the members of `System.Object` are available via an interface type variable, purely for convenience. In addition, as already discussed, it is impossible to instantiate an interface in the same way as a class. The following Try It Out provides an example of some class definitions, along with some code that uses them.

TRY IT OUT   Defining Classes: Ch09Ex01\Program.cs

1. Create a new Console Application called Ch09Ex01 and save it in the directory `C:\BeginningCSharpAndDotNET\Chapter09`.

2. Modify the code in `Program.cs` as follows:

```
namespace Ch09Ex01
{
    public abstract class MyBase {}
    internal class MyClass : MyBase {}
    public interface IMyBaseInterface {}
    internal interface IMyBaseInterface2 {}
    internal interface IMyInterface : IMyBaseInterface, IMyBaseInterface2 {}
    internal sealed class MyComplexClass : MyClass, IMyInterface {}
    class Program
    {
        static void Main(string[] args)
        {
            MyComplexClass myObj = new MyComplexClass();
            Console.WriteLine(myObj.ToString());
            Console.ReadKey();
        }
    }
}
```

3. Execute the project. Figure 9-1 shows the output.

FIGURE 9-1

How It Works

This project defines classes and interfaces in the inheritance hierarchy shown in Figure 9-2.

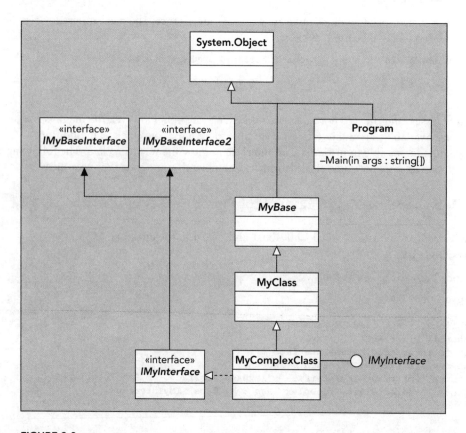

FIGURE 9-2

Program is included because it is a class defined in the same way as the other classes, even though it is not part of the main class hierarchy. The Main() method possessed by this class is the entry point for your application.

MyBase and IMyBaseInterface are public definitions, so they are available from other projects. The other classes and interfaces are internal, and only available in this project.

The code in `Main()` calls the `ToString()` method of `myObj`, an instance of `MyComplexClass`:

```
MyComplexClass myObj = new MyComplexClass();
Console.WriteLine(myObj.ToString());
```

`ToString()` is one of the methods inherited from `System.Object` (not shown in the diagram because members of this class are omitted for clarity) and simply returns the class name of the object as a string, qualified by any relevant namespaces.

This example does not do a lot, but you will return to it later in this chapter, where it is used to demonstrate several key concepts and techniques.

SYSTEM.OBJECT

Because all classes inherit from `System.Object`, all classes have access to the protected and public members of this class. Therefore, it is worthwhile to look at what is available there. `System.Object` contains the methods described in Table 9-2.

TABLE 9-2: Methods of System.Object

METHOD	RETURN TYPE	VIRTUAL	STATIC	DESCRIPTION
`Object()`	N/A	No	No	Constructor for the `System.Object` type. Automatically called by constructors of derived types.
`Finalize()`	N/A	No	No	Destructor for the `System.Object` type. Automatically called by destructors of derived types; cannot be called manually.
`Equals(object)`	bool	Yes	No	Compares the object for which this method is called with another object and returns `true` if they are equal. The default implementation checks whether the object parameter refers to the same object (because objects are reference types). This method can be overridden if you want to compare objects in a different way, for example, to compare the state of two objects.

continues

TABLE 9-2 (*continued*)

METHOD	RETURN TYPE	VIRTUAL	STATIC	DESCRIPTION
`Equals(object, object)`	`bool`	No	Yes	Compares the two objects passed to it and checks whether they are equal. This check is performed using the `Equals(object)` method. If both objects are null references, then this method returns `true`.
`ReferenceEquals (object, object)`	`bool`	No	Yes	Compares the two objects passed to it and checks whether they are references to the same instance.
`ToString()`	`string`	Yes	No	Returns a string corresponding to the object instance. By default, this is the qualified name of the class type, but this can be overridden to provide an implementation appropriate to the class type.
`MemberwiseClone()`	`object`	No	No	Copies the object by creating a new object instance and copying members. This member copying does not result in new instances of these members. Any reference type members of the new object refer to the same objects as the original class. This method is protected, so it can be used only from within the class or from derived classes.
`GetType()`	`System.Type`	No	No	Returns the type of the object in the form of a `System.Type` object.
`GetHashCode()`	`int`	Yes	No	Used as a hash function for objects where this is required. A hash function returns a value identifying the object state in some compressed form.

These are the basic methods that must be supported by object types in .NET, although you might never use some of them (or you might use them only in special circumstances, such as GetHashCode()).

GetType() is helpful when you are using polymorphism because it enables you to perform different operations with objects depending on their type, rather than the same operation for all objects, as is often the case. For example, if you have a function that accepts an object type parameter (meaning you can pass it just about anything), you might perform additional tasks if certain objects are encountered. Using a combination of GetType() and typeof (a C# operator that converts a class name into a System.Type object), you can perform comparisons such as the following:

```
if (myObj.GetType() == typeof(MyComplexClass))
{
    // myObj is an instance of the class MyComplexClass.
}
```

Another way to perform the same comparison is by using the "is" operator, which is introduced later in Chapter 11.

The System.Type object returned is capable of a lot more than that, but only this is covered here. It can also be especially useful to override the ToString() method, particularly in situations where the contents of an object can be easily represented with a single human-readable string. You will see these System.Object methods repeatedly in subsequent chapters, so you will learn more details as necessary.

CONSTRUCTORS AND DESTRUCTORS

When you define a class in C#, it is often unnecessary to define associated constructors and destructors because the compiler adds them for you when you build your code if you do not supply them. However, you can provide your own, if required, which enables you to initialize and clean up after your objects, respectively.

You can add a simple constructor to a class using the following syntax:

```
class MyClass
{
    public MyClass()
    {
        // Constructor code.
    }
}
```

This constructor has the same name as the class that contains it, has no parameters (making it the default constructor for the class), and is public so that objects of the class can be instantiated using this constructor (refer to Chapter 8 for more information about this).

You can also use a private default constructor, commonly utilized for classes that contain only static members. Setting the constructor to private means that instances of this class cannot be created using this constructor (it is *noncreatable*—again, see the discussion in Chapter 8):

```
class MyClass
{
    private MyClass()
    {
        // Constructor code.
    }
}
```

Finally, you can add nondefault constructors to your class in a similar way, simply by providing parameters:

```
class MyClass
{
    public MyClass()
    {
        // Default constructor code.
    }
    public MyClass(int myInt)
    {
        // Nondefault constructor code (uses myInt).
    }
}
```

You can supply an unlimited number of constructors (until you run out of memory or out of distinct sets of parameters, so maybe "almost unlimited" is more appropriate).

Destructors are declared using a slightly different syntax. The destructor used in .NET (and supplied by the System.Object class) is called Finalize(), but this isn't the name you use to declare a destructor. Instead of overriding Finalize(), you use the following:

```
class MyClass
{
    ~MyClass()
    {
        // Destructor body.
    }
}
```

Thus, the destructor of a class is declared by the class name (just as the constructor is), with the tilde (~) prefix. The code in the destructor is executed when garbage collection occurs, enabling you to free resources. After the destructor is called, implicit calls to the destructors of base classes also occur, including a call to Finalize() in the System.Object root class. This technique enables the .NET Framework to ensure that this occurs because overriding Finalize() would mean that base class calls would need to be explicitly performed, which is potentially dangerous (you learn how to call base class methods in the next chapter).

Constructor Execution Sequence

If you perform multiple tasks in the constructors of a class, it can be handy to have this code in one place, which has the same benefits as splitting code into functions, as shown in Chapter 6. You could do this using a method (see Chapter 10), but C# provides a nice alternative. You can configure any constructor to call any other constructor before it executes its own code.

First, though, you need to take a closer look at what happens by default when you instantiate a class instance. Apart from facilitating the centralization of initialization code, as noted previously, this is worth knowing about in its own right. During development, objects often don't behave quite as you expect them to due to errors during constructor calling—usually there is a base class somewhere in the inheritance hierarchy of your class that you are not instantiating correctly, or there is information that is not being properly supplied to base class constructors. Understanding what happens during this phase of an object's life cycle can make it much easier to solve this sort of problem.

For a derived class to be instantiated, its base class must be instantiated. For this base class to be instantiated, its own base class must be instantiated, and so on all the way back to `System.Object` (the root of all classes). As a result, whatever constructor you use to instantiate a class, `System.Object.Object()` is always called first.

Regardless of which constructor you use in a derived class (the default constructor or a nondefault constructor), unless you specify otherwise, the default constructor for the base class is used. (You will see how to change this behavior shortly.) Here is a short example illustrating the sequence of execution. Consider the following object hierarchy:

```
public class MyBaseClass
{
    public MyBaseClass()
    {
    }
    public MyBaseClass(int i)
    {
    }
}
public class MyDerivedClass : MyBaseClass
{
    public MyDerivedClass()
    {
    }
    public MyDerivedClass(int i)
    {
    }
    public MyDerivedClass(int i, int j)
    {
    }
}
```

You could instantiate `MyDerivedClass` as follows:

```
MyDerivedClass myObj = new MyDerivedClass();
```

In this case, the following sequence of events will occur:

➤ The `System.Object.Object()` constructor will execute.

➤ The `MyBaseClass.MyBaseClass()` constructor will execute.

➤ The `MyDerivedClass.MyDerivedClass()` constructor will execute.

Alternatively, you could use the following:

```
MyDerivedClass myObj = new MyDerivedClass(4);
```

The sequence is as follows:

➤ The `System.Object.Object()` constructor will execute.

➤ The `MyBaseClass.MyBaseClass()` constructor will execute.

➤ The `MyDerivedClass.MyDerivedClass(int i)` constructor will execute.

Finally, you could use this:

```
MyDerivedClass myObj = new MyDerivedClass(4, 8);
```

The result is the following sequence:

➤ The `System.Object.Object()` constructor will execute.

➤ The `MyBaseClass.MyBaseClass()` constructor will execute.

➤ The `MyDerivedClass.MyDerivedClass(int i, int j)` constructor will execute.

This system works fine most of the time, but sometimes you will want a little more control over the events that occur. For example, you might want to change the previous instantiation to the following sequence:

➤ The `System.Object.Object()` constructor will execute.

➤ The `MyBaseClass.MyBaseClass(int i)` constructor will execute.

➤ The `MyDerivedClass.MyDerivedClass(int i, int j)` constructor will execute.

Using this sequence, you could place the code that uses the `int i` parameter in `MyBaseClass(int i)`, which means that the `MyDerivedClass(int i, int j)` constructor would have less work to do—it would only need to process the `int j` parameter. (This assumes that the `int i` parameter has an identical meaning in both scenarios, which might not always be the case; but in practice, with this kind of arrangement, it usually is.) C# allows you to specify this kind of behavior if you want.

To do this, you can use a *constructor initializer*, which consists of code placed after a colon in the method definition. For example, you could specify the base class constructor to use in the definition of the constructor in your derived class, as follows:

```
public class MyDerivedClass : MyBaseClass
{
    ...
```

```
    public MyDerivedClass(int i, int j) : base(i)
    {
    }
}
```

The `base` keyword directs the .NET instantiation process to use the base class constructor, which has the specified parameters. Here, you are using a single `int` parameter (the value of which is the value passed to the `MyDerivedClass` constructor as the parameter i), so `MyBaseClass(int i)` will be used. Doing this means that `MyBaseClass()` will not be called, giving you the sequence of events listed prior to this example—exactly what you want here.

You can also use this `base` keyword to specify literal values for base class constructors, perhaps using the default constructor of `MyDerivedClass` to call a nondefault constructor of `MyBaseClass`:

```
public class MyDerivedClass : MyBaseClass
{
    public MyDerivedClass() : base(5)
    {
    }
    ...
}
```

This gives you the following sequence:

➤   The `System.Object.Object()` constructor will execute.

➤   The `MyBaseClass.MyBaseClass(int i)` constructor will execute.

➤   The `MyDerivedClass.MyDerivedClass()` constructor will execute.

As well as this `base` keyword, you can use one more keyword as a constructor initializer: `this`. This keyword instructs the .NET instantiation process to use another nondefault constructor on the current class before the specified constructor is called:

```
public class MyDerivedClass : MyBaseClass
{
    public MyDerivedClass() : this(5, 6)
    {
    }
    ...
    public MyDerivedClass(int i, int j) : base(i)
    {
    }
}
```

Here, using the `MyDerivedClass.MyDerivedClass()` constructor gives you the following sequence:

➤   The `System.Object.Object()` constructor will execute.

➤   The `MyBaseClass.MyBaseClass(int i)` constructor will execute.

➤   The `MyDerivedClass.MyDerivedClass(int i, int j)` constructor will execute.

➤   The `MyDerivedClass.MyDerivedClass()` constructor will execute.

The only limitation here is that you can specify only a single constructor using a constructor initializer. However, as demonstrated in the previous example, this isn't much of a limitation, because you can still construct sophisticated execution sequences.

> **NOTE** *If you do not specify a constructor initializer for a constructor, the compiler adds one for you:* base(). *This results in the default behavior described earlier in this section.*

Be careful not to accidentally create a circular reference when defining constructors. For example, consider this code:

```
public class MyBaseClass
{
    public MyBaseClass() : this(5)
    {
    }
    public MyBaseClass(int i) : this()
    {
    }
}
```

Using either one of these constructors requires the other to execute first, which in turn requires the other to execute first, and so on. This code will compile, but if you try to instantiate MyBaseClass you will receive an exception.

OOP TOOLS IN VISUAL STUDIO

Because OOP is such a fundamental aspect of .NET, several tools are provided by Visual Studio to aid development of OOP applications. This section describes some of these.

The Class View Window

In Chapter 2, you saw that the Solution Explorer window shares space with a window called Class View. This window shows you the class hierarchy of your application and enables you to see at a glance the characteristics of the classes you use. Figure 9-3 shows a view of the example project in the previous Try It Out.

The window is divided into two main sections; the bottom section shows members of types. Note that Figure 9-3 shows the display when all items in the Class View Settings drop-down, at the top of the Class View window, are checked. The Class View Settings drop-down is accessible by clicking the small arrow to the right of the image which resemble a gear.

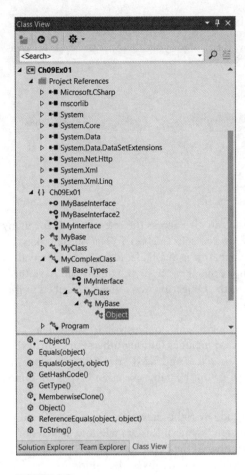

FIGURE 9-3

Many symbols can be used here, including the ones shown in Table 9-3.

TABLE 9-3: Class View Icons

ICON	MEANING	ICON	MEANING	ICON	MEANING
	Project		Property		Event
	Namespace		Field		Delegate
	Class		Struct		Assembly
	Interface		Enumeration		
	Method		Enumeration item		

Some of these are used for type definitions other than classes, such as enumerations and struct types.

Some of the entries can have other symbols placed below them, signifying their access level (no symbol appears for public entries). These are listed in Table 9-4.

TABLE 9-4: Additional Class View Icons

ICON	MEANING	ICON	MEANING	ICON	MEANING
🔒	Private	✦	Protected	♥	Internal

No symbols are used to denote abstract, sealed, or virtual entries.

As well as being able to look at this information here, you can also access the relevant code for many of these items. Double-clicking on an item, or right-clicking and selecting Go To Definition, takes you straight to the code in your project that defines the item, if it is available. If the code isn't available, such as code in an inaccessible base type (for example, System.Object), you instead have the option to select Browse Definition, which will take you to the Object Browser view (described in the next section).

One other entry that appears in Figure 9-3 is Project References. This enables you to see which assemblies are referenced by your projects, which in this case includes (among others) the core .NET types in mscorlib and System, data access types in System.Data, and XML manipulation types in System.Xml. The references here can be expanded, showing you the namespaces and types contained within these assemblies.

You can find occurrences of types and members in your code by right-clicking an item and selecting Find All References; a list of search results displays in the Find Symbol Results window, which normally appears at the bottom of the screen as a tabbed window in the Error List display area. You can also rename items using the Class View window. If you do this, you are given the option to rename references to the item wherever it occurs in your code. This means you have no excuse for spelling mistakes in class names because you can change them as often as you like!

In addition, you can navigate through your code with a view called *Call Hierarchy*, which is accessible from the Class View window through the View ➪ Call Hierarchy menu option, on the main menu navigation bar (Ctrl+W,K). This functionality is extremely useful for looking at how class members interact with each other, and you will look at it in the next chapter.

The Object Browser

The Object Browser is an expanded version of the Class View window, enabling you to view other classes available to your project, and even external classes. It is entered either automatically (for example, in the situation noted in the last section) or manually via View ➪ Object Browser. The view appears in the main window, and you can browse it in the same way as the Class View window.

This window provides the same information as Class View but also shows you more of the .NET types. When an item is selected, you also get information about it in a third window, as shown in Figure 9-4.

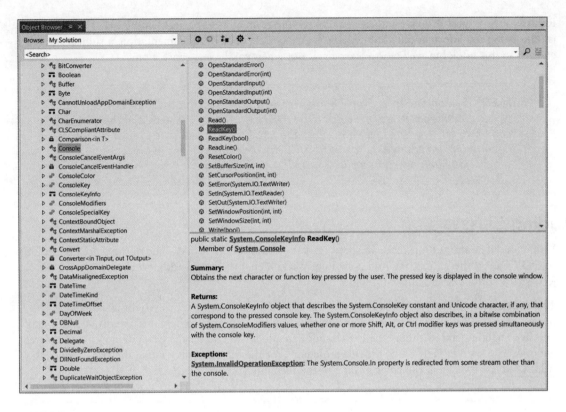

FIGURE 9-4

Here, the `ReadKey()` method of the `Console` class has been selected. (`Console` is found in the `System` namespace in the `mscorlib` assembly.) The information window in the bottom-right corner shows you the method signature, the class to which the method belongs, and a summary of the method function. This information can be useful when you are exploring the .NET types, or if you are just refreshing your memory about what a particular class can do.

Additionally, you can make use of this information window in types that you create. Make the following change to the code created previously in Ch09Ex01:

```
/// <summary>
/// This class contains my program!
/// </summary>
class Program
{
    static void Main(string[] args)
    {
        MyComplexClass myObj = new MyComplexClass();
        Console.WriteLine(myObj.ToString());
        Console.ReadKey();
    }
}
```

Return to the Object Browser and navigate to the Program class in project Ch09Ex01. The summary is reflected in the information window. This is an example of XML documentation, a subject not covered in this book but well worth learning about when you have a spare moment.

> **NOTE** *If you made this code change manually, then you noticed that simply typing the three slashes (///) causes the IDE to add most of the rest of the code for you. It automatically analyzes the code to which you are applying XML documentation and builds the basic XML documentation—more evidence, should you need any, that Visual Studio is a great tool to work with!*

Adding Classes

Visual Studio contains tools that can speed up some common tasks, and some of these are applicable to OOP. One of these tools, the Add New Item Wizard, enables you to add new classes to your project with a minimum amount of typing.

This tool is accessible through the Project ⇨ Add New Item menu item or by right-clicking your project in the Solution Explorer window and selecting the appropriate item. Either way, a dialog box appears, enabling you to choose the item to add. To add a class, select the Class item in the templates window, as shown in Figure 9-5, provide a filename for the file that will contain the class, and click Add. The class created is named according to the filename you provided.

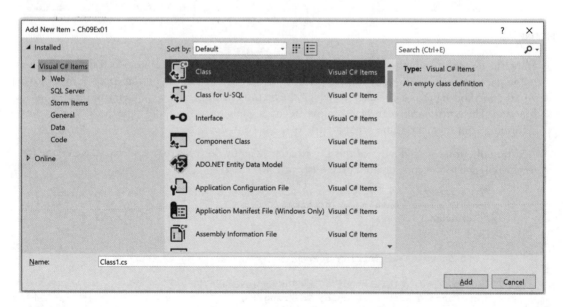

FIGURE 9-5

In the Try It Out earlier in this chapter, you added class definitions manually to your `Program.cs` file. Often, keeping classes in separate files makes it easier to keep track of your classes. Entering the information in the Add New Item dialog box when the Ch09Ex01 project is open results in the following code being generated in `MyNewClass.cs`:

```
using System;
using System.Collections.Generic;
using System.Linq;
using System.Text;
using System.Threading.Tasks;
namespace Ch09Ex01
{
    class MyNewClass
    {
    }
}
```

This class, `MyNewClass`, is defined in the same namespace as your entry point class, `Program`, so you can use it from code just as if it were defined in the same file. As shown in the code, the class generated for you contains no constructor. Recall that if a class definition does not include a constructor, then the compiler adds a default constructor when you compile your code.

Class Diagrams

One powerful feature of Visual Studio that you have not looked at yet is the capability to generate class diagrams from code and use them to modify projects. The class diagram editor in Visual Studio enables you to generate UML-like diagrams of your code with ease. You will see this in action in the following Try It Out when you generate a class diagram for the Ch09Ex01 project you created earlier.

> **NOTE** *Class Designer is an optional individual component that is not installed by default. To complete the next Try It Out, you need to install it. If you do not see the View Class Diagram option or you cannot add a new Class Diagram, you need to run the Visual Studio installer again and install "Class Designer."*

TRY IT OUT Generating a Class Diagram

1. Open the Ch09Ex01 project created earlier in this chapter.

2. In the Solution Explorer window, click the Ch09Ex01 project and then select the View ⇨ Class View menu item.

3. From within Class View, expand Ch09Ex01 ⇨ right-click {} Ch09Ex01 ⇨ select the View Class Diagram menu item ⇨ click {} Ch09Ex01, and drag it to the main window. A class diagram appears, called `ClassDiagram1.cd`.

4. Right-click `MyBase` and select Show Base Type from the context menu.

5. Move the objects in the drawing around by dragging them to achieve a more pleasing layout. At this point, the diagram should look a little like Figure 9-6.

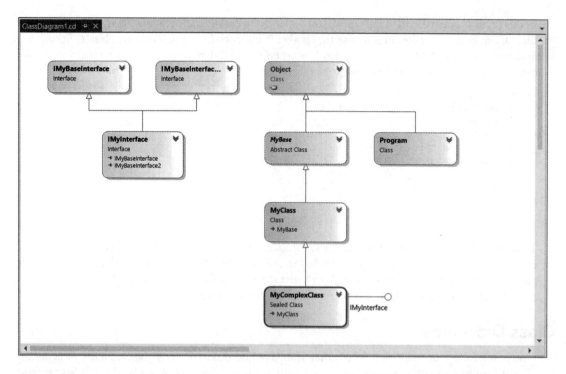

FIGURE 9-6

How It Works

With very little effort, you have created a class diagram not unlike the UML diagram presented in Figure 9-2 (without the color, of course). The following features are evident:

➤ Classes are shown including their names and types.
➤ Interfaces are shown including their names and types.
➤ Inheritance is shown with arrows with white heads (and in some cases, text inside class boxes).
➤ Classes implementing interfaces have lollipops.
➤ Abstract classes are shown with dotted outlines and italicized names.
➤ Sealed classes are shown with thick black outlines.

Clicking an object shows you additional information in a Class Details window at the bottom of the screen (right-click an object and select Class Details if this window doesn't appear). Here, you can see (and modify) class members. You can also see and modify class details in the Properties window.

From the Toolbox, you can add new items such as classes, interfaces, and enums to the diagram, and define relationships between objects in the diagram. When you do this, the code for the new items is automatically generated for you.

CLASS LIBRARY PROJECTS

As well as placing classes in separate files within your project, you can also place them in completely separate projects. A project that contains nothing but classes (along with other relevant type definitions, but no entry point) is called a *class library*.

Class library projects compile into .dll assemblies, and you can access their contents by adding references to them from other projects (which might be part of the same solution, but don't have to be). This extends the encapsulation that objects provide because class libraries can be revised and updated without touching the projects that use them. That means you can easily upgrade services provided by classes (which might affect multiple consumer applications).

The following Try It Out provides an example of a class library project and a separate project that makes use of the classes that it contains.

TRY IT OUT   Using a Class Library: Ch09ClassLib and Ch09Ex02\Program.cs

1. Create a new project of type Class Library called Ch09ClassLib, as shown in Figure 9-7, and save it in the directory C:\BeginningCSharpAndDotNET\Chapter09.

2. Rename the file Class1.cs to MyExternalClass.cs (by right-clicking the file in the Solution Explorer window and selecting Rename). Click Yes on the dialog box that appears.

3. The code in MyExternalClass.cs automatically changes to reflect the class name change:

    ```
    public class MyExternalClass
    {
    }
    ```

4. Add a new class to the project, using the filename MyInternalClass.cs.

5. Modify the code to make the class MyInternalClass explicitly internal:

    ```
    internal class MyInternalClass
    {
    }
    ```

6. Compile the project (this project has no entry point, so you cannot run it as normal—instead, you can build it by selecting Build ➪ Build Solution).

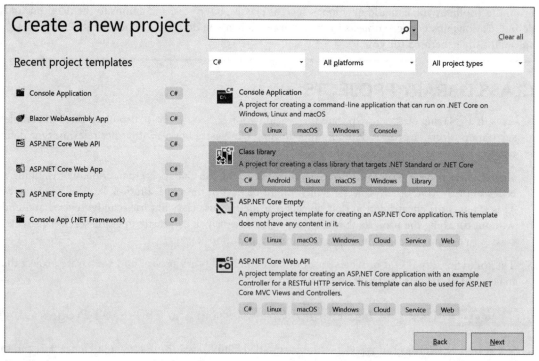

FIGURE 9-7

7. Create a new Console Application project called Ch09Ex02 and save it in the directory `C:\Beginning CSharpAndDotNET\Chapter09`.

8. Select Project ⇨ Add Project Reference menu item, or select the same option after right-clicking Dependencies in the Solution Explorer window.

9. Click the Browse option, then the Browse button. Navigate to `C:\BeginningCSharpAndDotNET\ Chapter09\Ch09ClassLib\bin\Debug\ net5.0\`, double-click `Ch09ClassLib.dll`, then click the OK button.

10. When the operation completes, confirm that a reference was added in the Solution Explorer window, as shown in Figure 9-8.

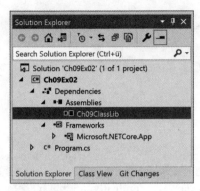

FIGURE 9-8

11. Open the Object Browser window and examine the new reference to see what objects it contains (see Figure 9-9).

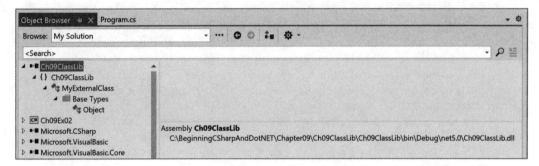

FIGURE 9-9

12. Modify the code in `Program.cs` as follows:

```
using System;
using Ch09ClassLib;
namespace Ch09Ex02
{
   class Program
   {
      static void Main(string[] args)
      {
         MyExternalClass myObj = new MyExternalClass();
         Console.WriteLine(myObj.ToString());
         Console.ReadKey();
      }
   }
}
```

13. Run the application. The result is shown in Figure 9-10.

```
C:\BeginningCSharpAndDotNET\Chapter09\Ch09Ex02\Ch09Ex02\bin\Debug\net5.0\Ch09Ex02.exe        —     □     ×
Ch09ClassLib.MyExternalClass
```

FIGURE 9-10

How It Works

This example created two projects: a class library project and a console application project. The class library project, Ch09ClassLib, contains two classes: MyExternalClass, which is publicly accessible, and MyInternalClass, which is internally accessible. Note that this class was implicitly internal by default when you created it, as it had no access modifier. It is good practice to be explicit about accessibility, though, because it makes your code more readable, which is why you add the internal keyword. The console application project, Ch09Ex02, contains simple code that makes use of the class library project.

> **NOTE** When an application uses classes defined in an external library, you can call that application a client application of the library. Code that uses a class that you define is often similarly referred to as client code.
>
> To use the classes in Ch09ClassLib, you added a reference to Ch09ClassLib.dll to the console application. For the purposes of this example, you simply point at the output file for the class library, although it would be just as easy to copy this file to a location local to Ch09Ex02, enabling you to continue development of the class library without affecting the console application. To replace the old assembly version with the new one, simply copy the newly generated DLL file over the old one.
>
> After adding the reference, you looked at the available classes using the Object Browser. Because the MyInternalClass is internal, you cannot see it in this display—it isn't accessible to external projects. However, MyExternalClass is accessible, and it is the one you use in the console application.
>
> You could replace the code in the console application with code attempting to use the internal class as follows:
>
> ```
> static void Main(string[] args)
> {
>     MyInternalClass myObj = new MyInternalClass();
>     Console.WriteLine(myObj.ToString());
>     Console.ReadKey();
> }
> ```
>
> If you attempt to compile this code, you receive the following compilation error:
>
> ```
> 'Ch09ClassLib.MyInternalClass'
>                 is inaccessible due to its protection level
> ```
>
> This technique of making use of classes in external assemblies is key to programming with C# and .NET. It is, in fact, exactly what you are doing when you use any of the classes in .NET because they are treated in the same way.

INTERFACES VERSUS ABSTRACT CLASSES

This chapter has demonstrated how you can create both interfaces and abstract classes (without members for now—you get to them in Chapter 10). The two types are similar in several ways, so it would be useful to know how to determine when you should use one technique or the other.

First the similarities: Both abstract classes and interfaces can contain members that can be inherited by a derived class. Neither interfaces nor abstract classes can be directly instantiated, but it is possible to declare variables of these types. If you do, you can use polymorphism to assign objects that inherit from these types to variables of these types. In both cases, you can then use the members of these types through these variables, although you do not have direct access to the other members of the derived object.

Now the differences: Derived classes can only inherit from a single base class, which means that only a single abstract class can be inherited directly (although it is possible for a chain of inheritance to include multiple abstract classes). Conversely, classes can use as many interfaces as they want, but this does not make a massive difference—similar results can be achieved either way. It's just that the interface way of doing things is slightly different.

Abstract classes can possess both *abstract members* (these have no code body and must be implemented in the derived class unless the derived class is itself abstract) and *nonabstract members* (these possess a code body and can be virtual so that they can be overridden in the derived class). *Interface members*, conversely, must be implemented on the class that uses the interface—they do not possess code bodies. Moreover, interface members are by definition public (because they are intended for external use), but members of abstract classes can also be private (as long as they aren't abstract), protected, internal, or protected internal (where protected internal members are accessible only from code within the application or from a derived class). In addition, interfaces cannot contain fields, constructors, destructors, static members, or constants.

> **NOTE** Abstract classes are intended for use as the base class for families of objects that share certain central characteristics, such as a common purpose and structure. Interfaces are intended for use by classes that might differ on a far more fundamental level but can still do some of the same things.

For example, consider a family of objects representing trains. The base class, Train, contains the core definition of a train, such as wheel gauge and engine type (which could be steam, diesel, and so on). However, this class is abstract because there is no such thing as a "generic" train. To create an "actual" train, you add characteristics specific to that train. For example, you derive classes such as PassengerTrain, FreightTrain, and 424DoubleBogey, as shown in Figure 9-11.

A family of car objects might be defined in the same way, with an abstract base class of Car and derived classes such as Compact, SUV, and PickUp. Car and Train might even derive from a common base class, such as Vehicle. This is shown in Figure 9-12.

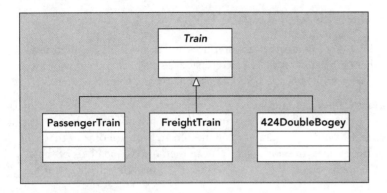

FIGURE 9-11

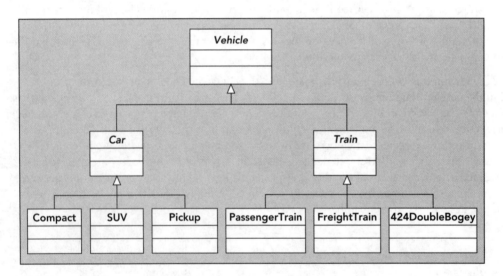

FIGURE 9-12

Some of the classes lower in the hierarchy can share characteristics because of their purpose, not just because of what they are derived from. For example, PassengerTrain, Compact, SUV, and Pickup are all capable of carrying passengers, so they might possess an IPassengerCarrier interface. FreightTrain and Pickup can carry heavy loads, so they might both have an IHeavy-LoadCarrier interface as well. This is illustrated in Figure 9-13.

By breaking down an object system in this way before going about assigning specifics, you can clearly see which situations should use abstract classes rather than interfaces, and vice versa. The result of this example could not be achieved using only interfaces or only abstract inheritance.

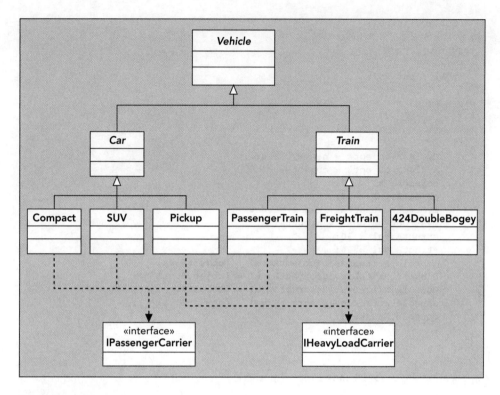

FIGURE 9-13

STRUCT TYPES

Chapter 8 noted that structs and classes are similar but that structs are value types and classes are reference types. What does this mean to you? Well, the easiest way of looking at this is with an example, such as the following Try It Out.

TRY IT OUT Classes versus Structs: Ch09Ex03\Program.cs

1. Create a new Console Application project called Ch09Ex03 and save it in the directory `C:\BeginningCSharpAndDotNET\Chapter09`.

2. Modify the code as follows:

```
namespace Ch09Ex03
{
    class MyClass
    {
```

```
            public int val;
        }
        struct myStruct
        {
            public int val;
        }
        class Program
        {
            static void Main(string[] args)
            {
                MyClass objectA = new MyClass();
                MyClass objectB = objectA;
                objectA.val = 10;
                objectB.val = 20;
                myStruct structA = new myStruct();
                myStruct structB = structA;
                structA.val = 30;
                structB.val = 40;
                Console.WriteLine($"objectA.val = {objectA.val}");
                Console.WriteLine($"objectB.val = {objectB.val}");
                Console.WriteLine($"structA.val = {structA.val}");
                Console.WriteLine($"structB.val = {structB.val}");
                Console.ReadKey();
            }
        }
    }
```

3.   Run the application. Figure 9-14 shows the output.

FIGURE 9-14

How It Works

This application contains two type definitions: one for a struct called myStruct, which has a single public int field called val, and one for a class called MyClass that contains an identical field (you look at class members such as fields in Chapter 10; for now, just understand that the syntax is the same here). Next, you perform the same operations on instances of both types:

1.   Declare a variable of the type.

2.   Create a new instance of the type in this variable.

3.   Declare a second variable of the type.

4.   Assign the first variable to the second variable.

5.   Assign a value to the `val` field in the instance in the first variable.

6.   Assign a new value to the `val` field in the instance in the second variable.

7.   Display the values of the `val` fields for both variables.

Although you are performing the same operations on variables of both types, the outcome is different. When you display the values of the `val` field, both object types have the same value, whereas the struct types have different values. What has happened?

Objects are *reference* types. When you assign an object to a variable you are assigning that variable with a *pointer* to the object to which it refers. A pointer, in real code terms, is an address in memory. In this case, the address is the point in memory where the object is found. When you assign the first object reference to the second variable of type `MyClass` with the following line, you are copying this address:

```
MyClass objectB = objectA;
```

This means that both variables contain pointers to the same object.

Structs are *value* types. Instead of the variable holding a pointer to the struct, the variable contains the struct itself. When you assign the first struct to the second variable of type `myStruct` with the following line, you are copying all the information from one struct to the other:

```
myStruct structB = structA;
```

You saw behavior like this earlier in this book for simple variable types such as `int`. The upshot is that the two `struct` type variables contain different structs. The entire technique of using pointers is hidden from you in managed C# code, making your code much simpler. It is possible to access lower-level operations such as pointer manipulation in C# using unsafe code, but that is an advanced topic not covered here.

SHALLOW COPYING VERSUS DEEP COPYING

Copying objects from one variable to another by value instead of by reference (that is, copying them in the same way as structs) can be quite complex. Because a single object can contain references to many other objects, such as field members and so on, a lot of processing can be involved. Simply copying each member from one object to another might not work because some of these members might be reference types in their own right.

The .NET Framework takes this into account. You can create a simple copy of an object where each member is copied to the new object by using the method `MemberwiseClone()`, inherited from `System.Object`. This is a protected method, but it would be easy to define a public method on an object that called this method. This copying method is known as a *shallow copy*, in that it doesn't take reference type members into account. This means that reference members in the new object refer to the same objects as equivalent members in the source object, which isn't ideal in many cases. If you want to create new instances of the members in question by copying the values across (rather than the references), you need to perform a *deep copy*.

There is an interface you can implement that enables you to deep copy in a standard way: `ICloneable`. If you use this interface, then you must implement the single method it contains, `Clone()`. This method returns a value of type `System.Object`. You can use whatever processing you want to obtain this object, by implementing the method body however you choose. That means you can implement a deep copy if you want to, although the exact behavior is not mandatory, so you could perform a shallow copy if desired. There are no rules or restrictions on what you actually return from this method, so many people recommend avoiding it. Instead, they recommend implementing your own deep-copy method. You take a closer look at this interface in Chapter 11.

EXERCISES

9.1 What is wrong with the following code?

```
public sealed class MyClass
{
    // Class members.
}
public class myDerivedClass : MyClass
{
    // Class members.
}
```

9.2 How would you define a noncreatable class?

9.3 Why are noncreatable classes still useful? How do you make use of their capabilities?

9.4 Write code in a class library project called `Vehicles` that implements the `Vehicle` family of objects discussed earlier in this chapter. There are nine objects and two interfaces that require implementation.

9.5 Create a console application project, Traffic, that references `Vehicles.dll` (created in Exercise 9.4). Include a function called `AddPassenger` that accepts any object with the `IPassengerCarrier` interface. To prove that the code works, call this function using instances of each object that supports this interface, calling the `ToString` method inherited from `System.Object` on each one and writing the result to the screen.

Answers to the exercises can be found in the Appendix.

▶ **WHAT YOU LEARNED IN THIS CHAPTER**

TOPIC	KEY CONCEPTS
Class and interface definitions	Classes are defined with the `class` keyword, and interfaces with the `interface` keyword. You can use the `public` and `internal` keywords to define class and interface accessibility, and classes can be defined as `abstract` or `sealed` to control inheritance. Parent classes and interfaces are specified in a comma-separated list after a colon following the class or interface name. Only a single parent class can be specified in a class definition, and it must be the first item in the list.
Constructors and destructors	Classes come ready-equipped with a default constructor and destructor implementation, and you rarely have to provide your own destructor. You can define constructors with an accessibility, the name of the class, and any required parameters. Constructors of base classes are executed before those of derived classes, and you can control the execution sequence within a class with the `this` and `base` constructor initializer keywords.
Class libraries	You can create class library projects that only contain class definitions. These projects cannot be executed directly; they must be accessed through client code in an executable application. Visual Studio provides various tools for creating, modifying, and examining classes.
Class families	Classes can be grouped into families that exhibit common behavior or that share common characteristics. You can do this by inheriting from a shared base class (which can be abstract), or by implementing interfaces.
Struct definitions	A struct is defined in a very similar way to a class, but remember that structs are value types whereas classes are reference types.
Copying objects	When you make a copy of an object, you must be careful to copy any objects that it might contain, rather than simply copying the references to those objects. Copying references is referred to as shallow copying, whereas a full copy is referred to as a deep copy. You can use the `ICloneable` interface as a framework for providing deep-copy capabilities in a class definition.

10

Defining Class Members

WHAT YOU WILL LEARN IN THIS CHAPTER

➤ Defining class members

➤ Controlling class member inheritance

➤ Defining nested classes

➤ Implementing interfaces

➤ Using partial class definitions

➤ Using the Call Hierarchy window

CODE DOWNLOADS FOR THIS CHAPTER

The code downloads for this chapter are found on the book page at `www.wiley.com`. Click the Downloads link. The code can also be found at `github.com/benperk/BeginningCSharpAndDotNET`. The code is in the Chapter10 folder and individually named according to the names throughout the chapter.

This chapter continues exploring class definitions in C# by looking at how you define field, property, and method class members. You start by examining the code required for each of these types and learn how to generate the structure of this code. You also learn how to modify members quickly by editing their properties.

After covering the basics of member definition, you'll learn some advanced techniques involving members: hiding base class members, calling overridden base class members, nested type definitions, and partial class definitions.

Finally, you will put theory into practice by creating a class library that you can build on and use in later chapters.

MEMBER DEFINITIONS

Within a class definition, you provide definitions for all members of the class, including fields, methods, and properties. All members have their own accessibility levels, defined in all cases by one of the following keywords:

➤ `public`—Members are accessible from any code.

➤ `private`—Members are accessible only from code that is part of the class (the default if no keyword is used).

➤ `internal`—Members are accessible only from code within the assembly (project) where they are defined.

➤ `protected`—Members are accessible only from code that is part of either the class or a derived class.

The last two of these can be combined, so `protected internal` members are also possible. These are only accessible from code within the project (more accurately, the assembly) or from code-derived classes within another assembly.

Fields, methods, and properties can also be declared using the keyword `static`, which means that they are static members owned by the class, rather than by object instances, as discussed in Chapter 8.

Defining Fields

Fields are defined using standard variable declaration format (with optional initialization), along with the modifiers discussed previously:

```
class MyClass
{
    public int MyInt;
}
```

> **NOTE** Public fields in the .NET Framework are named using PascalCasing, rather than camelCasing, and that is the casing methodology used here. That's why the field in this example is called `MyInt` instead of `myInt`. This is only a suggested casing scheme, but it makes a lot of sense. There is no recommendation for private fields, which are usually named using camelCasing.

Fields can also use the keyword `readonly`, meaning the field can be assigned a value only during constructor execution or by initial assignment:

```
class MyClass
{
    public readonly int MyInt = 17;
}
```

As noted in the chapter introduction, fields can be declared as static using the `static` keyword:

```
class MyClass
{
    public static int MyInt;
}
```

Static fields are accessed via the class that defines them (`MyClass.MyInt` in the preceding example), not through object instances of that class. You can use the keyword `const` to create a constant value. `const` members are static by definition, so you don't need to use the `static` modifier (in fact, it is an error to do so).

Defining Methods

Methods use standard function format, along with accessibility and optional `static` modifiers, as shown in this example:

```
class MyClass
{
    public string GetString() => "Here is a string.";
}
```

> **NOTE** *Like public fields, public methods in the .NET Framework are named using PascalCasing.*

Remember that if you use the `static` keyword, then this method is accessible only through the class, not an object instance. You can also use the following keywords with method definitions:

➤ `virtual`—The method can be overridden.

➤ `abstract`—The method must be overridden in nonabstract derived classes (only permitted in abstract classes).

➤ `override`—The method overrides a base class method (it must be used if a method is being overridden).

➤ `extern`—The method definition is found elsewhere.

Here is an example of a method override:

```
public class MyBaseClass
{
    public virtual void DoSomething()
    {
        // Base implementation.
    }
}
```

```
public class MyDerivedClass : MyBaseClass
{
    public override void DoSomething()
    {
        // Derived class implementation, overrides base implementation.
    }
}
```

If override is used, then sealed can also be used to specify that no further modifications can be made to this method in derived classes—that is, the method cannot be overridden by derived classes. Here is an example:

```
public class MyDerivedClass : MyBaseClass
{
    public override sealed void DoSomething()
    {
        // Derived class implementation, overrides base implementation.
    }
}
```

Using extern enables you to provide the implementation of a method externally to the project, but this is an advanced topic not covered here.

Defining Properties

Properties are defined in a similar way to fields, but there is more to them. Properties, as already discussed, are more involved than fields in that they can perform additional processing before modifying state—and, indeed, might not modify state at all. They achieve this by possessing two function-like blocks: one for getting the value of the property and one for setting the value of the property.

These blocks, also known as *accessors*, are defined using get and set keywords, respectively, and can be used to control the access level of the property. You can omit either of these blocks to create read-only or write-only properties (where omitting the get block gives you write-only access, and omitting the set block gives you read-only access). Of course, that only applies to external code because code elsewhere within the class will have access to the same data that these code blocks have. You can also include accessibility modifiers on accessors—making a get block public while the set block is protected, for example. You must include at least one of these blocks to obtain a valid property (and, let's face it, a property you can't read or change wouldn't be very useful).

The basic structure of a property consists of the standard access modifying keyword (public, private, and so on), followed by a type name, the property name, and one or both of the get and set blocks that contain the property processing:

```
public int MyIntProp
{
    get
    {
        // Property get code.
    }
    set
    {
        // Property set code.
    }
}
```

> **NOTE** *Public properties in .NET are also named using PascalCasing, rather than camelCasing; as with fields and methods, PascalCasing is used here.*

The first line of the definition is the bit that is similar to a field definition. The difference is that there is no semicolon at the end of the line; instead, you have a code block containing nested `get` and `set` blocks.

`get` blocks must have a return value of the type of the property. Simple properties are often associated with a single private field (also known as backing field) controlling access to that field, in which case the `get` block can return the field's value directly:

```
// Field used by property.
private int myInt;
// Property.
public int MyIntProp
{
    get { return myInt; }
    set { // Property set code. }
}
```

Code external to the class cannot access this `myInt` field directly due to its accessibility level (it is private). Instead, external code must use the property to access the field. The `set` function assigns a value to the field similarly. Here, you can use the keyword `value` to refer to the value received from the user of the property:

```
// Field used by property.
private int myInt;
// Property.
public int MyIntProp
{
    get { return myInt; }
    set { myInt = value; }
}
```

`value` equates to a value of the same type as the property, so if the property uses the same type as the field, then you never have to worry about casting in situations like this. To provide a default value in case the integer allows `null`, you can use an expression-bodied member function:

```
private int? myInt;
public int? MyIntProp
{
    get => myInt;
    set => myInt = value ?? 0;
}
```

This simple property does little more than shield direct access to the `myInt` field. The real power of properties is apparent when you exert a little more control over the proceedings. For example, you might implement your `set` block as follows:

```
set
{
```

```
        if (value >= 0 && value <= 10)
            myInt = value;
    }
```

Here, you modify `myInt` only if the value assigned to the property is between 0 and 10. In situations like this, you have an important design choice to make. What should you do if an invalid value is used? You have four options:

➤ Do nothing (as in the preceding code).

➤ Assign a default value to the field.

➤ Continue as if nothing went wrong but log the event for future analysis.

➤ Throw an exception.

In general, the last two options are preferable. Deciding between them depends on how the class will be used and how much control should be assigned to the users of the class. Exception throwing gives users a fair amount of control and lets them know what is going on so that they can respond appropriately. You can use one of the standard exceptions in the `System` namespace for this:

```
    set
    {
        if (value >= 0 && value <= 10)
            myInt = value;
        else
            throw (new ArgumentOutOfRangeException("MyIntProp", value,
                    "MyIntProp must be assigned a value between 0 and 10."));
    }
```

The exception created using `throw` can be handled using `try...catch...finally` logic in the implementing code that uses the property, as you saw in Chapter 7.

Logging data, perhaps to a text file or the Event Log, can be useful, such as in production code where problems really shouldn't occur. It enables developers to check on performance and perhaps debug existing code if necessary.

Properties can use the `virtual`, `override`, and `abstract` keywords just like methods, something that isn't possible with fields. Finally, as mentioned earlier, accessors can have their own accessibilities, as shown here:

```
    // Field used by property.
    private int myInt;
    // Property.
    public int MyIntProp
    {
        get { return myInt; }
        protected set { myInt = value; }
    }
```

Here, only code within the class or derived classes can use the `set` accessor.

The accessibilities that are permitted for accessors depend on the accessibility of the property, and it is forbidden to make an accessor more accessible than the property to which it belongs. This means that a private property cannot contain any accessibility modifiers for its accessors, whereas public properties can use all modifiers on their accessors.

There exists a feature called *expression-based properties* that is similar to the expression-based method discussed previously in Chapter 6. This feature reduces the extent of the property to a single line of code. For example, properties that return a one-line mathematical computation on a value can use the lambda arrow followed by the equation:

```
// Field used by property.
private int myDoubledInt = 5;
// Property.
public int MyDoubledIntProp => (myDoubledInt * 2);
```

The following Try It Out enables you to experiment with defining and using fields, methods, and properties.

TRY IT OUT Using Fields, Methods, and Properties: Ch10Ex01

1. Create a new Console Application called Ch10Ex01 and save it in the directory
   C:\\BeginningCSharpAndDotNET\Chapter10.

2. Add a new class called MyClass, using the Add Class shortcut, which will cause the new class to be defined in a new file called MyClass.cs.

3. Modify the code in MyClass.cs as follows:

```
public class MyClass
{
    public readonly string Name;
    private int intVal;
    public int Val
    {
        get { return intVal; }
        set {
            if (value >= 0 && value <= 10)
                intVal = value;
            else
                throw (new ArgumentOutOfRangeException("Val", value,
                    "Val must be assigned a value between 0 and 10."));
        }
    }
    public override string ToString() => "Name: " + Name + "\nVal: " + Val;
    private MyClass() : this("Default Name") { }
    public MyClass(string newName)
    {
        Name = newName;
        intVal = 0;
    }
    private int myDoubledInt = 5;
    public int myDoubledIntProp => (myDoubledInt * 2);
}
```

4. Modify the code in `Program.cs` as follows:

```
static void Main(string[] args)
{
    Console.WriteLine("Creating object myObj...");
    MyClass myObj = new MyClass("My Object");
    Console.WriteLine("myObj created.");
    for (int i = -1; i <= 0; i++)
    {
        try
        {
            Console.WriteLine($"\nAttempting to assign {i} to myObj.Val...");
            myObj.Val = i;
            Console.WriteLine($"Value {myObj.Val} assigned to myObj.Val.");
        }
        catch (Exception e)
        {
            Console.WriteLine($"Exception {e.GetType().FullName} thrown.");
            Console.WriteLine($"Message:\n\"{e.Message}\"");
        }
    }
    Console.WriteLine("\nOutputting myObj.ToString()...");
    Console.WriteLine(myObj.ToString());
    Console.WriteLine("myObj.ToString() Output.");
    Console.WriteLine("\nmyDoubledIntProp = 5...");
    Console.WriteLine($"Getting myDoubledIntProp of 5 is {myObj.myDoubledIntProp}");
    Console.ReadKey();
}
```

5. Run the application. The result is shown in Figure 10-1.

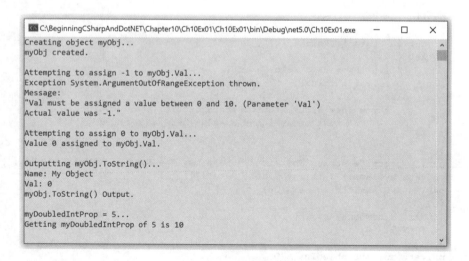

```
C:\BeginningCSharpAndDotNET\Chapter10\Ch10Ex01\Ch10Ex01\bin\Debug\net5.0\Ch10Ex01.exe    —    □    ×
Creating object myObj...
myObj created.

Attempting to assign -1 to myObj.Val...
Exception System.ArgumentOutOfRangeException thrown.
Message:
"Val must be assigned a value between 0 and 10. (Parameter 'Val')
Actual value was -1."

Attempting to assign 0 to myObj.Val...
Value 0 assigned to myObj.Val.

Outputting myObj.ToString()...
Name: My Object
Val: 0
myObj.ToString() Output.

myDoubledIntProp = 5...
Getting myDoubledIntProp of 5 is 10
```

FIGURE 10-1

How It Works

The code in `Main()` creates and uses an instance of the `MyClass` class defined in `MyClass.cs`. The code must instantiate this class by using a nondefault constructor because the default constructor of `MyClass` is private:

```
private MyClass() : this("Default Name") {}
```

Using `this("Default Name")` ensures that `Name` gets a value if this constructor is ever called, which is possible if this class is used to derive a new class. This is necessary because not assigning a value to the `Name` field could be a source of errors later.

The nondefault constructor used assigns values to the `readonly` field `Name` (you can only do this by assignment in the field declaration or in a constructor) and the private field `intVal`.

Next, `Main()` attempts two assignments to the `Val` property of `myObj` (the instance of `MyClass`). A `for` loop is used to assign the values –1 and 0 in two cycles, and a `try...catch` structure is used to check for any exception thrown. When –1 is assigned to the property, an exception of type `System.ArgumentOutOfRangeException` is thrown, and code in the `catch` block outputs information about the exception to the console window. In the next loop cycle, the value 0 is successfully assigned to the `Val` property, and through that property to the private `intVal` field.

Use the overridden `ToString()` method to output a formatted string representing the contents of the object:

```
public override string ToString() => "Name: " + Name + "\nVal: " + Val;
```

This method must be declared using the `override` keyword, because it is overriding the virtual `ToString()` method of the base `System.Object` class. The code here uses the property `Val` directly, rather than the private field `intVal`. There is no reason why you should not use properties from within classes in this way, although there may be a small performance hit (so small that you are unlikely to notice it). Of course, using the property also gives you the validation inherent in property use, which may be beneficial for code within the class as well.

Finally, you created and set a read-only property called `myDoubledInt` in `MyClass.cs` to 5. By using the expression-based property feature to return the value multiplied by 2:

```
public int MyDoubledIntProp => (myDoubledInt * 2);
```

when the property is accessed using `myObj.myDoubledIntProp` the output is 2 times 5 which is 10, as expected.

Tuple Deconstruction

In Chapter 6 you learned about tuples, which are useful for returning multiple results from a function. When using more complex objects like a class, structure, or array is unnecessary, using a `tuple` is a valid approach for handling this situation. Here is a simple example of a `tuple`:

```
var numbers = (1, 2, 3, 4, 5);
```

defining a function that returns multiple results:

```
private static (int max, int min, double average)
    GetMaxMin(IEnumerable<int> numbers) {...}
```

When your code consumes the GetMaxMin() function, the result must be parsed by the code to display the results. (Review Chapter 6 if you need a refresh on that specific approach.) Writing code to parse out the result is not required, however, if you implement tuple deconstruction. Tuple deconstruction is achieved by adding a function named Deconstruct() to any class that you want to support this feature. Examine, for example, the following class:

```
public class Location
{
  public Location(double latitude, double longitude)
      => (Latitude, Longitude) = (latitude, longitude);

  public double Latitude { get; }
  public double Longitude { get; }

  public void Deconstruct(out double latitude, out double longitude)
      => (latitude, longitude) = (Latitude, Longitude);
}
```

The Location class implements an expression-bodied constructer that accepts two variables of type double (latitude and longitude) that are used to set the values of the properties Latitude and Longitude. The Deconstruct() function has two out parameters: out double latitude and out double longitude. The expression then sets the two out parameters equal to the Latitude and Longitude properties populated when the Location class is initialized. You can then access the fields by assigning a tuple to Location:

```
var location = new Location(48.137154, 11.576124);
(double latitude, double longitude) = location;
```

It is then possible to reference the results directly without having to parse through the result.

Refactoring Members

One technique that comes in handy when adding properties is the capability to generate a property from a field. This is an example of *refactoring*, which means rewriting existing code to make it more manageable without changing its functionality. This can be accomplished by right-clicking a member in a class diagram or in code view.

For example, if the MyClass class contained this field:

```
public string myString;
```

you could right-click the field and select Quick Actions and Refactorings (Ctrl+ .). That would bring up the dialog box shown in Figure 10-2.

Accepting the default options modifies the code for MyClass as follows:

```
public string myString;
public string MyString { get => myString; set => myString = value; }
private string myString;
```

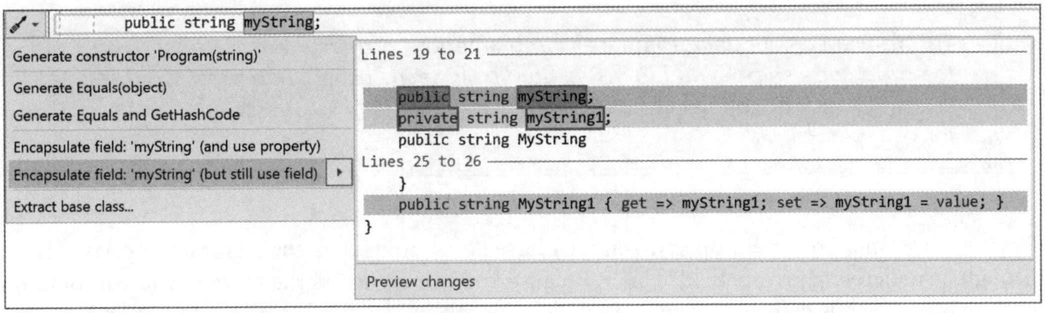

FIGURE 10-2

Here, the accessibility of the `myString` field has been changed to `private`, and a public property called `MyString` has been created and automatically linked to `myString`. Clearly, reducing the time required to monotonously create properties for fields is a big plus!

Automatic Properties

Properties are the preferred way to access the state of an object because they shield external code from the implementation of data storage within the object. They also give you greater control over how internal data is accessed, as you have seen several times in this chapter's code. However, you will typically define properties in a very standard way—that is, you will have a private member that is accessed directly through a public property. The code for this is almost invariably like the code in the previous section, which was autogenerated by the Visual Studio refactoring tool.

Refactoring certainly speeds things up when it comes to typing, but C# has another trick up its sleeve: automatic properties. With an *automatic property*, you declare a property with a simplified syntax and the C# compiler fills in the blanks for you. Specifically, the compiler declares a private field that is used for storage and uses that field in the `get` and `set` blocks of your property—without you having to worry about the details.

Use the following code structure to define an automatic property:

```
public int MyIntProp
{
   get;
   set;
}
```

You can even define an automatic property on a single line of code to save space, without making the property much less readable:

```
public int MyIntProp { get; set; }
```

You define the accessibility, type, and name of the property in the usual way, but you do not provide any implementation for the `get` or `set` block. Instead, the compiler provides the implementations of these blocks (and the underlying field).

> **TIP** *You can create an automatically implemented property template by using the prop code snippet within Visual Studio. Type in "prop" then press the Tab key twice and the following,* `public int MyProperty {get; set;}`, *is created for you.*

When you use an automatic property, you only have access to its data through the property, not through its underlying private field. This is because you cannot access the private field without knowing its name, which is defined during compilation. However, that is not really a limitation because using the property name directly is fine. The only limitation of automatic properties is that they must include both a `get` and a `set` accessor—you cannot define read- or write-only properties in this way. However, you can change the accessibility of these accessors. For example, this means you can create an externally read-only property as follows:

```
public int MyIntProp { get; private set; }
```

Here you can set the value of `MyIntProp` only from code in the class definition.

ADDITIONAL CLASS MEMBER TOPICS

Now you're ready to look at some more advanced member topics. This section tackles the following:

➤ Hiding base class methods

➤ Calling overridden or hidden base class methods

➤ Using nested type definitions

Hiding Base Class Methods

When you inherit a (non-abstract) member from a base class, you also inherit an implementation. If the inherited member is virtual, then you can override this implementation with the `override` keyword. Regardless of whether the inherited member is virtual, you also can *hide* the implementation. This is useful when, for example, a public inherited member does not work quite as you want it to.

You can do this simply by using code such as the following:

```
public class MyBaseClass
{
   public void DoSomething()
   {
      // Base implementation.
   }
}
public class MyDerivedClass : MyBaseClass
{
   public void DoSomething()
```

```
    {
        // Derived class implementation, hides base implementation.
    }
}
```

Although this code works fine, it generates a warning that you are hiding a base class member. That warning gives you the chance to correct it if you have accidentally hidden a member that you want to use. If you really do want to hide the member, you can use the new keyword to explicitly indicate that this is what you want to do:

```
public class MyDerivedClass : MyBaseClass
{
    new public void DoSomething()
    {
        // Derived class implementation, hides base implementation.
    }
}
```

This works in the same way but will not show a warning. At this point, it is worthwhile to note the difference between hiding and overriding base class members. Consider the following code:

```
public class MyBaseClass
{
    public virtual void DoSomething() => Console.WriteLine("Base imp");
}
public class MyDerivedClass : MyBaseClass
{
    public override void DoSomething() => Console.WriteLine("Derived imp");
}
```

Here, the overriding method replaces the implementation in the base class, such that the following code uses the new version even though it does so through the base class type (using polymorphism):

```
MyDerivedClass myObj = new MyDerivedClass();
MyBaseClass myBaseObj;
myBaseObj = myObj;
myBaseObj.DoSomething();
```

This results in the following output:

```
Derived imp
```

Alternatively, you could hide the base class method:

```
public class MyBaseClass
{
    public virtual void DoSomething() => Console.WriteLine("Base imp");
}
public class MyDerivedClass : MyBaseClass
{
    new public void DoSomething() => Console.WriteLine("Derived imp");
}
```

The base class method need not be virtual for this to work, but the effect is exactly the same and the preceding code only requires changes to one line. The result for a virtual or nonvirtual base class method is as follows:

```
Base imp
```

Although the base implementation is hidden, you still have access to it through the base class.

Calling Overridden or Hidden Base Class Methods

Whether you override or hide a member, you still have access to the base class member from the derived class. There are many situations in which this can be useful, such as the following:

➤ When you want to hide an inherited public member from users of a derived class but still want access to its functionality from within the class

➤ When you want to add to the implementation of an inherited virtual member rather than simply replace it with a new overridden implementation

To achieve this, you use the base keyword, which refers to the implementation of the base class contained within a derived class (in a similar way to its use in controlling constructors, as shown in the previous chapter):

```
public class MyBaseClass
{
    public virtual void DoSomething()
    {
        // Base implementation.
    }
}
public class MyDerivedClass : MyBaseClass
{
    public override void DoSomething()
    {
        // Derived class implementation, extends base class implementation.
        base.DoSomething();
        // More derived class implementation.
    }
}
```

This code executes the version of DoSomething() contained in MyBaseClass, the base class of MyDerivedClass, from within the version of DoSomething() contained in MyDerivedClass. As base works using object instances, it is an error to use it from within a static member.

The this Keyword

Besides using base in the previous chapter, you also used the this keyword. As with base, this can be used from within class members, and, like base, this refers to an object instance, although it is the current object instance (which means you can't use this keyword in static members because static members are not part of an object instance).

The most useful function of the `this` keyword is the capability to pass a reference to the current object instance to a method, as shown in this example:

```
public void doSomething()
{
    MyTargetClass myObj = new MyTargetClass();
    myObj.DoSomethingWith(this);
}
```

Here, the `MyTargetClass` instance that is instantiated (`myObj`) has a method called `DoSomethingWith()`, which takes a single parameter of a type compatible with the class containing the preceding method. This parameter type might be of this class type, a class type from which this class derives, an interface implemented by the class, or (of course) `System.Object`.

Another common use of the `this` keyword is to qualify local type members. For example:

```
public class MyClass
{
    private int someData;
    public int SomeData => this.someData;
}
```

Many developers like this syntax, which can be used with any member type, because it is immediately clear that you are referring to a member rather than a local variable.

Using Nested Type Definitions

You can define types such as classes in namespaces, and you can also define them inside other classes. Then you can use the full range of accessibility modifiers for the definition, rather than just `public` and `internal`, and you can use the `new` keyword to hide a type definition inherited from a base class. For example, the following code defining `MyClass` also defines a nested class called `MyNestedClass`:

```
public class MyClass
{
    public class MyNestedClass
    {
        public int NestedClassField;
    }
}
```

To instantiate `MyNestedClass` from outside `MyClass`, you must qualify the name, as shown here:

```
MyClass.MyNestedClass myObj = new MyClass.MyNestedClass();
```

However, you might not be able to do this, if for example, the nested class is declared as `private`. One reason for the existence of this feature is to define classes that are private to the containing class so that no other code in the namespace has access to them. Another reason is that nested classes have access to private and protected members of their containing class. The next Try it Out examines this feature.

TRY IT OUT   Using Nested Classes: Ch10Ex02

1.   Create a new Console Application called Ch10Ex02 and save it in the directory
     C:\BeginningCSharpAndDotNET\Chapter10.

2.   Modify the code in Program.cs as follows:

```
namespace Ch10Ex02
{
    public class ClassA
    {
        private int state = -1;
        public int State => state;
        public class ClassB
        {
            public void SetPrivateState(ClassA target, int newState)
            {
                target.state = newState;
            }
        }
    }
    class Program
    {
        static void Main(string[] args)
        {
            ClassA myObject = new ClassA();
            Console.WriteLine($"myObject.State = {myObject.State}");
            ClassA.ClassB myOtherObject = new ClassA.ClassB();
            myOtherObject.SetPrivateState(myObject, 999);
            Console.WriteLine($"myObject.State = {myObject.State}");
            Console.ReadKey();
        }
    }
}
```

3.   Run the application. The result is shown in Figure 10-3.

```
C:\BeginningCSharpAndDotNET\Chapter10\Ch10Ex02\Ch10Ex02\bin\Debug\net5.0\Ch10Ex02.exe    —    □    ×
myObject.State = -1
myObject.State = 999
```

FIGURE 10-3

How It Works

The code in Main() creates and uses an instance of ClassA, which has a read-only property called State.
Next, the code creates an instance of the nested class ClassA.ClassB. This class has access to the backing field for ClassA.State, which is the ClassA.state field, even though the field is private. Because of
this, the nested class method SetPrivateState() can change the value of the read-only State property
of ClassA.

It is important to reiterate that this is possible only because `ClassB` is defined as a nested class of `ClassA`. If you were to move the definition of `ClassB` outside of `ClassA`, then the code wouldn't compile due to this error:

```
'Ch10Ex02.ClassA.state' is inaccessible due to its protection level.
```

Being able to expose the internal state of your classes to nested classes can be extremely useful in some circumstances. However, most of the time it's enough to simply manipulate the internal state through methods that your class exposes.

INTERFACE IMPLEMENTATION

This section takes a closer look at how you go about defining and implementing interfaces. In the previous chapter, you learned that interfaces are defined in a similar way as classes, using code such as the following:

```
interface IMyInterface
{
    // Interface members.
}
```

You can define members using the `new` keyword if you want to hide members inherited from base interfaces:

```
interface IMyBaseInterface
{
    void DoSomething();
}
interface IMyDerivedInterface : IMyBaseInterface
{
    new void DoSomething();
}
```

This works the same way as hiding inherited class members.

Properties defined in interfaces define either or both of the access blocks—`get` and `set`—which are permitted for the property, as shown here:

```
interface IMyInterface
{
    int MyInt { get; set; }
}
```

Here the `int` property `MyInt` has both `get` and `set` accessors. Either of these can be omitted for a property with more restricted access.

> **NOTE** This syntax is similar to automatic properties, but remember that automatic properties are defined for classes, not interfaces, and that automatic properties must have both `get` and `set` accessors.

Interfaces do not specify how the property data should be stored. For example, interfaces cannot specify fields that might be used to store property data. Finally, interfaces, like classes, can be defined as members of classes (but not as members of other interfaces).

Implementing Interfaces in Classes

A class that implements an interface must contain implementations for all members of that interface, which must match the signatures specified (including matching the specified get and set blocks), and must be public, as shown here:

```
public interface IMyInterface
{
    void DoSomething();
    void DoSomethingElse();
}
public class MyClass : IMyInterface
{
    public void DoSomething() {}
    public void DoSomethingElse() {}
}
```

It is possible to implement interface members using the keyword virtual or abstract, static, or const. Interface members can also be implemented on base classes:

```
public interface IMyInterface
{
    void DoSomething();
    void DoSomethingElse();
}
public class MyBaseClass
{
    public void DoSomething() {}
}
public class MyDerivedClass : MyBaseClass, IMyInterface
{
    public void DoSomethingElse() {}
}
```

Inheriting from a base class that implements a given interface means that the interface is implicitly supported by the derived class. Here is an example:

```
public interface IMyInterface
{
    void DoSomething();
    void DoSomethingElse();
}
public class MyBaseClass : IMyInterface
{
    public virtual void DoSomething() {}
    public virtual void DoSomethingElse() {}
}
public class MyDerivedClass : MyBaseClass
{
    public override void DoSomething() {}
}
```

Clearly, it is useful to define implementations in base classes as virtual so that derived classes can replace the implementation, rather than hide it. If you were to hide a base class member using the new keyword, rather than override it in this way, the method `IMyInterface.DoSomething()` would always refer to the base class version even if the derived class were being accessed via the interface.

Explicit Interface Member Implementation

Interface members can also be implemented *explicitly* by a class. If you do that, the member can only be accessed through the interface, not the class. *Implicit* members, which you used in the code in the previous section, can be accessed either way.

For example, if the class `MyClass` implemented the `DoSomething()` method of `IMyInterface` implicitly, as in the preceding example, then the following code would be valid:

```
MyClass myObj = new MyClass();
myObj.DoSomething();
```

This would also be valid:

```
MyClass myObj = new MyClass();
IMyInterface myInt = myObj;
myInt.DoSomething();
```

Alternatively, if `MyDerivedClass` implements `DoSomething()` explicitly, then only the latter technique is permitted. The code for doing that is as follows:

```
public class MyClass : IMyInterface
{
    void IMyInterface.DoSomething() {}
    public void DoSomethingElse() {}
}
```

Here, `DoSomething()` is implemented explicitly, and `DoSomethingElse()` implicitly. Only the latter is accessible directly through an object instance of `MyClass`.

Additional Property Accessors

Earlier you learned that if you implement an interface with a property, you must implement matching get/set accessors. That isn't strictly true—it is possible to add a get block to a property in a class in which the interface defining that property only contains a set block, and vice versa. However, this is possible only if you implement the interface implicitly. Also, in most cases you will want to add the accessor with a more restrictive accessibility modifier than the one on the accessor defined in the interface. Because the accessor defined in the interface is, by definition, public, this means that you would add nonpublic accessors. Here's an example:

```
public interface IMyInterface
{
    int MyIntProperty { get; }
}
public class MyBaseClass : IMyInterface
{
    public int MyIntProperty { get; protected set; }
}
```

If you define the additional accessor as public, then code with access to the class implementing the interface can access it. However, code that has access only to the interface won't be able to access it.

PARTIAL CLASS DEFINITIONS

When you create classes with a lot of members of one type or another, the code can get quite confusing, and code files can get very long. One technique that can help is to use code outlining. By defining regions in code, you can collapse and expand sections to make the code easier to read. For example, you might have a class defined as follows:

```
public class MyClass
{
    #region Fields
    private int myInt;
    #endregion
    #region Constructor
    public MyClass() { myInt = 99; }
    #endregion
    #region Properties
    public int MyInt
    {
        get { return myInt; }
        set { myInt = value; }
    }
    #endregion
    #region Methods
    public void DoSomething()
    {
        // Do something..
    }
    #endregion
}
```

Here, you can expand and contract the regions, fields, properties, constructors, and methods for and around the class, enabling you to focus only on what you are interested in. It is even possible to nest regions this way, so some regions are visible only when the region that contains them is expanded.

An alternative to using regions is to use *partial class definitions*. Put simply, you use partial class definitions to split the definition of a class across multiple files. You can, for example, put the fields, properties, and constructors in one file, and the methods in another. To do that, you just use the `partial` keyword with the class in each file that contains part of the definition, as follows:

```
public partial class MyClass {  ...}
```

If you use partial class definitions, the `partial` keyword must appear in this position in every file containing part of the definition.

For example, a WPF window in a class called `MainWindow` has code stored in both `MainWindow`
`.xaml.cs` and `MainWindow.g.i.cs` (visible if Show All Files is selected in the Solution Explorer window if you drill down into the `obj\Debug\*` folder, where * represents the targeted framework

moniker). This enables you to concentrate on the functionality of your forms, without worrying about your code being cluttered with information that does not really interest you.

One final note about partial classes: Interfaces applied to one partial class part apply to the whole class, meaning that the definition

```
public partial class MyClass : IMyInterface1 {  ... }
public partial class MyClass : IMyInterface2 {  ... }
```

is equivalent to:

```
public class MyClass : IMyInterface1, IMyInterface2 { ... }
```

Partial class definitions can include a base class in a single partial class definition, or more than one partial class definition. If a base class is specified in more than one definition, though, it must be the *same* base class; recall that classes in C# can inherit only from a single base class.

PARTIAL METHOD DEFINITIONS

Partial classes can also define partial methods. Partial methods are defined in one partial class definition without a method body and implemented in another partial class definition. In both places, the partial keyword is used:

```
public partial class MyClass
{
    partial void MyPartialMethod();
}
public partial class MyClass
{
    partial void MyPartialMethod()
    {
        // Method implementation
    }
}
```

Partial methods can also be static, but they are implicitly private and can't have a return value. Any parameters they use cannot be out parameters, although they can be ref parameters. They also cannot use the virtual, abstract, override, new, sealed, or extern modifiers.

Given these limitations, it is not immediately obvious what purpose partial methods fulfill. In fact, they are important when it comes to code compilation, rather than usage. Consider the following code:

```
public partial class MyClass
{
    partial void DoSomethingElse();
    public void DoSomething()
    {
        Console.WriteLine("DoSomething() execution started.");
        DoSomethingElse();
        Console.WriteLine("DoSomething() execution finished.");
    }
}
```

```
public partial class MyClass
{
    partial void DoSomethingElse() =>
        Console.WriteLine("DoSomethingElse() called.");
}
```

Here, the partial method `DoSomethingElse()` is defined and called in the first partial class definition and implemented in the second. The output, when `DoSomething()` is called from a console application, is what you might expect:

```
DoSomething() execution started.
DoSomethingElse() called.
DoSomething() execution finished.
```

If you were to remove the second partial class definition or partial method implementation entirely (or comment out the code), the output would be as follows:

```
DoSomething() execution started.
DoSomething() execution finished.
```

You might assume that what is happening here is that when the call to `DoSomethingElse()` is made, the runtime discovers that the method has no implementation and therefore continues executing the next line of code. What happens is a little subtler. When you compile code that contains a partial method definition without an implementation, the compiler removes the method entirely. It also removes any calls to the method. When you execute the code, no check is made for an implementation because there is no call to check. This results in a slight—but nevertheless significant—improvement in performance.

As with partial classes, partial methods are useful when it comes to customizing autogenerated or designer-created code. The designer may declare partial methods that you can choose to implement or not depending on the situation. If you don't implement them, you incur no performance hit because effectively the method does not exist in the compiled code.

Consider at this point why partial methods cannot have a return type. If you can answer that to your own satisfaction, you can be sure that you fully understand this topic—so that is left as an exercise for you.

EXAMPLE APPLICATION

To illustrate some of the techniques you have been using so far, in this section you'll develop a class module that you can build on and make use of in subsequent chapters. The class module contains two classes:

➤   Card—Representing a standard playing card, with a suit of club, diamond, heart, or spade, and a rank that lies between ace and king

➤   Deck—Representing a full deck of 52 cards, with access to cards by position in the deck and the capability to shuffle the deck

You'll also develop a simple client to ensure that things are working, but you won't use the deck in a full card game application—yet.

Planning the Application

The class library for this application, Ch10CardLib, will contain your classes. Before you get down to any code, though, you should plan the required structure and functionality of your classes.

The Card Class

The Card class is basically a container for two read-only fields: suit and rank. The reason for making the fields read-only is that it doesn't make sense to have a "blank" card, and cards shouldn't be able to change once they have been created. To facilitate this, you'll make the default constructor private and provide an alternative constructor that builds a card from a supplied suit and rank.

Other than that, the Card class will override the ToString() method of System.Object, so that you can easily obtain a human-readable string representing the card. To make things a little simpler, you will provide enumerations for the two fields, suit and rank.

The Card class is shown in Figure 10-4.

FIGURE 10-4

The Deck Class

The Deck class will maintain 52 Card objects. You can use a simple array type for this. The array will not be directly accessible because access to the Card object is achieved through a GetCard() method, which returns the Card object with the given index. This class should also expose a Shuffle() method to rearrange the cards in the array. The Deck class is shown in Figure 10-5.

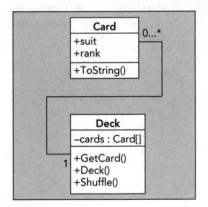

FIGURE 10-5

Writing the Class Library

For the purposes of this example, it is assumed that you are familiar enough with the IDE to bypass the standard Try It Out format, so the steps aren't listed explicitly, as they are the same steps you've used many times. The important thing here is a detailed look at the code. Nonetheless, several pointers are included to ensure that you do not run into any problems along the way.

Both your classes and your enumerations will be contained in a class library project called Ch10CardLib. This project will contain four .cs files: Card.cs, which contains the Card class definition, Deck.cs, which contains the Deck class definition, and the Suit.cs and Rank.cs files containing enumerations.

You can put together a lot of this code using the Visual Studio class diagram tool.

> **NOTE** *If you would prefer not to use the class diagram tool, do not worry. Each of the following sections also includes the code generated by the class diagram, so you will be able to follow along just fine.*

To get started, you need to do the following:

1. Create a new Class Library project called Ch10CardLib and save it in the directory C:\BeginningCSharpAndDotNET\Chapter10.

2. Remove Class1.cs from the project.

3. Open the class diagram for the project using the Solution Explorer window (right-click the project and then click Add ⇨ New Item ⇨ Class Diagram ⇨ Add). The class diagram should be blank to start with because the project contains no classes. This creates a file named ClassDiagram1.cd in the project for later use.

Adding the Suit and Rank Enumerations

With the ClassDiagram1.cd file opened, add an enumeration to the class diagram by dragging an Enum from the Toolbox into the diagram, and then filling in the New Enum dialog box that appears. For example, for the Suit enumeration, fill out the dialog box as shown in Figure 10-6.

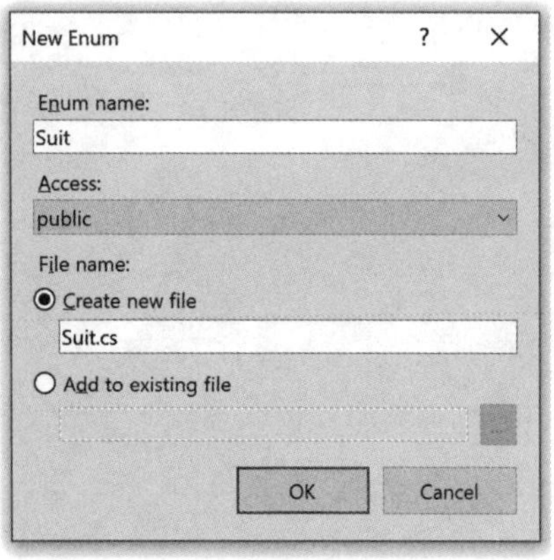

FIGURE 10-6

Next, add the members of the enumeration using the Class Details window (right-click the just added `Suit` Enum ⇨ Class Details within the `ClassDiagram1.cd` file). Figure 10-7 shows the values that are required.

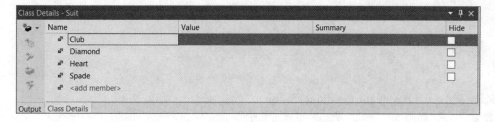

FIGURE 10-7

Add the `Rank` enumeration from the Toolbox in the same way. The values required are shown in Figure 10-8.

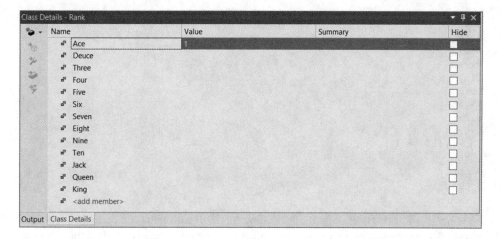

FIGURE 10-8

> **NOTE** *The value entry for the first member, `Ace`, is set to 1 so that the underlying storage of the Enum matches the rank of the card, such that Six is stored as 6, for example.*

You can find the code generated for these two enumerations in the code files, `Suit.cs` and `Rank.cs`. First, you can find the full code for this enumeration in `Ch10CardLib Suit.cs`:

```
using System;
using System.Collections.Generic;
```

```
using System.Text;
namespace Ch10CardLib
{
    public enum Suit
    {
        Club,
        Diamond,
        Heart,
        Spade,
    }
}
```

And you can find the full code for this enumeration in `Ch10CardLib Rank.cs`:

```
using System;
using System.Collections.Generic;
using System.Text;
namespace Ch10CardLib
{
    public enum Rank
    {
        Ace = 1,
        Deuce,
        Three,
        Four,
        Five,
        Six,
        Seven,
        Eight,
        Nine,
        Ten,
        Jack,
        Queen,
        King,
    }
}
```

Alternatively, you can add this code manually by adding `Suit.cs` and `Rank.cs` code files and then entering the code. Note that extra commas may get added by the code generator after the last enumeration member, but they do not prevent compilation and do not result in an additional "empty" member being created—although they are a little messy.

Adding the Card Class

To add the `Card` class, you will use a mix of the class designer and code editor. Adding a class in the class designer is much like adding an enumeration—you drag the appropriate entry from the Toolbox into the diagram. In this case, you drag a `Class` into the diagram and name the new class `Card`.

Use the Class Details window to add the fields `rank` and `suit`, and then use the Properties window to set the Constant Kind of the fields to `readonly`. You also need to add two constructors—a private default constructor and a public constructor that takes two parameters, `newSuit` and `newRank`, of types `Suit` and `Rank`, respectively. Finally, you override `ToString()`, which requires you to change the `Inheritance Modifier` in the Properties window to `override`.

Figure 10-9 shows the Class Details window and the `Card` class with all the information entered. (You can find this code in `Ch10CardLib\Card.cs`.)

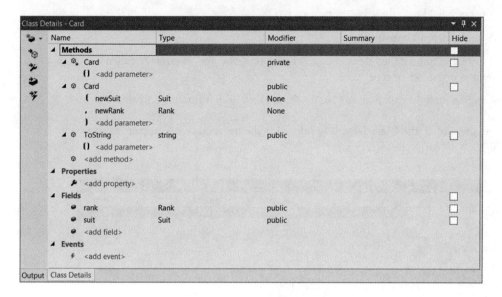

FIGURE 10-9

Next, if you didn't use the Class Diagram window to build the classes, modify the code for the class in `Card.cs` as follows (or add the code shown to a new class called `Card` in the `Ch10CardLib` namespace):

```csharp
public class Card
{
    public readonly Suit suit;
    public readonly Rank rank;
    public Card(Suit newSuit, Rank newRank)
    {
        suit = newSuit;
        rank = newRank;
    }
    private Card() {}
    public override string ToString() => "The " + rank + " of " + suit + "s";
}
```

The overridden `ToString()` method writes the string representation of the enumeration value stored to the returned string, and the nondefault constructor initializes the values of the `suit` and `rank` fields.

Adding the Deck Class

The `Deck` class needs the following members defined using the class diagram:

➤ A private field called `cards`, of type `Card[]`

➤ A public default constructor

➤ A public method called `GetCard()`, which takes one `int` parameter called `cardNum` and returns an object of type `Card`

➤ A public method called `Shuffle()`, which takes no parameters and returns `void`

When these are added, the Class Details window for the `Deck` class will appear as shown in Figure 10-10.

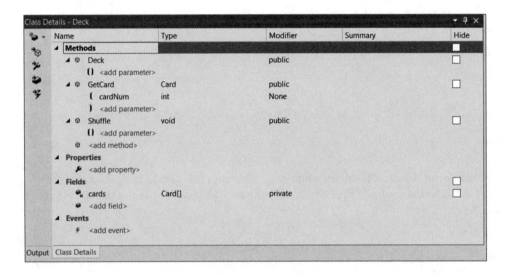

FIGURE 10-10

To make things clearer in the diagram, you can show the relationships among the members and types you have added. In the class diagram, right-click each of the following in turn and select Show as Association from the menu:

➤ `cards` in `Deck`

➤ `suit` in `Card`

➤ `rank` in `Card`

When you have finished, the diagram should look like Figure 10-11.

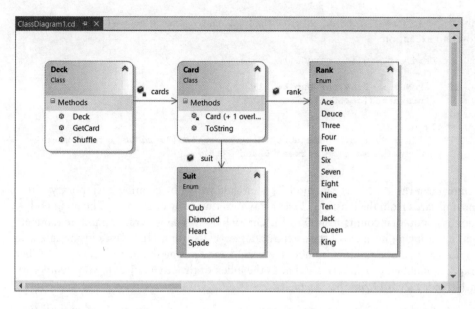

FIGURE 10-11

Next, modify the code in `Deck.cs` (if you are not using the class designer, you must add this class first with the code shown here). You can find this code in `Ch10CardLib\Deck.cs`. First you implement the constructor, which simply creates and assigns 52 cards in the `cards` field. You iterate through all combinations of the two enumerations, using each to create a card. This results in `cards` initially containing an ordered list of cards:

```
using System;
using System.Collections.Generic;
using System.Text;
namespace Ch10CardLib
{
    public class Deck
    {
        private Card[] cards;
        public Deck()
        {
            cards = new Card[52];
            for (int suitVal = 0; suitVal < 4; suitVal++)
            {
                for (int rankVal = 1; rankVal < 14; rankVal++)
                {
                    cards[suitVal * 13 + rankVal -1] = new Card((Suit)suitVal,
                                                                (Rank)rankVal);
                }
            }
        }
    }
}
```

Next, implement the GetCard() method, which either returns the Card object with the requested index or throws an exception:

```
public Card GetCard(int cardNum)
{
    if (cardNum >= 0 && cardNum <= 51)
        return cards[cardNum];
    else
        throw
            (new System.ArgumentOutOfRangeException("cardNum", cardNum,
                "Value must be between 0 and 51."));
}
```

Finally, you implement the Shuffle() method. This method works by creating a temporary card array and copying cards from the existing cards array into this array at random. The main body of this function is a loop that counts from 0 to 51. On each cycle, you generate a random number between 0 and 51, using an instance of the System.Random class from .NET. Once instantiated, an object of this class generates a random number between 0 and X, using the method Next(X). When you have a random number, you simply use that as the index of the Card object in your temporary array in which to copy a card from the cards array.

To keep a record of assigned cards, you also have an array of bool variables, and assign these to true as each card is copied. As you are generating random numbers, you check against this array to see whether you have already copied a card to the location in the temporary array specified by the random number. If so, you simply generate another.

This is not the most efficient way of doing things because many random numbers will be generated before finding a vacant slot into which a card can be copied. However, it works, it is quite simple, and C# code executes so quickly you will hardly notice a delay. The code is as follows:

```
public void Shuffle()
{
    Card[] newDeck = new Card[52];
    bool[] assigned = new bool[52];
    Random sourceGen = new Random();
    for (int i = 0; i < 52; i++)
    {
        int destCard = 0;
        bool foundCard = false;
        while (foundCard == false)
        {
            destCard = sourceGen.Next(52);
            if (assigned[destCard] == false)
                foundCard = true;
        }
        assigned[destCard] = true;
        newDeck[destCard] = cards[i];
    }
    newDeck.CopyTo(cards, 0);
}
```

The last line of this method uses the CopyTo() method of the System.Array class (used whenever you create an array) to copy each of the cards in newDeck back into cards. This means you are using the same set of `Card` objects in the same `cards` object, rather than creating any new instances. If you had instead used `cards = newDeck`, then you would be replacing the object instance referred to by `cards` with another. This could cause problems if code elsewhere were retaining a reference to the original `cards` instance—which would not be shuffled!

That completes the class library code.

A Client Application for the Class Library

To keep things simple, you can add a client console application to the solution containing the class library. To do so, simply right-click the solution in Solution Explorer and select Add ⇨ New Project. The new Console Application project is called `Ch10CardClient`.

To use the class library you have created from this new console application project, add a reference to your `Ch10CardLib` class library project. You can do that through the Projects tab of the Reference Manager dialog box (right-click the `Ch10CardClient` project then Add ⇨ Project Reference ⇨ Projects), as shown in Figure 10-12.

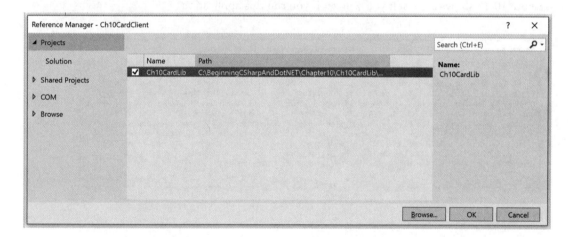

FIGURE 10-12

Select the project and click OK to add the reference.

Because this new project is the second one you've created, you also need to specify that it is the startup project for the solution, meaning the one that is executed when you click Run. To do so, simply right-click the project name in the Solution Explorer window and select the Set as StartUp Project menu option.

Next, add the code that uses your new classes. That does not require anything particularly special, so the following code will do (you can find this code in `Ch10CardClient\Program.cs`):

```
using System;
using Ch10CardLib;
namespace Ch10CardClient
{
```

```
class Program
{
    static void Main(string[] args)
    {
        Deck myDeck = new Deck();
        myDeck.Shuffle();
        for (int i = 0; i < 52; i++)
        {
            Card tempCard = myDeck.GetCard(i);
            Console.Write(tempCard.ToString());
            if (i != 51)
                Console.Write(", ");
            else
                Console.WriteLine();
        }
        Console.ReadKey();
    }
}
```

Figure 10-13 shows the result you will get if you run this application.

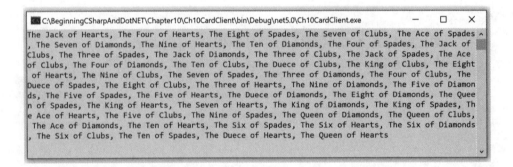

FIGURE 10-13

This is a random arrangement of the 52 playing cards in the deck. You'll continue to develop and use this class library in later chapters.

THE CALL HIERARCHY WINDOW

Now is a good time to take a quick look at another feature of Visual Studio: the Call Hierarchy window. This window enables you to interrogate code to find out where your methods are called from and how they relate to other methods. The best way to illustrate this is with an example.

Open the example application from the previous section and open the Deck.cs code file. Find the Shuffle() method, right-click it, and select the View Call Hierarchy menu item. The window that appears is shown in Figure 10-14 (which has some regions expanded).

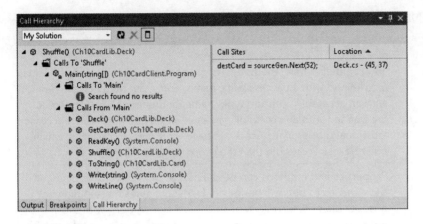

FIGURE 10-14

Starting from the `Shuffle()` method, you can drill into the tree view in the window to find all the code that calls the method. You can double-click the location to navigate instantly to the line of code that is referred to.

This window is useful when you are debugging or refactoring code, as it enables you to see at a glance how different pieces of code are related.

EXERCISES

10.1 Write code that defines a base class, `MyClass`, with the virtual method `GetString()`. This method should return the string stored in the protected field `myString`, accessible through the write-only public property `ContainedString`.

10.2 Derive a class, `MyDerivedClass`, from `MyClass`. Override the `GetString()` method to return the string from the base class, using the base implementation of the method, but add the text "`(output from derived class)`" to the returned string.

10.3 Partial method definitions must use the `void` return type. Provide a reason why this is so.

10.4 Write a class called `MyCopyableClass` that can return a copy of itself using the method `GetCopy()`. This method should use the `MemberwiseClone()` method inherited from `System.Object`. Add a simple property to the class and write client code that uses the class to confirm that everything is working.

10.5 Write a console client for the `Ch10CardLib` library that draws five cards at one time from a shuffled `Deck` object. If all five cards are the same suit, then the client should display the card names onscreen along with the text `Flush!`; otherwise, it should quit after 50 cards with the text `No flush`.

Answers to the exercises can be found in the Appendix.

▶ WHAT YOU LEARNED IN THIS CHAPTER

TOPIC	KEY CONCEPTS
Member definitions	You can define field, method, and property members in a class. Fields are defined with an accessibility, name, and type. Methods are defined with an accessibility, return type, name, and parameters. Properties are defined with an accessibility, name, and a `get` and/or `set` accessor. Individual property accessors can have their own accessibility, which must be less accessible than the property as a whole.
Member hiding and overrides	Properties and methods can be defined as `abstract` or `virtual` in base classes to define inheritance. Derived classes must implement abstract members, and can override virtual members, with the `override` keyword. They can also provide new implementations with the `new` keyword and prevent further overrides of `virtual` members with the `sealed` keyword. Base implementations can be called with the `base` keyword.
Interface implementation	A class that implements an interface must implement all the members defined by that interface. You can implement interfaces implicitly or explicitly, where explicit implementations are only available through an interface reference.
Partial definitions	You can split class definitions across multiple code files with the `partial` keyword. You can also create partial methods with the `partial` keyword.

11

Collections, Comparisons, and Conversions

WHAT YOU WILL LEARN IN THIS CHAPTER

➤ Defining and using collections

➤ Learning the types of collections that are available

➤ Comparing types and using the `is` operator

➤ Comparing values and overloading operators

➤ Defining and using conversions

➤ Using the `as` operator

CODE DOWNLOADS FOR THIS CHAPTER

The code downloads for this chapter are found on the book page at `www.wiley.com`. Click the Downloads link. The code can also be found at `github.com/benperk/BeginningCSharp-AndDotNET`. The code is in the Chapter11 folder and individually named according to the names throughout the chapter.

You have covered all the basic OOP techniques in C# by now, but there are some more advanced techniques that are worth becoming familiar with. These techniques relate to certain problems that you must solve regularly when you are writing code. Learning about them will make it much easier to progress and allow you to concentrate on other, potentially more important aspects of your applications. In this chapter, you will look at the following:

➤ **Collections**—Collections enable you to maintain groups of objects. Unlike arrays, which you have used in earlier chapters, collections can include more advanced functionality, such as controlling access to the objects they contain, searching and sorting, and more. You will learn how to use and create collection classes and learn about some powerful techniques for getting the most out of them.

➤ **Comparisons**—When dealing with objects, you often want to make comparisons between them. This is especially important in collections because it is how sorting is achieved. You will look at how to compare objects in a number of ways, including operator overloading, and how to use the IComparable and IComparer interfaces to sort collections.

➤ **Conversions**—Earlier chapters showed you how to cast objects from one type into another. In this chapter, you will learn how to customize type conversions to suit your needs.

COLLECTIONS

In Chapter 5, you learned how to use arrays to create variable types that contain several objects or values. Arrays, however, have their limitations. The biggest limitation is that once arrays have been created, they have a fixed size, so you cannot add new items to the end of an existing array without creating a new one. This often means that the syntax used to manipulate arrays can become overly complicated. OOP techniques enable you to create classes that perform much of this manipulation internally, simplifying the code that uses lists of items or arrays.

Arrays in C# are implemented as instances of the System.Array class and are just one type of what are known as *collection classes*. Collection classes in general are used for maintaining groups of objects, and they may expose more functionality than simple arrays. Much of this functionality comes through implementing interfaces from the System.Collections namespace, thus standardizing collection syntax. This namespace also contains some other interesting things, such as classes that implement these interfaces in ways other than System.Array.

Because the collection's functionality (including basic functions such as accessing collection items by using [index] syntax) is available through interfaces, you are not limited to using basic collection classes such as System.Array. Instead, you can create your own customized collection classes. These can be made more specific to the objects you want to enumerate (that is, the objects you want to maintain collections of). One advantage of doing this, as you will see, is that custom collection classes can be strongly *typed*. That is, when you extract items from the collection, you don't need to cast them into the correct type, because the items must already be cast to the type of object into which they are being stored. For example, you cannot store a Cow into a collection of Cards. If that is attempted, an exception is thrown and the code will not compile. Another advantage is the capability to expose specialized methods. For example, you can provide a quick way to obtain subsets of items. In the deck of cards example, you could add a method to obtain all Card items of a particular suit.

Several interfaces in the System.Collections namespace provide basic collection functionality:

➤ IEnumerable—Provides the capability to loop through items in a collection

➤ ICollection—Provides the capability to obtain the number of items in a collection and copy items into a simple array type (inherits from IEnumerable)

➤ IList—Provides a list of items for a collection along with the capabilities for accessing these items, and some other basic capabilities related to lists of items (inherits from IEnumerable and ICollection)

➤ IDictionary—Similar to IList, but provides a list of items accessible via a key value, rather than an index (inherits from IEnumerable and ICollection)

The System.Array class implements IList, ICollection, and IEnumerable. However, it does not support some of the more advanced features of IList, and it represents a list of items by using a fixed size.

Using Collections

One of the classes in the Systems.Collections namespace, System.Collections.ArrayList, also implements IList, ICollection, and IEnumerable, but does so in a more sophisticated way than System.Array. Whereas arrays are fixed in size (you can't add or remove elements), this class can be used to represent a variable-length list of items. To give you more of a feel for what is possible with such a highly advanced collection, the following Try It Out uses this class, as well as a simple array.

TRY IT OUT Arrays versus More Advanced Collections: Ch11Ex01

1. Create a new Console Application called Ch11Ex01 and save it in the directory C:\BeginningC-SharpAndDotNET\Chapter11.

2. Add three new classes, Animal, Cow, and Chicken, to the project by right-clicking the project in the Solution Explorer window and selecting Add ➪ Class for each.

3. Modify the code in Animal.cs as follows:

```
namespace Ch11Ex01
{
    public abstract class Animal
    {
        protected string name;
        public string Name
        {
            get { return name; }
            set { name = value; }
        }

        public Animal(string newName) => name = newName;

        public void Feed() => Console.WriteLine($"{name} has been fed.");
    }
}
```

4. Modify the code in Cow.cs as follows:

```
namespace Ch11Ex01
{
    public class Cow : Animal
    {
```

```
        public void Milk() => Console.WriteLine($"{name} has been milked.");
        public Cow(string newName) : base(newName) {}
    }
}
```

5. Modify the code in `Chicken.cs` as follows:

```
namespace Ch11Ex01
{
    public class Chicken : Animal
    {
        public void LayEgg() => Console.WriteLine($"{name} has laid an egg.");
        public Chicken(string newName) : base(newName) {}
    }
}
```

6. Modify the code in `Program.cs` as follows:

```
using System;
using System.Collections;
namespace Ch11Ex01
{
    class Program
    {
        static void Main(string[] args)
        {
            Console.WriteLine("Create an Array type collection of Animal " +
                        "objects and use it:");
            Animal[] animalArray = new Animal[2];
            Cow myCow1 = new Cow("Lea");
            animalArray[0] = myCow1;
            animalArray[1] = new Chicken("Noa");
            foreach (Animal myAnimal in animalArray)
            {
                Console.WriteLine($"New {myAnimal} object added to Array" +
                            $" collection, Name = {myAnimal.Name}");
            }
            Console.WriteLine($"Array collection contains {animalArray.Length} objects.");
            animalArray[0].Feed();
            ((Chicken)animalArray[1]).LayEgg();
            Console.WriteLine();
            Console.WriteLine("Create an ArrayList type collection of Animal " +
                        "objects and use it:");
            ArrayList animalArrayList = new ArrayList();
            Cow myCow2 = new Cow("Donna");
            animalArrayList.Add(myCow2);
            animalArrayList.Add(new Chicken("Andrea"));
            foreach (Animal myAnimal in animalArrayList)
            {
                Console.WriteLine($"New {myAnimal} object added to ArrayList " +
                            $" collection, Name = {myAnimal.Name}");
            }
            Console.WriteLine($"ArrayList collection contains {animalArrayList.Count} "
                        + "objects.");
            ((Animal)animalArrayList[0]).Feed();
```

```
((Chicken)animalArrayList[1]).LayEgg();
Console.WriteLine();
Console.WriteLine("Additional manipulation of ArrayList:");
animalArrayList.RemoveAt(0);
((Animal)animalArrayList[0]).Feed();
animalArrayList.AddRange(animalArray);
((Chicken)animalArrayList[2]).LayEgg();
Console.WriteLine($"The animal called {myCow1.Name} is at " +
                $"index {animalArrayList.IndexOf(myCow1)}.");
myCow1.Name = "Mary";
Console.WriteLine("The animal is now " +
                $" called {((Animal)animalArrayList[1]).Name }.");
Console.ReadKey();
        }
    }
}
```

7. Run the application. The result is shown in Figure 11-1.

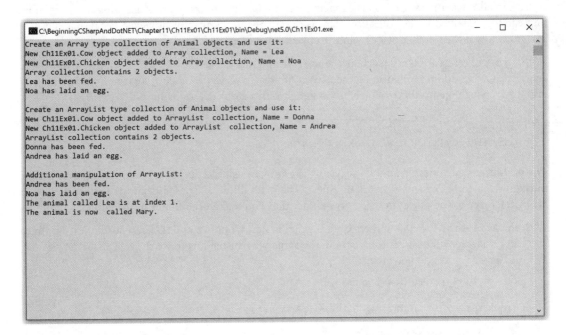

FIGURE 11-1

How It Works

This example creates two collections of objects: the first uses the System.Array class (that is, a simple array), and the second uses the System.Collections.ArrayList class. Both collections are of Animal objects, which are defined in Animal.cs. The Animal class is abstract, so it cannot be instantiated, although you can have items in your collection that are instances of the Cow and Chicken classes, which are derived from Animal. You achieve this by using polymorphism, discussed in Chapter 8.

Once created in the `Main()` method in `Program.cs`, these collections are manipulated to show their characteristics and capabilities. Several of the operations performed apply to both `Array` and `ArrayList` collections, although their syntax differs slightly. Some, however, are possible only by using the more advanced `ArrayList` type.

You'll learn the similar operations first, comparing the code and results for both collection types. You start with collection creation. With simple arrays you must initialize the array with a fixed size in order to use it. You do this to an array called `animalArray` by using the standard syntax shown in Chapter 5:

```
Animal[] animalArray = new Animal[2];
```

`ArrayList` collections, conversely, do not need a size to be initialized, so you can create your list (called `animalArrayList`) as follows:

```
ArrayList animalArrayList = new ArrayList();
```

You can use two other constructors with this class. The first copies the contents of an existing collection to the new instance by specifying the existing collection as a parameter; the other sets the capacity of the collection, also via a parameter. This capacity, specified as an `int` value, sets the initial number of items that can be contained in the collection. This is not an absolute capacity, however, because it is doubled automatically if the number of items in the collection ever exceeds this value.

With arrays of reference types (such as the `Animal` and `Animal`-derived objects), simply initializing the array with a size doesn't initialize the items it contains. To use a given entry, that entry needs to be initialized, which means that you need to assign initialized objects to the items:

```
Cow myCow1 = new Cow("Lea");
animalArray[0] = myCow1;
animalArray[1] = new Chicken("Noa");
```

The preceding code does this in two ways: by assignment using an existing `Cow` object and by assignment through the creation of a new `Chicken` object. The main difference here is that the former method creates a reference to the object in the array—a fact that you make use of later in the code.

With the `ArrayList` collection, there are no existing items, not even `null`-referenced ones. This means you can't assign new instances to indices in the same way. Instead, you use the `Add()` method of the `ArrayList` object to add new items:

```
Cow myCow2 = new Cow("Donna");
animalArrayList.Add(myCow2);
animalArrayList.Add(new Chicken("Andrea"));
```

Apart from the slightly different syntax, you can add new or existing objects to the collection in the same way. Once you have added items in this way, you can overwrite them by using syntax identical to that for arrays:

```
animalArrayList[0] = new Cow("Alma");
```

You will not do that in this example, though.

Chapter 5 showed how the `foreach` structure can be used to iterate through an array. This is possible because the `System.Array` class implements the `IEnumerable` interface, and the only method on this interface, `GetEnumerator()`, allows you to loop through items in the collection. You will look at this in more depth a little later in the chapter. In your code, you write out information about each `Animal` object in the array:

```
foreach (Animal myAnimal in animalArray)
{
    Console.WriteLine($"New {myAnimal} object added to Array " +
                    $"collection, Name = {myAnimal.Name}");
}
```

The `ArrayList` object you use also supports the `IEnumerable` interface and can be used with `foreach`. In this case, the syntax is identical:

```
foreach (Animal myAnimal in animalArrayList)
{
    Console.WriteLine($"New {myAnimal} object added to ArrayList " +
                    $"collection, Name = {myAnimal.Name}");
}
```

Next, you use the array's `Length` property to output to the screen the number of items in the array:

```
Console.WriteLine($"Array collection contains {animalArray.Length} objects.");
```

You can achieve the same thing with the `ArrayList` collection, except that you use the `Count` property that is part of the `ICollection` interface:

```
Console.WriteLine($"ArrayList collection contains {animalArrayList.Count} objects.");
```

Collections—whether simple arrays or more complex collections—are not very useful unless they provide access to the items that belong to them. Simple arrays are strongly typed—that is, they allow direct access to the type of the items they contain. This means you can call the methods of the item directly:

```
animalArray[0].Feed();
```

The type of the array is the abstract type `Animal`; therefore, you can't call methods supplied by derived classes directly. Instead you must use casting:

```
((Chicken)animalArray[1]).LayEgg();
```

The `ArrayList` collection is a collection of `System.Object` objects (you have assigned `Animal` objects via polymorphism). This means that you must use casting for all items:

```
((Animal)animalArrayList[0]).Feed();
((Chicken)animalArrayList[1]).LayEgg();
```

The remainder of the code looks at some of the `ArrayList` collection's capabilities that go beyond those of the `Array` collection. First, you can remove items by using the `Remove()` and `RemoveAt()` methods, part of the `IList` interface implementation in the `ArrayList` class. These methods remove items from a list based on an item reference or index, respectively. This example uses the latter method to remove the list's first item, the `Cow` object with a `Name` property of `Donna`:

```
animalArrayList.RemoveAt(0);
```

Alternatively, you could use

```
animalArrayList.Remove(myCow2);
```

because you already have a local reference to this object—you added an existing reference to the array via `Add()`, rather than create a new object. Either way, the only item left in the collection is the `Chicken` object, which you access as follows:

```
((Animal)animalArrayList[0]).Feed();
```

Any modifications to items in the `ArrayList` object resulting in N items being left in the list will be executed in such a way as to maintain indices from 0 to N-1. For example, removing the item with the index 0 results in all other items being shifted one place in the array, so you access the `Chicken` object with the index 0, not 1. You no longer have an item with an index of 1 (because you only had two items in the first place), so an exception would be thrown if you tried the following:

```
((Animal)animalArrayList[1]).Feed();
```

`ArrayList` collections enable you to add several items at once with the `AddRange()` method. This method accepts any object with the `ICollection` interface, which includes the `animalArray` array created earlier in the code:

```
animalArrayList.AddRange(animalArray);
```

To check that this works, you can attempt to access the third item in the collection, which is the second item in `animalArray`:

```
((Chicken)animalArrayList[2]).LayEgg();
```

The `AddRange()` method isn't part of any of the interfaces exposed by `ArrayList`. This method is specific to the `ArrayList` class and demonstrates the fact that you can exhibit customized behavior in your collection classes, beyond what is required by the interfaces you have looked at. This class exposes other interesting methods too, such as `InsertRange()`, for inserting a collection of objects at any point in the list, and methods for tasks such as sorting and reordering the array.

Finally, you make use of the fact that you can have multiple references to the same object. Using the `IndexOf()` method (part of the `IList` interface), you can see that `myCow1` (an object originally added to `animalArray`) is now part of the `animalArrayList` collection:

```
Console.WriteLine($"The animal called {myCow1.Name} is at index " +
                $"{animalArrayList.IndexOf(myCow1)}.");
```

As an extension of this, the next two lines of code rename the object via the object reference and display the new name via the collection reference:

```
myCow1.Name = "Mary";
Console.WriteLine($"The animal is now called {((Animal)animalArrayList[1]).Name}.");
```

Defining Collections

Now that you know what is possible using more advanced collection classes, it is time to learn how to create your own strongly typed collection. One way of doing this is to implement the required methods manually, but this can be a time-consuming and complex process. Alternatively, you can derive your collection from a class, such as `System.Collections.CollectionBase`, an abstract class that supplies much of the implementation of a collection for you. This option is strongly recommended.

The `CollectionBase` class exposes the interfaces `IEnumerable`, `ICollection`, and `IList` but provides only some of the required implementation—notably, the `Clear()` and `RemoveAt()` methods of `IList` and the `Count` property of `ICollection`. You need to implement everything else yourself if you want the functionality provided.

To facilitate this, `CollectionBase` provides two protected properties that enable access to the stored objects themselves. You can use `List`, which gives you access to the items through an `IList` interface, and `InnerList`, which is the `ArrayList` object used to store items.

For example, the basics of a collection class to store `Animal` objects could be defined as follows (you will see a fuller implementation shortly):

```
public class AnimalCollection : CollectionBase
{
    public void Add(Animal newAnimal) => List.Add(newAnimal);

    public void Remove(Animal oldAnimal) => List.Remove(oldAnimal);

}
```

Here, `Add()` and `Remove()` have been implemented as strongly typed methods that use the standard `Add()` method of the `IList` interface to access the items. The methods exposed will now only work with `Animal` classes or classes derived from `Animal`, unlike the `ArrayList` implementations shown earlier, which work with any object.

The `CollectionBase` class enables you to use the `foreach` syntax with your derived collections. For example, you can use code such as this:

```
Console.WriteLine("Using custom collection class AnimalCollection:");
AnimalCollection animalCollection = new AnimalCollection();
animalCollection.Add(new Cow("Lea"));
foreach (Animal myAnimal in animalCollection)
{
    Console.WriteLine($"New { myAnimal} object added to custom " +
                    $"collection, Name = {myAnimal.Name}");
}
```

You cannot, however, do the following:

```
animalCollection[0].Feed();
```

To access items via their indices in this way, you need to use an indexer.

Indexers

An *indexer* is a special kind of property that you can add to a class to provide array-like access. In fact, you can provide more complex access via an indexer, because you can define and use complex parameter types with the square bracket syntax as you want. Implementing a simple numeric index for items, however, is the most common usage.

You can add an indexer to the `AnimalCollection` collection of `Animal` objects as follows:

```
public class AnimalCollection : CollectionBase
{
    ...
    public Animal this[int animalIndex]
    {
        get { return (Animal)List[animalIndex]; }
        set { List[animalIndex] = value; }
    }
}
```

The `this` keyword is used along with parameters in square brackets, but otherwise, the indexer looks much like any other property. This syntax is logical because you access the indexer by using the name of the object followed by the index parameter(s) in square brackets (for example, `MyAnimals[0]`).

The indexer code uses an indexer on the `List` property (that is, on the `IList` interface that provides access to the `ArrayList` in `CollectionBase` that stores your items):

```
return (Animal)List[animalIndex];
```

Explicit casting is necessary here, as the `IList.List` property returns a `System.Object` object. The important point to note here is that you define a type for this indexer. This is the type that will be obtained when you access an item by using this indexer. This strong typing means that you can write code such as

```
animalCollection[0].Feed();
```

rather than

```
((Animal)animalCollection[0]).Feed();
```

This is another handy feature of strongly typed custom collections. In the following Try It Out, you expand the previous Try It Out to put this into action.

TRY IT OUT Implementing an AnimalCollection Collection: Ch11Ex02

1. Create a new Console Application called Ch11Ex02 and save it in the directory `C:\BeginningC-SharpAndDotNET\Chapter11`.

2. Right-click the project name in the Solution Explorer window and select Add ⇨ Existing Item.

3. Select the `Animal.cs`, `Cow.cs`, and `Chicken.cs` files from the `C:\BeginningCSharpAndDotNET\Chapter11\Ch11Ex01` directory, and click Add.

4. Modify the namespace declaration in the three files you added as follows:

   ```
   namespace Ch11Ex02
   ```

5. Add a new class called `AnimalCollection`.

6. Modify the code in `AnimalCollection.cs` as follows:

   ```
   using System;
   using System.Collections;
   namespace Ch11Ex02
   {
   ```

```csharp
public class AnimalCollection : CollectionBase
{
    public void Add(Animal newAnimal) =>
        List.Add(newAnimal);

    public void Remove(Animal newAnimal) =>
        List.Remove(newAnimal);

    public Animal this[int animalIndex]
    {
        get { return (Animal)List[animalIndex]; }
        set { List[animalIndex] = value; }
    }
}
```

7. Modify `Program.cs` as follows:

```csharp
static void Main(string[] args)
{
    AnimalCollection animalCollection = new AnimalCollection();
    animalCollection.Add(new Cow("Donna"));
    animalCollection.Add(new Chicken("Mary"));
    foreach (Animal myAnimal in animalCollection)
    {
        myAnimal.Feed();
    }
    Console.ReadKey();
}
```

8. Execute the application. The result is shown in Figure 11-2.

FIGURE 11-2

How It Works

This example uses code detailed in the previous section to implement a strongly typed collection of `Animal` objects in a class called `AnimalCollection`. The code in `Main()` simply instantiates an `AnimalCollection` object called `animalCollection`, adds two items (an instance of `Cow` and `Chicken`), and uses a `foreach` loop to call the `Feed()` method that both objects inherit from their base class, `Animal`.

Adding a CardCollection to CardLib

In the previous chapter, you created a class library project called `Ch10CardLib` that contained a `Card` class representing a playing card, and a `Deck` class representing a deck of cards—that is, a collection of `Card` classes. This collection was implemented as a simple array.

In this chapter, you will add a new class to this library, renamed `Ch11CardLib`. This new class, `CardCollection`, will be a custom collection of `Card` objects, giving you all the benefits described earlier in this chapter. Create a new Class Library (.NET Core) called `Ch11CardLib` in the `C:\BeginningCSharpAndDotNET\Chapter11` directory. Next, delete the autogenerated `Class1.cs` file; select Project ⇨ Add Existing Item; select the `Card.cs`, `Deck.cs`, `Suit.cs`, and `Rank.cs` files from the `C:\BeginningCSharpAndDotNET\Chapter10\Ch10CardLib` directory; and add the files to your project. As with the previous version of this project, introduced in Chapter 10, these changes are presented without using the standard Try It Out format. Should you want to jump straight to the code, feel free to open the version of this project included in the downloadable code for this chapter or on GitHub.

> **NOTE** *Do not forget that when copying the source files from* `Ch10CardLib` *to* `Ch11CardLib`, *you must change the namespace declarations to refer to* `Ch11CardLib`. *This also applies to the* `Ch10CardClient` *console application that you will use for testing.*

The downloadable code for this chapter includes a `Ch11CardLib` folder that contains all the code you need for the various expansions to the `Ch11CardLib` project. Because of this, you may notice some extra code that is not included in this example, but this will not affect how it works at this stage. Often you will find that code is commented out; however, when you reach the relevant example, you can uncomment the section you want to experiment with.

Add a new class called `CardCollection` and modify the code in `CardCollection.cs` as follows:

```
using System;
using System.Collections;
namespace Ch11CardLib
{
    public class CardCollection : CollectionBase
    {
        public void Add(Card newCard) => List.Add(newCard);

        public void Remove(Card oldCard) => List.Remove(oldCard);

        public Card this[int cardIndex]
        {
            get { return (Card)List[cardIndex]; }
            set { List[cardIndex] = value; }
        }
        /// <summary>
        /// Utility method for copying card instances into another CardCollection
        /// instance—used in Deck.Shuffle(). This implementation assumes that
        /// source and target collections are the same size.
        /// </summary>
        public void CopyTo(CardCollections targetCards)
        {
```

```
                for (int index = 0; index < this.Count; index++)
                {
                    targetCards[index] = this[index];
                }
            }
            /// <summary>
            /// Check to see if the CardCollection collection contains a particular card.
            /// This calls the Contains() method of the ArrayList for the collection,
            /// which you access through the InnerList property.
            /// </summary>
            public bool Contains(Card card) => InnerList.Contains(card);
        }
    }
```

Next, modify Deck.cs to use this new collection, rather than an array:

```
using System;
namespace Ch11CardLib
{
    public class Deck
    {
        private CardCollection cards = new CardCollection();
        public Deck()
        {
            // Line of code removed here
            for (int suitVal = 0; suitVal < 4; suitVal++)
            {
                for (int rankVal = 1; rankVal < 14; rankVal++)
                {
                    cards.Add(new Card((Suit)suitVal, (Rank)rankVal));
                }
            }
        }
        public Card GetCard(int cardNum)
        {
            if (cardNum >= 0 && cardNum <= 51)
                return cards[cardNum];
            else
                throw (new System.ArgumentOutOfRangeException("cardNum", cardNum,
                        "Value must be between 0 and 51."));
        }
        public void Shuffle()
        {
            CardCollection newDeck = new CardCollection();
            bool[] assigned = new bool[52];
            Random sourceGen = new Random();
            for (int i = 0; i < 52; i++)
            {
                int sourceCard = 0;
                bool foundCard = false;
                while (foundCard == false)
                {
```

```
                sourceCard = sourceGen.Next(52);
                if (assigned[sourceCard] == false)
                    foundCard = true;
            }
            assigned[sourceCard] = true;
            newDeck.Add(cards[sourceCard]);
        }
        newDeck.CopyTo(cards);
    }
  }
}
```

Not many changes are necessary here. Most of them involve changing the shuffling logic to allow for the fact that cards are added to the beginning of the new CardCollection collection, newDeck, from a random index in cards, rather than to a random index in newDeck from a sequential position in cards.

The client console application for the Ch10CardLib solution, Ch10CardClient, can be used with this new library with the same result as before, as the method signatures of Deck are unchanged. Clients of this class library can now make use of the CardCollection collection class, however, rather than rely on arrays of Card objects to define hands of cards in a card game application, for example.

Keyed Collections and IDictionary

Instead of implementing the IList interface, it is also possible for collections to implement the similar IDictionary interface, which allows items to be indexed via a key value (such as a string name), rather than an index. This is also achieved using an indexer, although here the indexer parameter used is a key associated with a stored item, rather than an int index, which can make the collection a lot more user-friendly.

As with indexed collections, there is a base class you can use to simplify implementation of the IDictionary interface: DictionaryBase. This class also implements IEnumerable and ICollection, providing the basic collection-manipulation capabilities that are the same for any collection.

DictionaryBase, like CollectionBase, implements some (but not all) of the members obtained through its supported interfaces. Like CollectionBase, the Clear and Count members are implemented, although RemoveAt() isn't because it's a method on the IList interface and doesn't appear on the IDictionary interface. IDictionary does, however, have a Remove() method, which is one of the methods you should implement in a custom collection class based on DictionaryBase.

The following code shows an alternative version of the Animals class, this time derived from DictionaryBase. Implementations are included for Add(), Remove(), and a key-accessed indexer:

```
public class Animals : DictionaryBase
{
    public void Add(string newID, Animal newAnimal) =>
        Dictionary.Add(newID, newAnimal);

    public void Remove(string animalID) =>
        Dictionary.Remove(animalID);
```

```
    public Animals() {}
    public Animal this[string animalID]
    {
        get { return (Animal)Dictionary[animalID]; }
        set { Dictionary[animalID] = value; }
    }
}
```

The differences in these members are as follows:

➤ Add()—Takes two parameters, a key and a value, to store together. The dictionary collection has a member called Dictionary inherited from DictionaryBase, which is an IDictionary interface. This interface has its own Add() method, which takes two object parameters. Your implementation takes a string value as a key and an Animal object as the data to store alongside this key.

➤ Remove()—Takes a key parameter, rather than an object reference. The item with the key value specified is removed.

➤ Indexer—Uses a string key value, rather than an index, which is used to access the stored item via the Dictionary inherited member. Again, casting is necessary here.

One other difference between collections based on DictionaryBase and collections based on CollectionBase is that foreach works slightly differently. The collection from the previous section allowed you to extract Animal objects directly from the collection. Using foreach with the DictionaryBase derived class gives you DictionaryEntry structs, another type defined in the System.Collections namespace. To get to the Animal objects themselves, you must use the Value member of this struct, or you can use the Key member of the struct to get the associated key. To get code equivalent to the earlier

```
foreach (Animal myAnimal in animalCollection)
{
    Console.WriteLine($"New {myAnimal} object added to custom " +
                    $"collection, Name = {myAnimal.Name}");
}
```

you need the following:

```
foreach (DictionaryEntry myEntry in animalCollection)
{
    Console.WriteLine($"New {myEntry.Value} object added to " +
                $"custom collection, Name = {((Animal)myEntry.Value).Name}");
}
```

It is possible to override this behavior so that you can access Animal objects directly through foreach. There are several ways to do this, the simplest being to implement an iterator.

Iterators

Earlier in this chapter, you saw that the IEnumerable interface enables you to use foreach loops. It is often beneficial to use your classes in foreach loops, not just collection classes such as those shown in previous sections.

However, overriding this behavior, or providing your own custom implementation of it, is not always simple. To illustrate this, it's necessary to take a detailed look at `foreach` loops. The following steps show you what actually happens in a `foreach` loop iterating through a collection called `collectionObject`:

1. `collectionObject.GetEnumerator()` is called, which returns an `IEnumerator` reference. This method is available through implementation of the `IEnumerable` interface.

2. The `MoveNext()` method of the returned `IEnumerator` interface is called.

3. If `MoveNext()` returns `true`, then the `Current` property of the `IEnumerator` interface is used to get a reference to an object, which is used in the `foreach` loop.

4. The preceding two steps repeat until `MoveNext()` returns `false`, at which point the loop terminates.

To enable this behavior in your classes, you must override several methods, keep track of indices, maintain the `Current` property, and so on. This can be a lot of work to achieve little.

A simpler alternative is to use an iterator. Effectively, using iterators generates a lot of the code for you behind the scenes and hooks it all up correctly. Moreover, the syntax for using iterators is much easier to get a grip on.

A good definition of an iterator is a block of code that supplies all the values to be used in a `foreach` block in sequence. Typically, this block of code is a method, although you can also use property accessors and other blocks of code as iterators. To keep things simple, you will just look at methods here.

Whatever the block of code is, its return type is restricted. Perhaps contrary to expectations, this return type is not the same as the type of object being enumerated. For example, in a class that represents a collection of `Animal` objects, the return type of the iterator block cannot be `Animal`. Two possible return types are the interface types mentioned earlier, `IEnumerable` or `IEnumerator`. You use these types as follows:

➤ To iterate over a class, use a method called `GetEnumerator()` with a return type of `IEnumerator`.

➤ To iterate over a class member, such as a method, use `IEnumerable`.

Within an iterator block, you select the values to be used in the `foreach` loop by using the `yield` keyword. The syntax for doing this is as follows:

```
yield return <value>;
```

That information is all you need to build a simple example, as follows (you can find this code in `SimpleIterators\Program.cs`):

```
using System.Collections;
public static IEnumerable SimpleList()
{
    yield return "string 1";
    yield return "string 2";
    yield return "string 3";
}
```

```
static void Main(string[] args)
{
    foreach (string item in SimpleList())
        Console.WriteLine(item);
    Console.ReadKey();
}
```

Here, the static method `SimpleList()` is the iterator block. Because it is a method, you use an `IEnumerable` return type. `SimpleList()` uses the `yield return` keyword to supply three values to the `foreach` block that uses it, each of which is written to the screen. The result is shown in Figure 11-3.

FIGURE 11-3

Obviously, this iterator is not a particularly useful one, but it does show how this works in action and how simple the implementation can be. Looking at the code, you might wonder how the code knows to return `string` type items. In fact, it doesn't; it returns `object` type values. As you know, `object` is the base class for all types, so you can return anything from the `yield` statements.

However, the compiler is intelligent enough that you can interpret the returned values as whatever type you want in the context of the `foreach` loop. Here, the code asks for `string` type values, so those are the values you get to work. Should you change one of the `yield` lines so that it returns, say, an integer, you would get a bad cast exception in the `foreach` loop.

One more thing about iterators. It is possible to interrupt the return of information to the `foreach` loop by using the following statement:

```
yield break;
```

When this statement is encountered in an iterator, the iterator processing terminates immediately, as does the `foreach` loop using it.

Now it's time for a more complicated—and useful!—example. In this Try It Out, you'll implement an iterator that obtains prime numbers.

TRY IT OUT Implementing an Iterator: Ch11Ex03

1. Create a new Console Application called Ch11Ex03 and save it in the directory `C:\BeginningCSharpAndDotNET\Chapter11`.

2. Add a new class called `Primes` and modify the code in `Primes.cs` as follows:

```
using System;
using System.Collections;
namespace Ch11Ex03
{
```

```csharp
public class Primes
{
    private long min;
    private long max;
    public Primes() : this(2, 100) {}
    public Primes(long minimum, long maximum)
    {
        if (minimum < 2)
            min = 2;
        else
            min = minimum;
        max = maximum;
    }
    public IEnumerator GetEnumerator()
    {
        for (long possiblePrime = min; possiblePrime <= max; possiblePrime++)
        {
            bool isPrime = true;
            for (long possibleFactor = 2; possibleFactor <=
                (long)Math.Floor(Math.Sqrt(possiblePrime)); possibleFactor++)
            {
                long remainderAfterDivision = possiblePrime % possibleFactor;
                if (remainderAfterDivision == 0)
                {
                    isPrime = false;
                    break;
                }
            }
            if (isPrime)
            {
                yield return possiblePrime;
            }
        }
    }
}
```

3. Modify the code in `Program.cs` as follows:

```csharp
static void Main(string[] args)
{
    Primes primesFrom2To1000 = new Primes(2, 1000);
    foreach (long i in primesFrom2To1000)
        Console.Write($"{i} ");
    Console.ReadKey();
}
```

4. Execute the application. The result is shown in Figure 11-4.

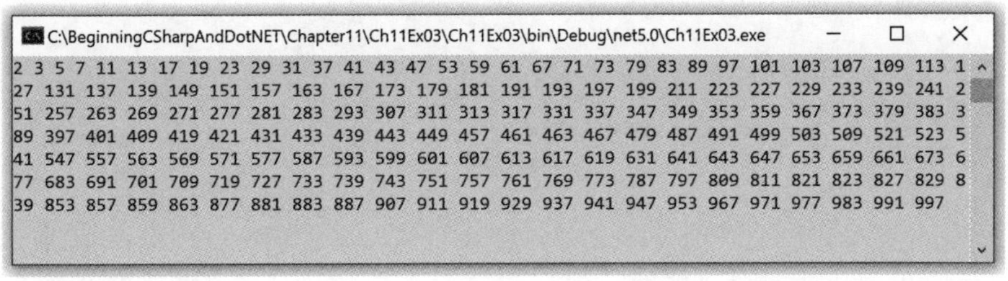

```
C:\BeginningCSharpAndDotNET\Chapter11\Ch11Ex03\Ch11Ex03\bin\Debug\net5.0\Ch11Ex03.exe        —    □    ×
2 3 5 7 11 13 17 19 23 29 31 37 41 43 47 53 59 61 67 71 73 79 83 89 97 101 103 107 109 113 1
27 131 137 139 149 151 157 163 167 173 179 181 191 193 197 199 211 223 227 229 233 239 241 2
51 257 263 269 271 277 281 283 293 307 311 313 317 331 337 347 349 353 359 367 373 379 383 3
89 397 401 409 419 421 431 433 439 443 449 457 461 463 467 479 487 491 499 503 509 521 523 5
41 547 557 563 569 571 577 587 593 599 601 607 613 617 619 631 641 643 647 653 659 661 673 6
77 683 691 701 709 719 727 733 739 743 751 757 761 769 773 787 797 809 811 821 823 827 829 8
39 853 857 859 863 877 881 883 887 907 911 919 929 937 941 947 953 967 971 977 983 991 997
```

FIGURE 11-4

How It Works

This example consists of a class that enables you to enumerate over a collection of prime numbers between an upper and lower limit. The class that encapsulates the prime numbers uses an iterator to provide this functionality.

The code for `Primes` starts off with the basics: two fields to hold the maximum and minimum values to search between, and constructors to set these values. Note that the minimum value is restricted—it can't be less than 2. This makes sense, because 2 is the lowest prime number. The interesting code is all in the `GetEnumerator()` method. The method signature fulfills the rules for an iterator block in that it returns an `IEnumerator` type:

```
public IEnumerator GetEnumerator()
{
```

To extract prime numbers between limits, you need to test each number in turn, so you start with a `for` loop:

```
for (long possiblePrime = min; possiblePrime <= max; possiblePrime++)
{
```

Because you do not know whether a number is prime, you first assume that it is and then check to see if it isn't. That means checking whether any number between 2 and the square root of the number to be tested is a factor. If this is `true`, then the number isn't prime, so you move on to the next one. If the number is indeed prime, then you pass it to the `foreach` loop using `yield`:

```
bool isPrime = true;
for (long possibleFactor = 2; possibleFactor <=
    (long)Math.Floor(Math.Sqrt(possiblePrime)); possibleFactor++)
{
    long remainderAfterDivision = possiblePrime % possibleFactor;
    if (remainderAfterDivision == 0)
    {
        isPrime = false;
        break;
```

```
            }
         }
         if (isPrime)
         {
            yield return possiblePrime;
         }
      }
   }
}
```

An interesting fact reveals itself through this code if you set the minimum and maximum limits to big numbers. When you execute the application, the results appear one at a time, with pauses in between, rather than all at once. This is evidence that the iterator code returns results one at a time, despite the fact that there is no obvious place where the code terminates between `yield` calls. Behind the scenes, calling `yield` does interrupt the code, which resumes when another value is requested—that is, when the `foreach` loop using the iterator begins a new cycle.

Iterators and Collections

Earlier you were promised an explanation of how iterators can be used to iterate over the objects stored in a dictionary-type collection without having to deal with `DictionaryItem` objects. In the downloadable code for this chapter, you will find the code for the next project in the `Dictionary-Animals` folder. Recall the collection class `Animals`:

```
public class Animals : DictionaryBase
{
   public void Add(string newID, Animal newAnimal) =>
      Dictionary.Add(newID, newAnimal);

   public void Remove(string animalID) =>
      Dictionary.Remove(animalID);

   public Animal this[string animalID]
   {
      get { return (Animal)Dictionary[animalID]; }
      set { Dictionary[animalID] = value; }
   }
}
```

You can add this simple iterator to the code to get the desired behavior. The `new` keyword in the method signature is used to implement a concept known as *method hiding*. This is an advanced topic, but note that this concept is used to make code more natural, readable, and understandable by avoiding seemingly duplicated code:

```
public new IEnumerator GetEnumerator()
{
   foreach (object animal in Dictionary.Values)
      yield return (Animal)animal;
}
```

Now you can use the following code to iterate through the `Animal` objects in the collection:

```
foreach (Animal myAnimal in animalCollection)
{
    Console.WriteLine($"New {myAnimal.ToString()} object added to " +
                      $" custom collection, Name = {myAnimal.Name}");
}
```

Deep Copying

Chapter 9 described how you can perform shallow copying with the `System.Object.Memberwise-Clone()` protected method, by using a method like the `GetCopy()` one shown here:

```
public class Cloner
{
    public int Val;
    public Cloner(int newVal) => Val = newVal;
    public object GetCopy() => MemberwiseClone();
}
```

Suppose you have fields that are reference types, rather than value types (for example, objects):

```
public class Content
{
    public int Val;
}
public class Cloner
{
    public Content MyContent = new Content();
    public Cloner(int newVal) => MyContent.Val = newVal;
    public object GetCopy() => MemberwiseClone();
}
```

In this case, the shallow copy obtained through `GetCopy()` has a field that refers to the same object as the original object. The following code, which uses this `Cloner` class, illustrates the consequences of shallow copying reference types:

```
Cloner mySource = new Cloner(5);
Cloner myTarget = (Cloner)mySource.GetCopy();
Console.WriteLine($"myTarget.MyContent.Val = {myTarget.MyContent.Val}");
mySource.MyContent.Val = 2;
Console.WriteLine($"myTarget.MyContent.Val = {myTarget.MyContent.Val}");
```

The fourth line, which assigns a value to `mySource.MyContent.Val`, the `Val` public field of the `MyContent` public field of the original object, also changes the value of `myTarget.MyContent.Val`. That is because `mySource.MyContent` refers to the same object instance as `myTarget.MyContent`. The output of the preceding code is as follows:

```
myTarget.MyContent.Val = 5
myTarget.MyContent.Val = 2
```

To get around this, you need to perform a deep copy. You could just modify the `GetCopy()` method used previously to do this, but it is preferable to use the standard .NET Framework way of doing things: implement the `ICloneable` interface, which has the single method `Clone()`. This method takes no parameters and returns an `object` type result, giving it a signature identical to the `GetCopy()` method used earlier.

To modify the preceding classes, try using the following deep copy code:

```
public class Content
{
   public int Val;
}
public class Cloner : ICloneable
{
   public Content MyContent = new Content();
   public Cloner(int newVal) => MyContent.Val = newVal;
   public object Clone()
   {
      Cloner clonedCloner = new Cloner(MyContent.Val);
      return clonedCloner;
   }
}
```

This created a new `Cloner` object by using the `Val` field of the `Content` object contained in the original `Cloner` object (`MyContent`). This field is a value type, so no deeper copying is necessary.

Using code like the example just shown to test the shallow copy—but using `Clone()` instead of `GetCopy()`—gives you the following result:

```
myTarget.MyContent.Val = 5
myTarget.MyContent.Val = 5
```

This time, the contained objects are independent. Note that sometimes calls to `Clone()` are made recursively, in more complex object systems. For example, if the `MyContent` field of the `Cloner` class also required deep copying, then you might need the following:

```
public class Cloner : ICloneable
{
   public Content MyContent = new Content();
   ...
   public object Clone()
   {
      Cloner clonedCloner = new Cloner();
      clonedCloner.MyContent = MyContent.Clone();
      return clonedCloner;
   }
}
```

You are calling the default constructor here to simplify the syntax of creating a new `Cloner` object. For this code to work, you would also need to implement `ICloneable` on the `Content` class.

Adding Deep Copying to CardLib

You can put this into practice by implementing the capability to copy `Card`, `CardCollection`, and `Deck` objects by using the `ICloneable` interface. This might be useful in some card games, where you might not necessarily want two decks with references to the same set of `Card` objects, although you might conceivably want to set up one deck to have the same card order as another.

Implementing cloning functionality for the `Card` class in `Ch11CardLib` is simple because shallow copying is sufficient (`Card` contains only value-type data, in the form of fields). Begin by making the following changes to the `class` definition:

```
public class Card : ICloneable
{
    public object Clone() => MemberwiseClone();
```

This implementation of `ICloneable` is just a shallow copy. There is no rule determining what should happen in the `Clone()` method, and this is sufficient for your purposes.

Next, implement `ICloneable` on the `CardCollection` collection class. This is slightly more complicated because it involves cloning every `Card` object in the original collection—so you need to make a deep copy:

```
public class CardCollection : CollectionBase, ICloneable
{
    public object Clone()
    {
        CardCollection newCards = new CardCollection();
        foreach (Card sourceCard in List)
        {
            newCards.Add((Card)sourceCard.Clone());
        }
        return newCards;
    }
}
```

Finally, implement `ICloneable` on the `Deck` class. Note a slight problem here: The `Deck` class in `Ch11CardLib` has no way to modify the cards it contains, short of shuffling them. There is no way, for example, to modify a `Deck` instance to have a given card order. To get around this, define a new private constructor for the `Deck` class that allows a specific `CardCollection` collection to be passed in when the `Deck` object is instantiated. Here is the code to implement cloning in this class:

```
public class Deck : ICloneable
{
    public object Clone()
    {
        Deck newDeck = new Deck(cards.Clone() as CardCollection);
        return newDeck;
    }
}
private Deck(CardCollection newCards) => cards = newCards;
```

Again, you can test this with some simple client code. As before, place this code within the `Main()` method of a client project for testing (you can find this code in `Ch11CardClient\Program.cs` in the chapter's online download):

```
Deck deck1 = new Deck();
Deck deck2 = (Deck)deck1.Clone();
Console.WriteLine($"The first card in the original deck is: {deck1.GetCard(0)}");
Console.WriteLine($"The first card in the cloned deck is: {deck2.GetCard(0)}");
deck1.Shuffle();
```

```
Console.WriteLine("Original deck shuffled.");
Console.WriteLine($"The first card in the original deck is: {deck1.GetCard(0)}");
Console.WriteLine($"The first card in the cloned deck is: {deck2.GetCard(0)}");
Console.ReadKey();
```

The output will be similar to what is shown in Figure 11-5.

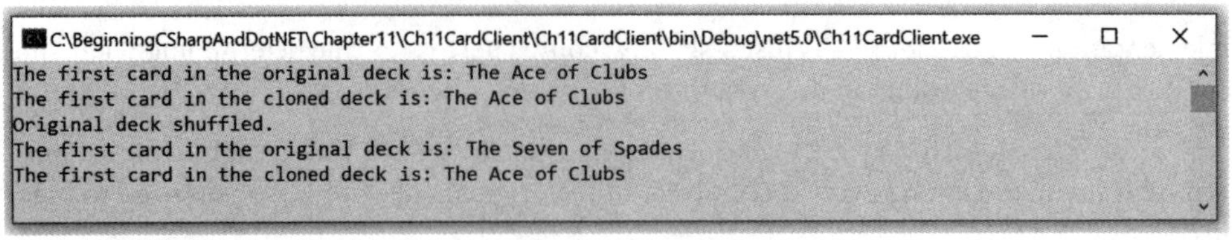

```
C:\BeginningCSharpAndDotNET\Chapter11\Ch11CardClient\Ch11CardClient\bin\Debug\net5.0\Ch11CardClient.exe    —    □    ×
The first card in the original deck is: The Ace of Clubs
The first card in the cloned deck is: The Ace of Clubs
Original deck shuffled.
The first card in the original deck is: The Seven of Spades
The first card in the cloned deck is: The Ace of Clubs
```

FIGURE 11-5

COMPARISONS

This section covers two types of comparisons between objects:

➤ Type comparisons

➤ Value comparisons

Type comparisons—that is, determining what an object is, or what it inherits from—are important in all areas of C# programming. Often when you pass an object—to a method, for example—what happens next depends on the type of the object. You've seen this in passing in this and earlier chapters, but here you will see some more useful techniques.

Value comparisons are also something you have seen a lot of, at least with simple types. When it comes to comparing values of objects, things get a little more complicated. You must define what is meant by a comparison for a start, and what operators such as > mean in the context of your classes. This is especially important in collections, for which you might want to sort objects according to some condition, perhaps alphabetically or according to a more complicated algorithm.

Type Comparisons

When comparing objects, you often need to know their type, which enables you to determine whether a value comparison is possible. In Chapter 9 you saw the GetType() method, which all classes inherit from System.Object, and how this method can be used in combination with the typeof() operator to determine (and take action depending on) object types:

```
if (myObj.GetType() == typeof(MyComplexClass))
{
    // myObj is an instance of the class MyComplexClass.
}
```

You've also seen how the default implementation of ToString(), also inherited from System.Object, will get you a string representation of an object's type. You can compare these strings too, although that's a rather messy way to accomplish this.

This section demonstrates a handy shorthand way of doing things: the `is` operator. This operator allows for much more readable code and, as you will see, has the advantage of examining base classes. Before looking at the `is` operator, though, you need to be aware of what often happens behind the scenes when dealing with value types (as opposed to reference types): *boxing* and *unboxing*.

Boxing and Unboxing

In Chapter 8, you learned the difference between reference types and value types, which was illustrated in Chapter 9 by comparing structs (which are value types) with classes (which are reference types). Boxing is the act of converting a value type into the `System.Object` type or to an interface type that is implemented by the value type. Unboxing is the opposite conversion.

For example, suppose you have the following struct type:

```
struct MyStruct
{
    public int Val;
}
```

You can box a struct of this type by placing it into an `object`-type variable:

```
MyStruct valType1 = new MyStruct();
valType1.Val = 5;
object refType = valType1;
```

Here, you create a new variable (`valType1`) of type `MyStruct`, assign a value to the `Val` member of this `struct`, and then box it into an `object`-type variable (`refType`).

The object created by boxing a variable in this way contains a reference to a copy of the value-type variable, not a reference to the original value-type variable. You can verify this by modifying the original struct's contents and then unboxing the struct contained in the object into a new variable and examining its contents:

```
valType1.Val = 6;
MyStruct valType2 = (MyStruct)refType;
Console.WriteLine($"valType2.Val = {valType2.Val}");
```

This code gives you the following output:

```
valType2.Val = 5
```

When you assign a reference type to an object, however, you get a different behavior. You can see this by changing `MyStruct` into a class (ignoring the fact that the name of this class is not appropriate now):

```
class MyStruct
{
    public int Val;
}
```

With no changes to the client code shown previously (again ignoring the misnamed variables), you get the following output:

```
valType2.Val = 6
```

You can also box value types into interface types, so long as they implement that interface. For example, suppose the `MyStruct` type implements the `IMyInterface` interface as follows:

```
interface IMyInterface {}
struct MyStruct : IMyInterface
{
    public int Val;
}
```

You can then box the struct into an `IMyInterface` type as follows:

```
MyStruct valType1 = new MyStruct();
IMyInterface refType = valType1;
```

You can unbox it by using the normal casting syntax:

```
MyStruct ValType2 = (MyStruct)refType;
```

As shown in these examples, boxing is performed without your intervention—that is, you do not have to write any code to make it possible. Unboxing a value requires an explicit conversion, however, and it requires you to make a cast (boxing is implicit and does not have this requirement).

You might be wondering why you would want to do this. There are two very good reasons why boxing is extremely useful. First, it enables you to use value types in collections (such as `ArrayList`) where the items are of type `object`. Second, it is the internal mechanism that enables you to call `object` methods on value types, such as `int`s and structs.

It is worth noting that you do not need to unbox to access members defined by an interface. An interface cannot define fields, so you do always need to unbox to access fields, but an interface can define properties.

The is Operator

Despite its name, the `is` operator isn't a way to determine whether an object is a certain type. Instead, the `is` operator enables you to check whether an object either is or *can be converted into* a given type. If this is the case, then the operator evaluates to `true`. In Object Oriented Programming (OOP) terms, `is` tests the "is-a" relationship.

Earlier examples showed a `Cow` and a `Chicken` class, both of which inherit from `Animal`. Using the `is` operator to compare objects with the `Animal` type will return `true` for objects of all three of these types, not just `Animal`. This is something you'd have a hard time achieving with the `GetType()` method and `typeof()` operator shown previously.

The `is` operator has the following syntax:

```
<operand> is <type>
```

The possible results of this expression are as follows:

➤   If `<type>` is a class type, then the result is `true` if `<operand>` is of that type, if it inherits from that type, or if it can be boxed into that type.

> ➤ If `<type>` is an interface type, then the result is `true` if `<operand>` is of that type or it is a type that implements the interface.

> ➤ If `<type>` is a value type, then the result is `true` if `<operand>` is of that type or it is a type that can be unboxed into that type.

The following Try It Out shows how this works in practice.

TRY IT OUT Using the is Operator: Ch11Ex04\Program.cs

1. Create a new Console Application called Ch11Ex04 in the directory `C:\BeginningCSharpAnd-DotNET\Chapter11`.

2. Modify the code in `Program.cs` as follows:

```
namespace Ch11Ex04
{
   class Checker
   {
      public void Check(object param1)
      {
         if (param1 is ClassA)
            Console.WriteLine("Variable can be converted to ClassA.");
         else
            Console.WriteLine("Variable can't be converted to ClassA.");
         if (param1 is IMyInterface)
            Console.WriteLine("Variable can be converted to IMyInterface.");
         else
            Console.WriteLine("Variable can't be converted to IMyInterface.");
         if (param1 is MyStruct)
            Console.WriteLine("Variable can be converted to MyStruct.");
         else
            Console.WriteLine("Variable can't be converted to MyStruct.");
      }
   }
   interface IMyInterface {}
   class ClassA : IMyInterface {}
   class ClassB : IMyInterface {}
   class ClassC {}
   class ClassD : ClassA {}
   struct MyStruct : IMyInterface {}
   class Program
   {
      static void Main(string[] args)
      {
         Checker check = new Checker();
         ClassA try1 = new ClassA();
         ClassB try2 = new ClassB();
```

```
            ClassC try3 = new ClassC();
            ClassD try4 = new ClassD();
            MyStruct try5 = new MyStruct();
            object try6 = try5;
            Console.WriteLine("Analyzing ClassA type variable:");
            check.Check(try1);
            Console.WriteLine("\nAnalyzing ClassB type variable:");
            check.Check(try2);
            Console.WriteLine("\nAnalyzing ClassC type variable:");
            check.Check(try3);
            Console.WriteLine("\nAnalyzing ClassD type variable:");
            check.Check(try4);
            Console.WriteLine("\nAnalyzing MyStruct type variable:");
            check.Check(try5);
            Console.WriteLine("\nAnalyzing boxed MyStruct type variable:");
            check.Check(try6);
            Console.ReadKey();
        }
    }
}
```

3. Execute the code. The result is shown in Figure 11-6.

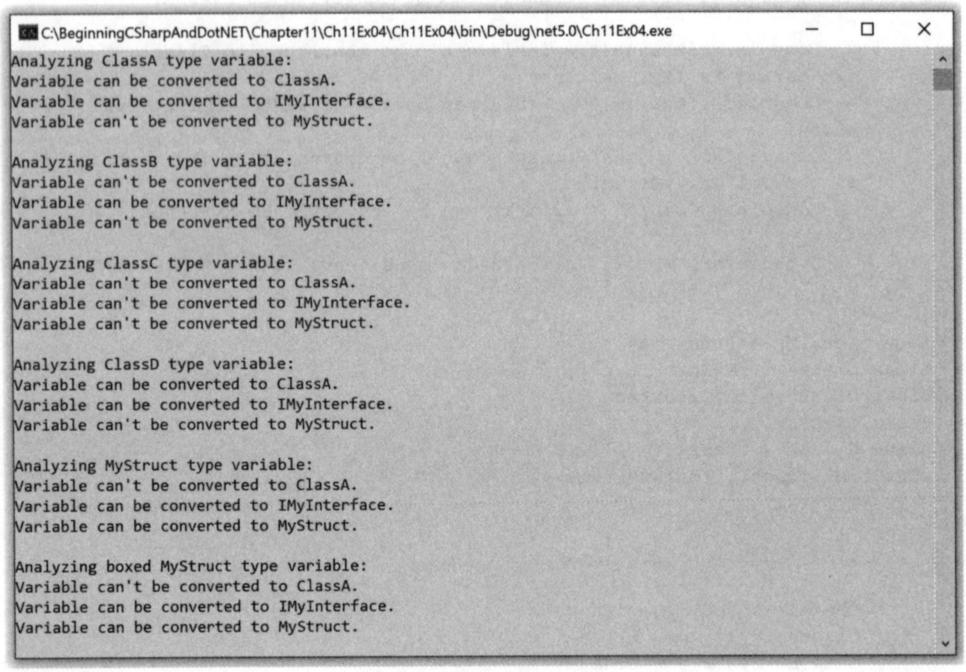

```
C:\BeginningCSharpAndDotNET\Chapter11\Ch11Ex04\Ch11Ex04\bin\Debug\net5.0\Ch11Ex04.exe        —   □   ×
Analyzing ClassA type variable:
Variable can be converted to ClassA.
Variable can be converted to IMyInterface.
Variable can't be converted to MyStruct.

Analyzing ClassB type variable:
Variable can't be converted to ClassA.
Variable can be converted to IMyInterface.
Variable can't be converted to MyStruct.

Analyzing ClassC type variable:
Variable can't be converted to ClassA.
Variable can't be converted to IMyInterface.
Variable can't be converted to MyStruct.

Analyzing ClassD type variable:
Variable can be converted to ClassA.
Variable can be converted to IMyInterface.
Variable can't be converted to MyStruct.

Analyzing MyStruct type variable:
Variable can't be converted to ClassA.
Variable can be converted to IMyInterface.
Variable can be converted to MyStruct.

Analyzing boxed MyStruct type variable:
Variable can't be converted to ClassA.
Variable can be converted to IMyInterface.
Variable can be converted to MyStruct.
```

FIGURE 11-6

How It Works

This example illustrates the various results possible when using the is operator. Four classes, an interface, and a structure are defined and used as parameters to a method of a class that uses the is operator to determine whether they can be converted into the ClassA type, the interface type, and the struct type.

Only the ClassA and ClassD (which inherits from ClassA) types are compatible with ClassA. Types that don't inherit from a class are not compatible with that class.

The ClassA, ClassB, and MyStruct types all implement IMyInterface, so these are all compatible with the IMyInterface type. ClassD inherits from ClassA, so it too is compatible. Therefore, only ClassC is incompatible.

Finally, only variables of type MyStruct itself and boxed variables of that type are compatible with MyStruct because you cannot convert reference types to value types (although, of course, you can unbox previously boxed variables).

Pattern Matching with the is Operator Pattern Expression

Recall from Chapter 4 where the switch statement was introduced and in Chapter 5 where it was expanded to include cases that support matching based on variable type (*string*, *int*, and so on). Once the type is known, you can access its properties and methods to further filter the matches.

The switch case approach is the more elegant way of pattern matching because the is operator commonly implements many if…else if… statements. As your pattern matching scenarios expand, the statements can get deep and long, making the code less legible. If that ever becomes the case, know that the alternative is the switch case pattern matching feature. However, for smaller code snippets, the is operator is a very valid and powerful tactic for matching patterns and filtering your data set. Take the following code, for example:

```
object[] data =
      { 1.6180, null, new Cow("Lea"), new Chicken("Rual"), "none" };

foreach (var item in data)
{
  if (item is 1.6180) Console.WriteLine("The Golden Ratio");
  else if (item is null) Console.WriteLine("The value is null");
  else if (item is Cow co) Console.WriteLine($"The cow is named {co.Name}.");
  else if (item is Chicken ch) Console.WriteLine("The chicken is named" +
          $" {ch.Name} and {ch.RunInCircles()}");
  else if (item is var catcher) Console.WriteLine("Catch all for" +
          $" {catcher.GetType().Name}");
}
```

The objects stored in the data variable consist of several different types. Looping through the object[] array using a foreach statement, you can check the type of the variable using the is operator and take an appropriate action when there is a match. The first pattern match is on 1.6180, which is a constant value and is an example of the *const pattern*, as is the `null` in the second pattern match. It is possible to use the `==` operator to achieve the same outcome when matching constants; however, the `is` operator is much easier to understand and is friendlier.

The last two objects in the `data` variable are of type `Cow` and `Chicken`. The *type pattern* assigns a new variable of the specified type when there is a pattern match. For example, when `Chicken` is matched, a new `ch` variable is created that contains a reference to the `Chicken` object, allowing the programmer to access properties and methods contained within the `Chicken` class (e.g., the property `Name` and a method named `RunInCircles()`).

Finally, you can use the *var pattern* to catch all the scenarios that did not match any of the `if…` `else if…` statements higher up in the code path. Then use the `catcher` variable to get the variable type via the `GetType().Name` property.

Value Comparisons

Consider two `Person` objects representing people, each with an integer `Age` property. You might want to compare them to see which person is older. You can simply use the following code:

```
if (person1.Age > person2.Age)
{
    . . .
}
```

This works fine, but there are alternatives. You might prefer to use syntax such as the following:

```
if (person1 > person2)
{
    . . .
}
```

This is possible using *operator overloading*, which you'll look at in this section. This is a powerful technique, but it should be used judiciously. In the preceding code, it is not immediately obvious that ages are being compared—it could be height, weight, IQ, or just general "greatness."

Another option is to use the `IComparable` and `IComparer` interfaces, which enable you to define how objects will be compared to each other in a standard way. This technique is supported by the various collection classes in the .NET Framework, making it an excellent way to sort objects in a collection.

Operator Overloading

Operator overloading enables you to use standard operators, such as +, >, and so on, with classes that you design. This is called "overloading" because you are supplying your own implementations for these operators when used with specific parameter types, in much the same way that you overload methods by supplying different parameters for methods with the same name.

Operator overloading is useful because you can perform whatever processing you want in the implementation of the operator overload, which might not be as simple as, for example, +, meaning "add these two operands together." Later, you'll see a good example of this in a further upgrade of the `CardLib` library, whereby you'll provide implementations for comparison operators that compare two cards to see which would beat the other in a trick (one round of card game play).

Because a trick in many card games depends on the ranks and suits of the cards involved, this isn't as straightforward as comparing the numbers on the cards. If the second card laid down is a different suit from the first, then the first card may win regardless of its rank. You can implement this by considering the order of the two operands. You can also take a trump suit into account, whereby trumps beat other suits even if that isn't the first suit laid down. This means that calculating that card1 > card2 is true (that is, card1 will beat card2 if card1 is laid down first), does not necessarily imply that card2 > card1 is false. If neither card1 nor card2 are trumps and they belong to different suits, then both comparisons will be true.

To start with, though, here is a look at the basic syntax for operator overloading. Operators can be overloaded by adding operator type members (which must be static) to a class. Some operators have multiple uses (such as -, which has unary and binary capabilities); therefore, you also specify how many operands you are dealing with and the types of these operands. In general, you will have operands that are the same type as the class in which the operator is defined, although it's possible to define operators that work on mixed types, as you'll see shortly.

As an example, consider the simple type AddClass1, defined as follows:

```
public class AddClass1
{
    public int val;
}
```

This is just a wrapper around an int value, but it illustrates the principles. With this class, code such as the following will fail to compile:

```
AddClass1 op1 = new AddClass1();
op1.val = 5;
AddClass1 op2 = new AddClass1();
op2.val = 5;
AddClass1 op3 = op1 + op2;
```

The error you get informs you that the + operator cannot be applied to operands of the AddClass1 type. This is because you have not defined an operation to perform yet. Code such as the following works, but it will not give you the result you might want:

```
AddClass1 op1 = new AddClass1();
op1.val = 5;
AddClass1 op2 = new AddClass1();
op2.val = 5;
bool op3 = op1 == op2;
```

Here, op1 and op2 are compared by using the == binary operator to determine whether they refer to the same object, not to verify whether their values are equal. op3 will be false in the preceding code, even though op1.val and op2.val are identical.

To overload the + operator, use the following code; note that an exception will occur if the operands are null:

```
public class AddClass1
{
    public int val;
```

```
      public static AddClass1 operator +(AddClass1 op1, AddClass1 op2)
      {
         AddClass1 returnVal = new AddClass1();
         returnVal.val = op1.val + op2.val;
         return returnVal;
      }
   }
```

As you can see, operator overloads look much like standard `static` method declarations, except that they use the keyword `operator` and the operator itself, rather than a method name. You can now successfully use the + operator with this class, as in the previous example:

```
   AddClass1 op3 = op1 + op2;
```

Overloading all binary operators fits the same pattern. Unary operators look similar but have only one parameter:

```
   public class AddClass1
   {
      public int val;
      public static AddClass1 operator +(AddClass1 op1, AddClass1 op2)
      {
         AddClass1 returnVal = new AddClass1();
         returnVal.val = op1.val + op2.val;
         return returnVal;
      }
      public static AddClass1 operator -(AddClass1 op1)
      {
         AddClass1 returnVal = new AddClass1();
         returnVal.val = -op1.val;
         return returnVal;
      }
   }
```

Both these operators work on operands of the same type as the class and have return values that are also of that type. Consider, however, the following class definitions:

```
   public class AddClass1
   {
      public int val;
      public static AddClass3 operator +(AddClass1 op1, AddClass2 op2)
      {
         AddClass3 returnVal = new AddClass3();
         returnVal.val = op1.val + op2.val;
         return returnVal;
      }
   }
   public class AddClass2
   {
      public int val;
   }
   public class AddClass3
   {
      public int val;
   }
```

This will allow the following code:

```
AddClass1 op1 = new AddClass1();
op1.val = 5;
AddClass2 op2 = new AddClass2();
op2.val = 5;
AddClass3 op3 = op1 + op2;
```

When appropriate, you can mix types in this way. Note, however, that if you added the same operator to `AddClass2`, then the preceding code would fail because it would be ambiguous as to which operator to use. You should, therefore, take care not to add operators with the same signature to more than one class.

In addition, if you mix types, then the operands must be supplied in the same order as the parameters to the operator overload. If you attempt to use your overloaded operator with the operands in the wrong order, the operation will fail. For example, you can't use the operator like

```
AddClass3 op3 = op2 + op1;
```

unless, of course, you supply another overload with the parameters reversed:

```
public static AddClass3 operator +(AddClass2 op1, AddClass1 op2)
{
   AddClass3 returnVal = new AddClass3();
   returnVal.val = op1.val + op2.val;
   return returnVal;
}
```

The following operators can be overloaded:

➤ **Unary operators**—+, -, !, ~, ++, --, `true`, `false`

➤ **Binary operators**—+, -, *, /, %, &, |, ^, <<, >>

➤ **Comparison operators**—==, !=, <, >, <=, >=

> **NOTE** *If you overload the* `true` *and* `false` *operators, then you can use classes in Boolean expressions, such as* `if(op1){}`.

You cannot overload assignment operators, such as +=, but these operators use their simple counterparts, such as +, so you don't have to worry about that. Overloading + means that += will function as expected. The = assignment operator can't be overloaded because it has such a fundamental usage, but this operator is related to the user-defined conversion operators, which you'll look at in the next section.

You also cannot overload && and ||, but these operators use the & and | operators to perform their calculations, so overloading these is enough. Both && and || operators are often referred to as *short-circuit evaluators*, which means that C# will stop its evaluation as soon as it determines the final true or false outcome. This prevents the unnecessary execution of code.

Some operators, such as < and >, must be overloaded in pairs. That is, you cannot overload < unless you also overload >. In many cases, you can simply call other operators from these to reduce the code required (and the errors that might occur), as shown in this example:

```
public class AddClass1
{
    public int val;
    public static bool operator >=(AddClass1 op1, AddClass1 op2)
            => (op1.val >= op2.val);
    public static bool operator <(AddClass1 op1, AddClass1 op2)
            => !(op1 >= op2);
    // Also need implementations for <= and > operators.
}
```

In more complex operator definitions, this can reduce the lines of code. It also means that you have less code to change if you later decide to modify the implementation of these operators.

The same applies to == and !=, but with these operators it is often worth overriding Object. Equals() and Object.GetHashCode(), because both of these functions can also be used to compare objects. By overriding these methods, you ensure that whatever technique users of the class use, they get the same result. This isn't essential, but it's worth adding for completeness. It requires the following nonstatic override methods:

```
public class AddClass1
{
    public int val;
    public static bool operator ==(AddClass1 op1, AddClass1 op2)
            => (op1.val == op2.val);
    public static bool operator !=(AddClass1 op1, AddClass1 op2)
            => !(op1 == op2);
    public override bool Equals(object op1) => val == ((AddClass1)op1).val;
    public override int GetHashCode() => val;
}
```

GetHashCode() is used to obtain a unique int value for an object instance based on its state. Here, using val is fine because it is also an int value.

Note that Equals() uses an object type parameter. You need to use this signature, or you will be overloading this method, rather than overriding it, and the default implementation will still be accessible to users of the class. Instead, you must use casting to get the required result. It is often worth checking the object type using the is operator discussed earlier, in code such as this:

```
public override bool Equals(object op1)
{
    if (op1 is AddClass1)
    {
        return val == ((AddClass1)op1).val;
    }
    else
    {
        throw new ArgumentException(
            "Cannot compare AddClass1 objects with objects of type "
            + op1.GetType().ToString());
    }
}
```

In this code, an exception is thrown if the operand passed to `Equals` is of the wrong type or cannot be converted into the correct type. Of course, this behavior might not be what you want. You might want to be able to compare objects of one type with objects of another type, in which case more branching would be necessary. Alternatively, you might want to restrict comparisons to those in which both objects are of the same type, which would require the following change to the first `if` statement:

```
if (op1.GetType() == typeof(AddClass1))
```

Adding Operator Overloads to CardLib

Now you will upgrade your `Ch11CardLib` project again, adding operator overloading to the `Card` class. Again, you can find the code for the classes that follow in the `Ch11CardLib` folder of this chapter's code download. First, though, you will add the extra fields to the `Card` class that allow for trump suits and an option to place aces high. You make these static, because when they are set, they apply to all `Card` objects:

```
public class Card
{
    /// <summary>
    /// Flag for trump usage. If true, trumps are valued higher
    /// than cards of other suits.
    /// </summary>
    public static bool useTrumps = false;
    /// <summary>
    /// Trump suit to use if useTrumps is true.
    /// </summary>
    public static Suit trump = Suit.Club;
    /// <summary>
    /// Flag that determines whether aces are higher than kings or lower
    /// than deuces.
    /// </summary>
    public static bool isAceHigh = true;
```

These rules apply to all `Card` objects in every `Deck` in an application. It is not possible to have two decks of cards with cards contained in each that obey different rules. That's fine for this class library, however, as you can safely assume that if a single application wants to use separate rules, then it could maintain these itself, perhaps setting the static members of `Card` whenever decks are switched.

Because you have done this, it is worth adding a few more constructors to the `Deck` class to initialize decks with distinctive characteristics:

```
    /// <summary>
    /// Nondefault constructor. Allows aces to be set high.
    /// </summary>
    public Deck(bool isAceHigh) : this()
    {
        Card.isAceHigh = isAceHigh;
    }
    /// <summary>
    /// Nondefault constructor. Allows a trump suit to be used.
    /// </summary>
    public Deck(bool useTrumps, Suit trump) : this()
    {
```

```
        Card.useTrumps = useTrumps;
        Card.trump = trump;
    }
    /// <summary>
    /// Nondefault constructor. Allows aces to be set high and a trump suit
    /// to be used.
    /// </summary>
    public Deck(bool isAceHigh, bool useTrumps, Suit trump) : this()
    {
        Card.isAceHigh = isAceHigh;
        Card.useTrumps = useTrumps;
        Card.trump = trump;
    }
```

Each of these constructors is defined by using the `: this()` syntax shown in Chapter 9, so in all cases, the default constructor is called before the nondefault one, initializing the deck.

> **NOTE** The null condition operator (?.) implemented in the == and > operator overload method is discussed in more detail in Chapter 12. The ?. in the code segment `card1?.suit` of the `public static bool operator ==` method checks whether the `card1` object is null before attempting to retrieve the value stored in `suit`. This is important when you implement the method in later chapters.

Now add your operator overloads (and suggested overrides) to the `Card` class:

```
public static bool operator ==(Card card1, Card card2)
    => (card1?.suit == card2?.suit) && (card1?.rank == card2?.rank);
public static bool operator !=(Card card1, Card card2)
    => !(card1 == card2);
public override bool Equals(object card) => this == (Card)card;
public override int GetHashCode()
            => 13 * (int)suit + (int)rank;
public static bool operator >(Card card1, Card card2)
{
    if (card1.suit == card2.suit)
    {
        if (isAceHigh)
        {
            if (card1.rank == Rank.Ace)
            {
                if (card2.rank == Rank.Ace)
                    return false;
                else
                    return true;
            }
            else
            {
                if (card2.rank == Rank.Ace)
                    return false;
```

```
                else
                    return (card1.rank > card2?.rank);
            }
        }
        else
        {
            return (card1.rank > card2.rank);
        }
    }
    else
    {
        if (useTrumps && (card2.suit == Card.trump))
            return false;
        else
            return true;
    }
}
public static bool operator <(Card card1, Card card2)
        => !(card1 >= card2);
public static bool operator >=(Card card1, Card card2)
{
    if (card1.suit == card2.suit)
    {
        if (isAceHigh)
        {
            if (card1.rank == Rank.Ace)
            {
                return true;
            }
            else
            {
                if (card2.rank == Rank.Ace)
                    return false;
                else
                    return (card1.rank >= card2.rank);
            }
        }
        else
        {
            return (card1.rank >= card2.rank);
        }
    }
    else
    {
        if (useTrumps && (card2.suit == Card.trump))
            return false;
        else
            return true;
    }
}
public static bool operator <=(Card card1, Card card2)
        => !(card1 > card2);
```

There is not much to note here, except perhaps the slightly lengthy code for the > and >= overloaded operators. If you step through the code for >, you can see how it works and why these steps are necessary.

You are comparing two cards, card1 and card2, where card1 is assumed to be the first one laid down on the table. As discussed earlier, this becomes important when you are using trump cards, because a trump will beat a non-trump even if the non-trump has a higher rank. Of course, if the suits of the two cards are identical, then whether the suit is the trump suit or not is irrelevant, so this is the first comparison you make:

```
public static bool operator >(Card card1, Card card2)
{
    if (card1.suit == card2.suit)
    {
```

If the static isAceHigh flag is true, then you can't compare the cards' ranks directly via their value in the Rank enumeration, because the rank of ace has a value of 1 in this enumeration, which is less than that of all other ranks. Instead, use the following steps:

➤ If the first card is an ace, then check whether the second card is also an ace. If it is, then the first card won't beat the second. If the second card isn't an ace, then the first card wins:

```
if (isAceHigh)
{
    if (card1.rank == Rank.Ace)
    {
        if (card2.rank == Rank.Ace)
            return false;
        else
            return true;
    }
```

➤ If the first card is not an ace, then you also need to check whether the second one is. If it is, then the second card wins; otherwise, you can compare the rank values because you know that aces are not an issue:

```
    else
    {
        if (card2.rank == Rank.Ace)
            return false;
        else
            return (card1.rank > card2?.rank);
    }
}
```

➤ If aces are not high, then you just compare the rank values:

```
else
{
    return (card1.rank > card2.rank);
}
```

The remainder of the code concerns the case where the suits of card1 and card2 are different. Here, the static useTrumps flag is important. If this flag is true and card2 is of the trump suit, then you can say definitively that card1 isn't a trump (because the two cards have different suits); and trumps always win, so card2 is the higher card:

```
else
{
    if (useTrumps && (card2.suit == Card.trump))
        return false;
```

If card2 isn't a trump (or useTrumps is false), then card1 wins, because it was the first card laid down:

```
    else
        return true;
    }
}
```

Only one other operator (>=) uses code like this, and the other operators are very simple, so there's no need to go into more detail about them.

The following simple client code tests these operators. Simply place it in the Main() method of a client project to test it, like the client code shown earlier in the CardLib examples (you can find this code in Ch11CardClient\Program.cs):

```
Card.isAceHigh = true;
Console.WriteLine("Aces are high.");
Card.useTrumps = true;
Card.trump = Suit.Club;
Console.WriteLine("Clubs are trumps.");
Card card1, card2, card3, card4, card5;
card1 = new Card(Suit.Club, Rank.Five);
card2 = new Card(Suit.Club, Rank.Five);
card3 = new Card(Suit.Club, Rank.Ace);
card4 = new Card(Suit.Heart, Rank.Ten);
card5 = new Card(Suit.Diamond, Rank.Ace);
Console.WriteLine($"{card1} == {card2} ? {card1 == card2}");
Console.WriteLine($"{card1} != {card3} ? {card1 != card3}");
Console.WriteLine($"{card1}.Equals({card4}) ? " +
            $" { card1.Equals(card4)}");
Console.WriteLine($"Card.Equals({card3}, {card4}) ? " +
        $" { Card.Equals(card3, card4)}");
Console.WriteLine($"{card1} > {card2} ? {card1 > card2}");
Console.WriteLine($"{card1} <= {card3} ? {card1 <= card3}");
Console.WriteLine($"{card1} > {card4} ? {card1 > card4}");
Console.WriteLine($"{card4} > {card1} ? {card4 > card1}");
Console.WriteLine($"{card5} > {card4} ? {card5 > card4}");
Console.WriteLine($"{card4} > {card5} ? {card4 > card5}");
Console.ReadKey();
```

The results are as shown in Figure 11-7.

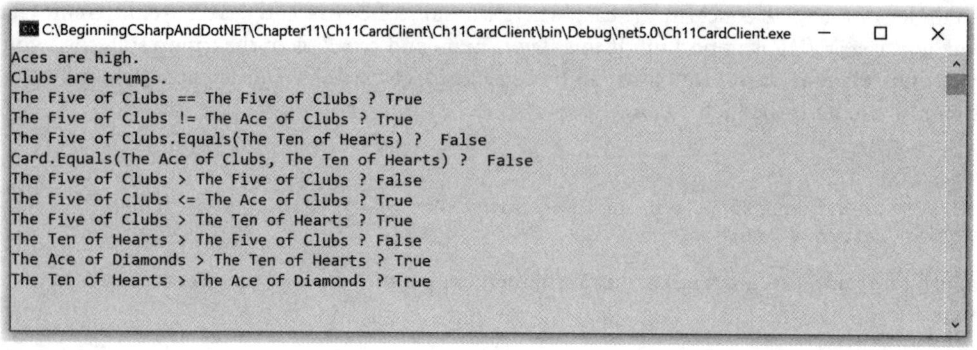

FIGURE 11-7

In each case, the operators are applied taking the specified rules into account. This is particularly apparent in the last four lines of output, demonstrating how trump cards always beat non-trumps.

The IComparable and IComparer Interfaces

The `IComparable` and `IComparer` interfaces are the standard way to compare objects in the .NET Framework. The difference between the interfaces is as follows:

➤ `IComparable` is implemented in the class of the object to be compared and allows comparisons between that object and another object.

➤ `IComparer` is implemented in a separate class, which allows comparisons between any two objects.

Typically, you give a class default comparison code by using `IComparable`, and nondefault comparisons using other classes.

`IComparable` exposes the single method `CompareTo()`, which accepts an object that returns a result less than zero, equal to zero, or greater than zero to indicate whether the first item is less than, equal to, or greater than the second object. You could, for example, implement it in a way that enables you to pass a `Person` object to it and determine whether that person is older or younger than the current person. In fact, this method returns an `int`, so you could also determine how much older or younger the second person is:

```
if (person1.CompareTo(person2) == 0)
{
    Console.WriteLine("Same age");
}
else if (person1.CompareTo(person2) > 0)
{
    Console.WriteLine("person 1 is Older");
}
else
{
    Console.WriteLine("person1 is Younger");
}
```

`IComparer` exposes the single method `Compare()`, which accepts two objects and returns an integer result just like `CompareTo()`. With an object supporting `IComparer`, you could use code like the following:

```
if (personComparer.Compare(person1, person2) == 0)
{
    Console.WriteLine("Same age");
}
else if (personComparer.Compare(person1, person2) > 0)
{
    Console.WriteLine("person 1 is Older");
}
else
{
    Console.WriteLine("person1 is Younger");
}
```

In both cases, the parameters supplied to the methods are of the type `System.Object`. This means that you can compare one object to another object of any other type, so you usually have to perform some type comparison before returning a result, and maybe even throw exceptions if the wrong types are used.

The .NET Framework includes a default implementation of the `IComparer` interface on a class called `Comparer`, found in the `System.Collections` namespace. This class can perform culture-specific comparisons between simple types, as well as any type that supports the `IComparable` interface. You can use it, for example, with the following code:

```
string firstString = "First String";
string secondString = "Second String";
Console.WriteLine($"Comparing '{firstString}' and '{secondString}', " +
                  $"result: {Comparer.Default.Compare(firstString, secondString)}");
int firstNumber = 35;
int secondNumber = 23;
Console.WriteLine($"Comparing '{firstNumber}' and '{ secondNumber }', " +
                  $"result: {Comparer.Default.Compare(firstNumber, secondNumber)}");
```

This uses the `Comparer.Default` static member to obtain an instance of the `Comparer` class, and then it uses the `Compare()` method to compare first two strings and then two integers.

The result is as follows:

```
Comparing 'First String' and 'Second String', result: -1
Comparing '35' and '23', result: 1
```

Because F comes before S in the alphabet, it is deemed "less than" S, so the result of the first comparison is –1. Similarly, 35 is greater than 23, hence the result of 1. Note that the results do not indicate the magnitude of the difference.

When using `Comparer`, you must use types that can be compared. Attempting to compare `firstString` with `firstNumber`, for instance, will generate an exception.

Here are a few more points about the behavior of this class:

➤ Objects passed to `Comparer.Compare()` are checked to determine whether they support `IComparable`. If they do, then that implementation is used.

➤ Null values are allowed and are interpreted as being "less than" any other object.

➤ Strings are processed according to the current culture. To process strings according to a different culture (or language), the `Comparer` class must be instantiated using its constructor, which enables you to pass a `System.Globalization.CultureInfo` object specifying the culture to use.

➤ Strings are processed in a case-sensitive way. To process them in a non–case-sensitive way, you need to use the `CaseInsensitiveComparer` class, which otherwise works exactly the same.

Sorting Collections

Many collection classes allow sorting, either by default comparisons between objects or by custom methods. `ArrayList` is one example. It contains the method `Sort()`, which can be used without parameters, in which case default comparisons are used, or it can be passed an `IComparer` interface to use to compare pairs of objects.

When you have an `ArrayList` filled with simple types, such as integers or strings, the default comparer is fine. For your own classes, you must either implement `IComparable` in your class definition or create a separate class supporting `IComparer` to use for comparisons.

Note that some classes in the `System.Collections` namespace, including `CollectionBase`, do not expose a method for sorting. If you want to sort a collection you have derived from this class, then you must do a bit more work and sort the internal `List` collection yourself.

The following Try It Out shows how to use a default and nondefault comparer to sort a list.

TRY IT OUT Sorting a List: Ch11Ex05

1. Create a new Console Application called Ch11Ex05 in the directory `C:\Beginning-CSharpAndDotNET\Chapter11`.

2. Add a new class called `Person` and modify the code in `Person.cs` as follows:

```
namespace Ch11Ex05
{
    public class Person : IComparable
    {
        public string Name;
        public int Age;
        public Person(string name, int age)
        {
            Name = name;
            Age = age;
        }
        public int CompareTo(object obj)
        {
```

```
            if (obj is Person)
            {
                Person otherPerson = obj as Person;
                return this.Age - otherPerson.Age;
            }
            else
            {
                throw new ArgumentException(
                    "Object to compare to is not a Person object.");
            }
        }
    }
}
```

3. Add another new class called `PersonNameComparer` and modify the code as follows:

```
using System;
using System.Collections;
namespace Ch11Ex05
{
    public class PersonNameComparer : IComparer
    {
        public static IComparer Default = new PersonNameComparer();
        public int Compare(object x, object y)
        {
            if (x is Person && y is Person)
            {
                return Comparer.Default.Compare(
                    ((Person)x).Name, ((Person)y).Name);
            }
            else
            {
                throw new ArgumentException(
                    "One or both objects to compare are not Person objects.");
            }
        }
    }
}
```

4. Modify the code in `Program.cs` as follows:

```
using System;
using System.Collections;
namespace Ch11Ex05
{
    class Program
    {
        static void Main(string[] args)
        {
            ArrayList list = new ArrayList();
            list.Add(new Person("Rual", 30));
            list.Add(new Person("Donna", 25));
            list.Add(new Person("Mary", 27));
            list.Add(new Person("Ben", 44));
            Console.WriteLine("Unsorted people:");
```

```
            for (int i = 0; i < list.Count; i++)
            {
                Console.WriteLine($"{(list[i] as Person).Name } ({(list[i] as Person).Age })");
            }
            Console.WriteLine();
            Console.WriteLine(
                "People sorted with default comparer (by age):");
            list.Sort();
            for (int i = 0; i < list.Count; i++)
            {
                Console.WriteLine($"{(list[i] as Person).Name } ({(list[i] as Person).Age })");
            }
            Console.WriteLine();
            Console.WriteLine(
                "People sorted with nondefault comparer (by name):");
            list.Sort(PersonNameComparer.Default);
            for (int i = 0; i < list.Count; i++)
            {
                Console.WriteLine($"{(list[i] as Person).Name } ({(list[i] as Person).Age })");
            }
            Console.ReadKey();
        }
    }
}
```

5. Execute the code. The result is shown in Figure 11-8.

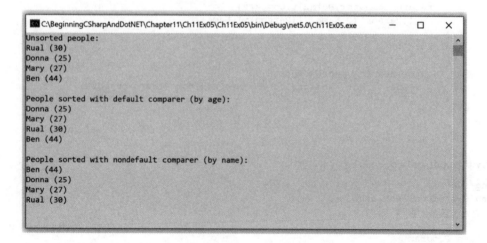

FIGURE 11-8

How It Works

An `ArrayList` containing `Person` objects is sorted in two different ways here. By calling the `ArrayList.Sort()` method with no parameters, the default comparison is used, which is the `CompareTo()` method in the `Person` class (because this class implements `IComparable`):

```
        public int CompareTo(object obj)
        {
```

```
        if (obj is Person)
        {
            Person otherPerson = obj as Person;
            return this.Age - otherPerson.Age;
        }
        else
        {
            throw new ArgumentException(
                "Object to compare to is not a Person object.");
        }
    }
```

This method first checks whether its argument can be compared to a `Person` object—that is, whether the object can be converted into a `Person` object. The `Age` properties of the two `Person` objects are compared; if there is a problem, then an exception is thrown.

Next, a nondefault comparison sort is performed using the `PersonNameComparer` class, which implements `IComparer`. This class has a `public static` field for ease of use:

```
        public static IComparer Default = new PersonNameComparer();
```

This enables you to get an instance using `PersonNameComparer.Default`, just like the `Comparer` class shown earlier. The `CompareTo()` method of this class is as follows:

```
        public int Compare(object x, object y)
        {
            if (x is Person && y is Person)
            {
                return Comparer.Default.Compare(
                    ((Person)x).Name, ((Person)y).Name);
            }
            else
            {
                throw new ArgumentException(
                    "One or both objects to compare are not Person objects.");
            }
        }
```

Again, arguments are first checked to determine whether they are `Person` objects. If they aren't, then an exception is thrown. If they are, then the default `Comparer` object is used to compare the two string `Name` fields of the `Person` objects.

CONVERSIONS

Thus far, you have used casting whenever you have needed to convert one type into another, but this is not the only way to do things. Just as an `int` can be converted into a `long` or a `double` implicitly as part of a calculation, you can define how classes you have created can be converted into other classes (either implicitly or explicitly). To do this, you overload conversion operators, much like other operators were overloaded earlier in this chapter. You will see how in the first part of this section. You will also see another useful operator, the `as` operator, which in general is preferable to casting when using reference types.

Overloading Conversion Operators

As well as overloading mathematical and logical operators, as shown earlier, you can define both implicit and explicit conversions between types. This is necessary if you want to convert between types that are not related—if there is no inheritance relationship between them and no shared interfaces, for example.

Suppose you define an implicit conversion between `ConvClass1` and `ConvClass2`. This means that you can write code such as the following:

```
ConvClass1 op1 = new ConvClass1();
ConvClass2 op2 = op1;
```

Alternatively, you can define an explicit conversion:

```
ConvClass1 op1 = new ConvClass1();
ConvClass2 op2 = (ConvClass2)op1;
```

As an example, consider the following code:

```
public class ConvClass1
{
    public int val;
    public static implicit operator ConvClass2(ConvClass1 op1)
    {
        ConvClass2 returnVal = new ConvClass2();
        returnVal.val = op1.val;
        return returnVal;
    }
}
public class ConvClass2
{
    public double val;
    public static explicit operator ConvClass1(ConvClass2 op1)
    {
        ConvClass1 returnVal = new ConvClass1();
        checked {returnVal.val = (int)op1.val;};
        return returnVal;
    }
}
```

Here, `ConvClass1` contains an `int` value and `ConvClass2` contains a `double` value. Because `int` values can be converted into `double` values implicitly, you can define an implicit conversion between `ConvClass1` and `ConvClass2`. The reverse is not true, however, and you should define the conversion operator between `ConvClass2` and `ConvClass1` as explicit.

You specify this using the `implicit` and `explicit` keywords as shown. With these classes, the following code is fine:

```
ConvClass1 op1 = new ConvClass1();
op1.val = 3;
ConvClass2 op2 = op1;
```

A conversion in the other direction, however, requires the following explicit casting conversion:

```
ConvClass2 op2 = new ConvClass2();
op2.val = 3;
ConvClass1 op1 = (ConvClass1)op2;
```

Because you have used the `checked` keyword in your explicit conversion, you will get an exception in the preceding code, as the `val` property of `op1` is too large to fit into the `val` property of `op2`.

The as Operator

The `as` operator converts a type into a specified reference type, using the following syntax:

```
<operand> as <type>
```

This is possible only in certain circumstances:

➤ If *<operand>* is of type *<type>*

➤ If *<operand>* can be implicitly converted to type *<type>*

➤ If *<operand>* can be boxed into type *<type>*

If no conversion from *<operand>* to *<type>* is possible, then the result of the expression will be `null`.

Conversion from a base class to a derived class is possible by using an explicit conversion, but it will not always work. Consider the two classes `ClassA` and `ClassD` from an earlier example, where `ClassD` inherits from `ClassA`:

```
class ClassA : IMyInterface {}
class ClassD : ClassA {}
```

The following code uses the `as` operator to convert from a `ClassA` instance stored in `obj1` into the `ClassD` type:

```
ClassA obj1 = new ClassA();
ClassD obj2 = obj1 as ClassD;
```

This will result in `obj2` being `null`.

However, it is possible to store `ClassD` instances in `ClassA`-type variables by using polymorphism. The following code illustrates this by using the `as` operator to convert from a `ClassA`-type variable containing a `ClassD`-type instance into the `ClassD` type:

```
ClassD obj1 = new ClassD();
ClassA obj2 = obj1;
ClassD obj3 = obj2 as ClassD;
```

This time the result is that `obj3` ends up containing a reference to the same object as `obj1`, not `null`.

This functionality makes the `as` operator especially useful, because the following code (which uses simple casting) results in an exception being thrown:

```
ClassA obj1 = new ClassA();
ClassD obj2 = (ClassD)obj1;
```

The `as` equivalent of this code results in a `null` value being assigned to `obj2`—no exception is thrown. This means that code such as the following (using two of the classes developed earlier in this chapter, `Animal` and a class derived from `Animal` called `Cow`) is common in C# applications:

```
public void MilkCow(Animal myAnimal)
{
    Cow myCow = myAnimal as Cow;
```

```
      if (myCow != null)
      {
          myCow.Milk();
      }
      else
      {
          Console.WriteLine($"{myAnimal.Name} isn't a cow, and so can't be milked.");
      }
  }
```

EXERCISES

11.1   Create a collection class called `People` that is a collection of the following `Person` class. The items in the collection should be accessible via a string indexer that is the name of the person, identical to the `Person.Name` property.

```
public class Person
{
    private string name;
    private int age;
    public string Name
    {
        get { return name; }
        set { name = value; }
    }
    public int Age
    {
        get { return age; }
        set { age = value; }
    }
}
```

11.2   Extend the `Person` class from the preceding exercise so that the `>`, `<`, `>=`, and `<=` operators are overloaded, and compare the `Age` properties of `Person` instances.

11.3   Add a `GetOldest()` method to the `People` class that returns an array of `Person` objects with the greatest `Age` property (one or more objects, as multiple items can have the same value for this property), using the overloaded operators defined in Exercise 11.2.

11.4   Implement the `ICloneable` interface on the `People` class to provide deep copying capability.

11.5   Add an iterator to the `People` class that enables you to get the ages of all members in a `foreach` loop as follows:

```
foreach (int age in myPeople.Ages)
{
    // Display ages.
}
```

Answers to the exercises can be found in the Appendix.

▶ **WHAT YOU LEARNED IN THIS CHAPTER**

KEY CONCEPT	DESCRIPTION
Defining collections	Collections are classes that can contain instances of other classes. You can define a collection by deriving from `CollectionBase`, or implement collection interfaces such as `IEnumerable`, `ICollection`, and `IList` yourself. Typically, you will define an indexer for your collection in order to use `collection[index]` syntax to access members.
Dictionaries	You can also define keyed collections, or dictionaries, whereby each item has an associated key. In this case, the key can be used to identify an item, rather than using the item's index. You can define a dictionary by implementing `IDictionary` or by deriving a class from `DictionaryBase`.
Iterators	You can implement an iterator to control how looping code obtains values in its loop cycles. To iterate over a class, implement a method called `GetEnumerator()` with a return type of `IEnumerator`. To iterate over a class member, such as a method, use a return type of `IEnumerable`. In iterator code blocks, return values with the `yield return` keyword.
Type comparisons	You can use the `GetType()` method to obtain the type of an object, or the `typeof()` operator to get the type of a class. You can then compare these type values. You can also use the `is` operator to determine whether an object is compatible with a certain class type.
Value comparisons	If you want to make classes whose instances can be operated upon using standard C# operators, you must overload those operators in the class definition. For other types of value comparison, you can use classes that implement the `IComparable` or `IComparer` interfaces. These interfaces are particularly useful for sorting collections.
The `as` operator	You can use the `as` operator to convert a value to a reference type. If no conversion is possible, the `as` operator returns a `null` value.

12

Generics

This chapter begins by looking at what generics are. You will learn about generics in abstract terms at first, because learning the concepts behind generics is crucial to being able to use them effectively.

Next, you will see some of the generic types in the .NET Framework in action. This will help you understand their functionality and power, as well as the new syntax required in your code. You will then move on to define your own generic types, including generic classes, interfaces, methods, and delegates. You will also learn additional techniques for further customizing generic types: the default keyword and type constraints.

Finally, you will look at covariance and contravariance, two forms of variance that were introduced in C# 4 and that allow greater flexibility when using generic classes.

WHAT ARE GENERICS?

To best illustrate what generics are, and why they are so useful, recall the collection classes from the previous chapter. You saw how basic collections can be contained in classes such as `ArrayList`, but that such collections suffer from being untyped. This requires that you cast `object` items into whatever type of objects you actually stored in the collection. Because anything that inherits from `System .Object` (that is, practically anything) can be stored in an `ArrayList`, you need to be careful. Assuming that certain types are all that is contained in a collection can lead to exceptions being thrown, and code logic breaking down. You learned some techniques to deal with this, including the code required to check the type of an object.

However, you discovered that a much better solution is to use a strongly typed collection class initially. By deriving from `CollectionBase` and providing your own methods for adding, removing, and otherwise accessing members of the collection, you learned how you could restrict collection members to those derived from a certain base type or supporting a certain interface. This is where you encounter a problem. Every time you create a new class that needs to be held in a collection, you must do one of the following:

➤   Use a collection class you have already made that can contain items of the new type.

➤   Create a new collection class that can hold items of the new type, implementing all the required methods.

Typically, with a new type you need extra functionality, so more often than not, you need a new collection class anyway. Therefore, making collection classes can take up a fair amount of your time!

Generic classes, conversely, make coding a lot simpler. A generic class is built around whatever type, or types, you supply during instantiation, enabling you to strongly type an object with hardly any effort at all. In the context of collections, creating a "collection of type T objects" is as simple as saying it aloud—and achievable in a single line of code. Instead of code such as this:

```
CollectionClass items = new CollectionClass();
items.Add(new ItemClass());
```

you can use this:

```
CollectionClass<ItemClass> items = new CollectionClass<ItemClass>();
items.Add(new ItemClass());
```

The angle bracket syntax is the way you pass type parameters to generic types. In the preceding code, read `CollectionClass<ItemClass>` as `CollectionClass` of `ItemClass`. You will, of course, examine this syntax in more detail later in the chapter.

There's more to the subject of generics than just collections, but they are particularly suited to this area, as you will see later in the chapter when you look at the `System.Collections.Generic` namespace. By creating a generic class, you can generate methods that have a signature that can be strongly typed to any type you want, even catering to the fact that a type can be a value or reference type, and deal with individual cases as they occur. You can even allow only a subset of types to be used, by restricting the types used to instantiate a generic class to those that support a given interface or are derived from a certain type. Moreover, you're not restricted to generic classes—you can create generic interfaces, generic methods (which can be defined on nongeneric classes), and even generic delegates. All this adds a great deal of flexibility to your code, and judicious use of generics can eliminate hours of development time.

> **NOTE** *If you are familiar with C++, this is one difference between C++ templates and C# generic classes. In C++ the compiler detects where you used a specific type of template—for example,* A *of* B*—and compiles the code necessary to create this type. In C# everything happens at runtime.*

You are probably wondering how all this is possible. Usually, when you create a class, it is compiled into a type that you can then use in your code. You might think that when you create a generic class, it would have to be compiled into a plethora of types, so that you could instantiate it. Fortunately, that's not the case—and given the infinite amount of classes possible in .NET, that's just as well. Behind the scenes, the .NET runtime allows generic classes to be dynamically generated as and when you need them. A given generic class A of B won't exist until you ask for it by instantiating it.

USING GENERICS

Before you look at how to create your own generic types, it is worth looking at the ones supplied by the .NET Framework. These include the types in the `System.Collections.Generic` namespace, a namespace that you have seen several times in your code because it is included by default in console applications. You have not yet used any of the types in this namespace, but that is about to change. This section looks at the types in this namespace and how you can use them to create strongly typed collections and improve the functionality of your existing collections.

First, though, you will look at another simpler generic type that gets around a minor issue with value types: *nullable types*.

Nullable Types

In earlier chapters, you saw that one of the ways in which value types (which include most of the basic types such as `int` and `double` as well as all structs) differ from reference types (`string` and any class) is that they must contain a value. They, reference types, can exist in an unassigned state, just after they are declared and before a value is assigned, but you cannot make use of the value type in that state in any way. Conversely, reference types can be `null`.

There are times, and they crop up more often than you might think (particularly when you work with databases), when it is useful to have a value type that can be `null`. Generics give you a way to do this using the `System.Nullable<T>` type, as shown in this example:

```
System.Nullable<int> nullableInt;
```

This code declares a variable called `nullableInt`, which can have any value that an `int` variable can, plus the value `null`. This enables you to write code such as the following:

```
nullableInt = null;
```

If `nullableInt` were an `int` type variable, then the preceding code would not compile.

The preceding assignment is equivalent to the following:

```
nullableInt = new System.Nullable<int>();
```

As with any other variable, you cannot just use it before initialization, whether to `null` (through either syntax shown previously) or by assigning a value.

You can test nullable types to determine whether they are `null`, just like you test reference types:

```
if (nullableInt == null)
{
    ...
}
```

Alternatively, you can use the `HasValue` property:

```
if (nullableInt.HasValue)
{
    ...
}
```

This wouldn't work for reference types, even one with a `HasValue` property of its own, because having a `null`-valued reference type variable means that no object exists through which to access this property, and an exception would be thrown.

You can also look at the value of a nullable type by using the `Value` property. If `HasValue` is `true`, then you are guaranteed a non-null value for `Value`; but if `HasValue` is `false`—that is, `null` has been assigned to the variable—then accessing `Value` will result in an exception of type `System.InvalidOperationException`.

Note that nullable types are so useful that they have resulted in a modification of C# syntax. Rather than using the syntax shown previously to declare a nullable type variable, you can instead use the following:

```
int? nullableInt;
```

`int?` is simply a shorthand for `System.Nullable<int>` but is much more readable. In subsequent sections, you will use this syntax.

Operators and Nullable Types

With simple types, such as `int`, you can use operators such as +, -, and so on to work with values. With nullable type equivalents, there is no difference: The values contained in nullable types are implicitly converted to the required type and the appropriate operators are used. This also applies to structs with operators that you have supplied:

```
int? op1 = 5;
int? result = op1 * 2;
```

Note that here the `result` variable is also of type `int?`. The following code will not compile:

```
int? op1 = 5;
int result = op1 * 2;
```

To get this to work you must perform an explicit conversion or access the value through the `Value` property, which requires code such as this:

```
int? op1 = 5;
int result = (int)op1 * 2;
```

or this:

```
int? op1 = 5;
int result = op1.Value * 2;
```

This works fine if `op1` has a value—if it is `null`, then you will get an exception of type `System.InvalidOperationException`.

This raises the obvious question: What happens when one or both values in an operator evaluation that involves two nullable values are `null`, such as `op1` in the following code?

```
int? op1 = null;
int? op2 = 5;
int? result = op1 * op2;
```

The answer is that for all simple nullable types other than `bool?`, the result of the operation is `null`, which you can interpret as "unable to compute."

```
bool? maybe = null;
bool? yes = true;
bool? result = yes | maybe; // result is true.
```

For structs, you can define your own operators to deal with this situation (as shown later in this chapter), and for `bool?` there are operators defined for `&&` and `||` that might result in non-null return values. The results in the table make perfect sense logically—if there is enough information to work out the answer of the computation without needing to know the value of one of the operands, then it doesn't matter if that operand is `null`.

The ?? Operator

To further reduce the amount of code you need in order to deal with nullable types, and to make it easier to deal with variables that can be `null`, you can use the `??` operator. Known as the *null coalescing operator*, it is a binary operator that enables you to supply an alternative value to use for expressions that might evaluate to `null`. The operator evaluates to its first operand if the first operand is not `null`, or to its second operator if the first operand is `null`. Functionally, the following two expressions are equivalent:

```
op1 ?? op2
op1 == null ? op2 : op1
```

In this code, `op1` can be any nullable expression, including a reference type and, importantly, a nullable type. This means that you can use the `??` operator to provide default values to use if a nullable type is `null`, as shown here:

```
int? op1 = null;
int result = op1 * 2 ?? 5;
```

Because in this example op1 is null, op1 * 2 will also be null. However, the ?? operator detects this and assigns the value 5 to result. Importantly, note here that no explicit conversion is required to put the result in the int type variable result. The ?? operator handles this conversion for you. Alternatively, you can pass the result of a ?? evaluation into an int? with no problems:

```
int? result = op1 * 2 ?? 5;
```

This behavior makes the ?? operator a versatile one to use when dealing with nullable variables, and a handy way to supply defaults without using either a block of code in an if structure or the often confusing ternary operator.

The ?. Operator

This operator, which is called the null-conditional member access operator, is often referred to as the *Elvis operator*, and is helpful to overcome code ambiguity caused by burdensome null checking. For example, if you wanted to get the count of orders for a given customer, you would need to check for null before setting the count value:

```
int count = 0;
if (customer.orders ! = null)
{
    count = customer.orders.Count();
}
```

If you were to simply write this code and there were no orders existing for the customer (i.e., it is null), a System.ArgumentNullException is thrown:

```
int count = customer.orders.Count();
```

Using the ?. operator results in the int? count being set to null instead of an exception happening:

```
int? count = customer.orders?.Count();
```

Combining the null coalescing operator ?? discussed in the previous section with the null condition operator ?. makes it possible to set a default value when the result is null:

```
int? count = customer.orders?.Count() ?? 0;
```

Another use of the null conditional operator is to trigger events. Events are discussed in detail in Chapter 13. The most common way to trigger an event is by using this code pattern:

```
var onChanged = OnChanged;
if (onChanged != null)
{
    onChanged(this, args);
}
```

This pattern is not thread-safe because someone might unsubscribe the last event handler just after the null check is done. When that happens, an exception is thrown and the application crashes. Avoid this by either copying the delegate reference just before you check it (shown in the previous snippet var onChanged = onChanged;) or by using the null condition operator as shown here:

```
OnChanged?.Invoke(this, args);
```

> **NOTE** *If you utilize operator overload methods (for example, the ==) without checking for nulls, you may receive a* System.NullReferenceException.

As mentioned in Chapter 11, use the `?.` operator to check for nulls with the `==` operator overload in the `C:\BeginningCSharpAndDotNET\Chapter12\Ch12CardLib\Card.cs` class to prevent an exception from being thrown when using the method. For example:

```
public static bool operator ==(Card card1, Card card2)
        => (card1?.suit == card2?.suit) && (card1?.rank == card2?.rank);
```

By including the null condition operator in the statement, you are effectively expressing that if the object to the left is not null (in this case `card1` or `card2`), then retrieve what is to the right. If the object on the left is null (i.e., `card1` or `card2`), then terminate the access chain and return `null`.

Working with Nullable Types

Use the following Try It Out to experiment with a nullable `Vector` type.

TRY IT OUT   Nullable Types: Ch12Ex01

1. Create a new Console Application project called Ch12Ex01 and save it in the directory `C:\BeginningCSharpAndDotNET\Chapter12`.

2. Add a new class called `Vector`.

3. Modify the code in `Vector.cs` as follows:

```
using System;
using static System.Math;
public class Vector
{
    public double? R = null;
    public double? Theta = null;
    public double? ThetaRadians => (Theta * Math.PI / 180.0);
    public Vector(double? r, double? theta)
    {
        // Normalize.
        if (r < 0)
        {
            r = -r;
            theta += 180;
        }
        theta = theta % 360;
        // Assign fields.
        R = r;
        Theta = theta;
    }
    public static Vector operator +(Vector op1, Vector op2)
    {
        try
        {
            // Get (x, y) coordinates for new vector.
            double newX = op1.R.Value * Sin(op1.ThetaRadians.Value)
                + op2.R.Value * Sin(op2.ThetaRadians.Value);
            double newY = op1.R.Value * Cos(op1.ThetaRadians.Value)
                + op2.R.Value * Cos(op2.ThetaRadians.Value);
            // Convert to (r, theta).
```

```
                double newR = Sqrt(newX * newX + newY * newY);
                double newTheta = Atan2(newX, newY) * 180.0 / PI;
                // Return result.
                return new Vector(newR, newTheta);
            }
            catch
            {
                // Return "null" vector.
                return new Vector(null, null);
            }
        }
        public static Vector operator -(Vector op1) => new Vector(-op1.R, op1.Theta);
        public static Vector operator -(Vector op1, Vector op2) => op1 + (-op2);
        public override string ToString()
        {
            // Get string representation of coordinates.
            string rString = R.HasValue ? R.ToString(): "null";
            string thetaString = Theta.HasValue ? Theta.ToString(): "null";
            // Return (r, theta) string.
            return string.Format($"({rString}, {thetaString})");
        }
    }
}
```

4. Modify the code in `Program.cs` as follows:

```
class Program
{
    static void Main(string[] args)
    {
        Vector v1 = GetVector("vector1");
        Vector v2 = GetVector("vector2");
        Console.WriteLine($"{v1} + {v2} = {v1 + v2}");
        Console.WriteLine($"{v1} - {v2} = {v1 - v2}");
        Console.ReadKey();
    }
    static Vector GetVector(string name)
    {
        Console.WriteLine($"Input {name} magnitude:");
        double? r = GetNullableDouble();
        Console.WriteLine($"Input {name} angle (in degrees):");
        double? theta = GetNullableDouble();
        return new Vector(r, theta);
    }
    static double? GetNullableDouble()
    {
        double? result;
        string userInput = Console.ReadLine();
        try
        {
            result = double.Parse(userInput);
        }
        catch
        {
            result = null;
        }
```

```
        return result;
    }
}
```

5. Execute the application and enter values for two vectors. The sample output is shown in Figure 12-1.

```
C:\BeginningCSharpAndDotNET\Chapter12\Ch12Ex01\Ch12Ex01\bin\Debug\net5.0\Ch12Ex01.exe   —   □   ×
Input vector1 magnitude:
5
Input vector1 angle (in degrees):
60
Input vector1 magnitude:
2.5
Input vector1 angle (in degrees):
180
(5, 60) + (2.5, 180) = (4.330127018922193, 90)
(5, 60) - (2.5, 180) = (6.614378277661476, 40.89339464913091)
```

FIGURE 12-1

6. Execute the application again, but this time skip at least one of the four values. The sample output is shown in Figure 12-2.

```
C:\BeginningCSharpAndDotNET\Chapter12\Ch12Ex01\Ch12Ex01\bin\Debug\net5.0\Ch12Ex01.exe   —   □   ×
Input vector1 magnitude:
5
Input vector1 angle (in degrees):
60
Input vector1 magnitude:

Input vector1 angle (in degrees):
180
(5, 60) + (null, 180) = (null, null)
(5, 60) - (null, 180) = (null, null)
```

FIGURE 12-2

How It Works

This example created a class called `Vector` that represents a vector with polar coordinates (that is, with a magnitude and an angle), as shown in Figure 12-3.

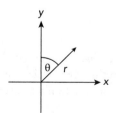

FIGURE 12-3

The coordinates *r* and θ are represented in code by the public fields R and Theta, where Theta is expressed in degrees. ThetaRadians is supplied to obtain the value of Theta in radians—this is necessary because the Math class uses radians in its static methods. Both R and Theta are of type double?, so they can be null:

```
public class Vector
{
    public double? R = null;
    public double? Theta = null;
    public double? ThetaRadians => (Theta * PI / 180.0);
```

The constructor for Vector normalizes the initial values of R and Theta and then assigns the public fields:

```
public Vector(double? r, double? theta)
{
    // Normalize.
    if (r < 0)
    {
        r = -r;
        theta += 180;
    }
    theta = theta % 360;
    // Assign fields.
    R = r;
    Theta = theta;
}
```

The main functionality of the Vector class is to add and subtract vectors using operator overloading, which requires some basic trigonometry not covered here. You might consider taking a look at onlinemathlearning.com/basic-trigonometry.html, or search for other resources on the Internet. The important point about the code is that if an exception is thrown when obtaining the Value property of R or ThetaRadians—that is, if either is null—then a "null" vector is returned:

```
public static Vector operator +(Vector op1, Vector op2)
{
    try
    {
        // Get (x, y) coordinates for new vector.
        ...
    }
    catch
    {
        // Return "null" vector.
        return new Vector(null, null);
    }
}
```

If either of the coordinates making up a vector is null, then the vector is invalid, which is signified here by a Vector class with null values for both R and Theta. The rest of the code in the Vector class overrides the other operators required to extend the addition functionality to include subtraction and overrides ToString() to obtain a string representation of a Vector object.

The code in `Program.cs` tests the `Vector` class by enabling the user to initialize two vectors, and then adds and subtracts them to and from one another. Should the user omit a value, it will be interpreted as `null`, and the rules mentioned previously apply.

The System.Collections.Generic Namespace

In practically every application used so far in this book, you have seen the `System` namespace. There are numerous other very common namespaces shown here and explained in the following list:

```
using System;
using System.Collections.Generic;
using System.Linq;
using System.Text;
using System.Threading.Tasks;
using static System.Console;
```

➤ The `System` namespace contains most of the basic types used in .NET applications.

➤ The `System.Collections.Generic` namespace contains generic types for dealing with collections, and it is likely to be used often with a `using` statement.

➤ You will look at the `System.Linq` namespace later in this book.

➤ The `System.Text` namespace includes types relating to string processing and encoding.

➤ The `System.Threading.Tasks` namespace contains types that help you to write asynchronous code, which is not covered in this book.

➤ The `using static System.Console` declaration is helpful when writing console applications. When this is manually added, you do not need to write `Console` before the `Write-Line()` and `ReadLine()` functions over and over again.

You will now look at some of the generic collection types, which are guaranteed to make your life easier. They make it possible for you to create strongly typed collection classes with hardly any effort. For example, Table 12-1 lists two types from the `System.Collections.Generic` namespace that are covered in this section. More of the types in this namespace are covered later in this chapter.

TABLE 12-1: Generic Collection Type

TYPE	DESCRIPTION
`List<T>`	Collection of type `T` objects
`Dictionary<K, V>`	Collection of items of type `V`, associated with keys of type `K`

This section also describes various interfaces and delegates used with these classes.

List<T>

Rather than derive a class from `CollectionBase` and implement the required methods as you did in the previous chapter, it can be quicker and easier to simply use the `List<T>` generic collection type. An added bonus here is that many of the methods you normally have to implement, such as `Add()`, are implemented for you.

Creating a collection of type `T` objects requires the following code:

```
List<T> myCollection = new List<T>();
```

That is it. You do not have to define any classes, implement any methods, or do anything else. You can also set a starting list of items in the collection by passing a `List<T>` object to the constructor. `List<T>` also has an `Item` property, enabling array-like access using its indexer:

```
T itemAtIndex2 = myCollectionOfT[2];
```

This class supports several other methods, but that's plenty to get you started. The following Try It Out demonstrates how to use `List<T>` in practice.

TRY IT OUT | **Using List<T>: Ch12Ex02**

1. Create a new Console Application called Ch12Ex02 and save it in the directory `C:\BeginningCSharpAndDotNET\Chapter12`.

2. Right-click the project name in the Solution Explorer window and select the Add ⇨ Existing Item option.

3. Select the `Animal.cs`, `Cow.cs`, and `Chicken.cs` files from the `C:\BeginningCSharpAndDotNET\Chapter11\Ch11Ex01\` directory and click Add.

4. Modify the namespace declaration in the three files you added as follows:

   ```
   namespace Ch12Ex02
   ```

5. Modify `Program.cs` as follows after adding `using System.Collections.Generic;` at the top of the file:

   ```
   static void Main(string[] args)
   {
       List<Animal> animalCollection = new List<Animal>();
       animalCollection.Add(new Cow("Donna"));
       animalCollection.Add(new Chicken("Mary"));
       foreach (Animal myAnimal in animalCollection)
       {
           myAnimal.Feed();
       }
       Console.ReadKey();
   }
   ```

6. Execute the application. The result is exactly the same as the result for Ch11Ex02 in the previous chapter.

How It Works

There are only three differences between this example and Ch11Ex02. The first is that the line of code

```
AnimalCollection animalCollection = new AnimalCollection();
```

has been replaced with:

```
List<Animal> animalCollection = new List<Animal>();
```

The second, and more crucial, difference is that there is no longer an `AnimalCollection` collection class in the project. All that hard work you did earlier to create this class was achieved in a single line of code by using a generic collection class.

An alternative way to get the same result is to leave the code in `Program.cs` as it was in the previous chapter, and use the following definition of `Animals`:

```
public class Animals : List<Animal> {}
```

Doing this has the advantage that the code in `Program.cs` is slightly easier to read, plus you can add members to the `Animals` class as you see fit.

Sorting and Searching Generic Lists

Sorting a generic list is much the same as sorting any other list. The previous chapter described how you can use the `IComparer` and `IComparable` interfaces to compare two objects and thereby sort a list of that type of object. The only difference here is that you can use the generic interfaces `IComparer<T>` and `IComparable<T>`, which expose slightly different, type-specific methods. Table 12-2 explains these differences.

TABLE 12-2: Sorting with Generic Types

GENERIC METHOD	NON-GENERIC METHOD	DIFFERENCE
`int IComparable<T>.CompareTo(T otherObj)`	`int IComparable.CompareTo(object otherObj)`	Strongly typed in generic versions.
`bool IComparable<T>.Equals(T otherObj)`	N/A	Does not exist on a non-generic interface; can override inherited `object.Equals()` instead.
`int IComparer<T>.Compare(T objectA, T objectB)`	`int IComparer.Compare(object objectA, object objectB)`	Strongly typed in generic versions.
`bool IComparer<T>.Equals(T objectA, T objectB)`	N/A	Does not exist on a non-generic interface; can override inherited `object.Equals()` instead.
`int IComparer<T>.GetHashCode(T objectA)`	N/A	Doesn't exist on a non-generic interface; can override inherited `object.GetHashCode()` instead.

To sort a `List<T>`, you can supply an `IComparable<T>` interface on the type to be sorted or supply an `IComparer<T>` object. Alternatively, you can supply a *generic delegate* as a sorting method. From the perspective of seeing how the code works, this is far more interesting because implementing the interfaces described here takes no more effort than implementing their non-generic cousins.

In general terms, all you need to sort a list is a method that compares two objects of type `T`; and to search, all you need is a method that checks an object of type `T` to determine whether it meets certain criteria. It is a simple matter to define such methods, and to aid you there are two generic delegate types that you can use:

➤ `Comparison<T>`—A delegate type for a method used for sorting, with the following return type and parameters:

```
int method(T objectA, T objectB)
```

➤ `Predicate<T>`—A delegate type for a method used for searching, with the following return type and parameters:

```
bool method(T targetObject)
```

You can define any number of such methods and use them to "snap-in" to the searching and sorting methods of `List<T>`. The next Try It Out illustrates this technique.

TRY IT OUT   Sorting and Searching List<T>: Ch12Ex03

1. Create a new Console Application called Ch12Ex03 and save it in the directory `C:\BeginningCSharpAndDotNET\Chapter12`.

2. Right-click the project name in the Solution Explorer window and select the Add Existing Item option.

3. Add the `Vector.cs` file from the `C:\BeginningCSharpAndDotNET\Chapter12\Ch12Ex01` directory.

4. Modify the namespace declaration in the file you added as follows:

```
namespace Ch12Ex03
```

5. Add a new class called `VectorList`.

6. Modify `VectorList.cs` as follows:

```
public class VectorList : List<Vector>
{
    public VectorList()
    {
    }
    public VectorList(IEnumerable<Vector> initialItems)
    {
        foreach (Vector vector in initialItems)
        {
            Add(vector);
        }
    }
    public string Sum()
```

```
        {
            StringBuilder sb = new StringBuilder();
            Vector currentPoint = new Vector(0.0, 0.0);
            sb.Append("origin");
            foreach (Vector vector in this)
            {
                sb.AppendFormat($" + {vector}");
                currentPoint += vector;
            }
            sb.AppendFormat($" = {currentPoint}");
            return sb.ToString();
        }
    }
```

7. Add a new class called `VectorDelegates`.

8. Modify `VectorDelegates.cs` as follows:

```
public static class VectorDelegates
{
    public static int Compare(Vector x, Vector y)
    {
        if (x.R > y.R)
        {
            return 1;
        }
        else if (x.R < y.R)
        {
            return -1;
        }
        return 0;
    }
    public static bool TopRightQuadrant(Vector target)
    {
        if (target.Theta >= 0.0 && target.Theta <= 90.0)
        {
            return true;
        }
        else
        {
            return false;
        }
    }
}
```

9. Modify `Program.cs` as follows:

```
static void Main(string[] args)
{
    VectorList route = new VectorList();
    route.Add(new Vector(2.0, 90.0));
    route.Add(new Vector(1.0, 180.0));
    route.Add(new Vector(0.5, 45.0));
    route.Add(new Vector(2.5, 315.0));
    Console.WriteLine(route.Sum());
    Comparison<Vector> sorter = new Comparison<Vector>(
```

```
            VectorDelegates.Compare);
        route.Sort(sorter);
        Console.WriteLine(route.Sum());
        Predicate<Vector> searcher =
            new Predicate<Vector>(VectorDelegates.TopRightQuadrant);
        VectorList topRightQuadrantRoute = new VectorList(route.FindAll(searcher));
        Console.WriteLine(topRightQuadrantRoute.Sum());
        Console.ReadKey();
    }
```

10. Execute the application. The result is shown in Figure 12-4.

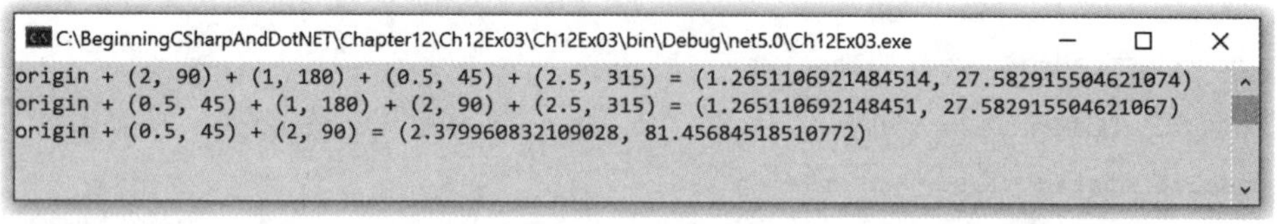

```
C:\BeginningCSharpAndDotNET\Chapter12\Ch12Ex03\Ch12Ex03\bin\Debug\net5.0\Ch12Ex03.exe          —    □    ×
origin + (2, 90) + (1, 180) + (0.5, 45) + (2.5, 315) = (1.2651106921484514, 27.582915504621074)
origin + (0.5, 45) + (1, 180) + (2, 90) + (2.5, 315) = (1.265110692148451, 27.582915504621067)
origin + (0.5, 45) + (2, 90) = (2.379960832109028, 81.45684518510772)
```

FIGURE 12-4

How It Works

In this example, you created a collection class, VectorList, for the Vector class created in Ch12Ex01. You could just use a variable of type List<Vector>, but because you want additional functionality, you use a new class, VectorList, and derive from List<Vector>, which enables you to add whatever additional members you want.

One member, Sum(), returns a string listing each vector in turn, along with the result of summing them all together (using the overloaded + operator from the original Vector class). Because each vector can be thought of as a direction and a distance, this effectively constitutes a route with an endpoint:

```
public string Sum()
{
    StringBuilder sb = new StringBuilder();
    Vector currentPoint = new Vector(0.0, 0.0);
    sb.Append("origin");
    foreach (Vector vector in this)
    {
        sb.AppendFormat($" + {vector}");
        currentPoint += vector;
    }
    sb.AppendFormat($" = {currentPoint}");
    return sb.ToString();
}
```

This method uses the handy StringBuilder class, found in the System.Text namespace, to build the response string. This class has members such as Append() and AppendFormat() (used here), which make it easy to assemble a string—the performance is better than concatenating individual strings. You use the ToString() method of this class to obtain the resultant string.

You also create two methods to be used as delegates, as static members of `VectorDelegates.Compare()`, which is used for comparison (sorting), and `TopRightQuadrant()` for searching. You will look at these as you review the code in `Program.cs`.

The code in `Main()` starts with the initialization of a `VectorList` collection, to which are added several `Vector` objects (you can find this code in `Ch12Ex03\Program.cs`):

```
VectorList route = new VectorList();
route.Add(new Vector(2.0, 90.0));
route.Add(new Vector(1.0, 180.0));
route.Add(new Vector(0.5, 45.0));
route.Add(new Vector(2.5, 315.0));
```

The `VectorList.Sum()` method is used to write out the items in the collection as noted earlier, this time in their initial order:

```
Console.WriteLine(route.Sum());
```

Next, you create the first of your delegates, `sorter`. This delegate is of type `Comparison<Vector>` and, therefore, can be assigned a method with the following return type and parameters:

```
int method(Vector objectA, Vector objectB)
```

This matches `VectorDelegates.Compare()`, which is the method you assign to the delegate:

```
Comparison<Vector> sorter = new Comparison<Vector>(
    VectorDelegates.Compare);
```

`Compare()` compares the magnitudes of two vectors as follows:

```
public static int Compare(Vector x, Vector y)
{
    if (x.R > y.R)
    {
        return 1;
    }
    else if (x.R < y.R)
    {
        return -1;
    }
    return 0;
}
```

This enables you to order the vectors by magnitude:

```
route.Sort(sorter);
Console.WriteLine(route.Sum());
```

The output of the application gives the result you'd expect—the result of the summation is the same because the endpoint of following the "vector route" is the same regardless of the order in which you carry out the individual steps.

Next, you obtain a subset of the vectors in the collection by searching. This uses `VectorDelegates.TopRightQuadrant()`:

```
public static bool TopRightQuadrant(Vector target)
{
    if (target.Theta >= 0.0 && target.Theta <= 90.0)
    {
        return true;
    }
    else
    {
        return false;
    }
}
```

This method returns `true` if its `Vector` argument has a value of `Theta` between 0 and 90 degrees—that is, if it points up and/or right in a diagram of the sort shown earlier.

In the `Main()` method, you use this method via a delegate of type `Predicate<Vector>` as follows:

```
Predicate<Vector> searcher =
    new Predicate<Vector>(VectorDelegates.TopRightQuadrant);
VectorList topRightQuadrantRoute = new VectorList(route.FindAll(searcher));
Console.WriteLine(topRightQuadrantRoute.Sum());
```

This requires the constructor defined in `VectorList`:

```
public VectorList(IEnumerable<Vector> initialItems)
{
    foreach (Vector vector in initialItems)
    {
        Add(vector);
    }
}
```

Here, you initialize a new `VectorList` collection using an interface of `IEnumerable<Vector>`, which is necessary because `List<Vector>.FindAll()` returns a `List<Vector>` instance, not a `VectorList` instance.

The result of the searching is that only a subset of `Vector` objects is returned, so (again, as you would expect) the result of the summation is different. The use of these generic delegate types to sort and search generic collections can take a little while to get used to, but the result is code that is streamlined and efficient, and which has a highly logical structure. It is well worth investing the time to learn the techniques presented in this section.

As an aside to this example, note that the code

```
Comparison<Vector> sorter = new Comparison<Vector>(
    VectorDelegates.Compare);
route.Sort(sorter);
```

can be simplified to the following:

```
route.Sort(VectorDelegates.Compare);
```

This removes the necessity to implicitly reference the `Comparison<Vector>` type. In fact, an instance of this type is still created, but it is created implicitly. The `Sort()` method obviously needs an instance of this type to work, but the compiler realizes this and creates one for you from the method that you supply. In this situation, the reference to `VectorDelegates.Compare()` (without the parentheses) is referred to as a *method group*. There are many situations in which you can use method groups to implicitly create delegates in this way, which can make your code more readable.

Dictionary<K, V>

The `Dictionary<K, V>` type enables you to define a collection of key-value pairs. Unlike the other generic collection types you have looked at in this chapter, this class requires instantiating two types: the types for both the key and the value that represents each item in the collection.

Once a `Dictionary<K, V>` object is instantiated, you can perform operations on it similar to the ones for a class that inherits from `DictionaryBase`, but with type-safe methods and properties already in place. You can, for example, add key-value pairs using a strongly typed `Add()` method:

```
Dictionary<string, int> things = new Dictionary<string, int>();
things.Add("Green Things", 29);
things.Add("Blue Things", 94);
things.Add("Yellow Things", 34);
things.Add("Red Things", 52);
things.Add("Brown Things", 27);
```

Initializing key-value pairs without using the `Add()` method can also be achieved and looks a little more elegant:

```
Dictionary<string, int> things = new Dictionary<string, int>(){
    {"Green Things", 29},
    {"Blue Things", 94},
    {"Yellow Things", 34},
    {"Red Things", 52},
    {"Brown Things", 27}
};
```

Iterate through keys and values in the collection by using the `Keys` and `Values` properties:

```
foreach (string key in things.Keys)
{
    Console.WriteLine(key);
}
foreach (int value in things.Values)
{
    Console.WriteLine(value);
}
```

In addition, iterate through items in the collection by obtaining each as a KeyValuePair<K, V> instance, much like you can with the DictionaryEntry objects shown in the previous chapter:

```
foreach (KeyValuePair<string, int> thing in things)
{
    Console.WriteLine($"{thing.Key} = {thing.Value}");
}
```

One point to note about Dictionary<K, V> is that the key for each item must be unique. Attempting to add an item with an identical key will cause an ArgumentException exception to be thrown. Because of this, Dictionary<K, V> allows you to pass an IComparer<K> interface to its constructor. This might be necessary if you use your own classes as keys and they don't support an IComparable or IComparable<K> interface, or if you want to compare objects using a nondefault process. For instance, in the preceding example, you could use a case-insensitive method to compare string keys:

```
Dictionary<string, int> things =
    new Dictionary<string, int>(StringComparer.CurrentCultureIgnoreCase);
```

Now you will get an exception if you use keys such as this:

```
things.Add("Green Things", 29);
things.Add("Green things", 94);
```

You can also pass an initial capacity (with an int) or a set of items (with an IDictionary<K, V> interface) to the constructor.

Instead of using the Add() method or the more elegant approach to populate a Dictionary<K, V> type, consider using *index initializers*, which supports the initialization of indices inside the object initializer:

```
var things = new Dictionary<string, int>()
{
    ["Green Things"] = 29,
    ["Blue Things"] = 94,
    ["Yellow Things"] = 34,
    ["Red Things"] = 52,
    ["Brown Things"] = 27
};
```

Index initializers can be streamlined as in many cases there is no need for a temporary variable as shown previously via var things. Using *expression-bodied methods*, the preceding example leads to a cascading effect of simplification and ultimate elegance for the initialization of a Dictionary<K, V> type:

```
public Dictionary<string, int>
    SomeThings() => new Dictionary<string, int>
    { ["Green Things"] = 29, ["Blue Things"] = 94 };
```

Modifying CardLib to Use a Generic Collection Class

One simple modification you can make to the CardLib project you have been building over recent chapters is to change the CardCollection collection class to use a generic collection class, thus saving many lines of code. The required modification to the class definition for CardCollection is as follows (you can find this code in Ch12CardLib\CardCollection.cs):

```
public class CardCollection : List<Card>, ICloneable { ... }
```

You can also remove all the methods of CardCollection except Clone(), which is required for ICloneable, and CopyTo(), because the version of CopyTo() supplied by List<Card> works with an array of Card objects, not a CardCollection collection. Clone() requires a minor modification because the List<T> class does not define a List property to use:

```
public object Clone()
{
    CardCollection newCards = new CardCollection();
    foreach (Card sourceCard in this)
    {
        newCards.Add((Card)sourceCard.Clone());
    }
    return newCards;
}
```

Rather than show the code here for what is a very simple modification, the updated version of CardLib, called Ch12CardLib, is included in the downloadable code for this chapter, along with the client code from the previous chapter.

DEFINING GENERIC TYPES

You have now learned enough about generics to create your own. You have seen plenty of code involving generic types and have had plenty of practice using generic syntax. This section looks at defining the following:

➤   Generic classes

➤   Generic interfaces

➤   Generic methods

➤   Generic delegates

You'll also look at the following more advanced techniques for dealing with the issues that come up when defining generic types:

➤   The default keyword

➤   Constraining types

➤   Inheriting from generic classes

➤   Generic operators

Defining Generic Classes

To create a generic class, merely include the angle bracket syntax in the class definition:

```
class MyGenericClass<T> { ... }
```

Here, T can be any identifier you like, following the usual C# naming rules, such as not starting with a number and so on. Typically, though, you can just use T. A generic class can have any number of type parameters in its definition, separated by commas:

```
class MyGenericClass<T1, T2, T3> { ... }
```

Once these types are defined, you can use them in the class definition just like any other type. You can use them as types for member variables, return types for members such as properties or methods, and parameter types for method arguments:

```
class MyGenericClass<T1, T2, T3>
{
    private T1 innerT1Object;
    public MyGenericClass(T1 item)
    {
        innerT1Object = item;
    }
    public T1 InnerT1Object
    {
        get { return innerT1Object; }
    }
}
```

Here, an object of type T1 can be passed to the constructor, and read-only access is permitted to this object via the property InnerT1Object. Note that you can make practically no assumptions as to what the types supplied to the class are. The following code, for example, will not compile:

```
class MyGenericClass<T1, T2, T3>
{
    private T1 innerT1Object;
    public MyGenericClass()
    {
        innerT1Object = new T1();
    }
    public T1 InnerT1Object
    {
        get { return innerT1Object; }
    }
}
```

Because you don't know what T1 is, you can't use any of its constructors—it might not even have any, or it might have no publicly accessible default constructor. Without more complicated code involving the techniques shown later in this section, you can make only the following assumption about T1: you can treat it as a type that either inherits from or can be boxed into System.Object.

Without using *reflection*, which is an advanced technique used to examine types at runtime (reflection is discussed in Chapter 13), you're limited to code that's no more complicated than the following:

```
public string GetAllTypesAsString()
{
    return "T1 = " + typeof(T1).ToString()
        + ", T2 = " + typeof(T2).ToString()
        + ", T3 = " + typeof(T3).ToString();
}
```

There is a bit more that you can do, particularly in terms of collections, because dealing with groups of objects is a pretty simple process and doesn't need any assumptions about the object types—which is one good reason why the generic collection classes you've seen in this chapter exist.

Another limitation that you need to be aware of is that using the operator `==` or `!=` is permitted only when comparing a value of a type supplied to a generic type to `null`. That is, the following code works fine:

```
public bool Compare(T1 op1, T1 op2)
{
    if (op1 != null && op2 != null)
    {
        return true;
    }
    else
    {
        return false;
    }
}
```

Here, if `T1` is a value type, then it is always assumed to be non-`null`, so in the preceding code `Compare` will always return `true`. However, attempting to compare the two arguments `op1` and `op2` fails to compile:

```
public bool Compare(T1 op1, T1 op2)
{
    if (op1 == op2)
    {
        return true;
    }
    else
    {
        return false;
    }
}
```

That is because this code assumes that `T1` supports the `==` operator. In short, to do anything interesting with generics, you need to know a bit more about the types used in the class.

The default Keyword

One of the most basic things you might want to know about types used to create generic class instances is whether they are reference types or value types. Without knowing this, you cannot even assign null values with code such as this:

```
public MyGenericClass()
{
    innerT1Object = null;
}
```

If T1 is a non-nullable value type, then innerT1Object cannot have the value null, so this code will not compile. Luckily, this problem has been addressed, resulting in a new use for the default keyword (which you have seen being used in switch structures earlier in the book). This is used as follows:

```
public MyGenericClass()
{
    innerT1Object = default(T1);
}
```

The result of this is that innerT1Object is assigned a value of null if it is a reference type or a nullable value type, or a default value if it is a value type. This default value is 0 for numeric types, while structs have each of their members initialized to 0 or null in the same way. The default keyword gets you a bit further in terms of doing a little more with the types you are forced to use, but to truly get ahead, you need to constrain the types that are supplied.

Constraining Types

The types you have used with generic classes until now are known as *unbounded types* because no restrictions are placed on what they can be. By *constraining types*, it is possible to restrict the types that can be used to instantiate a generic class. There are several ways to do this. For example, it is possible to restrict a type to one that inherits from a certain type. Referring back to the Animal, Cow, and Chicken classes used earlier, you could restrict a type to one that was or inherited from Animal, so this code would be fine:

```
MyGenericClass<Cow> = new MyGenericClass<Cow>();
```

The following, however, would fail to compile:

```
MyGenericClass<string> = new MyGenericClass<string>();
```

In your class definitions this is achieved using the where keyword:

```
class MyGenericClass<T> where T : constraint { ... }
```

Here, constraint defines what the constraint is. You can supply a number of constraints in this way by separating them with commas:

```
class MyGenericClass<T> where T : constraint1, constraint2 { ... }
```

You can define constraints on any or all of the types required by the generic class by using multiple where statements:

```
class MyGenericClass<T1, T2> where T1 : constraint1 where T2 : constraint2
{ ... }
```

Any constraints that you use must appear after the inheritance specifiers:

```
class MyGenericClass<T1, T2> : MyBaseClass, IMyInterface
    where T1 : constraint1 where T2 : constraint2 { ... }
```

The available constraints are shown in Table 12-3.

TABLE 12-3: Generic Type Constraints

CONSTRAINT	DEFINITION	EXAMPLE USAGE
Struct	Type must be a non-nullable value type.	In a class that requires value types to function—for example, where a member variable of type T being 0 means something
Class	Type can be a nullable or non-nullable reference type.	In a class that requires reference types to function—for example, where a member variable of type T being null means something
base-class	Type must be, or inherit from, base-class. You can supply any class name as this constraint.	In a class that requires certain baseline functionality inherited from base-class in order to function
Interface	Type must be, or implement, interface.	In a class that requires certain baseline functionality exposed by interface in order to function
new()	Type must have a public, parameterless constructor.	In a class where you need to be able to instantiate variables of type T, perhaps in a constructor

> **NOTE** If new() is used as a constraint, it must be the last constraint specified for a type.

It is possible to use one type parameter as a constraint on another through the *base-class* constraint as follows:

```
class MyGenericClass<T1, T2> where T2 : T1 { ... }
```

Here, T2 must be the same type as T1 or inherit from T1. This is known as a *naked type constraint*, meaning that one generic type parameter is used as a constraint on another.

Circular type constraints, as shown here, are forbidden:

```
class MyGenericClass<T1, T2> where T2 : T1 where T1 : T2 { ... }
```

This code will not compile. In the following Try It Out, you will define and use a generic class that uses the `Animal` family of classes shown in earlier chapters.

TRY IT OUT Defining a Generic Class: Ch12Ex04

1. Create a new Console Application called Ch12Ex04 and save it in the directory `C:\BeginningCSharpAndDotNET\Chapter12`.

2. Right-click the project name in the Solution Explorer window and select the Add Existing Item option.

3. Select the `Animal.cs`, `Cow.cs`, and `Chicken.cs` files from the `C:\BeginningCSharpAndDotNET\Chapter12\Ch12Ex02` directory and click Add.

4. Modify the namespace declaration in the file you have added as follows:

```
namespace Ch12Ex04
```

5. Modify `Animal.cs` as follows:

```
public abstract class Animal
{
    ...
    public abstract void MakeANoise();
}
```

6. Modify `Chicken.cs` as follows:

```
public class Chicken : Animal
{
    ...
    public override void MakeANoise()
    {
        Console.WriteLine($"{name} says 'cluck!';");
    }
}
```

7. Modify `Cow.cs` as follows:

```
public class Cow : Animal
{
    ...
    public override void MakeANoise()
    {
        Console.WriteLine($"{name} says 'moo!'");
    }
}
```

8. Add a new class called `SuperCow` and modify the code in `SuperCow.cs` as follows:

```
public class SuperCow : Cow
{
    public void Fly()
    {
        Console.WriteLine($"{name} is flying!");
    }
```

```csharp
        public SuperCow(string newName) : base(newName)
        {
        }
        public override void MakeANoise()
        {
            Console.WriteLine(
                $"{name} says 'here I come to save the day!'");
        }
    }
```

9. Add a new class called `Farm` and modify the code in `Farm.cs` as follows:

```csharp
using System;
using System.Collections;
using System.Collections.Generic;
using System.Text;
namespace Ch12Ex04
{
    public class Farm<T> : IEnumerable<T>
        where T : Animal
    {
        private List<T> animals = new List<T>();
        public List<T> Animals
        {
            get { return animals; }
        }
        public IEnumerator<T> GetEnumerator() => animals.GetEnumerator();
        IEnumerator IEnumerable.GetEnumerator() => animals.GetEnumerator();
        public void MakeNoises()
        {
            foreach (T animal in animals)
            {
                animal.MakeANoise();
            }
        }
        public void FeedTheAnimals()
        {
            foreach (T animal in animals)
            {
                animal.Feed();
            }
        }
        public Farm<Cow> GetCows()
        {
            Farm<Cow> cowFarm = new Farm<Cow>();
            foreach (T animal in animals)
            {
                if (animal is Cow)
                {
                    cowFarm.Animals.Add(animal as Cow);
                }
            }
            return cowFarm;
        }
    }
}
```

10. Modify `Program.cs` as follows:

```
static void Main(string[] args)
{
    Farm<Animal> farm = new Farm<Animal>();
    farm.Animals.Add(new Cow("Lea"));
    farm.Animals.Add(new Chicken("Donna"));
    farm.Animals.Add(new Chicken("Mary"));
    farm.Animals.Add(new SuperCow("Ben"));
    farm.MakeNoises();
    Farm<Cow> dairyFarm = farm.GetCows();
    dairyFarm.FeedTheAnimals();
    foreach (Cow cow in dairyFarm)
    {
        if (cow is SuperCow)
        {
            (cow as SuperCow)?.Fly();
        }
    }
    Console.ReadKey();
}
```

11. Execute the application. The result is shown in Figure 12-5.

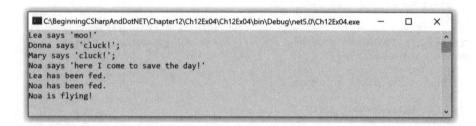

FIGURE 12-5

How It Works

In this example, you created a generic class called `Farm<T>`, which, rather than inheriting from a generic list class, exposes a generic list as a public property. The type of this list is determined by the type parameter `T` that is passed to `Farm<T>` and is constrained to be, or inherit from, `Animal`:

```
public class Farm<T> : IEnumerable<T>
    where T : Animal
{
    private List<T> animals = new List<T>();
    public List<T> Animals
    {
        get { return animals; }
    }
}
```

`Farm<T>` also implements `IEnumerable<T>`, where `T` is passed into this generic interface and is therefore also constrained in the same way. You implement this interface to make it possible to iterate through the items contained in Farm<T> without needing to explicitly iterate over Farm<T>.Animals. This is simple to achieve: you simply return the enumerator exposed by Animals, which is a List<T> class that also implements IEnumerable<T>:

```
public IEnumerator<T> GetEnumerator() => animals.GetEnumerator();
```

Because IEnumerable<T> inherits from IEnumerable, you also need to implement IEnumerable. GetEnumerator():

```
IEnumerator IEnumerable.GetEnumerator() => animals.GetEnumerator();
```

Next, Farm<T> includes two methods that make use of methods of the abstract Animal class:

```
public void MakeNoises()
{
    foreach (T animal in animals)
    {
        animal.MakeANoise();
    }
}
public void FeedTheAnimals()
{
    foreach (T animal in animals)
    {
        animal.Feed();
    }
}
```

Because T is constrained to Animal, this code compiles fine—you are guaranteed to have access to the MakeANoise() and Feed() methods, whatever type T actually is.

The next method, GetCows(), is more interesting. This method simply extracts all the items in the collection that are of type Cow (or that inherit from Cow, such as the new SuperCow class):

```
public Farm<Cow> GetCows()
{
    Farm<Cow> cowFarm = new Farm<Cow>();
    foreach (T animal in animals)
    {
        if (animal is Cow)
        {
            cowFarm.Animals.Add(animal as Cow);
        }
    }
    return cowFarm;
}
```

What is interesting here is that this method seems a bit wasteful. If you wanted other methods of the same sort, such as GetChickens() and so on, you would need to implement them explicitly, too. In a system with many more types, you would need many more methods. A far better solution is to use a *generic method,* which you'll implement a little later in the chapter.

The client code in Program.cs simply tests the various methods of Farm and does not contain much you haven't already seen, so there's no need to examine this code in any greater detail—despite the flying cow.

Inheriting from Generic Classes

The `Farm<T>` class in the preceding example, as well as several other classes you have seen in this chapter, inherit from a generic type. In the case of `Farm<T>`, this type was an interface: `IEnumerable<T>`. Here, the constraint on `T` supplied by `Farm<T>` resulted in an additional constraint on `T` used in `IEnumerable<T>`. This can be a useful technique for constraining otherwise unbounded types. However, you do need to follow some rules.

First, you cannot "un-constrain" types that are constrained in a type from which you are inheriting. In other words, a type `T` that is used in a type you are inheriting from must be constrained at least as much as it is in that type. For example, the following code is fine:

```
class SuperFarm<T> : Farm<T>
    where T : SuperCow {}
```

This works because `T` is constrained to `Animal` in `Farm<T>` and constraining it to `SuperCow` is constraining `T` to a subset of these values. However, the following will not compile:

```
class SuperFarm<T> : Farm<T>
    where T : struct{}
```

Here, you can say definitively that the type `T` supplied to `SuperFarm<T>` cannot be converted into a `T` usable by `Farm<T>`, so the code will not compile.

Even situations in which the constraint is a superset have the same problem:

```
class SuperFarm<T> : Farm<T>
    where T : class{}
```

Even though types such as `Animal` would be allowed by `SuperFarm<T>`, other types that satisfy the class constraint will not be allowed in `Farm<T>`. Again, compilation will fail. This rule applies to all the constraint types shown earlier in this chapter.

Also note that if you inherit from a generic type, then you must supply all the required type information, either in the form of other generic type parameters, as shown, or explicitly. This also applies to non-generic classes that inherit from generic types, as you have seen elsewhere. Here is an example:

```
public class CardCollection : List<Card>, ICloneable{}
```

This is fine, but attempting the following will fail:

```
public class CardCollection : List<T>, ICloneable{}
```

Here, no information is supplied for `T`, so no compilation is possible.

> **NOTE** *If you supply a parameter to a generic type, as in* `List<Card>`, *then you can refer to the type as closed. In contrast, inheriting from* `List<T>` *is inheriting from an open generic type.*

Generic Operators

Operator overrides are implemented in C# just like other methods and can be implemented in generic classes. For example, you could define the following implicit conversion operator in `Farm<T>`:

```
public static implicit operator List<Animal>(Farm<T> farm)
{
    List<Animal> result = new List<Animal>();
    foreach (T animal in farm)
    {
        result.Add(animal);
    }
    return result;
}
```

This allows the `Animal` objects in a `Farm<T>` to be accessed directly as a `List<Animal>` should you require it. This comes in handy if you want to add two `Farm<T>` instances together, such as with the following operators:

```
public static Farm<T> operator +(Farm<T> farm, List<T> list)
{
    Farm<T> result = new Farm<T>();
    foreach (T animal in farm)
    {
        result.Animals.Add(animal);
    }
    foreach (T animal in list)
    {
        if (!result.Animals.Contains(animal))
        {
            result.Animals.Add(animal);
        }
    }
    return result;
}
public static Farm<T> operator +(Farm<T> farm, List<T> list)
        => farm + list;
```

You could then add instances of `Farm<Animal>` and `Farm<Cow>` as follows:

```
Farm<Animal> newFarm = farm + dairyFarm;
```

In this code, `dairyFarm` (an instance of `Farm<Cow>`) is implicitly converted into `List<Animal>`, which is usable by the overloaded + operator in `Farm<T>`.

You might think that this could be achieved simply by using the following:

```
public static Farm<T> operator +(Farm<T> farm1, Farm<T> farm2){ ... }
```

However, because `Farm<Cow>` cannot be converted into `Farm<Animal>`, the summation will fail. To take this a step further, you could solve this using the following conversion operator:

```
public static implicit operator Farm<Animal>(Farm<T> farm)
{
    Farm <Animal> result = new Farm <Animal>();
    foreach (T animal in farm)
```

```
    {
        result.Animals.Add(animal);
    }
    return result;
}
```

With this operator, instances of `Farm<T>`, such as `Farm<Cow>`, can be converted into instances of `Farm<Animal>`, solving the problem. You can use either of the methods shown, although the latter is preferable for its simplicity.

Generic Structs

You learned in earlier chapters that structs are essentially the same as classes, barring some minor differences and the fact that a struct is a value type, not a reference type. Because this is the case, *generic structs* can be created in the same way as generic classes, as shown here:

```
public struct MyStruct<T1, T2>
{
    public T1 item1;
    public T2 item2;
}
```

Defining Generic Interfaces

You have now seen several generic interfaces in use—namely, those in the `Systems.Collections.Generic` namespace such as `IEnumerable<T>` used in the previous example. Defining a generic interface involves the same techniques as defining a generic class:

```
interface MyFarmingInterface<T>
    where T : Animal
{
    bool AttemptToBreed(T animal1, T animal2);
    T OldestInHerd { get; }
}
```

Here, the generic parameter `T` is used as the type of the two arguments of `AttemptToBreed()` and the type of the `OldestInHerd` property.

The same inheritance rules apply as for classes. If you inherit from a base generic interface, you must obey the rules, such as keeping the constraints of the base interface generic type parameters.

Defining Generic Methods

The previous Try It Out used a method called `GetCows()`, and in the discussion of the example it was stated that you could make a more general form of this method using a *generic method*. In this section you will see how this is possible. A generic method is one in which the return and/or parameter types are determined by a generic type parameter or parameters:

```
public T GetDefault<T>() => default(T);
```

This trivial example uses the `default` keyword you looked at earlier in the chapter to return a default value for a type T. This method is called as follows:

```
int myDefaultInt = GetDefault<int>();
```

The type parameter T is provided at the time the method is called.

This T is quite separate from the types used to supply generic type parameters to classes. In fact, generic methods can be implemented by non-generic classes:

```
public class Defaulter
{
    public T GetDefault<T>() => default(T);
}
```

If the class is generic, though, then you must use different identifiers for generic method types. The following code won't compile:

```
public class Defaulter<T>
{
    public T GetDefault<T>() => default(T);
}
```

The type T used by either the method or the class must be renamed.

Constraints can be used by generic method parameters in the same way that they are for classes, and in this case you can make use of any class type parameters:

```
public class Defaulter<T1>
{
    public T2 GetDefault<T2>()
        where T2 : T1
    {
        return default(T2);
    }
}
```

Here, the type T2 supplied to the method must be the same as, or inherit from, T1 supplied to the class. This is a common way to constrain generic methods.

In the `Farm<T>` class shown earlier, you could include the following method (included, but commented out, in the downloadable code for `Ch12Ex04`):

```
public Farm<U> GetSpecies<U>() where U : T
{
    Farm<U> speciesFarm = new Farm<U>();
    foreach (T animal in animals)
    {
        if (animal is U)
        {
            speciesFarm.Animals.Add(animal as U);
        }
    }
    return speciesFarm;
}
```

This can replace GetCows() and any other methods of the same type. The generic type parameter used here, U, is constrained by T, which is in turn constrained by the Farm<T> class to Animal. This enables you to treat instances of T as instances of Animal, should you want to do so.

In the client code for Ch12Ex04, in Program.cs, using this new method requires one modification:

```
Farm<Cow> dairyFarm = farm.GetSpecies<Cow>();
```

In a similar vein, you could write:

```
Farm<Chicken> poultryFarm = farm.GetSpecies<Chicken>();
```

You can take this same approach with any class that inherits from Animal.

Note here that having generic type parameters on a method changes the signature of the method. This means you can have several overloads of a method differing only in generic type parameters, as shown in this example:

```
public void ProcessT<T>(T op1){ ... }
public void ProcessT<T, U>(T op1){ ... }
```

Which method should be used is determined by the amount of generic type parameters specified when the method is called.

Defining Generic Delegates

The last generic type to consider is the *generic delegate*. You saw these delegates in action earlier in the chapter when you learned how to sort and search generic lists. You used the Comparison<T> and Predicate<T> delegates, respectively, for this.

Chapter 6 described how to define delegates using the parameters and return type of a method, the delegate keyword, and a name for the delegate:

```
public delegate int MyDelegate(int op1, int op2);
```

To define a generic delegate, you simply declare and use one or more generic type parameters:

```
public delegate T1 MyDelegate<T1, T2>(T2 op1, T2 op2) where T1: T2;
```

As you can see, constraints can be applied here, too. You will learn a lot more about delegates in the next chapter, including how you can use them in a common C# programming technique—events.

VARIANCE

Variance is the collective term for *covariance* and *contravariance*. The easiest way to grasp what these terms mean is to compare them with polymorphism. Polymorphism, as you will recall, is what enables you to put objects of a derived type into variables of a base type. For example:

```
Cow myCow = new Cow("Mary");
Animal myAnimal = myCow;
```

Here, an object of type Cow has been placed into a variable of type Animal—which is possible because Cow derives from Animal.

However, the same cannot be said for interfaces. That is to say, the following code will not work:

```
IMethaneProducer<Cow> cowMethaneProducer = myCow;
IMethaneProducer<Animal> animalMethaneProducer = cowMethaneProducer;
```

The first line of code is fine, assuming that Cow supports the interface IMethaneProducer<Cow>. However, the second line of code presupposes a relationship between the two interface types that does not exist, so there is no way of converting one into the other. Or is there? There certainly is not a way using the techniques you have seen so far in this chapter, as all the type parameters for generic types have been *invariant*. However, it is possible to define variant type parameters on generic interfaces and generic delegates that cater to exactly the situation illustrated in the previous code.

To make the previous code work, the type parameter T for the IMethaneProducer<T> interface must be *covariant*. Having a covariant type parameter effectively sets up an inheritance relationship between IMethaneProducer<Cow> and IMethaneProducer<Animal>, so that variables of one type can hold values of the other, just like with polymorphism (although a little more complicated).

To round off this introduction to variance, you need to look at the other kind, *contravariance*. This is similar but works in the other direction. Rather than being able to place a generic interface value into a variable that includes a base type as in covariance, contravariance enables you to place that interface into a variable that uses a derived type. For example:

```
IGrassMuncher<Cow> cowGrassMuncher = myCow;
IGrassMuncher<SuperCow> superCowGrassMuncher = cowGrassMuncher;
```

At first glance this seems a little odd, as you could not do the same with polymorphism. However, this is a useful technique in certain circumstances, as you will see in the section called "Contravariance."

In the next two sections, you will look at how to implement variance in generic types and how the .NET Framework uses variance to make your life easier.

> **NOTE** All the code in this section is included in a demo project called
> VarianceDemo *if you want to work through it as you go along.*

Covariance

To define a generic type parameter as covariant, you use the out keyword in the type definition, as shown in the following example:

```
public interface IMethaneProducer<out T>{ ... }
```

For interface definitions, covariant type parameters can be used only as return values of methods or property get accessors.

A good example of how this is useful is found in the .NET Framework, in the IEnumerable<T> interface that you have used previously. The item type T in this interface is defined as being covariant. This means that you can put an object that supports, say, IEnumerable<Cow> into a variable of type IEnumerable<Animal>.

This enables the following code:

```
static void Main(string[] args)
{
    List<Cow> cows = new List<Cow>();
    cows.Add(new Cow("Rual"));
    cows.Add(new SuperCow("Donna"));
    ListAnimals(cows);
    Console.ReadKey();
}
static void ListAnimals(IEnumerable<Animal> animals)
{
    foreach (Animal animal in animals)
    {
        Console.WriteLine(animal.ToString());
    }
}
```

Here the cows variable is of type List<Cow>, which supports the IEnumerable<Cow> interface. This variable can, through covariance, be passed to a method that expects a parameter of type IEnumerable<Animal>. Recalling what you know about how foreach loops work, you know that the GetEnumerator() method is used to get an enumerator of IEnumerator<T>, and the Current property of that enumerator is used to access items. IEnumerator<T> also defines its type parameter as covariant, which means that it is okay to use it as the get accessor of a parameter, and everything works perfectly.

Contravariance

To define a generic type parameter as contravariant, you use the in keyword in the type definition:

```
public interface IGrassMuncher<in T>{ ... }
```

For interface definitions, contravariant type parameters can be used only as method parameters, not as return types.

Again, the best way to understand this is to look at an example of how contravariance is used in .NET. One interface that has a contravariant type parameter, again one that you have already used, is IComparer<T>. You might implement this interface for animals as follows:

```
public class AnimalNameLengthComparer : IComparer<Animal>
{
    public int Compare(Animal x, Animal y)
        => x.Name.Length.CompareTo(y.Name.Length);
}
```

This comparer compares animals by name length, so you could use it to sort, for example, an instance of List<Animal>. However, through contravariance, you can also use it to sort an instance of List<Cow>, even though the List<Cow>.Sort() method expects an instance of IComparer<Cow>:

```
List<Cow> cows = new List<Cow>();
cows.Add(new Cow("Lea"));
cows.Add(new SuperCow("Donna"));
```

```
cows.Add(new Cow("Mary"));
cows.Add(new Cow("Ben"));
cows.Sort(new AnimalNameLengthComparer());
```

In most circumstances, contravariance is something that simply happens—and it has been worked into .NET to help with just this sort of operation. The good thing about both types of variance, though, is that you can now implement them with the techniques shown in this section whenever you need them.

EXERCISES

12.1 Which of the following can be generic?

    a. Classes

    b. Methods

    c. Properties

    d. Operator overloads

    e. Structs

    f. Enumerations

12.2 Extend the `Vector` class in `Ch12Ex01` such that the `*` operator returns the dot product of two vectors.

> **NOTE** *The dot product of two vectors is defined as the product of their magnitudes multiplied by the cosine of the angle between them.*

12.3 What is wrong with the following code? Fix it.

```
public class Instantiator<T>
{
    public T instance;
    public Instantiator()
    {
        instance = new T();
    }
}
```

12.4 What is wrong with the following code? Fix it.

```
public class StringGetter<T>
{
    public string GetString<T>(T item) => item.ToString();
}
```

12.5 Create a generic class called ShortList<T> that implements IList<T> and consists of a collection of items with a maximum size. This maximum size should be an integer that can be supplied to the constructor of ShortList<T> or defaults to 10. The constructor should also be able to take an initial list of items via an IEnumerable<T> parameter. The class should function exactly like List<T> but throw an exception of type IndexOutOfRangeException if an attempt is made to add too many items to the collection, or if the IEnumerable<T> passed to the constructor contains too many items.

12.6 Will the following code compile? If not, why not?

```
public interface IMethaneProducer<out T>
{
    void BelchAt(T target);
}
```

Answers to the exercises can be found in the Appendix.

▶ **WHAT YOU HAVE LEARNED IN THIS CHAPTER**

TOPIC	KEY CONCEPTS
Using generic types	Generic types require one or more type parameters to work. You can use a generic type as the type of a variable by passing the type parameters you require when you declare a variable. You do this by enclosing a comma-separated list of type names in angle brackets.
Nullable types	Nullable types are types that can take any value of a specified value type or the value `null`. You can use the syntax `Nullable<T>` or `T?` to declare a nullable type variable.
The `??`, `?.`, and `?[]` operators	The null coalescing operator, `??`, returns either the value of its first operand, or, if the first operand is `null`, its second operand. The member access `?.` and element access `?[]` null-conditional operators evaluate whether an object is null before performing an action on it.
Generic collections	Generic collections are extremely useful as they come with strong typing built in. You can use `List<T>`, `Collection<T>`, and `Dictionary<K, V>` among other collection types. These also expose generic interfaces. To sort and search generic collections, you use the `IComparer<T>` and `IComparable<T>` interfaces.
Defining generic types	You define a generic type much like any other type, with the addition of generic type parameters where you specify the type name. As with using generic types, you specify these as a comma-separated list enclosed in angle brackets. You can use the generic type parameters in your code anywhere you would use a type name; for example, in method return values and parameters.
Generic type parameter constraints	In order to use generic type parameters more effectively in your generic type code, you can constrain the types that can be supplied when the type is used. You can constrain type parameters by base class, supported interface, whether they must be value or reference types, and whether they support parameterless constructors. Without such constraints, you must use the `default` keyword to instantiate a variable of a generic type.

continues

(continued)

TOPIC	KEY CONCEPTS
Other generic types	As well as classes, you can define generic interfaces, delegates, and methods.
Variance	Variance is a concept similar to polymorphism but applied to type parameters. It allows you to use one generic type in place of another, where those generic types vary only in the generic type parameters used. Covariance allows conversion between two types where the target type has a type parameter that is a base class of the type parameter of the source type. Contravariance allows conversion where this relationship is inverted. Covariant type parameters are defined with the `out` parameter and can only be used as return types and property `get` accessor types. Contravariant type parameters are defined with the `in` parameter and can only be used as method parameters.

13

Additional C# Techniques

CODE DOWNLOADS FOR THIS CHAPTER

The code downloads for this chapter are found on the book page at www.wiley.com. Click the Downloads link. The code can also be found at github.com/benperk/BeginningCSharpAnd-DotNET. The code is in the Chapter13 folder and individually named according to the names throughout the chapter.

In this chapter, you continue exploring the C# language by looking at a few bits and pieces that have not quite fit in elsewhere. Anders Hejlsberg (the inventor of C#) and others at Microsoft continue to update and refine the language. At the time of this writing, the most recent changes are part of version 9 of the C# language. At this point in the book, you might be wondering what else could be needed; indeed, previous versions of C# lack little in terms of functionality. However, this does not mean that it is not possible to make some aspects of C# programming easier, or that the relationships between C# and other technologies can't be streamlined.

You will also make some final modifications to the `CardLib` code that you have been building in the last few chapters, and even use `CardLib` to create a card game.

THE :: OPERATOR AND THE GLOBAL NAMESPACE QUALIFIER

The `::` operator provides an alternative way to access types in namespaces. This might be necessary if you want to use a namespace alias and there is ambiguity between the alias and the actual namespace hierarchy. If that is the case, then the namespace hierarchy is given priority over the namespace alias. To see what this means, consider the following code:

```
using MyNamespaceAlias = MyRootNamespace.MyNestedNamespace;
namespace MyRootNamespace
{
    namespace MyNamespaceAlias
    {
        public class MyClass {}
    }
    namespace MyNestedNamespace
    {
        public class MyClass {}
    }
}
```

Code in `MyRootNamespace` might use the following to refer to a class:

```
MyNamespaceAlias.MyClass
```

The class referred to by this code is the `MyRootNamespace.MyNamespaceAlias.MyClass` class, not the `MyRootNamespace.MyNestedNamespace.MyClass` class. That is, the namespace `MyRootNamespace.MyNamespaceAlias` has hidden the alias defined by the `using` statement, which refers to `MyRootNamespace.MyNestedNamespace`. You can still access the `MyRootNamespace.MyNestedNamespace` namespace and the class contained within, but it requires different syntax:

```
MyNestedNamespace.MyClass
```

Alternatively, you can use the `::` operator:

```
MyNamespaceAlias::MyClass
```

Using this operator forces the compiler to use the alias defined by the `using` statement, and therefore the code refers to `MyRootNamespace.MyNestedNamespace.MyClass`.

You can also use the keyword `global` with the `::` operator, which is essentially an alias to the top-level, root namespace. This can be useful to make it clearer which namespace you are referring to, as shown here:

```
global::System.Collections.Generic.List<int>
```

This is the class you would expect it to be, the generic `List<T>` collection class. It is not the class defined with the following code:

```
namespace MyRootNamespace
{
    namespace System
    {
        namespace Collections
        {
            namespace Generic
            {
                class List<T> {}
            }
        }
    }
}
```

Of course, you should avoid giving your namespaces names that already exist as .NET namespaces, although similar problems can arise in large projects, particularly if you are working as part of a large team. Using the `::` operator and the `global` keyword might be the only way you can access the types you want.

CUSTOM EXCEPTIONS

Chapter 7 covered exceptions and explained how you can use `try...catch...finally` blocks to act on them. You also saw several standard .NET exceptions, including the base class for exceptions, `System.Exception`. Sometimes it is useful to derive your own exception classes from this base class for use in your applications, instead of using the standard exceptions. This enables you to be more specific with the information you send to whatever code catches the exception, and it enables catching code to be more specific about which exceptions it handles. For example, you might add a new property to your exception class that permits access to some underlying information, making it possible for the exception's receiver to make the required changes, or just provide more information about the exception's cause.

> **NOTE** Two fundamental exception classes exist in the `System` namespace and derive from `Exception`: `ApplicationException` and `SystemException`. `SystemException` is used as the base class for exceptions that are predefined by the .NET Framework. `ApplicationException` was provided for developers to derive their own exception classes, but more recent best practice dictates that you should not derive your exceptions from this class; you should use `Exception` instead.

Adding Custom Exceptions to CardLib

How to use custom exceptions is, once again, best illustrated by upgrading the CardLib project. The Deck.GetCard() method currently throws a standard .NET exception if an attempt is made to access a card with an index less than 0 or greater than 51, but you'll modify that to use a custom exception.

First, you need to create a new class library project called Ch13CardLib, save it in the Beginning-CSharpAndDotNET\Chapter13 directory, and copy the classes from Ch12CardLib as before, changing the namespace to Ch13CardLib as applicable. Next, define the exception. You do this with a new class defined in a new class file called CardOutOfRangeException.cs, which you can add to the Ch13CardLib project with Project ➪ Add Class (you can find this code in Ch13CardLib\CardOutOf-RangeException.cs):

```
public class CardOutOfRangeException : Exception
{
    private Cards deckContents;
    public Cards DeckContents
    {
        get { return deckContents; }
    }
    public CardOutOfRangeException(Cards sourceDeckContents)
       : base("There are only 52 cards in the deck.")
    {
        deckContents = sourceDeckContents;
    }
}
```

An instance of the Cards class is required for the constructor of this class. It allows access to this Cards object through a DeckContents property and supplies a suitable error message to the base Exception constructor so that it is available through the Message property of the class.

Next, add code to throw this exception to Deck.cs, replacing the old standard exception (you can find this code in Ch13CardLib\Deck.cs):

```
public Card GetCard(int cardNum)
{
    if (cardNum >= 0 && cardNum <= 51)
        return cards[cardNum];
    else
        throw new CardOutOfRangeException(cards.Clone() as Cards);
}
```

The DeckContents property in the CardOutOfRangeException class is initialized with a deep copy of the current contents of the Deck object, in the form of a Cards object. This means that you see the contents at the point where the exception was thrown, so subsequent modification to the deck contents will not "lose" this information.

To test this, use the following client code (you can find this code in Ch13CardClient\Program.cs):

```
Deck deck1 = new Deck();
try
{
    Card myCard = deck1.GetCard(60);
}
```

```
catch (CardOutOfRangeException e)
{
    Console.WriteLine(e.Message);
    Console.WriteLine(e.DeckContents[0]);
}
Console.ReadKey();
```

After adding a reference dependency to `Ch13CardLib.dll` and using `Ch13CardLib`, executing the code results in the output shown in Figure 13-1.

C:\BeginningCSharpAndDotNET\Chapter13\Ch13CardClient\Ch13CardClient\bin\Debug\net5.0\Ch13CardClient.exe — □ ×
There are only 52 cards in the deck.
The Ace of Clubs

FIGURE 13-1

Here, the catching code has written the exception `Message` property to the screen. You also displayed the first card in the `Cards` object obtained through `DeckContents`, just to prove that you can access the `Cards` collection through your custom exception object.

EVENTS

This section covers one of the most frequently used OOP techniques in .NET: *events*. You will start, as usual, with the basics—looking at what events are. After that, you will see some simple events in action and learn what you can do with them. Then, you will learn how you can create and use events of your own.

In this chapter, you will complete your `CardLib` class library by adding an event. Finally, because this is the last port of call before arriving at some advanced topics, you will have a bit of fun creating a card game application that uses this class library.

What Is an Event?

Events are like exceptions in that they are *raised* (thrown) by objects, and you can supply code that acts on them. However, there are several important differences, the most important of which is that there is no equivalent to the `try . . . catch` structure for handling events. Instead, you must *subscribe* to them. Subscribing to an event means supplying code that will be executed when an event is raised, in the form of an *event handler*.

Many handlers can be subscribed to a single event, all of which are called when the event is raised. This can include event handlers that are part of the class of the object that raises the event, but event handlers are just as likely to be found in other classes. Take notice that event handlers are called arbitrarily, which means you cannot rely on them being called in any specific order.

Event handlers themselves are simply methods. The only restriction on an event handler method is that it must match the return type and parameters required by the event. This restriction is part of the definition of an event and is specified by a *delegate*.

> **NOTE** *The fact that delegates are used in events is one of the reasons why delegates are so useful. This is why some space was devoted to them in Chapter 6. You might want to review that material to refresh your memory about delegates and how you use them.*

The basic sequence of processing is as follows: First, an application creates an object that can raise an event. For example, suppose an instant messaging application creates an object that represents a connection to a remote user. That connection object might raise an event when a message arrives through the connection from the remote user (see Figure 13-2).

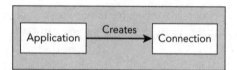

FIGURE 13-2

Next, the application subscribes to the event. Your instant messaging application would do this by defining a method that could be used with the delegate type specified by the event, and then passing a reference to this method to the event. The event handler method might be a method on another object, such as an object representing a display device to show instant messages when they arrive (see Figure 13-3).

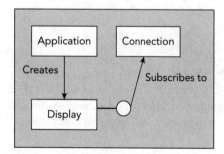

FIGURE 13-3

When the event is raised, the subscriber is notified. When an instant message arrives through the connection object, the event handler method on the display device object is called. Because you are using a standard method, the object that raises the event can pass any relevant information via parameters, making events very versatile. In the example case, one parameter might be the text of the instant message, which the event handler could display on the display device object. This is shown in Figure 13-4.

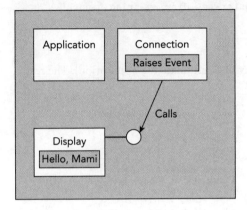

FIGURE 13-4

Handling Events

As previously discussed, to handle an event you need to subscribe to it by providing an event handler method whose return type and parameters match those of the delegate specified for use with the event. The following Try It Out uses a simple timer object to raise events, which results in a handler method being called.

TRY IT OUT   Handling Events: Ch13Ex01

1. Create a new Console Application called Ch13Ex01 and save it in the directory
   `C:\BeginningCSharpAndDotNET\Chapter13`.

2. Modify the code in `Program.cs` as follows:

```
using System;
using System.Timers;
namespace Ch13Ex01
{
   class Program
   {
      static int counter = 0;

      static string displayString =
                       "This string will appear one letter at a time. ";
      static void Main(string[] args)
      {
         Timer myTimer = new Timer(100);
         myTimer.Elapsed += new ElapsedEventHandler(WriteChar);
         myTimer.Start();
         System.Threading.Thread.Sleep(200);
         Console.ReadKey();
```

```
        }
        static void WriteChar(object source, ElapsedEventArgs e)
        {
            Console.Write(displayString[counter++ % displayString.Length]);
        }
    }
}
```

3.   Run the application (once it is running, pressing a key will terminate the application). The result, after a short period, is shown in Figure 13-5.

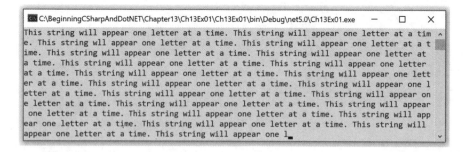

FIGURE 13-5

How It Works

The object you are using to raise events is an instance of the `System.Timers.Timer` class. This object is initialized with a time period (in milliseconds). When the `Timer` object is started using its `Start()` method, a stream of events is raised, spaced out in time according to the specified time period. `Main()` initializes a `Timer` object with a timer period of 100 milliseconds, so it will raise events 10 times a second when started:

```
static void Main(string[] args)
{
    Timer myTimer = new Timer(100);
```

The `Timer` object possesses an event called `Elapsed`, and the event handler required by this event must match the return type and parameters of the `System.Timers.ElapsedEventHandler` delegate type, which is one of the standard delegates defined in the .NET Framework. This delegate specifies the following return type and parameters:

```
void <MethodName>(object source, ElapsedEventArgs e);
```

The `Timer` object sends a reference to itself in the first parameter and an instance of an `ElapsedEvent-Args` object in its second parameter. It is safe to ignore these parameters for now; you'll take a look at them a little later.

In your code you have a suitable method:

```
static void WriteChar(object source, ElapsedEventArgs e)
{
    Console.Write(displayString[counter++ % displayString.Length]);
}
```

This method uses the two static fields of `Program`, `counter` and `displayString`, to display a single character. Every time the method is called, a different character is displayed.

The next task is to hook this handler up to the event—to subscribe to it. To do this, you use the `+=` operator to add a handler to the event in the form of a new delegate instance initialized with your event handler method:

```
static void Main(string[] args)
{
    Timer myTimer = new Timer(100);
    myTimer.Elapsed += new ElapsedEventHandler(WriteChar);
```

This command (which uses slightly strange-looking syntax, specific to delegates) adds a handler to the list that will be called when the `Elapsed` event is raised. You can add as many handlers as you like to this list if they all meet the criteria required. Each handler is called when the event is raised.

All that remains for `Main()` to do is start the timer running:

```
    myTimer.Start();
```

You do not want the application terminating before you have handled any events, so you put the `Main()` method on hold. The simplest way to do this is to request user input, as this command won't finish processing until the user has pressed a key:

```
    Console.ReadKey();
```

Although processing in `Main()` effectively ceases here, processing in the `Timer` object continues. When it raises events it calls the `WriteChar()` method, which runs concurrently with the `Console.ReadLine()` statement. The `System.Threading.Thread.Sleep(200)` statement is included to give the timer the opportunity to start sending messages to the console application.

Note that the syntax for adding an event handler can be simplified slightly using the method group concept introduced in the previous chapter, as follows:

```
    myTimer.Elapsed += WriteChar;
```

The result is the same, but you do not have to explicitly specify the delegate type; it is inferred by the compiler from the context in which you use it. However, many programmers dislike this syntax because it reduces readability—it is no longer possible to tell at a glance what delegate type you are using. Feel free to use this syntax if you prefer, but in this chapter all the delegates you use will be referenced explicitly to make things clearer.

Defining Events

Now it is time to define and use your own events. The following Try It Out implements an example version of the instant messaging scenario introduced earlier in this chapter, creating a `Connection` object that raises events that are handled by a `Display` object.

TRY IT OUT Defining Events: Ch13Ex02

1. Create a new Console Application called Ch13Ex02 and save it in the directory `C:\BeginningC-SharpAndDotNET\Chapter13`.

2. Add a new class called `Connection` and modify `Connection.cs` as follows:

```
using System;
using System.Timers;
namespace Ch13Ex02
{
    public delegate void MessageHandler(string messageText);
    public class Connection
    {
        public event MessageHandler MessageArrived;
        private Timer pollTimer;
        public Connection()
        {
            pollTimer = new Timer(100);
            pollTimer.Elapsed += new ElapsedEventHandler(CheckForMessage);
        }
        public void Connect() => pollTimer.Start();
        public void Disconnect() => pollTimer.Stop();
        private static Random random = new Random();
        private void CheckForMessage(object source, ElapsedEventArgs e)
        {
            Console.WriteLine("Checking for new messages.");
            if ((random.Next(9) == 0) && (MessageArrived != null))
            {
                MessageArrived("Hello Donna!");
            }
        }
    }
}
```

3. Add a new class called `Display` and modify `Display.cs` as follows:

```
namespace Ch13Ex02
{
    public class Display
    {
        public void DisplayMessage(string message)
            => Console.WriteLine($"Message arrived: {message}");
    }
}
```

4. Modify the code in `Program.cs` as follows:

```
static void Main(string[] args)
{
    Connection myConnection = new Connection();
    Display myDisplay = new Display();
    myConnection.MessageArrived +=
            new MessageHandler (myDisplay.DisplayMessage);
    myConnection.Connect();
    Console.ReadKey();
}
```

5. Run the application. The result is shown in Figure 13-6.

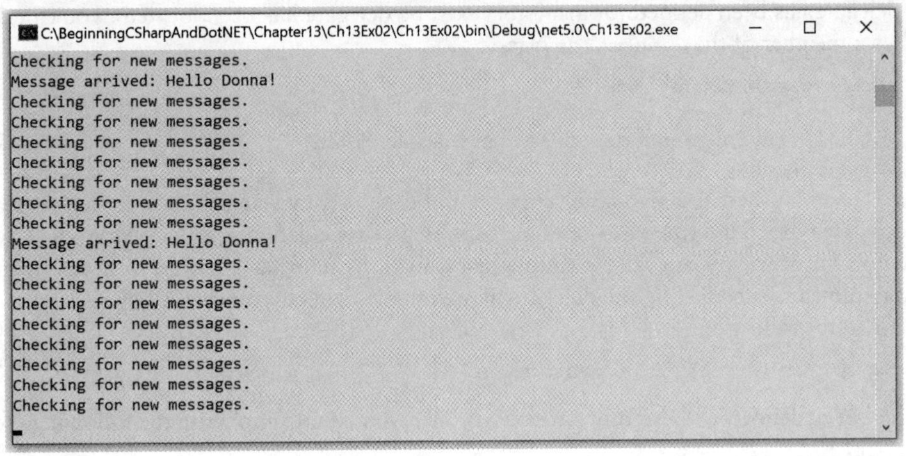

```
C:\BeginningCSharpAndDotNET\Chapter13\Ch13Ex02\Ch13Ex02\bin\Debug\net5.0\Ch13Ex02.exe       —    □    ×
Checking for new messages.
Message arrived: Hello Donna!
Checking for new messages.
Checking for new messages.
Checking for new messages.
Checking for new messages.
Checking for new messages.
Checking for new messages.
Message arrived: Hello Donna!
Checking for new messages.
Checking for new messages.
Checking for new messages.
Checking for new messages.
Checking for new messages.
Checking for new messages.
Checking for new messages.
Checking for new messages.
```

FIGURE 13-6

How It Works

The `Connection` class does most of the work in this application. Instances of this class make use of a `Timer` object much like the one shown in the first example of this chapter, initializing it in the class constructor and providing access to its state (enabled or disabled) via `Connect()` and `Disconnect()`:

```
public class Connection
{
    private Timer pollTimer;
    public Connection()
    {
        pollTimer = new Timer(100);
        pollTimer.Elapsed += new ElapsedEventHandler(CheckForMessage);
    }
    public void Connect() => pollTimer.Start();
    public void Disconnect() => pollTimer.Stop();
    ...
}
```

Also in the constructor, you register an event handler for the `Elapsed` event, just as you did in the first example. The handler method, `CheckForMessage()`, raises an event once every 10 times it is called. You will look at the code for this, but first it would be useful to look at the event definition itself.

Before you define an event, you must define a delegate type to use with the event—that is, a delegate type that specifies the return type and parameters to which an event handling method must conform. You do this using standard delegate syntax, defining it as public inside the `Ch13Ex02` namespace to make the type available to external code:

```
namespace Ch13Ex02
{
    public delegate void MessageHandler(string messageText);
```

This delegate type, called `MessageHandler` here, is a `void` method that has a single `string` parameter. You can use this parameter to pass an instant message received by the `Connection` object to the `Display` object. Once a delegate has been defined (or a suitable existing delegate has been located), you can define the event itself, as a member of the `Connection` class:

```
public class Connection
{
    public event MessageHandler MessageArrived;
```

You simply name the event (here it is `MessageArrived`) and declare it by using the `event` keyword and specifying the delegate type to use (the `MessageHandler` delegate type defined earlier). After you have declared an event in this way, you can raise it simply by calling it by name as if it were a method with the return type and parameters specified by the delegate. For example, you could raise this event using the something similar to the following:

```
MessageArrived("This is a message.");
```

If the delegate had been defined without any parameters, then you could simply use the following:

```
MessageArrived();
```

Alternatively, you could define more parameters, which would require more code to raise the event. The `CheckForMessage()` method looks like this:

```
private static Random random = new Random();
private void CheckForMessage(object source, ElapsedEventArgs e)
{
    Console.WriteLine("Checking for new messages.");
    if ((random.Next(9) == 0) && (MessageArrived != null))
    {
        MessageArrived("Hello Donna!");
    }
}
```

You use an instance of the `Random` class shown in earlier chapters to generate a random number between 0 and 8 and raise an event if the number generated is 0, which should happen 10 percent of the time. This simulates polling the connection to determine whether a message has arrived, which will not be the case every time you check. To separate the timer from the instance of `Connection`, you use a private static instance of the `Random` class.

Note that you supply additional logic. You raise an event only if the expression `MessageArrived != null` evaluates to `true`. This expression, which again uses the delegate syntax in a slightly unusual way, means "Does the event have any subscribers?" If there are no subscribers, then `MessageArrived` evaluates to `null`, and there is no point in raising the event to generate a null reference exception.

The class that will subscribe to the event is called `Display` and contains the single method, `DisplayMessage()`, defined as follows:

```
public class Display
{
    public void DisplayMessage(string message)
        => Console.WriteLine($"Message arrived: {message}");
}
```

All that is left now is for the code in `Main()` to initialize instances of the `Connection` and `Display` classes, hook them up, and start things going. The code required here is like the first example:

```
static void Main(string[] args)
{
    Connection myConnection = new Connection();
    Display myDisplay = new Display();
    myConnection.MessageArrived +=
            new MessageHandler(myDisplay.DisplayMessage);
    myConnection.Connect();
    System.Threading.Thread.Sleep(200);
    Console.ReadKey();
}
```

Again, you call `Console.ReadKey()` to pause the processing of `Main()` once you have started things moving with the `Connect()` method of the `Connection` object and inserted a short delay.

Multipurpose Event Handlers

The delegate you saw earlier, for the `Timer.Elapsed` event, contained two parameters that are of a type often seen in event handlers:

➤ `object source`—A reference to the object that raised the event

➤ `ElapsedEventArgs e`—Parameters sent by the event

The reason the `object` type parameter is used in this event, and indeed in many other events, is that you often use a single event handler for several identical events generated by different objects and are still able to tell which object generated the event.

To explain and illustrate this concept, the next Try It Out extends the last example a little.

TRY IT OUT   Using a Multipurpose Event Handler: Ch13Ex03

1. Create a new Console Application called Ch13Ex03 and save it in the directory `C:\BeginningC-SharpAndDotNET\Chapter13`.

2. Copy the code across for `Program.cs`, `Connection.cs`, and `Display.cs` from Ch13Ex02, making sure that you change the namespaces in each file from `Ch13Ex02` to `Ch13Ex03`.

3. Add a new class called `MessageArrivedEventArgs` and modify `MessageArrivedEventArgs.cs` as follows:

```
namespace Ch13Ex03
{
    public class MessageArrivedEventArgs : EventArgs
    {
        private string message;
        public string Message
        {
```

```
            get { return message; }
        }
        public MessageArrivedEventArgs() =>
            message = "No message sent.";

        public MessageArrivedEventArgs(string newMessage) =>
            message = newMessage;
    }
}
```

4. Modify Connection.cs as follows:

```
namespace Ch13Ex03
{
    // delegate definition removed
    public class Connection
    {
        public event EventHandler<MessageArrivedEventArgs> MessageArrived;
        public string Name { get; set; }
        ...
        private void CheckForMessage(object source, EventArgs e)
        {
            Console.WriteLine("Checking for new messages.");
            if ((random.Next(9) == 0) && (MessageArrived != null))
            {
                MessageArrived(this, new MessageArrivedEventArgs("Hello Mami!"));
            }
        }
        ...
    }
}
```

5. Modify Display.cs as follows:

```
public void DisplayMessage(object source, MessageArrivedEventArgs e)
{
    Console.WriteLine($"Message arrived from: {((Connection)source).Name}");
    Console.WriteLine($"Message Text: {e.Message}");
}
```

6. Modify Program.cs as follows:

```
static void Main(string[] args)
{
    Connection myConnection1 = new Connection();
    myConnection1.Name = "First connection.";
    Connection myConnection2 = new Connection();
    myConnection2.Name = "Second connection.";
    Display myDisplay = new Display();
    myConnection1.MessageArrived += myDisplay.DisplayMessage;
    myConnection2.MessageArrived += myDisplay.DisplayMessage;
    myConnection1.Connect();
    myConnection2.Connect();
    System.Threading.Thread.Sleep(200);
    Console.ReadKey();
}
```

7. Run the application. The result is shown in Figure 13-7.

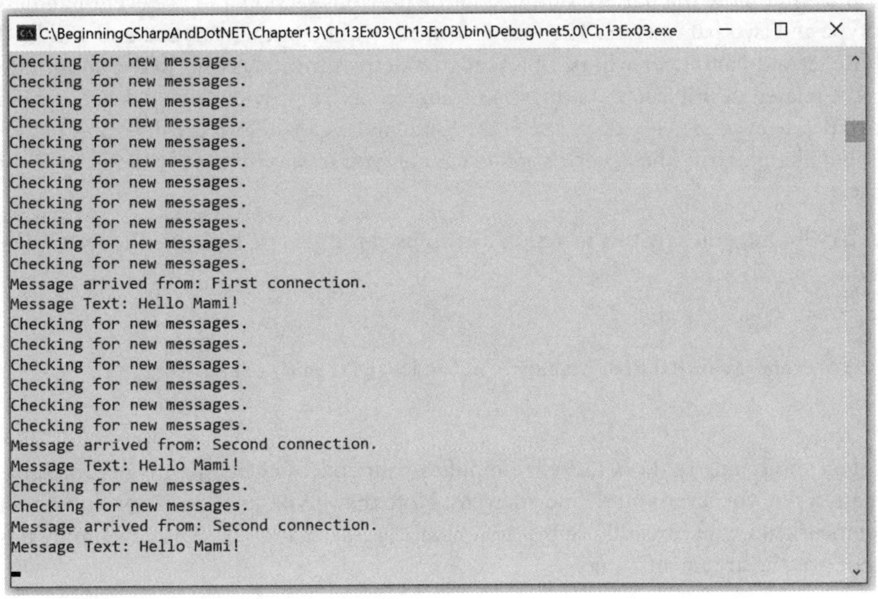

```
C:\BeginningCSharpAndDotNET\Chapter13\Ch13Ex03\Ch13Ex03\bin\Debug\net5.0\Ch13Ex03.exe       —    □    ×
Checking for new messages.
Checking for new messages.
Checking for new messages.
Checking for new messages.
Checking for new messages.
Checking for new messages.
Checking for new messages.
Checking for new messages.
Checking for new messages.
Checking for new messages.
Checking for new messages.
Message arrived from: First connection.
Message Text: Hello Mami!
Checking for new messages.
Checking for new messages.
Checking for new messages.
Checking for new messages.
Checking for new messages.
Message arrived from: Second connection.
Message Text: Hello Mami!
Checking for new messages.
Checking for new messages.
Message arrived from: Second connection.
Message Text: Hello Mami!
```

FIGURE 13-7

How It Works

By sending a reference to the object that raises an event as one of the event handler parameters, you can customize the response of the handler to individual objects. The reference gives you access to the source object, including its properties.

By sending parameters that are contained in a class that inherits from `System.EventArgs` (as `Elapsed-EventArgs` does), you can supply whatever additional information is necessary as parameters (such as the `Message` parameter on the `MessageArrivedEventArgs` class).

In addition, these parameters benefit from polymorphism. You could define a handler for the `MessageArrived` event such as this:

```
public void DisplayMessage(object source, EventArgs e)
{
    Console.WriteLine($"Message arrived from: {((Connection)source).Name}");
    Console.WriteLine($"Message Text: {((MessageArrivedEventArgs)e).Message}");
}
```

The application will execute exactly as it did before, but the `DisplayMessage()` method is now more versatile (in theory at least—more implementation is needed to make this production quality). This same handler could work with other events, such as the `Timer.Elapsed`, although you would have to modify the internals of the handler a bit more such that the parameters sent when this event is raised are handled properly. (Casting them to `Connection` and `MessageArrivedEventArgs` objects in this way will cause an exception; you should use the `as` operator instead and check for `null` values.)

The EventHandler and Generic EventHandler<T> Types

In most cases, you will follow the pattern outlined in the previous section and use event handlers with a `void` return type and two parameters. The first parameter will be of type `object` and will be the event source. The second parameter will be of a type that derives from `System.EventArgs` and will contain any event-related information. As this is so common, .NET provides two delegate types to make it easier to define events: `EventHandler` and `EventHandler<T>`. Both are delegates that use the standard event handler pattern. The generic version enables you to specify the type of event argument you want to use.

In the previous Try It Out, you saw this in action as you used the generic `EventHandler<T>` delegate type as follows:

```
public class Connection
{
    public event EventHandler<MessageArrivedEventArgs> MessageArrived;
    ...
}
```

This is obviously a good thing to do because it simplifies your code. In general, it is best practice to use these delegate types whenever you define an event. Note that if you have an event that does not need event argument data, you can still use the `EventHandler` delegate type. You can simply pass `EventArgs.Empty` as the argument value.

Return Values and Event Handlers

All the event handlers you have seen so far have had a return type of `void`. It is possible to provide a return type for an event, but this can lead to problems because a given event can result in several event handlers being called. If all these handlers return a value, then it can be unclear which value was actually returned.

The system deals with this by allowing you access to only the last value returned by an event handler. That will be the value returned by the event handler to subscribe to an event. Although this functionality might be of use in some situations, it is recommended that you use `void` type event handlers, and avoid `out` type parameters (which would lead to the same ambiguity regarding the source of the value returned by the parameter).

Anonymous Methods

Instead of defining event handler methods, you can choose to use *anonymous methods*. An anonymous method does not actually exist as a method in the traditional sense—that is, it isn't a method on any particular class. Instead, an anonymous method is created purely for use as a target for a delegate.

To create an anonymous method, you need the following code:

```
delegate (parameters)
{
    // Anonymous method code.
};
```

parameters is a list of parameters matching those of the delegate type you are instantiating, as used by the anonymous method code:

```
delegate(Connection source, MessageArrivedEventArgs e)
{
    // Anonymous method code matching MessageHandler event in Ch13Ex03.
};
```

For example, you could use this code to completely bypass the `Display.DisplayMessage()` method in Ch13Ex03:

```
myConnection1.MessageArrived +=
    delegate(object source, MessageArrivedEventArgs e)
    {
        Console.WriteLine($"Message arrived from: {((Connection)source).Name}");
        Console.WriteLine($"Message Text: {e.Message}");
    };
```

An interesting point about anonymous methods is that they are effectively local to the code block that contains them, and they have access to local variables in this scope. If you use such a variable, then it becomes an *outer* variable. Outer variables are not disposed of when they go out of scope as other local variables are; instead, they live on until the anonymous methods that use them are destroyed. This might be some time later than you expect, so it is definitely something to be careful about. If an outer variable takes up a large amount of memory, or if it uses resources that are expensive in other ways (for example, resources that are limited in number), then this could cause memory or performance problems.

EXPANDING AND USING CARDLIB

Now that you have had a look at defining and using events, you can use them in Ch13CardLib. The event you will add to your library will be generated when the last `Card` object in a `Deck` object is obtained by using `GetCard`, and it will be called `LastCardDrawn`. The event enables subscribers to reshuffle the deck automatically, cutting down on the processing necessary by a client. The event will use the `EventHandler` delegate type and will pass as its source a reference to the `Deck` object, such that the `Shuffle()` method will be accessible from wherever the handler is. Add the following code to `Deck.cs` (you can find this code in `Ch13CardLib\Deck.cs`) to define and raise the event:

```
namespace Ch13CardLib
{
    public class Deck : ICloneable
    {
        public event EventHandler LastCardDrawn;
        ...
        public Card GetCard(int cardNum)
        {
            if (cardNum >= 0 && cardNum <= 51)
            {
                if ((cardNum == 51) && (LastCardDrawn != null))
```

```
                         LastCardDrawn(this, EventArgs.Empty);
                   return cards[cardNum];
               }
            else
               throw new CardOutOfRangeException((Cards)cards.Clone());
        }
        ...
   }
```

This is all the code required to add the event to the Deck class definition.

After spending all this time developing the CardLib library, it would be a shame not to use it. Before finishing this section on OOP in C# and the .NET Framework, it's time to have a little fun and write the basics of a card game application that uses the familiar playing card classes.

As in previous chapters, you will add a client console application to the Ch13CardLib solution, add a reference to the Ch13CardLib project, and make it the startup project. This application will be called Ch13CardClient.

To begin, you will create a new class called Player in a new file in Ch13CardClient, Player.cs. You can find this code in Ch13CardClient\Player.cs in this chapter's online download. This class will contain two automatic properties: Name (a string) and PlayHand (of type Cards). Both properties have private set accessors, but despite this, the PlayHand object provides write access to its contents, which enables you to modify the cards in the player's hand.

You'll also hide the default constructor by making it private and supply a public nondefault constructor that accepts an initial value for the Name property of Player instances.

Finally, you'll provide a bool type method called HasWon(), which returns true if all the cards in the player's hand are the same suit (a simple winning condition, but that doesn't matter too much).

Here is the code for Player.cs:

```
using System;
using System.Collections.Generic;
using System.Linq;
using System.Text;
using System.Threading.Tasks;
using Ch13CardLib;
namespace Ch13CardClient
{
    public class Player
    {
        public string Name { get; private set; }
        public Cards PlayHand { get; private set; }
        private Player() {}
        public Player(string name)
        {
            Name = name;
            PlayHand = new Cards();
        }
        public bool HasWon()
        {
            bool won = true;
```

```
              Suit match = PlayHand[0].suit;
              for (int i = 1; i < PlayHand.Count; i++)
              {
                  won &= PlayHand[i].suit == match;
              }
              return won;
          }
       }
   }
```

Next, define a class that will handle the card game itself, called `Game`. This class is found in the file `Game.cs` of the Ch13CardClient project. The class has four private member fields:

➤ `playDeck`—A `Deck` type variable containing the deck of cards to use

➤ `currentCard`—An `int` value used as a pointer to the next card in the deck to draw

➤ `players`—An array of `Player` objects representing the players of the game

➤ `discardedCards`—A `Cards` collection for the cards that have been discarded by players but not shuffled back into the deck

The default constructor for the class initializes and shuffles the `Deck` stored in `playDeck`, sets the `currentCard` pointer variable to 0 (the first card in `playDeck`), and wires up an event handler called `LastCardDrawnEventHandler()` to the `playDeck.LastCardDrawn` event. The handler simply shuffles the deck, initializes the `discardedCards` collection, and resets `currentCard` to 0, ready to read cards from the new deck.

The `Game` class also contains two utility methods: `SetPlayers()` for setting the players for the game (as an array of `Player` objects) and `DealHands()` for dealing hands to the players (seven cards each). The allowed number of players is restricted to between two and seven to ensure that there are enough cards to go around.

Finally, there is a `PlayGame()` method that contains the game logic itself. You'll come back to this method shortly, after you've looked at the code in `Program.cs`. The rest of the code in `Game.cs` is as follows (you can find this code in `Ch13CardClient\Game.cs`):

```csharp
using System;
using System.Collections.Generic;
using System.Linq;
using System.Text;
using System.Threading.Tasks;
using Ch13CardLib;
namespace Ch13CardClient
{
    public class Game
    {
        private int currentCard;
        private Deck playDeck;
        private Player[] players;
        private Cards discardedCards;
        public Game()
        {
            currentCard = 0;
```

```
        playDeck = new Deck(true);
        playDeck.LastCardDrawn += LastCardDrawnEventHandler;
        playDeck.Shuffle();
        discardedCards = new Cards();
    }
    private void LastCardDrawnEventHandler(object source, EventArgs args)
    {
        Console.WriteLine("Discarded cards reshuffled into deck.");
        ((Deck)source).Shuffle();
        discardedCards.Clear();
        currentCard = 0;
    }
    public void SetPlayers(Player[] newPlayers)
    {
        if (newPlayers.Length > 7)
            throw new ArgumentException(
                "A maximum of 7 players may play this game.");
        if (newPlayers.Length < 2)
            throw new ArgumentException(
                "A minimum of 2 players may play this game.");
        players = newPlayers;
    }
    private void DealHands()
    {
        for (int p = 0; p < players.Length; p++)
        {
            for (int c = 0; c < 7; c++)
            {
                players[p].PlayHand.Add(playDeck.GetCard(currentCard++));
            }
        }
    }
    public int PlayGame()
    {
        // Code to follow.
    }
  }
}
```

Program.cs contains the Main() method, which initializes and runs the game. This method performs the following steps:

1. An introduction is displayed.

2. The user is prompted for a number of players between 2 and 7.

3. An array of Player objects is set up accordingly.

4. Each player is prompted for a name, which is used to initialize one Player object in the array.

5. A Game object is created, and players are assigned using the SetPlayers() method.

6. The game is started by using the PlayGame() method.

7. The int return value of PlayGame() is used to display a winning message (the value returned is the index of the winning player in the array of Player objects).

The code for this follows with comments added for clarity (you can find this code in `Ch13CardClient\Program.cs`):

```csharp
static void Main(string[] args)
{
    // Display introduction.
    Console.WriteLine("BenjaminCards: a new and exciting card game.");
    Console.WriteLine("To win you must have 7 cards of the same suit in" +
                      " your hand.");
    Console.WriteLine();
    // Prompt for number of players.
    bool inputOK = false;
    int choice = -1;
    do
    {
        Console.WriteLine("How many players (2-7)?");
        string input = Console.ReadLine();
        try
        {
            // Attempt to convert input into a valid number of players.
            choice = Convert.ToInt32(input);
            if ((choice >= 2) && (choice <= 7))
                inputOK = true;
        }
        catch
        {
            // Ignore failed conversions, just continue prompting.
        }
    } while (inputOK == false);
    // Initialize array of Player objects.
    Player[] players = new Player[choice];
    // Get player names.
    for (int p = 0; p < players.Length; p++)
    {
        Console.WriteLine($"Player {p + 1}, enter your name:");
        string playerName = Console.ReadLine();
        players[p] = new Player(playerName);
    }
    // Start game.
    Game newGame = new Game();
    newGame.SetPlayers(players);
    int whoWon = newGame.PlayGame();
    // Display winning player.
    Console.WriteLine($"{players[whoWon].Name} has won the game!");
    Console.ReadKey();
}
```

Now you come to `PlayGame()`, the main body of the application. Space limitations preclude us from providing a lot of detail about this method, but the code is commented to make it more comprehensible. None of the code is complicated; there is just quite a bit of it.

Play proceeds with each player viewing his or her cards and an upturned card on the table. They can either pick up this card or draw a new one from the deck. After drawing a card, each player must discard one, replacing the card on the table with another one if it has been picked up, or placing the discarded card on top of the one on the table (also adding the discarded card to the discardedCards collection).

As you consider this code, bear in mind how the Card objects are manipulated. The reason why these objects are defined as reference types, rather than value types (using a struct), should now be clear. A given Card object can appear to exist in several places at once because references can be held by the Deck object, the hand fields of the Player objects, the discardedCards collection, and the playCard object (the card currently on the table). This makes it easy to keep track of the cards and is used in the code that draws a new card from the deck. The card is accepted only if it is not in any player's hand or in the discardedCards collection.

The code is as follows:

```csharp
public int PlayGame()
{
    // Only play if players exist.
    if (players == null)
        return -1;
    // Deal initial hands.
    DealHands();
    // Initialize game vars, including an initial card to place on the
    // table: playCard.
    bool GameWon = false;
    int currentPlayer;
    Card playCard = playDeck.GetCard(currentCard++);
    discardedCards.Add(playCard);
    // Main game loop, continues until GameWon == true.
    do
    {
        // Loop through players in each game round.
        for (currentPlayer = 0; currentPlayer < players.Length;
            currentPlayer++)
        {
            //Write out current player, player hand, and the card on the
            // table.
            Console.WriteLine($"{players[currentPlayer].Name}'s turn.");
            Console.WriteLine("Current hand:");
            foreach (Card card in players[currentPlayer].PlayHand)
            {
                Console.WriteLine(card);
            }
            Console.WriteLine($"Card in play: {playCard}");
            // Prompt player to pick up card on table or draw a new one.
            bool inputOK = false;
            do
            {
                Console.WriteLine("Press T to take card in play or D to draw:");
                string input = Console.ReadLine();
                if (input.ToLower() == "t")
```

```
            {
                // Add card from table to player hand.
                Console.WriteLine($"Drawn: {playCard}");
                // Remove from discarded cards if possible (if deck
                // is reshuffled it won't be there any more)
                if (discardedCards.Contains(playCard))
                {
                    discardedCards.Remove(playCard);
                }
                players[currentPlayer].PlayHand.Add(playCard);
                inputOK = true;
            }
            if (input.ToLower() == "d")
            {
                // Add new card from deck to player hand.
                Card newCard;
                // Only add card if it isn't already in a player hand
                // or in the discard pile
                bool cardIsAvailable;
                do
                {
                    newCard = playDeck.GetCard(currentCard++);
                    // Check if card is in discard pile
                    cardIsAvailable = !discardedCards.Contains(newCard);
                    if (cardIsAvailable)
                    {
                        // Loop through all player hands to see if newCard
                        // is already in a hand.
                        foreach (Player testPlayer in players)
                        {
                            if (testPlayer.PlayHand.Contains(newCard))
                            {
                                cardIsAvailable = false;
                                break;
                            }
                        }
                    }
                } while (!cardIsAvailable);
                // Add the card found to player hand.
                Console.WriteLine($"Drawn: {newCard}");
                players[currentPlayer].PlayHand.Add(newCard);
                inputOK = true;
            }
        } while (inputOK == false);
        // Display new hand with cards numbered.
        Console.WriteLine("New hand:");
        for (int i = 0; i < players[currentPlayer].PlayHand.Count; i++)
        {
            Console.WriteLine($"{i + 1}: " +
                            $"{ players[currentPlayer].PlayHand[i] }");
```

```
        }
        // Prompt player for a card to discard.
        inputOK = false;
        int choice = -1;
        do
        {
            Console.WriteLine("Choose card to discard:");
            string input = Console.ReadLine();
            try
            {
                // Attempt to convert input into a valid card number.
                choice = Convert.ToInt32(input);
                if ((choice > 0) && (choice <= 8))
                    inputOK = true;
            }
            catch
            {
                // Ignore failed conversions, just continue prompting.
            }
        } while (inputOK == false);
        // Place reference to removed card in playCard (place the card
        // on the table), then remove card from player hand and add
        // to discarded card pile.
        playCard = players[currentPlayer].PlayHand[choice - 1];
        players[currentPlayer].PlayHand.RemoveAt(choice - 1);
        discardedCards.Add(playCard);
        Console.WriteLine($"Discarding: {playCard}");
        // Space out text for players
        Console.WriteLine();
        // Check to see if player has won the game, and exit the player
        // loop if so.
        GameWon = players[currentPlayer].HasWon();
        if (GameWon == true)
            break;
    }
} while (GameWon == false);
// End game, noting the winning player.
return currentPlayer;
}
```

Figure 13-8 shows a game in progress.

As a final exercise, have a close look at the code in Player.HasWon(). Can you think of a way that you could make this code more efficient, perhaps without having to examine every card in the player's hand every time this method is called?

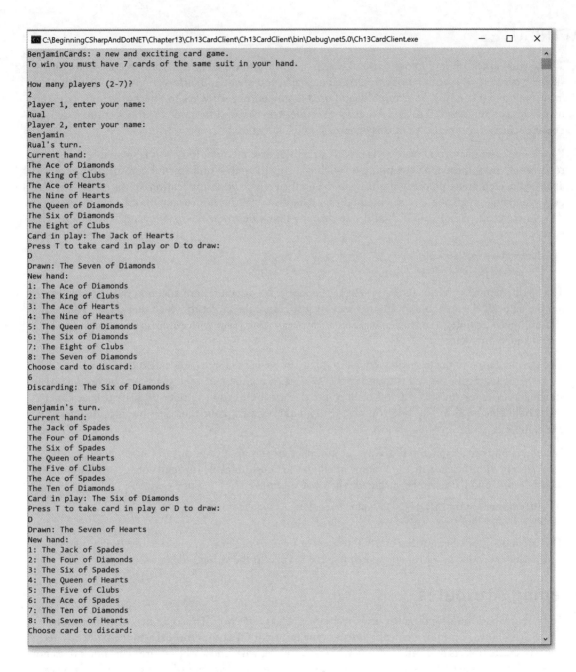

```
C:\BeginningCSharpAndDotNET\Chapter13\Ch13CardClient\Ch13CardClient\bin\Debug\net5.0\Ch13CardClient.exe        —    □    ×
BenjaminCards: a new and exciting card game.
To win you must have 7 cards of the same suit in your hand.

How many players (2-7)?
2
Player 1, enter your name:
Rual
Player 2, enter your name:
Benjamin
Rual's turn.
Current hand:
The Ace of Diamonds
The King of Clubs
The Ace of Hearts
The Nine of Hearts
The Queen of Diamonds
The Six of Diamonds
The Eight of Clubs
Card in play: The Jack of Hearts
Press T to take card in play or D to draw:
D
Drawn: The Seven of Diamonds
New hand:
1: The Ace of Diamonds
2: The King of Clubs
3: The Ace of Hearts
4: The Nine of Hearts
5: The Queen of Diamonds
6: The Six of Diamonds
7: The Eight of Clubs
8: The Seven of Diamonds
Choose card to discard:
6
Discarding: The Six of Diamonds

Benjamin's turn.
Current hand:
The Jack of Spades
The Four of Diamonds
The Six of Spades
The Queen of Hearts
The Five of Clubs
The Ace of Spades
The Ten of Diamonds
Card in play: The Six of Diamonds
Press T to take card in play or D to draw:
D
Drawn: The Seven of Hearts
New hand:
1: The Jack of Spades
2: The Four of Diamonds
3: The Six of Spades
4: The Queen of Hearts
5: The Five of Clubs
6: The Ace of Spades
7: The Ten of Diamonds
8: The Seven of Hearts
Choose card to discard:
```

FIGURE 13-8

ATTRIBUTES

This section takes a brief look at a useful way to provide additional information to code that consumes types that you create: *attributes*. Attributes give you a way to mark sections of code with information that can be read externally and used in any number of ways to affect how your types are used. This is often referred to as *decorating* the code. You can find the code for this section in `CustomAttributes\Program.cs` in this chapter's online download.

For example, let's say you create a class with a really simple method. In fact, it is so simple that you really aren't that interested in stepping through it. Unfortunately—and to your considerable annoyance—you keep doing precisely that as you debug the code in your application. In this situation, it's possible to add an attribute to the method that tells Visual Studio not to step into the code when you debug it; instead, Visual Studio should step through it and on to the next statement. The code for this is as follows:

```
[DebuggerStepThrough]
public void DullMethod() { ... }
```

The attribute in this code is `[DebuggerStepThrough]`. All attributes are added in this way, by enclosing the name of the attribute in square brackets just before the target to which they apply. You can add multiple attributes to a single target either by separating them with commas or by enclosing each one in square brackets.

The attribute used in the preceding code is actually implemented in a class called `Debugger-StepThroughAttribute`, and is found in the `System.Diagnostics` namespace, so you need a `using` statement for that namespace if you want to use this attribute. You can refer to this attribute either by its full name or, as in the code you saw, with an abbreviated name that does not include the suffix `Attribute`.

When you add an attribute in this way, the compiler creates an instance of the attribute class and associates it with the class method. Some attributes are customizable through constructor parameters or properties, and these can be specified when you add the attribute. For example:

```
[DoesInterestingThings(1000, WhatDoesItDo = "voodoo")]
public class DecoratedClass {}
```

This attribute is passing a value of 1000 to the constructor of `DoesInterestingThingsAttribute` and setting the value of a property called `WhatDoesItDo` to the string `"voodoo"`.

Reading Attributes

To read attribute values, you must use a technique called *reflection*. This is a fairly advanced technique that allows you to dynamically inspect type information at runtime, even to the point where you can create objects and call methods without knowing what those objects are. This book does not cover this technique in detail, but you do need to know some basics in order to use attributes. Visit docs.microsoft.com/en-us/dotnet/framework/reflection-and-codedom/reflection for more information about this technique.

Essentially, reflection involves using information stored in `Type` objects (which you have seen in several places in this book) along with types in the `System.Reflection` namespace to work with type information. You have already seen a quick way to get type information from a class with the `typeof` operator, and from an object instance using the `GetType()` method. Using reflection, you can proceed to interrogate member information from the `Type` object. You can then obtain attribute information from the class or its various members.

The simplest way to do this—and the only way you'll see in this book—is to use the `Type.GetCustomAttributes()` method. This method takes up to two parameters and returns an array of `object` instances, each of which is an attribute instance. First, you can optionally pass the type or types of attributes you are interested in (any other attributes will be ignored). If you omit this parameter, then all attributes will be returned. Second, you must pass a Boolean value indicating whether to look just at the class or at the class and all classes that the class derives from.

For example, the following code would list the attributes of a class called `DecoratedClass`:

```
Type classType = typeof(DecoratedClass);
object[] customAttributes = classType.GetCustomAttributes(true);
foreach (object customAttribute in customAttributes)
{
    Console.WriteLine($"Attribute of type {customAttribute} found.");
}
```

Once you have found attributes in this way, you can take whatever action is appropriate for the attribute. This is exactly what Visual Studio does when it encounters the `DebuggerStepThroughAttribute` attribute discussed earlier.

Creating Attributes

You can create your own attributes simply by deriving from the `System.Attribute` class. Sometimes, you do not need to do anything else, as no additional information is required if your code is interested only in the presence or absence of your attribute. However, you can supply nondefault constructors and/or writeable properties if you want the attribute to be customizable.

You also need to decide two things about your attribute: what type of target it can be applied to (class, property, and so on) and whether it can be applied more than once to the same target. You specify this information through an attribute that you apply to your attribute (this has a certain Zen feeling of correctness to it!) called `AttributeUsageAttribute`. This attribute has a constructor parameter of type `AttributeTargets`, which is an enum that allows you to combine its values with the | operator. It also has a Boolean property called `AllowMultiple` that specifies whether the attribute can be applied more than once.

For example, the following code specifies an attribute that can be applied (once) to a class or property:

```
[AttributeUsage(AttributeTargets.Class | AttributeTargets.Method,
                AllowMultiple = false)]
class DoesInterestingThingsAttribute : Attribute
{
    public DoesInterestingThingsAttribute(int howManyTimes)
    {
        HowManyTimes = howManyTimes;
    }
```

```
        public string WhatDoesItDo { get; set; }
        public int HowManyTimes { get; private set; }
    }
```

This attribute, `DoesInterestingThingsAttribute`, can be used as in the earlier code snippet:

```
[DoesInterestingThings(1000, WhatDoesItDo = "karma")]
public class DecoratedClass {}
```

And by modifying the code in the previous section, you can gain access to the properties of the attribute:

```
Type classType = typeof(DecoratedClass);
object[] customAttributes = classType.GetCustomAttributes(true);
foreach (object customAttribute in customAttributes)
{
    Console.WriteLine($"Attribute of type {customAttribute} found.");
    DoesInterestingThingsAttribute interestingAttribute =
        customAttribute as DoesInterestingThingsAttribute;
    if (interestingAttribute != null)
    {
        Console.WriteLine($"This class does {interestingAttribute.WhatDoesItDo} x " +
                        $"{interestingAttribute.HowManyTimes}!");
    }
}
```

Putting everything in this section together and using this code would give you the result shown in Figure 13-9.

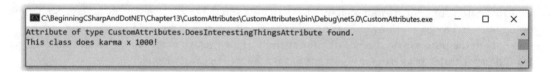

FIGURE 13-9

Attributes can be extremely useful and crop up all over .NET applications—and WPF and Universal Windows applications in particular. You will encounter them repeatedly throughout the remainder of this book.

INITIALIZERS

Up to now you have learned to instantiate and initialize objects in various ways. Invariably, that has required you either to add code to class definitions to enable initialization or to instantiate and initialize objects with separate statements. You have also learned how to create collection classes of various types, including generic collection classes. Again, you might have noticed that there was no easy way to combine the creation of a collection with adding items to the collection.

Object initializers provide a way to simplify your code by enabling you to combine instantiation and initialization of objects. Collection initializers give you a simple, elegant syntax to create and populate collections in a single step. This section explains how to use both of these features.

Object Initializers

Consider the following simple class definition:

```
public class Animal
{
    public string Name { get; set; }
    public int Age { get; set; }
    public double Weight { get; set; }
}
```

This class has three properties that are defined using the automatic property syntax shown in Chapter 10. If you want to instantiate and initialize an object instance of this class, you must execute several statements:

```
Animal animal = new Animal();
animal.Name = "Benjamin";
animal.Age = 42;
animal.Weight = 185.4;
```

This code uses the default, parameterless constructor that is supplied by the C# compiler if you do not include a constructor in your class definition. To simplify this initialization, you can supply an appropriate nondefault constructor:

```
public class Animal
{
    public Animal(string name, int age, double weight)
    {
        Name = name;
        Age = age;
        Weight = weight;
    }
    ...
}
```

That enables you to write code that combines instantiation with initialization:

```
Animal animal = new Animal("Noa", 5, 45.2);
```

This works fine, although it forces code that uses this class to use this constructor. However, this would prevent the previous code, which used a parameterless constructor, from working. Often, particularly when classes must be serializable, it is necessary to provide a parameterless constructor:

```
public class Animal
{
    public Animal() {}
    ...
}
```

Now you have a situation where you can instantiate and initialize the `Animal` class any way you like. However, you have added several lines of code to the initial class definition that do not do anything much other than provide the basic plumbing required for this flexibility.

Enter *object initializers*, which are a way to instantiate and initialize objects without having to add code (such as the constructors detailed here) to a class. When you instantiate an object, you supply values for publicly accessible properties or fields using a name/value pair for each property you want to initialize. The syntax for this is as follows:

```
<ClassName> <variableName> = new <ClassName>
{
    <propertyOrField1> = <value1>,
    <propertyOrField2> = <value2>,
    ...
    <propertyOrFieldN> = <valueN>
};
```

For example, you could rewrite the code shown earlier, which instantiates and initializes an object of type `Animal`, as follows:

```
Animal animal = new Animal
{
    Name = "Lea",
    Age = 14,
    Weight = 35.2
};
```

Often you can put code like that on a single line without seriously degrading readability.

When you use an object initializer, you do not have to explicitly call a constructor of the class. If you omit the constructor parentheses (as in the previous code), the default parameterless constructor is called automatically. This happens before any parameter values are set by the initializer, which enables you to provide default values for parameters in the default constructor if desired. Alternatively, you can call a specific constructor. Again, this constructor is called first, so any initialization of public properties that takes place in the constructor might be overridden by values that you provide in the initializer. You must have access to the constructor that you use (or the default one if you are not explicit) in order for object initializers to work.

If one of the properties you want to initialize with an object initializer is more complex than the simple types used in this example, then you might find yourself using a *nested object initializer*. That simply means using the exact same syntax you have already seen:

```
Animal animal = new Animal
{
    Name = "Rual",
    Age = "80",
    Weight = 172.7,
    Origin = new Farm
    {
        Name = "Circle Perk Ranch",
        Location = "Ann Road",
        Rating = 15
    }
};
```

Here, a property called `Origin` of type `Farm` (not shown here) is initialized. The code initializes three properties of the `Origin` property—`Name`, `Location`, and `Rating`—with values of type `string`, `string`, and `int`, respectively. This initialization uses a nested object initializer.

Note that object initializers are not a replacement for nondefault constructors. The fact that you can use object initializers to set property and field values when you instantiate an object does not mean that you will always know what state needs initializing. With constructors, you can specify exactly which values are required for an object to function and then execute code in response to those values immediately.

Also, in the previous example there is another (admittedly quite subtle) difference between using a nested object initializer and using constructors. This difference is the order in which objects get created. With a nested initializer, the top-level object (`Animal`) gets created first. Next, the nested object (`Farm`) is created and assigned to the property `Origin`. If you used a constructor, you would reverse this construction order and pass the `Farm` instance to the constructor of `Animal`. In this simple example, there is no practical difference, but in some circumstances, this might be significant.

Collection Initializers

Chapter 5 described how arrays can be initialized with values using the following syntax:

```
int[] myIntArray = new int[5] { 5, 9, 10, 2, 99 };
```

This is a quick and easy way to combine the instantiation and initialization of an array. Collection initializers simply extend this syntax to collections:

```
List<int> myIntCollection = new List<int> { 5, 9, 10, 2, 99 };
```

By combining object and collection initializers, it is possible to configure collections with simple and elegant code. Rather than code like this:

```
List<Animal> animals = new List<Animal>();
animals.Add(new Animal("Donna", 72, 116));
animals.Add(new Animal("Mary", 53, 132));
animals.Add(new Animal("Andrea", 49, 109.1));
```

You can use the following:

```
List<Animal> moreAnimals = new List<Animal>
{
    new Animal
    {
        Name = "Donna",
        Age = 72,
        Weight = 116
    },
    new Animal
    {
        Name   = "Mary",
        Age    = 53,
        Weight = 132
    },
```

```
        new Animal
        {
            Name   = "Andrea",
            Age    = 49,
            Weight = 109.1
        }
    };
```

This works very well for types that are primarily used for data representation, and as such, collection initializers are a great accompaniment to the LINQ technology described later in the book.

The following Try It Out illustrates how you can use object and collection initializers.

TRY IT OUT | Using Initializers: Ch13Ex04

1. Create a new Console Application called Ch13Ex04 and save it in the directory `C:\BeginningC-SharpAndDotNET\Chapter13`.

2. Right-click the project name in the Solution Explorer window and select the Add Existing Item option.

3. Select the `Animal.cs`, `Cow.cs`, `Chicken.cs`, `SuperCow.cs`, and `Farm.cs` files from the `C:\BeginningCSharpAndDotNET\Chapter12\Ch12Ex04` directory, and click Add.

4. Modify the `namespace` declaration in the file you have added as follows:

```
namespace Ch13Ex04
```

5. Remove the constructors from the `Cow`, `Chicken`, and `SuperCow` classes.

6. Modify the code in `Program.cs` as follows:

```
static void Main(string[] args)
{
    Farm<Animal> farm = new Farm<Animal>
    {
        new Cow { Name="Lea" },
        new Chicken { Name="Noa" },
        new Chicken(),
        new SuperCow { Name="Andrea" }
    };
    farm.MakeNoises();
    Console.ReadKey();
}
```

7. Build the application. You should receive the build errors shown in Figure 13-10 because there is no `Add(T animal)` method definition in the `Farm` class. It is added in the next step.

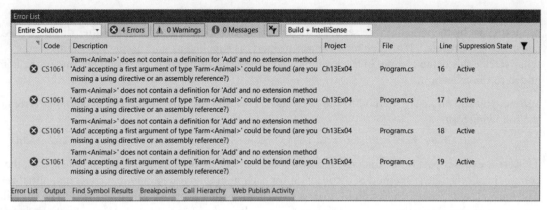

FIGURE 13-10

8. Add the following code to `Farm.cs`:

```
public class Farm<T> : IEnumerable<T> where T : Animal
{
    public void Add(T animal) => animals.Add(animal);
    ...
```

9. Run the application. The result is shown in Figure 13-11.

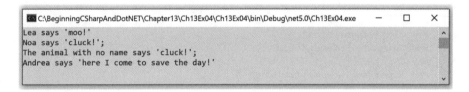

```
Lea says 'moo!'
Noa says 'cluck!';
The animal with no name says 'cluck!';
Andrea says 'here I come to save the day!'
```

FIGURE 13-11

How It Works

This example combines object and collection initializers to create and populate a collection of objects in a single step. It uses the farmyard collection of objects that you have seen in previous chapters, although two modifications are necessary for initializers to be used with these classes.

First, you remove the constructors from the classes derived from the base `Animal` class. You can remove these constructors because they set the animal's `Name` property, which you will do with object initializers instead. Alternatively, you could have added default constructors. In either case, when using default constructors, the `Name` property is initialized according to the default constructor in the base class, which has code as follows:

```
public Animal()
{
    name = "The animal with no name";
}
```

However, when an object initializer is used with a class that derives from `Animal`, recall that any properties set by the initializer are set after the object is instantiated, and therefore after this base class constructor is executed. If a value for the `Name` property is supplied as part of an object initializer, it will override this default value. In the example code, the `Name` property is set for all but one of the items added to the collection.

Second, you add an `Add()` method to the `Farm` class. This is in response to a series of compiler errors of the following form:

```
'Ch13Ex04.Farm<Ch13Ex04.Animal>' does not contain a definition for 'Add'
```

This error exposes part of the underlying functionality of collection initializers. Behind the scenes, the compiler calls the `Add()` method of a collection for each item that you supply in a collection initializer. The `Farm` class exposes a collection of `Animal` objects through a property called `Animals`. The compiler cannot guess that this is the property you want to populate (through `Animals.Add()`), so the code fails. To correct this problem, you add an `Add()` method to the class, which is initialized through the object initializer.

Alternatively, you could modify the code in the example to provide a nested initializer for the `Animals` property as follows:

```
static void Main(string[] args)
{
    Farm<Animal> farm = new Farm<Animal>
    {
        Animals =
        {
            new Cow { Name="Lea" },
            new Chicken { Name="Noa" },
            new Chicken(),
            new SuperCow { Name="Andrea" }
        }
    };
    farm.MakeNoises();
    Console.ReadKey();
}
```

With this code, there is no need to provide an `Add()` method for the `Farm` class. This alternative technique is appropriate when you have a class that contains multiple collections. In this case, there is no obvious candidate for a collection to add to with an `Add()` method of the containing class.

TYPE INFERENCE

Earlier in this book you saw how C# is a *strongly typed* language, which means that every variable has a fixed type and can be used only in code that takes that type into account. In every code example you have seen so far, you have declared variables in one of two ways:

```
<type> <varName>;
<type> <varName> = <value>;
```

The following code shows at a glance what type of variable `<varName>` is:

```
int myInt = 5;
Console.WriteLine(myInt);
```

You can also see that the IDE is aware of the variable type simply by hovering the mouse pointer over the variable identifier, as shown in Figure 13-12.

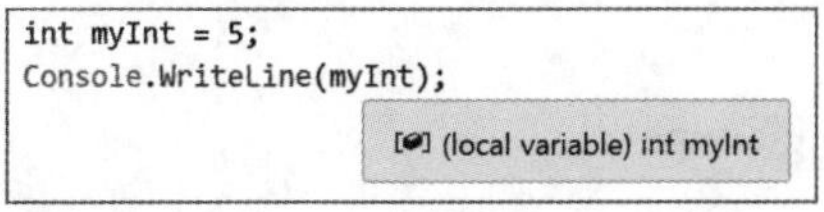

```
int myInt = 5;
Console.WriteLine(myInt);
            [●] (local variable) int myInt
```

FIGURE 13-12

You can use the `var` keyword as an alternative for the explicit type in the preceding code:

```
var <varName> = <value>;
```

In this code, the variable `<varName>` is *implicitly typed* to the type of `<value>`. Note that there is no type called `var`. In the code

```
var myVar = 5;
```

`myVar` is a variable of type `int`, not of type `var`. Again, as shown in Figure 13-13, the IDE is aware of this.

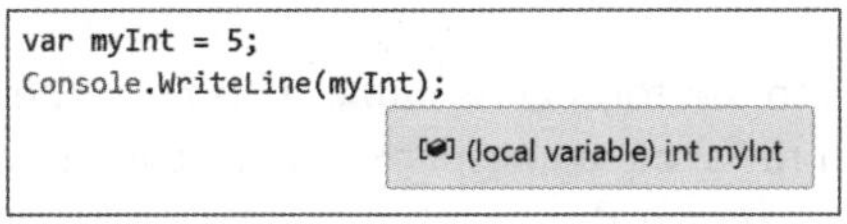

```
var myInt = 5;
Console.WriteLine(myInt);
            [●] (local variable) int myInt
```

FIGURE 13-13

This is an extremely important point. When you use `var` you are not declaring a variable with no type, or even a type that can change. If that were the case, C# would no longer be a strongly typed language. All you are doing is relying on the compiler to determine the type of the variable.

> **NOTE** *The introduction of dynamic types stretched the definition of C# being a strongly typed language, as you will see in the section "Dynamic Lookup" later in this chapter.*

If the compiler is unable to determine the type of variable declared using `var`, then your code will not compile. Therefore, you cannot declare a variable using `var` without initializing the variable at the same time. If you do this, there is no value that the compiler can use to determine the type of the variable. The following code, therefore, will not compile:

```
var myVar;
```

The `var` keyword can also be used to infer the type of an array through the array initializer:

```
var myArray = new[] { 4, 5, 2 };
```

In this code, the type of `myArray` is implicitly `int []`. When you implicitly type an array in this way, the array elements used in the initializer must be one of the following:

➤ All the same type

➤ All the same reference type or `null`

➤ All elements that can be implicitly converted to a single type

If the last of these rules is applied, then the type that elements can be converted to is referred to as the *best* type for the array elements. If there is any ambiguity as to what this best type might be—that is, if there are two or more types that all the elements can be implicitly converted to—your code will not compile. Instead, you receive the error indicating that no best type is available, as in the following code:

```
var myArray = new[] { 4, "not an int", 2 };
```

Note also that numeric values are never interpreted as nullable types, so the following code will not compile:

```
var myArray = new[] { 4, null, 2 };
```

You can, however, use a standard array initializer to make this work:

```
var myArray = new int?[] { 4, null, 2 };
```

A final point: The identifier `var` is not a forbidden identifier to use for a class name. This means, for example, that if your code has a class called `var` in scope (in the same namespace or in a referenced namespace), then you cannot use implicit typing with the `var` keyword.

In itself, type inference is not particularly useful because in the code you've seen in this section it only serves to complicate things. Using `var` makes it more difficult to see at a glance the type of a given variable. However, as you will see later in this chapter, the concept of inferred types is important because it underlies other techniques. The next subject, anonymous types, is one for which inferred types are essential.

ANONYMOUS TYPES

After programming for a while, you might find, especially in database applications, that you spend a lot of time creating simple, dull classes for data representation. It is not unusual to have families of classes that do absolutely nothing other than expose properties. The `Animal` class shown earlier in this chapter is a perfect example:

```
public class Animal
{
    public string Name { get; set; }
    public int Age { get; set; }
    public double Weight { get; set; }
}
```

This class does not do anything—it merely stores structured data. In database or spreadsheet terms, you could think of this class as representing a row in a table. A collection class that could hold instances of this class would be a representation of multiple rows in a table or spreadsheet.

This is a perfectly acceptable use of classes, but writing the code for these classes can become monotonous, and any modifications to the underlying data schema requires you to add, remove, or modify the code that defines the classes.

Anonymous types are a way to simplify this programming model. The idea behind anonymous types is that rather than define these simple data storage types, you can instead use the C# compiler to automatically create types based on the data that you want to store in them.

The preceding `Animal` type can be instantiated as follows:

```
Animal animal = new Animal
{
    Name = "Benjamin",
    Age = 49,
    Weight = 185.4
};
```

Alternatively, you could use an anonymous type, as in the following code:

```
var animal = new
{
    Name = "Lea",
    Age = 14,
    Weight = 35.2
};
```

There are two differences here. First, the `var` keyword is used. That is because anonymous types do not have a type identifier that you can use. Internally they do have an identifier, as you will see in a moment, but it is not available to you in your code. Second, no type name is specified after the `new` keyword. That is how the compiler knows you want to use an anonymous type.

The IDE detects the anonymous type definition and updates IntelliSense accordingly. With the preceding declaration, you can see the anonymous type, as shown in Figure 13-14.

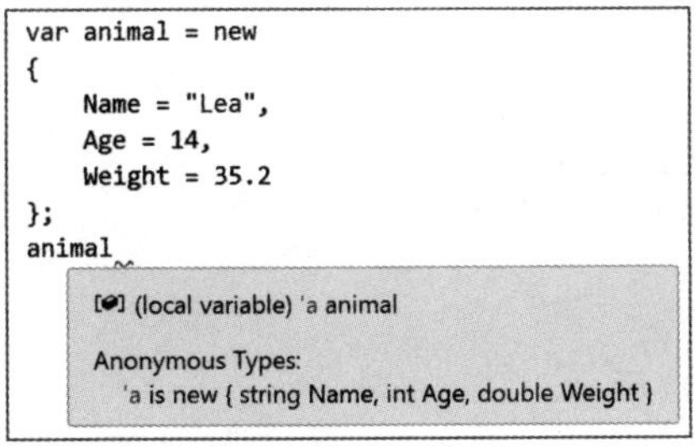

```
var animal = new
{
    Name = "Lea",
    Age = 14,
    Weight = 35.2
};
animal
```

[●] (local variable) 'a animal

Anonymous Types:
    'a is new { string Name, int Age, double Weight }

FIGURE 13-14

Here, internally, the type of the variable `animal` is a. Obviously, you can't use this type in your code—it's not even a legal identifier name. The ' is simply the symbol used to denote an anonymous type in IntelliSense. IntelliSense also enables you to inspect the members of the anonymous type, as shown in Figure 13-15.

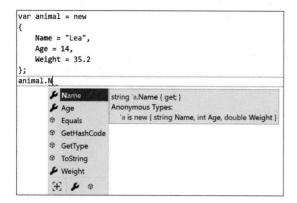

FIGURE 13-15

Note that the properties shown here are defined as *read-only* properties. This means that if you want to be able to change the values of properties in your data storage objects, you cannot use anonymous types.

The other members of anonymous types are implemented, as shown in the following Try It Out.

TRY IT OUT   Using Anonymous Types: Ch13Ex05

1. Create a new Console Application called Ch13Ex05 and save it in the directory `C:\BeginningC-SharpAndDotNET\Chapter13`.

2. Modify the code in `Program.cs` as follows:

```
static void Main(string[] args)
{
    var  animals = new[]
    {
        new { Name = "Benjamin",  Age = 49,  Weight = 185 },
        new { Name = "Benjamin",  Age = 49,  Weight = 185 },
        new { Name = "Andrea",  Age = 48,  Weight = 109 }
    };
    Console.WriteLine(animals[0].ToString());
    Console.WriteLine(animals[0].GetHashCode());
    Console.WriteLine(animals[1].GetHashCode());
    Console.WriteLine(animals[2].GetHashCode());
    Console.WriteLine(animals[0].Equals(animals[1]));
    Console.WriteLine(animals[0].Equals(animals[2]));
    Console.WriteLine(animals[0] == animals[1]);
    Console.WriteLine(animals[0] == animals[2]);
    Console.ReadKey();
}
```

3. Run the application. The result is shown in Figure 13-16.

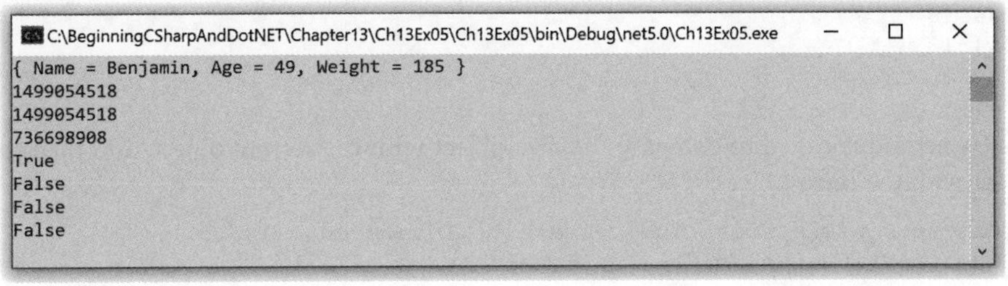

```
C:\BeginningCSharpAndDotNET\Chapter13\Ch13Ex05\Ch13Ex05\bin\Debug\net5.0\Ch13Ex05.exe          —    □    ✕
{ Name = Benjamin, Age = 49, Weight = 185 }
1499054518
1499054518
736698908
True
False
False
False
```

FIGURE 13-16

How It Works

In this example, you create an array of anonymous type objects that you then proceed to use to perform tests of the members supplied by anonymous types. The code to create the array of anonymously typed objects is as follows:

```
var  animals = new[]
{
   new {  Name = "Benjamin",  Age = 49,  Weight = 185 },
   ...
};
```

This uses an array that is implicitly typed to an anonymous type, using a combination of syntax from this section and the "Type Inference" section earlier in this chapter. The result is that the animals variable contains three instances of an anonymous type.

The first thing the code does after creating this array is output the result of calling ToString() on the first anonymous object type:

```
Console.WriteLine(animals[0].ToString());
```

This results in the following output:

```
{ Name = Benjamin, Age = 49, Weight = 185 }
```

The implementation of ToString() in an anonymous type outputs the values of each property defined for the type.

The code next calls GetHashCode() on each of the array's three objects:

```
Console.WriteLine(animals[0].GetHashCode());
Console.WriteLine(animals[1].GetHashCode());
Console.WriteLine(animals[2].GetHashCode());
```

When implemented, GetHashCode() should return a unique integer for an object based on the object's state. The first two objects in the array have the same property values, and therefore the same state. The result of these calls is the same integer for each of these objects, but a different integer for the third object. The output will be something similar as the following. The first two numbers may not be what you see here but they should be the same:

```
1499054518
1499054518
736698908
```

Next, the `Equals()` method is called to compare the first object with the second object, and then to compare the first object with the third object:

```
Console.Console.WriteLine(animals[0].Equals(animals[1]));
Console.WriteLine(animals[0].Equals(animals[2]));
```

The result is as follows:

```
True
False
```

The implementation of `Equals()` in anonymous types compares the state of objects. The result is `true` where every property of one object contains the same value as the comparable property on another object.

That is not what happens when you use the `==` operator, however. The `==` operator, as shown in previous chapters, compares object references. The last section of code performs the same comparisons as the previous section of code but uses `==` instead of `Equals()`:

```
Console.WriteLine(animals[0] == animals[1]);
Console.WriteLine(animals[0] == animals[2]);
```

Each entry in the `animals` array refers to a different instance of the anonymous type, so the result is `false` in both cases. The output is as expected:

```
False
False
```

Interestingly, when you create instances of the anonymous types in this example, the compiler notices that the parameters are the same and creates three instances of the *same* anonymous type—not three separate anonymous types. However, this does not mean that when you instantiate an object from an anonymous type the compiler looks for a type to match it with. Even if you have defined a class elsewhere that has matching properties, if you use anonymous type syntax, then an anonymous type will be created (or reused as in this example).

DYNAMIC LOOKUP

The `var` keyword, as described earlier, is not in itself a type, and so it does not break the "strongly typed" methodology of C#. From the time `var` was introduced onward, though, things have become a little less fixed. There is another related concept referred to as *dynamic variables*, which, as their name suggests, are variables that do not have a fixed type.

The main motivation for this is that there are many situations where you will want to use C# to manipulate objects created by another language. This includes interoperability with older technologies such as the Component Object Model (COM), as well as dealing with dynamic languages such as JavaScript, Python, and Ruby. Without going into too much implementation detail, using C# to access methods and properties of objects created by these languages has, in the past, involved awkward syntax. For example, say you had code that obtained an object from JavaScript with a method called `Add()` that added two numbers. Without dynamic lookup, your code to call this method might look something like the following:

```
ScriptObject jsObj = SomeMethodThatGetsTheObject();
int sum = Convert.ToInt32(jsObj.Invoke("Add", 2, 3));
```

The `ScriptObject` type (not covered in depth here) provides a way to access a JavaScript object, but even this is unable to give you the capability to do the following:

```
int sum = jsObj.Add(2, 3);
```

Dynamic lookup changes everything—enabling you to write code just like the preceding. However, as you will see in the following sections, this power comes at a price.

Another situation in which dynamic lookup can assist you is when you are dealing with a C# object whose type you do not know. This might sound like an odd situation, but it happens more often than you might think. It is also an important capability when writing generic code that can deal with whatever input it receives. The "old" way to deal with this situation is called *reflection*, which involves using type information to access types and members. The syntax for using reflection to access type members such as methods is quite similar to the syntax used to access the JavaScript object, as shown in the preceding code. In other words, it's messy.

Under the hood, dynamic lookup is supported by the Dynamic Language Runtime (DLR) which is part of the .NET runtime, just as the CLR is. An exact description of the DLR and how it makes interoperability easier is beyond the scope of this book; here you're more interested in how to use it in C#. You can read more about DLR here: `docs.microsoft.com/en-us/dotnet/framework/reflection-and-codedom/dynamic-language-runtime-overview`.

The dynamic Type

The `dynamic` keyword, which you can use to define variables, is shown in this example:

```
dynamic myDynamicVar;
```

Unlike the `var` keyword introduced earlier, there really is a `dynamic` type, so there is no need to initialize the value of `myDynamicVar` when it is declared.

> **NOTE** Unusually, the `dynamic` type exists only at compile time; at runtime, the `System.Object` type is used instead. This is a minor implementation detail but one that is worth remembering, as it might clarify some of the discussion that follows.

Once you have a dynamic variable, you can proceed to access its members (the code to obtain a value for the variable is not shown here):

```
myDynamicVar.DoSomething("With this!");
```

Regardless of the value that `myDynamicVar` contains, this code will compile. However, if the requested member does not exist, you will get an exception when this code is executed, of type `Runtime-BinderException`.

In effect, what you are doing with code like this is providing a "recipe" that should be applied at runtime. The value of `myDynamicVar` will be examined, and a method called `DoSomething()` with a single string parameter will be located and called at the point where it is required.

This is best illustrated with an example.

> **WARNING** *The following example is for illustrative purposes only! In general, you should use dynamic types only when they are your only option—for example, when you are dealing with non-.NET objects.*

TRY IT OUT   Using Dynamic Types: Ch13Ex06

1. Create a new Console Application called Ch13Ex06 and save it in the directory `C:\BeginningC-SharpAndDotNET\Chapter13`.

2. Modify the code in `Program.cs` as follows:

```
using System;
using Microsoft.CSharp.RuntimeBinder;
namespace Ch13Ex06
{
    class MyClass1
    {
        public int Add(int var1, int var2) => var1 + var2;
    }
    class MyClass2 {}
    class Program
    {
        static int callCount = 0;
        static dynamic GetValue()
        {
            if (callCount++ == 0)
            {
                return new MyClass1();
            }
            return new MyClass2();
        }
        static void Main(string[] args)
        {
            try
            {
```

```
                dynamic firstResult = GetValue();
                dynamic secondResult = GetValue();
                Console.WriteLine($"firstResult is: {firstResult.ToString()}");
                Console.WriteLine($"secondResult is: {secondResult.ToString()}");
                Console.WriteLine($"firstResult call: {firstResult.Add(2, 3)}");
                Console.WriteLine($"secondResult call: {secondResult.Add(2, 3)}");
            }
            catch (RuntimeBinderException ex)
            {
                Console.WriteLine(ex.Message);
            }
            Console.ReadKey();
        }
    }
}
```

3. Run the application. The result is shown in Figure 13-17.

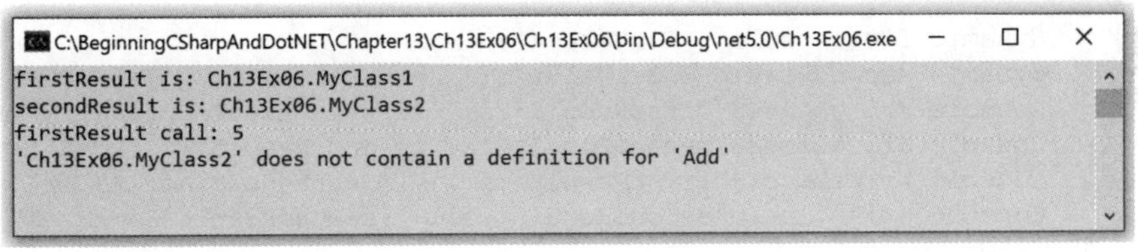

```
C:\BeginningCSharpAndDotNET\Chapter13\Ch13Ex06\Ch13Ex06\bin\Debug\net5.0\Ch13Ex06.exe   —   □   ×
firstResult is: Ch13Ex06.MyClass1
secondResult is: Ch13Ex06.MyClass2
firstResult call: 5
'Ch13Ex06.MyClass2' does not contain a definition for 'Add'
```

FIGURE 13-17

How It Works

In this example, you use a method that returns one of two types of objects to obtain a dynamic value, and then attempts to use the object obtained. The code compiles without any trouble, but an exception is thrown (and handled) when an attempt is made to access a nonexistent method.

To begin, you add a using statement for the namespace that contains the RuntimeBinderException exception:

```
using Microsoft.CSharp.RuntimeBinder;
```

Next, you define two classes, MyClass1 and MyClass2, where MyClass1 has an Add() method and MyClass2 has no members:

```
class MyClass1
{
    public int Add(int var1, int var2) => var1 + var2;
}
class MyClass2 { }
```

You also add a field (callCount) and a method (GetValue()) to the Program class to provide a way to obtain an instance of one of these classes:

```
static int callCount = 0;
static dynamic GetValue()
{
```

```
        if (callCount++ == 0)
        {
            return new MyClass1();
        }
        return new MyClass2();
    }
```

A simple call counter is used so that this method returns an instance of `MyClass1` the first time it is called, and instances of `MyClass2` thereafter. Note that the `dynamic` keyword can be used as a return type for a method.

Next, the code in `Main()` calls the `GetValue()` method twice and then attempts to call `GetString()` and `Add()` on both values returned in turn. This code is placed in a `try...catch` block to trap any exceptions of type `RuntimeBinderException` that occur:

```
static void Main(string[] args)
{
    try
    {
        dynamic firstResult = GetValue();
        dynamic secondResult = GetValue();
        Console.WriteLine($"firstResult is: {firstResult.ToString()}");
        Console.WriteLine($"secondResult is: {secondResult.ToString()}");
        Console.WriteLine($"firstResult call: {firstResult.Add(2, 3)}");
        Console.WriteLine($"secondResult call: {secondResult.Add(2, 3)}");
    }
    catch (RuntimeBinderException ex)
    {
        Console.WriteLine(ex.Message);
    }
    Console.ReadKey();
}
```

Sure enough, an exception is thrown when `secondResult.Add()` is called, as no such method exists on `MyClass2`. The exception message tells you exactly that.

The `dynamic` keyword can also be used in other places where a type name is required, such as for method parameters. You could rewrite the `Add()` method as follows:

```
public int Add(dynamic var1, dynamic var2) => var1 + var2;
```

This would have no effect on the result. In this case, at runtime the values passed to `var1` and `var2` are inspected to determine whether a compatible operator definition for + exists. In the case of two int values being passed, such an operator does exist. If incompatible values are used, a `RuntimeBinderException` exception is thrown. For example, if you try,

```
Console.WriteLine("firstResult call: {0}", firstResult.Add("2", 3));
```

the exception message will be as follows:

```
Cannot implicitly convert type 'string' to 'int'
```

The lesson to be learned here is that dynamic types are very powerful, but there's a warning to learn, too. These sorts of exceptions are entirely avoidable if you use strong typing instead of dynamic typing. For most C# code that you write, avoid the `dynamic` keyword. However, if a situation arises where you need to use it, use it and love it—and spare a thought for those poor programmers of the past who didn't have this powerful tool at their disposal.

ADVANCED METHOD PARAMETERS

There are numerous possibilities when defining and using method parameters. These were created primarily in response to a specific problem that arises when using interfaces defined externally, such as the Microsoft Office programming model. Here, certain methods expose a vast number of parameters, many of which are not required for every call. In the past, this has meant that a way to specify missing parameters has been necessary, or that a lot of nulls appear in code:

```
RemoteCall(var1, var2, null, null, null, null, null);
```

In this code, it is not at all obvious what the `null` values refer to, or why they have been omitted.

Perhaps, in an ideal world, there would be multiple overloads of this `RemoteCall()` method, including one that only required two parameters as follows:

```
RemoteCall(var1, var2);
```

However, this would require many more methods with alternative combinations of parameters, which in itself would cause more problems (more code to maintain, increased code complexity, and so on).

Languages such as Visual Basic have dealt with this situation in a different way, by allowing named and optional parameters. This became possible in C#, demonstrating one way in which the evolution of all .NET languages is converging.

In the following sections, you will see how to use these parameter types.

Optional Parameters

Often when you call a method, you pass in the same value for a particular parameter. This can be a Boolean value, for example, which might control a nonessential part of the method's operation. To be more specific, consider the following method definition:

```
public List<string> GetWords(string sentence, bool capitalizeWords)
{
    ...
}
```

Regardless of the value passed into the `capitalizeWords` parameter, this method will return a list of `string` values, each of which is a word from the input sentence. Depending on how this method was used, you might occasionally want to capitalize the list of words returned (perhaps you are formatting a heading such as the one for this section, "Optional Parameters"). In most cases, though, you might not want to do this, so most calls would be as follows:

```
List<string> words = GetWords(sentence, false);
```

To make this the "default" behavior, you might declare a second method as follows:

```
public List<string> GetWords(string sentence) => GetWords(sentence, false);
```

This method calls into the second method, passing a value of `false` for `capitalizeWords`.

There is nothing wrong with doing this, but you can probably imagine how complicated this would become in a situation where many more parameters were used.

An alternative is to make the `capitalizeWords` parameter an *optional parameter*. This involves defining the parameter as optional in the method definition by providing a default value that will be used if none is supplied, as follows:

```
public List<string> GetWords(string sentence, bool capitalizeWords = false)
{
    ...
}
```

If you were to define a method in this way, then you could supply either one or two parameters, where the second parameter is required only if you want `capitalizeWords` to be `true`. Overloaded methods must differ from those with optional parameters. For example, if a method takes two optional `int` parameters, then you cannot have overloaded versions that take no parameters, one `int`, or two `int`s because the compiler will not be able to tell whether to use them or the method with the optional parameters.

Optional Parameter Values

As described in the previous section, a method definition defines an optional parameter with syntax as follows:

```
<parameterType> <parameterName> = <defaultValue>
```

There are restrictions on what you can use for the `<defaultValue>` default value. Default values must be literal values, constant values, or default value type values. The following, therefore, will not compile:

```
public bool CapitalizationDefault;
public List<string> GetWords(string sentence,
    bool capitalizeWords = CapitalizationDefault)
{
    ...
}
```

To make this work, the `CapitalizationDefault` value must be defined as a constant:

```
public const bool CapitalizationDefault = false;
```

Whether it makes sense to do this depends on the situation; in most cases you will probably be better off providing a literal value as in the previous section.

The OptionalAttribute Attribute

As an alternative to the syntax described in the previous sections, you can define optional parameters using the `OptionalAttribute` attribute as follows:

```
[Optional] <parameterType> <parameterName>
```

This attribute is found in the `System.Runtime.InteropServices` namespace. Note that if you use this syntax there is no way to provide a default value for the parameter.

Optional Parameter Order

When you use optional values, they must appear at the end of the list of parameters for a method. No parameters without default values can appear after any parameters with default values.

The following code, therefore, is illegal:

```
public List<string> GetWords(bool capitalizeWords = false, string sentence)
{
    ...
}
```

Here, `sentence` is a required parameter, and must therefore appear before the optional `capital-izedWords` parameter.

Named Parameters

When you use optional parameters, you might find yourself in a situation where a particular method has several optional parameters. It's not beyond the realm of the imagination, then, to conceive of a situation where you want to pass a value to, say, only the third optional parameter. With just the syntax from the previous section there is no way to do this without supplying values for the first and second optional parameters.

Named parameters enable you to specify whichever parameters you want. This does not require you to do anything in particular to your method definition; it is a technique that you use when you are calling a method. The syntax is as follows:

```
MyMethod(
    <param1Name>: <param1Value>,
    ...
    <paramNName>: <paramNValue>);
```

The names of parameters are the names of the variables used in the method definition.

You can specify any number of parameters you like in this way, as long as the named parameters exist, and you can do so in any order. Named parameters can be optional as well.

You can, if you want, use named parameters for only some of the parameters in a method call. This is particularly useful when you have several optional parameters in a method signature, but some required parameters. You might specify the required parameters first, then finish off with named optional parameters. For example:

```
MyMethod(
    requiredParameter1Value,
    optionalParameter5: optionalParameter5Value);
```

If you mix named and positional parameters, though, note that you must include all positional parameters first before the named parameters. However, you can use a different order if you prefer as long as you use named parameters throughout, as in this example:

```
MyMethod(
    optionalParameter5: optionalParameter5Value,
    requiredParameter1: requiredParameter1Value);
```

If you do this, you must include values for all required parameters. Another reason to use named parameters is to make it easier to understand which values apply to which parameters. For example, if you have 10 parameters, then just listing them in order may make it hard to read.

In the following Try It Out, you will see how you can use named and optional parameters.

TRY IT OUT Using Named and Optional Parameters: Ch13Ex07

1. Create a new Console Application called Ch13Ex07 and save it in the directory `C:\BeginningC-SharpAndDotNET\Chapter13`.

2. Add a class called `WordProcessor` to the project and modify its code as follows:

```
public static class WordProcessor
{
    public static List<string> GetWords(
        string sentence,
        bool capitalizeWords = false,
        bool reverseOrder = false,
        bool reverseWords = false)
    {
        List<string> words = new List<string>(sentence.Split(' '));
        if (capitalizeWords)
            words = CapitalizeWords(words);
        if (reverseOrder)
            words = ReverseOrder(words);
        if (reverseWords)
            words = ReverseWords(words);
        return words;
    }
    private static List<string> CapitalizeWords(List<string> words)
    {
        List<string> capitalizedWords = new List<string>();
        foreach (string word in words)
        {
            if (word.Length == 0)
                continue;
            if (word.Length == 1)
                capitalizedWords.Add(
                    word[0].ToString().ToUpper());
            else
                capitalizedWords.Add(
                    word[0].ToString().ToUpper()
                    + word.Substring(1));
        }
        return capitalizedWords;
    }
```

```csharp
    private static List<string> ReverseOrder(List<string> words)
    {
        List<string> reversedWords = new List<string>();
        for (int wordIndex = words.Count - 1;
            wordIndex >= 0; wordIndex--)
          reversedWords.Add(words[wordIndex]);
        return reversedWords;
    }
    private static List<string> ReverseWords(List<string> words)
    {
        List<string> reversedWords = new List<string>();
        foreach (string word in words)
            reversedWords.Add(ReverseWord(word));
        return reversedWords;
    }
    private static string ReverseWord(string word)
    {
        StringBuilder sb = new StringBuilder();
        for (int characterIndex = word.Length - 1;
            characterIndex >= 0; characterIndex--)
          sb.Append(word[characterIndex]);
        return sb.ToString();
    }
}
```

3. Modify the code in Program.cs as follows:

```csharp
using System.Collections.Generic;
...
static void Main(string[] args)
{
    string sentence = "his gaze against the sweeping bars has "
        + "grown so weary";
    List<string> words;
    words = WordProcessor.GetWords(sentence);
    Console.WriteLine("Original sentence:");
    foreach (string word in words)
    {
        Console.Write(word);
        Console.Write(' ');
    }
    Console.WriteLine('\n');
    words = WordProcessor.GetWords(
        sentence,
        reverseWords: true,
        capitalizeWords: true);
    Console.WriteLine("Capitalized sentence with reversed words:");
    foreach (string word in words)
    {
        Console.Write(word);
        Console.Write(' ');
    }
    Console.ReadKey();
}
```

4. Run the application. The result is shown in Figure 13-18.

FIGURE 13-18

How It Works

In this example, you have created a utility class that performs some simple string manipulation, and used that class to modify a string. The single public method exposed by the class contains one required parameter and three optional ones:

```
public static List<string> GetWords(
    string sentence,
    bool capitalizeWords = false,
    bool reverseOrder = false,
    bool reverseWords = false)
{
    ...
}
```

This method returns a collection of `string` values, each of which is a word from the original input. Depending on which (if any) of the three optional parameters are specified, additional transformations can be made—on the string collection as a whole or on individual word values.

> **NOTE** You will not look at the functionality of the `WordProcessor` class in any more depth here; you are free to browse the code at your leisure. Along the way you might like to think about how this code might be improved. For example, should the word `his` be capitalized as `His`? How would you go about making that change?
>
> When this method is called, only two of the available optional parameters are used; the third parameter (`reverseOrder`) will have its default value of `false`:
>
> ```
> words = WordProcessor.GetWords(
>     sentence,
>     reverseWords: true,
>     capitalizeWords: true);
> ```
>
> Also, note that the two parameters specified are placed in a different order from how they are defined.

As a final point to note, IntelliSense can be quite handy when dealing with methods that have optional parameters. When entering the code for this Try It Out, you might have noticed the tooltip for the `GetWords()` method, shown in Figure 13-19 (you can also see this tooltip by hovering the mouse pointer over the method call as shown).

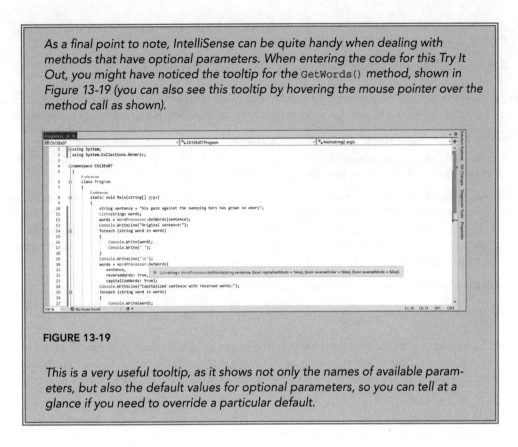

FIGURE 13-19

This is a very useful tooltip, as it shows not only the names of available parameters, but also the default values for optional parameters, so you can tell at a glance if you need to override a particular default.

LAMBDA EXPRESSIONS

Lambda expressions are a construct that you can use to simplify certain aspects of C# programming, in particular when combined with LINQ. They can be difficult to grasp at first, mainly because they are so flexible in their usage. Lambda expressions are extremely useful when combined with other C# language features, such as anonymous methods. Without looking at LINQ, a subject left until later in the book, anonymous methods are the best entry point for examining this subject. Start with a quick refresher.

Anonymous Methods Recap

Previously in this chapter you learned about anonymous methods—methods that you supply inline, where a delegate type variable would otherwise be required. When you add an event handler to an event, the sequence of events is as follows:

1. Define an event handler method whose return type and parameters match those of the delegate required for the event to which you want to subscribe.

2. Declare a variable of the delegate type used for the event.

3. Initialize the delegate variable to an instance of the delegate type that refers to the event handler method.

4. Add the delegate variable to the list of subscribers for the event.

In practice, things are a bit simpler than this because you typically won't bother with a variable to store the delegate—you will just use an instance of the delegate when you subscribe to the event.

This was the case when you previously used the following code:

```
Timer myTimer = new Timer(100);
myTimer.Elapsed += new ElapsedEventHandler(WriteChar);
```

This code subscribes to the `Elapsed` event of a `Timer` object. This event uses the `ElapsedEventHandler` delegate type, which is instantiated using a method identifier, `WriteChar`. The result here is that when the `Timer` raises the `Elapsed` event, the `WriteChar()` method is called. The parameters passed to `WriteChar()` depend on the parameter types defined by the `ElapsedEventHandler` delegate and the values passed by the code in `Timer` that raises the event.

In fact, the C# compiler can achieve the same result with even less code through method group syntax:

```
myTimer.Elapsed += WriteChar;
```

The C# compiler knows the delegate type required by the `Elapsed` event, so it can fill in the blanks. However, you should use this syntax with care because it can make it harder to read your code and know exactly what is happening. When you use an anonymous method, the sequence of events shown earlier is reduced to a single step:

Use an inline, anonymous method that matches the return type, and the parameters of the delegate required by an event to subscribe to that event.

The inline, anonymous method is defined by using the `delegate` keyword:

```
myTimer.Elapsed +=
    delegate(object source, ElapsedEventArgs e)
    {
        Console.WriteLine("Event handler called after {0} milliseconds.",
            (source as Timer).Interval);
    };
```

This code works just as well as using the event handler separately. The main difference is that the anonymous method used here is effectively hidden from the rest of your code. You cannot, for example, reuse this event handler elsewhere in your application. In addition, the syntax used here is, for want of a better description, a little clunky. The `delegate` keyword is immediately confusing because it is effectively being overloaded—you use it both for anonymous methods and for defining delegate types.

Lambda Expressions for Anonymous Methods

This brings you to lambda expressions. Lambda expressions are a way to simplify the syntax of anonymous methods. In fact, they are more than that, but this section will keep things simple for now. Using a lambda expression, you can rewrite the code at the end of the previous section as follows:

```
myTimer.Elapsed += (source, e) => Console.WriteLine("Event handler called after " +
                      $"{(source as Timer).Interval} milliseconds.");
```

At first glance, this looks. . .well, a little baffling (unless you are familiar with so-called functional programming languages such as Lisp or Haskell, that is). However, if you look closer you can see, or at least infer, how this works and how it relates to the anonymous method that it replaces. The lambda expression is made up of three parts:

➤   A list of (untyped) parameters in parentheses

➤   The => operator

➤   A C# statement

The types of the parameters are inferred from the context, using the same logic shown in the section "Anonymous Types" earlier in this chapter. The => operator simply separates the parameter list from the expression body. The expression body is executed when the lambda expression is called.

The compiler takes this lambda expression and creates an anonymous method that works exactly the same way as the anonymous method in the previous section. In fact, it will be compiled into the same or similar Common Intermediate Language (CIL) code.

The following Try It Out clarifies what occurs in lambda expressions.

TRY IT OUT   Using Simple Lambda Expressions: Ch13Ex08

1.   Create a new Console Application called Ch13Ex08 and save it in the directory C:\BeginningC-SharpAndDotNET\Chapter13.

2.   Modify the code in Program.cs as follows:

```
namespace Ch13Ex08
{
    delegate int TwoIntegerOperationDelegate(int paramA, int paramB);
    class Program
    {
        static void PerformOperations(TwoIntegerOperationDelegate del)
        {
            for (int paramAVal = 1; paramAVal <= 5; paramAVal++)
            {
                for (int paramBVal = 1; paramBVal <= 5; paramBVal++)
                {
```

```
            int delegateCallResult = del(paramAVal, paramBVal);
            Console.Write($"f({paramAVal}, " +
                $"{paramBVal})={delegateCallResult}");
            if (paramBVal != 5)
            {
                Console.Write(", ");
            }
        }
        Console.WriteLine();
    }
}
static void Main(string[] args)
{
    Console.WriteLine("f(a, b) = a + b:");
    PerformOperations((paramA, paramB) => paramA + paramB);
    Console.WriteLine();
    Console.WriteLine("f(a, b) = a * b:");
    PerformOperations((paramA, paramB) => paramA * paramB);
    Console.WriteLine();
    Console.WriteLine("f(a, b) = (a - b) % b:");
    PerformOperations((paramA, paramB) => (paramA - paramB)
        % paramB);
    Console.ReadKey();
}
}
}
```

3.   Run the application. The result is shown in Figure 13-20.

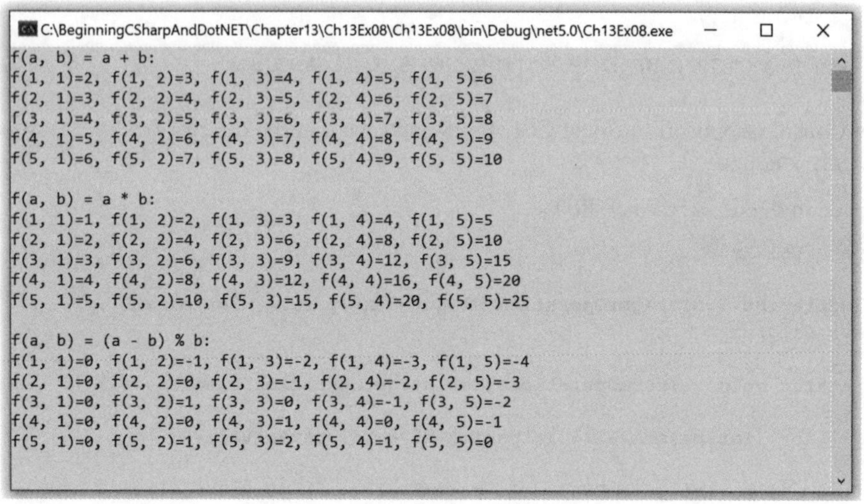

```
C:\BeginningCSharpAndDotNET\Chapter13\Ch13Ex08\Ch13Ex08\bin\Debug\net5.0\Ch13Ex08.exe      —    □    ×
f(a, b) = a + b:
f(1, 1)=2, f(1, 2)=3, f(1, 3)=4, f(1, 4)=5, f(1, 5)=6
f(2, 1)=3, f(2, 2)=4, f(2, 3)=5, f(2, 4)=6, f(2, 5)=7
f(3, 1)=4, f(3, 2)=5, f(3, 3)=6, f(3, 4)=7, f(3, 5)=8
f(4, 1)=5, f(4, 2)=6, f(4, 3)=7, f(4, 4)=8, f(4, 5)=9
f(5, 1)=6, f(5, 2)=7, f(5, 3)=8, f(5, 4)=9, f(5, 5)=10

f(a, b) = a * b:
f(1, 1)=1, f(1, 2)=2, f(1, 3)=3, f(1, 4)=4, f(1, 5)=5
f(2, 1)=2, f(2, 2)=4, f(2, 3)=6, f(2, 4)=8, f(2, 5)=10
f(3, 1)=3, f(3, 2)=6, f(3, 3)=9, f(3, 4)=12, f(3, 5)=15
f(4, 1)=4, f(4, 2)=8, f(4, 3)=12, f(4, 4)=16, f(4, 5)=20
f(5, 1)=5, f(5, 2)=10, f(5, 3)=15, f(5, 4)=20, f(5, 5)=25

f(a, b) = (a - b) % b:
f(1, 1)=0, f(1, 2)=-1, f(1, 3)=-2, f(1, 4)=-3, f(1, 5)=-4
f(2, 1)=0, f(2, 2)=0, f(2, 3)=-1, f(2, 4)=-2, f(2, 5)=-3
f(3, 1)=0, f(3, 2)=1, f(3, 3)=0, f(3, 4)=-1, f(3, 5)=-2
f(4, 1)=0, f(4, 2)=0, f(4, 3)=1, f(4, 4)=0, f(4, 5)=-1
f(5, 1)=0, f(5, 2)=1, f(5, 3)=2, f(5, 4)=1, f(5, 5)=0
```

FIGURE 13-20

How It Works

This example uses lambda expressions to generate functions that can be used to return the result of performing specific processing on two input parameters. Those functions then operate on 25 pairs of values and output the results to the console.

You start by defining a delegate type called `TwoIntegerOperationDelegate` to represent a method that takes two `int` parameters and returns an `int` result:

```
delegate int TwoIntegerOperationDelegate(int paramA, int paramB);
```

This delegate type is used later when you define your lambda expressions. These lambda expressions compile into methods whose return type and parameter types match this delegate type, as you will see shortly.

Next, you add a method called `PerformOperations()`, which takes a single parameter of type `TwoIntegerOperationDelegate`:

```
static void PerformOperations(TwoIntegerOperationDelegate del)
{
```

The idea behind this method is that you can pass it a delegate instance (or an anonymous method or lambda expression, because these constructs compile to delegate instances) and the method will call the method represented by the delegate instance with an assortment of values:

```
for (int paramAVal = 1; paramAVal <= 5; paramAVal++)
{
    for (int paramBVal = 1; paramBVal <= 5; paramBVal++)
    {
        int delegateCallResult = del(paramAVal, paramBVal);
```

The parameters and results are then output to the console:

```
Console.Write($"f({paramAVal}, " +
        $"{paramBVal})={delegateCallResult}");
if (paramBVal != 5)
{
    Console.Write(", ");
}
}
Console.WriteLine();
}
}
```

In the `Main()` method you create three lambda expressions and use them to call `PerformOperations()` in turn. The first of these calls is as follows:

```
Console.WriteLine("f(a, b) = a + b:");
PerformOperations((paramA, paramB) => paramA + paramB);
```

The lambda expression used here is as follows:

```
(paramA, paramB) => paramA + paramB
```

Again, this breaks down into three parts:

1. A parameter definition section. Here there are two parameters, `paramA` and `paramB`. These parameters are untyped, meaning the compiler can infer the types of these parameters according to the context. In this case, the compiler can determine that the `PerformOperations()` method call requires a delegate of type `TwoIntegerOperationDelegate`. This delegate type has two `int` parameters, so by inference both `paramA` and `paramB` are typed as `int` variables.

2. The `=>` operator. This separates the lambda expression parameters from the lambda expression body.

3. The expression body. This specifies a simple operation, which is the summation of `paramA` and `paramB`. Notice that there is no need to specify that this is a return value. The compiler knows that to create a method that can be used with `TwoIntegerOperationDelegate`, the method must have a return type of `int`. Because the operation specified, `paramA + paramB`, evaluates to an `int`, and no additional information is supplied, the compiler infers that the result of this expression should be the return type of the method.

In longhand then, you can expand the code that uses this lambda expression to the following code that uses an anonymous method:

```
Console.WriteLine("f(a, b) = a + b:");
PerformOperations(delegate(int paramA, int paramB)
    {
        return paramA + paramB;
    });
```

The remaining code performs operations using two different lambda expressions in the same way:

```
Console.WriteLine();
Console.WriteLine("f(a, b) = a * b:");
PerformOperations((paramA, paramB) => paramA * paramB);
Console.WriteLine();
Console.WriteLine("f(a, b) = (a - b) % b:");
PerformOperations((paramA, paramB) => (paramA - paramB)
    % paramB);
Console.ReadKey();
```

The last lambda expression involves more calculations but is no more complicated than the others. The syntax for lambda expressions enables you to perform far more complicated operations, as you will see shortly.

Lambda Expression Parameters

In the code you have seen so far, the lambda expressions have used type inference to determine the types of the parameters passed. In fact, this is not mandatory; you can define types if you want. For example, you could use the following lambda expression:

```
(int paramA, int paramB) => paramA + paramB
```

This has the advantage of making your code more readable, although you lose out in both brevity and flexibility. You could use the implicitly typed lambda expressions from the previous Try It Out for delegate types that used other numeric types, such as `long` variables.

Note that you cannot use implicit and explicit parameter types in the same lambda expression. The following lambda expressions will not compile because `paramA` is explicitly typed and `paramB` is implicitly typed:

```
(int paramA, paramB) => paramA + paramB
```

Parameter lists in lambda expressions always consist of a comma-separated list of either all implicitly typed parameters or all explicitly typed parameters. If you have only one implicitly typed parameter, then you can omit the parentheses; otherwise, they are required as part of the parameter list, as shown earlier. For example, you could have the following as a single-parameter, implicitly typed lambda expression:

```
param1 => param1 * param1
```

You can also define lambda expressions that have no parameters. This is denoted by using empty parentheses, `()`:

```
() => Math.PI
```

This could be used where a delegate requiring no parameters but returning a `double` value is required.

Lambda Expression Statement Bodies

In all the code that you have seen so far, a single expression has been used in the statement body of lambda expressions. You have also seen how this single expression has been interpreted as the return value of the lambda expression, which is, for example, how you can use the expression `paramA` `+ paramB` as the statement body for a lambda expression for a delegate with a return type of `int` (assuming both `paramA` and `paramB` are implicitly or explicitly typed to `int` values, as they were in the example code).

An earlier example showed how a delegate with a `void` return type was less fussy about the code used in the statement body:

```
myTimer.Elapsed += (source, e) => Console.WriteLine("Event handler called after " +
                   $"{(source as Timer).Interval} milliseconds.");
```

Here, the statement does not evaluate to anything, so it is simply executed without any return value being used anywhere.

Given that lambda expressions can be visualized as an extension of the anonymous method syntax, you might not be surprised to learn that you can also include multiple statements as a lambda expression statement body. To do so, you simply provide a block of code enclosed in curly braces, much like any other situation in C# where you must supply multiple lines of code:

```
(param1, param2) =>
{
    // Multiple statements ahoy!
}
```

If you use a lambda expression in combination with a delegate type that has a non-void return type, then you must return a value with the return keyword, just like any other method:

```
(param1, param2) =>
{
    // Multiple statements ahoy!
    return returnValue;
}
```

For example, earlier you saw how you could rewrite the following code from the previous Try It Out,

```
PerformOperations((paramA, paramB) => paramA + paramB);
```

as:

```
PerformOperations(delegate(int paramA, int paramB)
    {
        return paramA + paramB;
    });
```

Alternatively, you could rewrite the code as follows:

```
PerformOperations((paramA, paramB) =>
    {
        return paramA + paramB;
    });
```

This is more in keeping with the original code because it maintains implicit typing of the paramA and paramB parameters.

For the most part, lambda expressions are at their most useful—and certainly their most elegant—when used with single expressions. To be honest, if you require multiple statements, your code might read much better if you define a separate, non-anonymous method to use instead of a lambda expression; that also makes your code more reusable.

Lambda Expressions as Delegates and Expression Trees

You have already seen some of the differences between lambda expressions and anonymous methods where lambda methods have more flexibility—for example, implicitly typed parameters. At this point it is worth noting another key difference, although the implications of this will not become apparent until later in the book when you learn about LINQ.

You can interpret a lambda expression in two ways. The first way, which you have seen throughout this chapter, is as a delegate. That is, you can assign a lambda expression to a delegate type variable, as you did in the previous Try It Out.

In general terms, you can represent a lambda expression with up to eight parameters as one of the following generic types, all defined in the System namespace:

➤   Action for lambda expressions with no parameters and a return type of void

➤   Action<> for lambda expressions with up to eight parameters and a return type of void

➤   Func<> for lambda expressions with up to eight parameters and a return type that
     is not void

`Action<>` has up to eight generic type parameters, one for each parameter, and `Func<>` has up to nine generic type parameters, used for up to eight parameters and the return type. In `Func<>`, the return type is always the last in the list.

For example, the following lambda expression, which you saw earlier

```
(int paramA, int paramB) => paramA + paramB
```

can be represented as a delegate of type `Func<int, int, int>` because it has two parameters and a return type all of type `int`. Note that you can use these generic delegate types instead of defining your own in many circumstances. For example, you can use them instead of the `TwoIntegerOperation-Delegate` delegate you defined in the previous Try It Out.

The second way to interpret a lambda expression is as an *expression tree*. An expression tree is an abstract representation of a lambda expression; and as such, it cannot be executed directly. Instead, you can use the expression tree to analyze the lambda expression programmatically and perform actions in response to the lambda expression.

This is, obviously, a complicated subject. However, expression trees are critical to the LINQ functionality you will learn about later in this book. To give a more concrete example, the LINQ framework includes a generic class called `Expression<>`, which you can use to encapsulate a lambda expression. One of the ways in which this class is used is to take a lambda expression that you have written in C# and convert it into an equivalent SQL script representation for executing directly in a database. When you encounter this functionality later in the book, you will be better equipped to understand what is going on, as you now have a thorough grounding in the key concepts that the C# language provides.

Lambda Expressions and Collections

Now that you have learned about the `Func<>` generic delegate, you can understand some of the extension methods that the `System.Linq` namespace provides for array types (which you might have seen popping up in IntelliSense at various points during your coding). For example, there is an extension method called `Aggregate()`, which is defined with three overloads as follows:

```
public static TSource Aggregate<TSource>(
    this IEnumerable<TSource> source,
    Func<TSource, TSource, TSource> func);
public static TAccumulate Aggregate<TSource, TAccumulate>(
    this IEnumerable<TSource> source,
    TAccumulate seed,
    Func<TAccumulate, TSource, TAccumulate> func);
public static TResult Aggregate<TSource, TAccumulate,
                                Aggregate<TSource, TAccumulate, TResult>( TResult>(
    this IEnumerable<TSource> source,
    TAccumulate seed,
    Func<TAccumulate, TSource, TAccumulate> func,
    Func<TAccumulate, TResult> resultSelector);
```

As with the extension method shown earlier, this looks at first glance to be impenetrable, but if you break it down, you can work it out easily enough. The IntelliSense for this function tells you that it does the following:

```
Applies an accumulator function over a sequence.
```

This means that an accumulator function (which you can supply in the form of a lambda expression) will be applied to each element in a collection from beginning to end. This accumulator function must have two parameters and one return value. One input is the current element; the other input is either a seed value, the first value in the collection, or the result of the previous evaluation.

In the simplest of the three overloads, there is only one generic type specification, which can be inferred from the type of the instance parameter. For example, in the following code the generic type specification will be `int` (the accumulator function is left blank for now):

```
int[] myIntArray = { 2, 6, 3 };
int result = myIntArray.Aggregate(...);
```

This is equivalent to the following:

```
int[] myIntArray = { 2, 6, 3 };
int result = myIntArray.Aggregate<int>(...);
```

The lambda expression that is required here can be deduced from the extension method specification. Because the type `TSource` is `int` in this code, you must supply a lambda expression for the delegate `Func<int, int, int>`. For example, you could use one you've seen before:

```
int[] myIntArray = { 2, 6, 3 };
int result = myIntArray.Aggregate((paramA, paramB) => paramA + paramB);
```

This call results in the lambda expression being called twice, first with `paramA = 2` and `paramB = 6`, and once with `paramA = 8` (the result of the first calculation) and `paramB = 3`. The result assigned to the variable `result` will be the `int` value `11`—the summation of all the elements in the array.

The other two overloads of the `Aggregate()` extension method are similar, but enable you to perform slightly more complicated processing. This is illustrated in the following short Try It Out.

TRY IT OUT Using Lambda Expressions with Collections: Ch13Ex09

1. Create a new Console Application called Ch13Ex09 and save it in the directory `C:\BeginningCSharpAndDotNET\Chapter13`.

2. Modify the code in `Program.cs` as follows:

```
using System.Linq;
...
static void Main(string[] args)
{
    string[] people = { "Donna", "Mary", "Lea" };
    Console.WriteLine(people.Aggregate(
        (a, b) => a + " " + b));
    Console.WriteLine(people.Aggregate<string, int>(
        0,
        (a, b) => a + b.Length));
    Console.WriteLine(people.Aggregate<string, string, string>(
        "Some people:",
        (a, b) => a + " " + b,
        a => a));
```

```
        Console.WriteLine(people.Aggregate<string, string, int>(
            "Some people:",
            (a, b) => a + " " + b,
            a => a.Length));
        Console.ReadKey();
    }
```

3. Run the application. The result is shown in Figure 13-21.

C:\BeginningCSharpAndDotNET\Chapter13\Ch13Ex09\Ch13Ex09\bin\Debug\net5.0\Ch13Ex09.exe

```
Donna Mary Lea
12
Some people: Donna Mary Lea
27
```

FIGURE 13-21

How It Works

In this example, you experimented with each of the overloads of the `Aggregate()` extension method, using a string array with three elements as source data.

First, a simple concatenation is performed:

```
WriteLine(people.Aggregate((a, b) => a + " " + b));
```

The first pair of elements is concatenated into a string using simple syntax. After this first concatenation, the result is passed back into the lambda expression along with the third element in the array, in much the same way as you saw `int` values being summed earlier. The result is a concatenation of the entire array, with spaces separating entries. You can achieve this effect in a simpler way using the `string.Join()` method, but the remainder of the overloads illustrated in this example provide additional functionality that `string.Join()` doesn't.

The second overload of the `Aggregate()` function, which has the two generic type parameters `TSource` and `TAccumulate`, is used. In this case the lambda expression must be of the form `Func<TAccumulate, TSource, TAccumulate>`. In addition, a seed value of type `TAccumulate` must be specified. This seed value is used in the first call to the lambda expression, along with the first array element. Subsequent calls take the accumulator result of previous calls to the expression. The code used is as follows:

```
        Console.WriteLine(people.Aggregate<string, int>(
            0,
            (a, b) => a + b.Length));
```

The accumulator (and, by implication, the return value) is of type `int`. The accumulator value is initially set to the seed value of `0`, and with each call to the lambda expression it is summed with the length of an element in the array. The result is the sum of the lengths of each element in the array.

Next you come to the last overload of `Aggregate()`. This takes three generic type parameters and differs from the previous version only in that the return value can be a different type from both the type of the elements in the array and the accumulator value. First, this overload is used to concatenate the string elements with a seed string:

```
WriteLine(people.Aggregate<string, string, string>(
    "Some people:",
    (a, b) => a + " " + b,
    a => a));
```

The final parameter of this method, resultSelector, must be specified even if (as in this example) the accumulator value is simply copied to the result. This parameter is a lambda expression of type Func<TAccumulate, TResult>.

In the final section of code, the same version of Aggregate() is used again, but this time with an int return value. Here, resultSelector is supplied with a lambda expression that returns the length of the accumulator string:

```
Console.WriteLine(people.Aggregate<string, string, int>(
    "Some people:",
    (a, b) => a + " " + b,
    a => a.Length));
```

This example has not done anything spectacular, but it demonstrates how you can use more complicated extension methods that involve generic type parameters, collections, and seemingly complex syntax. You will see more of this later in the book.

EXERCISES

13.1 Write the code for an event handler that uses the general-purpose (object sender, EventArgs e) syntax that will accept either the Timer.Elapsed event or the Connection.MessageArrived event from the code shown earlier in this chapter. The handler should output a string specifying which type of event has been received, along with the Message property of the MessageArrivedEventArgs parameter or the SignalTime property of the ElapsedEventArgs parameter, depending on which event occurs.

13.2 Modify the card game example to check for the more interesting winning condition of the popular card game, rummy. This means that a player wins the game if his or her hand contains two "sets" of cards, one of which consists of three cards and one of which consists of four cards. A set is defined as either a sequence of cards of the same suit (such as 3H, 4H, 5H, 6H) or several cards of the same rank (such as 2H, 2D, 2S).

13.3 Why can't you use an object initializer with the following class? After modifying this class to enable the use of an object initializer, give an example of the code you would use to instantiate and initialize this class in one step:

```
public class Giraffe
{
    public Giraffe(double neckLength, string name)
    {
```

```
        NeckLength = neckLength;
        Name = name;
    }
    public double NeckLength {get; set;}
    public string Name {get; set;}
}
```

13.4 True or false: If you declare a variable of type `var`, you will then be able to use it to hold any object type.

13.5 When you use anonymous types, how can you compare two instances to determine whether they contain the same data?

13.6 Try to correct the following code for an extension method, which contains an error:

```
public string ToAcronym(this string inputString)
{
    inputString = inputString.Trim();
    if (inputString == "")
    {
        return "";
    }
    string[] inputStringAsArray = inputString.Split(' ');
    StringBuilder sb = new StringBuilder();
    for (int i = 0; i < inputStringAsArray.Length; i++)
    {
        if (inputStringAsArray[i].Length > 0)
        {
            sb.AppendFormat("{0}",
                inputStringAsArray[i].Substring(
                    0, 1).ToUpper());
        }
    }
    return sb.ToString();
}
```

13.7 How would you ensure that the extension method in Exercise 13.6 was available to your client code?

13.8 Rewrite the `ToAcronym()` method shown here as a single statement. The code should ensure that strings including multiple spaces between words do not cause errors. Hint: You will require the `?:` tertiary operator, the `string.Aggregate<string, string>()` extension method, and a lambda expression to achieve this.

Answers to the exercises can be found in the Appendix.

▶ **WHAT YOU LEARNED IN THIS CHAPTER**

TOPIC	KEY CONCEPTS
Namespace qualification	To avoid ambiguity in namespace qualification, you can use the :: operator to force the compiler to use aliases that you have created. You can also use the `global` namespace as an alias for the top-level namespace.
Custom exceptions	You can create your own exception classes by deriving from the root `Exception` class. This is helpful because it gives you greater control over catching specific exceptions, and allows you to customize the data that is contained in an exception in order to deal with it effectively.
Event handling	Many classes expose events that are raised when certain triggers occur in their code. You can write handlers for these events to execute code at the point where they are raised. This two-way communication is a great mechanism for responsive code, and prevents you from having to write what would otherwise be complex, convoluted code that might poll an object for changes.
Event definitions	You can define your own event types, which involves creating a named event and a delegate type for any handlers for the event. You can use the standard delegate type with no return type and custom event arguments that derive from `System.EventArgs` to allow for multipurpose event handlers. You can also use the `EventHandler` and `EventHandler<T>` delegate types to define events with simpler code.
Anonymous methods	Often, to make your code more readable, you can use an anonymous method instead of a full event handler method. This means defining the code to execute when an event is raised inline at the point where you add the event handler. You achieve this with the `delegate` keyword.
Attributes	Occasionally, either because the framework you are using demands it or because you choose to, you will make use of attributes in your code. You can add attributes to classes, methods, and other members using `[AttributeName]` syntax, and you can create your own attributes by deriving from `System.Attribute`. You can read attribute values through reflection.
Initializers	You can use initializers to initialize an object or collection at the same time as creating it. Both types of initializers consist of a block of code surrounded by curly brackets. Object initializers allow you to set property values by providing a comma-separated list of property name/value pairs. Collection initializers simply require a comma-separated list of values. When you use an object initializer, you can also use a nondefault constructor.

TOPIC	KEY CONCEPTS
Type inference	The `var` keyword allows you to omit the type of a variable when you declare it. However, this is possible only if the type can be determined at compile time. Using `var` does not break the strong typing methodology of C# as a variable declared with `var` has one and only one possible type.
Anonymous types	For many simple types used to structure data storage, defining a type is not necessary. Instead, you can use an anonymous type, whose members are inferred from usage. You define an anonymous type with object initializer syntax, and every property you set is defined as a read-only property.
Dynamic lookup	Use the `dynamic` keyword to define a dynamic type variable that can hold any value. You can then access members of the contained value with normal property or method syntax, and these are only checked at runtime. If, at runtime, you attempt to access a nonexistent member, an exception is thrown. This dynamic typing greatly simplifies the syntax required to access non-.NET types, or .NET types whose type information is not available at compile time. However, dynamic types must be used with caution as you lose compile-time code checking. You can control the behavior of dynamic lookup by implementing the `IDynamicMetaObjectProvider` interface. Read more about this at `docs.microsoft.com/en-us/dotnet/api/system.dynamic` `.idynamicmetaobjectprovider`.
Optional method parameters	Often, you can define a method with lots of parameters, many of which are only rarely used. Instead of forcing client code to specify values for rarely used parameters, you might provide multiple method overloads. Alternatively, you can define these parameters as optional (and provide default values for parameters that are not specified). Client code that calls your method can then specify only as many parameters as are required.
Named method parameters	Client code can specify method parameter values by position or by name (or a mix of the two where positional parameters are specified first). Named parameters can be specified in any order. This is particularly useful when combined with optional parameters.
Lambda expressions	Lambda expressions are essentially a shorthand way of defining anonymous methods, although they have additional capabilities such as implicit typing. You define a lambda expression with a single parameter, or zero or more parameters inside parentheses, the `=>` operator, and an expression. The expression can be a block of code enclosed in curly brackets. Lambda expressions with up to eight parameters and an optional return type can be represented with the `Action`, `Action<>`, and `Func<>` delegate types. Many LINQ extension methods that can be used with collections use lambda expression parameters.

PART II
Data Access

14

Files

WHAT YOU WILL LEARN IN THIS CHAPTER

➤ Discovering the `File` and `Directory` classes

➤ Understanding how .NET uses streams to access files

➤ Writing to and reading from a file

➤ Reading and writing compressed files

➤ Serializing and deserializing objects

➤ Monitoring files and directories for changes

CODE DOWNLOADS FOR THIS CHAPTER

The code downloads for this chapter are found on the book page at www.wiley.com. Click the Downloads link. The code can also be found at github.com/benperk/BeginningCSharpAnd-DotNET. The code is in the Chapter14 folder and individually named according to the names throughout the chapter.

Files can be a great way to store data between instances of your application, or they can be used to transfer data between applications. User and application configuration settings can be stored to be retrieved the next time your application is run.

This chapter shows you how to use files effectively in your applications, touching on the major classes used to create, read from and write to files, and the supporting classes used to manipulate the file system from C# code. Although you won't examine all of the classes in detail, this chapter goes into enough depth to give you a good idea of the concepts and fundamentals.

FILE CLASSES FOR INPUT AND OUTPUT

Reading and writing files is an essential way to get data into your C# program (*input*) and send data out of your program (*output*). Because files are used for input and output, the file classes are contained in the `System.IO` namespace. (*IO* is a common abbreviation for *Input/Output*.)

`System.IO` contains the classes for reading and writing data to and from files, and you can reference this namespace in your C# application to gain access to these classes without fully qualifying type names.

The classes covered in this chapter are described in Table 14-1.

TABLE 14-1: File System Access Classes

CLASS	DESCRIPTION
File	A static utility class that exposes many static methods for checking whether a file exists, reading and writing the contents, and moving, copying, and deleting files.
Directory	A static utility class that exposes many static methods for checking whether a directory exists and moving, copying, and deleting directories.
Path	A utility class used to manipulate path names.
FileInfo	Represents a physical file on disk and has methods to manipulate this file. For any reading from and writing to the file, a Stream object must be created.
DirectoryInfo	Represents a physical directory on disk and has methods to manipulate this directory.
FileSystemInfo	Serves as the base class for both FileInfo and DirectoryInfo, making it possible to deal with files and directories at the same time using polymorphism.
FileSystem Watcher	The most advanced class you examine in this chapter. It is used to monitor files and directories, and it exposes events that your application can catch when changes occur in these locations.

You'll also look at the `System.IO.Compression` namespace, which enables you to read from and write to compressed files (.ZIP extension). In particular, you will look at the following two stream classes:

➤ `DeflateStream`—Represents a stream in which data is compressed automatically when writing, or uncompressed automatically when reading. Compression is achieved using the Deflate algorithm.

➤ `GZipStream`—Represents a stream in which data is compressed automatically when writing, or uncompressed automatically when reading. Compression is achieved using the GZIP (GNU Zip) algorithm.

The File and Directory Classes

The `File` and `Directory` utility classes expose many static methods for manipulating, surprisingly enough, files and directories. These methods make it possible to move files, query and update attributes, and create `FileStream` objects. As you learned in Chapter 8, static methods can be called on classes without having to create instances of them.

Some of the most useful static methods of the `File` class are shown in the Table 14-2.

TABLE 14-2: Static Methods of the File Class

METHOD	DESCRIPTION
Copy()	Copies a file from a source location to a target location.
Create()	Creates a file in the specified path.
Delete()	Deletes a file.
Exists()	Checks whether a file exists.
Open()	Returns a `FileStream` object at the specified path.
Move()	Moves a specified file to a new location. You can specify a different name for the file in the new location.
ReadAllText()	Reads the contents of a text file into a string.
WriteAllText()	Writes the contents of a string into a text file.

Some useful static methods of the `Directory` class are shown in Table 14-3.

TABLE 14-3: Static Methods of the Directory Class

METHOD	DESCRIPTION
CreateDirectory()	Creates a directory with the specified path.
Delete()	Deletes the specified directory.
GetDirectories()	Returns an array of `string` objects that represent the names of the directories below the specified directory.
EnumerateDirectories()	Like `GetDirectories()`, but returns an `IEnumerable<string>` collection of directory names.
GetFiles()	Returns an array of `string` objects that represent the names of the files in the specified directory.
EnumerateFiles()	Like `GetFiles()`, but returns an `IEnumerable<string>` collection of filenames.
GetFileSystemEntries()	Returns an array of `string` objects that represent the names of the files and directories in the specified directory.
EnumerateFileSystemEntries()	Like `GetFileSystemEntries()`, but returns an `IEnumerable<string>` collection of file and directory names.
Move()	Moves the specified directory to a new location. You can specify a new name for the folder in the new location.

The three `EnumerateXxx()` methods provide better performance than their `GetXxx()` counterparts when a large amount of files or directories exist.

The FileInfo Class

Unlike the `File` class, the `FileInfo` class is not static and does not have static methods. This class is useful only when instantiated. A `FileInfo` object represents a file on a disk or a network location, and you can create one by supplying a path to a file:

```
FileInfo aFile = new FileInfo(@"C:\Log.txt");
```

> **NOTE** You will be working with strings representing the path of a file throughout this chapter, which means a lot of backslash (\) characters in your strings. Therefore, you should remember that you can precede a string value with @, which means that the string will be interpreted literally. Thus, \ will be interpreted as \ and not as an escape character. Without the @ prefix, you need to use \\ instead of \ to avoid having this character be interpreted as an escape character. In this chapter, you'll stick to the @ prefix for your strings.
>
> You can also use the forward slash (/) in path names, but that can cause conflicts when executing Windows commands that use the forward slash for command-line options.

You can also pass the name of a directory to the `FileInfo` constructor, although in practical terms that isn't particularly useful. Doing this causes the base class of `FileInfo`, which is `FileSystemInfo`, to be initialized with all the directory information, but none of the `FileInfo` methods or properties relating specifically to files will work.

Many of the methods exposed by the `FileInfo` class are similar to those of the `File` class, but because `File` is a static class, it requires a string parameter that specifies the file location for every method call. `FileInfo` does not have to refer to a file that actually exists. Therefore, the following calls do the same thing:

```
FileInfo aFile = new FileInfo("Data.txt");
if (aFile.Exists)
    Console.WriteLine("File Exists");
if (File.Exists("Data.txt"))
    Console.WriteLine("File Exists");
```

In this code, a check is made to see whether the file `Data.txt` exists. Note that no directory information is specified here, which means that the current *working directory* is the only location examined. This directory is the one containing the application that calls this code. You'll look at this in more detail a little later, in the section "Path Names and Relative Paths."

Most of the `FileInfo` methods mirror the `File` methods in this manner. In most cases, it doesn't matter which technique you use, although the following criteria can help you to decide which is more appropriate:

➤ It makes sense to use methods on the static `File` class if you are making only a single method call—the single call will be faster because the .NET Framework won't have to go through the process of instantiating a new object and then calling the method.

➤ If your application is performing several operations on a file, then it makes more sense to instantiate a `FileInfo` object and use its methods—this saves time because the object will already be referencing the correct file on the file system, whereas the static class has to find it every time.

The `FileInfo` class also exposes properties relating to the underlying file, some of which can be manipulated to update the file. Many of these properties are inherited from `FileSystemInfo`, and thus apply to both the `FileInfo` and `DirectoryInfo` classes. The properties of `FileSystemInfo` are shown in Table 14-4.

TABLE 14-4: FileSystemInfo Properties

PROPERTY	DESCRIPTION
Attributes	Gets or sets the attributes of the current file or directory, using the `FileAttributes` enumeration.
CreationTime, CreationTimeUtc	Gets or sets the creation date and time of the current file, available in coordinated universal time (UTC) and non-UTC versions.
Extension	Retrieves the extension of the file. This property is read-only.
Exists	Determines whether a file exists. This is a read-only abstract property, and is overridden in `FileInfo` and `DirectoryInfo`.
FullName	Retrieves the full path of the file. This property is read-only.
LastAccessTime, LastAccessTimeUtc	Gets or sets the date and time that the current file was last accessed, available in UTC and non-UTC versions.
LastWriteTime, LastWriteTimeUtc	Gets or sets the date and time that the current file was last written to, available in UTC and non-UTC versions.
Name	Retrieves the full path of the file. This is a read-only abstract property, and is overridden in `FileInfo` and `DirectoryInfo`.

The properties specific to `FileInfo` are shown in Table 14-5.

TABLE 14-5: FileInfo Properties

PROPERTY	DESCRIPTION
Directory	Retrieves a `DirectoryInfo` object representing the directory containing the current file. This property is read-only.
DirectoryName	Returns the path to the file's directory. This property is read-only.
IsReadOnly	Shortcut to the read-only attribute of the file. This property is also accessible via `Attributes`.
Length	Gets the size of the file in bytes, returned as a `long` value. This property is read-only.

The DirectoryInfo Class

The `DirectoryInfo` class works exactly like the `FileInfo` class except that it refers to directories, not files. It is an instantiated object that represents a single directory on a machine. Like the `FileInfo` class, many of the method calls are duplicated across `Directory` and `DirectoryInfo`. The guidelines for choosing whether to use the methods of `File` or `FileInfo` also apply to `DirectoryInfo` methods:

➤ If you are making a single call, use the static `Directory` class.

➤ If you are making a series of calls, use an instantiated `DirectoryInfo` object.

The `DirectoryInfo` class inherits most of its properties from `FileSystemInfo`, as does `FileInfo`, although these properties operate on directories instead of files. There are also two `DirectoryInfo`-specific properties, shown in Table 14-6.

TABLE 14-6: Properties Unique to the DirectoryInfo Class

PROPERTY	DESCRIPTION
Parent	Retrieves a `DirectoryInfo` object representing the directory containing the current directory. This property is read-only.
Root	Retrieves a `DirectoryInfo` object representing the root directory of the current volume—for example, the `C:\` directory. This property is read-only.

Path Names and Relative Paths

When specifying a path name in .NET code, you can use absolute or relative path names. An *absolute* path name explicitly specifies a file or directory from a known location—such as the `C:` drive. An example of this is `C:\Work\LogFile.txt`—this path defines exactly where the file is, with no ambiguity.

Relative path names are relative to a starting location. By using relative path names, no drive or known location needs to be specified. You saw this earlier, where the current working directory was the starting point, which is the default behavior for relative path names. For example, if your application is running in the `C:\Development\FileDemo` directory and uses the relative path `LogFile.txt`, the file references would be `C:\Development\FileDemo\LogFile.txt`. To move "up" a directory, the `..` string is used. Thus, in the same application, the path `..\Log.txt` points to the file `C:\Development\Log.txt`.

As shown earlier, the working directory is initially set to the directory in which your application is running. When you are developing with Visual Studio, this means the application is several directories beneath the project folder you created. It is usually located in *ProjectName*`\bin\Debug\net5.0`. To access a file in the root folder of the project, then, you have to move up *two* directories with `..\..\..\`. You will see this happen often throughout the chapter.

Should you need to, you can determine the working directory by using `Directory.GetCurrentDirectory()`, or you can set it to a new path by using `Directory.SetCurrentDirectory()`.

STREAMS

All input and output in the .NET Framework involves the use of *streams*. A stream is an abstract representation of a *serial device*. A serial device is something that stores and/or accesses data in a linear manner, that is, one byte at a time, sequentially. This device can be a disk file, a network channel, a memory location, or any other object that supports linear reading, writing, or both. By keeping the device abstract, the underlying destination/source of the stream can be hidden. This level of abstraction enables code reuse, and enables you to write more generic routines because you don't have to worry about the specifics of how data transfer actually occurs. Therefore, similar code can be transferred and reused when the application is reading from a file input stream, a network input stream, or any other kind of stream. Because you can ignore the physical mechanics of each device, you don't need to worry about, for example, hard disk heads or memory allocation when dealing with a file stream.

A stream can represent almost any source such as a keyboard, a physical disk file, a network location, a printer, or even another program, but this chapter focuses on reading and writing disk files. The concepts applied to reading/writing disk files apply to most devices, so you'll gain a basic understanding of streams and learn a proven approach that can be applied to many situations.

Classes for Using Streams

The classes for using streams are contained in the same `System.IO` namespace along with the `File` and `Directory` classes. These classes are listed in Table 14-7.

TABLE 14-7: Stream Classes

CLASS	DESCRIPTION
FileStream	Represents a file that can be written to, read from, or both. This file can be written to and read from asynchronously or synchronously.
StreamReader	Reads character data from a stream and can be created by using a `FileStream` as a base.
StreamWriter	Writes character data to a stream and can be created by using a `FileStream` as a base.

Let's look now at how to use each of these classes.

The FileStream Object

The `FileStream` object represents a stream pointing to a file on a disk or a network path. Although the class does expose methods for reading and writing bytes from and to the files, most often you will use a `StreamReader` or `StreamWriter` to perform these functions. That's because the `FileStream` class operates on bytes and byte arrays, whereas the `Stream` classes operate on character data. Character data is easier to work with, but certain operations, such as random file access (access to data at some point in the middle of a file), can be performed only by a `FileStream` object. You'll learn more about this later in the chapter.

There are several ways to create a `FileStream` object. The constructor has many different overloads, but the simplest takes just two arguments: the filename and a `FileMode` enumeration value:

```
FileStream aFile = new FileStream(filename, FileMode.<Member>);
```

The `FileMode` enumeration has several members that specify how the file is opened or created. You'll see the possibilities shortly. Another commonly used constructor is as follows:

```
FileStream aFile =
new FileStream(filename, FileMode.<Member>, FileAccess.<Member>);
```

The third parameter is a member of the `FileAccess` enumeration and is a way of specifying the purpose of the stream. The members of the `FileAccess` enumeration are shown in Table 14-8.

TABLE 14-8: FileAccess Enumeration Members

MEMBER	DESCRIPTION
Read	Opens the file for reading only
Write	Opens the file for writing only
ReadWrite	Opens the file for reading or writing

Attempting to perform an action other than that specified by the `FileAccess` enumeration member will result in an exception being thrown. This property is often used as a way to vary user access to the file based on the user's authorization level.

In the version of the `FileStream` constructor that doesn't use a `FileAccess` enumeration parameter, the default value is used, which is `FileAccess.ReadWrite`.

The `FileMode` enumeration members are shown in Table 14-9. What actually happens when each of these values is used depends on whether the filename specified refers to an existing file. Note that the entries in this table refer to the position in the file that the stream points to when it is created, a topic you'll learn more about in the next section. Unless otherwise stated, the stream points to the beginning of a file.

Both the `File` and `FileInfo` classes expose `OpenRead()` and `OpenWrite()` methods that make it easier to create `FileStream` objects. The first opens the file for read-only access, and the second allows write-only access. These methods provide shortcuts, so you do not have to provide all the information required in the form of parameters to the `FileStream` constructor. For example, the following line of code opens the `Data.txt` file for read-only access:

```
FileStream aFile = File.OpenRead("Data.txt");
```

The following code performs the same function:

```
FileInfo aFileInfo = new FileInfo("Data.txt");
FileStream aFile = aFileInfo.OpenRead();
```

File Position

The `FileStream` class maintains an internal file pointer that points to the location within the file where the next read or write operation will occur. In most cases, when a file is opened, it points to the beginning of the file, but this pointer can be modified. This enables an application to read or write

TABLE 14-9: Filemode Enumeration Members

MEMBER	FILE EXISTS BEHAVIOR	NO FILE EXISTS BEHAVIOR
Append	The file is opened, with the stream positioned at the end of the file. Can be used only in conjunction with `FileAccess.Write`.	A new file is created. Can be used only in conjunction with `FileAccess.Write`.
Create	The file is destroyed, and a new file is created in its place.	A new file is created.
CreateNew	An exception is thrown.	A new file is created.
Open	The file is opened, with the stream positioned at the beginning of the file.	An exception is thrown.
OpenOr Create	The file is opened, with the stream positioned at the beginning of the file.	A new file is created.
Truncate	The file is opened and erased. The stream is positioned at the beginning of the file. The original file creation date is retained.	An exception is thrown.

anywhere within the file, which in turn enables random access to a file and the capability to jump directly to a specific location in the file. This can save a lot of time when dealing with very large files because you can instantly move to the location you want.

The method that implements this functionality is the `Seek()` method, which takes two parameters. The first parameter specifies how far to move the file pointer, in bytes. The second parameter specifies where to start counting from, in the form of a value from the `SeekOrigin` enumeration. The `Seek-Origin` enumeration contains three values: `Begin`, `Current`, and `End`.

For example, the following line would move the file pointer eight bytes from the start of the file:

```
aFile.Seek(8, SeekOrigin.Begin);
```

The file pointer would now be positioned on the ninth byte of the file (because the first byte is byte 0). The following line would move the file pointer two bytes forward, starting from the current position. If this were executed directly after the previous line, then the file pointer would now point to the eleventh byte in the file:

```
aFile.Seek(2, SeekOrigin.Current);
```

When you read from or write to a file, the file pointer changes as well. After you have read 10 bytes, the file pointer will point to the byte after the tenth byte read.

You can also specify negative seek positions, which could be combined with the `SeekOrigin.End` enumeration value to seek near the end of the file. The following seeks to the fifth byte from the end of the file:

```
aFile.Seek(-5, SeekOrigin.End);
```

Files accessed in this manner are sometimes referred to as *random access files* because an application can access any position within the file. The `StreamReader` and `StreamWriter` classes described later access files sequentially and do not allow you to manipulate the file pointer in this way.

Reading Data

Reading data using the `FileStream` class is not as easy as using the `StreamReader` class, which you will look at later in this chapter. That's because the `FileStream` class deals exclusively with raw bytes. Working in raw bytes makes the `FileStream` class useful for any kind of data file, not just text files. By reading byte data, the `FileStream` object can be used to read files such as images or sound files. The cost of this flexibility is that you cannot use a `FileStream` to read data directly into a string as you can with the `StreamReader` class. However, several conversion classes make it fairly easy to convert byte arrays into character arrays, and vice versa.

The `FileStream.Read()` method is the primary means to access data from a file that a `FileStream` object points to. This method reads the data from a file and then writes this data into a `byte` array. There are three parameters, the first being a `byte` array passed in to accept data from the `File-Stream` object. The second parameter is the position in the `byte` array to begin writing data to—this is normally zero, to begin writing data from the file at the beginning of the array. The last parameter specifies how many bytes to read from the file.

The following Try It Out demonstrates reading data from a random access file. The file you will read from is actually the class file you create for the example.

TRY IT OUT   Reading Data from Random Access Files: ReadFile\Program.cs

1. Create a new Console Application called ReadFile and save it in the directory `C:\BeginningC-SharpAndDotNET\Chapter14`. Set the Target Framework to the Current version (.NET 5.0).

2. Add the following `using` directives to the top of the `Program.cs` file:

```
using System;
using System.Text;
using System.IO;
```

3. Add the following code to the `Main()` method:

```
static void Main(string[] args)
{
    byte[] byteData = new byte[200];
    char[] charData = new char[200];
    try
    {
        using (FileStream aFile = new FileStream(@"..\..\..\Program.cs", FileMode.Open))
        {
            aFile.Seek(88, SeekOrigin.Begin);
            aFile.Read(byteData, 0, 200);
        }
    }
    catch(IOException e)
    {
        Console.WriteLine("An IO exception has been thrown!");
        Console.WriteLine(e.ToString());
        Console.ReadKey();
        return;
    }
```

```
        Decoder d = Encoding.UTF8.GetDecoder();
        d.GetChars(byteData, 0, byteData.Length, charData, 0);
        Console.WriteLine(charData);
        Console.ReadKey();
    }
```

4. Run the application. The result is shown in Figure 14-1.

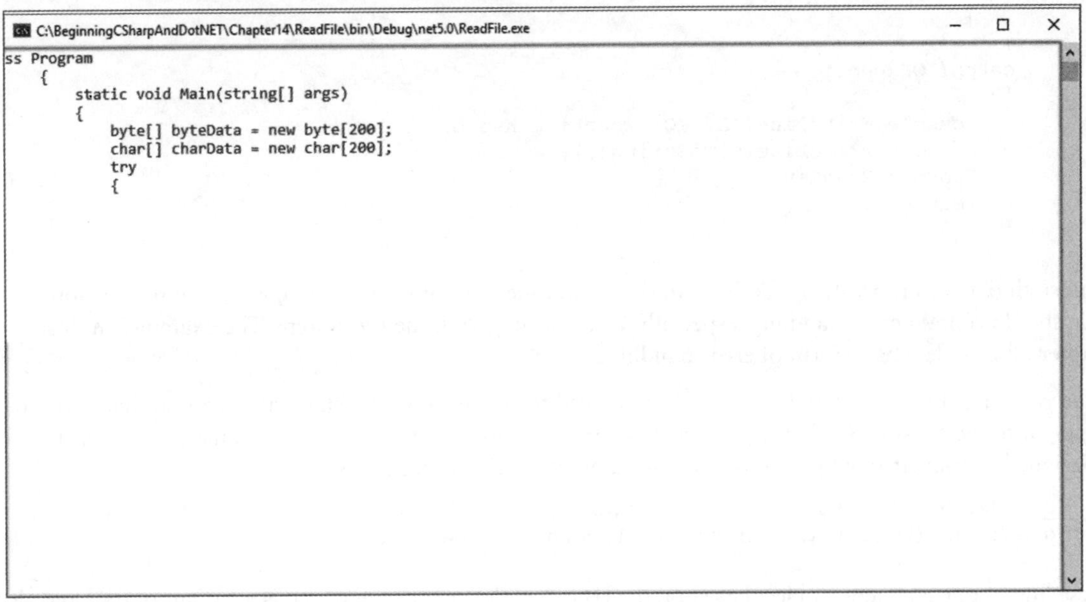

```
C:\BeginningCSharpAndDotNET\Chapter14\ReadFile\bin\Debug\net5.0\ReadFile.exe                    —    □    ×

ss Program
    {
        static void Main(string[] args)
        {
            byte[] byteData = new byte[200];
            char[] charData = new char[200];
            try
            {
```

FIGURE 14-1

How It Works

This application opens its own `.cs` file to read from. It does so by navigating three directories up the file structure with the `..` string in the following line:

```
using (FileStream aFile = new FileStream(@"..\..\..\Program.cs", FileMode.Open))
```

You'll notice we wrap the assignment of the `FileStream` with a `using(){}` block. You saw this mentioned in Chapter 8 in the discussion of the IDisposable interface. A file stream must be closed and disposed of after it is used to prevent operating system file handles from lying around and potentially causing memory leaks. The `using(){}` block is a handy syntax for ensuring this happens.

The two lines that implement the actual seeking and reading from a specific point in the file are as follows:

```
aFile.Seek(88, SeekOrigin.Begin);
aFile.Read(byteData, 0, 200);
```

The first line moves the file pointer to byte number 88 in the file. The second line reads the next 200 bytes into the `byte` array `byteData`.

Note that these two lines were enclosed in `try...catch` blocks to handle any exceptions that are thrown:

```
try
{
    using (FileStream aFile = new FileStream(@"..\..\..\Program.cs", FileMode.Open))
    {
        aFile.Seek(88, SeekOrigin.Begin);
        aFile.Read(byteData, 0, 200);
    }
}
catch(IOException e)
{
    Console.WriteLine("An IO exception has been thrown!");
    Console.WriteLine(e.ToString());
    Console.ReadKey();
    return;
}
```

Almost all operations involving file I/O can throw an exception of type `IOException`. All production code should contain error handling, especially when dealing with the file system. The examples in this chapter all include a basic form of error handling.

Once you have the `byte` array from the file, you need to convert it into a character array so that you can display it to the console. To do this, use the `Decoder` class from the `System.Text` namespace. This class is designed to convert raw bytes into more useful items, such as characters:

```
Decoder d = Encoding.UTF8.GetDecoder();
d.GetChars(byteData, 0, byteData.Length, charData, 0);
```

These lines create a `Decoder` object based on the UTF-8 encoding schema, which is a variant of the Unicode encoding schema. Then the `GetChars()` method is called, which takes an array of bytes and converts it to an array of characters. After that has been done, the character array can be written to the Console.

Writing Data

The process for writing data to a random access file is very similar; a byte array must be created. The easiest way to do this is to first build the character array you want to write to the file. Next, use the `Encoder` object to convert it to a byte array, very much as you used the `Decoder` object. Last, call the `Write()` method to send the array to the file.

The following Try It Out is a simple example to demonstrate how this is done.

TRY IT OUT   Writing Data to Random Access Files: WriteFile\Program.cs

1. Create a new Console Application called WriteFile and save it in the directory `C:\BeginningC-SharpAndDotNET\Chapter14`. Set the Target Framework to the Current version (.NET 5.0).

2. Add the following `using` directives to the top of the `Program.cs` file:

```
using System;
using System.Text;
using System.IO;
```

3. Add the following code to the `Main()` method:

```csharp
static void Main(string[] args)
{
    byte[] byteData;
    char[] charData;
    try
    {
        using (FileStream aFile = new FileStream("Temp.txt", FileMode.Create))
        {
            charData = "My pink half of the drainpipe.".ToCharArray();
            Encoder e = Encoding.UTF8.GetEncoder();
            byteData = new byte[e.GetByteCount(charData, true)];
            e.GetBytes(charData, 0, charData.Length, byteData, 0, true);
            // Move file pointer to beginning of file.
            aFile.Seek(0, SeekOrigin.Begin);
            aFile.Write(byteData, 0, byteData.Length);
        }
    }
    catch (IOException ex)
    {
        Console.WriteLine("An IO exception has been thrown!");
        Console.WriteLine(ex.ToString());
        Console.ReadKey();
        return;
    }
}
```

4. Run the application. It should run briefly and then close.

5. Navigate to the application directory—the file will have been saved there because you used a relative path. This is located in the `WriteFile\bin\Debug\net5.0` folder. Open the `Temp.txt` file. You should see text in the file, as shown in Figure 14-2.

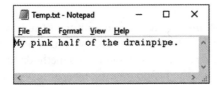

FIGURE 14-2

How It Works

This application opens a file in its own directory and writes a simple string to it. In structure, this example is similar to the previous example, except you use `Write()` instead of `Read()`, and `Encoder` instead of `Decoder`.

The following line creates a character array by using the `ToCharArray()` method of the `String` class. Because everything in C# is an object, the text `"My pink half of the drainpipe."` is actually a `string` object (albeit a slightly odd one), so these methods can be called even on a string of characters:

```csharp
CharData = "My pink half of the drainpipe.".ToCharArray();
```

The following lines show how to convert the character array to the correct byte array needed by the `FileStream` object:

```
Encoder e = Encoding.UTF8.GetEncoder();
byteData = new byte[e.GetByteCount(charData, true)];
e.GetBytes(charData, 0, charData.Length, byteData, 0, true);
```

This time, an `Encoder` object is created based on the UTF-8 encoding. You used Unicode for the decoding as well, and this time you need to encode the character data into the correct byte format before you can write to the stream. You get the byte count from the `Encoder` object using its `GetByteCount` method when populating the `byteData` array. The `GetBytes()` method is where the magic happens. It converts the character array to the byte array. It accepts a character array as the first parameter (`charData` in this example), and the index to start in that array as the second parameter (`0` for the start of the array). The third parameter is the number of characters to convert (`charData.Length`—the number of elements in the `charData` array). The fourth parameter is the byte array to place the data into (`byteData`), and the fifth parameter is the index to start writing from in the byte array (`0` for the start of the `byteData` array).

The sixth, and final, parameter determines whether the `Encoder` object should flush its state after completion. This reflects the fact that the `Encoder` object retains an in-memory record of where it was in the byte array. This aids in subsequent calls to the `Encoder` object but is meaningless when only a single call is made. The final call to the `Encoder` must set this parameter to `true` to clear its memory.

After that, it is a simple matter of writing the byte array to the `FileStream` by using the `Write()` method:

```
aFile.Seek(0, SeekOrigin.Begin);
aFile.Write(byteData, 0, byteData.Length);
```

Like the `Read()` method, the `Write()` method has three parameters: a byte array containing the data to write to the file stream, the index in the array to start writing from, and the number of bytes to write.

The StreamWriter Object

Working with arrays of bytes is not most people's idea of fun—having worked with the `FileStream` object, you might be wondering whether there is an easier way. Fear not, for once you have a `FileStream` object, you will usually create a `StreamWriter` or `StreamReader` and use its methods to manipulate the file. If you don't need the capability to change the file pointer to any arbitrary position, these classes make working with files much easier.

The `StreamWriter` class enables you to write characters and strings to a file, with the class handling the underlying conversions and writing to the `FileStream` object for you.

There are many ways to create a `StreamWriter` object. If you already have a `FileStream` object, then you can use it to create a `StreamWriter`:

```
FileStream aFile = new FileStream("Log.txt", FileMode.CreateNew);
StreamWriter sw = new StreamWriter(aFile);
```

A `StreamWriter` object can also be created directly from a file:

```
StreamWriter sw = new StreamWriter("Log.txt", true);
```

This constructor takes the filename and a Boolean value set as follows:

➤ If this is set to `false`, then a new file is created or the existing file is truncated and then opened.

➤ If it is set to `true`, then the file is opened and the data is retained. If there is no file, then a new one is created.

Unlike creating a `FileStream` object, creating a `StreamWriter` does not provide you with a similar range of options—other than the Boolean value to append or create a new file, you have no option for specifying the `FileMode` property as you did with the `FileStream` class. Nor do you have an option to set the `FileAccess` property, so you will always have read/write privileges to the file. To use any of the advanced parameters, you must first specify them in the `FileStream` constructor and then create a `StreamWriter` from the `FileStream` object, as you do in the following Try It Out.

TRY IT OUT Writing Data to an Output Stream: StreamWrite\Program.cs

1. Create a new Console Application called StreamWrite and save it in the directory `C:\BeginningC-SharpAndDotNET\Chapter14`. Set the Target Framework to the Current version (.NET 5.0).

2. You will be using the `System.IO` namespace again, so add the following `using` directives near the top of the `Program.cs` file:

```
using System;
using System.IO;
```

3. Add the following code to the `Main()` method:

```
static void Main(string[] args)
{
    try
    {
      using (FileStream aFile = new FileStream("Log.txt", FileMode.OpenOrCreate))
      {
          using (StreamWriter sw = new StreamWriter(aFile))
          {
            bool truth = true;
            // Write data to file.
            sw.WriteLine("Hello to you.");
            sw.Write($"It is now {DateTime.Now.ToLongDateString()}");
            sw.Write("and things are looking good.");
            sw.Write("More than that,");
            sw.Write($" it's {truth} that C# is fun.");
          }
      }
    }
    catch(IOException e)
    {
        Console.WriteLine("An IO exception has been thrown!");
        Console.WriteLine(e.ToString());
        Console.ReadLine();
        return;
    }
}
```

4. Build and run the project. If no errors are found, it should quickly run and close. Because you are not displaying anything on the console, it is not a very exciting program to watch.

5. Go to the application directory and find the `Log.txt` file. It is located in the `StreamWrite\bin\Debug\net5.0` folder because you used a relative path.

6. Open the file. You should see the text shown in Figure 14-3.

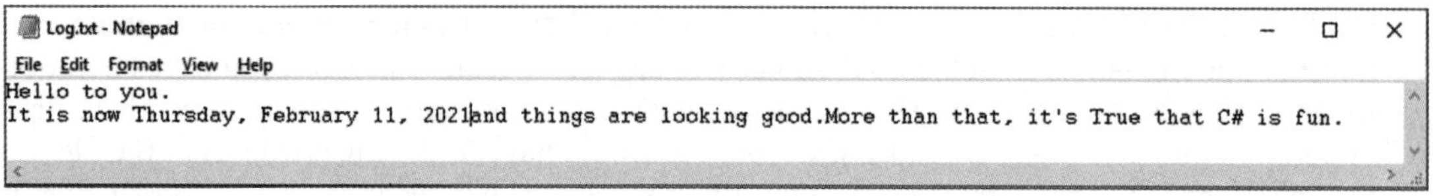

FIGURE 14-3

How It Works

This simple application demonstrates the two most important methods of the `StreamWriter` class, `Write()` and `WriteLine()`. Both of them have many overloaded versions for performing more advanced file output, but you used basic string output in this example.

The `WriteLine()` method writes the string passed to it, followed immediately by a newline character. You can see in the example that this causes the next write operation to begin on a new line:

```
sw.WriteLine("Hello to you.");
```

The `Write()` method simply writes the string passed to it to the file, without a newline character appended, enabling you to write a complete sentence or paragraph using more than one `Write()` statement. Just as you can write formatted data to the console, you can also write formatted data to files. For example, you can write out the value of variables to the file using interpolated string parameters:

```
sw.Write($"It is now {DateTime.Now.ToLongDateString()}");
```

`DateTime.Now` holds the current date; the `ToLongDateString()` method is used to convert this date into an easy-to-read form:

```
sw.Write("More than that,");
sw.Write(" it's {truth} that C# is fun.");
```

Again, you use interpolated string parameters, this time with `Write()` to display the Boolean value `truth`—you set this variable to `true` earlier, and its value is automatically converted into the string "True" for the formatting.

You can use `Write()` and format parameters to write comma-separated value (CSV) files:

```
[StreamWriter object].Write($"{100},{"A nice product"},{10.50}");
```

In a more sophisticated example, this data could come from a database or other data source.

Both the `FileStream` and `StreamWriter` objects are opened within a `using` block, which ensures that the resources associated with them are disposed of. This also ensures that the data is written to the file, which would otherwise require an explicit `sw.Flush()` or `sw.Close()` call at the end of the program.

The StreamReader Object

Input streams are used to read data from an external source. Often, this will be a file on a disk or network location, but remember that this source could be almost anything that can send data, such as a network application or even the Console.

The `StreamReader` class is the one that you will be using to read data from files. Like the `Stream-Writer` class, this is a generic class that can be used with any stream. In the next Try It Out, you again construct it around a `FileStream` object so that it points to the correct file.

`StreamReader` objects are created in much the same way as `StreamWriter` objects. The most common way to create one is to use a previously created `FileStream` object:

```
FileStream aFile = new FileStream("Log.txt", FileMode.Open);
StreamReader sr = new StreamReader(aFile);
```

Like `StreamWriter`, the `StreamReader` class can be created directly from a string containing the path to a particular file:

```
StreamReader sr = new StreamReader("Log.txt");
```

TRY IT OUT   Reading Data from an Input Stream: StreamRead\Program.cs

1. Create a new Console Application called StreamRead and save it in the directory C:\BeginningC-SharpAndDotNET\Chapter14. Set the Target Framework to the Current version (.NET 5.0).

2. Import the `System.IO` and `System.Console` namespaces by placing the following lines of code near the top of `Program.cs`:

```
using System;
using System.IO;
using static System.Console;
```

3. Add the following code to the `Main()` method:

```
static void Main(string[] args)
{
    string line;
    try
    {
        using (FileStream aFile = new FileStream("Log.txt", FileMode.Open))
        {
            using (StreamReader sr = new StreamReader(aFile))
            {
                line = sr.ReadLine();
                // Read data in line by line.
                while (line != null)
                {
                    WriteLine(line);
                    line = sr.ReadLine();
                }
            }
        }
    }
    catch (IOException e)
    {
```

```
            WriteLine("An IO exception has been thrown!");
            WriteLine(e.ToString());
            return;
        }
    }
```

4. Copy the `Log.txt` file, created in the previous example, into the `StreamRead\bin\Debug\net5.0` directory. If you don't have a file named `Log.txt`, the `FileStream` constructor will throw an exception when it doesn't find it.

5. Run the application. You should see the text of the file written to the console, as shown in Figure 14-4.

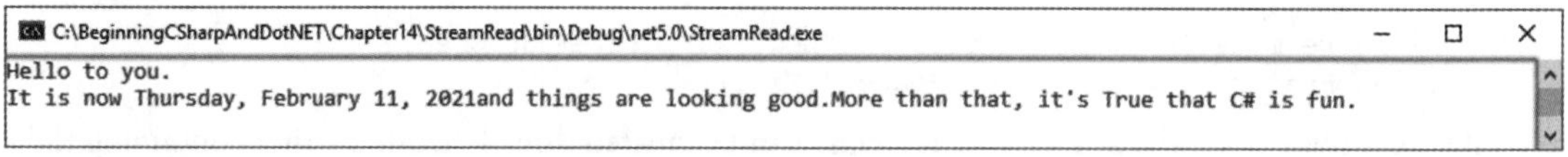

```
C:\BeginningCSharpAndDotNET\Chapter14\StreamRead\bin\Debug\net5.0\StreamRead.exe                    -   □   ×
Hello to you.
It is now Thursday, February 11, 2021and things are looking good.More than that, it's True that C# is fun.
```

FIGURE 14-4

How It Works

This application is very similar to the previous one, with the obvious difference being that it is reading a file, rather than writing one. As before, you must import the `System.IO` namespace to be able to access the necessary classes. You also use the `using` clause with both the `FileStream` and the `StreamReader` to ensure resources associated with these classes are disposed of.

You use the `ReadLine()` method to read text from the file. This method reads text until a new line is found and returns the resulting text as a string (without the ending newline character). The method returns a `null` when the end of the file has been reached, which you use to test for the end of the file. Note that you use a `while` loop, which ensures that the line read isn't null before any code in the body of the loop is executed—that way, only the genuine contents of the file are displayed:

```
line = sr.ReadLine();
while(line != null)
{
    WriteLine(line);
    line = sr.ReadLine();
}
```

Reading Data

The `ReadLine()` method is not the only way you can access data in a file. The `StreamReader` class has many methods for reading data.

The simplest of the reading methods is `Read()`. It returns the next character from the stream as a positive integer value or a `-1` if it has reached the end. This value can be converted into a character by using the `Convert` utility class. In the preceding example, the main parts of the program could be rewritten as follows:

```
StreamReader sr = new StreamReader(aFile);
int charCode;
```

```
    charCode = sr.Read();
    while(charCode != -1)
    {
        Write(Convert.ToChar(charCode));
        charCode = sr.Read();
    }
    sr.Close();
```

A very convenient method to use with smaller files is the `ReadToEnd()` method. It reads the entire file and returns it as a string. In this case, the earlier application could be simplified to the following:

```
    StreamReader sr = new StreamReader(aFile);
    line = sr.ReadToEnd();
    Console.WriteLine(line);
    sr.Close();
```

Although this might seem easy and convenient, be careful. By reading all the data into a string object, you are forcing the data in the file to exist in memory. Depending on the size of the data file, this can be prohibitive. If the data file is extremely large, then it is better to leave the data in the file and access it with the other methods of the `StreamReader`.

Another way to deal with large files, which was introduced in .NET 4, is to use the static `File.ReadLines()` method. There are, in fact, several static methods of `File` that you can use to simplify reading and writing file data, but this one is particularly interesting in that it returns an `IEnumerable<string>` collection. You can iterate through the strings in this collection to read the file one line at a time. Using this method, you can rewrite the previous example as follows:

```
    foreach (string alternativeLine in File.ReadLines("Log.txt"))
        WriteLine(alternativeLine);
```

There are, as you can see, several ways in .NET to achieve the same result—namely, reading data from a file. Choose the technique that suits you best.

Asynchronous File Access

Sometimes—for example, when you are performing a lot of file access operations in one go or are working with very large files—reading and writing file system data can be slow. If this is the case, you might want to perform other operations while you wait. This is especially important with desktop applications, where you want your application to remain responsive to users while you are doing work in the background.

To facilitate this, .NET 4.5 introduced asynchronous ways to work with streams. This applies to the `FileStream` class, as well as to `StreamReader` and `StreamWriter`. If you have browsed through the definitions of these classes, you might have noticed some methods that end with the suffix `Async`—for example, `StreamReader` has a method called `ReadLineAsync()`, which is an asynchronous version of `ReadLine()`. These methods are designed to be used with the task-based asynchronous programming model.

Asynchronous programming is an advanced technique that isn't covered in detail in this book. However, if asynchronous file system access is something you are interested in doing, then this is the place to start. You might also want to read *Professional C# 7.0 and .NET Core 2.0* by Christian Nagel (Wrox, 2018) for more details.

Reading and Writing Compressed Files

Often when dealing with files, quite a lot of space is used up on the hard disk. This is particularly true for graphics and sound files. You've probably come across utilities that enable you to compress and decompress files, which are handy when you want to move them around or email them. The System.IO.Compression namespace contains classes that enable you to compress files from your code, using either the GZIP or Deflate algorithm—both of which are publicly available and free for anyone to use.

There is a little bit more to compressing files than just compressing them, though. You've probably seen how commercial applications enable multiple files to be placed in a single compressed file, often called an *archive*. There are classes in the System.IO.Compression namespace that enable similar functionality. However, to keep things simple for this book you'll just look at one scenario: saving text data to a compressed file. While you are unlikely to be able to access this file with an external utility, you will see that the file will be much smaller than its uncompressed equivalent!

The two compression stream classes in the System.IO.Compression namespace that you'll look at here, DeflateStream and GZipStream, work very similarly. In both cases, you initialize them with an existing stream, which, in the case of files, will be a FileStream object. After this you can use them with StreamReader and StreamWriter just like any other stream. All you need to specify in addition to that is whether the stream will be used for compression (saving files) or decompression (loading files) so that the class knows what to do with the data that passes through it. This is best illustrated with the following Try It Out.

TRY IT OUT Reading and Writing Compressed Data: Compressor\Program.cs

1. Create a new Console Application called Compressor and save it in the directory C:\BeginningC-SharpAndDotNET\Chapter14. Set the Target Framework to the Current version (.NET 5.0).

2. Place the following lines of code near the top of Program.cs. You need to import the System.Console, System.IO, and System.IO.Compression namespaces to use the file and compression classes:

```
using System;
using System.Text;
using System.IO;
using System.IO.Compression;
using static System.Console;
```

3. Add the following methods into the body of Program.cs, before the Main() method:

```
static void SaveCompressedFile(string filename, string data)
    {
        using (FileStream fileStream =
            new FileStream(filename, FileMode.Create, FileAccess.Write))
        {
            using (GZipStream compressionStream =
                        new GZipStream(fileStream, CompressionMode.Compress))
            {
                using (StreamWriter writer = new StreamWriter(compressionStream))
                {
                    writer.Write(data);
```

```
                    }
                }
            }
        }
        static string LoadCompressedFile(string filename)
        {
            using (FileStream fileStream =
                new FileStream(filename, FileMode.Open, FileAccess.Read))
            {
                using (GZipStream compressionStream =
                    new GZipStream(fileStream, CompressionMode.Decompress))
                {
                    using (StreamReader reader = new StreamReader(compressionStream))
                    {
                        string data = reader.ReadToEnd();
                        return data;
                    }
                }
            }
        }
    }
```

4. Add the following code to the `Main()` method:

```
static void Main(string[] args)
{
    try
    {
        string filename = "compressedFile.gz";
        WriteLine(
            "Enter a string to compress (will be repeated 100 times):");
        string sourceString = ReadLine();
        StringBuilder sourceStringMultiplier =
            new StringBuilder(sourceString.Length * 100);
        for (int i = 0; i < 100; i++)
        {
            sourceStringMultiplier.Append(sourceString);
        }
        sourceString = sourceStringMultiplier.ToString();
        WriteLine($"Source data is {sourceString.Length} bytes long.");
        SaveCompressedFile(filename, sourceString);
        WriteLine($"\nData saved to {filename}.");
        FileInfo compressedFileData = new FileInfo(filename);
        Write($"Compressed file is {compressedFileData.Length}");
        WriteLine(" bytes long.");
        string recoveredString = LoadCompressedFile(filename);
        recoveredString = recoveredString.Substring(
            0, recoveredString.Length / 100);
        WriteLine($"\nRecovered data: {recoveredString}", recoveredString);
        ReadKey();
    }
    catch (IOException ex)
    {
        WriteLine("An IO exception has been thrown!");
        WriteLine(ex.ToString());
        ReadKey();
    }
}
```

5. Run the application and enter a suitably long string. An example result is shown in Figure 14-5.

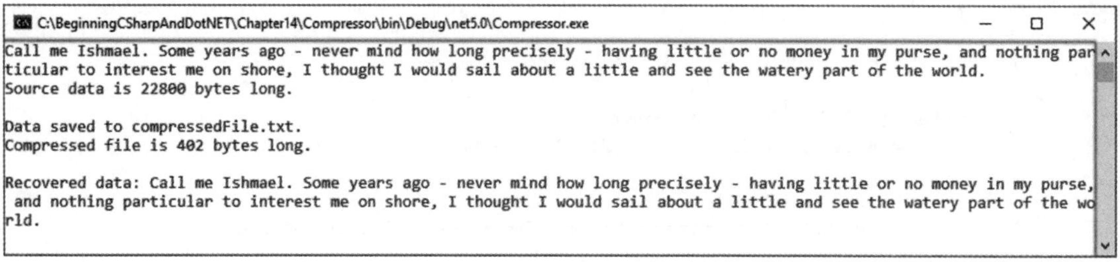

FIGURE 14-5

6. Open `compressedFile.gz` in Notepad. The text is shown in Figure 14-6.

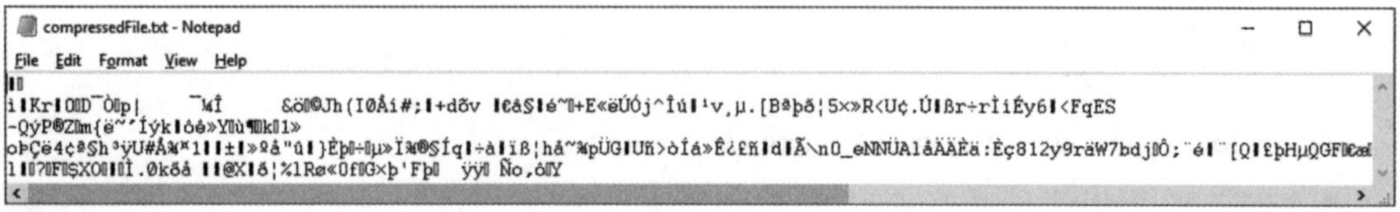

FIGURE 14-6

How It Works

In this example, you define two methods for saving and loading a compressed text file. The first of these, `SaveCompressedFile()`, is as follows:

```
static void SaveCompressedFile(string filename, string data)
{
    using (FileStream fileStream =
        new FileStream(filename, FileMode.Create, FileAccess.Write))
    {
        using (GZipStream compressionStream =
                new GZipStream(fileStream, CompressionMode.Compress))
        {
            using (StreamWriter writer = new StreamWriter(compressionStream))
            {
                writer.Write(data);
            }
        }
    }
}
```

The code starts by creating a `FileStream` object inside a `using` block and then uses it to create a `GZipStream` object. Each `Stream` and `Reader` object in turn is assigned with a `using` block to ensure it is disposed of and closed. Note that you could replace all occurrences of `GZipStream` in this code with `DeflateStream`—the classes work in the same way. You use the `CompressionMode.Compress` enumeration value to specify that data is to be compressed and then use a `StreamWriter` to write data to the file.

`LoadCompressedFile()` mirrors the `SaveCompressedFile()` method. Instead of saving to a filename, it loads a compressed file into a string:

```
static string LoadCompressedFile(string filename)
{
    using (FileStream fileStream =
        new FileStream(filename, FileMode.Open, FileAccess.Read))
    {
        using (GZipStream compressionStream =
            new GZipStream(fileStream, CompressionMode.Decompress))
        {
            using (StreamReader reader = new StreamReader(compressionStream))
            {
                string data = reader.ReadToEnd();
                return data;
            }
        }
    }
}
```

The differences are as you would expect. `FileMode`, `FileAccess`, and `CompressionMode` enumeration values that load and uncompress data are different, and the use of a `StreamReader` to get the uncompressed text out of the file is also different.

The code in `Main()` is a simple test of these methods. It simply asks for a string, duplicates the string 100 times to make things interesting, compresses it to a file, and then retrieves it. In the example, the first sentence of *Moby Dick* repeated 100 times is 22,800 characters long, but when compressed, it takes up only 402 bytes—that's a compression ratio of more than 50:1. Admittedly, this is a bit of a cheat—the GZIP algorithm works particularly well with repetitive data, but it does illustrate compression in action.

You also looked at the text stored in the compressed file. Obviously, it isn't easily readable, which has implications should you want to share data between applications, for example. However, because the file was compressed with a known algorithm, at least you know that it is possible for applications to uncompress it.

MONITORING THE FILE SYSTEM

Sometimes an application must do more than just read and write files to the file system. For example, it might be important to know when files or directories are being modified. It is easy to create custom applications that do just that in .NET.

The class that helps you to do this is the `FileSystemWatcher` class. It exposes several events that your application can catch. This enables your application to respond to file system events.

The basic procedure for using the `FileSystemWatcher` is simple. First, you must set a handful of properties, which specify where to monitor, what to monitor, and when it should raise the event that your application will handle. Then you give it the addresses of your custom event handlers, so that it can call these when significant events occur. Finally, you turn it on and wait for the events.

The properties that must be set before a `FileSystemWatcher` object is enabled are shown in Table 14-10.

TABLE 14-10: FileSystemWatcher Properties

PROPERTY	DESCRIPTION
Path	Must be set to the file location or directory to monitor.
NotifyFilter	A combination of `NotifyFilters` enumeration values that specify what to watch for within the monitored files. These represent properties of the file or folders being monitored. If any of the specified properties change, then an event is raised. The possible enumeration values are `Attributes`, `CreationTime`, `DirectoryName`, `FileName`, `LastAccess`, `LastWrite`, `Security`, and `Size`. Note that these can be combined using the binary OR operator.
Filter	A filter specifying which files to monitor—for example, `*.txt`.

Once these are set, you must write event handlers for four events: `Changed`, `Created`, `Deleted`, and `Renamed`. As shown in Chapter 13, this is simply a matter of creating your own method and assigning it to the object's event. By assigning your own event handler methods to these events, your method will be called when the event is fired. Each event will fire when a file or directory matching the `Path`, `NotifyFilter`, and `Filter` property is modified.

Once you have set the properties and the events, set the `EnableRaisingEvents` property to `true` to begin the monitoring. In the following Try It Out, you use `FileSystemWatcher` in a simple client application to keep tabs on a directory of your choice.

TRY IT OUT | Monitoring the File System: FileWatch

Here's a more sophisticated example using much of what you have learned in this chapter.

1. Create a new WPF Application called FileWatch and save it in the directory `C:\BeginningCSharp-AndDotNET\Chapter14`. Set the Target Framework to the Current version (.NET 5.0). WPF applications are covered in detail in Chapter 21. This sample is simple and you can just follow the steps.

2. Modify `MainWindow.xaml` as follows (the resulting window is shown in Figure 14-7):

```xml
<Window x:Class="FileWatch.MainWindow"
  xmlns="http://schemas.microsoft.com/winfx/2006/xaml/presentation"
  xmlns:x="http://schemas.microsoft.com/winfx/2006/xaml"
  Title="File Monitor" Height="160" Width="300">
  <Grid>
    <Grid.RowDefinitions>
      <RowDefinition Height="Auto" />
      <RowDefinition Height="Auto" />
      <RowDefinition />
    </Grid.RowDefinitions>
    <Grid Margin="4">
      <Grid.ColumnDefinitions>
        <ColumnDefinition />
        <ColumnDefinition Width="Auto" />
      </Grid.ColumnDefinitions>
      <TextBox Name="LocationBox" TextChanged="LocationBox_TextChanged" />
```

```
        <Button Name="BrowseButton" Grid.Column="1" Margin="4,0,0,0"
            Content="Browse…" Click="BrowseButton_Click" />
    </Grid>
    <Button Name="WatchButton" Content="Watch!" Margin="4" Grid.Row="1"
        Click="WatchButton_Click" IsEnabled="False" />
    <ListBox Name="WatchOutput" Margin="4" Grid.Row="2" />
  </Grid>
</Window>
```

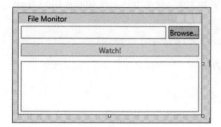

FIGURE 14-7

3. Add the following using directives to `MainWindow.xaml.cs`:

```
using System.IO;
using Microsoft.Win32;
```

4. Add a field of type `FileSystemWatcher` class to the `MainWindow` class:

```
namespace FileWatch
{
    /// <summary>
    /// Interaction logic for MainWindow.xaml
    /// </summary>
    public partial class MainWindow : Window
    {
        // File System Watcher object.
        private FileSystemWatcher watcher;
```

5. Add the following utility method to the class to allow messages to be added to the output from a background thread:

```
        private void AddMessage(string message)
        {
            Dispatcher.BeginInvoke(new Action(
                () => WatchOutput.Items.Insert(
                    0, message)));
        }
```

6. Just after the `InitializeComponent()` method call in the window constructor, add the following code. This code is needed to initialize the `FileSystemWatcher` object and associate the events to calls to `AddMessage()`:

```
        public MainWindow()
        {
            InitializeComponent();
            watcher = new FileSystemWatcher();
            watcher.Deleted += (s, e) =>
```

```
            AddMessage($"File: {e.FullPath} Deleted");
        watcher.Renamed += (s, e) =>
            AddMessage($"File renamed from {e.OldName} to {e.FullPath}");
        watcher.Changed += (s, e) =>
            AddMessage($"File: {e.FullPath} {e.ChangeType.ToString()}");
        watcher.Created += (s, e) =>
            AddMessage($"File: {e.FullPath} Created");
    }
```

7. Add the `Click` event handler for the `Browse` button. The code in this event handler opens the Open File dialog box, enabling the user to select a file to monitor:

```
private void BrowseButton_Click(object sender, RoutedEventArgs e)
{
    OpenFileDialog dialog = new OpenFileDialog();
    if (dialog.ShowDialog(this) == true)
    {
        LocationBox.Text = dialog.FileName;
    }
}
```

The `ShowDialog()` method returns a `bool?` value reflecting how the user exited the File Open dialog box (the user could have clicked OK or clicked the Cancel button). You need to confirm that the user did not click the Cancel button, so you compare the result from the method call to `true` before saving the user's file selection to the `TextBox`.

8. Add the `TextChanged` event handler for the `TextBox` to ensure the Watch! button is enabled when the `TextBox` contains text:

```
private void LocationBox_TextChanged(object sender, TextChangedEventArgs e)
{
    WatchButton.IsEnabled = !string.IsNullOrEmpty(LocationBox.Text);
}
```

9. Add the following code to the `Click` event handler for the Watch! button, which starts the `FileSystemWatcher`:

```
private void WatchButton_Click(object sender, RoutedEventArgs e)
{
    watcher.Path = System.IO.Path.GetDirectoryName(LocationBox.Text);
    watcher.Filter = System.IO.Path.GetFileName(LocationBox.Text);
    watcher.NotifyFilter = NotifyFilters.LastWrite |
        NotifyFilters.FileName | NotifyFilters.Size;
    AddMessage("Watching " + LocationBox.Text);
    // Begin watching.
    watcher.EnableRaisingEvents = true;
}
```

10. Create a directory called `C:\TempWatch` and a file in this directory called `temp.txt`.

11. Run the application. If everything builds successfully, click the Browse button and select `C:\Temp-Watch\temp.txt`.

12. Click the Watch! button to begin monitoring the file. The only change you will see in your application is a message confirming that the file is being watched.

13. Using Windows Explorer, navigate to `C:\TempWatch`. Open `temp.txt` in Notepad, add some text to the file, and save it.

14. Rename the file.

15. You should see a description of the changes to the file you selected to watch, as shown in Figure 14-8. Note that changes to the file after you rename it are ignored as the program is still watching the old file, so you'll need to rename it back or start watching the new name. You may see multiple events as the file size and its last write time change when it is saved.

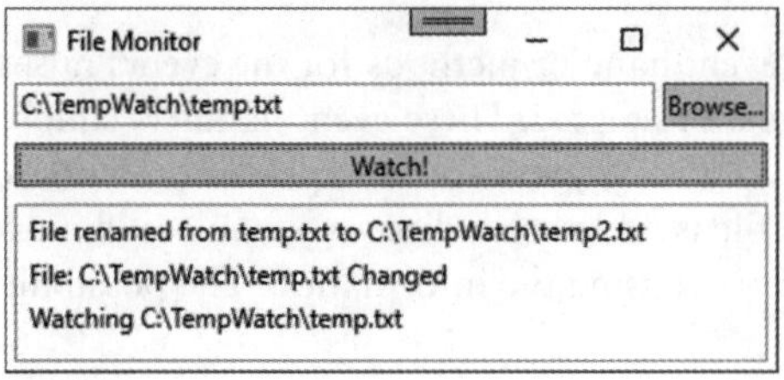

FIGURE 14-8

How It Works

This application is fairly simple, but it demonstrates how the `FileSystemWatcher` works. Try playing with the string you put into the monitor text box. If you specify `*.*` in a directory, it will monitor all changes in the directory.

Most of the code in the application is related to setting up the `FileSystemWatcher` object to watch the correct location:

```
watcher.Path = System.IO.Path.GetDirectoryName(LocationBox.Text);
watcher.Filter = System.IO.Path.GetFileName(LocationBox.Text);
watcher.NotifyFilter = NotifyFilters.LastWrite |
    NotifyFilters.FileName | NotifyFilters.Size;
AddMessage("Watching " + LocationBox.Text);
// Begin watching.
watcher.EnableRaisingEvents = true;
```

The code first sets the path to the directory to monitor. It uses a new object you have not looked at yet: `System.IO.Path`. This is a static class, much like the static `File` object. It exposes many static methods to manipulate and extract information out of file location strings. You first use it to extract the directory name the user typed in the text box, using the `GetDirectoryName()` method.

The next line sets the filter for the object. This can be an actual file, in which case it would only monitor the file, or it could be something like `*.txt`, in which case it would monitor all the `.txt` files in the directory specified. Again, you use the `Path` static object to extract the information from the supplied file location.

The `NotifyFilter` is a combination of `NotifyFilters` enumeration values that specify what constitutes a change. In this example, you have indicated that if the last write time stamp, the filename, or the size of the file changes, your application should be notified of the change. After updating the UI, you set the `EnableRaisingEvents` property to `true` to begin monitoring.

Before that, however, you have to create the object and set the event handlers:

```
watcher = new FileSystemWatcher();
watcher.Deleted += (s, e) =>
    AddMessage($"File: {e.FullPath} Deleted");
watcher.Renamed += (s, e) =>
    AddMessage($"File renamed from {e.OldName} to {e.FullPath}");
watcher.Changed += (s, e) =>
    AddMessage($"File: {e.FullPath} {e.ChangeType.ToString()}");
watcher.Created += (s, e) =>
    AddMessage($"File: {e.FullPath} Created");
```

This code uses lambda expressions to create anonymous event handler methods for the events raised by the watcher object when a file is deleted, renamed, changed, or created. These event handlers simply call the `AddMessage()` method with an informative message. Obviously, you could implement a more sophisticated response, depending on your application. When a file is added to a directory, you could move it somewhere else or read the contents and fire off a new process using the information. The possibilities are endless!

EXERCISES

14.1 Which namespace enables an application to work with files?

14.2 When would you use a `FileStream` object to write to a file instead of using a `StreamWriter` object?

14.3 Which methods of the `StreamReader` class enable you to read data from files and what does each one do?

14.4 Which class would you use to compress a stream by using the Deflate algorithm?

14.5 Which events does the `FileSystemWatcher` class expose and what are they for?

14.6 Modify the FileWatch application you built in this chapter by adding the capability to turn the file system monitoring on and off without exiting the application.

Answers to the exercises can be found in the Appendix.

▶ WHAT YOU LEARNED IN THIS CHAPTER

TOPIC	KEY CONCEPTS
Streams	A stream is an abstract representation of a serial device that you can read from or write to a byte at a time. Files are an example of such a device. There are two types of streams—input and output—for reading from and writing to devices, respectively.
File classes	There are numerous classes in the .NET Framework that abstract file system access, including `File` and `Directory` for dealing with files and directories through static methods, and `FileInfo` and `DirectoryInfo`, which can be instantiated to represent specific files and directories. The latter pair of classes is useful when you perform multiple operations on the same files and directories, as those classes don't require a path for every method call. Typical operations that you can perform on files and directories include interrogating and changing properties, creating, deleting, and copying.
File paths	File and directory paths can be absolute or relative. An absolute path gives a complete description of a location starting from the root of the drive that contains it; all parent directories are separated from child directories with backslashes. Relative directories are similar but start from a defined point in the file system, such as the directory where an application is executing (the working directory). To navigate the file system, you often use the `..` parent directory alias.
The `FileStream` object	The `FileStream` object provides access to the contents of a file, for reading and writing purposes. It accesses file data at the byte level and so is not always the best choice for accessing file data. A `FileStream` instance maintains a position byte index within a file so that you can navigate through the contents of a file. Accessing a file at any point in this way is known as *random access*.
Reading and writing to streams	An easier way to read and write file data is to use the `StreamReader` and `StreamWriter` classes in combination with a `FileStream`. These enable you to read and write character and string data rather than working with bytes. These types expose familiar methods for working with strings, including `ReadLine()` and `WriteLine()`. Because they work with string data, these classes make it easy to work with comma-delimited files, which are a common way to represent structured data.

TOPIC	KEY CONCEPTS
Compressed files	You can use the `DeflateStream` and `GZipStream` compressed stream classes to read and write compressed data from and to files. These classes work with byte data much like `FileStream`, but as with `FileStream` you can access data through `StreamReader` and `StreamWriter` classes to simplify your code.
Monitoring the file system	You can use the `FileSystemWatcher` class to monitor changes to file system data. You can monitor both files and directories, and provide a filter, if required, to be notified of changes to only those files that have a specific file extension. `FileSystemWatcher` instances notify you of changes by raising events that you can handle in your code.

15

XML and JSON

➤   XML basics

➤   JSON basics

➤   XML schemas

➤   XML Document Object Model

➤   Searching XML documents using XPath

➤   Serializing and Deserializing JSON

CODE DOWNLOADS FOR THIS CHAPTER

The code downloads for this chapter are found on the book page at www.wiley.com. Click the Downloads link. The code can also be found at github.com/benperk/BeginningCSharpAnd-DotNET. The code is in the Chapter15 folder and individually named according to the names throughout the chapter.

Just as programming languages like C# describe computer logic in a format that is readable by both machines and humans, XML and JSON are both *data languages*, which are used to store and retrieve data in a simple text format that can be read by both humans and nearly any computer.

Most C# .NET applications use XML in some form for storing data, such as .config files for storing configuration details and XAML files used in WPF and UWP applications. Because of this important fact, we'll spend the most time in this chapter on XML, with just a short look at JSON on the side.

During this chapter you will learn the basics of XML and JSON and then learn how to create XML documents and schemas. You will learn the basics of the `XmlDocument` class, how to read and write XML, how to insert and delete nodes, how to search for data in XML documents using XPath, and finally how to read and write JSON.

XML BASICS

Extensible Markup Language (XML) is a *data language*, which is a way of storing data in a simple text format that can be read by both humans and nearly any computer. It is a W3C standard format like HTML (`www.w3.org/XML`). It has been fully adopted by Microsoft in the .NET Framework and other Microsoft products. Even the document formats introduced with the newer versions of Microsoft Office are based on XML, although the Office applications themselves are not .NET applications.

The ins and outs of XML can be very complicated, so you won't look at every single detail here. Luckily, most tasks don't require a detailed knowledge of XML because Visual Studio typically takes care of most of the work—you will rarely have to write an XML document by hand. If you want to learn about XML in more depth, read a book such as *Beginning XML*, 5th Edition by Joe Fawcett, Danny Ayers, and Liam Quin (Wrox, 2021) or one of the many online tutorials such as `www.xml-news.org/docs/xml-basics.html` or `www.w3schools.com/xml`.

The basic format is very simple, as you can see in the following example that shows an XML format for sharing data about books:

```
<book>
  <title>Beginning C# and .NET</title>
  <author>Benjamin Perkins and Jon Reid</author>
  <code>978-1119795780</code>
</book>
<book>
  <title>Beginning XML</title>
  <author> Joe Fawcett et al </author>
  <code>978-1118162132</code>
</book>
<book>
  <title> Professional C# 7 and .NET Core =</title>
  <author>Christian Nagel</author>
  <code>978-1119449270</code>
</book>
```

In this example each book has a title, an author, and a unique code identifying the book. Each book's data is contained in a book *element* beginning with a `<book>` *tag* and ending with the `</book>` end tag. The `title`, `author`, and `code` values are stored in nested elements inside the book element.

Optionally, an element may also have *attributes* inside the tag itself. If the book code were an attribute of the book element instead of its own element, you'd see the book element beginning with something like this: `<book code=458685>`. To keep it simple we'll stick with elements in this chapter's examples. Generically both attributes and elements are called *nodes*, like the nodes of a tree.

JSON BASICS

Another data language you may encounter when developing C# applications is JSON. JSON stands for JavaScript Object Notation. Like XML, it is also a standard (`www.json.org`), though as you can tell from the name it is derived from the JavaScript language rather than C#. While not used throughout .NET like XML, it is a common format for transferring data from web services and web browsers.

JSON also has a very simple format. The same book data we showed previously in XML is presented here in JSON:

```
[
  {
    "title": "Beginning C# and .NET",
    "author": "Benjamin Perkins and Jon Reid",
    "code": "978-1119795780"
  },
  {
    "title": "Beginning XML",
    "author": "Joe Fawcett et al",
    "code": "978-1118162132"
  },
  {
    "title": "Professional C# 7 and .NET Core",
    "author": "Christian Nagel",
    "code": "978-1119449270"
  }
]
```

As with the previous XML example, we see books with title, author, and a unique code. JSON uses curly braces (`{}`) to delimit blocks of data and square brackets (`[]`) to delimit arrays and collections similar to the way C#, JavaScript, and other C-like languages use curly braces for blocks of code and square brackets to reference items in arrays and collections.

JSON is a more compact format than XML, but it is much harder for humans to read, especially as the curly braces and brackets become deeply nested in complex data.

XML SCHEMAS

An XML document may be described by a *schema*, which is another XML file describing what elements and attributes are allowed in a particular document. You can *validate* an XML document against a schema, ensuring that your program doesn't encounter data it isn't prepared to handle. The standard schema XML format used with C# is XML Schema Definition (XSD).

Figure 15-1 includes a long list of schemas recognized by Visual Studio (you can see this list by selecting XML ➪ Schemas from the Visual Studio menu). However, Visual Studio will not automatically remember schemas you've used. If you are using a schema repeatedly and don't want to browse for it every time you need it, you can copy it to the following location: `C:\Program Files (x86)\ Microsoft Visual Studio\2019\Community\Xml\Schemas`. Any schema copied to that location will show up on the XML Schemas dialog box.

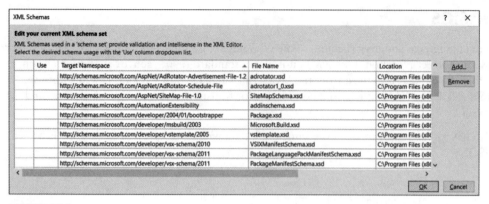

FIGURE 15-1

You can create an XML schema from an XML file and then use the schema to validate further changes, as demonstrated in the following Try It Out.

TRY IT OUT Creating an XML Document in Visual Studio: Chapter15\XML and Schema\GhostStories.xml

Follow these steps to create an XML document:

1. Open Visual Studio and select File ⇨ New ⇨ File from the menu. If you don't see this option, create a new project, right-click the project in the Solution Explorer, and choose to add a new item. Then select XML File from the dialog box.

2. In the New File dialog box, select XML File and click Open. Visual Studio creates a new XML document for you. Visual Studio adds an XML declaration, complete with an `encoding` attribute. (It also colors the attributes and elements.)

3. Save the file by pressing Ctrl+S or by selecting File ⇨ Save `XMLFile1.xml` from the File menu. Visual Studio asks you where to save the file and what to call the file; save it in the `BeginningCSharpAndDotNET\Chapter15\XML and Schemas` folder as `GhostStories.xml`.

4. Move the cursor to the line underneath the XML declaration, and type the text `<stories>`. Notice how Visual Studio automatically puts the end tag in as soon as you type the greater than sign to close the opening tag.

5. Type this XML file and then click Save:

```
<stories>
  <story>
    <title>A House in Aungier Street</title>
    <author>
        <name>Sheridan Le Fanu</name>
        <nationality>Irish</nationality>
    </author>
    <rating>eerie</rating>
  </story>
  <story>
```

```
        <title>The Signalman</title>
        <author>
            <name>Charles Dickens</name>
            <nationality>English</nationality>
        </author>
        <rating>atmospheric</rating>
    </story>
    <story>
        <title>The Turn of the Screw</title>
        <author>
            <name>Henry James</name>
            <nationality>American</nationality>
        </author>
        <rating>a bit dull</rating>
    </story>
</stories>
```

6. It is now possible to let Visual Studio create a schema that fits the XML you have written. Do this by selecting the Create Schema menu option from the XML menu. Save the resulting XSD file by clicking Save as GhostStories.xsd.

7. Return to the XML file and type the following XML before the ending </stories> tag:

```
<story>
    <title>Number 13</title>
    <author>
        <name>M.R. James</name>
        <nationality>English</nationality>
    </author>
    <rating>mysterious</rating>
</story>
```

You are now getting IntelliSense hints when you begin typing the starting tags. That's because Visual Studio knows to connect the newly created XSD schema to the XML file you are typing.

8. It is possible to create this link between XML and one or more schemas in Visual Studio. Select XML ➪ Schemas. That brings up the XML Schemas dialog box shown in Figure 15-2. At the top of the long list of schemas that Visual Studio recognizes, you will see GhostStories.xsd. To the left of it is a checkmark, which indicates that this schema is being used on the current XML document.

	Use	Target Namespace	File Name	Location	
▶	✓		GhostStories.xsd	C:\BeginningCSharpAndDotNET\Chapter15\XML and Schemas	

FIGURE 15-2

XML DOCUMENT OBJECT MODEL

The XML Document Object Model (XML DOM) is a set of classes used to access and manipulate XML in a very intuitive way. The DOM is perhaps not the quickest way to read XML data, but as soon as you understand the relationship between the classes and the elements of an XML document, you will find it very easy to use.

The classes that make up the DOM can be found in the namespace System.Xml. There are several classes and namespaces in this namespace, but this chapter focuses on only a few of the classes that enable you to easily manipulate XML. These classes are described in Table 15-1.

TABLE 15-1: Common DOM Classes

CLASS	DESCRIPTION
XmlNode	Represents a single node in a document tree. It is the base of many of the classes shown in this chapter. If this node represents the root of an XML document, you can navigate to any position in the document from it.
XmlDocument	Extends the XmlNode class, but is often the first object you use when using XML. That's because this class is used to load and save data from disk or elsewhere.
XmlElement	Represents a single element in the XML document. XmlElement is derived from XmlLinkedNode, which in turn is derived from XmlNode.
XmlAttribute	Represents a single attribute. Like the XmlDocument class, it is derived from the XmlNode class.
XmlText	Represents the text between a starting tag and a closing tag.
XmlComment	Represents a special kind of node that is not regarded as part of the document other than to provide information to the reader about parts of the document.
XmlNodeList	Represents a collection of nodes.

The XmlDocument Class

Usually, the first thing your application will want to do with XML is read it from disk. As described in Table 15-1, this is the domain of the XmlDocument class. You can think of the XmlDocument as an in-memory representation of the file on disk. Once you have used the XmlDocument class to load a file into memory, you can obtain the root node of the document from it and start reading and manipulating the XML:

```
using System.Xml;
.
.
.
XmlDocument document = new XmlDocument();
document.Load(@"C:\BeginningCSharpAndDotNET\Chapter15\XML and Schema\books.xml");
```

The two lines of code create a new instance of the XmlDocument class and load the file books .xml into it.

> **NOTE** *The folder name is an absolute path; your folder structure may differ, and if so, you should adjust the path following* document.Load *to reflect the actual folder path on your computer.*

Remember that the XmlDocument class is located in the System.Xml namespace, and you should insert a using System.Xml; directive in the using section at the beginning of the code.

In addition to loading and saving the XML, the XmlDocument class is also responsible for maintaining the XML structure itself. Therefore, you will find numerous methods on this class that are used to create, alter, and delete nodes in the tree. You will look at some of those methods shortly, but to present the methods properly, you need to know a bit more about another class: XmlElement.

The XmlElement Class

Now that the document has been loaded into memory, you want to do something with it. The DocumentElement property of the XmlDocument instance you created in the preceding code returns an instance of an XmlElement that represents the root element of the XmlDocument. This element is important because it gives you access to every bit of information in the document:

```
XmlDocument document = new XmlDocument();
document.Load(
        @"C:\BeginningCSharpAndDotNET\Chapter15\XML and Schema\books.xml");
XmlElement element = document.DocumentElement;
```

After you have the root element of the document, you are ready to use the information. The XmlElement class contains methods and properties for manipulating the nodes and attributes of the tree. Let's examine the properties for navigating the XML elements first, shown in Table 15-2.

TABLE 15-2: XmlElement Properties

PROPERTY	DESCRIPTION
FirstChild	Returns the first child element after this one. If you recall the books.xml file from earlier in the chapter, the root node of the document was called "books" and the next node after that was "book." In that document, then, the first child of the root node "books" is "book." <books> *Root node* <book> *FirstChild* FirstChild returns an XmlNode object, and you should test for the type of the returned node because it is unlikely to always be an XmlElement instance. In the books example, the child of the Title element is, in fact, an XmlText node that represents the text Beginning Visual C#.

continues

TABLE 15-2 (*continued*)

PROPERTY	DESCRIPTION

LastChild	Operates exactly like the FirstChild property except that it returns the last child of the current node. In the case of the books example, the last child of the "books" node will still be a "book" node, but it will be the node representing the "Beginning XML" book.
	
	\<books\> *Root node*
	  \<book\> *FirstChild*
	    \<title\>Beginning C# and .NET\</title\>
	    \<author\>Benjamin Perkins and Jon Reid\</author\>
	    \<code\>978-1119795780\</code\>
	  \</book\>
	  \<book\> *LastChild*
	    \<title\>Beginning XML\</title\>
	    \<author\>Joe Fawcett et al\</author\>
	    \<code\>978-1118162132\</code\>
	  \</book\>
	\</books\>

ParentNode	Returns the parent of the current node. In the books example, the "books" node is the parent of all three of the "book" nodes.
NextSibling	Where FirstChild and LastChild properties return their respective child nodes of the current node, the NextSibling node returns the next node that has the same parent node. In the case of the books example, that means getting the NextSibling of the title element will return the author element, and calling NextSibling on that will return the code element.
HasChildNodes	Enables you to check whether the current element has child elements without actually getting the value from FirstChild and examining that against null.

Using the five properties from Table 15-2, it is possible to run through an entire XmlDocument, as shown in the following Try It Out.

TRY IT OUT   Looping through All Nodes in an XML Document: Chapter15\ LoopThroughXmlDocument

In this example, you are going to create a small Windows Presentation Foundation (WPF) application that loops through all the nodes of an XML document and prints out the name of the element or the text contained in the element in the case of an XmlText element. This code uses Books.xml, which you saw in the "Schemas" section earlier; if you didn't create that file as you worked through that section, you can find it in Chapter15\XML and Schemas\ in this chapter's downloadable code.

1. Begin by creating a new WPF Application project by selecting File ➪ New ➪ Project. In the dialog box that appears, select C# ➪ WPF Application. Name the project **LoopThroughXmlDocument** and press Next. Set the Target Framework to the Current version (.NET 5.0). WPF applications are covered in detail in Chapter 21. This sample is simple and you can just follow the steps.

2. Design the form as shown in Figure 15-3 by dragging a `TextBlock` control and a `Button` control onto the form.

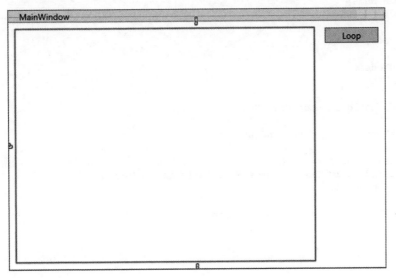

FIGURE 15-3

3. Name the `TextBlock` control **textBlockResults**, and name the button **buttonLoop**. Allow the `TextBlock` to fill all the space not used by the button.

4. Add the event handler for the `Click` event for the button, and enter the code that follows. Don't forget to add `using System.Xml;` to the using section at the top of the file:

```
private void buttonLoop_Click(object sender, RoutedEventArgs e)
{
  XmlDocument document = new XmlDocument();
  document.Load(booksFile);
  textBlockResults.Text =
  FormatText(document.DocumentElement as XmlNode, "", "");
}
private string FormatText(XmlNode node, string text, string indent)
{
  if (node is XmlText)
  {
    text += node.Value;
    return text;
  }
  if (string.IsNullOrEmpty(indent))
    indent = "";
  else
```

```
    {
        text += "\r\n" + indent;
    }
    if (node is XmlComment)
    {
        text += node.OuterXml;
        return text;
    }
    text += "<" + node.Name;
    if (node.Attributes.Count > 0)
    {
        AddAttributes(node, ref text);
    }
    if (node.HasChildNodes)
    {
        text += ">";
        foreach (XmlNode child in node.ChildNodes)
        {
            text = FormatText(child, text, indent + "  ");
        }
        if (node.ChildNodes.Count == 1 &&
            (node.FirstChild is XmlText || node.FirstChild is XmlComment))
            text += "</" + node.Name + ">";
        else
            text += "\r\n" + indent + "</" + node.Name + ">";
    }
    else
        text += "/>";
    return text;
}
private void AddAttributes(XmlNode node, ref string text)
{
    foreach (XmlAttribute xa in node.Attributes)
    {
        text += " " + xa.Name + "='" + xa.Value + "'";
    }
}
```

5. Add the private const that holds the location of the file that is loaded. You can change the location to reflect the location you put the file on your local system:

```
private const string booksFile =
        @"C:\BeginningCSharpAndDotNET\Chapter15\XML and Schema\Books.xml";
```

6. Run the application and click Loop. You should get a result like the one shown in Figure 15-4.

How It Works

When you click the button, the XmlDocument method Load is called. This method loads the XML from a file into the XmlDocument instance, which can then be used to access the elements of the XML. Then you call a method that enables you to loop through the XML recursively, passing the

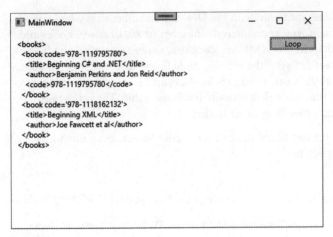

FIGURE 15-4

root node of the XML document to the method. The root element is obtained with the property
`DocumentElement` of the `XmlDocument` class. In the `FormatText` method, the first line to note is the
`if` sentence:

```
if (node is XmlText)
    {
       . . .
    }
```

Recall that the `is` operator enables you to examine the type of an object, and it returns `true` if the instance is
of the specified type. Even though the root node is declared as an `XmlNode`, that is merely the base type of the
objects you are going to work with. By using the `is` operator to test the type of the objects, you are able to
determine the type of the object at runtime and select the action to perform based on that.

Inside the `FormatText` method you generate the text for the text box. You have to know the type of the
current instance of root because the information you want to display is obtained differently for different
elements: You want to display the name of `XmlElements` and the value of `XmlText` elements.

Changing the Values of Nodes

Before you examine how to change the value of a node, it is important to realize that very rarely is the value
of a node a simple thing. In fact, you will find that although all of the classes that derive from `XmlNode`
include a property called `Value`, it very rarely returns anything useful to you. Although this can feel like a
bit of a letdown at first, you'll find it is actually quite logical. Examine the books example from earlier:

```
<books>
  <book>
    <title>Beginning C# and .NET</title>
    <author>Benjamin Perkins and Jon Reid</author>
    <code> 978-1119795780</code>
  </book>
  <book>
  . . .
</books>
```

Every single tag pair in the document resolves into a node in the DOM. Remember that when you looped through all the nodes in the document, you encountered a number of XmlElement nodes and three XmlText nodes. The XmlElement nodes in this XML are <books>, <book>, <title>, <author>, and <code>. The XmlText nodes are the text between the starting and closing tags of title, author, and code. Although it could be argued that the value of title, author, and code is the text between the tags, that text is itself a node; and it is that node that actually holds the value. The other tags clearly have no values associated with them other than other nodes.

The following line is in the if block near the top of the code in the earlier FormatText method. It executes when the current node is an XmlText node.

```
text += node.Value;
```

You can see that the Value property of the XmlText node instance is used to get the value of the node.

Nodes of the type XmlElement return null if you use their Value property, but it is possible to get the information between the starting and closing tags of an XmlElement if you use one of two other methods: InnerText and InnerXml. That means you are able to manipulate the values of nodes using two methods and a property, as described in Table 15-3.

TABLE 15-3: Three Ways to Get the Value of a Node

PROPERTY	DESCRIPTION
InnerText	Gets the text of all the child nodes of the current node and returns it as a single concatenated string. This means if you get the value of InnerText from the book node in the preceding XML, the string Beginning C# and .NETBenjamin Perkins and Jon Reid 978-1119795780 is returned. If you get the InnerText of the title node, only "Beginning C# and .NET" is returned. You can set the text using this method, but be careful if you do so because if you set the text of a wrong node you may overwrite information you did not want to change.

InnerXml	Returns the text like InnerText, but it also returns all of the tags. Therefore, if you get the value of InnerXml on the book node, the result is the following string:
	
	`<title>Beginning C# and .NET</title>`
	
	`<author>Benjamin Perkins and Jon Reid</author>`
	
	`<code>978-1119795780</code>`
	
	As you can see, this can be quite useful if you have a string containing XML that you want to inject directly into your XML document. However, you are entirely responsible for the string yourself, and if you insert badly formed XML, the application will generate an exception.

Value	The "cleanest" way to manipulate information in the document, but as mentioned earlier, only a few of the classes actually return anything useful when you get the value. The classes that will return the desired text are as follows: XmlText XmlComment XmlAttribute

Inserting New Nodes

Now that you've seen that you can move around in the XML document and even get the values of the elements, let's examine how to change the structure of the document by adding nodes to the books document you've been using.

To insert new elements in the list, you need to examine the new methods that are placed on the `XmlDocument` and `XmlNode` classes, shown in Table 15-4. The `XmlDocument` class has methods that enable you to create new `XmlNode` and `XmlElement` instances, which is nice because both of these classes have only a protected constructor, which means you cannot create an instance of either directly with new.

TABLE 15-4: Methods for Creating Nodes

METHOD	DESCRIPTION
CreateNode	Creates any kind of node. There are three overloads of the method, two of which enable you to create nodes of the type found in the `XmlNodeType` enumeration and one that enables you to specify the type of node to use as a string. Unless you are quite sure about specifying a node type other than those in the enumeration, use the two overloads that use the enumeration. The method returns an instance of `XmlNode` that can then be cast to the appropriate type explicitly.
CreateElement	A version of `CreateNode` that creates only nodes of the `XmlElement` variety.
CreateAttribute	A version of `CreateNode` that creates only nodes of the `XmlAttribute` variety.
CreateTextNode	Creates—yes, you guessed it—nodes of the type `XmlText`.
CreateComment	This method is included here to highlight the diversity of node types that can be created. This method doesn't create a node that is actually part of the data represented by the XML document, but rather is a comment meant for any human eyes that might have to read the data. You can pick up comments when reading the document in your applications as well.

The methods in Table 15-4 are all used to create the nodes themselves, but after calling any of them you have to do something with them before they become interesting. Immediately after creation, the nodes contain no additional information, and they are not yet inserted into the document. To do either, you should use methods that are found on any class derived from `XmlNode` (including `XmlDocument` and `XmlElement`), described in Table 15-5.

In the following Try It Out, you build on the previous example and insert a book node in the books .xml document. There is no code in the example to clean up the document (yet), so if you run it several times you will probably end up with a lot of identical nodes.

TABLE 15-5: Methods for Inserting Nodes

METHOD	DESCRIPTION
AppendChild	Appends a child node to a node of type XmlNode or a derived type. Remember that the node you append appears at the bottom of the list of children of the node on which the method is called. If you don't care about the order of the children, there's no problem; if you do care, remember to append the nodes in the correct sequence.
InsertAfter	Controls exactly where you want to insert the new node. The method takes two parameters—the first is the new node and the second is the node after which the new node should be inserted.
InsertBefore	Works exactly like InsertAfter, except that the new node is inserted before the node you supply as a reference.

TRY IT OUT   Creating Nodes: Chapter15\LoopThroughXmlDocument

This example builds on the LoopThroughXmlDocument project you created earlier. Follow these steps to add a node to the books.xml document:

1. Wrap the TextBlock in a ScrollViewer and set its VerticalScrollBarVisibility property to Auto.

2. Add a button beneath the existing button on the form and name it **buttonCreateNode**. Change its Content property to Create.

3. Add the Click event handler to the new button and enter the following code:

```
private void buttonCreateNode_Click(object sender, RoutedEventArgs e)
{
    // Load the XML document.
    XmlDocument document = new XmlDocument();
    document.Load(booksFile);
    // Get the root element.
    XmlElement root = document.DocumentElement;
    // Create the new nodes.
    XmlElement newBook = document.CreateElement("book");
    XmlElement newTitle = document.CreateElement("title");
    XmlElement newAuthor = document.CreateElement("author");
    XmlElement newCode = document.CreateElement("code");
    XmlText title = document.CreateTextNode("Professional C# 7 and .NET Core");
    XmlText author = document.CreateTextNode("Christian Nagel");
    XmlText code = document.CreateTextNode("978-1119449270");
    XmlComment comment = document.CreateComment("the Professional edition");
    // Insert the elements.
    newBook.AppendChild(comment);
    newBook.AppendChild(newTitle);
    newBook.AppendChild(newAuthor);
    newBook.AppendChild(newCode);
    newTitle.AppendChild(title);
    newAuthor.AppendChild(author);
```

```
        newCode.AppendChild(code);
        root.InsertAfter(newBook, root.LastChild);
        document.Save(booksFile);
    }
```

4. Run the application and click Create. Then click Loop, and you should see the window shown in Figure 15-5.

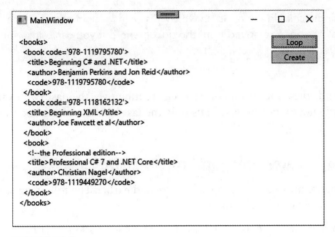

FIGURE 15-5

There is one important type of node that you didn't create in the preceding example: the XmlAttribute. That is left as an exercise at the end of the chapter.

How It Works

The code in the buttonCreateNode_Click method is where all the creation of nodes happens. It creates eight new nodes, four of which are of type XmlElement, three of type XmlText, and one of type XmlComment.

All of the nodes are created with the method of the encapsulating XmlDocument instance. The Xml-Element nodes are created with the CreateElement method, the XmlText nodes are created with the CreateTextNode method, and the XmlComment node is created with the CreateComment method.

After the nodes have been created, they still need to be inserted into the XML tree. This is done with the AppendChild method on the element to which the new node should become a child. The only exception to this is the book node, which is the root node of all of the new nodes. This node is inserted into the tree using the InsertAfter method of the root object. Whereas all of the nodes that are inserted using AppendChild always become the last node in the list of child nodes, InsertAfter enables you to position the node where you want it.

Deleting Nodes

Now that you've seen how to create new nodes, all that is left is to learn how to delete them again. All classes derived from XmlNode include two methods, shown in Table 15-6, that enable you to remove nodes from the document.

TABLE 15-6: Methods for Removing Nodes

METHOD	DESCRIPTION
RemoveAll	Removes all child nodes in the node on which it is called. What is slightly less obvious is that it also removes all attributes on the node because they are regarded as child nodes as well.
RemoveChild	Removes a single child in the node on which it is called. The method returns the node that has been removed from the document, but you can reinsert it if you change your mind.

The following short Try It Out extends the application you've been creating over the past two examples to include the capability to delete nodes. For now, it finds only the last instance of the book node and removes it.

TRY IT OUT Removing Nodes: Chapter15\LoopThroughXmlDocument

This example builds on the LoopThroughXmlDocument project you created earlier. The following steps enable you to find and remove the final instance of the book node:

1. Add a new button below the two that already exist and name it **buttonDeleteNode**. Set its Content property to Delete.

2. Double-click the new button and enter the following code:

```
private void buttonDeleteNode_Click(object sender, RoutedEventArgs e)
{
  // Load the XML document.
  XmlDocument document = new XmlDocument();
  document.Load(booksFile);
  // Get the root element.
  XmlElement root = document.DocumentElement;
  // Find the node. root is the <books> tag, find its last child
  // which will be the last <book> node.
  if (root.HasChildNodes)
  {
    XmlNode book = root.LastChild;
    // Delete the child.
    root.RemoveChild(book);
    // Save the document back to disk.
    document.Save(booksFile);
  }
}
```

3. Run the application. When you click the Delete Node button and then the Loop button, the last node in the tree will disappear.

How It Works

After the initial steps to load the XML into the XmlDocument object, you examine the root element to see whether there are any child elements in the XML you loaded. If there are, you use the LastChild property of the XmlElement class to get the last child. After that, removing the element is as simple as calling `RemoveChild`, which passes in the instance of the element you want to remove—in this case, the last child of the root element.

Selecting Nodes

You now know how to move back and forth in an XML document, how to manipulate the values of the document, how to create new nodes, and how to delete them again. Only one thing remains in this section: how to select nodes without having to traverse the entire tree.

The `XmlNode` class includes two methods, described in Table 15-7, commonly used to select nodes from the document without running through every node in it: `SelectSingleNode` and `SelectNodes`, both of which use a special query language, called XPath, to select the nodes. You will learn about that in the Try It Out in the next section.

TABLE 15-7: Methods for Selecting Nodes

METHOD	DESCRIPTION
`SelectSingleNode`	Selects a single node. If you create a query that fetches more than one node, only the first node will be returned.
`SelectNodes`	Returns a node collection in the form of an `XmlNodeList` class.

SEARCHING XML WITH XPATH

XPath is a query language for XML documents, much as SQL is for relational databases. It is used by the two methods described in Table 15-7 that enable you to avoid the hassle of walking the entire tree of an XML document. It does take a little getting used to, however, because the syntax is nothing like SQL or C#.

> **NOTE** *XPath is quite extensive, and only a small part of it is covered here so you can start selecting nodes. If you are interested in learning more, take a look at* www.w3.org/TR/xpath *and the Visual Studio help pages.*

To properly see XPath in action, you are going to use an XML file called `Elements.xml`, which contains a partial list of the chemical elements of the periodic table. You will find a subset of that XML listed in the "Selecting Nodes" Try It Out example later in the chapter, and it can be found in the download code for this chapter on this book's website as `Elements.xml`.

Table 15-8 lists some of the most common operations you can perform with XPath. If nothing else is stated, the XPath query example makes a selection that is relative to the node on which it is performed. When it is necessary to have a node name, you can assume the current node is the `<element>` node in the XML document.

TABLE 15-8: Common XPath Operations

PURPOSE	XPATH QUERY EXAMPLE
Select the current node.	`.`
Select the parent of the current node.	`..`
Select all child nodes of the current node.	`*`
Select all child nodes with a specific name—in this case, `title`.	`title`
Select an attribute of the current node.	`@Type`
Select all attributes of the current node.	`@*`
Select a child node by index—in this case, the second element node.	`element[2]`
Select all the text nodes of the current node.	`text()`
Select text node grandchildren of this node's element children.	`element/text()`
Select all nodes in the document with a particular name—in this case, all `mass` nodes.	`//mass`
Select all nodes in the document with a particular name and a particular parent name—in this case, the parent name is `element` and the node name is `name`.	`//element/name`
Select a node where a value criterion is met—in this case, the element whose name is `Hydrogen`.	`//element[name='Hydrogen']`
Select a node where an attribute value criterion is met—in this case, the `Type` attribute is `Noble Gas`.	`//element[@Type='Noble Gas']`

In the following Try It Out, you'll create a small application that enables you to execute and see the results of a number of predefined queries, as well as enter your own queries.

TRY IT OUT Selecting Nodes: Chapter15\XpathQuery\Elements.xml

As previously mentioned, this example uses an XML file called `Elements.xml`. You can download the file from the book's website or type part of it in from here:

```xml
<?xml version="1.0"?>
<elements>
  <!--First Non-Metal-->
  <element Type="Non-Metal">
    <name>Hydrogen</name>
    <symbol>H</symbol>
    <number>1</number>
    <specification>
```

```
      <mass>1.007825</mass>
      <density>0.0899 g/cm3</density>
    </specification>
  </element>
  <!--First Noble Gas-->
  <element Type="Noble Gas">
    <name>Helium</name>
    <symbol>He</symbol>
    <number>2</number>
    <specification>
      <mass>4.002602</mass>
      <density>0.1785 g/cm3</density>
    </specification>
  </element>
  <!--First Halogen-->
  <element Type="Halogen">
    <name>Fluorine</name>
    <symbol>F</symbol>
    <number>9</number>
    <specification>
      <mass>18.998404</mass>
      <density>1.696 g/cm3</density>
    </specification>
  </element>
  <element Type="Noble Gas">
    <name>Neon</name>
    <symbol>Ne</symbol>
    <number>10</number>
    <specification>
      <mass>20.1797</mass>
      <density>0.901 g/cm3</density>
    </specification>
  </element>
</elements>
```

Save the XML file as `Elements.xml`. Remember to change the path to the file in the code that follows. This example is a small query tool that you can use to test different queries on the XML provided with the code.

Follow these steps to create a WPF application with querying capability:

1. Create a new project. In the Create a New Project window, select C# ➪ WPF Application. Name the project **XPathQuery** and click Next. Set the Target Framework to the Current version (.NET 5.0).

2. Create the window shown in Figure 15-6. Name the controls as shown in the figure, except for the button, which should be named **buttonExecute**. Wrap the `TextBlock` in a `ScrollViewer` control and set its `VerticalScrollBarVisibility` property to `Auto`.

3. Go to the Code view and include the `using System.Xml` directive.

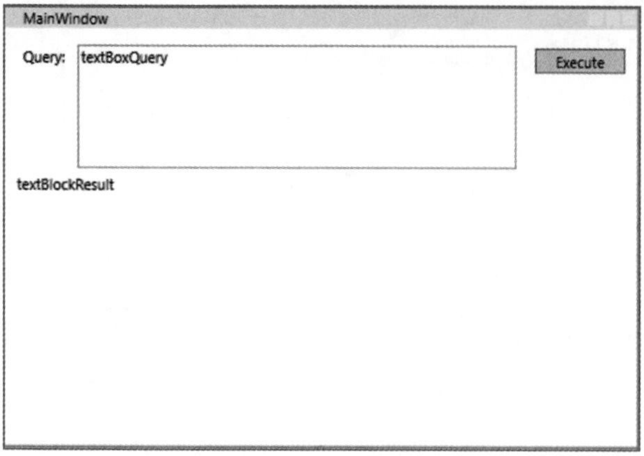

FIGURE 15-6

4. Add a private field to hold the document, and initialize it in the constructor:

```
private XmlDocument document;

public MainWindow()
{
  InitializeComponent();
  document = new XmlDocument();
  document.Load(@"C:\BeginningCSharpAndDotNET\Chapter15\XML and Schema\Elements.xml");
}
```

5. You need a few helper methods to display the result of the queries in the textBlockResult TextBlock:

```
private void Update(XmlNodeList nodes)
{
  if (nodes == null || nodes.Count == 0)
  {
    textBlockResult.Text = "The query yielded no results";
    return;
  }
  string text = "";
  foreach (XmlNode node in nodes)
  {
    text = FormatText(node, text, "") + "\r\n";
  }
  textBlockResult.Text = text;
}
```

6. Update the constructor to display the entire contents of the XML file when the application starts by adding the Update() method call on the last line as shown here:

```
public MainWindow()
{
  InitializeComponent();
  document = new XmlDocument();
  document.Load(@"C:\BeginningCSharpAndDotNET\Chapter15\XML and Schemas\Elements.xml");
  Update(document.DocumentElement.SelectNodes("."));
}
```

7. Copy and paste the two methods `FormatText` and `AddAttributes` from the previous LoopThroughXmlDocument Try It Out sections to the new project.

8. Finally, insert the code that executes the query that the user enters in the text box:

```
private void buttonExecute_Click(object sender, RoutedEventArgs e)
{
    try
    {
        XmlNodeList nodes = document.DocumentElement.SelectNodes(textBoxQuery.Text);
        Update(nodes);
    }
    catch (Exception err)
    {
        textBlockResult.Text = err.Message;
    }
}
```

9. Run the application and type the following query into the `textBoxQuery` text box to select the element node that contains a node with the text `Hydrogen`:

```
element[name='Hydrogen']
```

How It Works

The `buttonExecute_Click` method performs the queries. Because you can't know in advance if the queries typed into the `textBoxQuery` are going to yield a single node or multiple nodes, you must use the `SelectNodes` method. This will either return an `XmlNodeList` object or throw one of the exceptions regarding XPath if the query used is illegal.

The `Update` method is responsible for looping through the content of the `XmlNodeList` selected by `SelectNodes`. It calls `FormatText` from the earlier examples with each of the nodes, and `FormatText` is responsible for recursively traversing the node tree and creating readable text you can use in the `textBoxResult` control.

In the exercises at the end of the chapter, you will find a number of additional XPath queries to try. Before you enter them into the XPathQuery application to see the result, try to determine for yourself the query's outcome.

JSON SERIALIZATION AND DESERIALIZATION

We mentioned the JSON data language in the introduction to this chapter. The `System.Text.json` package provides support for JSON in the standard .NET libraries. The main purpose of this package is to provide fast *serialization* and *deserialization* of C# objects to and from the JSON format. Serialization is the conversion of an object to a character string format that can be transmitted over a network or saved to a file. Deserialization is the opposite of serialization, reading from the character string and creating objects for your code to work with. You can also serialize and deserialize to XML or binary data, but JSON is ideal for this as it is compact and yet readable by humans, which makes it easier to debug.

The following short Try It Out shows how to serialize a collection of objects to JSON, save to a file, and then read the file just created and deserialize to another collection of objects.

TRY IT OUT   Chapter15\SerializeJSON

1. In the Visual Studio menu, go to File ⇨ New ⇨ Project. Create a Console Application named SerializeJSON and save it in the directory C:\BeginningCSharpAndDotNET\Chapter15. Set the Target Framework to the Current version (.NET 5.0).

2. After the initial using System; import at the top of the file Program.cs., add the following using statements to import the System.Generic.Collections, System.IO, and System.Text.Json namespaces to serialize a collection of objects to a file:

```
using System.Collections.Generic;
using System.IO;
using System.Text.Json;
```

3. Add the following class definition for Book immediately following the namespace SerializeJSON declaration, preceding the Program class definition:

```
public class Book
{
    public string title { get; set; }
    public string author { get; set; }
    public string code { get; set; }
}
```

4. Replace the code in the Main method with the following code:

```
static void Main(string[] args)
{
    List<Book> books = new List<Book>();
    Book book1 = new Book {
        title = "Beginning C# and .NET",
        author = "Benjamin Perkins and Jon Reid",
        code = "978-1119795780"
    };
    Book book2 = new Book {
        title = "Beginning XML",
        author = "Joe Fawcett et al",
        code = "978-1118162132"
    };
    Book book3 = new Book {
        title = "Professional C# 7 and .NET Core",
        author = "Christian Nagel",
        code = "978-1119449270"
    };

    books.Add(book1);
    books.Add(book2);
    books.Add(book3);

    string jsonString1 = JsonSerializer.Serialize(books, typeof(List<Book>));
    File.WriteAllText("Books.json", jsonString1);
```

```
        string jsonString2 = File.ReadAllText("Books.json");
        List<Book> books2 = JsonSerializer.Deserialize<List<Book>>(jsonString2);
        foreach (Book b in books2)
        {
            Console.WriteLine("code: {0} title: {1} author: {2}", b.code, b.title, b.author);
        }

        Console.ReadKey();
    }
```

5. Run the application. Output of the book data read from the JSON file is shown in Figure 15-7.

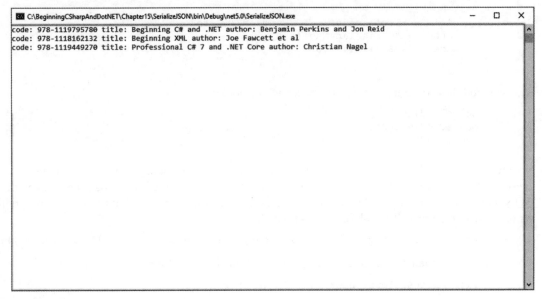

FIGURE 15-7

How It Works

First you define the Book class with the title, author, and code properties:

```
public class Book
{
    public string title { get; set; }
    public string author { get; set; }
    public string code { get; set; }
}
```

Then in the main program you create a collection of books (List<Book>) to represent a list of books in memory:

```
List<Book> books = new List<Book>();
```

Then you create three instances of the Book class:

```
Book book1 = new Book {
    title = "Beginning C# and .NET",
    author = "Benjamin Perkins and Jon Reid",
    code = "978-1119795780"
};
Book book2 = new Book {
    title = "Beginning XML",
    author = "Joe Fawcett et al",
    code = "978-1118162132"
};
Book book3 = new Book {
    title = "Professional C# 7 and .NET Core",
    author = "Christian Nagel",
    code = "978-1119449270"
};
```

Next you add these three instances to the collection of books:

```
books.Add(book1);
books.Add(book2);
books.Add(book3);
```

Now we are ready to serialize the books collection to a character string in JSON format. Simply declare the string jsonString1 and call the JsonSerializer.Serialize() method to load the string with the JSON data representing the books collection. You need to tell the serializer what object you are serializing (books) and the type of the object (List<Book>):

```
string jsonString1 = JsonSerializer.Serialize(books, typeof(List<Book>));
```

Now we can write the JSON character string to a file named Books.json:

```
File.WriteAllText("Books.json", jsonString1);
```

If you want to see the JSON content you're writing to file, set a debug breakpoint at the File .WriteAllText line and hover the cursor over jsonString1. You will see the JSON data in a very compact form with no formatting:

```
[{"title":"Beginning C# and .NET","author":"Benjamin Perkins and Jon
Reid","code":"978-1119795780"},{"title":"Beginning XML","author":"Joe
Fawcett et al","code":"978-1118162132"},{"title":"Professional C# 7 and .NET
Core","author":"Christian Nagel","code":"978-1119449270"}]
```

Next we read the JSON data back from the file we just created into a new character string variable jsonString2:

```
string jsonString2 = File.ReadAllText("Books.json");
```

Now we call the Deserialize() method of JsonSerializer to convert the JSON data back to a new collection of Book objects named books2:

```
List<Book> books2 = JsonSerializer.Deserialize<List<Book>>(jsonString2);
```

Now we can loop through the Book objects in the books2 collection and see they contain the same data we had originally set in the first collection:

```
foreach (Book b in books2)
{
        Console.WriteLine("code: {0} title: {1} author: {2}", b.code, b.title,
b.author);
}
```

As you can see, it is easy to serialize to the JSON format if you define the C# classes you want to serialize ahead of time and let the serializer do the work of conversion to JSON format and back—all you have to do is work with the C# objects you are familiar with without having to read and convert the contents of JSON files manually.

EXERCISES

15.1. Change the Insert example in the "Creating Nodes" Try It Out section to insert an attribute called Pages with the value 1000+ on the book node.

15.2. Determine the outcome of the following XPath queries and then verify your results by typing the queries into the XPathQuery application from the "Selecting Nodes" Try It Out. Remember that all of your queries are being executed on the DocumentElement, which is the elements node.

```
//elements
element
element[@Type='Noble Gas']
//mass
//mass/..
element/specification[mass='20.1797']
element/name[text()='Neon']
```

15.3. On many Windows systems the default viewer of XML is a web browser. If you are using Internet Explorer you will see a nicely formatted view of the XML when you load the Elements.xml file into it. Why would it not be ideal to display the XML from our queries in a browser control instead of a text box?

Answers to the exercises can be found in the Appendix.

▶ WHAT YOU LEARNED IN THIS CHAPTER

TOPIC	KEY CONCEPTS
XML basics	XML documents are created from an XML declaration, XML elements, and attributes. The XML declaration defines the XML version.
JSON basics	JSON is a data language most often used when transferring data between JavaScript and web services. JSON is more compact than the XML but harder to read.
XML schema	XML schemas are used to define the structure of XML documents. Schemas are especially useful when you need to exchange information with third parties. By agreeing on a schema for the data that is exchanged, you and the third party will be able to check that the documents are valid.
XML DOM	The Document Object Model (XML DOM) is the basis for .NET Framework classes provided for creating and manipulating XML.
JSON Serialization and Deserialization	You can use the `JsonSerializer` class in the `System.Text.Json` namespace to serialize C# objects to a string representation that you can save to a file and read later to recreate the C# objects.
XPath	XPath is one of the possible ways to query data in XML documents. To use XPath, you must be familiar with the structure of the XML document in order to be able to select individual elements from it. Although XPath can be used on any well-formed XML document, the fact that you must know the structure of the document when you create the query means that ensuring that the document is valid also ensures that the query will work from document to document, as long as the documents are valid against the same schema.

16

LINQ

WHAT YOU WILL LEARN IN THIS CHAPTER

- ➤ LINQ to XML
- ➤ LINQ providers
- ➤ LINQ query syntax
- ➤ LINQ method syntax
- ➤ Lambda expressions
- ➤ Ordering query results
- ➤ Aggregates (Count, Sum, Min, Max, Average)
- ➤ Distinct queries
- ➤ Group queries
- ➤ Joins

CODE DOWNLOADS FOR THIS CHAPTER

The code downloads for this chapter are found on the book page at www.wiley.com. Click the Downloads link. The code can also be found at github.com/benperk/BeginningCSharpAnd-DotNET. The code is in the Chapter16 folder and individually named according to the names throughout the chapter.

This chapter introduces Language INtegrated Query (LINQ). LINQ is an extension to the C# language that integrates data queries directly into the programming language itself.

Before LINQ this sort of work required writing a lot of looping code, and additional process-ing such as sorting or grouping the found objects required even more code that would differ depending on the data source. LINQ provides a portable, consistent way of querying, sorting, and grouping many different kinds of data (XML, JSON, SQL databases, collections of objects, web services, corporate directories, and more).

First you'll build on the previous chapter by learning the additional capabilities that the System .Xml.Linq namespace adds for creating XML. Then you'll get into the heart of LINQ by using query syntax, method syntax, lambda expressions, sorting, grouping, and joining related results.

LINQ is large enough that complete coverage of all its facilities and methods is beyond the scope of a beginning book. However, you will see examples of each of the different types of statements and operators you are likely to need as a user of LINQ, and you will be pointed to resources for more in-depth coverage as appropriate.

LINQ TO XML

LINQ to XML is an alternate set of classes for XML that enables the use of XML data with LINQ and also makes certain operations with XML easier even if you are not using LINQ. We will look at a couple of specific cases where LINQ to XML has advantages over the XML DOM (Document Object Model) introduced in the previous chapter.

LINQ to XML Functional Constructors

While you can create XML documents in code with the XML DOM, LINQ to XML provides an easier way to create XML documents called *functional construction*. In formal construction, the constructor calls can be nested in a way that naturally reflects the structure of the XML document. In the following Try It Out, you use functional constructors to make a simple XML document containing customers and orders.

TRY IT OUT   LINQ to XML: BeginningCSharpAndDotNET_16_1_
LinqtoXmlConstructors

Follow these steps to create the example in Visual Studio:

1. Create a new Console Application called BeginningCSharpAndDotNET_16_1_LinqToXmlConstructors in the directory C:\BeginningCSharpAndDotNET\Chapter16. Set the Target Framework to the Current version (.NET 5.0).

2. Open the main source file Program.cs.

3. Add references to the System.Xml.Linq and static System.Console namespaces to the beginning of Program.cs, as shown here:

```
using System;
using System.Xml.Linq;
using static System.Console;
```

4. Add the following code to the `Main()` method in `Program.cs`:

```
static void Main(string[] args)
{
    XDocument xdoc = new XDocument(
        new XElement("customers",
            new XElement("customer",
                new XAttribute("ID", "A"),
                new XAttribute("City", "New York"),
                new XAttribute("Region", "North America"),
                new XElement("order",
                    new XAttribute("Item", "Widget"),
                    new XAttribute("Price", 100)
                ),
                new XElement("order",
                    new XAttribute("Item", "Tire"),
                    new XAttribute("Price", 200)
                )
            ),
            new XElement("customer",
                new XAttribute("ID", "B"),
                new XAttribute("City", "Mumbai"),
                new XAttribute("Region", "Asia"),
                new XElement("order",
                    new XAttribute("Item", "Oven"),
                    new XAttribute("Price", 501)
                )
            )
        )
    );
    WriteLine(xdoc);
    Write("Program finished, press Enter/Return to continue:");

}
```

5. Compile and execute the program (you can just press F5 for Start Debugging). You will see the output shown here:

```
<customers>
  <customer ID="A" City="New York" Region="North America">
    <order Item="Widget" Price="100"/>
    <order Item="Tire" Price="200"/>
  </customer>
  <customer ID="B" City="Mumbai" Region="Asia">
    <order Item="Oven" Price="501"/>
  </customer>
</customers>
Program finished, press Enter/Return to continue:
```

The XML document shown on the output screen contains a very simplified set of customer/order data. Note that the root element of the XML document is `<customers>`, which contains two nested `<customer>` elements. These in turn contain a number of nested `<order>` elements. The `<customer>` elements have two attributes, `City` and `Region`, and the `<order>` elements have `Item` and `Price` attributes.

Press Enter/Return to exit the program and make the console screen disappear. If you used Ctrl+F5 (Start Without Debugging), you might need to press Enter/Return twice.

How It Works

The first step is to reference the `System.Xml.Linq` namespace. All of the XML examples in this chapter require that you add this line to your program:

```
using System.Xml.Linq;
```

Next we add a reference to the `static System.Console` namespace to make the code using console output methods shorter:

```
using static System.Console;
```

Next are the calls to the LINQ to XML constructors `XDocument()`, `XElement()`, and `XAttribute()`, which are nested inside one another as shown here:

```
XDocument xdoc = new XDocument(
    new XElement("customers",
        new XElement("customer",
            new XAttribute("ID", "A"),
            ...
```

Note that the code here looks like the XML itself, where the document contains elements and each element contains attributes and other elements. Take a look at each of these constructors in turn:

➤ `XDocument()`—The highest-level object in the LINQ to XML constructor hierarchy is `XDocument()`, which represents the complete XML document. It appears in your code here:

```
static void Main(string[] args)
{
    XDocument xdoc = new XDocument(
        ...
    );
```

The parameter list for `XDocument()` is omitted in the previous code fragment so you can see where the `XDocument()` call begins and ends. Like all the LINQ to XML constructors, `XDocument()` takes an array of objects (`object[]`) as one of its parameters so that a number of other objects created by other constructors can be passed to it. All the other constructors you call in this program are parameters in the one call to the `XDocument()` constructor. The first (and only) parameter you pass in this program is the `XElement()` constructor.

➤ `XElement()`—An XML document must have a root element, so in most cases the parameter list of `XDocument()` will begin with an `XElement` object. The `XElement()` constructor takes the name of the element as a string, followed by a list of the XML objects contained within that element. Here, the root element is `"customers"`, which in turn contains a list of `"customer"` elements:

```
new XElement("customers",
    new XElement("customer",
        ...
    ),
    ...
)
```

The `"customer"` element does not contain any other XML elements. Instead, it contains three XML attributes, which are constructed with the `XAttribute()` constructor.

➤ `XAttribute()`—Here you add three XML attributes to the `"customer"` element, named `"ID"`, `"City"`, and `"Region"`:

```
new XAttribute("ID", "A"),
new XAttribute("City", "New York"),
new XAttribute("Region", "North America"),
```

Because an XML attribute is by definition a leaf XML node containing no other XML nodes, the `XAttribute()` constructor takes only the name of the attribute and its value as parameters. In this case, the three attributes generated are `ID="A"`, `City="New York"`, and `Region="North America"`.

➤ Other LINQ to XML constructors—Although you do not call them in this program, there are other LINQ to XML constructors for all the XML node types, such as `XDeclaration()` for the XML declaration at the start of an XML document, `XComment()` for an XML comment, and so on. These other constructors are not used often but are available if you need them for precise control over formatting an XML document.

Finishing up the explanation of the first example, you add two child `"order"` elements to the `"customer"` element following the `"ID"`, `"City"`, and `"Region"` attributes:

```
new XElement("order=",
    new XAttribute("Item", "Widget"),
    new XAttribute("Price", 100)
),
new XElement("order",
    new XAttribute("Item", "Tire"),
    new XAttribute("Price", 200)
)
```

These order elements have `"Item"` and `"Price"` attributes but no other children.

Next, you display the contents of the `XDocument` to the console screen:

```
WriteLine(xdoc);
```

This prints the text of the XML document using the default `ToString()` method of `XDocument()`.

Finally, you pause the screen so you can see the console output, and then wait until the user presses Enter:

```
Write("Program finished, press Enter/Return to continue:");
```

After that your program exits the `Main()` method, which ends the program. The "Program finished" statement appears in all the following examples but isn't discussed again because it is the same for each one.

Working with XML Fragments

Unlike the XML DOM, LINQ to XML works with XML fragments (partial or incomplete XML documents) in very much the same way as complete XML documents. When working with a fragment, you simply work with `XElement` as the top-level XML object instead of `XDocument`.

> **NOTE** *The only restriction on working with XML fragments is that you cannot add some of the more esoteric XML node types that apply only to XML documents or XML fragments, such as* `XComment` *for XML comments,* `XDeclaration` *for the XML document declaration, and* `XProcessingInstruction` *for XML processing instructions.*

In the following Try It Out, you load, save, and manipulate an XML element and its child nodes, just as you did for an XML document.

TRY IT OUT Working with XML Fragments: BeginningCSharpAndDotNET_16_2_ XMLFragments

Follow these steps to create the example in Visual Studio:

1. Either modify the previous example or create a new Console Application called BeginningCSharp-AndDotNET_16_2_XMLFragments in the directory `C:\BeginningCSharpAndDotNET\Chapter16`. Set the Target Framework to the Current version (.NET 5.0).

2. Open the main source file `Program.cs`.

3. Add references to the `System.Xml.Linq` and `static System.Console` namespaces to the beginning of `Program.cs`, as shown here:

```
using System.Xml.Linq;
using static System.Console;
```

This will already be present if you are modifying the previous example.

4. Add the XML element without the containing XML document constructor used in the previous examples to the `Main()` method in `Program.cs`:

```
static void Main(string[] args)
{
    XElement xcust =
        new XElement("customers",
            new XElement("customer",
                new XAttribute("ID", "A"),
                new XAttribute("City", "New York"),
                new XAttribute("Region", "North America"),
                new XElement("order",
                    new XAttribute("Item", "Widget"),
                    new XAttribute("Price", 100)
                ),
                new XElement("order",
                    new XAttribute("Item", "Tire"),
                    new XAttribute("Price", 200)
                )
            ),
            new XElement("customer",
                new XAttribute("ID", "B"),
```

```
                              new XAttribute("City", "Mumbai"),
                              new XAttribute("Region", "Asia"),
                              new XElement("order",
                                    new XAttribute("Item", "Oven"),
                                    new XAttribute("Price", 501)
                              )
                        )
                  )
            ;
```

5. After the XML element constructor code you added in the previous step, add the following code to save, load, and display the XML element:

```
            string xmlFileName =
      @"c:\BeginningCSharpAndDotNET\Chapter16\BeginningCSharpAndDotNET_16_2_
      XMLFragments\fragment.xml";
                  xcust.Save(xmlFileName);
                  XElement xcust2 = XElement.Load(xmlFileName);
                  WriteLine("Contents of xcust:");
                  WriteLine(xcust2);
                  Write("Program finished, press Enter/Return to continue:");

      }
```

> **NOTE** The xmlFileName *is an absolute path; your folder structure may differ, and if so, you should adjust the path to reflect the actual folder path on your computer.*

6. Compile and execute the program (you can just press F5 for Start Debugging). You should see the following output in the console window:

```
Contents of XElement xcust2:
<customers>
  <customer ID="A" City="New York" Region="North America">
    <order Item="Widget" Price="100"/>
    <order Item="Tire" Price="200"/>
  </customer>
  <customer ID="B" City="Mumbai" Region="Asia">
    <order Item="Oven" Price="501"/>
  </customer>
</customers>
Program finished, press Enter/Return to continue:
```

Press Enter/Return to finish the program and make the console screen disappear. If you used Ctrl+F5 (Start Without Debugging), you might need to press Enter/Return twice.

How It Works

Both XElement and XDocument inherit from the LINQ to XML XContainer class, which implements an XML node that can contain other XML nodes. Both classes also implement Load() and Save(), so most operations that can be performed on an XDocument() in LINQ to XML can also be performed on an XElement instance and its children.

You simply create an XElement instance that has the same structure as the XDocument used in previous examples but omits the containing XDocument. All the operations for this particular program work the same with the XElement fragment.

XElement also supports the Load() and Parse() methods for loading XML from files and strings, respectively.

LINQ PROVIDERS

LINQ to XML is just one example of a *LINQ provider*. Visual Studio and .NET come with a number of built-in LINQ providers that provide query solutions for different types of data:

- ➤ **LINQ to Objects**—Provides queries on any kind of C# in-memory object, such as arrays, lists, and other collection types.

- ➤ **LINQ to XML**—As you have just seen, this provides creation and manipulation of XML documents using the same syntax and general query mechanism as the other LINQ varieties.

- ➤ **LINQ to Entities**—The Entity Framework is the newest set of data interface classes in .NET, recommended by Microsoft for new development.

- ➤ **LINQ to Data Set**—The DataSet object was introduced in the first version of the .NET Framework. This variety of LINQ enables legacy .NET data to be queried easily with LINQ.

- ➤ **LINQ to SQL**—This is an alternative LINQ interface that has been superseded by LINQ to Entities.

- ➤ **PLINQ**—PLINQ, or Parallel LINQ, extends LINQ to Objects with a parallel programming library that can split up a query to execute simultaneously on a multicore processor.

- ➤ **LINQ to JSON**—Supports creation and manipulation of JSON documents using the same syntax and general query mechanism as the other LINQ varieties.

With so many varieties of LINQ, it is impossible to cover them all in a beginning book, but the syntax and methods you will see apply to all. Next, let's look at the LINQ query syntax using the LINQ to Objects provider.

LINQ QUERY SYNTAX

In the following Try It Out, you use a LINQ query to find some data in a simple in-memory array of objects and print it to the console.

TRY IT OUT First LINQ Program: BeginningCSharpAndDotNET_16_3_
QuerySyntax\Program.cs

Follow these steps to create the example in Visual Studio:

1. Create a new Console Application called BeginningCSharpAndDotNET_16_3_QuerySyntax in the
directory C:\BeginningCSharpAndDotNET\Chapter16. Set the Target Framework to the Current
version (.NET 5.0), then open the main source file Program.cs.

2. Add the System.Linq and static System.Console namespaces in Program.cs:

```
using System.Linq;
using static System.Console;
```

3. Add the following code to the Main() method in Program.cs:

```
static void Main(string[] args)
{
    string[] names = { "Alonso", "Zheng", "Smith", "Jones", "Smythe",
        "Small", "Ruiz", "Hsieh", "Jorgenson", "Ilyich", "Singh",
"Samba", "Fatimah" };
    var queryResults =
        from n in names
        where n.StartsWith("S")
        select n;
    WriteLine("Names beginning with S:");
    foreach (var item in queryResults) {
        WriteLine(item);
    }
    Write("Program finished, press Enter/Return to continue:");

}
```

4. Compile and execute the program (you can just press F5 for Start Debugging). You will see the
names in the list beginning with S in the order they were declared in the array, as shown here:

```
Names beginning with S:
Smith
Smythe
Small
Singh
Samba
Program finished, press Enter/Return to continue:
```

Simply press Enter/Return to finish the program and make the console screen disappear. If you used
Ctrl+F5 (Start Without Debugging), you may need to press Enter/Return twice. That finishes the
program run.

How It Works

The first step is to reference the System.Linq namespace:

```
using System.Linq;
```

All the underlying base system support classes for LINQ reside in the `System.Linq` namespace.

Next we add the `static System.Console` namespace to make the code using console output methods shorter:

```
using static System.Console;
```

After that we create some data, which is done in this example by declaring and initializing the array of names:

```
string[] names = { "Alonso", "Zheng", "Smith", "Jones", "Smythe", "Small",
            "Ruiz", "Hsieh", "Jorgenson", "Ilyich", "Singh", "Samba", "Fatimah" };
```

This is a trivial set of data, but it is good to start with an example for which the result of the query is obvious. The actual LINQ query statement is the next part of the program:

```
var queryResults =
        from n in names
        where n.StartsWith("S")
        select n;
```

That is an odd-looking statement, isn't it? It almost looks like something from a language other than C#, and the `from...where...select` syntax is deliberately similar to that of the SQL database query language. However, this statement is not SQL; it is indeed C#, as you saw when you typed in the code in Visual Studio—the keywords `from`, `where`, and `select` are highlighted, and the odd-looking syntax is perfectly fine to the compiler.

The statement has four parts: the result variable declaration beginning with `var`, which is assigned using a *query expression* consisting of the `from` clause; the `where` clause; and the `select` clause. Let's look at each of these parts in turn.

Declaring a Variable for Results Using the var Keyword

The LINQ query starts by declaring a variable to hold the results of the query, which is usually done by declaring a variable with the `var` keyword:

```
var queryResult =
```

`var` is a keyword in C# created to declare a general variable type that is ideal for holding the results of LINQ queries. The `var` keyword tells the C# compiler to infer the type of the result based on the query. That way, you don't have to declare ahead of time what type of objects will be returned from the LINQ query—the compiler takes care of it for you. If the query can return multiple items, then it acts like a collection of the objects in the query data source (technically, it is not a collection; it just looks that way).

> **NOTE** *If you want to know the details, the query result will be a type that implements the* IEnumerable<T> *interface. The angle brackets with T(*<T>*) following* IEnumerable *indicate that it is a generic type. Generics are described in Chapter 12.*
>
> *In this particular case, the compiler creates a special LINQ data type that provides an ordered list of strings. If the query selected something else, like a new* Person *object, then the result would implement* IEnumerable<Person>.

By the way, the name queryResult is arbitrary—you can name the result anything you want. It could be namesBeginningWithS or anything else that makes sense in your program.

Specifying the Data Source: from Clause

The next part of the LINQ query is the from clause, which specifies the data you are querying:

```
from n in names
```

Your data source in this case is names, the array of strings declared earlier. The variable n is just a stand-in for an individual element in the data source, similar to the variable name following a foreach statement. By specifying from, you are indicating that you are going to *query* a subset of the collection.

Speaking of collections, a LINQ data source must be *enumerable*—that is, it must be an array or collection of items from which you can pick one or more elements to iterate through.

> **NOTE** *Enumerable means the data source must support the* IEnumerable<T> *interface, which is supported for any C# array or collection of items.*

The data source cannot be a single value or object, such as a single int variable. You already have such a single item, so there is no point in querying it!

Specify Condition: where Clause

In the next part of the LINQ query, you specify the condition for your query using the where clause, which looks like this:

```
where n.StartsWith("S")
```

Any Boolean (true or false) expression that can be applied to the items in the data source can be specified in the where clause. Actually, the where clause is optional and can even be omitted, but in almost all cases, you will want to specify a `where` condition to limit the results to only the data you want. The `where` clause is called a *restriction operator* in LINQ because it restricts the results of the query.

Here, you specify that the name `string` starts with the letter S, but you could specify anything else about the string instead—for example, a length greater than 10 (`where n.Length > 10`) or containing a Q (`where n.Contains("Q")`).

Selecting Items: select Clause

Finally, the `select` clause specifies which items appear in the result set. The `select` clause looks like this:

```
select n
```

The `select` clause is required because you must specify which items from your query appear in the result set. For this set of data, it is not very interesting because you have only one item, the name, in each element of the result set. You'll look at some examples with more complex objects in the result set where the usefulness of the `select` clause will be more apparent, but first, you need to finish the example.

Finishing Up: Using the foreach Loop

Now you print out the results of the query. As with the array used as the data source, the results of a LINQ query like this are *enumerable*, meaning you can iterate through the results with a `foreach` statement:

```
WriteLine("Names beginning with S:");
foreach (var item in queryResults) {
        WriteLine(item);
}
```

In this case, you matched five names—Smith, Smythe, Small, Singh, and Samba—so that is what you display in the `foreach` loop.

Deferred Query Execution

You may be thinking that the `foreach` loop really isn't part of LINQ itself—it's only looping through your results. While it's true that the `foreach` construct is not itself part of LINQ, nevertheless, it is the part of your code that actually executes the LINQ query! The assignment of the query results variable only saves a plan for executing the query; with LINQ, the data itself is not retrieved until the results are accessed. This is called *deferred query execution* or *lazy evaluation* of queries. Execution will be deferred for any query that produces a sequence—that is, a list—of results.

LINQ METHOD SYNTAX

There are multiple ways of doing the same thing with LINQ, as is often the case in programming. As noted, the previous example was written using the LINQ *query syntax*. In the next example, you will write the same program using LINQ's *method syntax* (also called *explicit syntax*, but the term method syntax is used here).

LINQ Extension Methods

LINQ is implemented as a series of extension methods to collections, arrays, query results, and any other object that implements the `IEnumerable<T>` interface. You can see these methods with the Visual Studio IntelliSense feature. For example, in Visual Studio, open the `Program.cs` file in the BeginningCSharpAndDotNET_16_3_QuerySyntax program you just completed and type in a new reference to the `names` array just below it:

```
string[] names = { "Alonso", "Zheng", "Smith", "Jones", "Smythe", "Small",
                   "Ruiz", "Hsieh", "Jorgenson", "Ilyich", "Singh", "Samba", "Fatimah" };
names.
```

Just as you type the period following `names`, you will see the methods available for `names` listed by the Visual Studio IntelliSense feature.

The `Where<T>` method and most of the other available methods are extension methods (as shown in the documentation appearing to the right of the `Where<T>` method, it begins with `extension`). You can see that they are LINQ extensions by commenting out the `using System.Linq` directive at the top. You will find that `Where<T>`, `Union<T>`, `Take<T>`, and most of the other methods in the list no longer appear. The `from...where...select` query expression you used in the previous example is translated by the C# compiler into a series of calls to these methods. When using the LINQ method syntax, you call these methods directly.

Query Syntax versus Method Syntax

The query syntax is the preferred way of programming queries in LINQ, as it is generally easier to read and is simpler to use for the most common queries. However, it is important to have a basic understanding of the method syntax because some LINQ capabilities either are not available in the query syntax or are just easier to use in the method syntax.

> **NOTE** As the Visual Studio online help recommends, use query syntax whenever possible and method syntax whenever necessary.

In this chapter, you will mostly use the query syntax, but the method syntax is pointed out in situations where it is needed, and you'll learn how to use the method syntax to solve the problem.

Most of the LINQ methods that use the method syntax require that you pass a method or function to evaluate the query expression. The method/function parameter is passed in the form of a delegate, which typically references an anonymous method.

Luckily, LINQ makes doing this much easier than it sounds! You create the method/function by using a *lambda expression*, which encapsulates the delegate in an elegant manner.

Lambda Expressions

A lambda expression is a simple way to create a method on-the-fly for use in your LINQ query. It uses the => operator, which declares the parameters for your method followed by the method logic all on a single line!

> **NOTE** The term "lambda expression" comes from lambda calculus, which is a mathematical field important in programming language theory. Look it up if you're mathematically inclined. Luckily, you don't need the math in order to use lambdas in C#!

For example, consider the lambda expression:

```
n => n < 0
```

This declares a method with a single parameter named n. The method returns *true* if n is less than zero, otherwise *false*. It's dead simple. You don't have to come up with a method name, put in a return statement, or wrap any code with curly braces.

Returning a true/false value like this is typical for methods used in LINQ lambdas, but it doesn't have to be done. For example, here is a lambda that creates a method that returns the sum of two variables. This lambda uses multiple parameters:

```
(a, b) => a + b
```

This declares a method with two parameters named a and b. The method logic returns the sum of a and b. You don't have to declare what type a and b are. They can be int, double, or string. The C# compiler infers the types.

Finally, consider this lambda expression:

```
n => n.StartsWith("S")
```

This method returns *true* if n starts with the letter S, otherwise *false*. Try this out in an actual program to see this more clearly.

TRY IT OUT   Using LINQ Method Syntax and Lambda Expressions: BeginningCSharpAndDotNET_16_4_MethodSyntax\Program.cs

Follow these steps to create the example in Visual Studio:

1. You can either modify the previous example or create a new Console Application called BeginningCSharpAndDotNET_16_4_MethodSyntax in the directory C:\BeginningCSharpAndDotNET\ Chapter16. Set the Target Framework to the Current version (.NET 5.0). Open the main source file Program.cs.

2. Add the System.Linq and static System.Console namespaces in Program.cs:

```
using System.Linq;
using static System.Console;
```

3.   Add the following code to the Main() method in Program.cs:

```
static void Main(string[] args)
{
    string[] names = { "Alonso", "Zheng", "Smith", "Jones", "Smythe", "Small",
        "Ruiz", "Hsieh", "Jorgenson", "Ilyich", "Singh", "Samba", "Fatimah" };
    var queryResults = names.Where(n => n.StartsWith("S"));
    WriteLine("Names beginning with S:");
    foreach (var item in queryResults) {
        WriteLine(item);
    }
    Write("Program finished, press Enter/Return to continue:");
}
```

4.   Compile and execute the program (you can just press F5). You will see the same output of names in the list beginning with S in the order they were declared in the array, as shown here:

```
Names beginning with S:
Smith
Smythe
Small
Singh
Samba
Program finished, press Enter/Return to continue:
```

How It Works

As before, we add the System.Linq and static System.Console namespaces:

```
using System.Linq;
using static System.Console;
```

The same source data as before is created again by declaring and initializing the array of names:

```
string[] names = { "Alonso", "Zheng", "Smith", "Jones", "Smythe", "Small",
    "Ruiz", "Hsieh", "Jorgenson", "Ilyich", "Singh", "Samba", "Fatimah" };
```

The part that is different is the LINQ query, which is now a call to the Where() method instead of a query expression:

```
var queryResults = names.Where(n => n.StartsWith("S"));
```

The C# compiler compiles the lambda expression n => n.StartsWith("S") into an anonymous method that is executed by Where() on each item in the names array. If the lambda expression returns true for an item, that item is included in the result set returned by Where(). The C# compiler infers that the Where() method should accept string as the input type for each item from the definition of the input source (the names array, in this case).

Well, a lot is going on in that one line, isn't it? For the simplest type of query like this, the method syntax is actually shorter than the query syntax because you do not need the from or select clauses; however, most queries are more complex than this.

The rest of the example is the same as the previous one—you print out the results of the query in a `foreach` loop and pause the output so you can see it before the program finishes execution:

```
foreach (var item in queryResults) {
    WriteLine(item);
}
Write("Program finished, press Enter/Return to continue:");
```

An explanation of these lines isn't repeated here because that was covered in the "How It Works" section following the first example in the chapter. Let's move on to explore how to use more of LINQ's capabilities.

ORDERING QUERY RESULTS

Once you have located some data of interest with a `where` clause (or `Where()` method invocation), LINQ makes it easy for you to perform further processing—such as reordering the results—on the resulting data. In the following Try It Out, you put the results from your first query in alphabetical order.

> **TRY IT OUT**   Ordering Query Results: BeginningCSharpAndDotNET_16_5_
> OrderQueryResults\Program.cs

Follow these steps to create the example in Visual Studio:

1. You can either modify the QuerySyntax example or create a new Console Application project called BeginningCSharpAndDotNET_16_5_OrderQueryResults in the directory `C:\Beginning-CSharpAndDotNET\Chapter16`. Set the Target Framework to the Current version (.NET 5.0).

2. Open the main source file `Program.cs`. As before, add the `System.Linq` and `static System.Console` namespaces in `Program.cs`:

    ```
    using System.Linq;
    using static System.Console;
    ```

3. Add the following code to the `Main()` method in `Program.cs`:

    ```
    static void Main(string[] args)
    {
            string[] names = { "Alonso", "Zheng", "Smith", "Jones", "Smythe", "Small",
                "Ruiz", "Hsieh", "Jorgenson", "Ilyich", "Singh", "Samba", "Fatimah" };
            var queryResults =
                from n in names
                where n.StartsWith("S")
                orderby n
                select n;
            WriteLine("Names beginning with S ordered alphabetically:");
            foreach (var item in queryResults) {
                WriteLine(item);
            }
            Write("Program finished, press Enter/Return to continue:");

    }
    ```

4. Compile and execute the program. You will see the names in the list beginning with S in alphabetical order, as shown here:

```
Names beginning with S:
Samba
Singh
Small
Smith
Smythe
Program finished, press Enter/Return to continue:
```

How It Works

This program is nearly identical to the previous example, except for one additional line added to the query statement:

```
var queryResults =
        from n in names
        where n.StartsWith("S")
        orderby n
        select n;
```

UNDERSTANDING THE ORDERBY CLAUSE

The orderby clause looks like this:

```
orderby n
```

Like the where clause, the orderby clause is optional. Just by adding one line, you can order the results of any arbitrary query, which would otherwise require additional code and possibly additional methods or collections to store the results of the reordered result, depending on the sorting algorithm you chose to implement. If multiple types needed to be sorted, you would have to implement a set of ordering methods for each one. With LINQ, you don't need to worry about any of that; just add one additional clause in the query statement and you're done.

By default, orderby orders in ascending order (A to Z), but you can specify descending order (from Z to A) simply by adding the descending keyword:

```
orderby n descending
```

This orders the example results as follows:

```
Smythe
Smith
Small
Singh
Samba
```

Plus, you can order by any arbitrary expression without having to rewrite the query; for example, to order by the last letter in the name instead of the normal alphabetical order, you just change the orderby clause to the following:

```
orderby n.Substring(n.Length - 1)
```

This results in the following output:

```
Samba
Smythe
Smith
Singh
Small
```

> **NOTE** *The last letters are in alphabetical order* (a, e, h, h, 1). *However, you will notice that the execution is implementation-dependent, meaning there's no guarantee of order beyond what is specified in the* orderby *clause. The last letter is the only letter considered, so, in this case, Smith came before Singh.*

QUERYING A LARGE DATA SET

All this LINQ syntax is well and good, you may be saying, but what is the point? You can see the expected results clearly just by looking at the source array, so why go to all this trouble to query something that is obvious by just looking? As mentioned earlier, sometimes the results of a query are not so obvious. In the following Try It Out, you create a very large array of numbers and query it using LINQ.

TRY IT OUT   Querying a Large Data Set: BeginningCSharpAndDotNET_16_6_ LargeNumberQuery\Program.cs

---

Follow these steps to create the example in Visual Studio:

1. Create a new Console Application called BeginningCSharpAndDotNET_16_6_LargeNumber-Query in the directory C:\BeginningCSharpAndDotNET\Chapter16. Set the Target Framework to the Current version (.NET 5.0). As before, add the System.Linq and static System.Console namespaces in Program.cs:

   ```
   using System.Linq;
   using static System.Console;
   ```

2. Add the following code to the Main() method:

   ```
   static void Main(string[] args)
   {
       int[] numbers = GenerateLotsOfNumbers(12045678);
         var queryResults =
             from n in numbers
             where n < 1000
             select n
           ;
         WriteLine("Numbers less than 1000:");
         foreach (var item in queryResults)
   ```

```
        {
            WriteLine(item);
        }
        Write("Program finished, press Enter/Return to continue:");
    }
```

3. Add the following method to generate the list of random numbers:

```
        private static int[] GenerateLotsOfNumbers(int count)
        {
            Random generator = new Random(0);
            int[] result = new int[count];
            for (int i = 0; i < count; i++)
            {
                result[i] = generator.Next();
            }
            return result;
        }
```

4. Compile and execute the program. You will see a list of numbers less than 1,000, as shown here:

```
Numbers less than 1000:
714
24
677
350
257
719
584
Program finished, press Enter/Return to continue:
```

How It Works

As before, you add the System.Linq and static System.Console namespaces. Make sure you keep the using System; line as you will use the System.Random() method to generate random numbers:

```
        using System.Linq;
        using static System.Console;
```

The next step is to create some data, which is done in this example by creating and calling the GenerateLotsOfNumbers() method:

```
        private static int[] GenerateLotsOfNumbers(int count)
        {
            Random generator = new Random(0);
            int[] result = new int[count];
            for (int i = 0; i < count; i++)
            {
                result[i] = generator.Next();
            }
            return result;
        }
        . . .
        int[] numbers = GenerateLotsOfNumbers(12345678);
```

This is not a trivial set of data—there are more than 12 million numbers in the array! In one of the exercises at the end of the chapter, you will change the `size` parameter passed to the `GenerateLotsOf-Numbers()` method to generate variously sized sets of random numbers and see how this affects the query results. As you will see when doing the exercises, the size of 12,345,678 shown here is just large enough for the program to generate some random numbers less than 1,000 in order to have results to show for this first query.

The values should be randomly distributed over the range of a signed integer (from zero to more than two billion). By creating the random number generator with a seed of 0, you ensure that the same set of random numbers is created each time and is repeatable, so you get the same query results as shown here, but what those query results are is unknown until you try some queries. Luckily, LINQ makes those queries easy!

The query statement itself is similar to what you did with the names before, selecting some numbers that meet a condition (in this case, numbers less than 1,000):

```
var queryResults =
    from n in numbers
    where n < 1000
    select n
```

The `orderby` clause isn't needed here and would add extra processing time (not noticeably for this query, but more so as you vary the conditions in the next example).

You print out the results of the query with a `foreach` statement just as in the previous example:

```
WriteLine("Numbers less than 1000:");
foreach (var item in queryResults)
{
    WriteLine(item);
}
```

It is very easy with LINQ to change the query conditions to explore different characteristics of the data set. However, depending on how many results the query returns, it may not make sense to print all the results each time. In the next section, you'll see how LINQ provides aggregate operators to deal with that issue.

USING AGGREGATE OPERATORS

Often, a query returns more results than you might expect. For example, if you were to change the condition of the large-number query program you just created to list the numbers greater than 1,000, rather than the numbers less than 1,000, there would be so many query results that the numbers would not stop printing!

Luckily, LINQ provides a set of aggregate operators that enable you to analyze the results of a query without having to loop through them all. Table 16-1 shows the most commonly used aggregate operators for a set of numeric results such as those from the large-number query. These may be familiar to you if you have used a database query language such as SQL.

TABLE 16-1: Aggregate Operators for Numeric Results

OPERATOR	DESCRIPTION
Count()	Count of results
Min()	Minimum value in results
Max()	Maximum value in results
Average()	Average value of numeric results
Sum()	Total of all of numeric results

There are more aggregate operators, such as `Aggregate()`, for executing arbitrary code in a manner that enables you to code your own aggregate function. However, those are for advanced users and therefore beyond the scope of this book.

In the following Try It Out, you modify the large-number query and use aggregate operators to explore the result set from the greater-than version of the large-number query using LINQ.

TRY IT OUT Numeric Aggregate Operators: BeginningCSharpAndDotNET_16_7_NumericAggregates\Program.cs

Follow these steps to create the example in Visual Studio:

1. For this example, you can either modify the previous example you just made or create a new console project named BeginningCSharpAndDotNET_16_7_NumericAggregates in the directory `C:\BeginningCSharpAndDotNET\Chapter16`.

2. As before, add the `System.Linq` and `static System.Console` namespaces after the `using System;` line at the top of the program. You just need to modify the `Main()` method as shown in the following code and in the rest of this Try It Out. As with the previous example, the `orderby` clause is not used in this query. However, the condition on the `where` clause is the opposite of the previous example (the numbers are greater than 1,000 (`n > 1000`), instead of less than 1,000):

```
static void Main(string[] args)
{
    int[] numbers = GenerateLotsOfNumbers(12345678);
    WriteLine("Numeric Aggregates");
    var queryResults =
        from n in numbers
        where n > 1000
        select n
    ;
    WriteLine("Count of Numbers > 1000");
    WriteLine(queryResults.Count());
    WriteLine("Max of Numbers > 1000");
    WriteLine(queryResults.Max());
    WriteLine("Min of Numbers > 1000");
    WriteLine(queryResults.Min());
    WriteLine("Average of Numbers > 1000");
```

```
WriteLine(queryResults.Average());
WriteLine("Sum of Numbers > 1000");
WriteLine(queryResults.Sum(n => (long) n));
Write("Program finished, press Enter/Return to continue:");

        }
```

3. If it is not already present, add the same `GenerateLotsOfNumbers()` method used in the previous example:

```
private static int[] GenerateLotsOfNumbers(int count)
{
    Random generator = new Random(0);
    int[] result = new int[count];
    for (int i = 0; i < count; i++)
    {
        result[i] = generator.Next();
    }
    return result;
}
```

4. Compile and execute. You will see the count, minimum, maximum, and average values as shown here:

```
Numeric Aggregates
Count of Numbers > 1000
12345671
Maximum of Numbers > 1000
2147483591
Minimum of Numbers > 1000
1034
Average of Numbers > 1000
1073643807.5029846
Sum of Numbers > 1000
13254853218619179
Program finished, press Enter/Return to continue:
```

This query produces many more results than the previous example (more than 12 million). Using `orderby` on this result set would definitely have a noticeable impact on performance! The largest number (maximum) in the result set is over two billion and the smallest (minimum) is just over one thousand, as expected. The average is around one billion, near the middle of the range of possible values. Looks like the `Random()` function generates a good distribution of numbers!

How It Works

The first part of the program is exactly the same as the previous example, with the reference to the `System.Linq` namespace and the use of the `GenerateLotsOfNumbers()` method to generate the source data:

```
int[] numbers = GenerateLotsOfNumbers(12345678);
```

The query is the same as the previous example, except for changing the `where` condition from less than to greater than:

```
var queryResults =
    from n in numbers
```

```
where n > 1000
select n;
```

As noted before, this query using the greater-than condition produces many more results than the less-than query (with this particular data set). By using the aggregate operators, you are able to explore the results of the query without having to print out each result or do a comparison in a `foreach` loop. Each one appears as a method that can be called on the result set, similar to methods on a collection type.

Look at the use of each aggregate operator:

➤ `Count()`:

```
WriteLine("Count of Numbers > 1000");
WriteLine(queryResults.Count());
```

`Count()` returns the number of rows in the query results—in this case, 12,345,671 rows.

➤ `Max()`:

```
WriteLine("Max of Numbers > 1000");
WriteLine(queryResults.Max());
```

`Max()` returns the maximum value in the query results—in this case, a number larger than two billion: 2,147,483,591, which is very close to the maximum value of an `int` (`int.MaxValue` or 2,147,483,647).

➤ `Min()`:

```
WriteLine("Min of Numbers > 1000");
WriteLine(queryResults.Min());
```

`min()` returns the minimum value in the query results—in this case, 1,034.

➤ `Average()`:

```
WriteLine("Average of Numbers > 1000");
WriteLine(queryResults.Average());
```

`Average()` returns the average value of the query results, which in this case is 1,073,643,807.5029846, a value very close to the middle of the range of possible values from 1,000 to more than two billion. This is rather meaningless with an arbitrary set of large numbers, but it shows the kind of query result analysis that is possible. You'll look at a more practical use of these operators with some business-oriented data in the last part of the chapter.

➤ `Sum()`:

```
WriteLine("Sum of Numbers > 1000");
WriteLine(queryResults.Sum(n => (long) n));
```

You passed the lambda expression `n => (long) n` to the `Sum()` method call to get the sum of all the numbers. Although `Sum()` has a no-parameter overload, like `Count()`, `Min()`, `Max()`, and so on, using that version of the method call would cause an overflow error because there are so many large numbers in the data set that the sum of all of them would be too large to fit into a standard 32-bit `int`, which is what the no-parameter version of `Sum()` returns. The lambda expression enables you to convert the result of `Sum()` to a long 64-bit integer, which is what you need to hold the total of over 13 quadrillion without overflow—13,254,853,218,619,179. Lambda expressions enable you to perform this kind of fix-up easily.

> **NOTE** *In addition to* Count(), *which returns a 32-bit* int, *LINQ also provides a* LongCount() *method that returns the count of query results in a 64-bit integer. That is a special case, however—all the other operators require a lambda or a call to a conversion method if a 64-bit version of the number is needed.*

USING THE SELECT DISTINCT QUERY

Another type of query that those of you familiar with the SQL data query language will recognize is the SELECT DISTINCT query, in which you search for the unique values in your data—that is, the query removes any repeated values from the result set. This is a fairly common need when working with queries.

Suppose you need to find the distinct regions in the customer data used in the XML examples earlier in this chapter. There is no separate region list in the data you just used, so you need to find the unique, nonrepeating list of regions from the customer list itself. LINQ provides a Distinct() method that makes it easy to find this data. You'll use it in the following Try It Out.

TRY IT OUT Projection: Select Distinct Query: BeginningCSharpAndDotNET_
16_8_SelectDistinctQuery\Program.cs

Follow these steps to create the example in Visual Studio:

1. Create a new Console Application called BeginningCSharpAndDotNET_16_8_SelectDistinctQuery in the directory C:\BeginningCSharpAndDotNET\Chapter16. Set the Target Framework to the Current version (.NET 5.0).

2. Enter this code to create the Customer class:

    ```
    class Customer
        {
            public string ID { get; set; }
            public string City { get; set; }
            public string Country { get; set; }
            public string Region { get; set; }
            public decimal Sales { get; set; }

            public override string ToString()
            {
                return "ID: " + ID + " City: " + City +
                    " Country: " + Country +
                    " Region: " + Region +
                    " Sales: " + Sales;
            }
        }
    ```

3. Enter this code in the Main() function to create a list of customers (List<Customer> customers) and initialize the list with values:

```
List<Customer> customers = new List<Customer> {
    new Customer { ID="A", City="New York", Country="USA",
        Region="North America", Sales=9999},
    new Customer { ID="B", City="Mumbai", Country="India",
        Region="Asia", Sales=8888},
    new Customer { ID="C", City="Karachi", Country="Pakistan",
        Region="Asia", Sales=7777},
    new Customer { ID="D", City="Delhi", Country="India",
        Region="Asia", Sales=6666},
    new Customer { ID="E", City="São Paulo", Country="Brazil",
        Region="South America", Sales=5555 },
    new Customer { ID="F", City="Moscow", Country="Russia",
        Region="Europe", Sales=4444 },
    new Customer { ID="G", City="Seoul", Country="Korea",
        Region="Asia", Sales=3333 },
    new Customer { ID="H", City="Istanbul", Country="Turkey",
        Region="Asia", Sales=2222 },
    new Customer { ID="I", City="Shanghai", Country="China",
        Region="Asia", Sales=1111 },
    new Customer { ID="J", City="Lagos", Country="Nigeria",
        Region="Africa", Sales=1000 },
    new Customer { ID="K", City="Mexico City", Country="Mexico",
        Region="North America", Sales=2000 },
    new Customer { ID="L", City="Jakarta", Country="Indonesia",
        Region="Asia", Sales=3000 },
    new Customer { ID="M", City="Tokyo", Country="Japan",
        Region="Asia", Sales=4000 },
    new Customer { ID="N", City="Los Angeles", Country="USA",
        Region="North America", Sales=5000 },
    new Customer { ID="O", City="Cairo", Country="Egypt",
        Region="Africa", Sales=6000 },
    new Customer { ID="P", City="Tehran", Country="Iran",
        Region="Asia", Sales=7000 },
    new Customer { ID="Q", City="London", Country="UK",
        Region="Europe", Sales=8000 },
    new Customer { ID="R", City="Beijing", Country="China",
        Region="Asia", Sales=9000 },
    new Customer { ID="S", City="Bogotá", Country="Colombia",
        Region="South America", Sales=1001 },
    new Customer { ID="T", City="Lima", Country="Peru",
        Region="South America", Sales=2002 }
};
```

4. In the `Main()` method, following the initialization of the `customers` list, enter the query as shown here:

```
var queryResults = customers.Select(c => c.Region).Distinct();
```

5. Finish the remaining code in the `Main()` method as shown here.

```
foreach (var item in queryResults)
{
    WriteLine(item);
}
Write("Program finished, press Enter/Return to continue:");
```

6. Compile and execute the program. You will see the unique regions where customers exist:

```
North America
Asia
South America
Europe
Africa
Program finished, press Enter/Return to continue:
```

How It Works

You create the `Customer` class and then initialize the `customers` list with values. In the query statement, you call the `Select()` method with a simple lambda expression to select the region from the `Customer` objects, and then you call `Distinct()` to return only the unique results from `Select()`:

```
var queryResults = customers.Select(c => c.Region).Distinct();
```

Because `Distinct()` is available only in method syntax, you make the call to `Select()` using method syntax. However, you can call `Distinct()` to modify a query made in the query syntax as well:

```
var queryResults = (from c in customers select c.Region).Distinct();
```

Because query syntax is translated by the C# compiler into the same series of LINQ method calls as used in the method syntax, you can mix and match if it makes sense for readability and style.

ORDERING BY MULTIPLE LEVELS

Now that you are dealing with objects with multiple properties, you might be able to envision a situation where ordering the query results by a single field is not enough. What if you wanted to query your customers and order the results alphabetically by region, but then order alphabetically by country or city name within a region? LINQ makes this very easy, as you will see in the following Try It Out.

TRY IT OUT   Ordering by Multiple Levels: BeginningCSharpAndDotNET_16_9_
MultiLevelOrdering\Program.cs

Follow these steps to create the example in Visual Studio:

1. Modify the previous example, BeginningCSharpAndDotNET_16_8_SelectDistinctQuery, or create a new Console Application called BeginningCSharpAndDotNET_16_9_MultiLevelOrdering in the directory C:\BeginningCSharpAndDotNET\Chapter16. Set the Target Framework to the Current version (.NET 5.0).

2. Create the `Customer` class and the initialization of the `customers` list (`List<Customer> customers`) as shown in the BeginningCSharpAndDotNET_16_8_SelectDistinctQuery example; this code is exactly the same as in previous examples.

3. In the `Main()` method, following the initialization of the `customers` list, enter the following query:

```
var queryResults =
    from c in customers
    orderby c.Region, c.Country, c.City
```

```
            select new { c.ID, c.Region, c.Country, c.City }
        ;
```

4. The results-processing loop and the remaining code in the `Main()` method are the same as in previous examples.

5. Compile and execute the program. You will see the selected properties from all customers ordered alphabetically by region first, then by country, and then by city, as shown here:

```
{ ID = O, Region = Africa, Country = Egypt, City = Cairo }
{ ID = J, Region = Africa, Country = Nigeria, City = Lagos }
{ ID = R, Region = Asia, Country = China, City = Beijing }
{ ID = I, Region = Asia, Country = China, City = Shanghai }
{ ID = D, Region = Asia, Country = India, City = Delhi }
{ ID = B, Region = Asia, Country = India, City = Mumbai }
{ ID = L, Region = Asia, Country = Indonesia, City = Jakarta }
{ ID = P, Region = Asia, Country = Iran, City = Tehran }
{ ID = M, Region = Asia, Country = Japan, City = Tokyo }
{ ID = G, Region = Asia, Country = Korea, City = Seoul }
{ ID = C, Region = Asia, Country = Pakistan, City = Karachi }
{ ID = H, Region = Asia, Country = Turkey, City = Istanbul }
{ ID = F, Region = Europe, Country = Russia, City = Moscow }
{ ID = Q, Region = Europe, Country = UK, City = London }
{ ID = K, Region = North America, Country = Mexico, City = Mexico City }
{ ID = N, Region = North America, Country = USA, City = Los Angeles }
{ ID = A, Region = North America, Country = USA, City = New York }
{ ID = E, Region = South America, Country = Brazil, City = São Paulo }
{ ID = S, Region = South America, Country = Colombia, City = Bogotá }
{ ID = T, Region = South America, Country = Peru, City = Lima }
Program finished, press Enter/Return to continue:
```

How It Works

The `Customer` class and `customers` list initialization are the same as in previous examples. In this query you have no `where` clause because you want to see all the customers, but you simply list the fields you want to sort by order in a comma-separated list in the `orderby` clause:

```
orderby c.Region, c.Country, c.City
```

Couldn't be easier, could it? It seems a bit counterintuitive that a simple list of fields is allowed in the `orderby` clause but not in the `select` clause, but that is how LINQ works. It makes sense if you realize that the `select` clause is creating a new object but the `orderby` clause, by definition, operates on a field-by-field basis.

You can add the `descending` keyword to any of the fields listed to reverse the sort order for that field. For example, to order this query by ascending region but descending country, simply add `descending` following `Country` in the list, like this:

```
orderby c.Region, c.Country descending, c.City
```

With `descending` added, you see the following output:

```
{ ID = J, Region = Africa, Country = Nigeria, City = Lagos }
{ ID = O, Region = Africa, Country = Egypt, City = Cairo }
{ ID = H, Region = Asia, Country = Turkey, City = Istanbul }
{ ID = C, Region = Asia, Country = Pakistan, City = Karachi }
```

```
{ ID = G, Region = Asia, Country = Korea, City = Seoul }
{ ID = M, Region = Asia, Country = Japan, City = Tokyo }
{ ID = P, Region = Asia, Country = Iran, City = Tehran }
{ ID = L, Region = Asia, Country = Indonesia, City = Jakarta }
{ ID = D, Region = Asia, Country = India, City = Delhi }
{ ID = B, Region = Asia, Country = India, City = Mumbai }
{ ID = R, Region = Asia, Country = China, City = Beijing }
{ ID = I, Region = Asia, Country = China, City = Shanghai }
{ ID = Q, Region = Europe, Country = UK, City = London }
{ ID = F, Region = Europe, Country = Russia, City = Moscow }
{ ID = N, Region = North America, Country = USA, City = Los Angeles }
{ ID = A, Region = North America, Country = USA, City = New York }
{ ID = K, Region = North America, Country = Mexico, City = Mexico City }
{ ID = T, Region = South America, Country = Peru, City = Lima }
{ ID = S, Region = South America, Country = Colombia, City = Bogotá }
{ ID = E, Region = South America, Country = Brazil, City = São Paulo }
Program finished, press Enter/Return to continue:
```

Note that the cities in India and China are still in ascending order even though the country ordering has been reversed.

USING GROUP QUERIES

A group query divides the data into groups and enables you to sort, calculate aggregates, and compare by group. These are often the most interesting queries in a business context (the ones that really drive decision-making). For example, you might want to compare sales by country or by region to decide where to open another store or hire more staff. You'll do that in the next Try It Out.

TRY IT OUT   Using a Group Query: BeginningCSharpAndDotNET_16_10_
GroupQuery\Program.cs

Follow these steps to create the example in Visual Studio:

1.   Create a new Console Application called BeginningCSharpAndDotNET_16_10_GroupQuery in the directory C:\BeginningCSharpAndDotNET\Chapter16. Set the Target Framework to the Current version (.NET 5.0).

2.   Create the Customer class and the initialization of the customers list (List<Customer> customers), as shown in the BeginningCSharpAndDotNET_16_8_SelectDistinctQuery example; this code is exactly the same as previous examples.

3.   In the Main() method, following the initialization of the customers list, enter two queries:

```
var queryResults =
    from c in customers
    group c by c.Region into cg
    select new { TotalSales = cg.Sum(c => c.Sales), Region = cg.Key }
;
```

```
var orderedResults =
    from cg in queryResults
    orderby cg.TotalSales descending
    select cg
;
```

4. Continuing in the `Main()` method, add the following print statement and `foreach` processing loop:

```
WriteLine("Total\t: By\nSales\t: Region\n-----\t ------");
foreach (var item in orderedResults)
{
    WriteLine($"{item.TotalSales}\t: {item.Region}");
}
```

5. The results-processing loop and the remaining code in the `Main()` method are the same as in previous examples. Compile and execute the program. Here are the group results:

```
Total  : By
Sales  : Region
-----    ------
52997  : Asia
16999  : North America
12444  : Europe
8558   : South America
7000   : Africa
```

How It Works

The `Customer` class and `customers` list initialization are the same as in previous examples.

The data in a group query is grouped by a key field, the field for which all the members of each group share a value. In this example, the key field is the `Region`:

```
group c by c.Region
```

You want to calculate a total for each group, so you group `into` a new result set named `cg`:

```
group c by c.Region into cg
```

In the `select` clause, you project a new anonymous type whose properties are the total sales (calculated by referencing the `cg` result set) and the key value of the group, which you reference with the special group `Key`:

```
select new { TotalSales = cg.Sum(c => c.Sales), Region = cg.Key }
```

The group result set implements the LINQ `IGrouping` interface, which supports the `Key` property. You almost always want to reference the `Key` property in some way in processing group results, because it represents the criteria by which each group in your data was created.

You want to order the result in descending order by the `TotalSales` field so you can see which region has the highest total sales, next highest, and so on. To do that, you create a second query to order the results from the group query:

```
var orderedResults =
    from cg in queryResults
    orderby cg.TotalSales descending
    select cg
;
```

The second query is a standard `select` query with an `orderby` clause, as you have seen in previous examples; it does not use any LINQ group capabilities except that the data source comes from the previous group query.

Next, you print out the results, with a little bit of formatting code to display the data with column headers and some separation between the totals and the group names:

```
WriteLine("Total\t: By\nSales\t: Region\n---\t ---");
foreach (var item in orderedResults)
{
    WriteLine($"{item.TotalSales}\t: {item.Region}");
};
```

This could be formatted in a more sophisticated way with field widths and by right-justifying the totals, but this is just an example so you don't need to bother—you can see the data clearly enough to understand what the code is doing.

USING JOINS

A data set such as the `customers` list you just created, with a shared key field (ID), enables a `join` query, whereby you can query related data in both lists with a single query, joining the results together with the key field. This is similar to the `JOIN` operation in the SQL data query language; and as you might expect, LINQ provides a `join` command in the query syntax, which you will use in the following Try It Out.

TRY IT OUT   Join Query: BeginningCSharpAndDotNET_16_11_JoinQuery\
Program.cs

Follow these steps to create the example in Visual Studio:

1. Create a new Console Application called BeginningCSharpAndDotNET_16_11_JoinQuery in the directory `C:\BeginningCSharpAndDotNET\Chapter16`. Set the Target Framework to the Current version (.NET 5.0).

2. Copy the code to create the `Customer` class and the initialization of the `customers` list (`List<Customer> customers`) from the previous example; this code is the same.

3. Add the following code for an `Order` class and an `orders` list:

```
class Order
{
    public string ID { get; set; }
    public decimal Amount { get; set; }
}
```

4. In the `Main()` method, add this code to initialize the `orders` list:

```
List<Order> orders = new List<Order> {
    new Order { ID="P", Amount=100 },
    new Order { ID="Q", Amount=200 },
```

```
              new Order { ID="R", Amount=300 },
              new Order { ID="S", Amount=400 },
              new Order { ID="T", Amount=500 },
              new Order { ID="U", Amount=600 },
              new Order { ID="V", Amount=700 },
              new Order { ID="W", Amount=800 },
              new Order { ID="X", Amount=900 },
              new Order { ID="Y", Amount=1000 },
              new Order { ID="Z", Amount=1100 }
            };
```

5. In the `Main()` method, following the initialization of the `customers` and `orders` lists, enter this query:

```
    var queryResults =
        from c in customers
        join o in orders on c.ID equals o.ID
        select new { c.ID, c.City, SalesBefore = c.Sales, NewOrder = o.Amount,
                            SalesAfter = c.Sales+o.Amount };
```

6. Finish the program using the standard `foreach` query processing loop and program-finished statement you used in earlier examples:

```
        foreach (var item in queryResults)
        {
            WriteLine(item);
        }
        Write("Program finished, press Enter/Return to continue:");
```

7. Compile and execute the program. Here's the output:

```
    { ID = P, City = Tehran, SalesBefore = 7000, NewOrder = 100, SalesAfter = 7100 }
    { ID = Q, City = London, SalesBefore = 8000, NewOrder = 200, SalesAfter = 8200 }
    { ID = R, City = Beijing, SalesBefore = 9000, NewOrder = 300, SalesAfter = 9300 }
    { ID = S, City = Bogotá, SalesBefore = 1001, NewOrder = 400, SalesAfter = 1401 }
    { ID = T, City = Lima, SalesBefore = 2002, NewOrder = 500, SalesAfter = 2502 }
    Program finished, press Enter/Return to continue:
```

How It Works

You declare and initialize the `Customer` class, the `Order` class, and the `customers` and `orders` lists.

The query uses the `join` keyword to unite the customers with their corresponding orders using the ID fields from the `Customer` and `Order` classes:

```
    var queryResults =
        from c in customers
        join o in orders on c.ID equals o.ID
```

The on keyword is followed by the name of the key field (`ID`), and the `equals` keyword indicates the corresponding field in the other collection. The query result only includes the data for objects that have the same ID field value as the corresponding ID field in the other collection.

The `select` statement projects a new data type with properties named so that you can clearly see the original sales total, the new order, and the resulting new total:

```
select new { c.ID, c.City, SalesBefore = c.Sales, NewOrder = o.Amount,
    SalesAfter = c.Sales+o.Amount };
```

Although you do not increment the sales total in the `customer` object in this program, you could easily do so in the business logic of your program.

The logic of the `foreach` loop and the display of the values from the query are exactly the same as in previous programs in this chapter.

EXERCISES

16.1 Modify the third example program (BeginningCSharpAndDotNET_16_3_QuerySyntax) to order the results in descending order.

16.2 Modify the number passed to the `GenerateLotsOfNumbers()` method in the large-number program example (BeginningCSharpAndDotNET_16_6_LargeNumberQuery) to create result sets of different sizes and see how query results are affected.

16.3 Add an `orderby` clause to the query in the large-number program example (Beginning-CSharpAndDotNET_16_6_LargeNumberQuery) to see how this affects performance.

16.4 Modify the query conditions in the large-number program example (BeginningCSharp-AndDotNET_16_6_LargeNumberQuery) to select larger and smaller subsets of the number list. How does this affect performance?

16.5 Modify the method syntax example (BeginningCSharpAndDotNET_16_4_MethodSyntax) to eliminate the `where` clause entirely. How much output does it generate?

16.6 Add aggregate operators to the third example program (BeginningCSharpAndDot-NET_16_3_QuerySyntax). Which simple aggregate operators are available for this non-numeric result set?

Answers to the exercises can be found in the Appendix.

▶ **WHAT YOU LEARNED IN THIS CHAPTER**

TOPIC	KEY CONCEPTS
What LINQ is and when to use it	LINQ is a query language built into C#. Use LINQ to query data from large collections of objects, XML, or databases.
Parts of a LINQ query	A LINQ query includes the `from`, `where`, `select`, and `orderby` clauses.
How to get the results of a LINQ query	Use the `foreach` statement to iterate through the results of a LINQ query.
Deferred execution	LINQ query execution is deferred until its result is needed. (By a loop, conversion method such as `ToArray`, aggregate method call, etc.).
Method syntax and query syntax	Use the query syntax for most LINQ queries and method queries when required. For any given query, the query syntax or the method syntax will give the same result.
Lambda expressions	Lambda expressions let you declare a method on-the-fly for use in a LINQ query using the method syntax.
Aggregate operators	Use LINQ aggregate operators to obtain information about a large data set without having to iterate through every result.
Group queries	Use group queries to divide data into groups, then sort, calculate aggregates, and compare by group.
Ordering	Use the `orderby` operator to order the results of a query.
Joins	Use the `join` operator to query related data in multiple collections with a single query.

17

Databases

WHAT YOU WILL LEARN IN THIS CHAPTER:

- ➤ Using databases
- ➤ Understanding the Entity Framework
- ➤ Code-First versus Database-First
- ➤ Migrations and Scaffolding
- ➤ Creating data with Code-First
- ➤ Using LINQ with databases
- ➤ Navigating database relationships
- ➤ Creating and querying XML from databases

CODE DOWNLOADS FOR THIS CHAPTER

The code downloads for this chapter are found on the book page at www.wiley.com. Click the Downloads link. The code can also be found at github.com/benperk/BeginningCSharpAnd-DotNet. The code is in the Chapter17 folder and individually named according to the names throughout the chapter.

The previous chapter introduced LINQ (Language INtegrated Query) and showed how LINQ works with objects and XML. This chapter teaches you how to store your objects in a database and use LINQ to query the data.

USING DATABASES

For the purposes of this book, a *database* is a persistent, structured storehouse for data. There are many kinds of databases, but the most common ones you will encounter for storing and querying business data are *relational databases* such as Microsoft SQL Server and Oracle. Relational databases use the SQL database language (SQL stands for *Structured Query Language*) to query and manipulate data. Relational databases store data in *tables* organized in *rows* and *columns*.

The relationships between tables, rows, and columns are traditionally shown in an *entity-relationship model*, where an *entity* is the abstract concept of a data object such as a customer, which is related to other entities such as orders and products (for example, a customer places an order for products) in a relational database.

Working with such a database directly requires understanding this model as well as knowing the SQL language. You would use SQL for embedding SQL statements in your programming language. You would also use it for passing strings containing SQL statements to API calls or methods in a SQL-oriented database class library.

Sounds complicated, doesn't it? Well, the good news is that we will show you how you can use the *Entity Framework* to generate the code you need to translate your C# classes into database objects, store your objects in a database, and use LINQ to query the objects without having to use another language such as SQL.

ENTITY FRAMEWORK

The main class library in .NET for working with databases is the *Entity Framework*. The name comes from the entity-relationship model mentioned in the introduction to this chapter.

The Entity Framework maps the C# objects in your program to the entities in a relational database. This is called *object-relational mapping (ORM)*. Object-relational mapping is code that maps your classes, objects, and properties in C# to the tables, rows, and columns that make up a relational database. Creating this mapping code by hand is tedious and time-consuming, but the Entity Framework makes it easy!

There are a couple of different versions of the Entity Framework for working with different versions of .NET. You will use the Entity Framework that works with the latest version of .NET, called `EntityFrameworkCore`.

CODE-FIRST VERSUS DATABASE-FIRST

The Entity Framework supports two ways of mapping C# objects to your database. The first approach we will look at is called *Code-First*, where you create your C# classes first and the Entity Framework generates database objects directly from your classes. The second approach is called *Database-First*, where you start with an existing database and the Entity Framework generates C# objects that map to the pre-existing tables, rows, and columns in the database. We'll start with Code-First (this is a C# book after all) and then briefly show Database-First at the end of the chapter.

MIGRATIONS AND SCAFFOLDING

The Entity Framework uses some terms you may be unfamiliar with at first, but they are simple enough to understand in the context of the Code-First and Database-First approaches.

The first term to understand is *migrations*. Migrations are used in the Code-First approach. A migration is a set of classes that create the database objects from your C# objects. You will create an initial migration to initialize the database with your first set of C# classes. After the initial migration, each time you make changes to your database-mapped C# classes, you will need to create a new migration to update the database with your changes. Luckily the Entity Framework makes this easy by including command-line tools to generate the code for you as needed. We'll show you how to run these commands in Visual Studio as part of the Try It Out examples.

The second term is *scaffolding*, which is used for the Database-First approach. Scaffolding also uses a command-line tool to generate C# code, but it goes in the opposite direction as migration, starting from the database and generating the classes needed in your C# code. We show you how to generate scaffolding as part of the last example in this chapter.

INSTALL SQL SERVER EXPRESS LOCALDB

In order to work with a specific database, the Entity Framework needs a *provider* for that database. Entity Framework providers are available for many different databases such as SQL Server, MySQL, Oracle, SQLite, and others. These providers have a consistent architecture so the techniques you will learn in this chapter will apply to all of them. However, in order to show you working code, we need to pick one for this chapter, and the one we have chosen is Microsoft SQL Server.

You will use Microsoft's SQL Server Express, the free lightweight version of Microsoft SQL Server. You will use the *LocalDB* option with SQL Server Express, which enables Visual Studio to create and open a database file locally on your development computer without the need to connect to a separate database server over the network.

SQL Server Express LocalDB is included with Visual Studio. If you specified the ASP.NET and Web Development workload or the Data Storage and Processing workload when installing Visual Studio, you already have SQL Express Server LocalDB installed. If you did not install these workloads, you can go back and install it under the Individual Components tab under the Cloud, Database, and Server section, or alternatively, you can download and install SQL Server Express LocalDB from this link: `go.microsoft.com/fwlink/?linkid=866658`.

> **NOTE** When you first use SQL Server from Visual Studio, it creates a local SQL Server instance for you called `(localdb)\MSSQLLocalDB`. If you had installed the localdb database with a previous version of Visual Studio, you might have to use the name `(localdb)\v11.0` in the Server Name field, as Microsoft has changed the default server name. Or if you have installed the SQL Server Express Edition, you might have to use `.\sqlexpress`, as the Entity Framework uses the first local SQL Server database it finds.

A CODE-FIRST DATABASE

In the following Try It Out, you create some objects in a database using Code-First with the Entity Framework and then query the objects you created using LINQ to Entities.

> **TRY IT OUT** Code-First Database: BeginningCSharpAndDotNet_17_1_ CodeFirstDatabase

Follow these steps to create the example in Visual Studio:

1. Create a new Console Application project called BeginningCSharpAndDotNet_17_1_CodeFirst-Database in the directory C:\BeginningCSharpAndDotNet\Chapter17.

2. Click Next to create the project. When prompted for the Target Framework, choose .NET 5.0 (Current).

3. To add the Entity Framework, go to Tools ⇨ NuGet Package Manager ⇨ Manage NuGetPackages for Solution as shown in Figure 17-1.

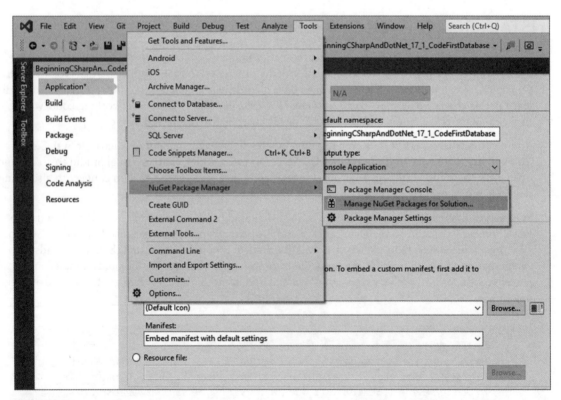

FIGURE 17-1

4. Click Browse in the Manage Packages for Solution window. Do not check the Include prelease box. Search for `EntityFrameworkCore`. You will see several EntityFrameworkCore packages listed as shown in Figure 17-2. You will use several of these packages. To start, select the top one named simply Microsoft.EntityFrameworkCore. Check the box next to Project to enable the Install button, and then click Install.

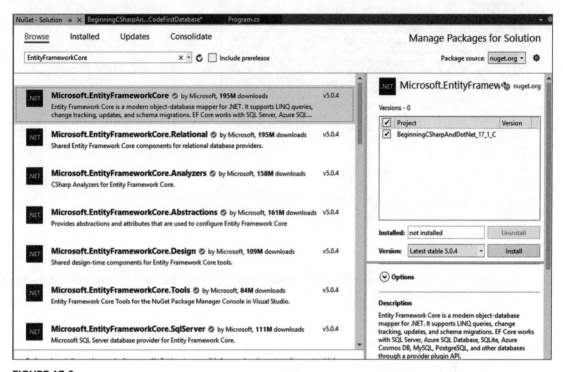

FIGURE 17-2

5. Microsoft.EntityFrameworkCore and several other required packages will be installed as shown on the Preview Changes dialog in Figure 17-3. Click OK.

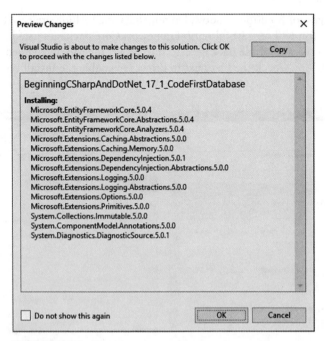

FIGURE 17-3

6. The License Acceptance dialog for the Microsoft.EntityFrameworkCore and some related packages will be displayed as shown in Figure 17-4. Click the I Accept button.

FIGURE 17-4

7. Repeat steps 4, 5, and 6 to install the Microsoft.EntityFrameworkCore.Design, Microsoft.Entity-FrameworkCore.Tools, and Microsoft.EntityFrameworkCore.SqlServer packages in your solution as well. Click Install, preview the changes, and accept the license agreement for each one.

Now the Entity Framework and related packages are added to your project. To see these, go to the Solution Explorer in your project. Expand the Dependencies node and then the Packages node. You should see all four packages: Microsoft.EntityFrameworkCore, Microsoft.EntityFrameworkCore.Design, Microsoft.EntityFrameworkCore.Tools, and Microsoft.EntityFrameworkCore.SqlServer, as shown in Figure 17-5.

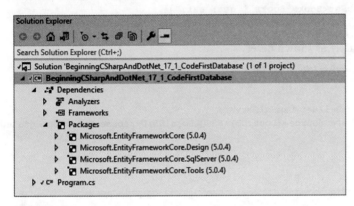

FIGURE 17-5

8. Open the main source file `Program.cs` and add the following code. First add the `using` clauses for the Microsoft.EntityFrameworkCore and Microsoft.EntityFrameworkCore.SqlServer namespaces at the top of the file:

```
using Microsoft.EntityFrameworkCore;
using Microsoft.EntityFrameworkCore.SqlServer;
```

9. Next, add `using` clauses for LINQ and Data Annotations following the `using System` directive as shown in the following snippet. The Data Annotations enable you to give hints to the Entity Framework on how to set up the database. Finally, add the `System.Console` namespace as with previous examples:

```
using System.Linq;
using System.ComponentModel.DataAnnotations;
using static System.Console;
```

10. Next, add a `Book` class with `Author`, `Title`, and `Code` similar to the example you used in Chapter 15. The `[Key]` attribute you see before the `Code` field is a data annotation, telling C# to use this field as the unique identifier for each object in the database:

```
namespace BeginningCSharpAndDotNet_17_1_CodeFirstDatabase
{
    public class Book
    {
```

```
public string Title { get; set; }
public string Author { get; set; }
[Key] public int Code { get; set; }
}
```

11. Now add a `BookContext` class that inherits from `DbContext` in order to connect your program to your database. In the `BookContext` class, add a `DbSet<Books>` class member that represents your collection of books:

```
public class BookContext : DbContext
{
    public DbSet<Book> Books { get; set; }
```

12. Inside the `BookContext` class, add an `OnConfiguring` method override using the `ContextOptionsBuilder` exactly as shown here:

```
protected override void OnConfiguring(DbContextOptionsBuilder optionsBuilder)
{
    optionsBuilder.UseSqlServer(
        @"Data Source=(LocalDB)\MSSQLLocalDB;Database=Books;Integrated Security=True");
}
}
```

> **NOTE** The `UseSqlServer` method takes a connection string parameter to specify how your program connects to your database. The connection string is a quoted string with clauses separated by semicolons. You will use this connection string:
>
> ```
> @"Server=(LocalDB)\MSSQLLocalDB;Database=Books;Integrated Security=True"
> ```
>
> The `Server` clause specifies the database server, which is your LocalDB SQL Server instance. The `Database` clause specifies the database name. The `Integrated Security` clause says to use the built-in security of your Windows login to connect to your database. If you were connecting to a different database than the one in the example, your connection string might specify a different SQL server name on the network, a database user and password, or other options.

13. Next, add code in the `Main()` function to create a couple of `Book` objects, and save the `Book` objects to the database:

```
class Program
{
    static void Main(string[] args)
    {
        using (var db = new BookContext())
        {
            Book book1 = new Book { Title = "Beginning C# and .NET",
                                    Author = "Perkins and Reid" };
```

```
                    db.Books.Add(book1);
                    Book book2 = new Book { Title = "Beginning XML",
                                            Author = "Fawcett, Quin, and Ayers"};
                    db.Books.Add(book2);
                    db.SaveChanges();
```

14. Finally, add the code for a simple LINQ query to list the books in the database after creation:

```
                    var query = from b in db.Books
                                orderby b.Title
                                select b;
                    WriteLine("All books in the database:");
                    foreach (var b in query)
                    {
                        WriteLine($"{b.Title} by {b.Author}, code={b.Code}");
                    }
                    WriteLine("Press a key to exit...");
                    ReadKey();
                }
```

The complete code for your program should now look like this:

```
        using Microsoft.EntityFrameworkCore;
        using Microsoft.EntityFrameworkCore.SqlServer;
        using System;
        using System.Linq;
        using System.ComponentModel.DataAnnotations;
        using static System.Console;

        namespace BeginningCSharpAndDotNet_17_1_CodeFirstDatabase
        {
            public class Book
            {
                public string Title { get; set; }
                public string Author { get; set; }
                [Key] public int Code { get; set; }
            }
            public class BookContext : DbContext
            {
                protected override void OnConfiguring(DbContextOptionsBuilder
    optionsBuilder)
                {
                    optionsBuilder.UseSqlServer(
                      @"Data Source=(LocalDB)\MSSQLLocalDB;Database=Books;Integra
    ted Security=True");
                }
                public DbSet<Book> Books { get; set; }
            }
            class Program
            {
                static void Main(string[] args)
                {
                    using (var db = new BookContext())
                    {
                        Book book1 = new Book
                        {
```

```
                    Title = "Beginning C# and .NET",
                    Author = "Perkins, Reid"
                };
                db.Books.Add(book1);
                Book book2 = new Book
                {
                    Title = "Beginning XML",
                    Author = "Fawcett, Quin, and Ayers"
                };
                db.Books.Add(book2);
                db.SaveChanges();
                var query = from b in db.Books
                            orderby b.Title
                            select b;
                WriteLine("All books in the database:");
                foreach (var b in query)
                {
                    WriteLine($"{b.Title} by {b.Author}, code={b.Code}");
                }
                WriteLine("Press a key to exit...");
                ReadKey();
            }
        }
    }
}
```

15. Build the program but do not run it yet. Before attempting to run the program, you must initialize your database. You will do this with some NuGet console commands that are available from the Microsoft.EntityFrameworkCore.Tools package that you referenced earlier. Go to Tools ➪ NuGet Package Manager ➪ Package Manager Console as shown in Figure 17-6.

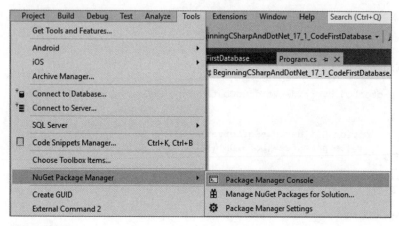

FIGURE 17-6

16. The Package Manager Console window will appear as shown in Figure 17-7.

```
Package Manager Console
Package source:  nuget.org          ▼  ⚙  | Default project:  BeginningCSharpAndDotNet_17_1_CodeFirstDa ▼ |
Each package is licensed to you by its owner. NuGet is not responsible for, nor does it grant any
additional licenses. Follow the package source (feed) URL to determine any dependencies.

Package Manager Console Host Version 5.8.1.7021

Type 'get-help NuGet' to see all available NuGet commands.

PM>
```

FIGURE 17-7

17. At the PM> command prompt, type in **Add-Migration Initialize** and then press Enter. The command will execute as shown here:

```
PM> Add-Migration Initial
Build started...
Build succeeded.
To undo this action, use Remove-Migration.
PM>
```

The Add-Migration Initialize command adds some *migration* classes to your project, as shown in Figure 17-8.

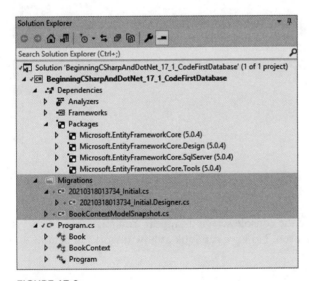

FIGURE 17-8

> **NOTE** *The migration classes contain code generated by the Entity Framework to migrate changes from your C# classes into your database. These classes manage the mapping from your C# objects to your relational database objects (tables, rows, and columns). You do not and should not modify the code in the Migration classes. Just accept them as part of the object-relational mapping magic that the Entity Framework handles for you.*

18. Next, at the PM> command prompt, type in **Update-Database** and then press Enter. The command will execute as shown here:

```
PM> Update-Database
Build started...
Build succeeded.
Applying migration '20210318013734_Initial'.
Done.
PM>
```

The Update-Database command actually creates the database objects specified in your program. We'll show how you can see the database objects later in the chapter.

19. Now that the mapping logic and the database have been created, you can finally compile and execute your program (you can just press F5 for Start Debugging). You will see the information for the Books database appear as shown in Figure 17-9.

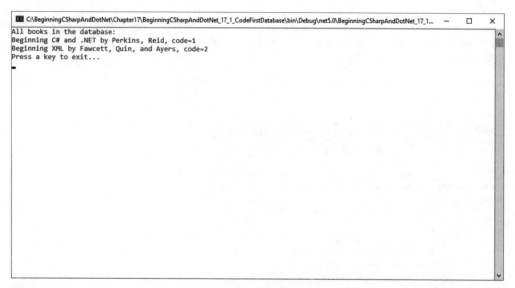

```
C:\BeginningCSharpAndDotNet\Chapter17\BeginningCSharpAndDotNet_17_1_CodeFirstDatabase\bin\Debug\net5.0\BeginningCSharpAndDotNet_17_1...   —   □   ×

All books in the database:
Beginning C# and .NET by Perkins, Reid, code=1
Beginning XML by Fawcett, Quin, and Ayers, code=2
Press a key to exit...
```

FIGURE 17-9

Press any key to finish the program and make the console screen disappear. You might need to press Enter/Return twice. That finishes the program run. Now we can look at how it works in detail.

How It Works

First you added the Microsoft.EntityFrameworkCore and Microsoft.EntityFrameworkCore.SqlServer using clauses at the top of the file in order to use the Entity Framework in your program:

```
using Microsoft.EntityFrameworkCore;
using Microsoft.EntityFrameworkCore.SqlServer;
```

Next you added the `using` clauses for the System.Linq namespace in order to use a LINQ query in your program:

```
using System.Linq;
```

Next you added the Entity Framework namespace at the top of the file below the other `using` clauses:

```
using System.Data.Entity;
```

After this you added the `using` clause for data annotations, so that you could add hints to tell the Entity Framework how to set up the database and identify key fields:

```
using System.ComponentModel.DataAnnotations;
```

Next you added the static `System.Console` namespace to make writing output to the console more convenient:

```
using static System.Console;
```

Then you added a `Book` class with `Author`, `Title`, and `Code` similar to the example used in Chapter 15. You used the `[Key]` attribute to identify the `Code` property as the unique identifier for each row in the database, enabled by your use of `System.ComponentModel.DataAnnotations`:

```
namespace BeginningCSharpAndDotNet_17_1_CodeFirstDatabase
{
    public class Book
    {
        public string Title { get; set; }
        public string Author { get; set; }
        [Key] public int Code { get; set; }
    }
}
```

Next you created the `BookContext` class inheriting from the Entity Framework's `DbContext` (Database Context) class for creating, updating, and deleting the book objects as needed in the database:

```
public class BookContext : DbContext
{
    public DbSet<Book> Books { get; set; }
```

You added the class member `DbSet<Book>` to represent a collection of all the `Book` entities in your database.

Next you added an `OnConfiguring` override method to be called by the Entity Framework to connect to your database. You passed a `DbContextOptionsBuilder` parameter to the `OnConfiguring` override method and called the `UseSqlServer` options method to specify that you will connect to a Microsoft SQL Server database. You passed a *connection string* with the details used to connect to your database, including your LocalDB database server name, your Books database, and your use of integrated Windows security:

```
protected override void OnConfiguring(DbContextOptionsBuilder optionsBuilder)
{
    optionsBuilder.UseSqlServer(
        @"Data Source=(LocalDB)\MSSQLLocalDB;Database=Books;Integrated Security=True");
}
}
```

You called the UseSqlServer method, which takes a *connection string* parameter to specify the location of your local SQL Server database. This is a quoted string with clauses separated by semicolons. You will use this connection string:

```
@"Server=(LocalDB)\MSSQLLocalDB;Database=Books;Integrated Security=True"
```

The Server clause specifies the database server, which is your LocalDB SQL Server instance. The Database clause specifies the database name. The Integrated Security clause says to use the built-in security of your Windows login.

Next you added code to use the BookContext to create two Book objects and save them to the database:

```
using (var db = new BookContext())
{
    Book book1 = new Book { Title = "Beginning C# and .NET",
                            Author = "Perkins, Reid" };
    db.Books.Add(book1);
    Book book2 = new Book { Title = "Beginning XML",
                            Author = "Fawcett, Quin, and Ayers"};
    db.Books.Add(book2);
    db.SaveChanges();
```

The using (var db = new BookContext()) clause lets you create a new BookContext instance for use in all the following code between the curly braces. Besides being a convenient shorthand, the using() clause ensures that the database connection and other underlying plumbing objects associated with the connection are closed and disposed of properly when the operations inside the using clause are finished, even if there is an exception or other unexpected event.

The Book creation and assignment statements such as

```
Book book = new Book { Title = "Beginning C# and .NET",
                       Author = "Perkins, Reid" };
```

are a fairly straightforward creation of Book objects; no database magic has occurred yet as these are simple objects in memory. You'll note that you did not assign any value for the Code property; at this point, the unassigned Code property simply contains a default value.

Next you saved the changes to BookContext db to the database:

```
db.SaveChanges();
```

Now some magic has happened; because you used the [Key] attribute to identify Code as a key, a unique value was assigned to the Code field when each object was saved to the database. You don't have to use this value or even care what it is because it is taken care of for you by the Entity Framework.

> **NOTE** *If you had not added the [Key] attribute to your object, you would have seen an exception like the one shown in Figure 17-10 when running your program.*

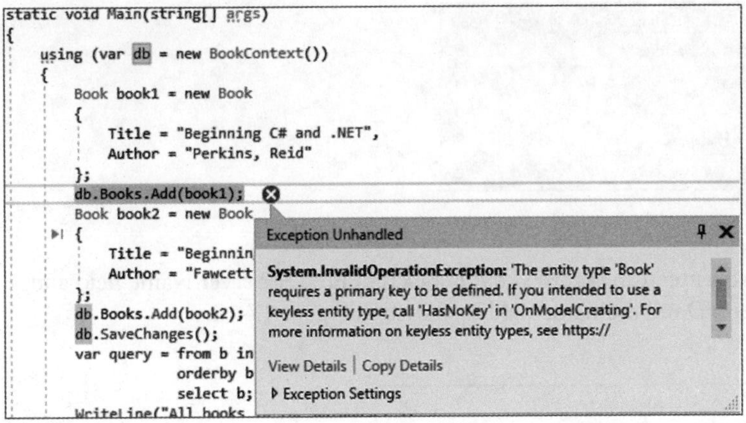

```
static void Main(string[] args)
{
    using (var db = new BookContext())
    {
        Book book1 = new Book
        {
            Title = "Beginning C# and .NET",
            Author = "Perkins, Reid"
        };
        db.Books.Add(book1);  ⊗
        Book book2 = new Book
▶ {
            Title = "Beginnin
            Author = "Fawcett
        };
        db.Books.Add(book2);
        db.SaveChanges();
        var query = from b in
                        orderby b
                        select b;
        WriteLine("All books
```

Exception Unhandled   ⊓ ✕

System.InvalidOperationException: 'The entity type 'Book'
requires a primary key to be defined. If you intended to use a
keyless entity type, call 'HasNoKey' in 'OnModelCreating'. For
more information on keyless entity types, see https://

View Details | Copy Details

▷ Exception Settings

FIGURE 17-10

Finally, you execute the code for a simple LINQ query to list the books in the database after creation:

```
var query = from b in db.Books
                orderby b.Title
                select b;
WriteLine("All books in the database:");
foreach (var b in query)
{
        WriteLine($"{b.Title} by {b.Author}, code={b.Code}");
}
WriteLine("Press a key to exit...");
ReadKey();
}
```

This LINQ query is very similar to the ones you used in the previous chapter, but instead of querying objects in memory using the LINQ to Objects provider, you are querying the database with the LINQ to Entities provider. LINQ infers the correct provider based on the types referenced in the query; you don't have to make any changes in your logic.

Finally, you just use the standard ReadKey() to pause the program before exiting so you can see the output.

That was easy, right? You created some objects, saved them to a database, and queried the database using LINQ.

EXPLORING YOUR DATABASE

But wait, you say. Where is the database you created? You never specified a file name or a folder location—it was all magic! You can see the database in Visual Studio through the Server Explorer. Go to Tools ⇨ Connect to Database. Choose Data Source and select Microsoft SQL Server, then click Continue to get the dialog shown in Figure 17-11.

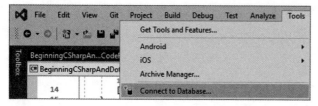

FIGURE 17-11

In the Add Connection wizard, enter `(localdb)\MSSQLLocalDB` into the Server Name field and **Books** into the Select or Enter a Database name field as shown in Figure 17-12.

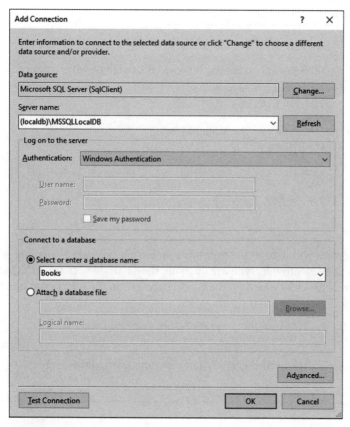

FIGURE 17-12

Click OK. You will see the Server Explorer with the Data Connections subtree as shown in Figure 17-13.

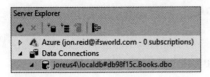

FIGURE 17-13

The Server Explorer will show the physical name of your local database, something like `YourComputerName\localdb###Books.dbo`. Click the expander next to the physical database name, and then expand the Tables subtree. You will see the Books table with the Title, Author, and Code fields as shown in Figure 17-14.

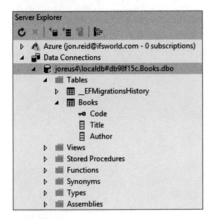

FIGURE 17-14

From here you can explore the database directly. For example, you can right-click the Books table and choose Show Table Data to see the data you entered, as shown in Figure 17-15.

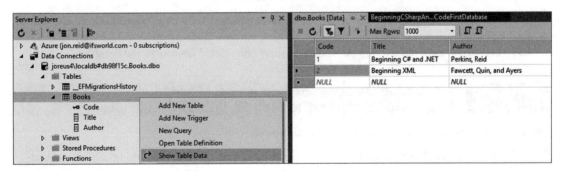

FIGURE 17-15

You will see another table listed called _EFMigrationsHistory. This was created when you used the Package Manager Console to create your initial migration and update the database. We'll explain more about migrations later in the chapter. But first, we'll explore database relationships.

NAVIGATING DATABASE RELATIONSHIPS

One of the most powerful aspects of the Entity Framework is its capability to automatically create LINQ objects to help you navigate relationships between related tables in the database.

In the following Try It Out, you add two new classes related to the Book class to make a simple bookstore inventory report. The new classes are called Store, to represent each bookstore, and Stock, to represent the inventory of books on hand (in the store on the shelf) and on order from the publisher. A diagram of these new classes and relationships is shown in Figure 17-16.

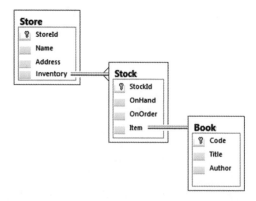

FIGURE 17-16

Each store has a name, address, and an Inventory collection consisting of one or more stock objects, one for each different book (title) carried by the store. The relationship between Store and Stock is one-to-many. Each stock record is related to exactly one book. The relationship between Stock and Book is one-to-one. You need the stock record because one store may have three copies of a particular book, but another store will have six copies of the same book.

You'll see how with Code-First, all you have to do is create the C# objects and collections, and the Entity Framework will create the database structure for you and let you easily navigate the relationships between your database objects and then query the related objects in the database.

TRY IT OUT Navigating Database Relationships: Modify BeginningCSharpAndDotNet_17_1_CodeFirstDatabase

Follow these steps to create the example in Visual Studio:

1. Open the project from the previous example in the chapter, named BeginningCSharpAndDot-Net_17_1_CodeFirstDatabase, in the directory `C:\BeginningCSharpAndDotNet\Chapter17`.

2. Open the main source file `Program.cs`. Following the declaration of the Book class, add declarations for new classes Store and Stock exactly as shown in the following code. Make sure to declare Inventory and Item as virtual. You'll see why in the How It Works section:

```
public class Book
{
```

```csharp
        public string Title { get; set; }
        public string Author { get; set; }
        [Key]
        public int Code { get; set; }
    }

    public class Store
    {
        [Key]
        public int StoreId { get; set; }
        public string Name { get; set; }
        public string Address { get; set; }
        public virtual List<Stock> Inventory { get; set; }
    }
    public class Stock
    {
        [Key]
        public int StockId { get; set; }
        public int OnHand { get; set; }
        public int OnOrder { get; set; }
        public virtual Book Item{ get; set; }

    }
```

3. Next add `Stores` and `Stocks` to the `DbContext` class:

```csharp
    public class BookContext : DbContext
    {
        public DbSet<Book> Books { get; set; }
        public DbSet<Store> Stores { get; set; }
        public DbSet<Stock> Stocks { get; set; }
```

4. Now add code to the `Main()` method to use the `BookContext` and create the two instances of the `Book` class:

```csharp
    class Program
    {
        static void Main(string[] args)
        {
            using (var db = new BookContext())
            {
                Book book1 = new Book
                {
                    Title = "Beginning C# and .NET",
                    Author = "Perkins, Reid"
                };
                db.Books.Add(book1);
                Book book2 = new Book
                {
                    Title = "Beginning XML",
                    Author = "Fawcett, Quin, and Ayers"
                };
                db.Books.Add(book2);
            }
```

5.   Now add an instance for the first store and its inventory, still inside the `using(var db = new`
     `BookContext())` clause:

```
var store1 = new Store
{
    Name = "Main St Books",
    Address = "117 Main St",
    Inventory = new List<Stock>()
};
db.Stores.Add(store1);
Stock store1book1 = new Stock
    { Item = book1, OnHand = 4, OnOrder = 6 };
store1.Inventory.Add(store1book1);
Stock store1book2 = new Stock
    { Item = book2, OnHand = 1, OnOrder = 9 };
store1.Inventory.Add(store1book2);
```

6.   Now add an instance for the second store and its inventory:

```
var store2 = new Store
{
    Name = "Campus Books",
    Address = "317 College Ave",
    Inventory = new List<Stock>()
};
db.Stores.Add(store2);
Stock store2book1 = new Stock
    { Item = book1, OnHand = 7, OnOrder = 17 };
store2.Inventory.Add(store2book1);
Stock store2book2 = new Stock
    { Item = book2, OnHand = 2, OnOrder = 8 };
store2.Inventory.Add(store2book2);
```

7.   Next, save the database changes as in the previous example:

```
db.SaveChanges();
```

8.   Now create a LINQ query on all the stores:

```
var query = from store in db.Stores
                orderby store.Name
                select store;
```

9.   Finally, add code to print out the results of the query and pause the output:

```
WriteLine("Bookstore Inventory Report:");
foreach (var store in query)
{
    WriteLine($"{store.Name} located at {store.Address}");
    foreach (Stock stock in store.Inventory)
    {
        WriteLine($"- Title: {stock.Item.Title}");
        WriteLine($"-- Copies in Store: {stock.OnHand}");
        WriteLine($"-- Copies on Order: {stock.OnOrder}");
    }
}
```

```
                                WriteLine("Press a key to exit...");
                                ReadKey();
                            }
                        }
                    }
                }
```

10. Build the program but do not run it yet. Before attempting to run the program, add a migration in order to update the database. Go to Tools ⇨ NuGet Package Manager ⇨ Package Manager Console, then run Add-Migration StoresAndStocks followed by Update-Database as shown here:

```
PM>
PM> Add-Migration StoresAndStocks
Build started...
Build succeeded.
To undo this action, use Remove-Migration.
PM> Update-Database
Build started...
Build succeeded.
Applying migration '20210321220025_StoresAndStocks'.
Done.
PM>
```

11. Compile and execute the program (you can just press F5 for Start Debugging). You will see the information for the bookstore inventory appear as shown in Figure 17-17.

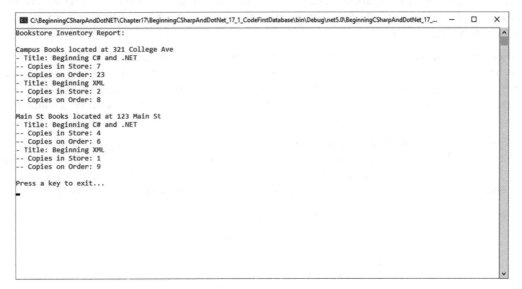

C:\BeginningCSharpAndDotNET\Chapter17\BeginningCSharpAndDotNet_17_1_CodeFirstDatabase\bin\Debug\net5.0\BeginningCSharpAndDotNet_17_...   —   □   ×

```
Bookstore Inventory Report:

Campus Books located at 321 College Ave
- Title: Beginning C# and .NET
-- Copies in Store: 7
-- Copies on Order: 23
- Title: Beginning XML
-- Copies in Store: 2
-- Copies on Order: 8

Main St Books located at 123 Main St
- Title: Beginning C# and .NET
-- Copies in Store: 4
-- Copies on Order: 6
- Title: Beginning XML
-- Copies in Store: 1
-- Copies on Order: 9

Press a key to exit...
```

FIGURE 17-17

Press any key to finish the program and make the console screen disappear. If you used Ctrl+F5 (Start Without Debugging), you might need to press Enter/Return twice. That finishes the program run. Now look at how it works in detail.

How It Works

The basics of the Entity Framework, DbContext, and data annotations were covered in the previous example, so here you'll concentrate on what is different.

The Store and Stock classes are similar to the original Book class, but you added some new virtual properties for Inventory and Item as shown here:

```
public class Store
{
    [Key]
    public int StoreId { get; set; }
    public string Name { get; set; }
    public string Address { get; set; }
    public virtual List<Stock> Inventory { get; set; }
}
public class Stock
{
    [Key]
    public int StockId { get; set; }
    public int OnHand { get; set; }
    public int OnOrder { get; set; }
    public virtual Book Item{ get; set; }
}
```

The Inventory property looks and behaves like a normal in-memory List<Stock> collection. However, because it is declared as virtual, the Entity Framework can override its behavior when storing to and retrieving from the database.

You used the migration tool in the Entity Framework to generate the migration StoresAndStocks to update the database with these new classes. The migration takes care of the database details such as adding a foreign key column to the Stocks table in the database to implement the Inventory relationship between a Store and its Stock records. Similarly, the migration adds another foreign key column to the Stock table in the database to implement the Item relationship between Stock and Book.

In the past, you would have had to decide how to map the collection in your program to foreign keys and columns in the database and keep that code up-to-date as your design changes. However, with the Entity Framework migration tools, you do not need to know these details; using Code-First, you simply work with C# classes and collections and let the framework take care of the plumbing for you.

Next you added the DbSet classes for Store and Stock to the BookContext:

```
public class BookContext : DbContext
{
    public DbSet<Book> Books { get; set; }
    public DbSet<Store> Stores { get; set; }
    public DbSet<Stock> Stocks { get; set; }
}
```

Then you used those DbSet classes to create instances of two books, two stores, and two stock records for each book under each store:

```
class Program
{
```

```
static void Main(string[] args)
{
    using (var db = new BookContext())
    {
        Book book1 = new Book
        {
            Title = "Beginning C# and .NET",
            Author = "Perkins, Reid "
        };
        db.Books.Add(book1);
        Book book2 = new Book
        {
            Title = "Beginning XML",
            Author = "Fawcett, Quin, and Ayers"
        };
        db.Books.Add(book2);
        var store1 = new Store
        {
            Name = "Main St Books",
            Address = "117 Main St",
            Inventory = new List<Stock>()
        };
        db.Stores.Add(store1);
        Stock store1book1 = new Stock
            { Item = book1, OnHand = 4, OnOrder = 6 };
        store1.Inventory.Add(store1book1);
        Stock store1book2 = new Stock
            { Item = book2, OnHand = 1, OnOrder = 9 };
        store1.Inventory.Add(store1book2);
        var store2 = new Store
        {
            Name = "Campus Books",
            Address = "317 College Ave",
            Inventory = new List<Stock>()
        };
        db.Stores.Add(store2);
        Stock store2book1 = new Stock
            { Item = book1, OnHand = 7, OnOrder = 17 };
        store2.Inventory.Add(store2book1);
        Stock store2book2 = new Stock
            { Item = book2, OnHand = 2, OnOrder = 8 };
        store2.Inventory.Add(store2book2);
```

After creating the objects, you saved the changes to the database:

```
db.SaveChanges();
```

Then you made a simple LINQ query to list all the stores' information:

```
var query = from store in db.Stores
            orderby store.Name
            select store;
```

The code to print out the results of the query is very straightforward because it simply deals with objects and collections, not database-specific code:

```
WriteLine("Bookstore Inventory Report:");
foreach (var store in query)
{
    WriteLine($"{store.Name} located at {store.Address}");
    foreach (Stock stock in store.Inventory)
    {
        WriteLine($"- Title: {stock.Item.Title}");
        WriteLine($"-- Copies in Store: {stock.OnHand}");
        WriteLine($"-- Copies on Order: {stock.OnOrder}");
    }
}
```

To print the inventory under each store, you simply use a `foreach` loop like with any collection. That's all for this example. Let's move on to querying data from an existing database!

> **NOTE** *This example is intended to be run only once to create the data shown. If you run the example multiple times, duplicate data will be created in your database and unexpected results may occur.*

CREATING AND QUERYING XML FROM AN EXISTING DATABASE

For the last example, you will combine all you have learned about LINQ, databases, and XML.

In the following Try It Out, you create a query to find some data in the previous example database, use LINQ to Entities to query the data, and then use LINQ to XML classes to convert the data to XML. This is an example of Database-First as opposed to Code-First programming where you take an existing database and generate C# objects from it.

TRY IT OUT Generating XML from Databases: BeginningCSharpAndDotNet_17_2_XMLfromDatabase

Follow these steps to create the example in Visual Studio:

1. Create a new Console Application called BeginningCSharpAndDotNet_17_2_XMLfromDatabase in the directory `C:\BeginningCSharpAndDotNet\Chapter17`. When prompted for the Target Framework, choose .NET 5.0 (Current).

2. As described in the first example, go to Tools ➪ NuGet Package Manager ➪ Manage NuGet Packages for Solution. Uncheck the Preview packages option, and then click Browse in the Manage Packages for Solution window. Search for `EntityFrameworkCore`. Install the Microsoft. EntityFrameworkCore, Microsoft.EntityFrameworkCore.Design, Microsoft.EntityFrameworkCore.

Tools, and Microsoft.EntityFrameworkCore.SqlServer packages in your solution as well. Click Install, preview the changes, and accept the license agreement for each one.

3. Now we will generate scaffolding from your database created in the previous examples. Go to Tools ⇨ NuGet Package Manager ⇨ Package Manager Console. At the PM> command prompt, type in `Scaffold-DbContext` followed by the connection string you used earlier in quotes and then the provider name Microsoft.EntityFrameworkCore.SqlServer *all on one line* as shown here:

```
PM> Scaffold-DbContext "Server=(LocalDB)\MSSQLLocalDB;Database=Books;Integrated
Security=True" Microsoft.EntityFrameworkCore.SqlServer
Build started...
Build succeeded.
PM>
```

You may see a warning about storing the connection string directly in your generated classes. Storing the connection string in the classes is not recommended for a business application with a shared database on the network, but since you have a local database and are not specifying a user or password directly in your connection string, this is not a concern.

4. After the scaffolding command runs, you will see new class files for `Book`, `BooksContext`, `Store`, and `Stock` in your Solution Explorer as shown in Figure 17-18.

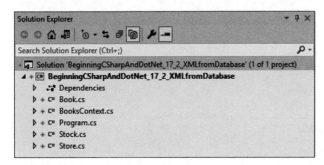

FIGURE 17-18

5. Open the main source file `Program.cs`.

6. Add references to the `System.Linq`, `System.Xml.Linq`, and static `System.Console` namespaces as shown here:

```
using System;
using System.Linq;
using System.Xml.Linq;
using static System.Console;
```

7. Add the following code to the `Main()` method in `Program.cs`:

```
static void Main(string[] args)
{
    using (var db = new BooksContext())
    {
        var query = from store in db.Stores
                    orderby store.Name
                    select store;
```

```
                        foreach (var s in query)
                        {
                            XElement storeElement = new XElement("store",
                                new XAttribute("name", s.Name),
                                new XAttribute("address", s.Address),
                                from stock in s.Stocks
                                select new XElement("stock",
                                        new XAttribute("StockID", stock.StockId),
                                        new XAttribute("onHand",
                                          stock.OnHand),
                                        new XAttribute("onOrder",
                                          stock.OnOrder),
                                new XElement("book",
                                new XAttribute("title",
                                    stock.ItemCodeNavigation.Title),
                                new XAttribute("author",
                                    stock.ItemCodeNavigation.Author)
                                )// end book
                              ) // end stock
                            ); // end store
                            WriteLine(storeElement);
                        }
                        Write("Program finished, press Enter/Return to continue:");
                        ReadLine();
                }
        }
```

8. Compile and execute the program (you can just press F5 for Start Debugging). You will see the output shown in Figure 17-19.

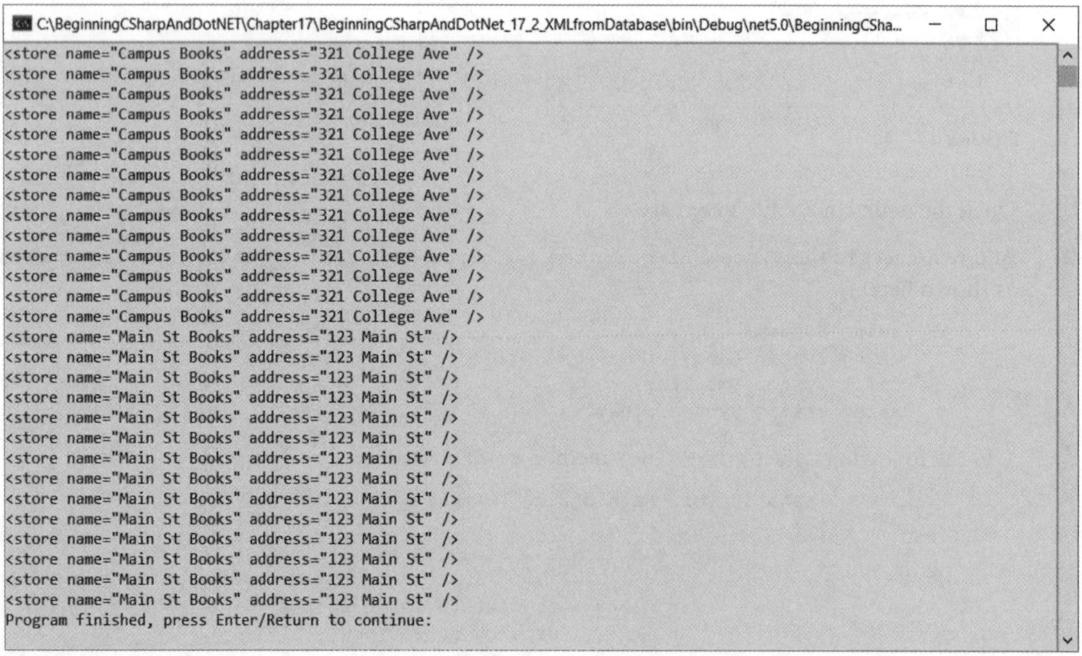

FIGURE 17-19

Simply press Enter/Return to exit the program and make the console screen disappear. If you used Ctrl+F5 (Start Without Debugging), you might need to press Enter/Return twice.

How It Works

Before writing your code in `Program.cs`, you ran the scaffolding command to generate C# classes from your database. This command generated new class files for `Books`, `BooksContext`, `Stores`, and `Stock`. Note that the generated `BooksContext` class contains the connection string you specified when running the `Scaffold-DbContext` command in the Package Manager Console.

In `Program.cs` you added the references to the `System.Linq`, `System.Xml.Linq`, and `static System.Console` namespaces in order to generate a LINQ query and then display the results in XML with the LINQ to XML constructor classes.

In the main program, you created an instance of the `BooksContext` database context class and used the same LINQ to Entities query used in previous examples:

```
using (var db = new BooksContext())
{
    var query = from store in db.Stores
                orderby store.Name
                select store;
```

When you processed the results of the query in a `foreach` loop, you used the LINQ to XML classes to transform the query results into XML using a nested set of LINQ to XML elements and attributes:

```
foreach (var s in query)
{
    XElement storeElement = new XElement("store",
        new XAttribute("name", s.Name),
        new XAttribute("address", s.Address),
        from stock in s.Stocks
        select new XElement("stock",
                new XAttribute("StockID", stock.StockId),
                new XAttribute("onHand",
                 stock.OnHand),
                new XAttribute("onOrder",
                 stock.OnOrder),
        new XElement("book",
        new XAttribute("title",
            stock. ItemCodeNavigation.Title),
        new XAttribute("author",
            stock.ItemCodeNavigation.Author)
        )// end book
      ) // end stock
    ); // end store
    WriteLine(storeElement);
}
```

Congratulations! You have combined your data access knowledge from Chapters 16 and 17 into a single program using the full power of LINQ and the Entity Framework!

EXERCISES

17.1   Modify the first example, BeginningCSharpAndDotNet_17_1_CodeFirstDatabase, to prompt the user for title and author and store the user-entered data into the database.

17.2   The first example, BeginningCSharpAndDotNet_17_1_CodeFirstDatabase, will create duplicate records if run repeatedly. Modify the example to not create duplicates.

17.3   The generated `BooksContext` class used in the last example, BeginningCSharpAndDot-Net_17_2_XMLfromDatabase, does not use the same relationship names as the previous example. Modify the `BookContext` class to use the same relationship names.

17.4   Create a database using Code-First to store the data found in the `GhostStories.xml` file used in Chapter 15.

Answers to the exercises can be found in the Appendix.

▶ **WHAT YOU LEARNED IN THIS CHAPTER**

TOPIC	KEY CONCEPTS
Using databases	A database is a persistent, structured storehouse for data. While there are many different kinds of databases, the most common type used for business data are relational databases.
Entity Framework	The Entity Framework is a set of .NET classes for object-relational mapping between C# objects and relational databases.
Code-First versus Database-First	The Code-First approach creates a database from your C# classes. The Database-First approach creates C# classes from a pre-existing database.
Migrations and scaffolding	Migrations are classes generated by the Entity Framework for Code-First to update your database as your C# classes evolve over time. Scaffolding is the method used by Database-First to generate C# classes from your existing database.
How to use LINQ with databases	LINQ enables powerful queries on databases using the same Entity Framework classes to create the data.
How to navigate database relationships	The Entity Framework enables creation and navigation of related entities in your database through the use of virtual properties and collections in your C# code.
How to create and query XML from databases	You can construct XML from databases by combining LINQ to Entities, LINQ to Objects, and LINQ to XML in a single query.

PART III
Additional Techniques

18

.NET and ASP.NET

WHAT YOU WILL LEARN IN THIS CHAPTER

➤ Cross-platform basics

➤ What was .NET Standard?

➤ Referencing and targeting .NET

➤ What was .NET Core?

➤ Porting from .NET Framework to .NET

➤ Overview of web applications

➤ Which ASP.NET to use and why

CODE DOWNLOADS FOR THIS CHAPTER

The code downloads for this chapter are found on the book page at www.wiley.com. Click the Downloads link. The code can also be found at github.com/benperk/BeginningCSharpAnd-DotNET. The code is in the Chapter18 folder and individually named according to the names throughout the chapter.

For many years, perhaps even for many decades, the Microsoft Windows operating system platform had such reach and usage that there was limited need for cross-platform support. Companies and developers would create software using the .NET Framework, which ran on Microsoft Windows, without much consideration of supporting Android, Apple, or Linux. With the rise of mobile, IoT, and touch-based devices, these other platforms gained in popularity, leading many firms to rethink their cross-platform support and opportunities.

Actually, the .NET Framework was designed from the beginning to run cross-platform, to function on different processor types (i.e., x86, ARM, or x64), and to interoperate with other programming languages. The way in which the .NET Framework was intended to run cross-platform was by compiling first into an intermediate language, frequently referred to as the Common Intermediate Language (CIL), previously called Microsoft Intermediate Language (MSIL). CIL, considered the lowest level of human-readable code, is then compiled into native code (native code is machine code [0s and 1s] that is executed directly by the processor). Once compiled into native code, the instructions can be run on the targeted platform and processor. Finally, the compilation of CIL into native code can be optimized on the type and version of processor. For example, the Intel Core i5 processor has some features and instruction sets that do not exist in older Pentium 4 processors.

> **NOTE** *How to configure the compiler options to optimize execution based on processor type is not discussed in this book. Consider performing an Internet search using ".NET Compiler Optimizations" to learn more about this advanced subject.*

There are two methods for compiling the CIL code into native code: just in time (JIT) or ahead of time (AOT). JIT compilation happens, as its name implies, only when the contents of the assembly are executed. This means that when you deploy your C# code onto a platform, it remains in CIL until a request to a specific method is invoked. The assembly (or `.dll`) is compiled a little bit at a time based on when/if it gets used. This contrasts with AOT, where you compile all assemblies into native code on the targeted platform and processor type prior to deployment. The tool that is used to AOT compile is called NGEN.

The prerequisite to the .NET Framework cross-platform support is having a Common Language Runtime (CLR) that can convert the CIL into the native code required to run on the targeted platform. The CLR is often referred to as a "virtual machine" (not to be confused with a VM created using Hyper-V or VMWare). Without a CLR virtual machine for Android, Apple OS, or Linux, the CIL cannot be compiled and run on those platforms. The fact that those virtual machines were not fully created or supported is the primary basis for the rise of Mono, Xamarin, and ultimately the creation of .NET Standard and .NET Core frameworks.

Finally, from an interoperational perspective, the .NET Framework library can be consumed using many languages like F#, PowerShell, Eiffel, COBOL, and Visual Basic .NET. The concept of *interoperate* means that if a module (e.g., a DLL file) is written in F#, then the objects and methods within that module can be consumed by a program written in any supported CLI language, i.e., C#. This consumption is achieved by adding the F# module as a reference in your C# project and then declaring the module with the `using` directive at the top of the `.cs` file.

You know now that the .NET Framework was originally designed to run cross-platform, and that was intended to be achieved with CIL and CLR virtual machines. The remainder of this chapter discusses reasons why the shift from the .NET Framework to .NET Core happened and it also shows some examples of how to create .NET Standard libraries and .NET Core projects. You begin by reading about some "must know" cross-platform and open-source terms in the next section.

CROSS-PLATFORM BASICS AND KEY "MUST KNOW" TERMS

A cross-platform program is one that can run on more than a single operating system, where an operating system is, for example, Microsoft Windows, Android, Mac OS, or Linux. The objective is that the program is written once, compiled on a supported OS, and when deployed, the code executes, performs, and behaves the same on each of the targeted operating systems. This has historically been very difficult to achieve, even when using an open-source library like Mono or Java and, as previously stated, is not truly viable using the full .NET Framework. Many of the complexities come from the way the cross-platform code interfaces and reacts to subtle differences in operating system services like disk I/O, security protocols, and network access.

As programmers begin to focus more effort toward writing C# code that can easily run cross-platform, consider these numerous "must know" concepts and terms to help build a solid foundation. These key terms are identified and described in Table 18-1.

TABLE 18-1: Cross-Platform Key Terms

KEY TERM	DESCRIPTION
.NET Native	Creates native code compiled AOT.
API	An Application Programming Interface (API) exposes classes, delegates, enumerations, interfaces, and structures for consumption via other programs.
Assembly	A `.dll` or `.exe` file that exposes APIs that can be utilized from other assemblies or executables.
BCL	Base Class Libraries (BCL) is a common collection of classes, interfaces, and value types. For example, the classes, interfaces, methods, and value types in the `System.*` directive.
CoreCLR	Same as the CLR but can run cross-platform. This is the Common Language Runtime engine for .NET Core.
CoreFX	The .NET Core `System.*` namespaces, which have strong dependencies on the runtime.
CoreRT	A runtime like the CoreCLR but without the JIT compiler. The program is compiled AOT (see .NET Native) and during which time all unnecessary code and metadata are removed.
Cross platform	Write code once and run on any supported hardware and software platform combination after the code is compiled to target the desired platform.
Dependencies	A specific group of assemblies required for a program to compile or for a task to be completed.
Ecosystem	The combination of community resources, development tools, and runtime software.

continues

TABLE 18-1 (*continued*)

KEY TERM	DESCRIPTION
Forking	Also referred to as a `branch` but implies a split in the development community as well. It is a copy of an existing source code repository to start new independent development. For example, .NET Core is a fork of the .NET Framework.
Framework/library	An inclusive collection of APIs used for the creation of programs focused on a specific vertical, in the form of an assembly.
GitHub	An online open-source code repository for sharing, updating, and forking publicly available and community supported code.
Hardware platform	X86, 64-bit, Itanium, ARM, and so on.
Metadata	Data that provides information about other data, for example: date created, author, and file size.
Metapackages	A group of interdependent packages but has no library or assembly of its own.
NuGet	A package manager for .NET that helps developers create and consume packages.
Open Source	Frameworks and code libraries that are written and supported by an open community of software developers. These libraries can be used based on the license for the specific open-source library.
Package	A group of assemblies and metadata.
PCL	Portable Class Library (PCL) is a class library that can run in numerous .NET verticals without recompilation.
Runtime	The Common Language Runtime (CLR). The CLR manages memory allocation (garbage collection), compilation, and execution.
Semantic versioning	A concept to describe the scale and type of change in this format: `[MAJOR].[MINOR].[PATCH]`. If the MAJOR number changes, the version is more impactful than if the MINOR changes.
Software platform	The operating system: Windows, Linux, Android, Mac OS, iOS, and so on.
Stack	Hardware, software, and ecosystem used together to build and run programs and/or solutions (e.g., Windows Stack, Linux Stack, and so on).
Standard	A formal specification of APIs, or a contract.
Target framework	The collection of APIs that a program relies on, for example: `dotnet-sdk-5.0.102-win-x64`.

KEY TERM	DESCRIPTION
TFM	Target Framework Moniker (TFM) is a condensed version of the target framework, for example: `netstandard2.1`, `netcoreapp3.1`, or `net5.0`. TFM is commonly used for targeting the program to a specific framework version.
Version	Each version of a framework contains new or enhanced APIs and possible bug fixes.
Verticals	Windows Forms, ASP.NET, WPF, WCF, and so on; often referred to as Application Models.

With a solid understanding of these key terms, it is time to jump into the new Microsoft cross-platform library and framework called .NET Standard and .NET Core.

WHAT WAS .NET STANDARD?

Before we begin, it is important to note that since the release of .NET 5 in 2020, that going forward, there is officially no more .NET Framework, .NET Core, and .NET Standard; hence, the past tense title of this section—"What Was .NET Standard?" The written discussions associated with these terms are remaining in the book because people learning C# and .NET will certainly run across them and will likely have some questions. The terms .NET Framework, .NET Core, and .NET Standard are not completely going away, however. Instead of having these three names, Microsoft has merged all of their respective capabilities into a single library and decided to refer to it as simply .NET. Going forward, only the term .NET is used when referencing .NET Framework, .NET Core, and .NET Standard. This reflects the most recent path Microsoft has chosen to take. In cases where references to the old way of doing things is made, the old name will be used.

A driving reason for merging all the capabilities into a single .NET library is illustrated in Figure 18-1. Notice there are numerous verticals or application models that developers and companies can target a program to run on. For example, Windows Forms, ASP.NET, and WPF are based on the full .NET Framework, while Windows Phone utilizes the .NET Compact Framework, and Universal Windows Apps is based on the .NET Native library.

The .NET Compact Framework, .NET Core, .NET Microframework, and others shown in Figure 18-1 all contain some type of Base Class Library (BCL) capabilities that were forked from the full .NET Framework.

> **NOTE** *Forking is an indicator that the base code has a solid foundation and is now being used for a separate, independent, and specifically tailored version of the code.*

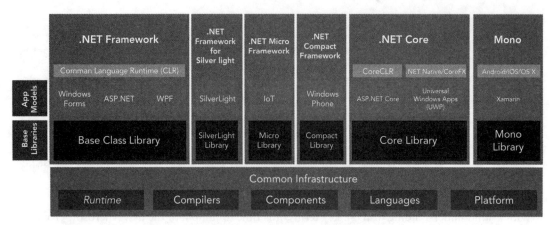

FIGURE 18-1

Take the .NET Microframework fork, for example. This fork, with a slimmed-down BCL, was created specifically to work within the confines of small Internet of Things (IoT) devices where the full .NET Framework footprint was simply too large to be a feasible library on that hardware platform. That framework version simply consumed too much drive and memory space for those small devices. The fork was made with reduced size and memory requirements so that it could fit and function on that platform. To reduce the size of the .NET Microframework, some of the features commonly found in the full .NET Framework were removed. The capabilities that were minimized and/or modified require the developer to learn the subtleties of the vertical BCL library for that specific framework. Each application model having a slightly different set of requirements was the reason for most of the forks made from the .NET Framework.

When a developer wanted a program to run on a Windows PC, a Windows Phone, and to function as a Universal Windows App, historically, it was necessary to have multiple projects and sources for each of the three verticals. As implied previously, in most cases the differences in the implementation of features were distinct per vertical BCL, specifically in the cases of security, networking, remoting, reflection, and file access, for example. This required the developer to learn, develop, and support the BCL confines for each vertical, which also resulted in additional costs for a company. The costs are incurred by having to develop, test, deploy, and support multiple versions of the same program.

> **NOTE** Most of the features that cannot be easily ported to different verticals are contained specifically in the `mscorlib.dll`.

Also note in Figure 18-1 that each .NET Framework runtime (Compact, Micro, Silverlight, Core, and so on) used by each application model remains necessary to successfully run the program on the targeted vertical and platform. When a developer decides to target a vertical, the target framework gets chosen during the creation of the solution and project in Visual Studio, for example. Therefore, each vertical will execute in its own runtime or virtual machine and must be compiled for the target app model, deployed with the dependent components, and programmed in a .NET Framework supported language. This remains the case also when targeting a .NET Standard class library.

Shared Project, PCL, and .NET Standard

Before .NET Standard and Portable Class Libraries (PCL), both of which are described later, there were *shared projects* where it was common to use the #if, #else, and #endif directives to identify which software or hardware platform the code is running on and then load the correct assembly(s) for the platform. The following code snippet, for example, checks whether the platform is .NET Framework 4.0. If it is, a reference to System.Net is used; if not, a reference to System.Net.Http occurs. (The code does assume there is no .NET Framework version older than 4.0.) Later in the code or class file, the developer must again check for platform dependencies and call the methods within those classes to achieve the objective of the program, such as using either the WebClient() or HttpClient() methods. Those methods handle outgoing or incoming HTTP requests and responses. Those two methods have different implementations depending on the version of the loaded .NET Framework.

```
#if NET40
    using System.Net;
#else
    using System.Net.Http;
    using System.Threading.Tasks;
#endif
```

In addition to software runtime validation, developers could also use those directives (#if, #else, and #endif) to determine different hardware platforms and load specific binaries based on the results:

```
#if PLATFORM_X64
    [DllImport("BLIB64.dll", CallingConvention=CallingConvention.Cdecl)]
#else
    [DllImport("BLIB32.dll", CallingConvention=CallingConvention.Cdecl)]
#endif
```

Using the directives #if, #else, and #endif to provide cross-platform support was never a solid, scalable, maintainable, or easily supportable approach. The program ended up with many code paths, and required much updating and complicated testing procedures when the components of the software or hardware were changed. As the need for targeting multiple verticals and platforms increased, a new solution for cross-platform support was in high demand. From that demand, the concept of Portable Class Libraries (PCL) was created. PCL helped resolve the scaling, maintaining, testing, and supportability issues to a considerable extent. When creating a PCL, a developer could select from a list of verticals to target (see Figure 18-2), and the tooling (e.g., Visual Studio) would generate the APIs into the specific BCL for each different application model. Notice that you can also install additional targets like Xamarin, Unity, and other supported versions of the full .NET Framework.

> **NOTE** *It is no longer recommended to use PCLs for new application development. This information is here for historical reasons. If you need to target .NET implementations that are running the .NET Framework, then .NET Standard can be used; otherwise, it is recommended to use .NET.*

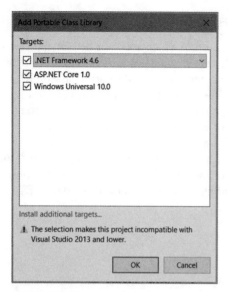

FIGURE 18-2

PCLs worked well if you remained on the Windows stack and ecosystem. The issue is that the Windows operating system has features that are unique to the operating system. One such feature is the registry that other operating systems either do not have or have something similar but different enough not to work with a PCL designed for reading and writing to the Windows registry. Additionally, Windows implements reflection differently than other operating systems and has a different concept when it comes to application domains (i.e., `AppDomain`), where an `AppDomain` is a layer of isolation within a process. Therefore, using a PCL helps resolve the issue of developing for multiple Windows verticals but does not achieve full software and hardware cross-platform support.

The solution was the creation of the .NET Standard library in combination with .NET Core. .NET Standard is a set of .NET APIs that are intended to be used across all .NET verticals. As shown in Figure 18-3, .NET Standard it replaces all the various BCL-specific implementation details per fork or framework vertical. A .NET Standard class library unifies the BCLs for all .NET Framework verticals.

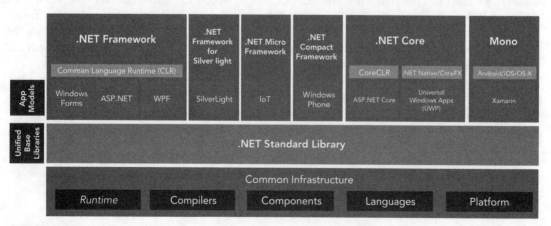

FIGURE 18-3

For a detailed look into .NET Standard 2.1 (which is the last supported version), have a look at this page: docs.microsoft.com/en-us/dotnet/standard/net-standard. You should now have some understanding of the purpose of .NET Standard class libraries and some history of the industry's evolution toward the open-source concept. In many ways, .NET Standard was a bridge that helped developers move toward this open-source, cross-platform solution. For example, if a developer utilized .NET Core 1.0 and found a missing capability, the solution was to create that in a .NET Standard class that targeted a .NET Framework. With each release, .NET Core contained more and more of the capabilities found in the .NET Framework. .NET Core 5 was the first version that was on par with the .NET Framework.

Building and Packaging a .NET Standard Library

A .NET Standard class library is a BCL that can be used to run across many different application verticals. In the following Try It Out, you will create a .NET Standard class library that contains classes required to deal a hand of cards.

TRY IT OUT   Create a .NET Standard Class Library

You will use Visual Studio to create a .NET Standard class library that contains the classes needed for the Card game example used throughout the book and package it in a NuGet package.

1. Create a new .NET Standard class library by creating a new project: select Class Library (see Figure 18-4) ⇨ press the Next button ⇨ name the Class Library `Ch18CardLibStandard`, set the Location to `C:\BeginningCSharpAndDotNET\Chapter18` ⇨ press the Create button.

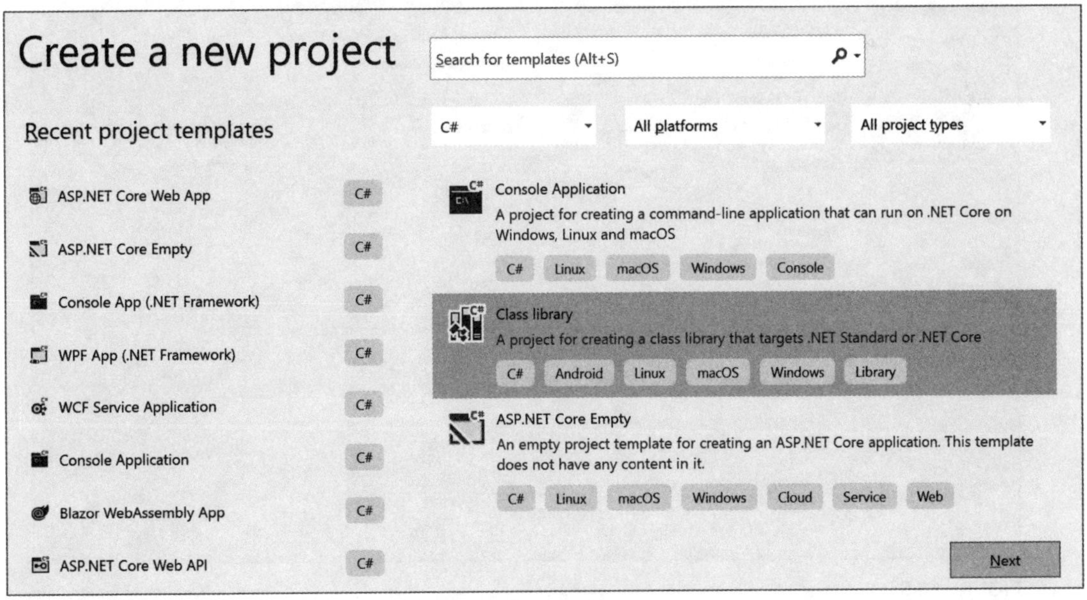

FIGURE 18-4

2.   Because the default class is not needed, right-click the `Class1.cs` file (which was created by default) ⇨ select the Delete menu item, which removes the class from the project.

3.   Download the `CardGame.cs` sample code from the online repository (the location is stated at the beginning of the chapter) and add it to the root of the `Ch18CardLibStandard` project. Add it by right-clicking the `Ch18CardLibStandard` project, then select Add ⇨ Existing Item, and select the `CardGame.cs` class from the downloaded example.

> **NOTE** The `CardGame.cs` class contains the classes from the `Ch13CardLib` exercise from earlier. Only a few modifications were implemented, such as the removal of the `WriteLine()` and `ReadLine()` methods, combining them into a single file and some other unneeded methods.

4.   As shown in Figure 18-5, set the project to Release mode, and on the Properties tab of the `Ch18CardLibStandard` project, confirm the Target framework is set to .NET Standard 2.1 by right-clicking the project and choosing Properties.

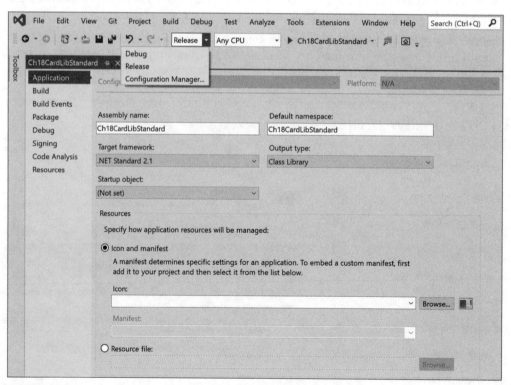

FIGURE 18-5

5. Click the Build sub-tab menu, also seen in Figure 18-5 directly under Application sub-tab ⇨ check the XML documentation file check box and then save.

6. Click the Package sub-tab menu, also seen in Figure 18-5 ⇨ check the Generate NuGet package on build check box.

7. Right-click Ch18CardLibStandard ⇨ Edit Project File ⇨ update the C# project file .csproj so it resembles the following. Feel free to change any of the attribute values, for example, Authors, PackageVersion, and PackageTags. Note that the line in the following snippet in bold is broken for presentation reasons; it should be a single line.

```xml
<Project Sdk="Microsoft.NET.Sdk">
  <PropertyGroup>
    <TargetFramework>netstandard2.1</TargetFramework>
    <GeneratePackageOnBuild>true</GeneratePackageOnBuild>
    <Version>2.0.0</Version>
    <PackageId>Ch18CardLibStandard</PackageId>
    <Authors>Benjamin Perkins</Authors>
    <Description>Beginning C# and .NET Standard CardLib</Description>
    <PackageRequireLicenseAcceptance>false</PackageRequireLicenseAcceptance>
    <PackageReleaseNotes>
      Beginning C# and .NET Standard CardLib for completing the Chapter 18 exercises
    </PackageReleaseNotes>
    <Copyright>Copyright 2021 (c). All rights reserved.</Copyright>
    <PackageTags>Beginning C# and .NET, CardLib</PackageTags>
  </PropertyGroup>

  <PropertyGroup Condition="'$(Configuration)|$(Platform)'=='Release|AnyCPU'">
    <DocumentationFile>
      C:\BeginningCSharpAndDotNET\Chapter18\Ch18CardLibStandard\
        Ch18CardLibStandard\Ch18CardLibStandard.xml
    </DocumentationFile>
  </PropertyGroup></Project>
```

8. Build/Rebuild the project by pressing SHIFT + F6 or by selecting Build ⇨ Build Ch18CardLib-Standard from the toolbar.

9. Right-click the Ch18CardLibStandard project ⇨ select Open Folder in File Explorer ⇨ view the output on the bin\Release\netstandard2.1 directory ⇨ confirm both the XML and DLL files were successfully produced from the build. You will also find the Ch18CardLibStandard.2.0.0.nupkg file in the bin\Release directory.

10. Copy the just created .NET Standard Ch18CardLibStandard.2.0.0.nupkg NuGet package into C:\Program Files (x86)\Microsoft SDKs\NuGetPackages. That directory is the location to store NuGet packages offline; you may need admin privileges in your computer to place a file in this directory.

11. To view the NuGet package offline, right-click Ch18CardLibStandard project ⇨ Manage NuGet Packages and select Microsoft Visual Studio Offline Packages from the Package Source drop-down list as shown in Figure 18-6.

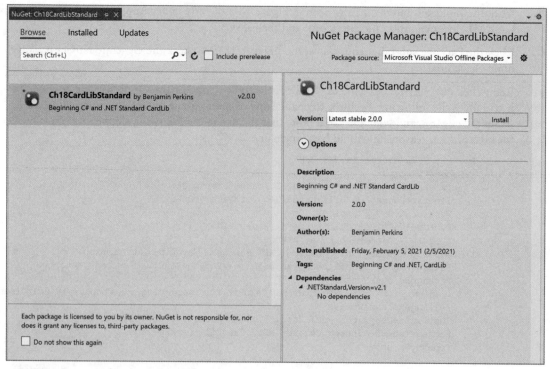

FIGURE 18-6

Congratulations! You have completed the creation of a .NET Standard class library and a NuGet package.

How It Works

Although this Try It Out targeted .NET Standard version 2.1, there are no APIs in the `CardLib` library that require APIs that exist in the frameworks supported only in 2.1. This means that realistically, the .NET Standard version can run on any version of .NET Standard and could therefore function on all operating systems.

Step 5 instructed you to enable the creation of the XML documentation file by placing a check in the check box. The information in the generated XML file is collected from the summary content within the class files. This information and the information provided in the `.csproj` file (step 7) are used for automated description generation during publishing and packaging of the NuGet package. For example, above the `Card` class within the `CardGame.cs` file, there is a summary like this:

```
/// <summary>
/// Class that describes a single card
/// </summary>
```

The content between the `/// <summary>` and `/// </summary>` tags represents the content of the XML documentation file. In a later exercise in this chapter, you will utilize the .NET Standard class from a Console Application.

> **NOTE** *Although the NuGet package in this example is deployed locally, the programmer can deploy the package to* Nuget.org *and make it public or private. NuGet is the current and future package manager for .NET and is used by many programmers and companies to get their product into the open. The .NET Standard* Ch18CardLibStandard *library is publicly hosted at* NuGet.org. *Anyone can browse for* Ch18CardLibStandard *within Visual Studio after selecting Manage NuGet Packages, or entering*
>
> ```
> Install-Package Ch18CardLibStandard
> ```
>
> *into the Package Manager Console. Then the package will be installed into the program. You open the Package Manager Console by selecting Tools ⇨ NuGet Package Manager ⇨ Package Manager Console.*

REFERENCING AND TARGETING .NET

The key factor when deciding which version of .NET Standard to target is determined by the platform and framework your class library must run on. Recognize, as shown in Table 18-2, that the higher the version of .NET Standard chosen, the more capabilities are available, but consequently the class will run on fewer platforms.

TABLE 18-2: Summary of .NET Standard Supported Version

FRAMEWORK						
.NET Standard	1.1	1.2	1.4	1.5	2.0	2.1
.NET	5.0	5.0	5.0	5.0	5.0	5.0
.NET Core	1.0	1.0	1.0	1.0	2.0	3.0
.NET Framework	4.5	4.5.1	4.6.1	4.6.1	4.6.1	none
Mono	4.6	4.6	4.6	4.6	5.4	6.4
Xamarin.iOS	10	10	10	10	10.14	12.16
Xamarin.Android	7.0	7.0	7.0	7.0	8.0	10.0
UWP	10	10	10	10	10	10

Envision a scenario where your .NET Standard class library needs to run, targeting the .NET Core 1.0, .NET Framework 4.5.1, and Xamarin.Android 7.0 frameworks. In that case, the .NET Standard class library must target .NET Standard version 1.2 because that is the version that supports all those frameworks. Consider a scenario where all the previous frameworks remain the same excluding the .NET Framework, which needs to target 4.6.1. The .NET Standard class library should therefore be targeted to version 1.4. Had the .NET Framework needed to focus on version 4.5, know that 4.5 features exist in 4.6.1; therefore, a backwards downgrade is not required as the APIs are rolled up into newer versions.

The capabilities found in different .NET Standard versions are vastly different. The probability of having access to the features required to execute a program is less when targeting 1.0 than when targeting 2.0. In many cases, these "older" shared projects or PCLs would target older .NET Framework versions, which are not ported to .NET Standard at all. That would mean that the code in those projects would not run as the capabilities either do not exist, have changed considerably, or are not supported at all. Remember that .NET Standard acted as bridge from .NET Framework to .NET Core to .NET. Each version of .NET Standard included additional features, each time getting a bit closer to supporting all capabilities found in the .NET Framework.

WHAT WAS .NET CORE?

In a previous section, you learned that .NET Standard was a class library for use across all the Windows application verticals, and one of those verticals is .NET Core. .NET Core was a fork of the full, feature-rich .NET Framework and was cross-platform and open source. In addition, .NET Core was optimized to run on the cloud platform, such as Microsoft Azure, and was highly performant, modularized, and adopted a true self-contained deployment model.

> **NOTE** *The full version on .NET Framework is still a supported option for running feature-rich Windows- and ASP.NET-based applications that target the Windows operating system. The final version of the .NET Framework is 4.8. No new features will be added to the .NET Framework; instead, all features will be added to .NET.*

.NET Core version 3.1 is the last version of that library. .NET 5.0, aka .NET, is the version that all new features and capabilities will be added to. It is the newest addition to the Microsoft development verticals and is destined to be the preferred framework for all future developments. From this point on, .NET contains all the capabilities and features available in the legacy .NET Framework version 4.8.

The remainder of this chapter discusses the specific elements that made .NET Core, and therefore .NET, worthy of a new Microsoft vertical final and, desirably, at some point in the future, the only vertical.

Cross Platform

As shown previously in Table 18-1, *cross platform* means that code is written once and can then run on any supported hardware and software platform. It is, though, necessary to target the hardware and software platform and compile the code for those specific platforms and include the specific runtimes. However, the code needs to be written only once. .NET can be downloaded for Windows, macOS, and Linux, as you will find, at this location: dotnet.microsoft.com/download/dotnet.

To use the .NET for Windows, MacOS, or Linux you need to have a computer that is running one of those operating systems and an IDE that supports .NET for use with your code. A popular IDE for development using .NET is Visual Studio Code, downloadable from code.visualstudio.com (see Figure 18-7). Visual Studio Code has a feature debugging capability and supports IntelliSense.

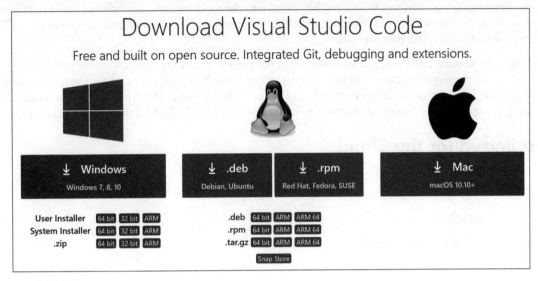

FIGURE 18-7

The exercises to this point in the book have used Visual Studio Community. Because this is a Microsoft-focused book, Visual Studio Community will continue to be used because the exercises are executed on a computer running the Windows operating system. But, have no doubt that the code written using .NET on a Windows computer using .NET targeting Windows can be compiled on a Mac or Linux machine and executed on those operating systems.

One topic that has been discussed already but is worth mentioning again is that operating system–specific features like those that would live in the System.IO namespace must be compiled against a System.IO.dll compiled for the targeted operating system. Therefore, if you create a project in Visual Studio Code on a Linux computer and include the System.IO namespace, it will be the one necessary to work on the Linux OS. NuGet, which is explained later in this section, will help ensure your project gets the correct platform version of the binary.

Open Source

The source code for .NET is located at github.com/dotnet/core. Any developer (or anyone who can read code) can view it and see specifically what it does. In addition, individuals can, in collaboration with others, search for, identify, and even fix bugs or problems with the code. Note that the source code for the full .NET Framework can be found at referencesource.microsoft.com, but it is not open source, and therefore, it is neither possible to fork it nor can you build/compile a version of that full framework. Do not assume that you need to clone or download the .NET GitHub repository, build, and compile it to use it. As mentioned previously, a stable compiled version created by Microsoft can be downloaded and installed here: dotnet.microsoft.com/download/dotnet.

If a method or class is found to be missing or if there is something your application needs to work optimally in the .NET source code—and this is the coolness of open source—you can add it. When making a fork, add the code optimization and make it known to the community that it was done. If the optimization is accepted, then it can be placed into the main branch and included in the next version. If the optimization is not accepted, it would be possible to compile and build a version of .NET just for that one project that needs it.

Finally, by making .NET open source, Microsoft has truly engaged the open community of developers and designers, giving them a terrific opportunity to contribute, make a name for themselves, and really use their existing skills to contribute and advance their careers. This kind of access to code written predominantly by Microsoft developers has historically been locked off to the open community.

Optimized for the Cloud

Cloud-optimized stacks consist of the following attributes:

➤   Portability

➤   Scalability

  ➤   Small and compact

  ➤   Modular (side-by-side execution)

➤   Resiliency

.NET is portable, and it is fully cross-platform compliant. It is also scalable due to its small footprint, certainly when compared to the full .NET Framework. When a .NET program is compiled, only the binaries required to run the program are packaged into the assembly or executable, making it very easy to copy and run on additional cloud hardware. Because .NET is a fork of the full .NET Framework, which is a time-tested and heavily engineered programming library, the code is resilient to transient blips and handled exceptions. Refer to the "Cloud Patterns and Best Practices" section in Chapter 19 for more on that.

The size and speed of the .NET runtime has also been optimized, which is especially important considering that in the cloud, customers are charged by what is used (i.e., consumption). Therefore, if the program takes up little space and runs fast, less compute power is required, and costs are reduced.

Performance

.NET offers many performance improvements compared to the full .NET Framework. Many ideas for optimization have come from the open-source community. Now, instead of working around performance issues, developers can view the source code causing the slowness and optimize it. Check the COREFX and CORECLR GitHub repositories for requests containing "performance" and you will find thousands of changes. Some examples are shown in Table 18-3.

TABLE 18-3: .NET Core Performance Improvements versus .NET Framework

NAMESPACE/MODULE	PERFORMANCE IMPROVEMENT
`System.Runtime.Serialization`	12x
`System.Security.Cryptography`	2x
`System.IO.Compression`	4x
`System.Linq`	Up to 30x
`System.Collections.Concurrent.CollectionBag<T>`	30%
`System.Collections.Generic.List<T>`	25%
`System.Collections.Generic.SortedSet<T>`	600x
`System.Collections.Generic.Queue<T>`	2x
`System.Text.RegularExpressions`	25%

There have been many optimizations, and the library will continue to get better and better as more developers and companies adopt it and contribute to it. Visit `devblogs.microsoft.com/dotnet/ performance-improvements-in-net-5` for a discussion of the performance improvements in .NET.

Modular Design

When a new .NET project is created, which is done in a later Try It Out, the project contains a "standard" set of dependencies found when you expand Dependencies ➪ Frameworks ➪ `Microsoft .NetCore.App`, as shown in Figure 18-8. Although the project contains over 100 assemblies, only those referenced and required by your program to run are included in the assembly or executable when it is compiled.

FIGURE 18-8

.NET is delivered via a set of NuGet packages. The "standard" or default project assemblies are present to support a scenario, for example, where a developer has a computer that is not connected to the Internet and is therefore not able to download and install the basic NuGet packages. However, these default assemblies ensure that there are no roadblocks with making progress once the .NET project is originally created.

Self-Contained Deployment Model

The full .NET Framework is most commonly installed on the computer or server that will run the program created by a developer. A benefit of doing this is that the framework is installed once and all applications can reference and use the framework as needed, saving local storage space. However, an undesirable situation can happen when all applications reference the same framework assemblies and unexpected updates are performed, breaking some code functions.

There are two distinguishable types of upgrades in the context of the full .NET Framework. They are side-by-side and in-place. Side-by-side is a major version change. For example, installing .NET Framework 2.0 and .NET Framework 4.0 would support programs targeting either 2.0 or 4.0. This is common when there are significant modifications or optimizations to the CLR and framework components. If a program targeted .NET Framework 2.0 and .NET Framework 4.0 was installed, the risk of impact is small because it is a side-by-side installation. In contrast, an in-place upgrade (for example, upgrading from .NET Framework 4.5 to .NET Framework 4.6.2), would likely contain changes to the mscorlib.dll and other .NET assemblies that would be run when programs are targeting .NET Framework 4.x.

.NET resolves this by being self-contained, also referred to as being an *application local framework*. What this means is that the assemblies referenced within the program are included with the module or executable, and when deployed, the program has all the required assemblies to run (the runtime, the compiler, and the referenced framework components). The program is no longer dependent on a machine-wide installation of any .NET Framework, and any modification to a machine-wide side-by-side or in-place .NET Framework version would have no impact on the .NET program. Finally, because the assemblies are small and compact (i.e., cloud optimized), they consume limited local storage space.

This means that as a developer and a company, once the product has shipped, high confidence can be held that the program will never stop working due to a framework upgrade on a computer or server. Historically, when breaking upgrades happened, the developers and IT support staff were called into escalation meetings to resolve this issue in a state of crisis. These were complicated situations in the enterprise as it is common for groups, teams, and processes to require many agreements and approvals to get changes made in a production environment. It is common practice that once the development is complete, the ownership of the code transfers to support, which is the basis for the complexities and approvals. Those constraints made the situation much more challenging.

> **NOTE** .NET upgrades and rollbacks in the development environment are simple when compared to .NET Framework machine-wide changes. To upgrade to the most current version of a .NET module, execute install-package System.Text.RegularExpressions. To roll back to the previous version, use the -Version parameter to identify the desired version.

When .NET is chosen as the target framework, this crisis mode situation will no longer happen. Instead, upgrades are made only at the application level where ample development, integration, and performance testing can happen in advance. If issues do come up during the development cycle when upgrading to a new assembly version, developers and companies then can decide on which actions to take. Deciding to upgrade the code to support the new version or roll back to the version that had worked well prior to the upgrade is much easier in a development environment than in production crisis mode.

The .NET Standard class library was created and packaged earlier; now it is time to consume it. Continue reading to learn how to do that. .NET is a cross-platform, open-source application framework. Using this framework in combination with the .NET Standard class library allows the programmer to code the BCL once and use it across all supported application verticals. In the .NET scenario, the benefit is true cross-platform support. In the following Try It Out, you will create a Console Application to consume the .NET Standard class library created in a previous section. The .NET console application will deal a hand of cards.

TRY IT OUT   Create a .NET Console Application

You will use Visual Studio to create a Console Application using the classes and methods within the .NET Standard class library `Ch18CardLibStandard`.

1. Create a new Console Application named `Ch18CardClientCore` ⇨ store it in `C:\BeginningC-SharpAndDotNET\Chapter18` ⇨ press the Next button ⇨ choose .NET 5.0 from the dropdown ⇨ press the Create button.

2. Right-click Dependencies ⇨ Manage NuGet Packages. If the .NET Standard NuGet package was placed into the directory `C:\Program Files (x86)\Microsoft SDKs\NuGetPackages`, as shown previously (Figure 18-6), the package is available offline.

3. Select either the local copy of the `Ch18CardLibStandard` NuGet package by selecting Microsoft Visual Studio Offline Packages from the Package source drop-down list (refer to Figure 18-6) or the public one, mentioned in step 3b. Perform either step a or b; both are not required. If for some reason the package does not show up in the offline list, you can execute the following snippet to install it manually. Make sure you are on the Browse tab and not Installed.

    ```
    Install-Package "C:\Program Files(x86)\MicrosoftSDKs\NuGetPackages\Ch18CardLib-
    Standard.2.0.0.nupkg"
    ```

    a. Install the local package by then selecting the `Ch18CardLibStandard` NuGet package from the offline package list ⇨ press the Install button.

    b. Install the public package (written by Benjamin Perkins) from the Package Manager Console and select the menu item Tools ⇨ NuGet Package Manager ⇨ Package Manager Console. Then execute the following command:

    ```
    Install-Package Ch18CardLibStandard
    ```

4. Open the `Program.cs` file and update the code so that it resembles the following:

    ```
    using System;
    using BeginningCSharp;
    ```

```
namespace Ch18CardClientCore
{
    class Program
    {
        static void Main(string[] args)
        {
            Player[] players = new Player[2];
            Console.Write("Enter the name of player #1: ");
            players[0] = new Player(Console.ReadLine());
            Console.Write("Enter the name of player #2: ");
            players[1] = new Player(Console.ReadLine());

            Game newGame = new Game();
            newGame.SetPlayers(players);
            newGame.DealHands();

            Console.WriteLine($"{players[0].Name} received this hand: ");
            foreach (var card in players[0].PlayHand)
            {
                Console.WriteLine($"{card.rank} of {card.suit}s");
            }

            Console.WriteLine($"{players[1].Name} received this hand: ");
            foreach (var card in players[1].PlayHand)
            {
                Console.WriteLine($"{card.rank} of {card.suit}s");
            }
            Console.WriteLine("Press enter to exit.");
            Console.ReadLine();
        }
    }
}
```

5. Execute the .NET Core application and enter names for two players as requested. The result and the dealt hands of cards will look like Figure 18-9.

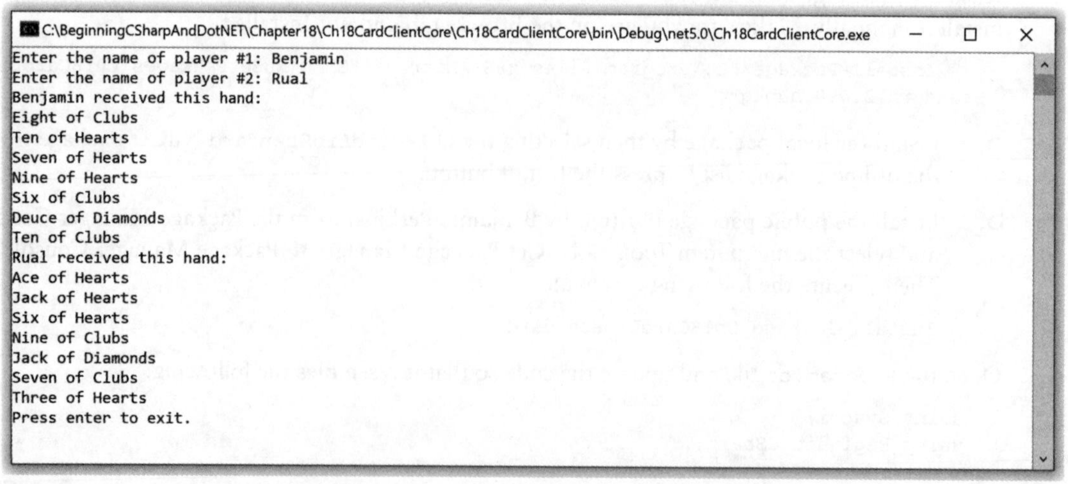

```
C:\BeginningCSharpAndDotNET\Chapter18\Ch18CardClientCore\Ch18CardClientCore\bin\Debug\net5.0\Ch18CardClientCore.exe    —    □    ×
Enter the name of player #1: Benjamin
Enter the name of player #2: Rual
Benjamin received this hand:
Eight of Clubs
Ten of Hearts
Seven of Hearts
Nine of Hearts
Six of Clubs
Deuce of Diamonds
Ten of Clubs
Rual received this hand:
Ace of Hearts
Jack of Hearts
Six of Hearts
Nine of Clubs
Jack of Diamonds
Seven of Clubs
Three of Hearts
Press enter to exit.
```

FIGURE 18-9

How It Works

When a Console Application project is rendered, a default `Program.cs` file is created with a `Console.WriteLine()` command including the string "Hello World." Take note of two things. First, notice that only the `using System` directive is included in the `Program` class file by default. This is another indication that the focus is on making the assembly as small as possible. This contrasts with a Console App (.NET Framework) project that includes many more modules by default.

When the code is executed, an array of the `Player[]` class expecting two elements is instantiated and named `players`. The names of both players are requested and retrieved from the console using the `Console.ReadLine()` method and stored into the `player[0]` and `player[1]` elements. A new `Game` class is instantiated called `newGame` and the players are allocated to the `Game` by calling the `SetPlayers()` method, passing the players array as a parameter. The `DealHands()` method in the `Game` class is called, and the results are looped through using `foreach` statements for each player. Look through the results and pick the winner.

To this point, discussions have been focused on creating new .NET Standard class libraries and .NET applications. The next section discusses some topics having to do with moving a program that originally targeted the full .NET Framework version to .NET so that it can run cross-platform.

PORTING FROM .NET FRAMEWORK TO .NET

After reading all the benefits of .NET, it is probable that you are wondering about how to use this new library. If an existing program is written using the full version of the .NET Framework, the possibility to port the code to .NET is achievable. Because each program has unique constraints and context, this section describes only some basic ideas and processes for porting. In many cases, for large, complicated programs, more analysis, planning, code development, and testing are surely required and recommended.

Microsoft has created a tool called the .NET Portability Analyzer, which you can read about on Docs and is downloadable on the Visual Studio Marketplace. The source code is also available on GitHub.

➤ `docs.microsoft.com/en-us/dotnet/standard/analyzers/portability-analyzer`

➤ `marketplace.visualstudio.com`

➤ `github.com/Microsoft/dotnet-apiport`

The .NET Portability Analyzer will analyze a program and its assemblies, then generate a report that identifies any APIs the program has that are not currently part of .NET. Once downloaded and installed from the Marketplace, you configure the analyzer by right-clicking your project and selecting Portability Analyzer Settings from the pop-up menu. The result is a window like the one illustrated in Figure 18-10.

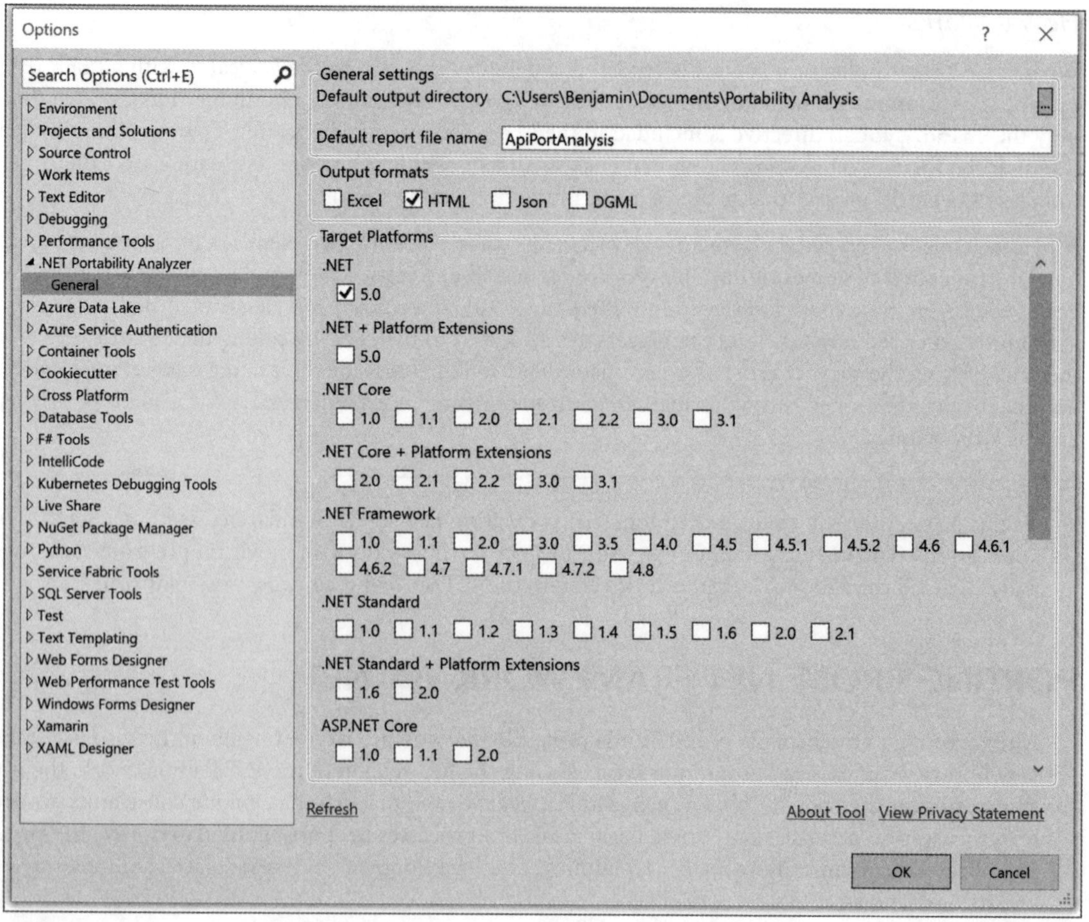

FIGURE 18-10

The source application in this example is a .NET Framework 4.7.2 console application, but the source application can be from any currently supported platform. As you see in Figure 8-10, the target platform is .NET. Press the OK button, then right-click the project and select Analyze Project Portability from the pop-up menu. The result will be a report that shows any incompatibility found with your current project and .NET. You will be presented with an overview of any detected issues and their descriptions. These descriptions are helpful for resolving each specifically identified issue. In addition to the .NET Portability Analyzer, there is a tool named .NET Upgrade Assistant that you should consider using as you plan a migration to .NET. Read more about that here: dotnet .microsoft.com/platform/upgrade-assistant.

Other points to consider when porting from .NET Framework to .NET are:

➤   Identifying any third-party dependencies

➤   Understanding which features are not available

➤   Upgrading the current .NET Framework target

Identifying Third-Party Dependencies

As previously mentioned, .NET runs cross-platform (Windows, Linux, or MacOS) and across multiple chipsets (x64, x86, ARM). .NET assemblies are designed to function and run on those platforms when compiled against those targets. However, this does not mean that all assemblies included in the project do so. It is possible that a third-party package only supports running in a 32-bit (x86) process mode or does not have a package that runs on a Linux OS. In that case, the developer must find an alternative or contact the third-party and ask if there are plans to provide this kind of support.

Understanding Which Features Are Not Available

If the third-party assembly utilizes Windows OS–specific technologies like AppDomains, Remoting, File Access, Security, Registry, and so on, then the included third-party assemblies will not function as expected. There is a comprehensive list of breaking changes here: `docs.microsoft.com/en-us/dotnet/core/compatibility/5.0`. By comparing this list and a review of the code contained in the .NET Framework program, you can gain more insight into the effort and feasibility of porting to .NET and realize the gain of running cross-platform.

Upgrading the Current .NET Framework Target

In addition to upgrading the development IDE to the most current available version of Visual Studio, you or the team planning the port to .NET should also consider targeting the most current version of the .NET Framework. You should consider doing this before you attempt to port the .NET. For example, if your application currently targets .NET Framework 4.5.1, you may have an easier time moving to .NET Framework 4.8 and then to .NET, instead of moving directly to .NET. This is because you reduce the number of complexities. By porting to .NET Framework 4.8 from 4.5.1, you would remain in the same runtime, so you would only experience problems with code library issues, instead of potentially code and runtime issues. Determining where an issue is coming from is complicated, so if you can reduce the number of places, you will have a higher probability of fixing it.

Another reason is that .NET Framework 4.8 is as close on par with the code found in .NET. Remember that .NET is open source and has been completely rewritten and that it also has a new runtime. If for some reason the API in the original project does not exist in .NET, there are these options:

➤ Refer to the previous section, "Understanding Which Features Are Not Available."

➤ Confirm the API is identified in the Portability Analyzer report.

➤ Remain on the current platform version until the API is added.

➤ Find an alternative API, a third-party assembly, or a NuGet package that helps resolve the issue and satisfies the requirement.

In conclusion, there are great complexities that exist when you attempt to port an application to a new platform. You should perform analysis of the existing program and map the features in the source program to the ones in the target platform. Then take small, logical steps, troubleshooting and resolving any issues until your code is running fully on the new version. Most migrations are unique, which is why only guidelines are provided here. It is common to hire individuals who specialize in planning, designing, testing, executing, and deploying migration projects. Depending on the complexity of your solution, you might consider this.

OVERVIEW OF WEB APPLICATIONS

Windows Presentation Foundation (WPF) and its predecessor Windows Forms are technologies for writing applications to run on the Windows operating system. Additionally, the Universal Windows App (UWA) application type, which has been deprecated, was the technology for writing apps that were downloadable from the Microsoft Store and targeted tablets or other mobile devices. With ASP. NET, developers create web applications that are hosted on an Internet or intranet web server and are mostly utilized using an Internet browser via the HTTP protocol.

This section provides an overview of programming web applications using ASP.NET Web Forms and ASP.NET Core. In addition, as there are numerous flavors of ASP.NET (e.g., MVC, Web Forms, Web Pages, and Web API), their differences and the scenarios for when to use each flavor are described. Additionally, the differences between ASP.NET Web Site and ASP.NET Web Application Projects are presented and dissected. In addition to a comparison of the ASP.NET flavors and project types, discussions covering topics with regard to web controls, input validation, state management, and authentication are provided. Start with reading about what a web application is, its benefits, and its unique properties and features in the next section.

A web application causes a web server to send graphics, HTML, and/or JavaScript code to a client. That code is typically displayed in a web browser, for example, Microsoft Edge, Chrome, or Firefox. When a user enters a web address (URL) into a browser and presses Enter, an HTTP request is sent to the web server. The HTTP request can contain a filename like `Default.aspx` along with additional information such as cookies, the languages that the client supports, security tokens, and additional data belonging to the request. The web server then returns an HTTP response that contains HTML code. This code is interpreted by the web browser and can display, for example, text boxes, buttons, and lists to the user. If JavaScript is included in the HTTP response, that code will run on the client while loading or perform validation prior to sending a further HTTP request. For example, the JavaScript might confirm that a value exists in a text box when a submit button is pressed. When the ASP.NET Web Form (ASPX) and ASP.NET Core applications are written later, take note of the ASP.NET `Page` object and its properties. In fact, two of the `Page` properties are `Request` and `Response`.

ASP.NET is a technology for dynamically creating web pages with server-side code. These web pages can be developed with many similarities to client-side Windows programs. Instead of dealing directly with the HTTP request and response and manually creating HTML code to send to the client, use ASP.NET controls such as `TextBox`, `Label`, `ComboBox`, and `Calendar`, which create HTML code. To create a `TextBox` server-side control, add the following to an ASP.NET Web Form (ASPX) file:

```
<asp:TextBox ID="player1TextBox" runat="server" />
```

To achieve the same using Razor syntax, which is introduced later in this chapter and again in Chapter 19, use this syntax:

```
@Html.TextBox("player1TextBox")
```

In each case, when an HTTP request is made to the file containing those code snippets, the code is executed, and an HTTP response is returned to the client containing an HTML representation of that control. Figure 18-11 illustrates how a request flows from a browser to an IIS server and back.

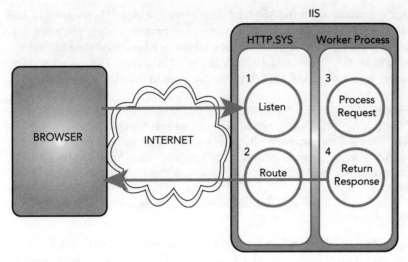

FIGURE 18-11

WHICH ASP.NET TO USE AND WHY

After a solution architect or a programmer has decided that the best platform to run their program on is a website, the next question is which flavor of ASP.NET to target. The first iteration of Microsoft's web development platform was Active Server Pages or ASP. Razor used ASP-like syntax contained within an `.asp` file and often included an embedded VB COM instantiated using the `Service.CreateObject()` for initialization that provided the reference to the methods exposed via the API. Although ASP is still a supported technology, it would not be a recommended application type for the creation of any new web-based program.

When the .NET Framework was created in the early 2000s, the natural evolution of ASP was to utilize that framework when updating ASP, which was renamed to ASP.NET. The major change was the split between the presentation layer (`.aspx` file) and the business logic layer (`aspx.cs` or `aspx.vb` file), commonly referred to as a code-behind. The supported languages in a code-behind are C# and VB.NET, and the ASP.NET model was referred to as Web Forms. ASP.NET Web Forms were and continue to be a valid and fully supported technology for creating feature-friendly and highly complex applications that target IIS and the Windows Server operating system. Over the many years of engineering and feature improvements, it became apparent that ASP.NET Web Forms was a little heavy. What "heavy" specifically means is described later, but this "heavy" stigma resulted in the development of a new ASP.NET flavor that is called ASP.NET MVC.

The MVC in ASP.NET MVC stands for Model-View-Controller. As mentioned previously, ASP.NET Web Forms split ASP code into two different layers: the presentation layer and the business logic layer. Now, MVC splits this out into three layers:

➤ **Model**—The business layer

➤ **View**—The presentation layer

➤ **Controller**—The input control layer

ASP.NET MVC was a logical iteration from the ASP.NET Web Form model, but be aware that ASP. NET MVC is significantly different in design, support concepts, and practices. Some programmers having an ASP.NET Web Form background might view the changes as a bit challenging from the beginning, but after digging in and using the model, clarity begins to take root. There is more on this in the sections of this chapter where each ASP.NET flavor is discussed in detail.

> **NOTE** *Each of the primary ASP.NET flavors (Web Forms and MVC) as well as ASP and ASP.NET Web APIs are handled by what is called a handler. A handler is most commonly a `.dll` assembly that is configured in IIS. The assembly parses the file and executes the code found within it and then returns HTML to the requesting client.*

The most recent addition to the ASP.NET family is ASP.NET Core, which aligns with .NET like ASP.NET aligned with the .NET Framework. ASP.NET Core, like .NET, is an open-source framework and platform that can target operating systems other than Microsoft Windows, for example, Linux or MacOS. ASP.NET Core supports both Web Applications and Web Applications (Model-View-Controller) project types. While ASP.NET Core Web Applications is like the ASP.NET Web Pages flavor and provides a simpler, less complex implementation for programmers of small web sites, ASP.NET Core Web Applications (MVC) provides full MVC capabilities for running web applications cross-platform.

Finally, an ASP.NET Web API is like a `.dll` that exposes an API. There is no presentation layer; only the ability to call the exposed API method and pass the required parameters is available. The result of the API method call is a string of data. In the context of an ASP.NET Web API, this string is in JSON format. The calling client then needs to parse and present the JSON data in a usable form. Now that the progression and evolution of the Microsoft web application frameworks are described, read on to learn why one should be used versus the other.

ASP.NET Web Forms

The reasons for choosing ASP.NET Web Forms over the other frameworks are that Web Forms are:

➤ Optimal for small to mid-sized development teams and projects

➤ Useful for web applications that need to maintain session and state over HTTP

➤ Based on a very initiative set of request pipeline events

When compared to the other ASP.NET flavors, ASP.NET Web Forms is the best and simplest way to get a feature-rich and highly performant web application developed and deployed rapidly. The separation between the presentation logic and the business logic aligns well with targeted skill sets of front-end, user interface developers and coders. This is optimal because the team can have specialists working on the various aspects of the project in parallel.

ASP.NET Web Forms is often considered "heavy" due to a feature called viewstate and is one way in which state is maintained in an ASP.NET Web Form. For example, consider a web application that requires a series of page completions and submits to place an order. If a client hits the back button at some point in the process, viewstate is how the contents in the previous form are repopulated with the originally entered values. The issue with the viewstate feature is that it can be abused (i.e., over-used), which results in an exceptionally large page size that moves back and forth between the client and the sever. As well, viewstate is enabled for the Page by default, instead of only on the web page controls that need to maintain state.

The best way to avoid problems with viewstate is to disable it at the page level by setting the EnableViewState property to false. If you need to then maintain state on a TextBox, for example, use the following snippet to enable it specifically. Additionally, monitor the size of the .aspx files to make sure they are not getting too big.

```
<asp:TextBox EnableViewState="true" ID="Name"  runat="server" />
```

It is not possible to maintain state without a session. Maintaining a session is a concept that comes from the era of client/server computing, where the connection between a computer and a server remained persistent. The HTTP protocol is synonymous with being stateless and is optimally suited for handling static (i.e., not dynamic) content.

> **NOTE** Sessions are restricted to a worker process (refer to Figure 18-11), which means values stored within them cannot be accessed between them. This is an important constraint when an ASP.NET application needs to run in the cloud or in a web farm.

ASP.NET Web Forms are dynamic because of the C# code in the code-behind file (e.g., Default.aspx.cs), which executes when the file is requested. The returned HTML delivered to the browser is most likely changed by the executing C# code based on the unique input from the client/user. The HTML can be different for each client based on the contents stored in the session cookie, as well. ASP.NET Web Form programmers store information in a session using the following syntax:

```
Session["username"] = TextBoxUID.Text;
```

The session variable with the name of username can then be accessed on subsequent HTTP requests using this code:

```
var username = Session["username"];
```

Lastly, events in the execution of an ASP.NET Web Forms request, such as BeginRequest, AuthenticateRequest, Init, Load, ProcessRequest, and EndRequest, to name a few, are completely intuitive by name. That is important because when a programmer wants to take some special action toward authenticating a client or clean up any data before the request is completed, it's easy to identify the location to place the code. The following continues with discussing a few important ASP.NET Web Form concepts in more detail. Each of the ASP.NET application flavors have aspects that make them unique (the specifics were discussed previously). After reading this section, you will have a solid understanding of the following ASP.NET Web Form features:

➤ Server controls

➤ Input validation

➤ State management

➤ Authentication and authorization

> **NOTE** *The remainder of this section covers these four points in more detail, but there is much more to ASP.NET Web Forms. Keep in mind that this is not an ASP.NET book, and therefore, if more information about any flavor of ASP. NET interests you, there are many books that cover each of them.*

Server Controls

In this section, you will learn about the server controls provided by the ASP.NET page framework. These controls are designed to provide a structured, event-driven, object-oriented model for programming web applications. Table 18-4 lists some of the principal web server controls available with ASP.NET and the HTML code returned by these controls.

TABLE 18-4: Examples of ASP.NET Server Controls

CONTROL	HTML	DESCRIPTION
Label	`<span>`	Returns a span element containing text.
TextBox	`<input type="text">`	Returns HTML `<input type="text">` whereby the user can enter some values. You can write a server-side event handler when the text changes.
Button	`<input type="submit">`	Sends form values to the server.
HyperLink	`<a>`	Creates a simple anchor tag referencing a web page.
DropDownList	`<select>`	Creates a select tag whereby the user sees one item and can select one of multiple items by clicking the drop-down list.

CONTROL	HTML	DESCRIPTION
CheckBox	`<input type="checkbox">`	Returns an `input` element of type `check box` to show a button that can be selected or deselected. Instead of using the `CheckBox`, you can use a `CheckBoxList`, which creates a table consisting of multiple `check box` elements.
RadioButton	`<input type="radio">`	Returns an `input` element of type `radio`. With a radio button, just one button of a group can be selected. Similar to the `CheckBoxList`, `RadioButtonList` provides a list of buttons.
Image	`<img src="">`	Returns an `img` tag to display a GIF or JPG file on the client.

There are many additional controls not shown in this table. However, these controls all have in common an ability to fire off events invoked by the user, either automatically or as part of the page event life cycle. These events execute server-side event handlers. You will find ASP.NET applications are largely structured based on this event-driven model.

Input Validation

When users enter data, it should be checked for validity. The check can happen on both the client and on the server. You can check the data on the client using JavaScript. However, if the data is checked on the client using JavaScript, it should also be checked on the server because you can never fully trust the client. It is possible to disable JavaScript in the browser, and hackers can use different JavaScript functions that accept incorrect input. Checking the data on the client leads to better performance, as no round-trips occur to the server until the data is validated on the client.

With ASP.NET it is not necessary to write the validation functions yourself. Many validation controls exist that create both client- and server-side validation. The following example shows the `Required-FieldValidator` validation control that is associated with the text box `player1TextBox`. All validator controls have the properties `ErrorMessage` and `ControlToValidate` in common. If the input is not correct, then `ErrorMessage` defines the message that is displayed. By default, the error message is displayed where the validator control is positioned. The property `ControlToValidate` defines the control where the input is checked.

```
<asp:TextBox ID="player1TextBox" runat="server"></asp:TextBox>
<asp:RequiredFieldValidator ID="RequiredFieldValidator1" runat="server"
    ErrorMessage="Enter a name for player 1" ControlToValidate="player1TextBox">
</asp:RequiredFieldValidator>
```

Table 18-5 lists and describes some validation controls.

TABLE 18-5: Examples of ASP.NET Validation Controls

CONTROL	DESCRIPTION
RequiredFieldValidator	Specifies that input is required with the control that is validated. If the control to validate has an initial value set, which the user must change, you can set this initial value with the `InitialValue` property of the validator control.
RangeValidator	Defines a minimum and maximum value that the user can enter. The specific properties of the control are `MinimumValue` and `MaximumValue`.
CompareValidator	Compares multiple values (such as passwords). Not only does this validator support comparing two values for equality, but additional options can also be set with the `Operator` property. The `Operator` property is of type `ValidationCompareOperator`, which defines enumeration values such as `Equal`, `NotEqual`, `GreaterThan`, and `DataTypeCheck`. Using `DataTypeCheck`, the input value can be checked to determine whether it is of a specific data type; for example, correct date input.

State Management

The HTTP protocol is stateless. The connection that is initiated from the client to the server is closed after every request. However, normally, it is necessary to remember some client information from one page to the other. There are several ways to accomplish this.

The main difference among the various ways to keep state is whether the state is stored on the client or on the server. Table 18-6 shows an overview of state management techniques and how long the state can be valid.

TABLE 18-6: ASP.NET Web Forms State Management Techniques

STATE TYPE	CLIENT OR SERVER RESOURCE	TIME VALID
View State	Client	Within a single page only.
Cookie	Client	Temporary cookies are deleted when the browser is closed; permanent cookies are stored on the disk of the client system.
Session	Server	Session state is associated with a browser session. The session is invalidated with a timeout (by default, 20 minutes).
Application	Server	Application state is shared among all clients. This state is valid until the server restarts.
Cache	Server	Like application state, cache is shared. Developers have control over when the cache can be invalidated.

Authentication and Authorization

To secure the web site, authentication is used to verify that the user has a valid logon, and authorization confirms that the user who was authenticated can use the resource. Commonly used authentication techniques for web applications are Forms and Windows authentication. Windows Authentication makes use of Windows accounts and IIS to authenticate users, while Forms requires a database that contains user access information.

ASP.NET has many classes for user authentication. With ASP.NET, many security controls, such as `Login` and `PasswordRecovery`, are available. These controls make use of the Membership API. With the Membership API, it is possible to create and delete users, validate logon information, or get information about currently logged-in users. The Membership API makes use of a membership provider. Since ASP.NET 4.5, different providers exist to access users in an Access database, a SQL Server database, or the Active Directory. It is also possible to create a custom provider that accesses an XML file or any custom store.

ASP.NET Web Site versus ASP.NET Web Applications

Historically, as shown in Figure 18-12, a new ASP.NET web application came in two types: Projects and Web Sites. The concept of Web Sites has been ported to a new model referred to as Single Page Applications, razor pages, and Blazor Apps, which is discussed later. The inclusion of Web Sites remains for historical reasons as there remain many Web Sites in a production capacity and knowledge of these differences can still add value. This information can also add value from a progressive perspective as you can realize where the technology has evolved from.

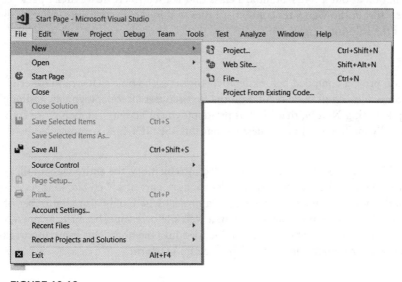

FIGURE 18-12

The differences between them are shown in Table 18-7.

TABLE 18-7: Differences between Projects and Web Sites

DIFFERENCE	PROJECTS	WEB SITES
File Structure	A C# project has a `.csproj` file, which contains a list of files and assembly references required to run the program.	There is no `.csproj` file for Web Sites created in C#. All files existing in the directory structure are included in the site.
Compiling	The code-behind files are compiled into a single assembly (`.dll`).	Source code is compiled dynamically when first requested. This usually results in multiple assemblies (`.dll`).
Deployment	The assembly (`.dll`), `.aspx`, and `.ascx` files are deployed to the web server where the application is consumed.	A copy of the web application source is deployed to the web server (`.aspx`, `.ascx`, and `.aspx.cs`).

File Structure

A `.csproj` (project file) for ASP.NET Projects provides the ability to remove from the project a file that will not be included in the deployment, but also will not be removed permanently. The file is excluded from the project but not deleted. This is helpful if there is a need to make a deployment but some of the files are not ready for it. Additionally, as you learned in the previous chapter, the project file is used to store information about a .NET Standard class that is used to create a NuGet package. Where there is no `.csproj` file, in the Web Sites context, all files within the directory structure of the site are considered part of the solution.

Compiling

Having the web application project compiled before deployment saves the time that would otherwise be spent compiling the `.aspx` file and its code-behind on the first request after deployment. Although web sites can be precompiled using NGEN, that kind of pre-deployment activity is much more complicated than simply manually making the first request so that the ASP.NET files are compiled by the ASP.NET Runtime.

When the compiled assembly or an ASP.NET Project is loaded into memory, the entire web application consumes the memory. On the other hand, only the files that are part of a Web Site that gets requested are compiled and loaded into memory. Therefore, a project where only a small number of the pages are ever used would consume more memory than a web site over time, because, as previously stated, only files that are requested get compiled and loaded into memory. This is an important concept when customers pay for resource consumption on a cloud platform.

Deployment

When a Web Site is deployed, the source code in the code-behind (`.aspx.cs`) is deployed as plain text and is human-readable. As long as the location where the web site is deployed is secure, that is not a problem, but still some developers or businesses might not want that. Instead, with a project, no human-readable code is deployed to the server as it is all compiled into an assembly (`.dll`).

> **WARNING** *Even though the code in the assembly is not human-readable, if access to the server is obtained, the code in the* .dll *can be captured and decompiled. Fiercely restrict access to servers running a program.*

To make a change to the project after the compiled assembly (.dll) that is part of the ASP.NET web application project is loaded into the ASP.NET Runtime, the ASP.NET Runtime process must be stopped and unloaded from memory for the change to become available to clients using the web site. If the process has a handle on the assembly, it cannot be changed and therefore must be stopped to release the handle. This is not the case with web sites where the .aspx.cs or .aspx files can be updated without stopping the ASP.NET Runtime and are compiled and loaded into memory the next time there is a request to them.

ASP.NET MVC/ASP.NET Core Web App MVC

Some reasons for choosing an ASP.NET MVC over other ASP.NET application types are that it is:

➤ Well suited for larger, more complicated web applications

➤ Tightly coupled with Entity Framework (EF) and model binding

➤ Deeply integrated with test-driven development (TDD)

In addition, it is important you know to choose ASP.NET Core for cross-platform support.

Where ASP.NET Web Forms was split into two separate modules, as stated previously, MVC is split into three: a Model, a View, and a Controller (see Figure 18-13).

For the same reason that such separation helped ASP.NET Web Forms, it also helps MVC. The separation of the components allows larger teams to be split by specialization and work in parallel on the application, which results in a more rapid development cycle.

Entity Framework (EF) is an Object Relationship Model (ORM) technology, discussed in Chapter 17, that is tightly coupled with the MVC architecture and model binding. ORMs, and therefore EF, give developers the power to design a database in an object-oriented way. For example, if an MVC application is intended to store information about people, then a Person class, like the following, can store and retrieve that information:

```
public class Person
{
  public string Name { get; set; }
  public int Age { get; set; }
}
```

Once the data model is designed, developers can deploy the model to a database (like SQL Server) and the data structure. The database tables and primary and foreign keys are generated using the description in the C# classes. When an MVC application is created in Visual Studio, part of the default solution is a folder named Models. This is the location where C# class representations of database tables reside. These classes are used to store the data from the database in memory for modification by the controller updating from the view, each of which also has a folder in a default ASP.NET MVC application named Controllers and Views.

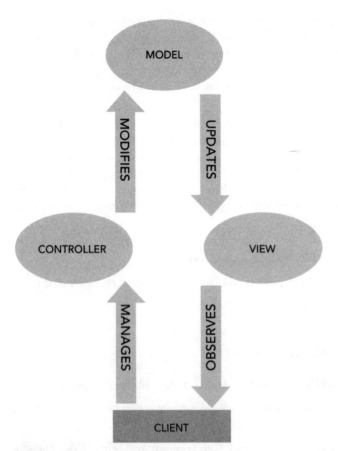

FIGURE 18-13

The *controller* is the location where a developer places the code to create, read, update, or delete contents of a database via EF logic through a bound Model object like a Person. The controller is also where any business logic, authentication, or any other activity the application needs is performed. The *view* is the presentation layer where the output of the actions triggered from the client and executed in the controller using an object-oriented model is presented back to the client.

MVC is deeply integrated with test-driven development techniques and is much simpler to unit test when compared to ASP.NET Web Forms. As shown in Figure 18-14, once you create the ASP.NET application, you can add a Unit Test Project to the solution, which is tightly bound to the ASP.NET MVC model.

By placing test code in the Tests project, dependencies such as IIS, databases, and external classes can be abstracted away from the test cases. This is an important and beneficial feature as data is often different between production instances, and the build of a server running IIS may also deliver inconsistent behavior between production and testing environments. Removing these dependencies—by testing only the logic within the controller, regardless of the dependency state—improves the speed and efficiency of testing. The reason is that instead of keeping all the dependencies in a valid and stable testing state, which can be very time consuming, a developer can focus only on making sure the testing scenarios complete successfully.

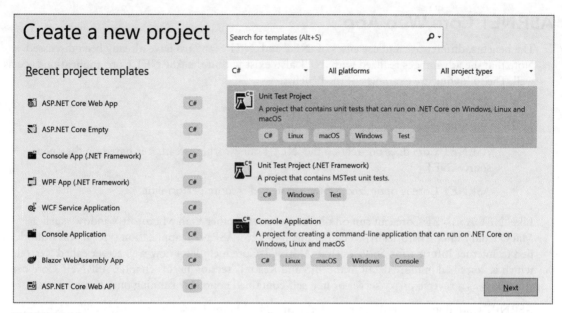

FIGURE 18-14

> **NOTE** It is common for dependencies to change; however, those changes would be coded into the testing scenarios as well. The point is that instead of troubleshooting an issue that comes from inconsistent data or a platform issue, these are avoided because of TDD.

MVC utilizes *extension-less URLs*: No specific filename is placed into the request. .aspx files are requested for ASP.NET Web Form applications, but this is not the case for MVC. MVC uses the concept of *routes* or *routing* where URL segments instead of a filename are used to route the request to the correct controller and view. For example, a request to /Home/About would execute the About() method in a controller named HomeController, which is found in the Controllers folder. The results of the About() method are presented to the client, using the view named About.cshtml located in the Views\Home directory.

ASP.NET Core Web API

The benefits of choosing an ASP.NET Web API are like those for an ASP.NET MVC application in that the application type is tightly coupled with EF, deeply integrated into the TDD concepts, and well suited for large and complicated web applications. The primary difference is that there is no View component or Views folder in a ASP.NET Web API Visual Studio project. This makes perfect sense simply based on the API concept where a client calls a method, exposed by the API, that returns some data. The client is responsible for consuming, reacting to, and/or presenting the result of the API, which is typically in the JSON format.

ASP.NET Core Web App

The benefits, differences, and use cases of .NET and .NET Standard have already been discussed. Note that the advantages realized with .NET also exist within the ASP.NET Core application type as well. The following are examples of the benefits:

➤   ASP.NET Core runs across platforms.

➤   ASP.NET Core is not dependent on IIS.

➤   ASP.NET Core does not rely on the .NET Framework; instead, it is based on the open-source .NET.

➤   ASP.NET Core is optimized for the cloud and is more performant.

Like .NET, ASP.NET Core can run on operating systems other than Microsoft Windows such as MacOS and Linux. Historically, when talking about any ASP.NET application type, it was doubtlessly tied to Internet Information Services (IIS). ASP.NET Core includes a new web server called Kestrel, which is described in more detail in the "IIS and Kestrel" section in this chapter. ASP.NET Core can run on IIS as a reverse proxy server or in a self-contained container running only Kestrel.

ASP.NET Core does not need nor rely on the full .NET Framework library. Instead, like .NET, only the assemblies required to perform the function of the program are included in the application deployment package. The modularized, highly performant, and self-contained application package is what gets deployed to a server or cloud platform for execution and consumption. Due to the optimizations in size and code execution paths with ASP.NET Core on Kestrel, performance when compared to ASP.NET 4.8 Web Forms experiences an increase of 5.5x in its ability to handle requests per second. When compared to Node.js, ASP.NET Core on Kestrel exceeds the performance by a factor of three, as described in Table 18-8.

TABLE 18-8: Baseline ASP.NET Core on Kestrel performance

STACK	REQUESTS PER SECOND (RPS)
ASP.NET Web Forms 4.6	~57,000
ASP.NET Core on Kestrel	~310,000
Node.js	~105,000

The RPS performance tests were performed on the same Windows Server operating system, with the same amount of RAM, CPU speed/type, and network interface card. Therefore, the performance is due specifically to the optimizations and execution efficiencies existing in the application type.

This section discusses numerous ASP.NET Core concepts. The most important concept to take away from the section is that ASP.NET Core can be run cross-platform. Like .NET applications, ASP.NET Core web sites can run on Linux and MacOS in addition to Microsoft Windows. Therefore, if the web application needs to run cross-platform, this is the ASP.NET flavor to develop in. Regardless of whether a web application is targeted to run only on Microsoft Windows, you should target ASP.NET Core applications, as shown in Figure 18-15.

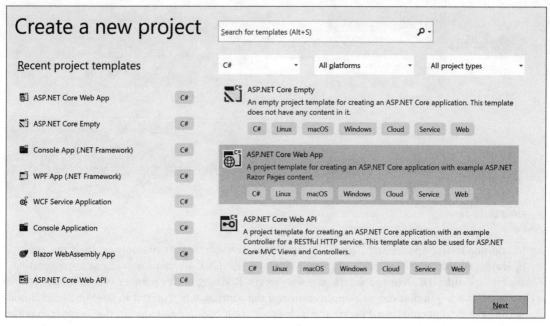

FIGURE 18-15

You will learn about the following ASP.NET Core specifics in this section:

- ➤ IIS and Kestrel
- ➤ Blazor App and Razor Pages
- ➤ Input Validation
- ➤ State Management
- ➤ Authentication and Authorization
- ➤ Dependency Injection

IIS and Kestrel

Up to now, when developers spoke about an ASP.NET flavor, it was understood that the web application would run on a Microsoft Windows server with Internet Information Services (IIS), a Microsoft-developed web server that responds to HTTP and HTTPS requests from clients. However, because IIS will not run on Linux or MacOS, there needs to be a way for IIS to send requests to a web server that can run on those operating systems. The answer is to use Kestrel, a new cross-platform web server included with ASP.NET Core projects.

As shown in Figure 18-16, when Kestrel is configured to run with IIS, the clients' HTTP request is simply forwarded to the Kestrel web server. Kestrel then interacts with the ASP.NET Core source code by passing the HttpContext class, which contains the HTTP-specific information about the HTTP request (for example, session management information, query string, culture information, client certificates, and much, much more).

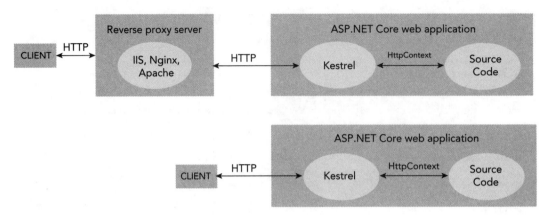

FIGURE 18-16

In addition to IIS, Apache and Nginx are functional web servers that run only on their targeted operating system like Windows, Linux, or MacOS. ASP.NET Core can run without any operating system–specific web server, as Kestrel is a web server. Running in this manner is commonly referred to as *self-hosting* in that the web application and the components required to operate are enclosed within a dedicated container. Having the web application bundled together in this manner makes it easily deployable using, for example, XCOPY, and portability is a fundamental characteristic of a cloud optimized program, as described in more detail in Chapter 19.

Blazor App and Razor Pages

Technology constantly evolves, and as a result, the tools used to interface with those technical advancements must also evolve. You would have learned by reading this chapter about the earliest Microsoft web coding pattern called App Server Pages (ASP), then to ASP.NET Web Forms, and finally, all the way up to where we are today at ASP.NET Core. Those evolutions are more than just a change in name; behind the scenes, you will find a lot of changes in the approaches for binding and presenting data. An example of a change from the early web application era was the need to perform some activities after the code had been executed with C# and rendered on the browser. Another was the separation of presentation and business logic code, making a web application more manageable. That separation of a web application into these different components was implemented using the Model-View-Controller (MVC) model.

The View or Pages engines of a web application is where you would historically find Razor syntax; it is what you use when working with ASP.NET Core applications. In Chapter 19, you will create an ASP.NET Core Web Application and add some Razor syntax to an `Index.cshtml` file. When referencing variables in a page, prior to Razor, the markup syntax in the presentation layer resembled `<%= %>`, which is five characters. The improvement with Razor is that the @ sign is used to denote the starting point of code or for setting a reference to a variable. You will find a similar implementation using @ `code` in Blazor, which is used to represent the code on the page that needs execution. The remainder of this section will discuss the differences between these two syntaxes and present some more details about Blazor, so that you better understand the benefits of each and when either should be used:

➤ Blazor versus Razor

➤ Blazor Server versus WebAssembly

The best way to begin a comparison of Blazor and Razor is to define them. Razor syntax increases the speed in which developers can create applications running the Model-View-Controller model. The Razor syntax allows you to reference dependencies with similar C# syntax as shown here:

```
@using BeginningCSharp
```

Then later in the same .cshtml file, you can reference the classes and methods found within the referenced assembly:

```
<label id="labelPlayer1">Player2: @player2 </label>
@foreach (Card card in players[0].PlayHand)
{
  <img width="75" height="100" alt="cardImage"
      src="https://deckofcards.blob.core.windows.net/carddeck/@card.imageLink"/>
}
```

This is a faster and more efficient way than existed previously. Notice in the previous code snippet that there is a label with an ID of labelPlayer1. Prior to Razor, the setting of its value to the name of player2 would have been done with C# in a code-behind page by using something like the following:

```
labelPlayer1.Text = "Benjamin";
```

That is relatively easy when you have only a single label. With more complex pages, which include text boxes, buttons, links, and so forth, getting all the names to match the values you need to set them to wound up taking too much time. With Razor, the C# code retrieved the necessary data and passed it to the .cshtml page, and Razor did the rest. Razor fundamentally broke the link between the code-behind page and the page that rendered the HTML.

Blazor, on the other hand, does include Razor-like syntax, but it targets a different web application model. This model is called a Single-Page Application (SPA), and when compared to the multi-paged applications such as those common to MVC applications, you can easily see the difference. This is not the only difference, however. As alluded to previously, some web applications require code to be executed on the client, after the result has been rendered in the browser. Historically, this has been achieved using JavaScript or one of its numerous libraries. With Blazor, you can use C#, which leads nicely into the comparison between Blazor Server and WebAssembly. Blazor Server is, for the most part, an ASP.NET Core application, and as the name implies, the C# code runs on the server and returns render-able text for client-side pages using Razor pages, which have a file extension of .razor. The extension of the file that contains the Razor-like syntax is an easy way to determine if you are discussing Razor or Blazor; otherwise, it can be a bit complicated. The following code snippet illustrates how you would instantiate the Player and Game classes in a Blazor page:

```
@code {
    private Player[] players = new Player[2];
```

```
    private Game newGame = new Game();

    protected override void OnInitialized()
    {
        players[0] = new Player("Benjamin");
        players[1] = new Player("Rual");
        newGame.SetPlayers(players);
        newGame.DealHands();
    }
}
```

The code snippet also sets the name of the `players` and deals them each a hand of cards. The rendering of the hand of cards into the browser is the same for both Razor and Blazor, shown earlier using the `@foreach` statement and HTML.

A Blazor WebAssembly makes me think of legacy technologies like ActiveX or Silverlight where in all three cases, the browser will download an assembly and run it on the client. Running a Blazor WebAssembly application typically means that the bulk of the business logic is referenced using APIs over the HTTP protocol. REST API and ASP.NET Web API concepts are discussed further in Chapter 20. This means that the code within the Blazor WebAssembly commonly performs client-side tasks—tasks that historically have been done using JavaScript, such as input validations or authentication. Activities like data manipulation or business processes that require complex algorithms remain server-side. The remainder of this chapter focuses on ASP.NET Core Web Applications.

Input Validation

Validation for an ASP.NET Core application is configured using validation attributes existing within the `System.ComponentModel.DataAnnotations` namespace. The validators are configured in the class definition for a specific model:

```
public class Player
{
    [StringLength(20, MinimumLength = 3)]
    [Required]
    public string Name { get; set; }
}
```

When a request is made to the page that binds with the defined `Player` model, the ASP.NET Core runtime generates jQuery client-side validation syntax. Then, if a user attempts to submit a form without a value for `Name`, validation happens on the client and an error is rendered.

Table 18-9 lists and describes some ASP.NET Core data annotation validation attributes. Data annotations are built-in validation attributes that get applied at design time to enforce the expected validation. Take a look at the previous code snippet and you will see the `[Required]` data annotation. This means that you are required to provide the `Name` of the player when you instantiate it.

TABLE 18-9: Examples of ASP.NET Core Validation Attributes

CONTROL	DESCRIPTION
Required	Indicates that the property is required.
StringLength	Defines a maximum and an optional minimum value that the user must satisfy.
Range	For a numeric field, maximum and minimum values can be set.
EmailAddress	Confirms that the entered value has a valid email address format.
DataType	Confirms that the entered value is a specific type like Date or Currency.
RegularExpression	Confirms that the entered value matches regular expression syntax.

State Management

As previously mentioned, the HTTP protocol is stateless, which means that once the request has been successfully responded to by the server, no information is stored about the client that made the request. The connection is closed and forgotten after every request. However, it does often happen that some information about the client needs to be persisted and reused when managing multiple requests from a client. As is true with other ASP.NET flavors, there are several ways to implement the management of state-full information when using HTTP. Table 18-10 shows an overview of state management techniques and how long the state can be valid.

TABLE 18-10: ASP.NET Core State Management Techniques

STATE TYPE	CLIENT OR SERVER RESOURCE	TIME VALID
TempData	Server	Removed once the data is read by the application.
Query strings	Both	Passed between client and server as URL elements and are accessible only during a single request.
Cookie	Client	Temporary cookies are deleted when the browser is closed; permanent cookies are stored on the disk of the client system.
HttpContext.Items	Both	Passed between client and server, stored in the HttpContext object, and accessible only during a single request.
Cache	Server	Like application state, cache is shared. However, there is much better control over when the cache should be invalidated.
Session	Server	Session state is associated with a browser session. The session is invalidated with a configurable timeout setting.
Application	Server	Application state is shared among all clients. This state is valid until the server restarts.

Authentication and Authorization

Since ASP.NET Core is not focused on a single operating system, the authentication and authorization protocols must also work cross-platform. The most popular open-source authentication providers are OWIN and OAuth. OWIN, which stands for Open Web Interface for .NET, is not an authentication provider per se; however, it is commonly associated with Katana, which is. OWIN is a specification that details how web servers and web applications should be decoupled from each other. OWIN removes the dependency of ASP.NET Core from IIS and helps make the self-hosting concept via Kestrel a reality. The Katana NuGet package contains the libraries necessary for implementing the many types of authentication like Windows and Forms, for example.

OAuth is an interface exposed by companies like Microsoft, Facebook, Twitter, Google, and others for web applications to authenticate against. It is common for applications running on a mobile device or in a browser to prompt the client to use Facebook or Microsoft credentials to access the web site. In those cases, OAuth is the protocol being used. The classes and methods for implementing OAuth into an ASP.NET Core web application are found in the `Microsoft.AspNetCore.Authentication` namespace. A client that uses OAuth for authentication uses a bearer token that is in the JSON Web Token (JWT) format.

Authentication is the process of confirming that individuals are really who they say they are. Usually when someone creates a new account, it is linked to an email address and a password. A verification email is sent to the provided email, and once clicked, the registration is completed. Using that email and password from then on to access a resource validates that it really is the one who created the account. The other portion of the process is authorization. *Authorization* is the process of defining what features or content the authorized person has access to. This is commonly referred to as *claims*.

In the simplest form, some source code checks for the existence of a claim, for example to a `Deal-Card()` method, and if the claim exists, the method can be called from the requesting card dealer:

```
principle.FindFirst(c => c.Type == "DealerID");
```

Claims can also be represented by name-value pairs that provide more granular access to a resource:

```
policy.RequireClaim("DealerID", "1", "2", "3", "4", "5"));
```

This shows that the `DealCard()` method is only available for a card dealer with a `DealerID` equal to 1, 2, 3, 4, or 5.

Dependency Injection

Dependency Injection (DI) is a very advanced topic, but it is a fundamental concept on which ASP.NET Core is built, so it will be touched on here. The basic point to understand when it comes to DI is the avoidance of the `new` keyword:

```
Player[] players = new Player[2];
```

The reason for avoiding `new` is that it permanently binds the program to the class it refers to. There are cases where using `new` is acceptable when the likelihood that the class will need to be modified is very slim, in which case using the keyword is a design decision. The alternative is the implementation of an interface, which was discussed in Chapters 9, 10, and 12. An interface loosely couples or decouples the consumer from the provider, where the program is the consumer, and the class is the provider. As seen in the following code snippet, a `Player` is used without using the new keyword:

```
public interface ICardGameClient
{
    void Player(string Name);
}
public class PlaySomeCards
{
    private readonly ICardGameClient _cardGameClient;
    public PlaySomeCards(ICardGameClient cardGameClient)
    {
        _cardGameClient = cardGameClient;
    }
    public PlayHand
    {
        _cardGameClient.Player("Benjamin");
    }
}
```

DI takes it one step further by using what is known as a factory or container. ASP.NET Core supports DI by default and is configured into the `Startup.cs` file, which is created with an ASP.NET Core web application. This file contains a method named `ConfigureServices()` and is the place where the providers are configured:

```
public void ConfigurServices(IServiceCollection services)
{
    services.AddMvc();
    services.AddDbContext<className>(options => ...
    services.AddIdentity<className1,className2>()...
    ...
}
```

The configured service providers contained in the `ConfigureServices()` method provide the `className` when it is requested from the code running within the program.

▶ WHAT YOU LEARNED IN THIS CHAPTER

TOPIC	KEY CONCEPTS
Key cross-platform terms	See Table 18-1 for a list of important cross-platform terms you should know.
.NET Standard APIs	A group of classes and methods found in .NET Framework namespaces for consumption inside cross-platform or cross-vertical programs.
Targeting	The higher the version, the fewer the platforms, but the greater the number of APIs; it is a trade-off.
.NET	A cross-platform and open-source programming vertical. .NET was referred to as .NET Core until the .NET evolved to be an equivalent open-source version of the .NET Framework.
Open Source	Code or frameworks written and supported by an open community of developers.
NuGet Packages	A modular approach for installing program dependencies. In contrast to creating a reference to an assembly, install the NuGet assembly.
ASP.NET flavors	There are numerous ASP.NET application types; each have specific use cases and benefits for use.
Projects versus Web Sites	Projects are compiled into a `.dll` and deployed, while Web Sites deploy the source code and are compiled when requested for the first time.
Server controls and the `HtmlHelper`	Web Server Controls are server-side controls that generate HTML code for ASP.NET Web Forms applications. The `HtmlHelper` class provides the means to create objects such as `Label`, `Textbox`, and so on with Razor pages.
Verifying user input with validation controls and Data Annotations	ASP.NET offers several validation controls that can easily be used to validate user input on both the client and server sides. Validation on the client is done for performance reasons, but because the web client can never be trusted, validation must happen on the server as well.
State management	With web applications, it is necessary to think about where to store state. State can be stored on the client with cookies or view state, and on the server with session, cache, and application objects.

TOPIC	KEY CONCEPTS
Authentication and Authorization	Authentication is the process that determines whether clients really are who they say they are. Authorization provides access to features and services the authenticated client has access to.
Kestrel	Kestrel is a new web server that can self-host ASP.NET Core web applications and can run cross-platform.
Dependency Injection (DI)	DI decouples consumers and providers.

19

Basic Cloud Programming

WHAT YOU WILL LEARN IN THIS CHAPTER

➤ Understanding the cloud, cloud programming, and the cloud optimized stack

➤ Programming for the cloud using cloud design patterns

➤ Using Microsoft Azure C# libraries to create a storage container

➤ Creating an ASP.NET Core Web Application that uses the storage container

CODE DOWNLOADS FOR THIS CHAPTER

The code downloads for this chapter are found on the book page at www.wiley.com. Click the Downloads link. The code can also be found at github.com/benperk/BeginningCSharp-AndDotNet. The code is in the Chapter19 folder and individually named according to the names throughout the chapter.

In this book, the basics of C# programming are conveyed mostly using console applications and desktop applications with WPF. Although these are viable and compelling development techniques, they are not suitable examples of programs to host and run in the cloud. These kinds of programs are classically deployed to and run on a user's computer, tablet, or mobile device. These programs are compiled into executables or dynamic linked libraries that have dependencies on preinstalled software like .NET, for example. These dependencies are generally assumed to be present on the location where they are installed, or they get included in the installation procedure. By contrast, an Internet application that is run in the cloud, based on ASP.NET, for instance, cannot rely on any such library or dependency being present on the computer or device from which the program is accessed. All dependencies instead are installed on the server hosting the Internet application and are accessed by a device using protocols such as HTTP, WS (web socket), FTP, or SMTP. Although console and desktop apps can have dependencies in the cloud, like databases, storage containers, or web services, they themselves are generally not hosted there.

Programs that are accessed via web browsers and respond to REST API or gRPC service requests are good candidates for running in the cloud. Development techniques used for creating those program types do not require any built-in dependency on the device from which they are called. In typical cases, those program types merely exchange information between themselves and render data in a legible and user-friendly fashion. Additionally, programs that receive and process large amounts of data are good candidates for running in the cloud because utilizing the hyper-scalability of resources to accept and process the data is a fundamental feature of the cloud itself.

This chapter provides an overview of what the cloud is, some examples of patterns and techniques for successfully running a program in the cloud, and an example of creating and using cloud resources from an ASP.NET Core Web Application.

THE CLOUD, CLOUD COMPUTING, AND THE CLOUD OPTIMIZED STACK

If you have not already, it is only a matter of time before you begin creating applications that run completely or partially in the cloud. It is no longer a question of "if" but "when." Deciding which components of your program will run in the cloud, the cloud type, and the cloud service model requires some investigation, understanding, and planning. For starters, you need to be clear on what the cloud is. The cloud is simply a large amount of commoditized computer hardware running inside a datacenter that can run programs and store large amounts of data. The differentiator is elasticity, which is the ability to scale up (for example, increase CPU and memory) and/or scale out (for example, increase number of virtual server instances) dynamically, then scale back down with seemingly minimal to no effort. This is an enormous difference from the current IT operational landscape where differentiated computer resources often go partially or completely unused in one area of the company, while in other areas there is a serious lack of computer resources. The cloud resolves this issue by providing access to computer resources as you need them, and when you don't need them those resources are given to someone else. For individual developers, the cloud is a place to deploy your program and expose it to the world. If by chance the program becomes a popular one, you can scale to meet your resource needs; if the program is a flop, then you are not out much money or time spent on setting up dedicated computer hardware and infrastructure.

Let's explore cloud type and cloud service models in more detail now. The common cloud types are public, private, and hybrid and are described in the following bullet points and illustrated in Figure 19-1.

➤ *Public cloud* is shared computer hardware and infrastructure owned and operated by a cloud provider like Microsoft Azure, Amazon AWS, Rackspace, or Google Cloud. This cloud type is ideal for small and medium businesses that need to manage fluctuations in customer and user demands.

➤ *Private cloud* is dedicated computer hardware and infrastructure that exists onsite or in an outsourced data center. This cloud type is ideal for larger companies or those that must deliver a higher level of data security or government compliance.

➤ *Hybrid cloud* is a combination of both public and private cloud types whereby you choose which segments of your IT solution run on the private cloud and which run on the public cloud. The ideal solution is to run your businesses-critical programs that require a greater level of security in the private cloud and run nonsensitive, possibly spiking tasks in the public cloud.

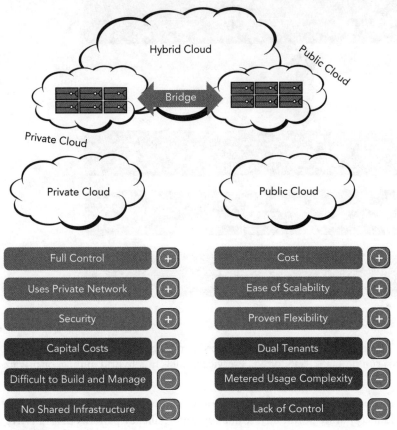

FIGURE 19-1

The number of cloud service models continues to increase, but the most common cloud service models are described in the following bullet points and illustrated in Figure 19-2.

➤ **Infrastructure as a Service (IaaS)**—You are responsible from the operating system upward. You are not responsible for the hardware or network infrastructure; however, you are responsible for operating system patches and third-party dependent libraries.

➤ **Platform as a Service (PaaS)**—You are responsible only for your program running on the chosen operating system and its dependencies. You are not responsible for operating system maintenance, hardware, or network infrastructure.

➤ **Software as a Service (SaaS)**—A software program or service used from a device that is accessed via the Internet; for example, O365, Salesforce, OneDrive, or Box, all of which are accessible from anywhere with an Internet connection and do not require software to be installed on the client to function. You are only responsible for the software running on the platform and nothing else.

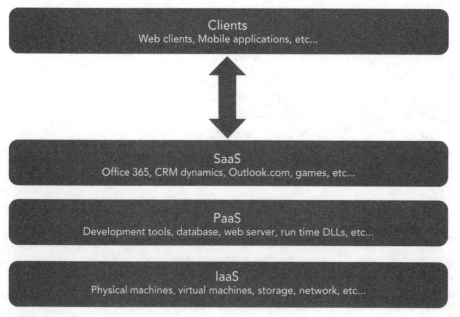

FIGURE 19-2

In summary, the cloud is an elastic structure of commoditized computer hardware for running programs. These programs run on IaaS, PaaS, or SaaS service models in a hybrid, public, or private cloud type.

Cloud programming is the development of code logic that runs on any of the cloud service models. The cloud program should incorporate portability, scalability, and resiliency patterns that improve the performance and stability of the program. Programs that do not implement these portability, scalability, and resiliency patterns would likely run in the cloud, but some circumstances such as a hardware failure or a network latency issue may cause the program to execute an unexpected code path and terminate.

> **NOTE** *Cloud programming patterns and best practices are discussed in the next section.*

Reflecting back to the elasticity of the cloud as being one of its most favorable benefits, it is important that not only the platform is able to scale, but the cloud program can as well. For example, does the code rely on backend resources such as databases, read or open files, or parse through large data objects? These kinds of functional actions within a cloud program can reduce its ability to scale and therefore have a low support for throughput. Make sure your cloud program manages code paths that execute long running methods and perhaps place them into an offline process mechanism.

The cloud optimized stack is a concept used to refer to code that can handle high throughput, makes a small footprint, can run side-by-side with other applications on the same server, and is cross-platform enabled. A *small footprint* refers to packaging into your cloud program only the components for which a dependency exists, making the deployment size as small as possible. Consider whether the cloud program requires the entire .NET Framework to function. If not, then instead of packaging the entire .NET Framework, include only the libraries required to run your cloud program, and then compile your cloud program into a self-contained application to support side-by-side execution. The cloud program can run alongside any other cloud program because it contains the needed dependencies within the binaries package itself. Finally, by using an open source such as .NET Core or ASP.NET Core, the cloud program can be packaged, compiled, and deployed onto operating systems in addition to Microsoft—for example, Mac OS or Linux. Both .NET Framework and .NET Core are used here on purpose in an attempt to call out the differences between their uses. As mentioned in earlier chapters, as of .NET 5, the features in .NET Framework and .NET Core are on par with each other, and the library is now referred to as simply .NET.

CLOUD PATTERNS AND BEST PRACTICES

In the cloud, very brief moments of increased latency or downtime are expected, and your code must be prepared for this and include logic to successfully recover from these platform exceptions. This is a significant mind shift if you have historically been coding for onsite or on-premise program executions. You need to unlearn a lot of what you know about managing exceptions and learn to embrace failure and create your code to recover from such failures.

In the previous section, words like portability, scalability, and resiliency were mentioned in the context of integrating those concepts into your program slated to run in the cloud. But what does *portability* specifically mean here? A program is portable if it can be moved or executed on multiple platforms, for example, Windows, Linux, and Mac OS. Take, for example, some ASP.NET Core features that sit on a new stack of open-source technologies that provide the developer with options to compile code into binaries capable of running on any of those platforms. Traditionally, a developer who wrote a program using ASP.NET, with C# in the background, would run it on a Windows server using Internet Information Server (IIS). However, from a core cloud-centric perspective, the ability of your program and all its dependencies to move from one virtual machine to another, without manual or programmatic intervention, is the most applicable form of portability in this context. Remember that failures in the cloud are expected, and the virtual machine (VM) on which your program is running can be wiped out at any given time and then be rebuilt fresh on another VM. Therefore, your program needs to be portable and able to recover from such an event.

Scalability means that your code responds well when multiple customers use it. For example, if you have 1,500 requests per minute, that would be roughly 25 concurrent requests per second, if the request is completed and responded to in 1 second. However, if you have 15,000 requests per minute, that would mean 250 concurrent requests per second. Will the cloud program respond in the same manner with 25 or 250 concurrent requests? How about 2,550? The following are a few cloud programming patterns that are useful for managing scalability:

➤ **Command and Query Responsibility Segregation (CQRS) pattern**—This pattern concerns the separation of operations that read data from operations that modify or update the data.

➤ **Materialized View pattern**—This modifies the storage structure to reflect the data query pattern. For example, creating views for specific highly used queries can make for more efficient querying.

➤ **Sharding pattern**—This breaks your data into multiple horizontal or vertical shards that contain a distinct subset of the data as opposed to vertical scaling via the addition of hardware capacity.

➤ **Valet Key pattern**—This gives clients direct access to the data store for streaming of or uploading of large files. Instead of having a web client manage the gatekeeping to the data store, it provides a client with a Valet Key and direct access to the data store.

> **NOTE** *These patterns cover some advanced C# coding techniques, and therefore, only descriptions of the patterns are provided. If you are interested in seeing the actual C# code to implement the patterns, it certainly exists and can be found by searching for it on the Internet.*

Resiliency refers to how well your program responds and recovers from service faults and exceptions. Historically, IT infrastructures have been focused on failure prevention where the acceptance of downtime was minimal, and 99.99% or 99.999% SLAs (service-level agreements) were the expectation. Running a program in the cloud, however, requires a reliability mind shift, one that embraces failure and is clearly oriented toward recovery and not prevention. Having multiple dependencies such as database, storage, network, and third-party services, some of which have no SLA, requires this shift in perspectives. User-friendly reactions in response to outages or situations that are not considered normal operation make your cloud program resilient. Here are a few cloud programming patterns that are useful for embedding resiliency into your cloud program:

➤ **Circuit Breaker pattern**—This is a code design that is aware of the state of remote services and will only attempt to make the connection if the service is available. This avoids attempting a request and wasting CPU cycles when it is already known the remote service is unavailable via previous failures.

➤ **Health Endpoint Monitoring pattern**—This checks that cloud-based applications are functionally available via the implementation of endpoint monitoring.

➤ **Retry pattern**—This retries the request after transient exceptions or failure. This pattern retries a number of times within a given time frame and stops when the retry attempt threshold is breached.

➤ **Throttling pattern**—This manages the consumption of a cloud program so that SLAs can be met, and the program remains functional under high load.

Using one or more of the patterns described in this section will help make your cloud migration more successful. The discussed patterns enhance usability of your program by improving the scalability and resiliency of it. This in turn makes for a more pleasant user or customer experience.

USING MICROSOFT AZURE C# LIBRARIES TO CREATE A STORAGE CONTAINER

Although there are numerous cloud providers, the cloud provider used for the examples in this and the next chapter is Microsoft. The cloud platform provided by Microsoft is called Azure. Azure has many different kinds of features. For example, the IaaS offering is called Azure VM, and the PaaS offering is called Azure App Services. Additionally, Microsoft has SQL Azure for database, Azure Active Directory for user authentication, and Azure storage for storing BLOBs, for example.

> **NOTE** *The exercise in the next Try It Out requires that you have a Microsoft Azure subscription. If you do not have one, you can sign up for a 12-month free trial with up to $200 in free products here:* `azure.microsoft.com`.

The following two exercises walk through the creation of an Azure storage account and an Azure storage container. Once created, images of 52 playing cards are stored in the container using the Azure Storage SDK for .NET. Then in the next section, you will create an ASP.NET Core Web Application to access the images stored in the Azure storage container. Then, following along with the card game theme in the book, the ASP.NET Core Web Application will deal a hand of playing cards. The card images are the blobs stored in the Azure storage container.

TRY IT OUT Create an Azure Storage Account

1. Access the Microsoft Azure Portal at `portal.azure.com`.

2. Click the three horizontal lines button on the top left of the browser ⇨ click + Create a resource ⇨ then Storage account, as shown in Figure 19-3. If you cannot find the Storage account entry, search for Storage account in the Marketplace.

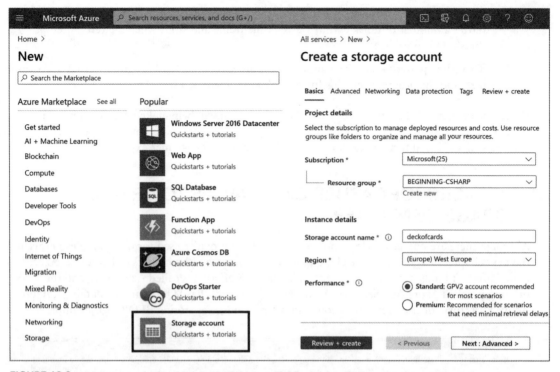

FIGURE 19-3

3. Enter the Subscription, Resource group, Storage account name, and Region ⇨ click the Review + create button ⇨ click the Create button. Once the storage account has been provisioned, you will find something similar to what is shown in Figure 19-4 in your Storage account list. In this example, the Azure storage account is deckofcards. Give your Azure storage account a different name. Remember the name of this storage account, as it is used in the next Try It Out exercise.

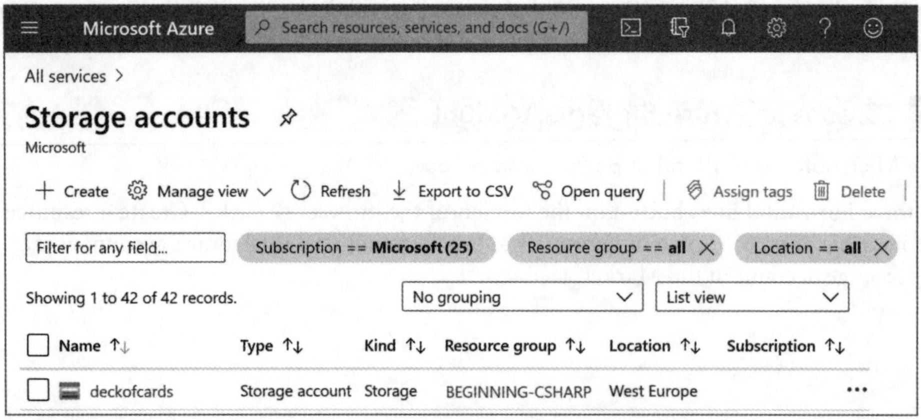

FIGURE 19-4

4. You have now successfully created an Azure storage account.

> **NOTE** *Storage accounts can be used for storing BLOBs, tables, queues, and files. Some example items that can be stored here include database backups, Azure Web App IIS logs, VM machine images, documents, or images, with a limit of 100 TB per storage account.*

How It Works

The Microsoft Azure management console itself runs on the Microsoft Azure platform in the PaaS cloud service model. The management portal is written by a product team within Microsoft and supported by additional Microsoft support staff. All the features you find on the left-hand side navigation bar can be created and utilized; see Figure 19-3. Provisioning an Azure storage account with your subscriptions allocates storage space and a globally accessible URL for accessing the contents of the `deckofcards` storage account (for example: `https://deckofcards.blob.core.windows.net`).

TRY IT OUT Create an Azure Storage Container Using the Microsoft Azure Storage Client Library

You will create a console application using Visual Studio and the Azure Storage client libraries to create an Azure storage container and upload the 52 cards into it.

1. Open Visual Studio ➪ click the Create a new project box ➪ select Console Application as seen in Figure 19-5 ➪ click the Next button ➪ name the project `Ch19Ex01` and save it in the directory `C:\BeginningCSharpAndDotNET\Chapter19` ➪ click the Next button ➪ select .NET 5.0 from the drop down and click the Create button.

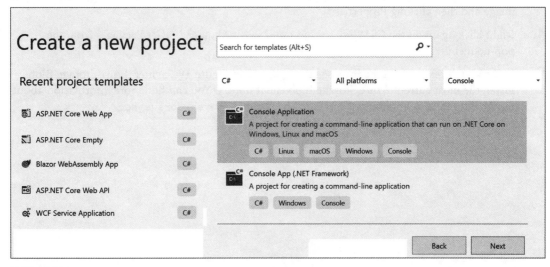

FIGURE 19-5

2. Add a directory named `Cards` to the project by right-clicking Ch19Ex01 ➪ Add ➪ New Folder. Add the 52 card images to the directory, as shown in Figure 19-6. The images are available on GitHub (`github.com/benperk/BeginningCSharpAndDotNET/tree/main/Chapter19/Ch19Ex01/Ch19Ex01/Cards`) and are named from `0-1.PNG` to `3-13.PNG`.

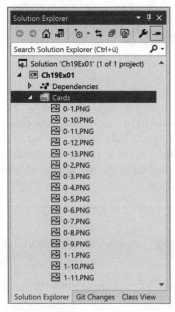

FIGURE 19-6

3. Copy the `Cards` directory into `C:\BeginningCSharpAndDotNET\Chapter19\Ch19Ex01\bin\Debug\net5.0\` so that the compiled executable can find them when run. You can also manually set the Copy to Output Directory property to Copy Always for each image by right-clicking each image and then clicking Properties.

4. Right-click again on the Ch19Ex01 project and select Manage NuGet Packages from the pop-up menu.

5. In the search text box on the Browse tab, as shown in Figure 19-7, enter **Azure Storage Blobs** and install the most current Azure Storage Blob client library. You can find more information about the Azure Storage SDK library here: `github.com/Azure/azure-storage-net`.

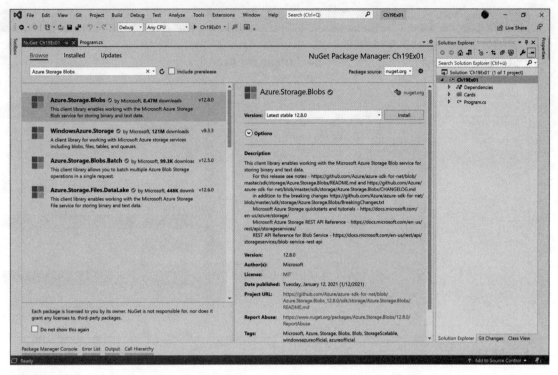

FIGURE 19-7

6. Accept the user agreements. Once the NuGet package and its dependencies are installed, you should see a ============== Finished================= message in the Output window of Visual Studio. Expand the `Dependencies/Packages` folder and you can view the newly added binaries.

7. Copy the Azure Storage Connection string by again accessing the Microsoft Azure management portal (`portal.azure.com`) and then navigate to your Azure storage account, which you created in the previous Try It Out. As seen in Figure 19-8, within the Settings section ➪ click Access keys. Click the Show keys button, which changes to Hide keys after clicking ➪ copy the Connection string for `Key1` and place it in a safe place. I removed the Key value; you would see one in that text box.

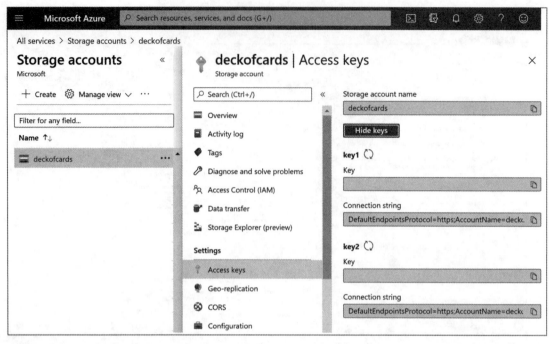

FIGURE 19-8

8. Open a Command Prompt ⇨ add the following command ⇨ click the Enter key. Replace `<yourConnectionString>` with the Connection string from the previous step. Restart Visual Studio so that it can get access to the newly created Environment Variable.

```
setx AZURE_STORAGE_CONNECTION_STRING "<yourConnectionString>"
```

9. Now add the code that creates the container, uploads the images, lists them, and if desired, deletes them. First add the assembly references and the `try{}...catch{}` C# framework to the `Main()` method, as shown here:

```
using System;
using System.IO;
using Azure;
using Azure.Storage.Blobs;
using Azure.Storage.Blobs.Models;

namespace Ch19Ex01
{
  class Program
  {
    static void Main(string[] args)
    {
      try {}
      catch (RequestFailedException rfe)
      {
```

```
        Console.WriteLine($"RequestFailedException: {rfe.Message}");
      }
      catch (Exception ex)
      {
        Console.WriteLine($"Exception: {ex.Message}");
      }
      Console.WriteLine("Press enter to exit.");
      Console.ReadLine();
    }
  }
}
```

10. Next, add the code within the `try{}` code block that creates the container, as shown here. Look at the parameter passed to the `blobServiceClient.CreateBlobContainer("carddeck")`. This `carddeck` is the name used for the Azure storage container. Content within this container can then be accessed via `deckofcards.blob.core.windows.net/carddeck/0-1.PNG`, for example. You can choose any desired container name as long as it meets the naming requirements (for example, it must be 3 to 63 characters long, must be lowercase, and must begin with a letter or number). If you provide a container name that does not meet the naming requirements, a 400 HTTP status error is returned.

```
    string connectionString = Environment.GetEnvironmentVariable("AZURE_STORAGE_
CONNECTION_STRING");
    BlobServiceClient blobServiceClient = new BlobServiceClient(connectionString);
```

11. Add this code following the code that creates the identified container in step 10, which uploads the card images stored in the `Cards` folder:

```
    BlobContainerClient containerClient = blobServiceClient.CreateBlobContainer(
"carddeck");
    containerClient.SetAccessPolicy(PublicAccessType.Blob);

    int numberOfCards = 0;
    DirectoryInfo dir = new DirectoryInfo(@"Cards");
    foreach (FileInfo f in dir.GetFiles("*.*"))
    {
      BlobClient blob = containerClient.GetBlobClient(f.Name);
      using (var fileStream = System.IO.File.OpenRead(@"Cards\" + f.Name))
      {
        blob.Upload(fileStream);
        Console.WriteLine($"Uploading: '{f.Name}' which " +
                          $"is {fileStream.Length} bytes.");
      }
      numberOfCards++;
    }
    Console.WriteLine($"Uploaded {numberOfCards.ToString()} cards.");
    Console.WriteLine();
```

12. Now that the images are uploaded, just to check that all went well, add this code to list the blobs stored in the newly created Azure storage container, named `carddeck`, after the code from step 11:

```
      numberOfCards = 0;
      foreach (BlobItem item in containerClient.GetBlobs())
      {
```

```
            Console.WriteLine($"Card image url '{containerClient.Uri}/{item.Name}' with length " +
                      $"of {item.Properties.ContentLength}");
          numberOfCards++;
        }
        Console.WriteLine($"Listed {numberOfCards.ToString()} cards.");
```

13. Now, if desired, you can delete the images that were just uploaded:

```
        Console.WriteLine("If you want to delete the container and its contents enter: " +
                      "'Yes' and press the Enter key");
        var delete = Console.ReadLine();
        if (delete == "Yes")
        {
          containerClient.Delete();
          Console.WriteLine("Container deleted.");
        }
        Console.WriteLine("All done, press the Enter key to exit.");
        Console.ReadLine();
```

14. Run the console application and review the output. You should see something like what is shown in Figure 19-9 ⇨ access the Microsoft Azure management console ⇨ click Storage Accounts ⇨ click the account you created ⇨ scroll down to the blob service ⇨ click Containers ⇨ click the folder, for example, carddeck as shown in Figure 19-10, to view its contents.

FIGURE 19-9

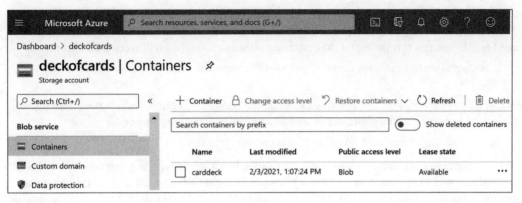

FIGURE 19-10

How It Works

It is programmatically possible to create a Microsoft Azure storage account, but the security aspect of that creation is relatively complex. That step was performed in the previous exercise from within the Microsoft Azure Management portal instead. Once an Azure storage account is provisioned, you can then create multiple containers within the account. In this example, you created a container called carddeck. There is only a limit on the number of storage accounts per Microsoft Azure subscription and no limit on the number of containers within the storage account. You can create as much and as many as you want, but keep in mind that each comes with a cost, which will be deducted from any credit you have with the trial subscription.

The code is split into four sections (create the container, upload the images to the container, list the blobs in the container, and optionally delete the contents of the container). The first action taken was to set up the try{}...catch{} framework for the console application. This is a good practice because uncaught or unhandled exceptions typically crash the process (EXE), which is something that should always be avoided. The first catch() expression is the RequestFailedexception and captures exceptions thrown specifically from methods within the Azure namespace:

```
catch (RequestFailedException rfe)
```

Then there is a catch all exceptions expression that handles all other unexpected exceptions and writes the exception message for them to the console:

```
catch (Exception ex)
```

The first two lines within the try{} code block retrieve the Azure storage account Access key from an Environment Variable, which is used to create an instance of the BlobServiceClient:

```
string connectionString = Environment.GetEnvironmentVariable("AZURE_
STORAGE_CONNECTION_STRING");
    BlobServiceClient blobServiceClient = new BlobServiceClient(connection
String);
```

Next, you create a client that manages the interface with a specific blob container within the storage account. Then the code creates the container and gets a reference to it; in this example, the container is named `carddeck`. If you run this code and the container already exists, you will receive an exception.

```
BlobContainerClient containerClient = blobServiceClient.CreateBlobContainer(
    "carddeck");
```

Containers can be `Private` or `Public`. For this example, the container is public, which means an access key is not required to access it. The container is set to be public by executing this code:

```
containerClient.SetAccessPolicy(PublicAccessType.Blob);
```

At this point, the container is created and publicly accessible, but it is empty. Using `System.IO` methods like `DirectoryInfo` and `FileInfo`, you created a `foreach` loop that added each of the card images to the `carddeck` storage container. The `GetBlobClient()` method is used to set the reference to the specific image name to be added to the container. Then using the filename and path, the `System.IO.File.OpenRead()` method opens the actual file as a `FileStream`, and it is uploaded to the container via the `Upload()` method:

```
BlobClient blob = containerClient.GetBlobClient(f.Name);
using (var fileStream = System.IO.File.OpenRead(@"Cards\" + f.Name))
{
    blob.Upload(fileStream);
    Console.WriteLine($"Uploading: '{f.Name}' which " +
                      $"is {fileStream.Length} bytes.");
}
```

All of the files in the `Cards` directory are looped through and uploaded to the container. Using the same object created during the initial creation of the `carddeck` container, by calling the `GetBlobs()` method, a list of existing blobs is returned as a `Pageable<BlobItem>`. You then loop through the list and write them to the console.

```
foreach (BlobItem item in containerClient.GetBlobs())
{
Console.WriteLine($"Card image url '{containerClient.Uri}/{item.Name}' with length " +
                  $"of {item.Properties.ContentLength}");
    numberOfCards++;
}
```

To delete the blobs and the container, use the `Delete()` method from the `BlobContainerClient` class. It is prudent to ask for confirmation before performing such a delete.

```
containerClient.Delete();
```

Now that the Microsoft Azure storage account and container are created and loaded with the images of a 52-card deck, you can create an ASP.NET Core Web Application to reference the Microsoft Azure storage container.

CREATING AN ASP.NET CORE WEB APPLICATION THAT USES THE STORAGE CONTAINER

We have examined the topic of ASP.NET in the previous chapter, so in case you skipped that one, you might consider reading it before continuing forward from here. To reiterate some important topics from the previous chapter, remember that a web application causes a web server to send HTML code to a client. That code is displayed in a web browser such as Microsoft Edge or Google Chrome. When a user enters a URL string in the browser, an HTTP request is sent to the web server. The HTTP request contains the filename that is requested along with additional information such as a string identifying the application, the languages that the client supports, and additional data belonging to the request. The web server returns an HTTP response that contains HTML code, which is interpreted by the web browser to display text boxes, buttons, and lists to the user.

ASP.NET is a technology for dynamically creating web pages with server-side code. These web pages can be developed with many similarities to client-side Windows programs. Instead of dealing directly with the HTTP request and response and manually creating HTML code to send to the client, you can use controls such as `TextBox`, `Label`, `ComboBox`, and `Calendar`, which create HTML code.

Using ASP.NET for web applications on the client system requires only a simple web browser. You can use Internet Explorer, Edge, Chrome, Firefox, or any other web browser that supports HTML. The client system does not require .NET to be installed.

On the server system, the ASP.NET runtime is needed. If you have Internet Information Services (IIS) on the system, the ASP.NET runtime is configured with the server when .NET is installed. During development, there is no need to work with IIS because Visual Studio delivers its own IIS Express server that you can use for testing and debugging the application locally.

To understand how the ASP.NET runtime goes into action, consider a typical web request from a browser (see Figure 19-11). The client requests a file, such as `default.aspx` or `index.cshtml`, from the server. ASP.NET Web Form pages usually have the file extension `.aspx`, (ASP.NET MVC has no file extension, aka extensionless), and `.cshtml` is used for Razor Pages. Because these file extensions are registered with IIS or known by IIS Express, the ASP.NET runtime and the ASP.NET worker process enter the picture. The IIS worker process is named `w3wp.exe` and is host to your application on the web server. With the first request to the `index.cshtml` file, the ASP.NET parser starts, and the compiler compiles the file together with the C# code, which is associated with the `.cshtml` file, and creates an assembly. Then the assembly is compiled to native code by the just-in-time (JIT) compiler of the .NET runtime. The assembly is kept for subsequent requests, though, so it is not necessary to compile the assembly again.

Now that you have the basic understanding of what web applications and ASP.NET are, perform the steps in the following Try It Out.

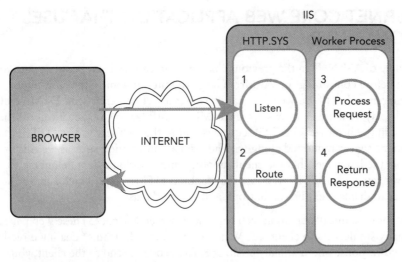

FIGURE 19-11

Create an ASP.NET Core Web Application that deals two hands of cards

You will use Visual Studio to create an ASP.NET Web Site that requests the names of two players, and then when the page is submitted, two hands of cards are dealt. Those cards are downloaded from the Microsoft Azure storage container created earlier, and the cards are displayed on the web page.

1. Open Visual Studio ➪ click the Create a new project box ➪ select ASP.NET Core Web App as seen in Figure 19-12 ➪ click the Next button ➪ name the project Ch19Ex02 and save it in the directory C:\BeginningCSharpAndDotNET\Chapter19 ➪ click the Next button ➪ select .NET 5.0 from the drop-down (leave the other as the default setting) ➪ click the Create button.

2. Download the file CardGame.cs from the GitHub repository located here: github.com/benperk/ BeginningCSharpAndDotNET/tree/main/Chapter19/Ch19Ex02/Ch19Ex02/Models ➪ right-click the project ➪ select Add ➪ select New Folder and name it Models ➪ add the CardGames.cs to the Models folder by right-clicking on the folder ➪ select Add ➪ select Existing Item ➪ navigate to the location of the downloaded file CardGame.cs ➪ select and add the file.

3. Open the index.cshtml file in the Pages folder and place the following code at the top of the page:

```
@page
@model Ch19Ex02.Pages.IndexModel
@addTagHelper*, Microsoft.AspNetCore.Mvc.TagHelpers
@using BeginningCSharp
@{
```

```
            Player[] players = new Player[2];
            string player1 = "", player2 = "";

            if (Model.Request.Method == "POST")
            {
                player1 = Model.Request.Form["PlayerName1"];
                player2 = Model.Request.Form["PlayerName2"];
                players[0] = new Player(player1);
                players[1] = new Player(player2);
                Game newGame = new Game();
                newGame.SetPlayers(players);
                newGame.DealHands();
            }
        }
```

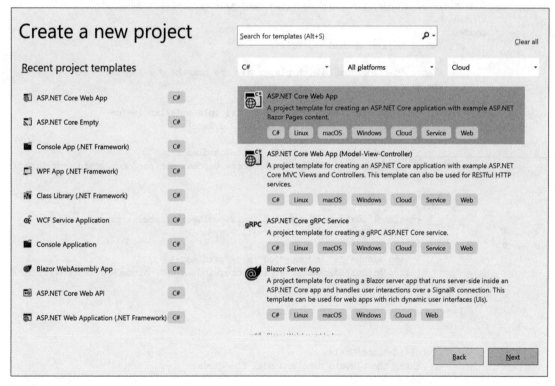

FIGURE 19-12

4. Next, add this syntax under the code you added in step 3. Pay close attention to the `@card` `.imageLink`, which is the newly added parameter to the `Card` class.

```
            <html lang="en">
            <head>
```

```html
        <meta charset="utf-8"/>
        <style>
            body {
                font-family: Verdana;
                margin-left: 50px;
                margin-top: 50px;
            }

            div {
                border: 1px solid black;
                width: 40%;
                margin: 1.2em;
                padding: 1em;
            }
        </style>
        <title>BensCards: a new and exciting card game. </title>
    </head>
    <body>
        @if (Model.Request.Method == "POST")
        {
            <label id="labelGoal">Which player has the best hand.</label>
            <br/>
            <div>
                <p><label id="labelPlayer1">Player1: @player1</label></p>
                @foreach (Card card in players[0].PlayHand)
                {
                  <img width="75" height="100" alt="cardImage"
                  src="https://deckofcards.blob.core.windows.net/carddeck/@card.imageLink"/>
                }
            </div>
            <div>
                <p><label id="labelPlayer1">Player2: @player2</label></p>
                @foreach (Card card in players[1].PlayHand)
                {
                  <img width="75" height="100" alt="cardImage"
                  src="https://deckofcards.blob.core.windows.net/carddeck/@card.imageLink"/>
                }
            </div>
        }
        else
        {
            <label id="labelGoal">
                Enter the players name and deal the cards.
            </label>
            <br/><br/>
            <form method="post">
                <div>
                    <p>Player 1:  @Html.TextBox("PlayerName1")</p>
                    <p>Player 2:  @Html.TextBox("PlayerName2")</p>
                    <p><input type="submit" value="Deal Cards" asp-page-handler="Submit"
class="submit"></p>
            </div>
```

```
            </form>
        }
    </body>
</html>
```

5. Open the `Startup.cs` file and add the following to the end of the `ConfigureServices()` method:

```
services.AddMvc(options =>
{
  options.EnableEndpointRouting = false;
});
```

6. In the `Startup.cs` file, add the following to the end of the `Configure()` method:

```
app.UseMvc();
```

7. Now, run the Web App by pressing F5, or click the Run button within Visual Studio. A browser will start up and you should see a page rendered similar to the one illustrated in Figure 19-13. First you are prompted to enter in the Player names. Enter any two names.

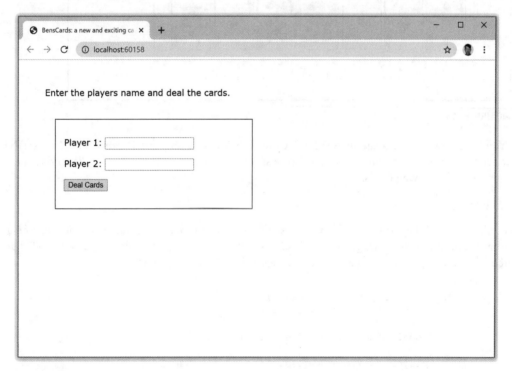

FIGURE 19-13

8. After entering the names ⇨ click the Deal Cards button, and a hand of cards is dealt to each player. You would see something similar to what is shown in Figure 19-14.

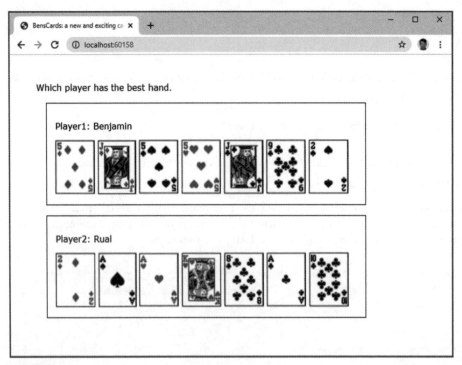

FIGURE 19-14

You have now created a simple ASP.NET Core Web Application using Razor Pages. The ASP.NET Core Web Application connects to the Azure storage account and container for displaying the images of the playing cards.

How It Works

You certainly noticed the term Razor that was used in the previous exercise. Razor is a view engine and, as you have seen, uses C#-like language that is placed within a @{ ... } code block and is compiled and executed when the page is requested from a browser. Take a look at this code:

```
@{
    Player[] players = new Player[2];
    string player1 = "", player2 = "";

    if (Model.Request.Method == "POST")
    {
        player1 = Model.Request.Form["PlayerName1"];
        player2 = Model.Request.Form["PlayerName2"];
        players[0] = new Player(player1);
        players[1] = new Player(player2);
        Game newGame = new Game();
        newGame.SetPlayers(players);
        newGame.DealHands();
    }
}
```

The code is encapsulated within a @{...} code block and is compiled and executed by the Razor engine when accessed. When the page is accessed, an array of type Player[] is created and two empty strings named player1 and player2. If the page is not a post back, which means the page was simply requested (GET) instead of a button click (POST), then the code within the if(Model.Request.Method == "POST"){} code block does not execute. If the request to the page is a POST, which happens when you click the Deal Cards button, the Players are populated, by adding the values entered on the form into the player1 and player2 strings. Then a new game is started, and the hands of cards get dealt.

The initial request to the index.cshtml file executes this code path because it is not a POST:

```
else
{
  <label id="labelGoal">
    Enter the players name and deal the cards.
  </label>
  <br/><br/>
  <form method="post">
   <div>
      <p>Player 1:  @Html.TextBox("PlayerName1")</p>
      <p>Player 2:  @Html.TextBox("PlayerName2")</p>
      <p><input type="submit" value="Deal Cards" asp-page-handler="Submit"
class="submit"></p>
   </div>
   </form>
}
```

The code renders two HTML TextBox controls that request the player names and a button. Once the information is entered, clicking the Deal Cards button executes a POST and the following code path is executed. The code loops through the cards dealt to each player of the game.

```
@if (Model.Request.Method == "POST")
{
  <label id="labelGoal">Which player has the best hand.</label>
  <br/>
  <div>
  <p><label id="labelPlayer1">Player1: @player1</label></p>
  @foreach (Card card in players[0].PlayHand)
  {
    <img width="75" height="100" alt="cardImage"
    src="https://deckofcards.blob.core.windows.net/carddeck/@card.imageLink"/>
  }
  </div>
   <div>
    <p><label id="labelPlayer1">Player2: @player2</label></p>
    @foreach (Card card in players[1].PlayHand)
    {
     <img width="75" height="100" alt="cardImage"
      src="https://deckofcards.blob.core.windows.net/carddeck/@card.imageLink"/>
    }
   </div>
}
```

Notice that within both foreach loops, there is a reference to the Azure storage account URL and the container created in the previous exercise.

> **NOTE** *The Azure storage account URL and container are for example only. You should replace* deckofcards *with your Azure storage account and* carddeck *with your Azure storage container.*

EXERCISES

19.1   What information would you need to pass between the browser and the server to play the card game?

19.2   As web applications are stateless, describe some ways to store this information so it can be included with a web request.

19.3   Instead of consuming the ASP.NET Web API from a Blazor App, try consuming it from another program type like a Console Application or a WPF Application.

Answers to the exercises can be found in the Appendix.

▶ **WHAT YOU LEARNED IN THIS CHAPTER**

TOPIC	KEY CONCEPTS
Defining the cloud	The cloud is an elastic structure of commoditized computer hardware for running programs. These programs run on IaaS, PaaS, or SaaS service models in a Hybrid, Public, or Private Cloud type.
Defining the cloud optimized stack	The cloud optimized stack is a concept used to refer to code that can handle high throughput, makes a small footprint, can run side-by-side with other applications on the same server, and is cross-platform enabled.
Creating a storage account	A storage account can contain an infinite number of containers. The storage account is the mechanism for controlling access to the containers created within it.
Creating a storage container with C#	A storage container exists within a storage account and contains the blobs, files, or data that are accessible from any place where an Internet connection exists.
Referencing the storage container from ASP.NET Razor	It is possible to reference a storage container from C# code. You use the storage account name, the container name, and the name of the blog, file, or data you need to access.

20

Basic Web API and WCF Programming

WHAT YOU WILL LEARN IN THIS CHAPTER:

➤ Creating an ASP.NET Core Web API

➤ Consuming an ASP.NET Core Web API

➤ What is REST?

➤ What is WCF?

➤ WCF concepts

➤ Understanding WCF programming

CODE DOWNLOADS FOR THIS CHAPTER

The code downloads for this chapter are found on the book page at www.wiley.com. Click the Downloads link. The code can also be found at github.com/benperk/BeginningCSharpAnd-DotNET. The code is in the Chapter20 folder and individually named according to the names throughout the chapter. Now that you know a bit about the cloud and cloud programming, let's move forward and write some C# code that is a little more complex than what you did in the previous chapter. In this chapter, you explore ASP.NET Core Web APIs and Blazor Apps.

CREATING AN ASP.NET CORE WEB API

The *Application Programming Interface* (API) computer programming concept has been around for many decades and is generally described as a module that contains a set of functions useful for building software programs. Originally, from a Windows client application perspective, these modules were dynamic linked libraries (.dll) that revealed programmatically accessible interfaces that exposed internal functions to other programs. In such a system, when a consuming program uses an API, it becomes dependent on the pattern of the interface. Changes to the interface cause exceptions and failures within the consuming program because the current procedure to access and execute the functions within the module is no longer valid. Once programs become dependent on an interface, it should not be changed. When it is changed, that event is commonly referred to as DLL Hell. For more information about DLL Hell, read this article: en.wikipedia.org/wiki/DLL_Hell.

As time moved on and the implementation of Internet and intranet solutions became mainstream, dependencies on technologies such as web services and Windows Communication Foundation (WCF) were made. Both web services and WCF exposed formal contractual interfaces that exposed the functions contained within them to other programs. As opposed to the previously mentioned DLL API where the module exists on the same computer as the one consuming it, the web service and WCF are hosted on a web server. As a result of being hosted on an Internet or intranet web server, access to the web interface is no longer confined to a single computer and is possible from any device, from any place with an Internet or networked intranet connection.

Recall from the previous chapter where the analysis of the cloud optimized stack took place. From that discussion, you learned that to be considered *cloud optimized*, a program must have a small footprint, be able to handle high throughput, and be cross-platform enabled. An ASP.NET Core Web API is based on the ASP.NET MVC (Model-View-Controller) concept, which aligns directly with the new cloud optimized stack definition. If you have created and/or used web services or WCF in the past, you will realize how much simpler and compact an ASP.NET Core Web API is in comparison. If you have never used either, take my word for it: It is.

In the following Try It Out, you will create an ASP.NET Core Web API that deals a hand of cards.

TRY IT OUT   Create an ASP.NET Core Web API

You will use Visual Studio to create an ASP.NET Core Web API that accepts a player's name and returns a hand of cards for that player.

1. Create a new ASP.NET Core Web API by selecting Create a new project within Visual Studio. In the Create a new project dialog box (see Figure 20-1), select the ASP.NET Core Web API template ⇨ click the Next button. Change the path to C:\BeginningCSharpAndDotNET\Chapter20 ⇨ name the Web API Ch20Ex01 ⇨ click the Next button.

2. Select .NET 5.0 from the Target Framework dropdown box ⇨ leave the remaining defaults (see Figure 20-2) ⇨ click the Create button.

3. Install the public package (written by Benjamin Perkins) from the Package Manager Console ⇨ select the menu item Tools ⇨ NuGet Package Manager ⇨ Package Manager Console ⇨ execute the following command:

```
Install-Package Ch18CardLibStandard
```

4. Next add a controller by right-clicking the Controllers folder ⇨ select Add ⇨ Controller. . . ⇨ select MVC Controller - Empty ⇨ Add (Figure 20-3).

5. Name the controller HandOfCardsController ⇨ click the Add button.

6. Add using BeginningCSharp; at the top of the HandOfCardsController.cs file.

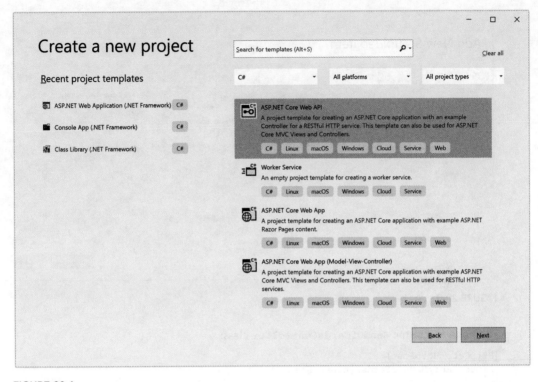

FIGURE 20-1

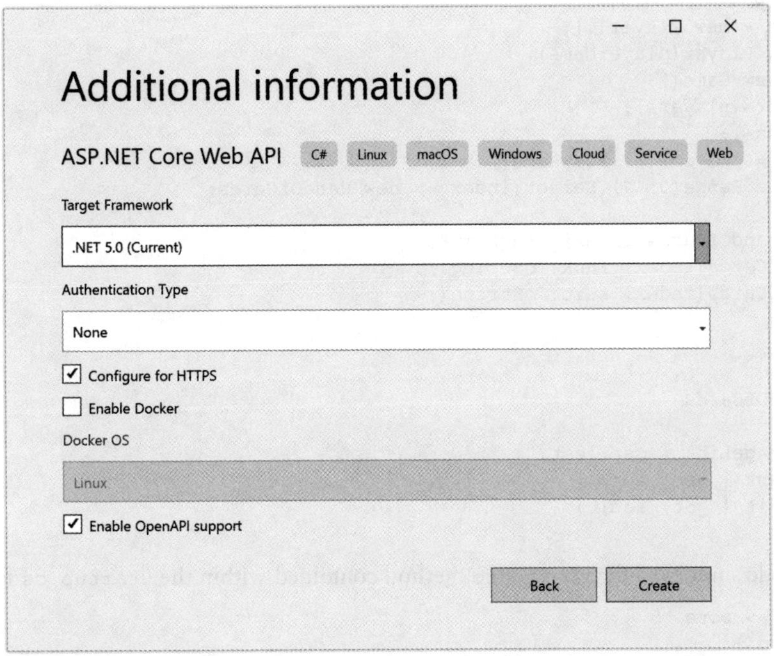

FIGURE 20-2

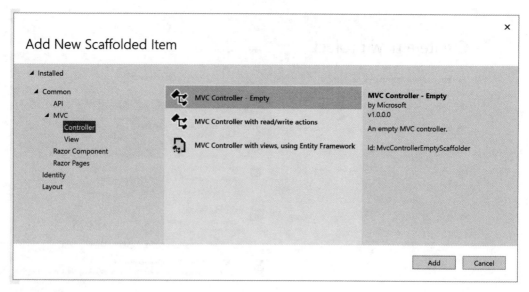

FIGURE 20-3

7. Add this code into the `HandOfCardsController` class:

```
[HttpGet, HttpPost]
[Route("api/HandOfCards/{playerName}")]

public async Task<IEnumerable<HandOfCards>> GetHandOfCards(string playerName)
{
 Player[] players = new Player[1];
 players[0] = new Player(playerName);
 Game newGame = new Game();
 newGame.SetPlayers(players);
 newGame.DealHands();
 var handOfCards = players[0].PlayHand;
 return Enumerable.Range(0, 7).Select(index => new HandOfCards
 {
    imageLink = handOfCards[index].imageLink,
    rank = handOfCards[index].rank.ToString(),
    suit = handOfCards[index].suit.ToString()
 }).ToArray();
}

public class HandOfCards
{
 public string imageLink { get; set; }
 public string rank { get; set; }
 public string suit { get; set; }
}
```

8. Add the following code snippet to the `Configure` method contained within the `Startup.cs` file:

```
app.UseCors(cors => cors
   .AllowAnyMethod()
```

```
        .AllowAnyHeader()
        .SetIsOriginAllowed(origin => true)
        .AllowCredentials()
    );
```

9. Run the project and a browser will open rendering something similar to what is shown in Figure 20-4. The default project includes a `WeatherForecast` controller. You can ignore or delete that one.

FIGURE 20-4

Congratulations! You have completed the creation of an ASP.NET Core Web API that returns some JSON that contains a link to an image, the rank of the card (for example, an ace), and the suit. At this point, if you run the application, you will see only the JSON text and not a hand of cards. You will make that happen later when you consume this API.

How It Works

The first item you may notice that is unfamiliar is this thing called Swagger. Swagger is a language that is useful for describing, building, and documenting Web APIs that use the JSON syntax. Read more about Swagger here: `swagger.io`.

When you create a new ASP.NET Core Web API, you are prompted with a few options; see Figure 20-3. The method that this Try It Out described was the Empty one. The fact that you selected Empty from the

Scaffold selection window meant that the project would contain nothing other than the bare necessities required to create an ASP.NET Core Web API. This resulted in very few configuration files and binaries being added to the solution; the footprint for this Web API is therefore small and is just what is needed to run optimally and to be very portable.

The other possible selections would include additional configuration files, many additional references, and a basic example of an ASP.NET Core MVC application. As this Try It Out is relatively small and did not require most of the MVC features, the Empty scaffold was chosen. If additional functionalities and examples are needed in a future project of your own, consider selecting a more feature-rich Web API scaffold because it constructs data pipelines and provides many proven coding pattern examples to build your solution on top of.

You installed the Ch18CardLibStandard NuGet package, which provides the programming logic to play the card game. The package provides the capability to instantiate the Player array, creates a new Game, sets the Players, adds the playerName, deals the hand of cards, and returns a JSON file for a consumer to request.

```
[HttpGet, HttpPost]
[Route("api/HandOfCards/{playerName}")]
```

The HttpGet and HttpPost annotations describe which kinds of requests can be made to the Web API. In this case, a GET and a POST are supported. The Route annotation is how ASP.NET decides which Web API method responds to which request. As you will come to realize, when you attempt to consume this Web API, there is no specific file requested when you interface with an ASP.NET Web API. Unlike an ASP.NET Web Forms application where a request is sent to a file with an .aspx extension, the same is not true when calling a Web API (or an ASP.NET MVC application for that matter). A Web API request is sent to a web server, where the parameters are in the requested URL, separated by forward slashes. For example: "http://localhost:445348/api/{controllerName}/Parameter1/Parameter2/etc...".

Another concept introduced in this exercise has to do with the app.UseCors() configurations. This is related to a security feature called cross-origin resource sharing (CORS). CORS makes sure that, when a page is being rendered in a browser, any call to any other server is approved. It is intended to make sure no scripts are executed on your client machine unless it is expected to do so. To keep the scenario simple in this example, this configuration you made allows all methods, headers, and domains to work with this API. This is not something you would do in a live production environment. For more details about CORS, read the following article: en.wikipedia.org/wiki/Cross-origin_resource_sharing.

Now that the ASP.NET Core Web API is created, move on to the next section to learn about the consumption of the Web API.

CONSUMING AN ASP.NET CORE WEB API

When you ran the ASP.NET Core Web API in the last exercise, you could use the Swagger page to try out the API. You could also enter the URL directly into a browser, while the application is running, and you would receive the output of the JSON response. A request to https://localhost:44348/api/HandOfCards/Benjamin would output something like that shown in Figure 20-5. Make sure to change the port number, which is the series of numbers after the semicolon, to match the one you see in your browser. The name Benjamin is the name of the player for whom you would like the hand of cards.

FIGURE 20-5

There is also a utility called CURL, which is helpful when you are working with Web APIs. As shown in Figure 20-6, executing the following command will also give you the JSON output of the Web API. The application must be running for this to work via Visual Studio:

```
curl https://localhost:44348/api/HandOfCards/Benjamin
```

```
Command Prompt                                                    —    □    ×

C:\Users\Benjamin>curl https://localhost:44348/api/HandOfCards/Benjamin
[{"imageLink":"3-1.PNG","rank":"Ace","suit":"Spade"},{"imageLink":"2-9.PNG","rank":"Nine","suit":"Heart"
},{"imageLink":"1-5.PNG","rank":"Five","suit":"Diamond"},{"imageLink":"0-1.PNG","rank":"Ace","suit":"Clu
b"},{"imageLink":"1-9.PNG","rank":"Nine","suit":"Diamond"},{"imageLink":"3-10.PNG","rank":"Ten","suit":"
Spade"},{"imageLink":"0-12.PNG","rank":"Queen","suit":"Club"}]
```

FIGURE 20-6

Just seeing the content of the JSON file does not add much value; it needs to be used in some way. The name of the playing card image, for example 3-1.PNG, can be used to show the images for the dealt hand, instead of or in addition to its rank and suit. That makes the game a bit more appealing. You can deploy the ASP.NET Core Web API onto a server in the cloud, like Azure, or you can consume it locally on your own client. Consuming the API locally is what will be done in this next exercise. In the exercise, you will create a Blazor WebAssembly App that will call the ASP.NET Core Web API, parse the JSON, and use its contents to display a hand of cards.

TRY IT OUT Consume the Web API from a Blazor WebAssembly App

You will use Visual Studio to create a Blazor WebAssembly App that consumes an ASP.NET Core Web API. The Web API accepts a player's name and returns a hand of cards for that player.

1. Open Visual Studio ⇨ select Create a new project ⇨ select Blazor WebAssembly App ⇨ click the Next button ⇨ name the project Ch20Ex02 ⇨ change the Location to C:\BeginningCSharpAnd-DotNET\Chapter20 ⇨ click the Next button. Configure the settings like those shown in Figure 20-7 and click the Create button.

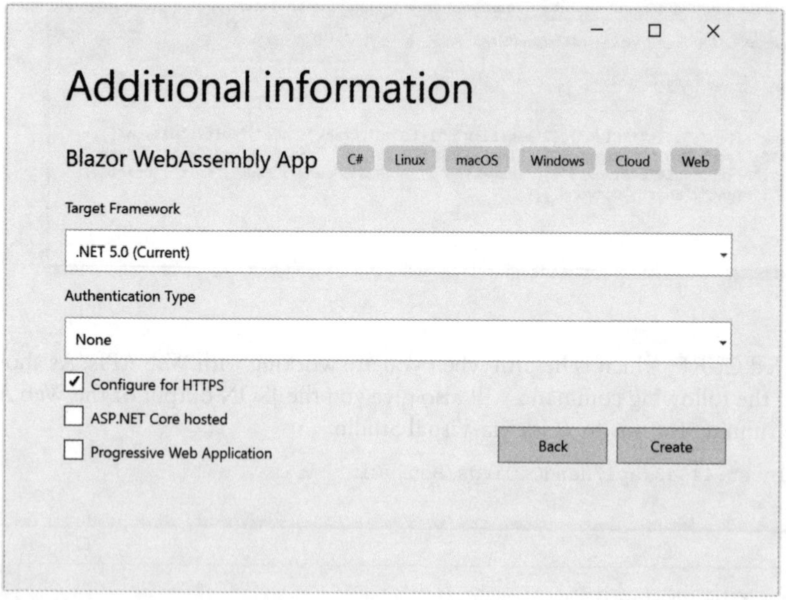

FIGURE 20-7

> **NOTE** *The output of an ASP.NET Web API is a JSON file, the format of which follows a standard format, making it easily parsed. The most common means for parsing a JSON file is using the* `Newtonsoft.Json` *libraries.*

2. To install the `Newtonsoft.Json` libraries used for parsing the JSON response, right-click the `Ch20Ex02` project ➪ select Manage NuGet Packages, which opens a tab in Visual Studio like that shown in Figure 20-8.

3. Browse for and select `Newtonsoft.Json` from the Package list ➪ click the Install button. You will find the `Newtonsoft.Json` binary reference in the Dependencies ➪ Packages directory.

4. Open the `Index.razor` file located in the `Pages` folder. Add these directives to the top of the file:

```
@page "/"
@inject HttpClient Http
@using Newtonsoft.Json;
@using System.IO;
@using Microsoft.AspNetCore.Components.Rendering
```

5. Directly beneath that code, enter the following, which creates a text box to enter a name and a button to pass the name to the code that calls the Web API and displays the hand of cards:

```
<h1>BensCards: a new and exciting card game.</h1>
<br/>
Enter your name:
<input type="text" @bind="player.PlayerName"/>
<br/><br/>
```

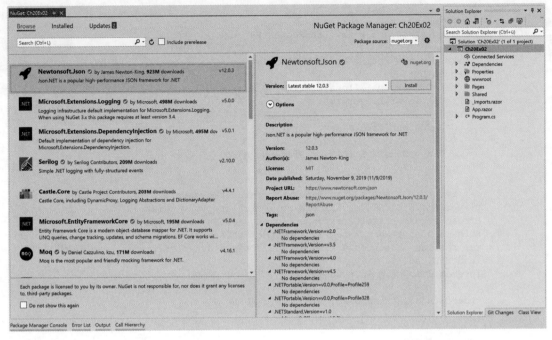

FIGURE 20-8

```
<button @onclick="PostRequest">Deal Cards</button>
<br/><br/>
<h2>@playerName</h2>
<br/>
<p>@responseBody</p>
@if (cards.Count > 0)
{
    ShowHand(__builder);
    cards.Clear();
}
```

6. Next, enter this code, which will contain the executable code within the Blazor App; this code also instantiates some variables required to deal the hand of cards:

```
@code{

    private string responseBody;
    private string playerName;
    Player player = new Player();
    List<string> cards = new List<string>();
}
```

7. Notice that in step 5 you added a button that calls a method named PostRequest when clicked. Add the PostRequest method within the @code brackets. Change the URL so that it matches the one that is in your browser, or the URL you used with curl earlier. The change will likely only be to the number after the semicolon:

```
private async Task PostRequest()
{
```

```
      try
      {
        var requestMessage = new HttpRequestMessage()
        {
          Method = new HttpMethod("POST"),
          RequestUri =
            new Uri("https://localhost:44348/api/HandOfCards/"
                + player.PlayerName),
          Content =
            JsonContent.Create(new Player
            {
              PlayerName = $"{player.PlayerName}"
            })
        };
        var response = await Http.SendAsync(requestMessage);
        playerName = $"{player.PlayerName}, here are your cards.";
        Stream stream = await response.Content.ReadAsStreamAsync();
        StreamReader reader = new StreamReader(stream);
        var results = JsonConvert.DeserializeObject<dynamic>(reader.ReadLine());
        reader.Close();
        foreach (var card in results)
        {
          cards.Add((string)card.imageLink);
        }
      }
      catch (Exception ex)
      {
        responseBody = ex.Message + " - " + ex.StackTrace;
      }
    }
```

8. Finally, add the `ShowHand()` method and the `Player` class within the `@code` brackets:

```
private void ShowHand(RenderTreeBuilder __builder)
{
    <div>
    @foreach (string card in cards)
    {
      <img width="75"
           height="100"
           alt="cardImage"
           src="https://deckofcards.blob.core.windows.net/carddeck/@card" />
    }
    </div>
}
public class Player
{
    public string PlayerName { get; set; }
}
```

9. Run the Blazor App by pressing F5 ⇨ make sure the ASP.NET Core Web API project is also running. Once rendered, enter a name ⇨ click the Deal Hand button. The code in the Blazor App consumes the ASP.NET Web API and renders a hand of cards, like that shown in Figure 20-9.

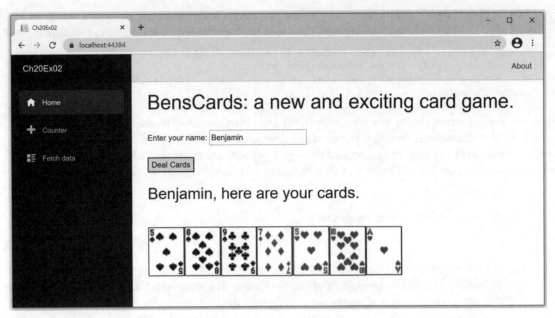

FIGURE 20-9

How It Works

When the Index.razor page is initially rendered, the ShowHand() is not executed because the cards list has not yet been populated with the contents of the JSON response. Instead, only the portion of HTML code that contains the input text to capture the player name and a Button to trigger the posting of the page back to itself are displayed.

Once a player name is entered and the Deal Hand button is clicked, the PostRequest method is executed.

```
var requestMessage = new HttpRequestMessage()
{
  Method = new HttpMethod("POST"),
  RequestUri =
    new Uri("https://localhost:44348/api/HandOfCards/"
      + player.PlayerName),
  Content =
    JsonContent.Create(new Player
    {
      PlayerName = $"{player.PlayerName}"
    })
};
var response = await Http.SendAsync(requestMessage);
```

The web address stored in the RequestUri is the Internet, intranet, or localhost location of the ASP.NET Core Web API and is used as a parameter to build the HttpRequestMessage. The SendAsync method of the `HttpClient` class takes the `responseMessage` parameters and returns the `response`, which is formatted in JSON. Then `ReadAsStreamAsync()` is used to place the response into a `Stream` object:

```
Stream stream = await response.Content.ReadAsStreamAsync();
StreamReader reader = new StreamReader(stream);
var results = JsonConvert.DeserializeObject<dynamic>(reader.ReadLine());
reader.Close();
```

The `Stream` object is then passed as a parameter to the `StreamReader` constructor. Using the `ReadLine()` method of the `StreamReader` class as a parameter to deserialize the JSON using the `Newtonsoft.Json` libraries, the `results` can then be enumerated through a `foreach` statement and added to a `List<string>` container named `cards`. The `cards` list can then be accessed for usage later in the page rendering process:

```
foreach (var card in results)
{
  cards.Add((string)card.imageLink);
}
```

> **NOTE** Review the `dynamic` type discussed previously in Chapter 13. It is common practice to use the `dynamic` type with JSON files as the structure contained within it is not always castable to a strongly typed class.

Once the parsed results of the JSON response are loaded into the `cards` container, the markup code within the `ShowHand()` method gets executed. The `foreach` loop reads through the `cards` container and concatenates the image name with the link to the Microsoft Azure Blob Container created in Chapter 19:

```
@foreach (string card in cards)
{
  <img width="75"
       height="100"
       alt="cardImage"
       src="https://deckofcards.blob.core.windows.net/carddeck/@card" />
}
```

That concludes the discussion concerning the Web API. Keep in mind that this information is intended to provide you a gateway into the world of coding web applications. The remainder of this chapter will cover the predecessor of this REST-based Web API concept called the *Windows Communication Foundation* (WCF). WCF will not be migrated to the cross-platform version of .NET and will remain on .NET Framework 4.8. Since there remain many implementations of this technique in the IT industry, it is worth having this information available for those who need it. Prior to WCF, there was something called a *web service*. A web service is like a website that is used by a computer instead of a person. For example, instead of browsing to a website about your favorite TV program, you might instead use a desktop application that pulls in the same information via a web service. The advantage here is that the same web service could be used by all sorts of applications and, indeed, by websites. Also, you can write your own application or website that uses third-party web services. Perhaps you might combine information about your favorite TV program with a mapping service to show filming locations.

The .NET Framework has supported web services for a long time now. However, in the more recent versions of the framework, web services have been combined with another technology, called *remoting*, to create a WCF service, which is a generic infrastructure for communication between applications. Remoting makes it possible to create instances of objects in one process and use them from another process—even if the object is created on a computer other than the one that is using it. However, remoting on its own is limited and is not the easiest thing for a beginner programmer to learn.

WCF takes concepts such as services and platform-independent Simple Object Access Protocol (SOAP) messaging from web services and combines these with concepts such as host server applications and advanced binding capabilities from remoting. The result is a technology you can think of as a superset that includes both web services and remoting, but that is much more powerful than web services and much easier to use than remoting. Using WCF, you can move from simple applications to applications that use a *service-oriented architecture* (SOA). SOA means that you decentralize processing and make use of distributed processing by connecting to services and data as you need them across local networks and the Internet.

This chapter walks you through how to create and consume WCF services from your application code. But just as importantly, it also covers the principles behind WCF, so you understand why things work the way they do. But before we delve into WCF, here is a brief overview of what REST is and what it has to do with Web APIs.

WHAT IS REST?

The *representational state transfer* (REST) is a style of software architecture that sets the standard of communication between a client and a server over HTTP. In comparison to WCF, you would consider the fact that WCF is Windows only, while REST can be used cross-platform. The same goes for an ASP.NET Web API; notice the missing "Core" from that product name. An ASP.NET Core Web API is cross-platform, whereas the version of ASP.NET Web API that targets the .NET Framework is not.

Recall from the previous exercises where you created and consumed an ASP.NET Core Web API. Whether you knew it or not, you were using REST under the hood there. When you created the message to send to the API, the message was formatted into a JSON document that contained a player name. The response from the API also came in the form of JSON, and you used Newtonsoft to deserialize the response and parse out the content it contained. This might be a bit clearer if you look at Figure 20-6 again to see the response of the API.

The simplicity of REST is what makes it such a useful technique, especially when you compare it to what existed before. Web services that used SOAP and even WCF are platform dependent and somewhat complicated to configure and support. Also consider what preceded those, which was something called *Electronic Data Interchange* (EDI), which really was not an industry standard. Instead, it was an agreement only between a specific client and server that the file would be in a decipherable format; for example, a comma-delimited text file. You might consider reading more about REST at this location: en.wikipedia.org/wiki/Representational_state_transfer.

WHAT IS WCF?

WCF is a technology that enables you to create services that you can access from other applications across process, machine, and network boundaries. You can use these services to share functionality across multiple applications, to expose data sources, or to abstract complicated processes. The functionality that WCF services offer is encapsulated as individual methods that are exposed by the service. Each method—or, in WCF terminology, each *operation*—has an endpoint that you exchange data with to use it. This data exchange can be defined by one or more protocols, depending on the network that you use to connect to the service and your specific requirements.

In WCF, an endpoint can have multiple *bindings*, each of which specifies a means of communication. Bindings can also specify additional information, such as which security requirements must be met to communicate with the endpoint. A binding might require username and password authentication or a Windows user account token, for example. When you connect to an endpoint, the protocol that the binding uses may affect the address that you use, as you will see shortly.

Once you have connected to an endpoint, you can communicate with it by using SOAP or REST messages. The form of the messages that you use depends on the operation you are using and the data structures that are required to send messages to (and receive messages from) that operation. WCF uses *contracts* to specify all of this. You can discover contracts through metadata exchange with a service. One commonly used format for service discovery is the Web Service Description Language (WSDL), which was originally used for web services, although WCF services can also be described in other ways.

> **NOTE** *WCF is something of a chameleon in how it can be used and set up. It is possible to create REST services using WCF. These services rely on simple HTTP requests to communicate between the client and the server, and because of this, they can have a smaller footprint than the SOAP messages.*

When you have identified a service and endpoint that you want to use, and after you know which binding you use and which contracts to adhere to, you can communicate with a WCF service as easily as with an object that you have defined locally. Communications with WCF services can be simple, one-way transactions, request/response messages, or full-duplex communications that can be initiated from either end of the communication channel. You can also use message payload optimization techniques, such as Message Transmission Optimization Mechanism (MTOM), to package data if required.

The WCF service itself might be running in one of several different processes on the computer where it is hosted. Unlike web services, which always run in Internet Information Services (IIS), you can choose a host process that is appropriate to your situation. You can use IIS to host WCF services, but you can also use Windows services or executables. If you are using TCP to communicate with a WCF service over a local network, there is no need even to have IIS installed on the PC that is hosting the service. The WCF framework has been designed to enable you to customize nearly everything you have read about in this section. However, this is an advanced subject, and you will only be using the techniques provided by default in .NET 4.8 in this chapter.

Now that you have learned the basics about WCF services, you will further explore these concepts in the following sections.

WCF CONCEPTS

This section describes the following aspects of WCF:

➤ WCF communication protocols

➤ Addresses, endpoints, and bindings

➤ Contracts

➤ Message patterns

➤ Behaviors

➤ Hosting

WCF Communication Protocols

As described earlier, you can communicate with WCF services through a variety of transport protocols. In fact, five are defined in the .NET 4.8 Framework:

➤ **HTTP**—Enables you to communicate with WCF services from anywhere, including across the Internet. You can use HTTP communications to create WCF web services.

➤ **TCP**—Enables you to communicate with WCF services on your local network or across the Internet if you configure your firewall appropriately. TCP is more efficient than HTTP and has more capabilities, but it can be more complicated to configure.

➤ **UDP**—User Datagram Protocol is like TCP in that it enables communications via the local network or Internet, but it's implemented in a subtly different way. One of the consequences of this implementation is that a service can broadcast messages to multiple clients simultaneously.

➤ **Named pipe**—Enables you to communicate with WCF services that are on the same machine as the calling code but reside in a separate process.

➤ **MSMQ**—Microsoft Message Queuing is a queuing technology that enables messages sent by an application to be routed through a queue to arrive at a destination. MSMQ is a reliable messaging technology that ensures that a message sent to a queue will reach that queue. MSMQ is also inherently asynchronous, so a queued message will be processed only when messages ahead of it in the queue have been processed and a processing service is available.

These protocols often enable you to establish secure connections. For example, you can use the HTTPS protocol to establish a TLS connection across the Internet. TCP offers extensive possibilities for security in a local network by using the Windows security framework. UDP does not support security. To connect to a WCF service, you must know where it is. In practice, this means knowing the address of an endpoint.

Addresses, Endpoints, and Bindings

The type of address you use for a service depends on the protocol that you are using. Service addresses are formatted for the three protocols described in this chapter (MSMQ is not covered) as follows:

➤ **HTTP**—Addresses for the HTTP protocol are URLs of the familiar form `http://<server>:<port>/<service>`. For TLS connections, you can also use `https://<server>:<port>/<service>`. If you are hosting a service in IIS, `<service>` will be a file with a .svc extension. IIS addresses will probably include more subdirectories than this example—that is, more sections separated by / characters before the .svc file.

➤ **TCP**—Addresses for TCP are of the form `net.tcp://<server>:<port>/<service>`.

➤ **UDP**—Addresses for UDP are of the form `soap.udp://<server>:<port>/<service>`. Certain `<server>` values are required for multicast communications, but this is beyond the scope of this chapter.

➤ **Named pipe**—Addresses for named pipe connections are similar but have no port number. They are of the form `net.pipe://<server>/<service>`.

The address for a service is a base address that you can use to create addresses for endpoints representing operations. For example, you might have an operation at this location:
`net.tcp://<server>:<port>/<service>/operation1`.

Imagine you create a WCF service with a single operation that has bindings for all three protocols listed here. You might use the following base addresses:

```
http://www.mydomain.com/services/amazingservices/mygreatservice.svc
net.tcp://myhugeserver:8080/mygreatservice
net.pipe://localhost/mygreatservice
```

You could then use the following addresses for operations:

```
http://www.mydomain.com/services/amazingservices/mygreatservice.svc/greatop
net.tcp://myhugeserver:8080/mygreatservice/greatop
net.pipe://localhost/mygreatservice/greatop
```

It is possible to use default endpoints for operations, without having to explicitly configure them. This simplifies configuration, especially in situations where you want to use standard endpoint addresses, as in the preceding examples. Bindings, as mentioned earlier, specify more than just the transport protocol that will be used by an operation. You can also use them to specify the security requirements for communication over the transport protocol, transactional capabilities of the endpoint, message encoding, and much more. Because bindings offer such a great degree of flexibility, the .NET Framework provides some predefined bindings that you can use. You can also use these bindings as starting points, tweaking them to obtain exactly the type of binding you want—up to a point. The predefined bindings have certain capabilities to which you must adhere. Each binding type is represented by a class in the `System.ServiceModel` namespace. Table 20-1 lists the most used bindings, along with some basic information about them.

TABLE 20-1: Binding Types

BINDING	DESCRIPTION
BasicHttpBinding	The simplest HTTP binding, and the default binding used by web services. It has limited security capabilities and no transactional support.
WSHttpBinding	A more advanced form of HTTP binding that is capable of using all the additional functionality that was introduced in WSE.
WSDualHttpBinding	Extends WSHttpBinding capabilities to include duplex communication capabilities. With duplex communication, the server can initiate communications with the client in addition to ordinary message exchange.
WSFederationHttpBinding	Extends WSHttpBinding capabilities to include federation capabilities. Federation enables third parties to implement single sign-on and other proprietary security measures. This is an advanced topic not covered in this chapter.
NetTcpBinding	Used for TCP communications, and enables you to configure security, transactions, and so on.
NetNamedPipeBinding	Used for named pipe communications, and enables you to configure security, transactions, and so on.
NetMsmqBinding	Used with MSMQ, which is not covered in this chapter.
NetPeerTcpBinding	Used for peer-to-peer binding, which is not covered in this chapter.
WebHttpBinding	Used for web services that use HTTP requests instead of SOAP messages.
UdpBinding	Allows binding to the UDP protocol.

Many of the binding classes have similar properties that you can use for additional configuration. For example, they have properties that you can use to configure timeout values. You will learn more about this when you look at code later in this chapter.

Endpoints have default bindings that vary according to the protocol used. These defaults are shown in Table 20-2.

TABLE 20-2: NET Default Bindings

PROTOCOL	DEFAULT BINDING
HTTP	BasicHttpBinding
TCP	NetTcpBinding
UDP	UdpBinding
Named pipe	NetNamedPipeBinding

Contracts

Contracts define how WCF services can be used. Several types of contracts can be defined:

➤ **Service contract**—Contains general information about a service and the operations exposed by a service. This includes, for example, the namespace used by service. Services have unique namespaces that are used when defining the schema for SOAP messages in order to avoid possible conflicts with other services.

➤ **Operation contract**—Defines how an operation is used. This includes the parameter and return types for an operation method along with additional information, such as whether a method will return a response message.

➤ **Message contract**—Enables you to customize how information is formatted inside SOAP messages—for example, whether data should be included in the SOAP header or SOAP message body. This can be useful when creating a WCF service that must integrate with legacy systems.

➤ **Fault contract**—Defines faults that an operation can return. When you use .NET clients, faults result in exceptions that you can catch and deal with, in the normal way.

➤ **Data contract**—If you use complex types, such as user-defined structs and objects, as parameters or return types for operations, then you must define data contracts for these types. Data contracts define the types in terms of the data that they expose through properties.

You typically add contracts to service classes and methods by using attributes, as you will see later in this chapter.

Message Patterns

In the previous section, you saw that an operation contract can define whether an operation returns a value. You have also read about duplex communications that are made possible by the WSDualHttp-Binding binding. These are both forms of message patterns, of which there are three types:

➤ **Request/response messaging**—The "ordinary" way of exchanging messages, whereby every message sent to a service results in a response being sent back to the client. This does not necessarily mean that the client waits for a response, as you can call operations asynchronously in the usual way.

➤ **One-way, or simplex, messaging**—Messages are sent from the client to the WCF operation, but no response is sent.

➤ **Two-way, or duplex, messaging**—A more advanced scheme whereby the client effectively acts as a server as well as a client, and the server as a client as well as a server. Once set up, duplex messaging enables both the client and the server to send messages to each other, which might not have responses.

You will see how these message patterns are used in practice later in this chapter.

Behaviors

Behaviors are a way to apply additional configuration to services and operations. By adding a behavior to a service, you can control how it is instantiated and used by its hosting process, how it participates in transactions, how multithreading issues are dealt with in the service, and so on. Operation behaviors can control whether impersonation is used in the operation execution, how the individual operation affects transactions, and more.

You can specify default behaviors at various levels, so that you don't have to specify every aspect of every behavior for every service and operation. Instead, you can provide defaults and override settings where necessary, which reduces the amount of configuration required.

Hosting

At the beginning of this section, you learned that WCF services can be hosted in several different processes. Your options are as follows:

➤ **Web server**—IIS-hosted WCF services are the closest thing to pure web services that WCF offers. However, you can use advanced functionality and security features in WCF services that are much more difficult to implement in web services. You can also integrate with IIS features such as IIS security.

➤ **Executable**—You can host a WCF service in any application type that you can create in .NET, such as console applications, Windows Forms applications, and WPF applications.

➤ **Windows service**—You can host a WCF service in a Windows service and take advantage of the useful features that Windows services provide, such as automatic startup and fault recovery.

➤ **Windows Process Activation Service (WAS)**—Designed specifically to host WCF services, WAS is basically a simple version of IIS that you can use where IIS is not available.

Two of the options in the preceding list—IIS and WAS—provide useful features for WCF services such as activation, process recycling, and object pooling. If you use either of the other two hosting options, a WCF service is said to be *self-hosted*. You will occasionally self-host services for testing purposes, but there can be good reasons for creating self-hosted production-grade services. For example, you could be in a situation where you are not allowed to install a web server on the computer on which your service should run. This might be the case if the service runs on a domain controller or if the local policy of your organization simply prohibits running IIS. In this case you can host the service in a Windows service and it will work every bit as well as it would otherwise.

WCF PROGRAMMING

Now that you have covered all the basics, it is time to get started with some code. In this section, you will start by looking at a simple web server–hosted WCF service and a console application client. After looking at the structure of the code created, you will learn about the basic structure of WCF services and client applications. Then you will look at some key topics in a bit more detail:

➤ Defining WCF service contracts

➤ Self-hosted WCF services

In the following Try It Out, you create a simple WCF service that exposes two methods and a client to consume them.

TRY IT OUT A Simple WCF Service and Client: Ch20Ex03Client

1. Create a new WCF Service Application project called Ch20Ex03 in the directory C:\BeginningC-SharpAndDotNET\Chapter20. If you do not see a WCF project template, you need to install the Windows Communication Foundation template via the Visual Studio Installer as seen in Figure 20-10.

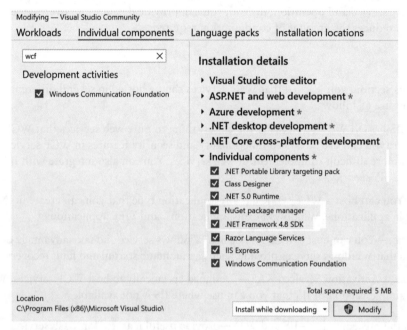

FIGURE 20-10

2. Right-click the Solution ⇨ Add ⇨ New Project ⇨ Console App (.NET Framework) called Ch20Ex-03Client to the solution that targets .NET Framework 4.8.

3. On the Build menu, click Build Solution.

4. Right-click the Ch20Ex03Client project ⇨ Add ⇨ Service Reference ⇨ in the Add Service Reference dialog box ⇨ click Discover.

5. When the development web server has started and information about the WCF service has been loaded, expand the reference to look at its details. Notice that there are two methods in the service: GetData and GetDataUsingDataContract, as illustrated in Figure 20-11.

6. Click the OK button to add the service reference.

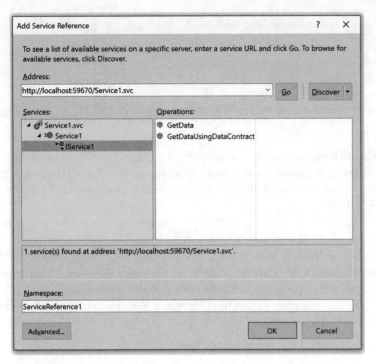

FIGURE 20-11

7. Modify the code in `Program.cs` in the Ch20Ex03Client application as follows:

```
using Ch20Ex03Client.ServiceReference1;

namespace Ch20Ex03Client
{
  class Program
  {
    static void Main(string[] args)
    {
      int intParam;
      do
      {
        Console.WriteLine("Enter an integer and press enter to call the WCF service.");
      } while (!int.TryParse(Console.ReadLine(), out intParam));
      Service1Client client = new Service1Client();
      Console.WriteLine(client.GetData(intParam));
      Console.WriteLine("Press an key to exit.");
      Console.ReadKey();
    }
  }
}
```

8. Right-click the Ch20Ex03Client project in the Solution Explorer ➪ select Set as Startup Project ➪ run the application (F5) ➪ enter a number in the console application window ➪ press Enter. The result is shown in Figure 20-12.

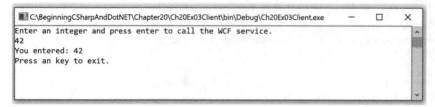

FIGURE 20-12

9.   Exit the application ⇨ right-click the `Service1.svc` file in the Ch20Ex03 project in the Solution Explorer ⇨ click View in Browser ⇨ review the information in the window ⇨ click the link at the top of the web page for the service to view the WSDL. Do not panic—you do not need to understand all the stuff in the WSDL file!

How It Works

In this example, you created a simple web server–hosted WCF service and console application client. You used the default Visual Studio template for a WCF service project, which meant that you did not have to add any code. Instead, you used one of the operations defined in this default template, `GetData()`. For the purposes of this example, the actual operation used is not important; here, you are focusing on the structure of the code and the plumbing that makes things work.

First, look at the server project, Ch20Ex03. This consists of the following:

➤   A `Service1.svc` file that defines the hosting for the service
➤   A class definition, `CompositeType`, that defines a data contract used by the service (located in the `IService1.cs` code file)
➤   An interface definition, `IService1`, that defines the service contract and two operation contracts for the service
➤   A class definition, `Service1`, that implements `IService1` and defines the functionality of the service (located in the `Service1.svc.cs` code file)
➤   A `<system.serviceModel>` configuration section (in `Web.config`) that configures the service

The `Service1.svc` file contains the following line of code (to see this code, right-click the file in the Solution Explorer and select View Markup):

```
<%@ ServiceHost Language="C#" Debug="true" Service="Ch20Ex03.Service1"
    CodeBehind="Service1.svc.cs" %>
```

This is a `ServiceHost` instruction that is used to tell the web server (the development web server in this case, although this also applies to IIS) what service is hosted at this address. The class that defines the service is declared in the `Service` attribute, and the code file that defines this class is declared in the `CodeBehind` attribute. This instruction is necessary to obtain the hosting features of the web server as defined in the previous sections.

This file is not required for WCF services that are not hosted in a web server. You will learn how to self-host WCF services later in this chapter.

Next, the data contract CompositeType is defined in the IService1.cs file. You can see from the code that the data contract is simply a class definition that includes the DataContract attribute on the class definition and DataMember attributes on class members:

```
[DataContract]
public class CompositeType
{
    bool boolValue = true;
    string stringValue = "Hello ";
    [DataMember]
    public bool BoolValue
    {
        get { return boolValue; }
        set { boolValue = value; }
    }
    [DataMember]
    public string StringValue
    {
        get { return stringValue; }
        set { stringValue = value; }
    }
}
```

This data contract is exposed to the client application through metadata (if you looked through the WSDL file in the example you might have seen this). This enables client applications to define a type that can be serialized into a form that can be deserialized by the service into a CompositeType object. The client does not need to know the actual definition of this type; in fact, the class used by the client might have a different implementation. This simple way of defining data contracts is surprisingly powerful and enables the exchange of complex data structures between the WCF service and its clients.

The IService1.cs file also contains the service contract for the service, which is defined as an interface with the ServiceContract attribute. Again, this interface is completely described in the metadata for the service and can be re-created in client applications. The interface members constitute the operations exposed by the service, and each is used to create an operation contract by applying the Operation-Contract attribute. The example code includes two operations, one of which uses the data contract you looked at earlier:

```
[ServiceContract]
public interface IService1
{
    [OperationContract]
    string GetData(int value);
    [OperationContract]
    CompositeType GetDataUsingDataContract(CompositeType composite);
}
```

All four of the contract-defining attributes that you have seen so far can be further configured with attributes, as shown in the next section. The code that implements the service looks much like any other class definition:

```
public class Service1 : IService1
{
    public string GetData(int value)
```

```
        {
            return string.Format($"You entered: {value}");
        }
        public CompositeType GetDataUsingDataContract(CompositeType composite)
        {
            ...
        }
    }
}
```

Note that this class definition does not need to inherit from a particular type and does not require any particular attributes. All it needs to do is implement the interface that defines the service contract. In fact, you can add attributes to this class and its members to specify behaviors, but these are not mandatory.

The separation of the service contract (the interface) from the service implementation (the class) works extremely well. The client does not need to know anything about the class, which could include much more functionality than just the service implementation. A single class could even implement more than one service contract.

Finally, you come to the configuration in the `Web.config` file. Configuration of WCF services in `.config` files works with all types of WCF services (hosted or self-hosted) as well as clients of WCF services (as shown in a moment).

WCF configuration code is contained in the `<system.serviceModel>` configuration section of `Web.config` or `app.config` files. In this example, there is little service configuration, as default values are used. In the `Web.config` file, the configuration section consists of a single subsection that supplies overrides to default values for the service behavior `<behaviors>`. The code for the `<system.serviceModel>` configuration section in `Web.config` (with comments removed for clarity) is as follows:

```
<system.serviceModel>
  <behaviors>
    <serviceBehaviors>
      <behavior>
        <serviceMetadata httpGetEnabled="true" httpsGetEnabled="true" />
        <serviceDebug includeExceptionDetailInFaults="false" />
      </behavior>
    </serviceBehaviors>
  </behaviors>
</system.serviceModel>
```

This section can define one or more behaviors in `<behavior>` child sections, which can be reused on multiple other elements. A `<behavior>` section can be given a name to facilitate this reuse (so that it can be referenced from elsewhere) or can be used without a name (as in this example) to specify overrides to default behavior settings.

> **NOTE** *If a nondefault configuration were being used, you would expect to see a* `<services>` *section inside* `<system.serviceModel>`, *containing one or more* `<services>` *child sections. In turn, the* `<service>` *sections can contain child* `<endpoint>` *sections, each of which (you guessed it) defines an endpoint for the service. In fact, the endpoints defined are base endpoints for the service. Endpoints for operations are inferred from these.*

One of the default behavior overrides in `Web.config` is as follows:

```
<serviceDebug includeExceptionDetailInFaults="false"/>
```

This setting can be set to `true` to expose exception details in any faults that are transmitted to the client, which is something you would usually allow only in development.

Another default behavior override in `Web.config` relates to metadata. Metadata is used to enable clients to obtain descriptions of WCF services. The default configuration defines two default endpoints for services. One is the endpoint that clients use to access the service; the other is an endpoint used to obtain metadata from the service. This can be disabled in the `Web.config` file as follows:

```
<serviceMetadata httpGetEnabled="false"
httpsGetEnabled="false" />
```

Alternatively, you could remove this line of configuration code entirely, as the default behavior does not enable metadata exchange.

If you try disabling this in the example, it will not stop your client from being able to access the service because it has already obtained the metadata it needed when you added the service reference. However, disabling metadata will prevent other clients from using the Add Service Reference tool for this service. Typically, web services in a production environment will not need to expose metadata, so you should disable this functionality after the development phase is complete.

Now that you've looked at the WCF service code, it's time to look at the client, and in particular at what using the Add Service Reference tool actually did. You will notice in the Solution Explorer that the client includes a folder called Service References, and if you expand that, you will see an item called `Service-Reference1`, which is the default name given to a service reference if you do not provide one yourself.

The Add Service Reference tool creates all the classes you require to access the service. This includes a proxy class for the service that contain methods for all the operations exposed by the service (`Service-1Client`) and a client-side class generated from the data contract (`CompositeType`).

> **NOTE** You can browse through the code that is generated by the Add Service Reference tool if you want (by displaying all files in the project, including the hidden ones).

The tool also adds a configuration file to the project, `app.config`. This configuration defines two things:

➤ Binding information for the service endpoint
➤ The address and contract for the endpoint

The binding information is taken from the service description:

```
<configuration>
  <system.serviceModel>
    <bindings>
      <basicHttpBinding>
        <binding name="BasicHttpBinding_IService1" />
      </basicHttpBinding>
    </bindings>
```

This binding is used in the endpoint configuration, along with the base address of the service (which is the address of the .svc file for web server–hosted services) and the client-side version of the contract IService1:

```
<client>
  <endpoint address="http://localhost:49227/Service1.svc"
    binding="basicHttpBinding"
    bindingConfiguration="BasicHttpBinding_IService1"
    contract="ServiceReference1.IService1"
    name="BasicHttpBinding_IService1" />
</client>
</system.serviceModel>
</configuration>
```

If you remove the <bindings> section as well as the bindingConfiguration attribute from the <endpoint> element, then the client will use the default binding configuration.

The <binding> element, which has the name BasicHttpBinding_IService1, is included so that you can use it to customize the configuration of the binding. There are several configuration settings that you might use here, ranging from timeout settings to message size limits and security settings. If these had been specified in the service project to be nondefault values, then you would have seen them in the app.config file, since they would have been copied across. In order for the client to communicate with the service, the binding configurations must match. You won't look at WCF service configuration in great depth in this chapter.

This example has covered a lot of ground, and it is worth summarizing what you have learned before moving on:

➤ WCF service definitions:
> ➤ Services are defined by a service contract interface that includes operation contract members.
>
> ➤ Services are implemented in a class that implements the service contract interface.
>
> ➤ Data contracts are simply type definitions that use data contract attributes.

➤ WCF service configuration:
> ➤ You can use configuration files (Web.config or app.config) to configure WCF services.

➤ WCF web server hosting:
> ➤ Web server hosting uses .svc files as service base addresses.

➤ WCF client configuration:
> ➤ You can use configuration files (Web.config or app.config) to configure WCF service clients.

The following section explores contracts in more detail.

The WCF Test Client

In the previous Try It Out, you created both a service and a client in order to look at how the basic WCF architecture works and how configuration of WCF services is achieved. In practice, though, the client application you want to use might be complex, and it can be tricky to test services properly. To ease the development of WCF services, Visual Studio provides a test tool you can use to ensure that your WCF operations work correctly. This tool is automatically configured to work with your WCF service projects, so if you run your project, the tool will appear. All you need to do is ensure that the service you want to test (that is, the .svc file) is set to be the startup page for the WCF service project. The tool enables you to invoke service operations and inspect the service in some other ways. The following Try It Out illustrates this.

TRY IT OUT Using the WCF Test Client

1. Open the WCF Service Application project from the previous Try It Out, Ch20Ex03 ⇨ right-click the Service1.svc service in Solution Explorer ⇨ click Set As Start Page ⇨ right-click the Ch20Ex03 project in Solution Explorer and click Set As Startup Project.

2. Metadata must be enabled, so if you have disabled it, re-enable it in the web.config file like this:

```
<serviceMetadata httpGetEnabled="true" httpsGetEnabled="true" />
```

3. Run the application. The WCF test client appears.

4. In the left pane of the test client, double-click Config File. The config file used to access the service is displayed in the right pane ⇨ in the left pane, double-click the GetDataUsingDataContract() operation.

5. In the pane that appears on the right, change the value of BoolValue to True ⇨ change String-Value to Test String ⇨ click Invoke.

6. If a security prompt dialog box appears, click OK to confirm that you are happy to send information to the service ⇨ the operation result appears, as shown in Figure 20-13.

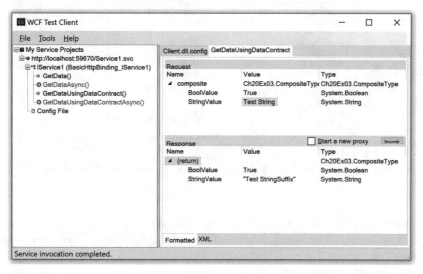

FIGURE 20-13

7. Click the XML tab at the bottom to view the request and response XML ⇨ close the WCF Test Client. This will stop debugging in Visual Studio.

How It Works

In this example, you used the WCF test client to inspect and invoke an operation on the service you created in the previous Try It Out. The first thing you probably noticed is a slight delay while the service is loaded. This is because the test client has to inspect the service to determine its capabilities. This discovery uses the same metadata as the Add Service Reference tool, which is why you must ensure that metadata is available. Once discovery is complete, you can view the service and its operations in the left pane of the tool.

Next, you looked at the configuration used to access the service. As with the client application from the previous Try It Out, this is generated automatically from the service metadata, and contains the same code. You can edit this configuration file through the tool if you need to by right-clicking the Config File item and clicking Edit with SvcConfigEditor. An example of this configuration is shown in Figure 20-14, which includes the binding configuration options mentioned earlier in this chapter.

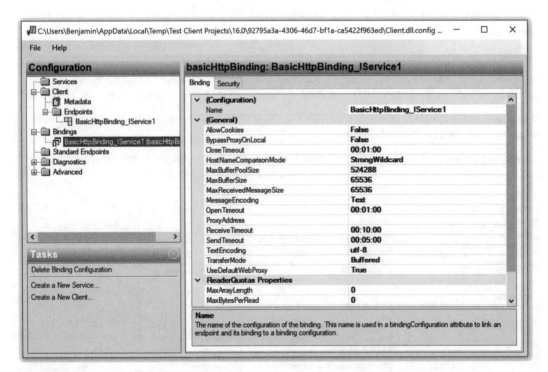

FIGURE 20-14

Finally, you invoked an operation. The test client allows you to enter the parameters to use and invoke the method, then displays the result, all without you writing any client code. You also saw how to view the actual XML that is sent and received to obtain the result. This information is quite technical, but it can be absolutely critical when debugging more complex services.

Defining WCF Service Contracts

The previous examples showed how the WCF infrastructure makes it easy for you to define contracts for WCF services with a combination of classes, interfaces, and attributes. This section takes a deeper look at this technique.

Data Contracts

To define a data contract for a service, you apply the `DataContractAttribute` attribute to a class definition. This attribute is found in the `System.Runtime.Serialization` namespace. You can configure this attribute with the properties shown in Table 20-3.

TABLE 20-3: DataContractAttribute Properties

PROPERTY	DESCRIPTION
Name	Names the data contract with a different name than the one you use for the class definition. This name will be used in SOAP messages and client-side data objects that are defined from service metadata.
Namespace	Defines the namespace that the data contract uses in SOAP messages.
IsReference	Affects the way that objects are serialized. If this is set to `true`, then an object instance is serialized only once even if it is referenced several times, which can be important is some situations. The default is `false`.

The `Name` and `Namespace` properties are useful when you need interoperability with existing SOAP message formats (as are the similarly named properties for other contracts), but otherwise, you will probably not require them.

Each class member that is part of a data contract must use the `DataMemberAttribute` attribute, which is also found in the `System.Runtime.Serialization` namespace. Table 20-4 lists this attribute's properties.

TABLE 20-4: DataMemberAttribute Properties

PROPERTY	DESCRIPTION
Name	Specifies the name of the data member when serialized (the default is the member name).
IsRequired	Specifies whether the member must be present in a SOAP message.
Order	An `int` value specifying the order of serializing or deserializing the member, which might be required if one member must be present before another. Lower `Order` members are processed first.
EmitDefaultValue	Set this to `false` to prevent members from being included in SOAP messages if their value is the default value for the member.

Service Contracts

Service contracts are defined by applying the `System.ServiceModel.ServiceContractAttribute` attribute to an interface definition. You can customize the service contract with the properties shown in Table 20-5.

TABLE 20-5: ServiceContractAttribute Properties

PROPERTY	DESCRIPTION
Name	Specifies the name of the service contract as defined in the `<portType>` element in WSDL.
Namespace	Defines the namespace of the service contract used by the `<portType>` element in WSDL.
ConfigurationName	The name of the service contract as used in the configuration file.
HasProtectionLevel	Determines whether messages used by the service have explicitly defined protection levels. Protection levels enable you to sign, or sign and encrypt, messages.
ProtectionLevel	The protection level to use for message protection.
SessionMode	Determines whether sessions are enabled for messages. If you use sessions, then you can ensure that messages sent to different endpoints of a service are correlated—that is, they use the same service instance and so can share state, and so on.
CallbackContract	For duplex messaging the client exposes a contract as well as the service. This is because, as discussed earlier, the client in duplex communications also acts as a server. This property enables you to specify which contract the client uses.

Operation Contracts

Within interfaces that define service contracts, you define members as operations by applying the `System.ServiceModel.OperationContractAttribute` attribute. This attribute has the properties described in Table 20-6.

TABLE 20-6: OperationContractAttribute Properties

PROPERTY	DESCRIPTION
Name	Specifies the name of the service operation. The default is the member name.
IsOneWay	Specifies whether the operation returns a response. If you set this to `true`, then clients won't wait for the operation to complete before continuing.
AsyncPattern	If set to `true`, the operation is implemented as two methods that you can use to call the operation asynchronously: `Begin<methodName>()` and `End<methodName>()`.
HasProtection Level	See the previous section.
ProtectionLevel	See the previous section.

PROPERTY	DESCRIPTION
`IsInitiating`	If sessions are used, then this property determines whether calling this operation can start a new session.
`IsTerminating`	If sessions are used, then this property determines whether calling this operation terminates the current session.
`Action`	If you are using addressing (an advanced capability of WCF services), then an operation has an associated action name, which you can specify with this property.
`ReplyAction`	As with `Action`, but specifies the action name for the operation response.

> **NOTE** *When you add a service reference, Visual Studio also generates asynchronous proxy methods to call the service, regardless of whether* `Async-cPattern` *is set to true. These methods, which have the suffix* `Async`, *use the asynchronous techniques and are asynchronous only from the point of view of the calling code. Internally, they call the synchronous WCF operations.*

Message Contracts

The earlier example did not use message contract specifications. If you use these, then you do so by defining a class that represents the message and applying the `MessageContractAttribute` attribute to the class. You then apply `MessageBodyMemberAttribute`, `MessageHeaderAttribute`, or `MessageHeaderArrayAttribute` attributes to members of this class. All these attributes are in the `System.ServiceModel` namespace. You are unlikely to want to do this unless you need a high degree of control over the SOAP messages used by WCF services, so details are not provided here.

Fault Contracts

If you have a particular exception type—for example, a custom exception—that you want to make available to client applications, then you can apply the `System.ServiceModel.FaultContractAttribute` attribute to the operation that might generate this exception.

TRY IT OUT **WCF Contracts: Ch20Ex04Contracts**

1. Create a new WCF Service Application project called Ch20Ex04 in the directory `C:\BeginningCSharpAndDotNET\Chapter20`.

2. Add a Class Library (.NET Framework) project called Ch20Ex04Contracts to the solution ⇨ remove the `Class1.cs` file.

3. Add references to the `System.Runtime.Serialization.dll` and `System.ServiceModel.dll` assemblies to the Ch20Ex04Contracts project.

4. Add a class called `Player` to the Ch20Ex04Contracts project and modify the code in `Player.cs` as follows:

```
using System.Runtime.Serialization;

namespace Ch20Ex04Contracts
{
  [DataContract]
  public class Player
  {
    [DataMember]
    public string Name { get; set; }
    [DataMember]
    public int Level { get; set; }
  }
}
```

5. Add an interface called `IGameService` to the Ch20Ex04Contracts project and modify the code in `IGameService.cs` as follows:

```
using System.ServiceModel;

namespace Ch20Ex04Contracts
{
  [ServiceContract(SessionMode = SessionMode.Required)]
  public interface IGameService
  {
    [OperationContract(IsOneWay = true, IsInitiating = true)]
    void SetPlayerLevel(int playerLevel);
    [OperationContract]
    Player[] GetProfessionalPlayer(Player[] playerToTest);
  }
}
```

6. In the Ch20Ex04 project, add a reference to the Ch20Ex04Contracts project by right-clicking References ➪ Add Reference ➪ Projects ➪ Ch20Ex04Contracts ➪ click the OK button.

7. Remove `IService1.cs` and `Service1.svc` from the Ch20Ex04 project.

8. Add a new WCF service called `GameService` to Ch20Ex04 ➪ remove the `IGameService.cs` file from the Ch24Ex04 project ➪ modify the code in `GameService.svc.cs` as follows:

```
using System.Collections.Generic;
using Ch20Ex04Contracts;
namespace Ch20Ex04
{
  public class GameService : IGameService
  {
    private int playerLevel;
    public void SetPlayerLevel(int playerLevel)
    {
      this.playerLevel = playerLevel;
    }
    public Player[] GetProfessionalPlayer(Player[] playerToTest)
    {
      List<Player> result = new List<Player>();
      foreach (Player player in playerToTest)
      {
```

```
          if (player.Level > playerLevel)
          {
            result.Add(player);
          }
        }
      return result.ToArray();
    }
  }
}
```

9. Modify the service configuration section in `Web.config` in project Ch20Ex04 as follows:

```xml
<system.serviceModel>
  <protocolMapping>
    <add scheme="http" binding="wsHttpBinding" />
  </protocolMapping>
  ...
</system.serviceModel>
```

10. Open the project properties for Ch20Ex04 by right-clicking the project ➪ select Properties from the pop-up menu. In the Web section, make a note of the port used in the hosting settings, ex: `http://localhost:52262/`.

11. Add a new Console App (.NET Framework) project called Ch20Ex04Client to the solution ➪ set it as the startup project ➪ add references to the `System.ServiceModel.dll` assembly and the Ch20Ex04Contracts project to the Ch20Ex04Client project ➪ modify the code in `Program.cs` in Ch20Ex04Client as follows (ensure that you use the port number you obtained earlier as the parameter for the `EndpointAddress` constructor; the example code uses port 52262):

```csharp
using System;
using System.ServiceModel;
using Ch20Ex04Contracts;


namespace Ch20Ex04Client
{
  class Program
  {
    static void Main(string[] args)
    {
      Player [] players = new Player[]
      {
        new Player { Level = 46, Name="Benamin" },
        new Player { Level = 73, Name="Jon" },
        new Player { Level = 92, Name="Rual" },
        new Player { Level = 24, Name="Mary" }
      };
      Console.WriteLine("Player:");
      OutputPlayers(players);
      IGameService client = ChannelFactory<IGameService>.CreateChannel(
          new WSHttpBinding(),
          new EndpointAddress("http://localhost:52262/GameService.svc"));
      client.SetPlayerLevel(70);
      Player[] professionalPlayers = client.GetProfessionalPlayer(players);
      Console.WriteLine();
      Console.WriteLine("Professional players:");
      OutputPlayers(professionalPlayers);
```

```
        Console.ReadKey();
      }
      static void OutputPlayers(Player[] players)
      {
        foreach (Player player in players)
          Console.WriteLine($"{player.Name}, level: {player.Level}");
      }
    }
  }
```

12. To test the WCF Service, right-click the `GameService.svc` file in Ch20Ex04 ⇨ View in Browser, which will render the service details similar to that illustrated in Figure 20-15.

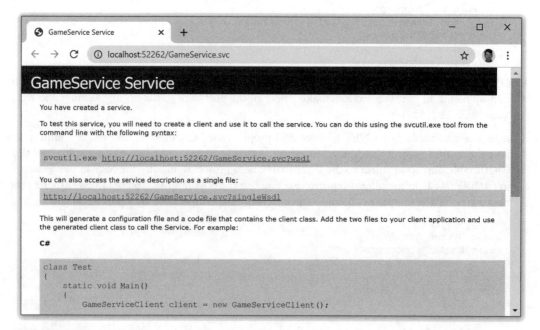

FIGURE 20-15

13. Right-click Ch20Ex04Client ⇨ select Set as Startup Project again ⇨ press F5 or click the Start button on the menu. The result is shown in Figure 20-16.

```
C:\BeginningCSharpAndDotNET\Chapter20\Ch20Ex04Client\bin\Debug\Ch20Ex04Client.exe        —  □  ×
Player:
Benamin, level: 46
Jon, level: 73
Rual, level: 92
Mary, level: 24

Professional players:
Jon, level: 73
Rual, level: 92
```

FIGURE 20-16

How It Works

In this example, you created a set of contracts in a class library project and used that class library in both a WCF service and a client. The service, as in the previous example, is hosted in a web server. The configuration for this service is reduced to the bare minimum.

The main difference in this example is that no metadata is required by the client, as the client has access to the contract assembly. Instead of generating a proxy class from metadata, the client obtains a reference to the service contract interface through an alternative method. Another point to note about this example is the use of a session to maintain state in the service, which requires the WSHttpBinding binding instead of the BasicHttpBinding binding.

The data contract used in this example is for a simple class called Person, which has a string property called Name and an int property called Level. You used the DataContractAttribute and DataMember-Attribute attributes with no customization.

The service contract is defined by applying the ServiceContractAttribute attribute to the IGame-Service interface. The SessionMode property of this attribute is set to SessionMode.Required, as this service requires state:

```
[ServiceContract(SessionMode=SessionMode.Required)]
public interface IGameService
{
```

The first operation contract, SetPlayerLevel(), is the one that sets state, and therefore has the IsIni-tiating property of OperationContractAttribute set to true. This operation does not return anything, so it is defined as a one-way operation by setting IsOneWay to true:

```
[OperationContract(IsOneWay=true,IsInitiating=true)]
void SetPlayerLevel(int playerLevel);
```

The other operation contract, GetProfessionalPlayer(), does not require any customization and uses the data contract defined earlier:

```
[OperationContract]
Person[] GetProfessionalPlayer(Player[] playerToTest);
}
```

Remember that these two types, Player and IGameService, are available to both the service and the client. The service implements the IGameService contract in a type called GameService, which does not contain any remarkable code. The only difference between this class and the service class you saw earlier is that it is stateful. This is permissible, as a session is defined to correlate messages from a client.

To ensure that the service uses the WSHttpBinding binding, you added the following to Web.config for the service:

```
<protocolMapping>
  <add scheme="http" binding="wsHttpBinding" />
</protocolMapping>
```

This overrides the default mapping for HTTP binding. Alternatively, you could configure the service manually and keep the existing default, but this override is much simpler. However, be aware that this type of override is applied to all services in a project. If you have more than one service in a project, then you would have to ensure that this binding is acceptable to each of them.

The client is more interesting, primarily because of this code:

```
IGameService client = ChannelFactory<IGameService>.CreateChannel(
    new WSHttpBinding(),
    new EndpointAddress("http://localhost:52262/GameService.svc"));
```

The client application has no `app.config` file to configure communications with the service, and no proxy class defined from metadata to communicate with the service. Instead, a proxy class is created through the `ChannelFactory<T>.CreateChannel()` method. This method creates a proxy class that implements the `IGameService` client, although behind the scenes the generated class communicates with the service just like the metadata-generated proxy shown earlier.

> **NOTE** *If you create a proxy class with* `ChannelFactory<T>.CreateChannel()`, *the communication channel will, by default, time out after a minute, which can lead to communication errors. There are ways to keep connections alive, but they are beyond the scope of this chapter.*

> **NOTE** *Creating proxy classes in this way is an extremely useful technique that you can use to quickly generate a client application on-the-fly.*

Self-Hosted WCF Services

So far in this chapter you have seen WCF services that are hosted in web servers. This enables you to communicate across the Internet, but for local network communications it is not the most efficient way of doing things. For one thing, you need a web server on the computer that hosts the service. In addition, the architecture of your applications might be such that having an independent WCF service is not desirable.

Instead, you might want to use a self-hosted WCF service. A *self-hosted* WCF service exists in a process that you create, rather than in the process of a specially made hosting application such as a web server. This means, for example, that you can use a console application or Windows application to host your service.

To self-host a WCF service, you use the `System.ServiceModel.ServiceHost` class. You instantiate this class with either the type of the service you want to host or an instance of the service class. You can configure a service host through properties or methods, or (and this is the clever part) through a configuration file. In fact, host processes, such as web servers, use a `ServiceHost` instance to do their hosting. The difference when self-hosting is that you interact with this class directly. However, the configuration you place in the `<system.serviceModel>` section of the `app.config` file for your host application uses the same syntax as the configuration sections you've already seen in this chapter.

You can expose a self-hosted service through any protocol that you like, although typically you will use TCP or named pipe binding in this type of application. Services accessed through HTTP are more likely to live inside web server processes because you get the additional functionality that web servers offer, such as security and other features.

If you want to host a service called `MyService`, you could use code such as the following to create an instance of `ServiceHost`:

```
ServiceHost host = new ServiceHost(typeof(MyService));
```

If you want to host an instance of `MyService` called `myServiceObject`, you could code as follows to create an instance of `ServiceHost`:

```
MyService myServiceObject = new MyService();
ServiceHost host = new ServiceHost(myServiceObject);
```

> **WARNING** *Hosting a service instance in a* `ServiceHost` *works only if you configure the service so that calls are always routed to the same object instance. To do this, you must apply a* `ServiceBehaviorAttribute` *attribute to the service class and set the* `InstanceContextMode` *property of this attribute to* `InstanceContextMode.Single`.

After creating a `ServiceHost` instance, you can configure the service and its endpoints and binding through properties. Alternatively, if you put your configuration in a `.config` file, the `ServiceHost` instance will be configured automatically.

To start hosting a service once you have a configured `ServiceHost` instance, you use the `Service-Host.Open()` method. Similarly, you stop hosting the service through the `ServiceHost.Close()` method. When you first start hosting a TCP-bound service, you might, if you have it enabled, receive a warning from the Windows Firewall service, as it will block the TCP port by default. You must open the TCP port for the service to begin listening on the port.

In the following Try it Out, you use self-hosting techniques to expose some functionality of a WPF application through a WCF service.

TRY IT OUT Self-Hosted WCF Services: Ch20Ex05

1. Create a new WPF App (.NET Framework) called Ch20Ex05 in the directory `C:\BeginningC-SharpAndDotNET\Chapter20`.

2. Add a new WCF Service to the Solution by right-clicking the Solution ➪ Add ➪ New Item ➪ select WCF Service ➪ name AppControlService ➪ click the Add button.

3. Modify the code in `MainWindow.xaml` as follows:

```
<Window x:Class="Ch20Ex05.MainWindow"
        xmlns="http://schemas.microsoft.com/winfx/2006/xaml/presentation"
        xmlns:x="http://schemas.microsoft.com/winfx/2006/xaml"
        xmlns:d="http://schemas.microsoft.com/expression/blend/2008"
        xmlns:mc="http://schemas.openxmlformats.org/markup-compatibility/2006"
```

```xml
          xmlns:local="clr-namespace:Ch20Ex05"
          Loaded="Window_Loaded" Closing="Window_Closing"
          Title="Stellar Evolution" Height="450" Width="430"
          mc:Ignorable="d">
  <Grid Height="400" Width="400" HorizontalAlignment="Center"
    VerticalAlignment="Center">
    <Rectangle Fill="Black" RadiusX="20" RadiusY="20"
      StrokeThickness="10">
      <Rectangle.Stroke>
        <LinearGradientBrush EndPoint="0.358,0.02"
          StartPoint="0.642,0.98">
          <GradientStop Color="#FF121A5D" Offset="0" />
          <GradientStop Color="#FFB1B9FF" Offset="1" />
        </LinearGradientBrush>
      </Rectangle.Stroke>
    </Rectangle>
    <Ellipse Name="AnimatableEllipse" Stroke="{x:Null}" Height="0"
      Width="0" HorizontalAlignment="Center"
      VerticalAlignment="Center">
      <Ellipse.Fill>
        <RadialGradientBrush>
          <GradientStop Color="#FFFFFFFF" Offset="0" />
          <GradientStop Color="#FFFFFFFF" Offset="1" />
        </RadialGradientBrush>
      </Ellipse.Fill>
      <Ellipse.Effect>
        <DropShadowEffect ShadowDepth="0" Color="#FFFFFFFF"
          BlurRadius="50" />
      </Ellipse.Effect>
    </Ellipse>
  </Grid>
</Window>
```

4. Modify the code in `MainWindow.xaml.cs` as follows:

```csharp
using System;
using System.Windows;
using System.Windows.Media;
using System.Windows.Shapes;
using System.ServiceModel;
using System.Windows.Media.Animation;

namespace Ch20Ex05
{
  public partial class MainWindow : Window
  {
    private AppControlService service;
    private ServiceHost host;
    public MainWindow()
    {
      InitializeComponent();
    }
    private void Window_Loaded(object sender, RoutedEventArgs e)
    {
      service = new AppControlService(this);
```

```
                host = new ServiceHost(service);
                host.Open();
            }
            private void Window_Closing(object sender,
                System.ComponentModel.CancelEventArgs e)
            {
                host.Close();
            }
            internal void SetRadius(double radius, string foreTo,
                TimeSpan duration)
            {
                if (radius > 200)
                {
                    radius = 200;
                }
                Color foreToColor = Colors.Red;
                try
                {
                    foreToColor = (Color)ColorConverter.ConvertFromString(foreTo);
                }
                catch
                {
                    // Ignore color conversion failure.
                }
                Duration animationLength = new Duration(duration);
                DoubleAnimation radiusAnimation = new DoubleAnimation(
                    radius * 2, animationLength);
                ColorAnimation colorAnimation = new ColorAnimation(
                    foreToColor, animationLength);
                AnimatableEllipse.BeginAnimation(Ellipse.HeightProperty,
                    radiusAnimation);
                AnimatableEllipse.BeginAnimation(Ellipse.WidthProperty,
                    radiusAnimation);
                ((RadialGradientBrush)AnimatableEllipse.Fill).GradientStops[1]
                    .BeginAnimation(GradientStop.ColorProperty, colorAnimation);
            }
        }
    }
```

5. Modify the code in `IAppControlService.cs` as follows:

```
[ServiceContract]
public interface IAppControlService
{
    [OperationContract]
    void SetRadius(int radius, string foreTo, int seconds);
}
```

6. Modify the code in `AppControlService.cs` as follows:

```
[ServiceBehavior(InstanceContextMode=InstanceContextMode.Single)]
public class AppControlService : IAppControlService
{
    private MainWindow hostApp;
    public AppControlService(MainWindow hostApp)
    {
```

```
        this.hostApp = hostApp;
    }
    public void SetRadius(int radius, string foreTo, int seconds)
    {
        hostApp.SetRadius(radius, foreTo, new TimeSpan(0, 0, seconds));
    }
}
```

7. Modify the code in app.config as follows:

```
<configuration>
    <startup>
        <supportedRuntime version="v4.0" sku=".NETFramework,Version=v4.8" />
    </startup>
  <system.serviceModel>
    <services>
      <service name="Ch20Ex05.AppControlService">
        <endpoint address="net.tcp://localhost:8081/AppControlService"
            binding="netTcpBinding"
            contract="Ch20Ex05.IAppControlService" />
      </service>
    </services>
  </system.serviceModel>
</configuration>
```

8. Build the Ch20Ex05 project by pressing F6 or select Build ⇨ Build Solution from the menu ⇨ add a new Console App (.NET Framework) to the Solution named Ch20Ex05Client ⇨ right-click the Project ⇨ select Set as Startup Project ⇨ add references to System.ServiceModel.dll from both Ch20Ex05 and Ch20Ex05Client projects. In the CH20Ex05Client project, add reference to Ch20Ex05 by right-clicking the References ⇨ Add Reference ⇨ Projects Ch20Ex05 ⇨ click the OK button.

9. Configure the solution to have multiple startup projects by right-clicking the Solution ⇨ select Properties ⇨ expand Common Properties ⇨ select Startup Project ⇨ select Multiple startup projects ⇨ select Start from the Action drop-down list for both projects as shown in Figure 20-17 ⇨ click the OK button.

10. Modify the Ch20Ex05Client code in Program.cs as follows:

```
using Ch20Ex05;
using System.ServiceModel;
using System;

namespace Ch20Ex05Client
{
  class Program
  {
    static void Main(string[] args)
    {
      Console.WriteLine("Press enter to begin.");
      Console.ReadLine();
      Console.WriteLine("Opening channel.");
      IAppControlService client =
          ChannelFactory<IAppControlService>.CreateChannel(
              new NetTcpBinding(),
              new EndpointAddress(
                  "net.tcp://localhost:8081/AppControlService"));
```

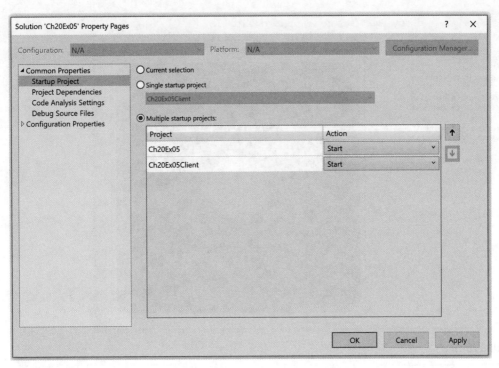

FIGURE 20-17

```
            Console.WriteLine("Creating sun.");
            client.SetRadius(100, "yellow", 3);
            Console.WriteLine("Press enter to continue.");
            Console.ReadLine();
            Console.WriteLine("Growing sun to red giant.");
            client.SetRadius(200, "Red", 5);
            Console.WriteLine("Press enter to continue.");
            Console.ReadLine();
            Console.WriteLine("Collapsing sun to neutron star.");
            client.SetRadius(50, "AliceBlue", 2);
            Console.WriteLine("Finished. Press enter to exit.");
            Console.ReadLine();
        }
    }
}
```

11. Run the solution. If prompted, unblock the Windows Firewall TCP port so that the WCF can listen for connections ⇨ when both the WPF window and the Console App are displayed, press Enter in the console ⇨ the result is shown in Figure 20-18.

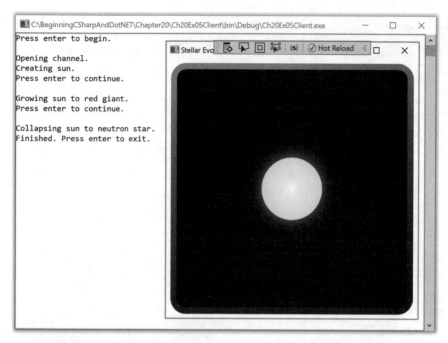

FIGURE 20-18

12. Continue pressing Enter in the console window to continue the stellar evolution cycle ➪ close the WPF window.

How It Works

In this example, you have added a WCF service to a WPF application and used it to control the animation of an Ellipse control. You have created a simple client application to test the service. Do not worry too much about the XAML code in this example if you are not familiar with WPF yet; it's the WCF plumbing that is of interest here.

The WCF service, AppControlService, exposes a single operation, SetRadius(), which clients call to control the animation. This method communicates with an identically named method defined in the Window1 class for the WPF application. For this to work, the service needs a reference to the application, so you must host an object instance of the service. As discussed previously, this means that the service must use a behavior attribute:

```
[ServiceBehavior(InstanceContextMode=InstanceContextMode.Single)]
public class AppControlService : IAppControlService
{
    ...
}
```

In Window1.xaml.cs, the service instance is created in the Windows_Loaded() event handler. This method also begins hosting by creating a ServiceHost object for the service and calling its Open() method:

```
public partial class Window1 : Window
```

```
    {
        private AppControlService service;
        private ServiceHost host;
        ...
        private void Window_Loaded(object sender, RoutedEventArgs e)
        {
            service = new AppControlService(this);
            host = new ServiceHost(service);
            host.Open();
        }
```

When the application closes, hosting is terminated in the `Window_Closing()` event handler.

The configuration file is again about as simple as it can be. It defines a single endpoint for the WCF service that listens at a `net.tcp` address, on port 8081, and uses the default `NetTcpBinding` binding:

```
<service name="Ch20Ex05.AppControlService">
  <endpoint address="net.tcp://localhost:8081/AppControlService"
    binding="netTcpBinding"
    contract="Ch20Ex05.IAppControlService" />
</service>
```

This matches up with code in the client app:

```
IAppControlService client =
    ChannelFactory<IAppControlService>.CreateChannel(
        new NetTcpBinding(),
        new EndpointAddress(
            "net.tcp://localhost:8081/AppControlService"));
```

When the client has created a client proxy class, it can call the `SetRadius()` method with radius, color, and animation duration parameters, and these are forwarded to the WPF application through the service. Simple code in the WPF application then defines and uses animations to change the size and color of the ellipse.

This code would work across a network if you used a machine name, rather than `localhost`, and if the network permitted traffic on the specified port. Alternatively, you could separate the client and host application further, and connect across the Internet. Either way, WCF services provide an excellent means of communication that doesn't take much effort to set up.

EXERCISES

20.1. Which of the following applications can host WCF services?

a. Web applications

b. Windows Forms applications

c. Windows services

d. COM+ applications

e. Console applications

20.2. Which type of contract would you implement if you wanted to exchange parameters of type `MyClass` with a WCF service? Which attributes would you require?

20.3. If you host a WCF service in a web application, what extension will the base endpoint for the service use?

20.4. When self-hosting WCF services, you must configure the service by setting properties and calling methods of the `ServiceHost` class. True or false?

20.5. Provide the code for a service contract, IMusicPlayer, with operations defined for `Play()`, `Stop()`, and `GetTrackInformation()`. Use one-way methods where appropriate. What other contracts might you define for this service to work?

Answers to the exercises can be found in the Appendix.

▶ WHAT YOU LEARNED IN THIS CHAPTER

TOPIC	KEY CONCEPTS
REST	REST is an architecture style that provides a standard for communications between a client and a server. It is an alternative to WCF and web services, which use SOAP.
Web API	A Web API is a REST implementation of ASP.NET that has no user interface and returns only a data payload in the form of a JSON document.
JSON	This data file format is an open standard for sending and receiving data between a client and server. It is an alternative to XML or HTML formats.
WCF fundamentals	WCF provides a framework for creating and communicating with remote services. It combines elements of the web service and remoting architectures along with new technologies to achieve this.
Communication protocols	You can communicate with a WCF service by any one of several protocols, including HTTP and TCP. This means that you can use services that are local to your client application, or that are separated by machine or network boundaries. To do this, you access a specific endpoint for the service through a binding corresponding to the protocol and features that you require. You can control these features, such as using session state or exposing metadata, through behaviors. .NET includes many default settings to make it very easy to define a simple service.
Communication payload	Typically, calls to responses from WCF services are encoded as SOAP messages. However, there are alternatives, such as plain HTTP messages, and you can define your own payload types from scratch if you need to.
Hosting	WCF services might be hosted in IIS or in a Windows service, or they can be self-hosted. Using a host such as IIS enables you to make use of the host's built-in capabilities, including security and application pooling. Self-hosting is more flexible, but it can require more configuration and coding.
Contracts	You define the interface between a WCF service and client code through contracts. Services themselves, along with any operations they expose, are defined with service and operation contracts. Data types are defined with data contracts. Further customization of communications is achieved with message and fault contracts.
Client applications	Client applications communicate with WCF services by means of a proxy class. Proxy classes implement the service contract interface for the service, and any calls to operation methods of this interface are redirected to the service. You can generate a proxy by using the Add Service Reference tool, or you can create one programmatically through channel factory methods. In order for communications to succeed, the client must be configured to match the service configuration.

21

Basic Desktop Programming

WHAT YOU WILL LEARN IN THIS CHAPTER

- ➤ Using the WPF designer
- ➤ Using controls for displaying information to the user, such as the `Label` and `TextBlock` controls
- ➤ Using controls for triggering events, such as the `Button` control
- ➤ Using the controls that enable users of your application to enter text, such as the `TextBox` control
- ➤ Using controls that enable you to inform users of the current state of the application and allow the user to change that state, such as the `RadioButton` and `CheckButton` controls
- ➤ Using controls that enable you to display lists of information, such as the `ListBox` and `ComboBox` controls
- ➤ Using panels to lay out your user interfaces
- ➤ Using routed commands instead of events
- ➤ Working with styling controls and applications using XAML styles
- ➤ Creating menus using the `Menu` control and routed commands
- ➤ Creating value converters
- ➤ Using timelines to create animations
- ➤ Defining and referencing static and dynamic resources
- ➤ Creating user controls when the common controls are not enough

CODE DOWNLOADS FOR THIS CHAPTER

The code downloads for this chapter are found on the book page at www.wiley.com. Click the Downloads link. The code can also be found at github.com/benperk/BeginningCSharpAndDotNET. The code is in the Chapter21 folder and individually named according to the names throughout the chapter.

The first part of this book has concerned itself with the ins and outs of C#, but now it is time to move away from the details of the programming language and into the world of the graphical user interface (GUI).

Over the years, Visual Studio has provided the Windows developers with a couple of choices for creating user interfaces: Windows Forms, which is a basic tool for creating applications that target classic Windows, and Windows Presentation Foundation (WPF), which provides a wider range of application types and attempts to solve a number of problems with Windows Forms. In this chapter you are going to learn how to use WPF to create classic Windows applications.

At the heart of the development of most graphical Windows applications is the Window Designer. You create a user interface by dragging and dropping controls from a Toolbox to your window, placing them where you want them to appear when you run the application. With WPF this is only partly true, as the user interface is in fact written entirely in another language called Extensible Application Markup Language (XAML, pronounced *zammel*). Visual Studio allows you to do both and as you get more comfortable with WPF, you are likely going to combine dragging and dropping controls with writing raw XAML.

In this chapter, you work with the Visual Studio WPF designer to create a number of windows for the card game that you wrote in previous chapters. You learn to use some of the many controls that ship with Visual Studio that cover a wide range of functionality. Through the design capabilities of Visual Studio, developing user interfaces and handling user interaction is very straightforward—and fun! Presenting all of Visual Studio's controls is impossible within the scope of this book, so this chapter looks at some of the most commonly used controls, ranging from labels and text boxes to menu bars and layout panels.

XAML

XAML is a language that uses XML syntax and enables controls to be added to a user interface in a declarative, hierarchical way. That is to say, you can add controls in the form of XML elements, and specify control properties with XML attributes. You can also have controls that contain other controls, which is essential for both layout and functionality.

> **NOTE** *XML is covered in detail in Chapter 15. If you want a quick introduction to the basics of XML at this point, it might be a good idea to go back and review the first few pages of that chapter.*

XAML is designed with today's powerful graphics cards in mind, and as such it enables you to use all the advanced capabilities that these graphics cards offer. The following lists some of these capabilities:

➤ Floating-point coordinates and vector graphics to provide layout that can be scaled, rotated, and otherwise transformed with no loss of quality

➤ 2D and 3D capabilities for advanced rendering

➤ Advanced font processing and rendering

➤ Solid, gradient, and texture fills with optional transparency for UI objects

➤ Animation storyboarding that can be used in all manner of situations, including user-triggered events such as mouse clicks on buttons

➤ Reusable resources that you can use to dynamically style controls

Separation of Concerns

One problem that exists with maintaining Windows applications that have been written over the years is that they very often mix the code that generates the user interface and the code that executes based on users' actions. This makes it difficult for multiple developers and designers to work on the same project. WPF solves this in two ways. First, by using XAML to describe the GUI rather than C#, the GUI becomes platform independent, and you can in fact render XAML without any code what-soever. Second, this means that it feels natural to place the C# code in a different file than you place the GUI code. Visual Studio utilizes something called *code-behind* files, which are C# files that are dynamically linked to the XAML files.

Because the GUI is separated from the code, it is possible to create tailor-made applications for designing the GUI, and this is exactly what Microsoft has done. The design tool Blend for Visual Studio is the favored tool used by designers when creating GUIs for WPF. This tool can load the same projects as Visual Studio, but where Visual Studio targets the developer more than the designer, the opposite is true in Blend. This means that on large projects with designers and developers, everyone can work together on the same project, using their preferred tool without fear of inadvertently influencing the others.

XAML in Action

As stated, XAML is XML, which means that as long as the files are fairly small, it is possible to see immediately what they are describing. Take a look at this small example and see if you can tell what it does:

```
<Window x:Class="Ch21Ex01.MainWindow"
        xmlns="http://schemas.microsoft.com/winfx/2006/xaml/presentation"
        xmlns:x="http://schemas.microsoft.com/winfx/2006/xaml"
        xmlns:d="http://schemas.microsoft.com/expression/blend/2008"
        xmlns:mc="http://schemas.openxmlformats.org/markup-compatibility/2006"
        xmlns:local="clr-namespace:WpfApp1"
        mc:Ignorable="d"
        Title="Hello World" Height="350" Width="525">
```

```
<Grid>
    <Button Content="Hello World"
        HorizontalAlignment="Left"
        Margin="220,151,0,0"
        VerticalAlignment="Top"
        Width="75"/>

</Grid>
</Window>
```

The XAML in this example creates a window with a single button on it. Both the window and the button display the text "Hello World". XML allows you to place tags inside other tags as long as you close them properly. When an element is placed inside another in XAML, this element becomes the content of the enclosing element, meaning that the Button could also have been written like this:

```
<Button HorizontalAlignment="Left"
        Margin="220,151,0,0"
        VerticalAlignment="Top"
        Width="75">
    Hello World
        </Button>
```

Here, the Content property of the Button has been removed and the text is now a child node of the Button control. Content can be just about anything in XAML, which is also demonstrated in this example: The Button element is the content of the Grid element, which is itself the content of the Window element.

Most controls can have content, and there are very few limits to what you can do to change the appearance of the built-in controls.

Namespaces

The Window element of the previous example is the root element of the XAML file. This element usually includes a number of namespace declarations. By default, the Visual Studio designer includes two namespaces that you should be aware of: http://schemas.microsoft.com/winfx/2006/xaml/presentation and http://schemas.microsoft.com/winfx/2006/xaml. The first one is the default namespace of WPF and declares a lot of controls that you are going to use to create user interfaces. The second one declares the XAML language itself. Namespaces don't have to be declared on the root tag, but doing so ensures that their content can be easily accessed throughout the XAML file, so there is rarely any need to move the declarations.

> **NOTE** The namespaces look like they might be URLs, but this is deceiving. In fact, they are what is known as Uniform Resource Identifiers (URIs). A URI can be any string as long as it uniquely identifies a resource. Microsoft has chosen to specify the URIs in a form that is normally used for URLs, but there is no guarantee that there is a page to be displayed if you were to type the address into a browser.

When you create a new window in Visual Studio, the presentation namespace is always declared as the default and the language namespace as `xmlns:x`. As seen with the `Window`, `Button`, and `Grid` tags, this ensures that you don't have to prefix the controls you add to the window, but the language elements you specify must be prefixed with an x.

The last namespace that you will see quite often is the system namespace: `xmlns:sys="clr-namespace:System;assembly=mscorlib"`. This namespace allows you to use the built-in types of the .NET Framework in your XAML. By doing this, the markup you write can explicitly declare the types of elements you are creating. For example, it is possible to declare an array in markup and state that the members of the array are strings:

```
<Window.Resources>
  <ResourceDictionary>
    <x:Array Type="sys:String" x:Key="localArray">
      <sys:String>"Benjamin Perkins"</sys:String>
      <sys:String>"Jon D. Reid"</sys:String>
    </x:Array>
  </ResourceDictionary>
</Window.Resources>
```

Code-Behind Files

Although XAML is a powerful way to declare user interfaces, it is not a programming language. Whenever you want to do more than presentation, you need C#. It is possible to embed C# code directly into XAML, but mixing code and markup is never recommended and you will not see it done in this book. What you will see quite a lot is the use of code-behind files. These files are normal C# files that have the same name as the XAML file, plus a `.cs` extension. Although you can call them whatever you like, it's best to stick to this naming convention. Visual Studio creates code-behind files automatically when you create a new window in your application, because it expects you to add code to the window. It also adds the `x:Class` property to the `Window` tag in the XAML:

```
<Window x:Class="Ch21Ex01.MainWindow"
```

This tells the compiler that it can find the code for this window in, not a file, but the class `Ch21Ex01.MainWindow`. Because you can specify only the fully qualified class name, and not the assembly in which the class is found, it is not possible to put the code-behind file somewhere outside of the project in which the XAML is defined. Visual Studio puts the code-behind files in the same directory as the XAML files so you never have to worry about this while working in Visual Studio.

THE PLAYGROUND

Now that you know enough about how WPF is constructed to start getting your hands dirty, it's time to look at the editor. Start by creating a new WPF project by selecting File ⇨ New ⇨ Project. From the Create a New Project dialog box, narrow the choices by C#, Windows, and Desktop to the Windows Classic Desktop node under Visual C# and select the project template WPF Application. Figure 21-1 shows the Create a new project Dialog with the proper template selected.

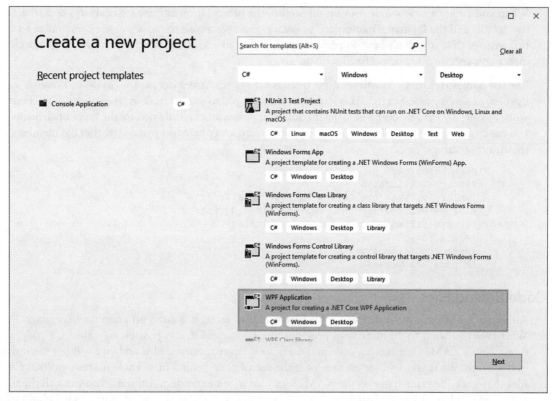

FIGURE 21-1

To be able to reuse this example with the next examples, name the project Ch21Ex01. Click Next. For the Target Framework choose .NET 5 (Current).

Visual Studio now displays an empty window and a number of panels around it. The greater part of the screen is divided in two sections. The upper section, known as the Design View, displays a WYSIWYG (What You See Is What You Get) representation of the window you are designing and the lower section, known as the XAML View, displays a textual representation of the same window.

To the right of the Design View, you see the Solution Explorer that you have seen in previous projects and a Properties panel that displays information about the current selection in the Design and XAML Views. It is worth noting that the selection in the Properties panel, XAML View, and Design View are always in sync, so if you move the cursor in the XAML View you will see the selection change in the other two.

Collapsed to the left of the Design View are a number of panels, one of which is the Toolbox. This chapter shows you how to use many of the controls from the Toolbox panel to create dialog boxes for the card game, so expand it and pin it open by clicking the pin in the top-right corner. While you are at it, expand the Common WPF Controls node in the panel as well. You will be using most of the controls shown here in this chapter.

WPF Controls

Controls combine prepackaged code and a GUI that can be reused to create more complex applications. They can define how they draw themselves by default and a set of standard behaviors. Some controls, such as the `Label`, `Button`, and `TextBox` controls are easily recognizable and have been used in Windows applications for decades. Others, such as `Canvas` and `StackPanel`, don't display anything and simply help you organize the GUI.

Out-of-the-box controls look exactly as you would expect a control to look in a standard Windows app and use the current Windows Theme to draw themselves. All of this is highly customizable and with only a few clicks you can completely change how a control is displayed. This customization is done using properties that are defined on the controls. WPF uses normal properties that you have seen before and adds a new type of property called a *dependency property*. These are examined in detail later in this chapter, but for now it is enough to know that many of the properties of WPF do more than just get and set a value; for one, they are able to notify observers of changes.

Besides defining how something looks on the screen, controls also define standard behavior, such as the ability to click a button and select something in a list. You can change what happens when a user performs an action on a control by "handling" the events that the control defines. When and how you implement the event handler will vary from application to application and from control to control, but generally speaking you will always handle the `Click` event for a button; for a `ListBox` control, you often have to react when the user changes the selection and so the `SelectionChanged` event should be handled. On other controls, such as the `Label` or `TextBlock` controls, you will rarely implement any event.

> **WARNING** *Although users are often happy when you take the time to provide a more interesting user interface than the standard Windows display, you must be careful when changing the standard behavior of controls. Imagine that you change a* `Button` *control to work only when users right-click it. Your users will think that your application is broken if nothing happens when they left-click the button. In fact, even if there are good reasons for changing the button like this, it is likely that you should be using another type of control instead of the* `Button` *control.*

You can add controls to a window in a number of ways, but the most common way is to drag and drop them from the Toolbox onto the Design View or the XAML View. In the following Try It Out you work through a simple example.

TRY IT OUT Adding Controls to a Window

As you work your way through this chapter, you will add controls to the Design View by dragging them from the Toolbox panel or by typing the XAML manually.

1. Start by dragging a `Button` control from the Toolbox onto the Design View. Notice how the text in the XAML View is updated to reflect the change you made.

2. Now drag another `Button`, but this time drop it in the XAML View below the first `Button`, but above the `</Grid>` tag.

How It Works

The result you see in the Design View might be somewhat surprising—the second button expands to fill the entire window. When you drop a control onto the Design View, Visual Studio will try to set properties and insert child elements to allow the controls to display themselves in a standard way. This does not happen when you drag controls into the XAML View, where only the tag that is used to define the control is inserted.

There are times when you want to position a control at a specific location on your window and it is difficult to drop it at exactly the right spot. When this happens, you might want to drop the control directly in the XAML View or type it manually.

> **NOTE** If you want the behavior of the Design View when you drop a control, but can't hit the right spot, just drop it anywhere and then cut and paste the XAML that was generated for you into the correct position.

Properties

As mentioned, all controls have a number of properties that are used to manipulate the behavior of the control. Some of these are easy to understand such as `Height` and `Width`, whereas others are less obvious such as `RenderTransform`. All of them can be set using the Properties panel, directly in XAML, or by manipulating the control on the Design View. The following Try It Out demonstrates setting control properties in the Design View.

> **NOTE** Visual Studio will create a default namespace for your classes when you create a new project. That namespace is subsequently used when you add new classes or windows to your project. You can change the namespace by double-clicking Properties in the Solution Explorer. If you find that your classes get a different namespace than given in the examples, it can be helpful to change the default namespace to the namespace from the book. The change will only affect new classes, not anything already in the project.

TRY IT OUT   Manipulating Properties: Ch21Ex01\MainWindow.xaml

Return to the previous example and follow these steps. As you change the properties, notice how your changes affect the XAML and Design Views. You are going to change the window to look like Figure 21-2.

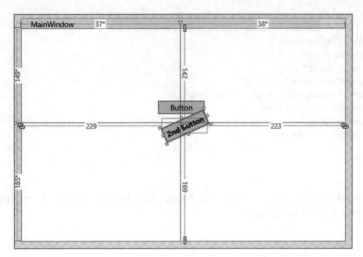

FIGURE 21-2

1. Start by selecting the second `Button` control in Design View; this is the button that is currently filling the entire window.

2. You can change the name of the control in the Properties panel at the very top. Change it to `rotatedButton`.

3. Under the Common node, change the `Content` to `2nd Button`.

4. Under Layout, change width to 75 and height to 22.

5. Expand the Text node and change the text to bold by clicking the B icon.

6. Select the first button and drag it to a position above the second button. Visual Studio will assist with the positioning by snapping the control.

7. Select the second button again, and hover the mouse pointer over the top-left corner of it. The pointer changes to double-arrow. If you move the mouse slightly down or right, then it changes to a quarter-circle with arrows on both ends. Drag down until the button is tilted down.

8. The XAML code for the window should now look like this:

```
<Window x:Class="Ch21Ex01.MainWindow"
        xmlns="http://schemas.microsoft.com/winfx/2006/xaml/presentation"
        xmlns:x="http://schemas.microsoft.com/winfx/2006/xaml"
        xmlns:d="http://schemas.microsoft.com/expression/blend/2008"
```

```
                 xmlns:mc="http://schemas.openxmlformats.org/markup-compatibility/2006"
                 xmlns:local="clr-namespace:Ch21Ex01"
                 mc:Ignorable="d"
                 Title="MainWindow" Height="350" Width="525">
        <Grid>
            <Button Content="Button" HorizontalAlignment="Left" Margin="221,115,0,0"
                VerticalAlignment="Top" Width="75"/>
            <Button x:Name="rotatedButton" Content="2nd Button" Width="75" Height="22"
                FontWeight="Bold" RenderTransformOrigin="0.5,0.5" >
                <Button.RenderTransform>
                    <TransformGroup>
                        <ScaleTransform/>
                        <SkewTransform/>
                        <RotateTransform Angle="-32.744"/>
                        <TranslateTransform/>
                    </TransformGroup>
                </Button.RenderTransform>
            </Button>
        </Grid>
    </Window>
```

9. Run the application by pressing F5. Try to resize the window. Notice that the second button moves with the window, whereas the first button stays fixed.

How It Works

Any change that you apply in any of the three views is reflected in the other views, but some things are easier to do in certain views. Changing something trivial like the text displayed on a button can be done quickly in XAML View, but adding the information needed to perform a render transformation is much quicker from Design View.

In this exercise, you began by changing the name of the button, which added the x:Name property to the button. If a control has a name, then the control name must be unique within the scope of the namespace, so you can use the name for only one control.

Next you changed the Content property, set the Height and Width of the control, and then changed the font to bold. Doing so changed the way the control displayed itself within the window. It used to fill all the space of its container, but now you have limited it to a specific size.

Then you dragged the first button to a specific position on the Design View. As you see later in this chapter, this action will not always yield the same results but is dependent on the container in which the control is placed. In this case, with the Grid container, the control can be dragged to a specific position. The action sets the Margin property on the control. Two other properties should be mentioned here: HorizontalAlignment="Left" and VerticalAlignment="Top". With these two properties set, the margin becomes relative to the top-left corner of the window and thus the control is pushed to the position you placed it in the grid. If you compare the first and second buttons at this point, you will notice that the second control has none of these properties set. By omitting the alignment properties as well as the margin properties, the control is placed at the center of the container, even at runtime. This means that the first button with the margin and alignments set is fixed when the window resizes, but the second button always stays centered.

Finally, you performed a little bit of a party trick. By dragging the control when the Rotate mouse pointer is displayed, you can rotate the control. This is a standard feature of XAML and WPF and can be applied to all controls, although there are a few controls that fail to change their content when the control itself is rotated. This includes controls that rely on Windows Forms or old Windows controls to display content.

Dependency Properties

Actions that users take on a dialog, such as selecting something from a list, should often cause other controls to change and update their display or content. For the most part, normal .NET properties are simple getters and setters, and they do not have the ability to inform other controls that they have changed. A *dependency property* is a property that is registered with the WPF property system in a way that allows extended functionality. This extended functionality includes, but is not limited to, automatic property change notifications. Specifically, dependency properties have the following features:

➤ You can use styles to change the values of dependency properties.

➤ You can set the value of a dependency property by using resources or by data binding.

➤ You can change dependency property values in an animation.

➤ You can set dependency properties hierarchically in XAML—that is, a value for a dependency property that you set on a parent element can be used to set the default value for the same dependency property of its child elements.

➤ You can configure notifications for property value changes using a well-defined coding pattern.

➤ You can configure sets of related properties so that they all update in response to a change to one of them. This is known as *coercion*. The changed property is said to *coerce* the values of the other properties.

➤ You can apply metadata to a dependency property to specify other behavior characteristics. For example, you might specify that if a given property changes, then it might be necessary to rearrange the user interface.

In practice, because of the way in which dependency properties are implemented, you might not notice much of a difference compared to ordinary properties. However, when you create your own controls, you will quickly find that a lot of functionality suddenly disappears when you use ordinary .NET properties.

Attached Properties

An *attached property* is a property that is made available to each child object of an instance of the class that defines the property. For example, as you will see later in this chapter, the Grid control that you used in the previous examples allows you to define columns and rows for ordering the child controls of the `Grid`. Each child control can then use the attached properties `Column` and `Row` to specify where it belongs in the grid:

```
<Grid HorizontalAlignment="Left" Height="167" VerticalAlignment="Top" Width="290">
    <Button Content="Button" HorizontalAlignment="Left" Margin="10,10,0,0"
                VerticalAlignment="Top" Width="75" Grid.Column="0" Grid.Row="0"
                Height="22" />
    ...
        </Grid>
```

Here, the attached property is referred to using the name of the parent element, a period, and the name of the attached property.

In WPF, attached properties serve a variety of uses. You will see a lot of attached properties shortly, when you look at how to position controls in the "Control Layout" section. You will learn how container controls define attached properties that enable child controls to define, for example, which edges of the container to dock to.

Events

In Chapter 13, you learned what events are and how to use them. This section covers particular kinds of events—specifically, the events generated by WPF controls—and introduces *routed events*, which are usually associated with user actions. For example, when the user clicks a button, that button generates an event indicating what just happened to it. Handling the event is the means by which the programmer can provide some functionality for that button.

Many of the events you handle are exposed by most of the controls that you work with in this book. This includes events such as `LostFocus` and `MouseEnter`. This is because the events themselves are inherited from base classes such as `Control` or `ContentControl`. Other events such as the `CalendarOpened` event of the `DatePicker` are more specific and only found on specialized controls. Some of the most used events are listed in Table 21-1.

TABLE 21-1: Common Control Events

EVENT	DESCRIPTION
Click	Occurs when a control is clicked. In some cases, this event also occurs when a user presses the Enter or space keys.
Drop	Occurs when a drag-and-drop operation is completed—in other words, when an object has been dragged over the control, and the user releases the mouse button.
DragEnter	Occurs when an object being dragged enters the bounds of the control.
DragLeave	Occurs when an object being dragged leaves the bounds of the control.
DragOver	Occurs when an object has been dragged over the control. This event occurs repeatedly as long as the dragged object remains over the control.

EVENT	DESCRIPTION
`KeyDown`	Occurs when a key is pressed while the control has focus. This event always occurs before `KeyPress` and `KeyUp`.
`KeyUp`	Occurs when a key is released while a control has focus. This event always occurs after `KeyDown` event.
`GotFocus`	Occurs when a control receives focus. Do not use this event to perform validation of controls. Use `Validating` and `Validated` instead.
`LostFocus`	Occurs when a control loses focus. Do not use this event to perform validation of controls. Use `Validating` and `Validated` instead.
`MouseDoubleClick`	Occurs when a control is double-clicked.
`MouseDown`	Occurs when the mouse pointer is over a control and a mouse button is pressed. This is not the same as a `Click` event because `MouseDown` occurs as soon as the button is pressed and *before* it is released.
`MouseMove`	Occurs continually as the mouse travels over the control.
`MouseUp`	Occurs when the mouse pointer is over a control and a mouse button is released.

You will see many of these events in the examples in this chapter.

Handling Events

There are two basic ways to add a handler for an event. One way is to use the Events list in the Properties window, shown in Figure 21-3, which is displayed when you click the lightning bolt button.

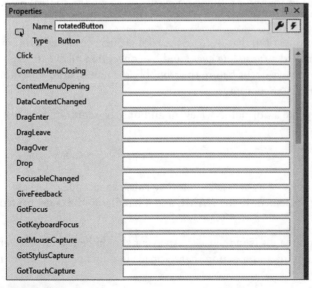

FIGURE 21-3

To add a handler for a particular event, double-click to the right of the event name in the Events list. This causes the event to be added to the XAML tag. The method signature to handle the event is added to the C# code-behind file.

```
    <Button x:Name="rotatedButton" Content="2nd Button" Width="75"
            Height="22" FontWeight="Bold" Margin="218,138,224,159"
            RenderTransformOrigin="0.5,0.5"
            Click="rotatedButton_Click">

        ...
    </Button>
private void rotatedButton_Click(object sender, RoutedEventArgs e)
    {
    }
```

You can also type the name of the event directly in XAML and add the name of the handler there. If you do this, Visual Studio will display a New Event Handler menu as you type. Selecting this will give the event the default name and create the handler in the code-behind file. If you type the name yourself, you can later right-click the event and select Go To Definition to generate the event handler in code.

Routed Events

WPF uses events that are called *routed events*. A standard .NET event is handled by the code that has explicitly subscribed to it and it is sent only to those subscribers. Routed events are different in that they can send the event to all controls in the hierarchy in which the control participates.

A routed event can travel up and down the hierarchy of the control on which the event occurred. So, if you right-click a button, the MouseRightButtonDown event will first be sent to the button itself, then to the parent of the control—in the case of the earlier example, the Grid control. If this doesn't handle it, then the event is finally sent to the window. If, on the other hand you don't want the event to travel further up the hierarchy, then you simply set the RoutedEventArgs property Handled to true, and no additional calls will be made at that point. When an event travels up the control hierarchy like this, it is called a *bubbling event*.

Routed events can also travel in the other direction, that is, from the root element to the control on which the action was performed. This is called a *tunneling event* and by convention all events like this are prefixed with the word Preview and always occur before their bubbling counterparts. An example of this is the PreviewMouseRightButtonDown event.

Finally, a routed event can behave exactly like a normal .NET event and only be sent to the control on which the action was made.

Routed Commands

Routed commands serve much the same purpose as events in that they cause some code to execute. Where events are bound directly to a single element in the XAML and a handler in the code, routed commands are more sophisticated.

The key difference between events and commands is in their use. An event should be used whenever you have a piece of code that has to respond to a user action that happens in only one place in your application. An example of such an event could be when the user clicks OK in a window to save and close it. A command can be used when you have code that will be executed to respond to actions that happen in many locations. An example of this is when the content of an application is saved. There is often a menu with a Save command that can be selected, as well as a toolbar button for the same purpose. It is possible to use event handlers to do this, but it would mean implementing the same code in many locations—a command allows you to write the code just once.

When you create a command, you must also implement code that can respond to the question, "Should this code be available to the user at the moment?" This means that when a command is associated with a button, that button can ask the command if it can execute and set its state accordingly.

A command is much more complicated to implement than an event, so you are not going to see them in use until later in this chapter, where they will be used with menu items. In the next Try It Out you add event handlers to the examples from earlier in this chapter to demonstrate the routed events.

TRY IT OUT   Routed Events: Ch21Ex01\MainWindow.xaml

This example builds on the example from earlier in the chapter. If you set the rows and columns earlier, you should remove them to match the XAML in this example.

1. Select the button `rotatedButton` and add the event `KeyDown`. You can do this by double-clicking the event in the Properties panel or by typing the XAML directly. If you type the name yourself, give it the name `rotatedButton_KeyDown`.

2. Select the `Grid` by clicking on the tag in the XAML View, and add the same event to it. Name it `Grid_KeyDown`.

3. Select the `Window` tag in the XAML View and add the event again. Name it `Window_KeyDown`.

4. Repeat steps 1 through 3, but replace the event with `PreviewKeyDown` and change the name of the event to reflect that it is the `Preview` handler. The XAML should look like this:

```xaml
<Window x:Class="Ch21Ex01.MainWindow"
        xmlns="http://schemas.microsoft.com/winfx/2006/xaml/presentation"
        xmlns:x="http://schemas.microsoft.com/winfx/2006/xaml"
        xmlns:d="http://schemas.microsoft.com/expression/blend/2008"
        xmlns:mc="http://schemas.openxmlformats.org/markup-compatibility/2006"
        xmlns:local="clr-namespace:Ch21Ex01"
        mc:Ignorable="d"
        Title="MainWindow" Height="350" Width="525" KeyDown="Window_KeyDown"
        PreviewKeyDown="Window_PreviewKeyDown">
    <Grid KeyDown="Grid_KeyDown" PreviewKeyDown="Grid_PreviewKeyDown">
        <Button Content="Button" HorizontalAlignment="Left" Margin="221,115,0,0"
            VerticalAlignment="Top" Width="75 "/>
        <Button x:Name="rotatedButton" Content="2nd Button" Width="75" Height="22"
            FontWeight="Bold" RenderTransformOrigin="0.5,0.5" KeyDown="rotatedButton_
            KeyDown" PreviewKeyDown="rotatedButton_PreviewKeyDown" >
            <Button.RenderTransform>
                <TransformGroup>
                    <ScaleTransform/>
                    <SkewTransform/>
```

```
                <RotateTransform Angle="-32.744" />
                <TranslateTransform/>
            </TransformGroup>
        </Button.RenderTransform>
    </Button>
</Grid>
</Window>
```

5. If you typed the XAML directly, right-click each of the events and add the event handler to the code-behind by selecting the Go To Definition menu item.

6. Add this code to the event handlers:

```csharp
private void Grid_KeyDown(object sender, KeyEventArgs e)
{
  MessageBox.Show("Grid handler, bubbling up");
}
private void Grid_PreviewKeyDown(object sender, KeyEventArgs e)
{
  MessageBox.Show("Grid handler, tunneling down");
}
private void rotatedButton_KeyDown(object sender, KeyEventArgs e)
{
  MessageBox.Show("rotatedButton handler, bubbling up");
}
private void rotatedButton_PreviewKeyDown(object sender, KeyEventArgs e)
{
  MessageBox.Show("rotatedButton handler, tunneling down");
}
private void Window_KeyDown(object sender, KeyEventArgs e)
{
  MessageBox.Show("Window handler, bubbling up");
}
private void Window_PreviewKeyDown(object sender, KeyEventArgs e)
{
  MessageBox.Show("Window handler, tunneling down");
}
```

7. Run the application by pressing F5.

8. Select the rotated button by clicking it and pressing any key except Enter or the spacebar key. Observe the events being executed in turn.

9. Stop the application.

10. Go to the `Grid_PreviewKeyDown` event handler and add this line below the `MessageBox` line:

```csharp
e.Handled = true;
```

11. Repeat steps 7 and 8.

How It Works

The `KeyDown` and `PreviewKeyDown` events demonstrate bubbling and tunneling events. When you press a key with `rotatedButton` selected, you see each of the event handlers executing, one after another.

First the `Preview` events execute, starting with the handler on `Window`, then the `Grid`, and finally the `rotatedButton`. Then the `KeyDown` events execute, but in the opposite order, starting with the event handler on the `rotatedButton` and finishing with the handler on `Window`.

The Enter and Space keys are handled specially by the button control. Both of these are treated as a Click, and you will therefore only see the Preview events fired for these keys.

Then you added this line:

```
e.Handled = true;
```

This changed the behavior dramatically. By setting the `Handled` property of the `RoutedEventArgs` you not only stopped the execution of the tunneling events, but also of the bubbling events. This is generally true for all events like this.

Control Types

WPF has a lot of controls to choose from. Two types of interest are the Content and Items controls. Content controls, such as the `Button` control, have a `Content` property that can be set to numbers, strings, and objects, as well as any other control. This means that you can specify how the control is displayed, but you must specify zero or exactly one control directly in the content. That being said, you can specify an Items control, which is a control that allows you to insert multiple controls as content. An example of an Items control is the `Grid` control. When you are creating user interfaces, you are continually combining these two control types.

In addition to Content and Items controls, there are a number of other types of controls that don't allow you to use other controls as their content. One example of this is the `Image` control, which is used to display an image. Changing that behavior defeats the purpose of the control.

CONTROL LAYOUT

So far in this chapter, you have used the `Grid` element to lay out a few controls, primarily because that is the control supplied by default when you create a new WPF application. However, you haven't yet examined the full capabilities of this class, nor have you learned about the other layout containers that you can use to achieve alternative layouts. This section looks at control layout in more detail, as it is a fundamental concept of WPF.

Basic Layout Concepts

In WPF you use layout controls to assist you with the layout of the items on a window. There are a number of these controls, but before you start using them, there are a few basic concepts and a visual aid provided by Visual Studio that you should know about.

Stack Order

When a container control contains multiple child controls, they are drawn in a specific stack order. You might be familiar with this concept from drawing packages. The best way to think of stack order is to imagine that each control is contained in a plate of glass, and the container contains a stack of these plates of glass. The appearance of the container, therefore, is what you would see if you looked down from the top through these layers of glass. The controls contained by the container overlap, so what you see is determined by the order of the glass plates. If a control is higher up the stack, then it will be the control that you see in the overlap area. Controls lower down may be partially or completely hidden by controls above them.

This also affects *hit testing* such as when you click on a control with the mouse. The target control will always be the one that is uppermost in the stack when considering overlapping controls. The stack order of controls is determined by the order in which they appear in the list of children for a container. The first child in a container is placed on the lowest layer in the stack, and the last child on the topmost layer. The children between the first and last child are placed on increasingly higher layers. The stack order of controls has additional implications for some of the layout controls that you can use in WPF, as you will see shortly.

Alignment, Margins, Padding, and Dimensions

Earlier examples used the `Margin`, `HorizontalAlignment`, and `VerticalAlignment` properties to position controls in a `Grid` container, but without going into much detail about their use. You have also seen how you can use `Height` and `Width` to specify dimensions. These properties, along with `Padding`, which you haven't looked at yet, are useful for all of the layout controls (or most of them, as you will see), but in different ways. Different layout controls can also set default values for these properties. You'll see a lot of this by example in subsequent sections, but before doing that, it is worth covering the basics.

The two alignment properties, `HorizontalAlignment` and `VerticalAlignment`, determine how the control is aligned. `HorizontalAlignment` can be set to `Left`, `Right`, `Center`, or `Stretch`. `Left` and `Right` tend to position controls to the left or right edges of the container, `Center` positions controls in the middle, and `Stretch` changes the width of the control so that its edges reach to the sides of the container. `VerticalAlignment` is similar, and has the values `Top`, `Bottom`, `Center`, or `Stretch`.

`Margin` and `Padding` specify the space to leave blank around the edges of controls and inside the edges of controls, respectively. Earlier examples used `Margin` to position controls relative to the edges of a window. This worked because with `HorizontalAlignment` set to `Left` and `VerticalAlignment` set to `Top`, the control is positioned tight against the top-left corner, and `Margin` inserted a gap around the edge of the control. `Padding` is used similarly, but spaces out the content of a control from its edges. This is particularly useful for `Border`, as you will see in the next section. Both `Padding` and `Margin` can be specified in four parts (in the form `leftAmount, topAmount, rightAmount, bottomAmount`) or as a single value (a `Thickness` value).

Later, you will see how `Height` and `Width` are often controlled by other properties. For example, with `HorizontalAlignment` set to `Stretch`, the `Width` property of a control changes as the width of its container changes.

Border

The `Border` control is a very simple, and very useful, container control. It holds a single child, not multiple children like the more complicated controls you'll look at in a moment. This child will be sized to completely fill the `Border` control. This might not seem particularly useful, but remember that you can use the `Margin` and `Padding` properties to position the `Border` within its container, and the content of the `Border` within the edges of the `Border`. You can also set, for example, the `Back-ground` property of a `Border` so that it is visible. You will see this control in action shortly.

Visual Debugging Tools

When you run a WPF app in debug mode, Visual Studio overlays the application with a small 4-point menu at the top center of the window. Three of the four menu items toggle debugging functionality on and off, and the remaining item opens the Live Visual Tree. The next Try It Out continues on the previous example and demonstrates the visual tools.

TRY IT OUT   Using Visual Debugging Tools: Ch21Ex01\MainWindow.xaml

Return to the first Try It Out example in this chapter and follow these steps.

1. Run the app in debug mode by pressing F5.

2. Toggle Enable Selection on by clicking the Select Element menu item.

3. Click the button with the "2nd button" text. Note how a red dotted outline is displayed on the button when the mouse is over the control.

4. Open the Live Visual Tree by clicking the left-most menu item.

5. In Visual Studio, the Live Visual Tree is a tab on the left; click it to expand it.

6. Depending on where you clicked the button, the Live Visual Tree will have selected the `rotated-Button` or a close-by element.

7. Right-click the `rotatedButton` in the Live Visual Tree and select Show Properties. This opens the Live Properties Explorer. In this you can see and modify the properties of the control as they are during runtime.

8. Click the `MainWindow` to bring the running app back up in front of Visual Studio.

9. Click the right-most menu item, which is named Track Focused Element.

10. Click the button with the text "Button" and notice that the values in the Live Properties Explorer change to reflect the new selection. If you toggle the Track Focused Element off, then the explorer will no longer change its content when you select something.

11. Finally, toggle the Display Layout Adorners menu item.

12. Hover the mouse over different elements in the display, and notice how Visual Studio displays lines that indicate how the margins are applied when you click them (note you may need to click the Track Focuses Element option to see this).

How It Works

The Visual Debugging tools are useful for examining how the UI of an app is behaving at runtime. It can be very hard to determine why elements of a UI behave in a certain way at runtime, and these tools will allow you to dig down and examine the properties of controls as they are actually applied as the app executes.

Layout Panels

All content layout controls derive from the abstract `Panel` class. This class simply defines a container that can hold a collection of objects derived from `UIElement`. All WPF controls derive from `UIElement`. You cannot use the `Panel` class directly for control layout, but you can derive from it if you want to. Alternatively, you can use one of the layout controls that derive from `Panel`. Table 21-2 describes the most common panels.

TABLE 21-2: Common Layout Panels

PANEL	DESCRIPTION
Canvas	This control enables you to position child controls any way you see fit. It doesn't place any restrictions on child control positioning, nor does it provide any assistance in positioning.
DockPanel	This control enables you to dock child controls against one of its four edges. The last child control fills the remaining space.
Grid	This control enables flexible positioning of child controls. You can divide the layout of this control into rows and columns, which enables you to align controls in a grid layout.
StackPanel	This control positions its child controls in a sequential horizontal or vertical layout.
WrapPanel	This control positions its child controls in a sequential horizontal or vertical layout as `StackPanel`, but rather than a single row or column of controls, this control wraps its children into multiple rows or columns according to the space available.

Canvas

The `Canvas` control provides complete freedom over control positioning. Another thing about `Canvas` is that the `HorizontalAlignment` and `VerticalAlignment` properties used with a child element will have no effect whatsoever over the positioning of those elements.

You can use `Margin` to position elements in a `Canvas` as it was done in earlier examples, but a better way is to use the `Canvas.Left`, `Canvas.Top`, `Canvas.Right`, and `Canvas.Bottom` attached properties that the `Canvas` class exposes:

```
<Canvas...>
  <Button Canvas.Top="10" Canvas.Left="10"...>Button1</Button>
</Canvas>
```

The preceding code positions a `Button` so that its top edge is 10 pixels from the top edge of the `Canvas`, and its left edge is 10 pixels from the left edge of the `Canvas`. Note that the `Top` and `Left` properties take precedence over `Bottom` and `Right`. For example, if you specify both `Top` and `Bottom`, then the `Bottom` property is ignored.

Figure 21-4 shows two Rectangle controls positioned in a Canvas control, with the window resized to two sizes.

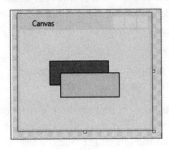
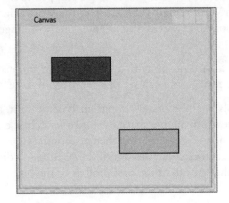

FIGURE 21-4

> **NOTE** All of the example layouts in this section can be found in the Layout-Examples project in the downloadable code for this chapter. See the "CODE DOWNLOADS FOR THIS CHAPTER" section at the beginning of this chapter for information on how to download this chapter's code.

One Rectangle is positioned relative to the top-left corner, and one is positioned relative to the bottom-right corner. As you resize the window, these relative positions are maintained. You can also see the importance of the stacking order of the Rectangle controls. The bottom-right Rectangle is higher up in the stacking order, so when they overlap this is the control that you see.

The code for this example is as follows (you can find it in the downloadable code LayoutExamples\Canvas.xaml):

```
<Window x:Class="LayoutExamples.Canvas"
        xmlns="http://schemas.microsoft.com/winfx/2006/xaml/presentation"
        xmlns:x="http://schemas.microsoft.com/winfx/2006/xaml"
        xmlns:d="http://schemas.microsoft.com/expression/blend/2008"
        xmlns:mc="http://schemas.openxmlformats.org/markup-compatibility/2006"
        xmlns:local="clr-namespace:LayoutExamples"
        mc:Ignorable="d"
        Title="Canvas" Height="300" Width="300">
    <Canvas Background="AliceBlue">
        <Rectangle Canvas.Left="50" Canvas.Top="50" Height="40" Width="100"
    Stroke="Black" Fill="Chocolate" />
        <Rectangle Canvas.Right="50" Canvas.Bottom="50" Height="40" Width="100"
    Stroke="Black" Fill="Bisque" />
    </Canvas>
</Window>
```

DockPanel

The DockPanel control, as its name suggests, enables you to dock controls to its edges. This sort of layout should be familiar to you, even if you've never stopped to notice it before. It is how, for example, the Ribbon control in Word remains at the top of the Word window, or how the various windows in Visual Studio are positioned. In Visual Studio you can also change the docking of windows by dragging them around.

DockPanel has a single attached property that child controls can use to specify the edge to which controls dock: DockPanel.Dock. You can set this property to Left, Top, Right, or Bottom.

The stack order of controls in a DockPanel is extremely important, as every time you dock a control to an edge you also reduce the available space of subsequent child controls. For example, you might dock a toolbar to the top of a DockPanel and then a second toolbar to the left of the DockPanel. The first control would stretch across the entire top of the DockPanel display area, but the second control would only stretch from the bottom of the first toolbar to the bottom of the DockPanel along the left edge.

The last child control you specify will (usually) fill the area that remains after all the previous children have been positioned. (You can control this behavior, which is why this statement is qualified.)

When you position a control in a DockPanel, the area occupied by the control might be smaller than the area of the DockPanel that is reserved for the control. For example, if you dock a Button with a Width of 100, a Height of 50, and a HorizontalAlignment of Left to the top of a DockPanel, then there will be space to the right of the Button that isn't used by other docked children. In addition, if the Button control has a Margin of 20, then a total of 90 pixels at the top of the DockPanel will be reserved (the height of the control plus the top and bottom margins). You need to take this behavior into account when you use DockPanel for layout; otherwise, you can end up with unexpected results.

Figure 21-5 shows a sample DockPanel layout.

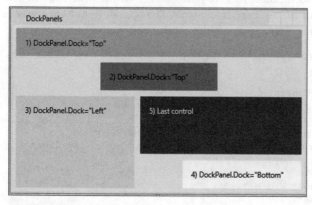

FIGURE 21-5

The code for this layout is as follows (you can find it in the downloadable code
`LayoutExamples\DockPanels.xaml`):

```xml
<Window x:Class="LayoutExamples.DockPanels"
        xmlns="http://schemas.microsoft.com/winfx/2006/xaml/presentation"
        xmlns:x="http://schemas.microsoft.com/winfx/2006/xaml"
        xmlns:d="http://schemas.microsoft.com/expression/blend/2008"
        xmlns:mc="http://schemas.openxmlformats.org/markup-compatibility/2006"
        xmlns:local="clr-namespace:LayoutExamples"
        mc:Ignorable="d"
        Title="DockPanels" Height="300" Width="500">
    <DockPanel Background="AliceBlue">
        <Border DockPanel.Dock="Top" Padding="10" Margin="5"
Background="Aquamarine" Height="45">
            <Label>1) DockPanel.Dock="Top"</Label>
        </Border>
        <Border DockPanel.Dock="Top" Padding="10" Margin="5"
Background="PaleVioletRed" Height="45" Width="200">
            <Label>2) DockPanel.Dock="Top"</Label>
        </Border>
        <Border DockPanel.Dock="Left" Padding="10" Margin="5"
Background="Bisque" Width="200">
            <Label>3) DockPanel.Dock="Left"</Label>
        </Border>
        <Border DockPanel.Dock="Bottom" Padding="10" Margin="5"
Background="Ivory" Width="200" HorizontalAlignment="Right">
            <Label>4) DockPanel.Dock="Bottom"</Label>
        </Border>
        <Border Padding="10" Margin="5" Background="BlueViolet">
            <Label Foreground="White">5) Last control</Label>
        </Border>
    </DockPanel>
</Window>
```

This code uses the `Border` control introduced earlier to clearly mark out the docked control regions in the example layout, along with `Label` controls to output simple informative text. To understand the layout, you must read it from top to bottom, looking at each control in turn:

1. The first `Border` control is docked to the top of the `DockPanel`. The total area taken up in the `DockPanel` is the top 55 pixels (`Height` + 2 × `Margin`). Note that the `Padding` property does not affect this layout, as it is inside the edge of the `Border`, but this property does control the positioning of the embedded `Label` control. The `Border` control fills any available space along the edge it is docked to if not constrained by `Height` or `Width` properties, which is why it stretches across the `DockPanel`.

2. The second `Border` control is also docked to the top of the `DockPanel`, and takes up another 55 pixels from the top of the display area. This `Border` control also includes a `Width` property, which causes the border to take up only a portion of the width of the `DockPanel`. It is positioned centrally, as the default value for `HorizonalAlignment` in a `DockPanel` is `Center`.

3. The third `Border` control is docked to the left of the `DockPanel` and takes up 210 pixels of the left of the display.

4. The fourth `Border` control is docked to the bottom of the `DockPanel` and takes up 30 pixels plus the height of the `Label` control it contains (whatever that is). This height is determined by the `Margin`, `Padding`, and contents of the `Border` control, as it is not specified explicitly. The `Border` control is locked to the bottom-right corner of the `DockPanel`, as it has a `HorizontalAlignment` of `Right`.

5. The fifth and final `Border` control fills the remaining space.

Run this example and experiment with resizing content. Note that the further up the stacking order a control is, the more priority is given to its space. By shrinking the window, the fifth `Border` control can be completely obscured by controls further up the stacking order. Be careful when using `Dock-Panel` control layout to avoid this, perhaps by setting minimum dimensions for the window.

StackPanel

You can think of `StackPanel` as being a slimmed down version of `DockPanel`, where the edge, to which child controls are docked, is fixed for those controls. The other difference between these controls is that the last child control of a `StackPanel` doesn't fill the remaining space. However, controls will, by default, stretch to the edges of the `StackPanel` control.

The direction in which controls are stacked is determined by three properties. `Orientation` can be set to `Horizontal` or `Vertical`, and `HorizontalAlignment` and `VerticalAlignment` can be used to determine whether control stacks are positioned next to the top, bottom, left, or right edge of the `StackPanel`. You can even make the stacked controls stack at the center of the `StackPanel` using the `Center` value for the alignment property you use.

Figure 21-6 shows two `StackPanel` controls, each of which contains three buttons. The top `Stack-Panel` has its `Orientation` property set to `Horizontal` and the bottom one has `Orientation` set to `Vertical`.

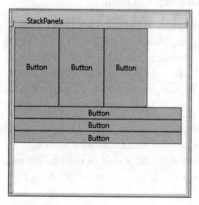

FIGURE 21-6

The code used here is as follows (you can find it in the downloadable code
`LayoutExamples\StackPanels.xaml`):

```
<Window x:Class="LayoutExamples.StackPanels"
        xmlns="http://schemas.microsoft.com/winfx/2006/xaml/presentation"
        xmlns:x="http://schemas.microsoft.com/winfx/2006/xaml"
        xmlns:d="http://schemas.microsoft.com/expression/blend/2008"
        xmlns:mc="http://schemas.openxmlformats.org/markup-compatibility/2006"
        xmlns:local="clr-namespace:LayoutExamples"
        mc:Ignorable="d"
        Title="StackPanels" Height="300" Width="300">
    <Grid>
        <StackPanel HorizontalAlignment="Left" Height="128" VerticalAlignment="Top"
Width="284" Orientation="Horizontal">
            <Button Content="Button" Height="128" VerticalAlignment="Top"
                Width="75"/>
            <Button Content="Button" Height="128" VerticalAlignment="Top"
                Width="75"/>
            <Button Content="Button" Height="128" VerticalAlignment="Top"
                Width="75"/>
        </StackPanel>
        <StackPanel HorizontalAlignment="Left" Height="128" VerticalAlignment="Top"
Width="284" Margin="0,128,0,0" Orientation="Vertical">
            <Button Content="Button" HorizontalAlignment="Left" Width="284"/>
            <Button Content="Button" HorizontalAlignment="Left" Width="284"/>
            <Button Content="Button" HorizontalAlignment="Left" Width="284"/>
        </StackPanel>
    </Grid>
</Window>
```

WrapPanel

`WrapPanel` is essentially an extended version of `StackPanel`; controls that "don't fit" are moved to
additional rows (or columns). Figure 21-7 shows a `WrapPanel` control containing multiple shapes,
with the window resized to two sizes.

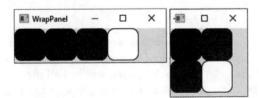

FIGURE 21-7

The code to achieve this effect is shown here (you can find it in the downloadable code `LayoutExamples\WrapPanel.xaml`):

```
<Window x:Class="LayoutExamples.WrapPanel"
        xmlns="http://schemas.microsoft.com/winfx/2006/xaml/presentation"
        xmlns:x="http://schemas.microsoft.com/winfx/2006/xaml"
        xmlns:d="http://schemas.microsoft.com/expression/blend/2008"
```

```
          xmlns:mc="http://schemas.openxmlformats.org/markup-compatibility/2006"
          xmlns:local="clr-namespace:LayoutExamples"
          mc:Ignorable="d"
          Title="WrapPanel" Height="92" Width="260">
    <WrapPanel Background="AliceBlue">
        <Rectangle Fill="#FF000000" Height="50" Width="50" Stroke="Black"
    RadiusX="10" RadiusY="10" />
        <Rectangle Fill="#FF111111" Height="50" Width="50" Stroke="Black"
    RadiusX="10" RadiusY="10" />
        <Rectangle Fill="#FF222222" Height="50" Width="50" Stroke="Black"
    RadiusX="10" RadiusY="10"/>
        <Rectangle Fill="#FFFFFFFF" Height="50" Width="50" Stroke="Black"
    RadiusX="10" RadiusY="10" />
    </WrapPanel>
    </Window>
```

WrapPanel controls are a great way to create a dynamic layout that enables users to control exactly how content should be viewed.

Grid

Grid controls can have multiple rows and columns that you can use to lay out child controls. You have used Grid controls several times already in this chapter, but in all cases you used a Grid with a single row and a single column. To add more rows and columns, you must use the RowDefinitions and ColumnDefinitions properties, which are collections of RowDefinition and ColumnDefinition objects, respectively, and are specified using property element syntax:

```
<Grid>
  <Grid.RowDefinitions>
    <RowDefinition />
    <RowDefinition />
  </Grid.RowDefinitions>
  <Grid.ColumnDefinitions>
    <ColumnDefinition />
    <ColumnDefinition />
  </Grid.ColumnDefinitions>
  ...
  </Grid>
```

This code defines a Grid control with two rows and two columns. Note that no extra information is required here; with this code, each row and column is dynamically resized automatically as the Grid control resizes. Each row will be half of the height of the Grid, and each column will be half the width. You can display lines between cells in a Grid by setting the ShowGridlines property to True.

> **NOTE** You can also define rows and columns in the grid by clicking the edges of the grid in the Design View. If you move the mouse pointer to the edge of the grid, a line is drawn across the Design View; if you click the edge, the necessary XAML is inserted. When you do this, the Width and Height properties of the rows and columns are always set by the designer, but you can delete them or drag the lines to suit your needs.

You can control the resizing with the `Width`, `Height`, `MinWidth`, `MaxWidth`, `MinHeight`, and `MaxHeight` properties. For example, setting the `Width` property of a column ensures that the column stays at that width. You can also set the `Width` property of a column to `*`, which means "fill the remaining space after calculating the width of all other columns." This is actually the default. When you have multiple columns with a `Width` of `*`, then the remaining space is divided between them equally. The `*` value can also be used with the `Height` property of rows. The other possible value for `Height` and `Width` is `Auto`, which sizes the row or column according to its content. You can also use `GridSplitter` controls to enable users to customize the dimensions of rows and columns by clicking and dragging.

You can also use numbered `*`s to use proportional spacing. For example, if two rows have heights `*` and `2*`, then the first gets one share and the second gets two shares of the remaining space. If those are all of the rows, then the first gets 1/3 of the space and the second gets 2/3.

Child controls of a `Grid` control can use the attached `Grid.Column` and `Grid.Row` properties to specify which cell they are contained in. Both these properties default to `0`, so if you omit them, then the child control is placed in the top-left cell. Child controls can also use `Grid.ColumnSpan` and `Grid.RowSpan` to be positioned over multiple cells in a table, where the upper-left cell is specified by `Grid.Column` and `Grid.Row`.

In the following Try It Out you will use the properties of the `Grid` to create rows and columns and use a `GridSplitter` to change these properties at runtime.

TRY IT OUT   Using Rows and Columns: Ch21Ex01\MainWindow.xaml

Return to the example from the beginning of the chapter with the two buttons and follow these steps.

1. Select the `Grid` control by clicking in the XAML View.

2. Move the mouse pointer to the top edge of the grid in Design View; you'll see a line appear across the surface of the grid. Allow room for a button and click to create two columns.

3. Repeat step 2 on the left edge of the grid, creating two rows.

4. Select the first of the two buttons. Note that the action of adding the rows and columns automatically added the `Grid.Row` and `Grid.Column` properties to the button. Change the `Grid.Row` and `Grid.Column` attached properties to `0`.

5. Adjust the `Margin` property to make the button fully visible in the cell.

6. The second button has also been adjusted. For example, a `Margin` has been added. Now delete the `Margin` property from the button.

7. Add a `GridSplitter` control to the XAML View just before the closing tag of the `Grid` control and set its properties like this:

    ```
    <GridSplitter Grid.RowSpan="2" Width="3" BorderThickness="2" BorderBrush="Black"/>
    ```

8. Run the application. The complete XAML should look like this:

    ```
    <Window x:Class="Ch21Ex01.MainWindow"
            xmlns="http://schemas.microsoft.com/winfx/2006/xaml/presentation"
    ```

```
          xmlns:x="http://schemas.microsoft.com/winfx/2006/xaml"
          xmlns:d="http://schemas.microsoft.com/expression/blend/2008"
          xmlns:mc="http://schemas.openxmlformats.org/markup-compatibility/2006"
          xmlns:local="clr-namespace:Ch21Ex01"
          mc:Ignorable="d"
          Title="MainWindow" Height="350" Width="525" KeyDown="Window_KeyDown"
          PreviewKeyDown="Window_PreviewKeyDown">
    <Grid KeyDown="Grid_KeyDown" PreviewKeyDown="Grid_PreviewKeyDown">
      <Grid.RowDefinitions>
        <RowDefinition Height="109*"/>
        <RowDefinition Height="210*"/>
      </Grid.RowDefinitions>
      <Grid.ColumnDefinitions>
        <ColumnDefinition Width="191*"/>
        <ColumnDefinition Width="326*"/>
      </Grid.ColumnDefinitions>
      <Button x:Name="button" Content="Button" HorizontalAlignment="Left"
              Margin="27,4,0,0" VerticalAlignment="Top" Width="75" Grid.Column="0"
              Grid.Row="0"/>
      <Button x:Name="rotatedButton" Content="2nd Button" Width="75" Height="22"
              FontWeight="Bold" RenderTransformOrigin="0.5,0.5"
              KeyDown="rotatedButton_KeyDown"
              PreviewKeyDown="rotatedButton_PreviewKeyDown" Grid.Column="1"
              Grid.Row="1" >
        <Button.RenderTransform>
          <TransformGroup>
            <ScaleTransform/>
            <SkewTransform/>
            <RotateTransform Angle="-23.896"/>
            <TranslateTransform/>
          </TransformGroup>
        </Button.RenderTransform>
      </Button>
      <GridSplitter Grid.RowSpan="2" Width="3" BorderThickness="2"
                    BorderBrush="Black" />
    </Grid>
</Window>
```

Figure 21-8 shows the application running with the splitter pushed to two positions.

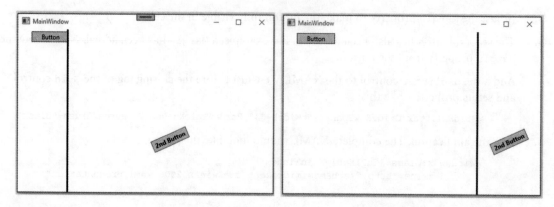

FIGURE 21-8

How It Works

By dividing the grid into two columns and two rows, you have changed how the controls can be positioned in the grid. When you set the `Grid.Row` and `Grid.Column` to `0` for the first button, you move it from its previous position on the form to the top-left section.

The second button more or less stays put, but when you drag the `GridSplitter` slider, you see that the margin of the button is now relative to the left edge of the column in which it is placed, meaning that it slides across the window as you move the slider.

THE GAME CLIENT

Now that you know the basics of what it means to work with WPF and Visual Studio, it is time to start working with the controls to create something useful. The remaining sections of this chapter are dedicated to writing a game client for the card game you have been developing over the previous chapters. You are going to use a lot of controls and you are even going to write one yourself.

In this chapter, you are going to write the supporting dialog boxes of the game—this includes the About, Options, and New Game windows.

The About Window

An About window, or About box as it's sometimes called, is used to display information about the developer of the application and the application itself. Some About windows are quite complex, like the one found in Microsoft Office applications and Visual Studio, and display version and licensing information. The About window is often accessible from the Help menu where it is usually the last item on the list.

Figure 21-9 shows a screenshot of the finished dialog box that you are about to create.

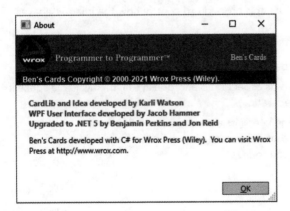

FIGURE 21-9

Designing the User Interface

An About window is not something that the user is going to see very often. In fact, the reason that it is usually located on the Help menu is that it is very often only used when the user needs to find information about the version of the application or who to contact when something is wrong. But this also means that it is something the user has a specific purpose for visiting and if you include such a window in your application, you should treat it as important.

Whenever you are designing an application, you should strive to keep the look and feel as consistent as possible. This means that you should stick to a few select colors and use the same styling of controls everywhere in the application. In the case of Ben's Cards, you are going to work with three main colors—red, black, and white.

If you look at Figure 21-9, you will see that the top-left corner of the window is occupied by a Wrox Press logo. You have not used images before, but adding a few select images to your applications can make the user interface look more professional.

The Image Control

Image is a very simple control that can be used to great effect. It allows you to display a single image and to resize this image as you see fit. The control exposes two key properties, as shown in Table 21-3.

TABLE 21-3: Image Control Properties

PROPERTY	DESCRIPTION
Source	Use this property to specify the location of the image. This can be a location on disk or somewhere on the web. As you will see later in this chapter, it is also possible to create a static resource and use it as the source.
Stretch	It's actually pretty rare to have an image that is exactly the right size for your purpose, and sometimes the size of the image must change as the application window is resized. You can use this property to control how the image behaves. There are four possibilities:
	None—The image doesn't resize.
	Fill—The image resizes to fill the entire space. This may contort the image.
	Uniform—The image keeps its aspect ratio and doesn't fill the available space if this would change the aspect ratio.
	UniformToFill—The image keeps its aspect ratio and fills the available space. If keeping the ratio means that some of the image is too large for the space available, the image is clipped to fit.

The Label Control

You have already seen this most simple of controls used in some of the previous examples. It displays simple text information to the user and in some cases relays information about shortcut keys. The control uses the Content property to display its text. The Label control displays text on a single line.

If you prefix a letter with an underscore "_" character, the letter will become underlined and it will then be possible to access the control directly by using the prefixed letter and Alt. For example, _Name assigns the shortcut Alt+N to any control directly following the label.

The TextBlock Control

Like `Label`, this control displays simple text without any complicated formatting. Unlike the `Label`, the `TextBlock` control is capable of displaying multiple lines of text. It is not possible to format individual parts of the text.

The `TextBlock` displays the text even if it will not fit in the space granted to the control. The control itself does not provide any scrollbars in this case, but it can be wrapped in a handy view control when needed: the `ScrollViewer`.

The Button Control

Like the `Label` control, you have already seen quite a bit of the `Button` control. This control is used everywhere and is easily recognized on a user interface. Your users will expect that they can left-click it to perform an action—no more and no less. Altering this behavior will most likely lead to bad interface design and frustrated users.

By default, the button displays itself with a single short line of text or an image that describes what happens when you click it.

The button does not contain any properties to display images or text, but you can use the `Content` property to display simple text or embed an `Image` control in the content to display an image. You can find this code in the downloadable code `Ch21Ex01\ImageButton.xaml`:

```
<Button HorizontalAlignment="Left" VerticalAlignment="Top" Width="75" Margin="10" >
    <StackPanel Orientation="Horizontal">
        <Image Source=".\Images\Delete_black_32x32.png" Stretch="UniformToFill"
Width="16" Height="16" />
        <TextBlock>Delete</TextBlock>
    </StackPanel>
      </Button>
```

> **NOTE** The image for the button is included in the code download in
> `Ch21Ex01\Images`.

Figure 21-10 shows the Delete button with text and an image.

FIGURE 21-10

> **NOTE** To complete the following example, you need an image for a
> banner. This image is included in the download for this chapter in
> `BensCards.WPF\Images\Banner.png`.

TRY IT OUT   Creating the About Window: BensCards Gui\AboutWindow.xaml

Before you can start the About window, you need a project to work on. This is just one of many windows you are going to make in this chapter, so go ahead and create a new WPF Application project and name it `BensCards.WPF`. Name the solution `BensCards`.

1. In the Solution Explorer, right-click the BensCards.WPF project and select Add ➪ Window (WPF). Name the window `AboutWindow.xaml`.

2. Resize the window by clicking and dragging it or by setting these properties:

```
Height="300" Width="434" MinWidth="434" MinHeight="300"
ResizeMode="CanResizeWithGrip"
```

3. Select the `Grid` and create four rows by clicking at the edges of the grid. Don't worry too much about the exact positioning of the rows; instead, change the values like this:

```xml
<Grid.RowDefinitions>
    <RowDefinition Height="58"/>
    <RowDefinition Height="20"/>
    <RowDefinition />
    <RowDefinition Height="42"/>
</Grid.RowDefinitions>
```

4. Drag a `Canvas` control from the Toolbox into the top-most row. Remove any properties inserted by Visual Studio and add this:

```
Grid.Row="0" Background="#C40D42"
```

5. Right-click the project and Select Add ➪ New Folder. Create a directory called `Images`.

6. Right-click the new directory in the Solution Explorer and select Add ➪ Existing Item. Browse to the images of this chapter. Select them all and click Add. The banner is now displayed in Design View.

7. Drag an image control onto the canvas. Change its properties like so:

```
Height="56" Canvas.Left="0" Canvas.Top="0" Stretch="UniformToFill"
Source=".\Images\Banner.png"
```

8. Select the `Canvas` control and drag a `Label` control onto it. Change its properties like this:

```
Canvas.Right="10" Canvas.Top="25" Content="Ben's Cards" Foreground="#FFF7EFEF"
FontFamily="Times New Roman"
```

9. Select the `Grid` control and drag a new `Canvas` control onto it. Change its properties to:

```
Grid.Row="1" Background="Black"
```

10. Select the new `Canvas` control and drag a `Label` onto it. Change its properties like this (note you can use `(c)` instead of © if that is easier):

```
Canvas.Left="5" Canvas.Top="0" FontWeight="Bold" FontFamily="Arial"
Foreground="White"
Content="Ben's Cards © Copyright 2020 - 2021 Wrox Press (Wiley)"
```

11. Select the Grid control again, and drag the last Canvas into the bottom-most row. Change its properties like this:

```
Grid.Row="3"
```

12. Select the new Canvas control and drag a Button onto it. Change its properties to this:

```
Content="_OK" Canvas.Right="12" Canvas.Bottom="10" Width="75"
```

13. Select the Grid again, and drag a StackPanel into the third row. Change its properties to:

```
Grid.Row="2"
```

14. Select the StackPanel and drag two Label controls and one TextBlock into it, in that order.

15. Change the top-most Label like this:

```
Content="CardLib and Idea developed by Ben's Watson" HorizontalAlignment="Left"
VerticalAlignment="Top" Padding="20,20,0,0" FontWeight="Bold"
Foreground="#FF8B6F6F"
```

16. Change the next Label like this:

```
Content="WPF User Interface developed by Jacob Hammer"
HorizontalAlignment="Left" Padding="20,0,0,0" VerticalAlignment="Top"
FontWeight="Bold" Foreground="#FF8B6F6F"
```

17. Change TextBlock like this:

```
Text="Ben's Cards developed with C# for Wrox Press (Wiley).
You can visit Wrox Press at http://www.wrox.com."
Margin="0,10,0,0" Padding="20,0,0,0" TextWrapping="Wrap"
HorizontalAlignment="Left" VerticalAlignment="Top" Height="39"
```

18. Double-click the button and, in the event handler, add this code:

```
private void Button_Click(object sender, RoutedEventArgs e)
{
   this.Close();
}
```

19. In the Solution Explorer, double-click the App.xaml file and change the StartupUri property from MainWindow.xaml to AboutWindow.xaml.

20. Run the application.

How It Works

You begin by setting some properties on the window. By setting MinWidth and MinHeight, you prevent the user from resizing the window to a point where it obscures the content. The ResizeMode is set to CanResizeWithGrip, which displays a small grip section in the bottom-right corner of the window that indicates to the user that the window can be resized.

Next you add four rows to the grid. By doing this, you define the basic structure of the window. By setting rows 1, 2, and 4 to fixed heights, you ensure that only the third row can change height; this is the row that holds the content.

Then you add the first `Canvas` control. This provides you with a handy place to set the background color of the first row. By ensuring that the canvas has no specific size, you force the canvas to fill the top row in the grid.

The `Image` control that is added to the canvas is fixed to the left and top edges of the canvas. This ensures that as the window resizes, the image stays put. You also gave the image a fixed height, but left the width open. With the `Stretch` property set to `UniformToFill`, this allows the `Image` control to use the height as a guide for the aspect ratio. The control simply changes its width to match the scale specified by the height and aspect ratio.

For the final part of the first row, you add a single `Label` control and bind it to the top-right edge of the canvas, ensuring that when the window resizes, the `Label` moves with the right edge.

Then you start on the second row, which is filled by another `Canvas` control that has a `Label` added to it.

The bottom `Canvas` is more of the same, but this time you add a button to it and bind that button to the bottom-right side of the canvas. This ensures that when the window is resized, the button sticks to the bottom-right side of the window. The underscore "_" before the text "OK" creates an Alt+O shortcut for the button.

Finally, you add a `StackPanel` to the third row and add `Label` controls and a `TextBlock` control to it. By setting the `Padding` of the first label to 20,0,0,0 you push the content of the control down from the row above by 20 pixels and out from the left edge, also by 20 pixels.

The padding of the next label is set to 20,0,0,0 which pushes the content out from the edge because the space between the two labels is fine and doesn't need any extra space.

The `TextBlock` was then introduced. The property `TextWrapping` is set to `Wrap`, which causes the text to wrap if it can't fit on a single line. As the window resizes and the line becomes longer, the text is automatically fitted into as few lines as needed. Both the `Margin` and `Padding` properties are used here. The `Margin` property is set so it pushes the entire control down 10 pixels from the labels above, and the `Padding` is set so it pushes the content of the control in by 20 pixels from the left edge.

The code in the event handler closes the window. In this case, this is the same as closing the entire application, because in step 19 you changed the startup window to be the About window, so closing it is the same as closing the application.

The Options Window

The next window you are going to create is the Options window. This window will allow the players to set a number of parameters that will alter the game play. It will also allow you to use some controls that you haven't used yet: the `CheckBox`, `RadioButton`, `ComboBox`, `TextBox`, and `TabControl` controls.

Figure 21-11 shows the window with the first tab selected. At first glance the window looks much like the About window, but there is a lot more to do on this window.

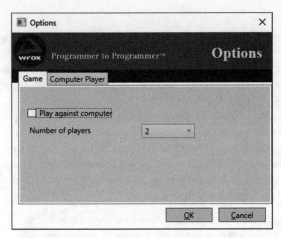

FIGURE 21-11

The TextBox Control

Previously in this chapter you used the `Label` and `TextBlock` controls. These controls are designed exclusively for displaying text to the user. The `TextBox` control allows the user to type text into the application. Although it can just display text as well, you should not use it for this purpose unless the user is allowed to edit the displayed text (or copy/paste the text). If you decide that you want to display text using a text box, be sure to set its `IsReadOnly` property to `false` to prevent users from being able to edit it.

You control how the text is displayed and can be entered into the `TextBox` using a number of properties shown in Table 21-4.

TABLE 21-4: TextBox Properties

PROPERTY	DESCRIPTION
`Text`	The text currently displayed in the `TextBox` control.
`IsEnabled`	When this is set to `true`, the user can edit the text in the `TextBox`. When it is `false`, the text is grayed out and the user cannot give focus to the control.
`IsReadOnly`	When this is set to `true`, the user can copy the text in the `TextBox` but cannot alter it.

continues

TABLE 21-4 (*continued*)

PROPERTY	DESCRIPTION
TextWrapping	Sometimes you want the TextBox to display only a single line of text. In this case, you can set this property to NoWrap. This is the default. If you want your text to be displayed on multiple lines, you can set it to either Wrap or WrapWithOverflow. Wrap will cause the text that extends beyond the edge of the box to be moved to the line below. WrapWithOverflow will in some cases allow very long words to extend beyond the edge if no suitable breakpoint can be determined.
VerticalScrollBarVisibility	If your TextBox allows the user to enter multiple lines of text, then the user can potentially type text that will disappear below the lower edge of the box. In that case, it's a good idea to display a scrollbar. Set this to Auto if you want the scrollbar to appear only if the text is too long to be displayed. Set it to Visible to always display it, and Hidden or Disabled to never display a scrollbar.
AcceptsReturn	This property controls how text can be entered into the control. If you set this to false, which is the default, then the user can't break the line with a Return. This also affects the default button. If there is a default button and you press Return while focus is on the text box, then it either enters a new line or triggers the default button.

The CheckBox Control

CheckBox controls present the users with options that they can select or clear. You should use a CheckBox if you want to present an option to the users that can be turned on or off, or want the users to answer yes or no to a question. For example, in the Options dialog box, you want the user to decide whether they should play against the computer. To this end a CheckBox with the text "Play Against Computer" is used.

A CheckBox is designed to be used as a single entity that is unaffected by other CheckBox controls on the view. You will sometimes see CheckBox controls used in a way that links them together so that selecting one causes another to become cleared, but this is not the intended use for this control. If you want this functionality, you should use a RadioButton, described in the next section.

CheckBox controls can also display a third state, which is known as "indeterminate" and is supposed to indicate that the yes/no answer could not be answered. This state is commonly used when a CheckBox is used to show information about something else. For example, CheckBox controls are sometimes used to indicate whether all child nodes in a tree view are selected. In this case, the Check-Box will be selected if all nodes are selected, cleared if none are, and indeterminate if some, but not all, are selected.

Table 21-5 lists the properties commonly used to control the CheckBox control.

TABLE 21-5: CheckBox Properties

PROPERTY	DESCRIPTION
Content	The CheckBox is a Content control and its display can therefore be heavily customized. Adding text to the Content property yields the default view.
IsThreeState	Used to indicate if the control can have two or three states. The default is false, meaning that only two possible values exist.
IsChecked	This is either true or false. By default, setting it to true displays a checkmark. If IsThreeState is true, null is possible and indicates that the state is indeterminate.

The RadioButton Control

RadioButtons are used with other RadioButton controls to allow users to choose between multiple options where only one can be selected at any time. You should use RadioButton controls when you want the users to answer a question that has a very limited number of possible values. If there are more than four or five possible values, you should consider using a ListBox or a ComboBox instead. In the Options window you will create shortly, the user can choose the skill level of the computer player. There are three options: Dumb, Good, and Cheats. Only one should ever be selected at any given time.

When more than one RadioButton is displayed in the same view they will by default know about each other and as soon as any one of them is selected, all the others are cleared. If you have multiple unrelated RadioButton controls on the same view, they can be grouped together to avoid controls clearing the values of unrelated controls.

You can control the RadioButton with the properties listed in Table 21-6.

TABLE 21-6: RadioButton Properties

PROPERTY	DESCRIPTION
Content	RadioButtons are Content controls and can therefore have their display modified. By default, you enter text (a string) in the Content.
IsChecked	This is either true or false. If IsThreeState is true, null is possible and indicates that the state is indeterminate.
GroupName	The name of the group the control belongs to. By default, this is empty and any RadioButton controls without a GroupName are considered in the same group.

The ComboBox Control

Like the RadioButton control, ComboBox controls allow users to select exactly one option. However, ComboBox controls are fundamentally different in two ways:

➤ ComboBox controls display the possible choices in a drop-down list.

➤ It is possible to allow the users to type new values.

ComboBox controls are commonly used to display long lists of values, such as country or state names, but they can be used for many purposes. In the Options dialog box, a ComboBox is used to display a list from which the user can choose the number of players. Although this could just as well have been done using a Slider or set of RadioButton controls, the use of a ComboBox saves space in the view.

A ComboBox can be changed to display itself with a TextBox at the top that allows the users to type any values that they feel are missing. One of the exercises of this chapter asks you to add a ComboBox to the Options dialog box from which the users can either type their name or select it from a list.

The two properties—IsReadOnly and IsEditable—are very important for the behavior of the control and work together to provide four possible ways for the user to select the value of the ComboBox using the keyboard (see Table 21-7).

TABLE 21-7: IsReadOnly and IsEditable Combinations

	ISREADONLY IS TRUE	ISREADONLY IS FALSE
IsEditable is true	The TextBox is displayed but the control does not react to key presses. If a selection is made in the list, the text can be selected in the TextBox.	The TextBox is displayed and the user can type anything she wishes. If something is typed that is in the list, it is selected. The control will display the best possible match as the user is typing.
IsEditable is false	When IsEditable is false, IsReadOnly no longer has any effect because the TextBox is not displayed. When the control is selected, the user can select a value from the list by typing, but it is not possible to type a value that isn't in the list.	

A ComboBox is an Items control, which means that you can add multiple items to it. Table 21-8 shows additional properties for the ComboBox control.

TABLE 21-8: Other ComboBox Properties

COMBOBOX PROPERTY	DESCRIPTION
Text	Represents the text displayed at the head of the ComboBox. It is either an element of the list or a new character string typed by the user.
SelectedIndex	Represents the index of the selected item in the list. If this is –1, then no selection is made. This is also the case if the user has typed something that was not in the list.
SelectedItem	Represents the actual item of the list, not just the index or the text. If nothing is selected or the user has typed something new, this returns null.

The TabControl

The TabControl is radically different than the other controls presented in this section. It is a layout control that is used to group controls on pages that can be selected by clicking them.

Tab controls are used when you want to display a lot of information in a single window but don't want to clutter the view too much. In this case, you should divide the information into groups of related items and create a single page for each group. Generally speaking, you should never allow controls on one page to affect controls on another page. If you do so anyway, the user will not realize that something has changed on another page and will be confused when settings change behind her back.

By default, each page is constructed of TabItem controls that, by default, are populated by a single Grid control, but you can change the Grid to any other control as you see fit. On each tab, you can lay out your UI and, by selecting the TabItems, you can change between the tabs. Each TabItem has a Header that can be used to display the tab itself. This can be used as a Content control, meaning that you can customize how the header is displayed so that it can be more than just a character string.

TRY IT OUT Designing the Options Window: BensCards.WPF \OptionsWindow.xaml

The first thing that you probably notice when you see the Options window is that it looks remarkably like the About window, and that is true. Because of that, it is possible to reuse at least some of the code from the previous example.

1. Right-click the project in the Solution Explorer and choose Add ➪ Window (WPF). Name the window OptionsWindow.xaml.

2. Delete the Grid control that is inserted by default.

3. Open the `AboutWindow.xaml` window described earlier, copy the `Grid` control and all its content, and paste it into the new `OptionsWindow.xaml` file.

4. Change the window properties like this:

   ```
   Title="Options" Height="345" Width="434" ResizeMode="NoResize"
   ```

5. Delete the `StackPanel` and all of its content.

6. Delete the `Canvas` control with the `Grid.Row` property set to 3 and all of its content.

7. Delete the `Label` control from the `Canvas` control with the `Grid.Row` property set to 1.

8. Change the `Label` control in the `Canvas` with the `Grid.Row` property set to 0 like this:

   ```
   <Label Canvas.Right="10" Canvas.Top="13" Content="Options"
   Foreground="#FFF7EFEF"
                   FontFamily="Times New Roman" FontSize="24" FontWeight="Bold" />
   ```

9. Drag a `StackPanel` into the bottom row and set its properties to this:

   ```
   Grid.Row="3" Orientation="Horizontal" FlowDirection="RightToLeft"
   ```

10. Add two buttons to the `StackPanel` like this:

    ```
    <Button Content="_Cancel" Height="22" Width="75" Margin="10,0,0,0"
            Name="cancelButton" />
    <Button Content="_OK" Height="22" Width="75" Margin="10,0,0,0"
            Name="okButton" />
    ```

11. Drag a `TabControl` into the canvas control in the grid's second row and set its properties like this:

    ```
    Grid.RowSpan="2" Canvas.Left="10" Canvas.Top="2" Width="408" Height="208"
    Grid.Row="1"
    ```

12. Change the `Header` property of each of the two `TabItem` controls to `Game` and `Computer Player`, respectively.

    Your window now looks like Figure 21-12, and it is time to insert some content into the tab items.

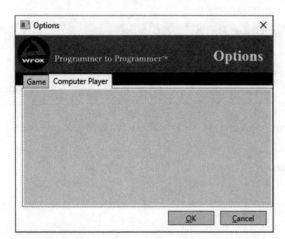

FIGURE 21-12

13. Select the Game `TabItem` and drag a `CheckBox` control onto it. Set its properties like this:

```
Content="Play against computer" HorizontalAlignment="Left" Margin="11,33,0,0"
VerticalAlignment="Top" Name="playAgainstComputerCheck"
```

14. Drag a `Label` control and then a `ComboBox` control into the `TabItem` and set their properties like this:

```
<Label Content="Number of players" HorizontalAlignment="Left"
Margin="10,54,0,0" VerticalAlignment="Top" />
    <ComboBox HorizontalAlignment="Left" Margin="196,58,0,0"
VerticalAlignment="Top" Width="86" Name="numberOfPlayersComboBox"
SelectedIndex="0"  >
        <ComboBoxItem>2</ComboBoxItem>
        <ComboBoxItem>3</ComboBoxItem>
        <ComboBoxItem>4</ComboBoxItem>
    </ComboBox>
```

15. Select the second `TabItem` with the header `Computer Player`. Drag a `Label` and three `RadioButtons` onto the `Grid` and set their properties like this:

```
<Label Content="Skill Level" HorizontalAlignment="Left"
Margin="10,10,0,0" VerticalAlignment="Top"/>
    <RadioButton Content="Dumb" HorizontalAlignment="Left"
Margin="37,41,0,0" VerticalAlignment="Top" IsChecked="True"
Name="dumbAIRadioButton"/>
    <RadioButton Content="Good" HorizontalAlignment="Left"
Margin="37,62,0,0" VerticalAlignment="Top" Name="goodAIRadioButton"/>
    <RadioButton Content="Cheats" HorizontalAlignment="Left"
Margin="37,83,0,0" VerticalAlignment="Top"
Name="cheatingAIRadioButton"/>
```

16. The layout of the window is now complete. The final XAML should look like this:

```
<Window x:Class="BensCards.WPF.OptionsWindow"
        xmlns="http://schemas.microsoft.com/winfx/2006/xaml/presentation"
        xmlns:x="http://schemas.microsoft.com/winfx/2006/xaml"
        xmlns:d="http://schemas.microsoft.com/expression/blend/2008"
        xmlns:mc="http://schemas.openxmlformats.org/markup-compatibility/2006"
        xmlns:local="clr-namespace:BensCards.WPF"
        mc:Ignorable="d"
        Title="Options" Height="345" Width="434" ResizeMode="NoResize">
    <Window.Resources>
        <local:InversedBoolConverter x:Key="inverseBool" />
    </Window.Resources>
    <Grid>
        <Grid.RowDefinitions>
            <RowDefinition Height="58"/>
            <RowDefinition Height="20"/>
            <RowDefinition />
            <RowDefinition Height="42"/>
        </Grid.RowDefinitions>
        <Canvas Grid.Row="0" Background="#C40D42" >
            <Image Height="56" Canvas.Left="0" Canvas.Top="0" Stretch="UniformToFill"
                        Source=".\Images\Banner.png"/>
```

```xml
        <Label Canvas.Right="10" Canvas.Top="13" Content="Options" Foreground="#FFF7EFEF"
                FontFamily="Times New Roman" FontSize="24" FontWeight="Bold" />
</Canvas>
<Canvas Grid.Row="1" Background="Black" >
    <Canvas.Resources>
        <local:NumberOfPlayers x:Key="numberOfPlayersData" />
    </Canvas.Resources>
    <TabControl Grid.RowSpan="2" Canvas.Left="10" Canvas.Top="2" Width="408"
            Height="208" Grid.Row="1">
        <TabItem Header="Game">
            <Grid Background="#FFE5E5E5">
                <CheckBox Content="Play against computer"
                    HorizontalAlignment="Left"
                    Margin="11,33,0,0" VerticalAlignment="Top"
                    Name="playAgainstComputerCheck"
                    IsChecked="{Binding Path=PlayAgainstComputer}" />
                <Label Content="Number of players" HorizontalAlignment="Left"
                    Margin="10,54,0,0" VerticalAlignment="Top" />
                <ComboBox HorizontalAlignment="Left"
                    Margin="196,58,0,0" VerticalAlignment="Top"
                    Width="86" Name="numberOfPlayersComboBox"
                    ItemsSource=
                    "{Binding Source={StaticResource numberOfPlayersData}}"
                    SelectedValue="{Binding Path=NumberOfPlayers}"
                    IsEnabled="{Binding ElementName=playAgainstComputerCheck,
                    Path=IsChecked, Converter={StaticResource inverseBool}}"/>
            </Grid>
        </TabItem>
        <TabItem Header="Computer Player">
            <Grid Background="#FFE5E5E5">
                <Label Content="Skill Level" HorizontalAlignment="Left"
                    Margin="10,10,0,0" VerticalAlignment="Top" />
                <RadioButton Content="Dumb" HorizontalAlignment="Left"
                    Margin="37,41,0,0" VerticalAlignment="Top" IsChecked="True"
                    Name="dumbAIRadioButton" Checked="dumbAIRadioButton_Checked"/>
                <RadioButton Content="Good" HorizontalAlignment="Left"
                    Margin="37,62,0,0" VerticalAlignment="Top" Name="goodAIRadioButton"
                    Checked="goodAIRadioButton_Checked"/>
                <RadioButton Content="Cheats" HorizontalAlignment="Left"
                    Margin="37,83,0,0" VerticalAlignment="Top"
                    Name="cheatingAIRadioButton"
                    Checked="cheatingAIRadioButton_Checked"/>
            </Grid>
        </TabItem>
    </TabControl>
</Canvas>
<StackPanel Grid.Row="3" Orientation="Horizontal" FlowDirection="RightToLeft">
    <Button Content="_Cancel" Height="22" Width="75" Margin="10,0,0,0"
        Name="cancelButton" Click="cancelButton_Click" />
```

```
                    <Button Content="_OK" Height="22" Width="75" Margin="10,0,0,0"
                        Name="okButton" Click="okButton_Click" />
            </StackPanel>
        </Grid>
    </Window>
```

17. Open the `App.xaml` file and change `StartupUri` to `OptionsWindow.xaml`.

18. Run the application.

How It Works

The window's `ResizeMode` is set to `NoResize`. You can therefore position the controls without regard to what happens if the window changes size, because the user can no longer resize the window. While it is better if the controls can arrange and size themselves to fit, sometimes it is better to limit what the user can do.

The `StackPanel` in step 9 has a new property, `FlowDirection`, which is set to `RightToLeft`. This causes the two buttons that are added to it to cling to the right edge of the dialog box rather than the left edge that is the default. Interestingly, this also changes the meaning of the `Margin` property of the two buttons, causing `Left` and `Right` to be swapped.

The `RadioButtons` on the second tab are set up without specifying a `GroupName`, which causes them to be grouped together. You set the `IsChecked` property to `true` on the first one, which makes this the default selection.

Handling Events in the Options Window

The window looks fine at this point, and there are even a few things users can do with it, although nothing happens when a setting is changed. Users expect that the options they choose are stored and used by the application. You could do this by storing the values of the controls in the window, but this is not very flexible and mixes the data of the application with the GUI, which is not a good idea. Instead, you should create a class to hold the selections made by the users.

In the following Try It Out you add event handlers to the Options window that are executed as the user interacts with the controls.

TRY IT OUT Handling Events: BensCards.WPF\OptionsWindow.xaml

In this example, you will add a new class to the project that will contain the selections made by the user and handle events that happen as the user changes selections.

1. Add a new class to the project and name it `GameOptions.cs`.

2. Enter this code:

```
using System;
namespace BensCards.WPF
{
```

```
[Serializable]
public class GameOptions
{
  public bool PlayAgainstComputer { get; set; }
  public int NumberOfPlayers { get; set; }
  public int MinutesBeforeLoss { get; set; }
  public ComputerSkillLevel ComputerSkill { get; set; }
}
[Serializable]
public enum ComputerSkillLevel
{
  Dumb,
  Good,
  Cheats
}
}
```

3. Return to the OptionsWindow.xaml.cs code-behind file and add a private field to hold the GameOptions instance:

```
private GameOptions gameOptions;
```

4. Add this code to the constructor:

```
using System.IO;
using System.Windows;
using System.Xml.Serialization;
namespace BensCards.WPF
{

  public partial class OptionsWindow : Window
  {
  private GameOptions gameOptions;
  public OptionsWindow()
  {
    if (gameOptions == null)
    {
      if (File.Exists("GameOptions.xml"))
      {
        using (var stream = File.OpenRead("GameOptions.xml"))
        {
          var serializer = new XmlSerializer(typeof(GameOptions));
          gameOptions = serializer.Deserialize(stream) as GameOptions;
        }
      }
      else
        gameOptions = new GameOptions();
    }
    InitializeComponent();
  }
```

5. Go to Design View and double-click each of the three RadioButtons to add the Checked event handler to the code-behind file. Change the handlers like this:

```
private void dumbAIRadioButton_Checked(object sender, RoutedEventArgs e)
{
  gameOptions.ComputerSkill = ComputerSkillLevel.Dumb;
}
```

```
private void goodAIRadioButton_Checked(object sender, RoutedEventArgs e)
{
    gameOptions.ComputerSkill = ComputerSkillLevel.Good;
}
private void cheatingAIRadioButton_Checked(object sender, RoutedEventArgs e)
{
    gameOptions.ComputerSkill = ComputerSkillLevel.Cheats;
}
```

6. Double-click the OK and Cancel buttons and add this code to the handler methods:

```
private void okButton_Click(object sender, RoutedEventArgs e)
{
    using (var stream = File.Open("GameOptions.xml", FileMode.Create))
    {
        var serializer = new XmlSerializer(typeof(GameOptions));
        serializer.Serialize(stream, gameOptions);
    }
    Close();
}

private void cancelButton_Click(object sender, RoutedEventArgs e)
{
    gameOptions = null;
    Close();
}
```

7. Run the application.

How It Works

The new class is currently just a number of properties that store the values from the Options window. It is marked as `Serializable` to make it possible to save it to a file.

The `Checked` event of a `RadioButton` is raised whenever the user selects it. You handle this event in order to set the value of the `ComputerSkillLevel` property of the `GameOptions` instance.

Data Binding

Data binding is a way of declaratively connecting controls with data. In the Options window, you handled the `Checked` event of the `RadioButtons` in order to set the value of the `Computer-SkillLevel` property in the `GameOptions` class. This works well, and you can use code and event handling to set all the values you have in a window, but very often it is better to bind the properties of your controls directly to the data.

A binding consists of four components:

➤ The binding target, which specifies the object on which the binding is used

➤ The target property, which specifies the property to set

➤ The binding source, which specifies the object used by the binding

➤ The source property, which specifies which property holds the data

You don't always set all of these elements explicitly; in particular, the binding target is very often implicitly specified by the fact that you are setting a binding to a property on a control.

The binding source is always set in order to make a binding work, but it can be set in several ways. In the following sections, you are going to see several ways of binding data from sources.

The DataContext

A DataContext control defines a data source that can be used for data binding on all descendant elements of an element. You will often have a single instance of a class that holds most of the data that is used in a view. If this is the case, you can set the DataContext of the window to the instance of that object, which makes you able to bind properties from that class in your view. This is demonstrated in the "Dynamic Binding to External Objects" section.

Binding to Local Objects

You can bind to any .NET object that has the data you need as long as the compiler can locate the object. If the object is found in the same context, that is, the same XAML block, as the control using the object, you can specify the binding source by setting the ElementName property of the binding. Take a look at this changed ComboBox from the Options window:

```
<ComboBox HorizontalAlignment="Left" Margin="196,58,0,0" VerticalAlignment="Top"
Width="86" Name="numberOfPlayersComboBox" SelectedIndex="0"
IsEnabled="{Binding ElementName=playAgainstComputerCheck, Path=IsChecked}" >
```

Notice the IsEnabled property. Instead of specifying true or false, there is now lengthy text within a couple of curly brackets. This way of specifying property values is called *markup extension syntax*, and is shorthand for specifying properties. The same could have been written like this:

```
                    <ComboBox HorizontalAlignment="Left" Margin="196,58,0,0"
VerticalAlignment="Top" Width="86" Name="numberOfPlayersComboBox"
SelectedIndex="0" >
            <ComboBox.IsEnabled>
                <Binding ElementName="playAgainstComputerCheck"
Path="IsChecked" />
            </ComboBox.IsEnabled>
```

Both examples set the binding source to the playAgainstComputerCheck CheckBox. The source property is specified in the Path to be the IsChecked property.

The binding target is set to the IsEnabled property. Both examples do this by specifying the binding as the content of the property—they just do it using different syntax. Finally, the binding target is implicitly specified by the fact that the binding is done on the ComboBox.

The binding in this example causes the IsEnabled property of the ComboBox to be set or cleared depending on the value of the IsChecked property of the CheckBox. The result is that without any code, the ComboBox is enabled and disabled when the user changes the value of the CheckBox.

Static Binding to External Objects

It is possible to create object instances on the fly by specifying that a class is used as a resource in the XAML. This is done by adding a namespace to the XAML to allow the class to be located and then declaring the class as a resource on an element in the XAML.

The following Try It Out shows how to create resource references on parent elements of the object that you want to data bind.

> **NOTE** *If you changed the* `ComboBox` *as described in the previous sections, you should revert the changes by removing the* `IsEnabled` *binding.*

TRY IT OUT   Creating a Static Data Binding: BensCards.WPF\NumberOfPlayers.cs

In this example, you create a new class to hold the data for the `ComboBox` in the Options window and bind it to the control.

1. Add a new class to the project and name it `NumberOfPlayers.cs`.

2. Add this code:

    ```
    using System.Collections.ObjectModel;

    namespace BensCards.WPF
    {
        public class NumberOfPlayers : ObservableCollection<int>
        {
            public NumberOfPlayers()
              : base()
            {
                Add(2);
                Add(3);
                Add(4);
            }
        }
    }
    ```

3. In the `OptionsWindow.xaml`, select the `Canvas` control that is the grandparent of the `TabControl`. Place the following code inside the `Canvas` control's opening tag and above the `TabControl` declaration:

    ```
    <Canvas.Resources>
      <local:NumberOfPlayers x:Key="numberOfPlayersData" />
    </Canvas.Resources>
    ```

4. Select the `ComboBox` and remove the three `ComboBoxItems` from it.

5. Add this property to it:

    ```
    ItemsSource="{Binding Source={StaticResource numberOfPlayersData}}"
    ```

How It Works

There is a lot happening in this example. The class `NumberOfPlayers` derives from a special collection named `ObservableCollection`. This base class is a collection that has been extended to make it work better with WPF. In the constructor of the class, you add the values to the collection.

Next you create a new resource on the `Grid`. You could have created this resource on any ancestor element of the `ComboBox`. When a resource is specified on an element, all descendant elements can use it.

Finally, you set the `ItemsSource` to a binding. The `ItemsSource` property is specifically designed to allow you to specify a binding for the collection of items on an Items control. In the binding you just need to specify the binding source. The binding target, target property, and source property settings are handled by the `ItemsSource` property.

Note that at this point the binding is defined, but there's no `numberOfPlayersData` to bind to so this can't run. We'll get to that next.

Dynamic Binding to External Objects

Now you can bind to objects that are created on the fly as they are needed in order to provide some data. What if you already have an instantiated object that you want to use for data binding? In that case, you need to do a little plumbing in the code.

In the case of the Options window, you don't want the options to be cleared every time the window is opened, and you want the selections the user made to persist and be used in the rest of the application.

In the following Try It Out you set the `DataContext` to an instance of the `GameOptions` class, which allows you to use dynamic bindings of the properties of that class.

TRY IT OUT   Creating Dynamic Bindings: BensCards.WPF\GameOptions.cs

In this example, you bind the remaining controls to the `GameOptions` instance in the Options window.

1. Go to the `OptionsWindow.xaml.cs` code-behind file.

2. At the bottom of the constructor, but above `InitializeComponent()`, add this line:

```
DataContext = gameOptions;
```

3. Go to the `GameOptions` class and change it like this:

```
using System;
using System.ComponentModel;

namespace BensCards.WPF
{
    [Serializable]
    public class GameOptions
    {
        private bool playAgainstComputer = true;
        private int numberOfPlayers = 2;
```

```
                private ComputerSkillLevel computerSkill = ComputerSkillLevel.Dumb;

                public int NumberOfPlayers
                {
                    get { return numberOfPlayers; }
                    set
                    {
                        numberOfPlayers = value;
                        OnPropertyChanged(nameof(NumberOfPlayers));
                    }
                }
                public bool PlayAgainstComputer
                {
                    get { return playAgainstComputer; }
                    set
                    {
                        playAgainstComputer = value;
                        OnPropertyChanged(nameof(PlayAgainstComputer));
                    }
                }
                public ComputerSkillLevel ComputerSkill
                {
                    get { return computerSkill; }
                    set
                    {
                        computerSkill = value;
                        OnPropertyChanged(nameof(ComputerSkill));
                    }
                }
                public event PropertyChangedEventHandler PropertyChanged;
                private void OnPropertyChanged(string propertyName)
                {
                    PropertyChanged?.Invoke(this, new
                        PropertyChangedEventArgs(propertyName));
                }
            }

            [Serializable]
            public enum ComputerSkillLevel
            {
                Dumb,
                Good,
                Cheats
            }
        }
```

4. Return to `OptionsWindow.xaml` and select the `CheckBox`. Add the `IsChecked` property like this:

```
IsChecked="{Binding Path=PlayAgainstComputer}"
```

5. Select the `ComboBox` and change it like this, removing the `SelectedIndex` property and changing the `ItemsSource` and `SelectedValue` properties:

```
<ComboBox HorizontalAlignment="Left" Margin="196,58,0,0" VerticalAlignment="Top"
```

```
        Width="86" Name="numberOfPlayersComboBox"
        ItemsSource="{Binding Source={StaticResource numberOfPlayersData}}"
            SelectedValue="{Binding Path=NumberOfPlayers}" />
```

6. Run the application.

How It Works

Setting the `DataContext` of the window to an instance of `GameOptions` allows you to bind to this instance simply by specifying the property to use in the binding. This is done in steps 4 and 5. Note that the `ComboBox` is filled with items from a static resource, but the selected value is set in the `GameOptions` instance.

The `GameOptions` class is changed quite a bit. In order to notify WPF that a property has changed, you have to call the subscribers to the `PropertyChanged` event defined by the interface. For this to happen, the property setters have to actively call them, which is done using the helper method `OnPropertyChanged`.

When the `OnPropertyChanged` method is called, we use a new expression introduced by C# 6: `nameof`. When we call `nameof(...)` with an expression, it will retrieve the name of the final identifier. This is particularly useful in the case of the `OnPropertyChanged` method because it takes the name of the property that is being changed as a string.

The OK button event handler saves the settings to disk using an `XmlSerializer`. The `Cancel` event handler sets the game options field to `null`, ensuring that the selections made by the user are cleared. Both event handlers close the window.

Starting a Game with the ListBox Control

You are now only one window short of having created all the supporting windows in the game. The last window before creating the game board is a window where the player can add new players and select the players who will be participating in a new game. This window will use a `ListBox` to display the names of the players.

`ListBox` and `ComboBox` controls can often be used for the same purpose, but where a `ComboBox` normally allows you to select only a single entry, `ListBox` controls often allow the user to select multiple items. Another key difference is that a `ListBox` will display its content in a list that is always expanded. This means that it takes up more real estate on the window, but it allows the user to see the options available right away.

Table 21-9 lists a few particularly interesting properties for the `ListBox` control.

In the next Try It Out, you create the window that is displayed when the user wants to start a new game.

TABLE 21-9: Interesting ListBox Properties

PROPERTY	DESCRIPTION
SelectionMode	Controls how the user can select items from the list. There are three possible values: Single, which allows the user to select only one item, Multiple, which allows the user to select multiple items without holding down the Ctrl key, and Extended, which allows the user to select multiple consecutive items by holding down the Shift key, and non-consecutive items by holding down the Ctrl key.
SelectedItem	Gets or sets the first selected item or null if nothing is selected. Even if multiple items are selected, only the first item is returned.
SelectedItems	Gets a list containing the items that are currently selected.
SelectedIndex	Works like SelectedItem, but returns the index instead of the item itself and −1 instead of null if nothing is selected.

TRY IT OUT **Creating the Start Game Window:**
BensCards.WPF\StartGameWindow.xaml

This window is displayed to the players when a new game starts. It will allow the players to enter their names and select them from a list of known players.

1. Create a new window and name it StartGameWindow.xaml.

2. Delete the Grid element from the window and copy the main Grid and its content from the OptionsWindow.xaml window instead.

3. Remove all the content from the Canvas control that has its Grid.Row property set to 1.

4. Change the window title to "Start New Game" and set these properties:

    ```
    Height="345" Width="445" ResizeMode="NoResize"
    ```

5. Change the content of the label in grid row 0 to "New Game."

6. Open the GameOptions.cs file and add these fields at the top of the class:

    ```
    private ObservableCollection<string> playerNames =
            new ObservableCollection<string>();
    public List<string> SelectedPlayers { get; set; } = new List<string>();
    ```

7. The previous code used System.Collections.Generic and the System.Collections.Object-Model namespaces, so include these:

    ```
    using System.Collections.Generic;
    using System.Collections.ObjectModel;
    ```

8. Add a property and two methods to the class like this:

```
public ObservableCollection<string> PlayerNames
{
    get
    {
        return playerNames;
    }
    set
    {
        playerNames = value;
        OnPropertyChanged("PlayerNames");
    }
}
public void AddPlayer(string playerName)
{
    if (playerNames.Contains(playerName))
        return;
    playerNames.Add(playerName);
    OnPropertyChanged("PlayerNames");
}
```

9. Return to the StartGameWindow.xaml window.

10. Add a ListBox, two Label controls, a TextBox, and a Button to the grid below the Canvas in grid row 1 (set Grid.Row to 2) and change the controls to look like those shown in Figure 21-13.

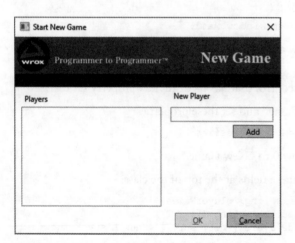

FIGURE 21-13

11. Set the `Name` properties of the controls as shown in Table 21-10.

TABLE 21-10: The Name Property

CONTROL	NAME
TextBox	newPlayerTextBox
Button	addNewPlayerButton
ListBox	playerNamesListBox

12. Set the `ItemsSource` of the `ListBox` like this:

```
ItemsSource="{Binding Path=PlayerNames}"
```

13. Add the `ListBox`'s `SelectionChanged` event handler to the code-behind file:

```
private void playerNamesListBox_SelectionChanged(object sender,
SelectionChangedEventArgs e)
    {
      if (gameOptions.PlayAgainstComputer)
        okButton.IsEnabled = (playerNamesListBox.SelectedItems.Count == 1);
      else
        okButton.IsEnabled = (playerNamesListBox.SelectedItems.Count ==
gameOptions.NumberOfPlayers);
    }
```

14. Add this field to the top of the `StartGameWindow` class:

```
private GameOptions gameOptions;
```

15. Set the `IsEnabled` property of the OK button to `false`.

16. Copy the constructor from the `OptionsWindow.xaml.cs` code-behind (though not the name) and add these lines to the end after `InitializeComponent` (Note: You will need to add using declarations for `System.IO` and `System.Xml.Serialization`):

```
        if (gameOptions.PlayAgainstComputer)
            playerNamesListBox.SelectionMode = SelectionMode.Single;
        else
            playerNamesListBox.SelectionMode = SelectionMode.Extended;
```

17. Select the Add button and add the `Click` event handler. Add this code:

```
        private void addNewPlayerButton_Click(object sender, RoutedEventArgs e)
        {
            if (!string.IsNullOrWhiteSpace(newPlayerTextBox.Text))
                gameOptions.AddPlayer(newPlayerTextBox.Text);
            newPlayerTextBox.Text = string.Empty;
        }
```

18. Copy the event handler for the OK and Cancel buttons from the `OptionsWindow.xaml.cs` code-behind files to this code-behind.

19. Add these lines to the top of the OK button handler:

```
foreach (string item in playerNamesListBox.SelectedItems)
    {
        gameOptions.SelectedPlayers.Add(item);
    }
```

20. Go to the `App.xaml` file and change the `StartupUri` to `StartGameWindow.xaml`.

21. Run the application.

How It Works

You started by adding code to the `GameOptions` class that holds information about all the known players and the current selection made in the `StartGame` window.

The `ListBox`'s `ItemsSource` property is the same as you saw on the `ComboBox` earlier. But while you were able to bind the selected value of the `ComboBox` directly to a value, it is more complicated with a `ListBox`. If you try to bind the `SelectedValues` property you will find that it is read-only and therefore can't be used for data binding. The workaround used here is to use the OK button to store the values through code. Note that the cast to `IList<string>` works here because the content of the `ListBox` is strings at the moment, but if you decided to change the default behavior and display something else, then this selection of items must be changed as well.

The `ListBox`'s `SelectionChanged` event is raised whenever something happens that changes the selection. In this case you want to handle this event to check if the number of items selected is correct. If the game is to be played against a computer, then there can only be one human player; otherwise, the correct number of human players must be selected.

CREATING AND STYLING CONTROLS

One of the best features of WPF is the complete control it provides designers over the look and feel of user interfaces. Central to this is the capability to style controls however you want, in two or three dimensions. Until now, you have been using the basic styling for controls that is supplied with .NET, but the actual possibilities are endless.

This section describes two basic techniques:

➤ **Styles**—Sets of properties that are applied to a control as a batch

➤ **Templates**—The controls that are used to build the display for a control

There is some overlap here, as styles can contain templates.

Styles

WPF controls have a property called `Style` (inherited from `FrameworkElement`) that can be set to an instance of the `Style` class. The `Style` class is quite complex and is capable of advanced styling functionality, but at its heart it is a set of `Setter` objects. Each `Setter` object is responsible for setting the value of a property according to its `Property` property (the name of the property to set) and its `Value` property (the value to set the property to). You can either fully qualify the name you use in `Property` to the control type (for example, `Button.Foreground`) or set the `TargetType` property of the `Style` object (for example, `Button`) so that it is capable of resolving property names.

The following code shows how to use a `Style` object to set the `Foreground` property of a `Button` control:

```
<Button>
  Click me!
  <Button.Style>
    <Style TargetType="Button">
      <Setter Property="Foreground">
        <Setter.Value>
          <SolidColorBrush Color="Purple" />
        </Setter.Value>
      </Setter>
    </Style>
  </Button.Style>
</Button>
```

Obviously, in this case it would be far easier to simply set the `Foreground` property of the button in the usual way. Styles become much more useful when you turn them into resources because resources can be reused.

Templates

Controls are constructed using templates, which you can customize. A template consists of a hierarchy of controls used to build the display of a control, which may include a content presenter for controls such as buttons that display content.

The template of a control is stored in its `Template` property, which is an instance of the `ControlTemplate` class. The `ControlTemplate` class includes a `TargetType` property that you can set to the type of control for which you are defining a template.

Typically, you set the template for a class by using a style. This simply involves providing controls to use for the `Template` property in the following way:

```
<Button>
  Click me!
  <Button.Style>
    <Style TargetType="Button">
      <Setter Property="Template">
        <Setter.Value>
          <ControlTemplate TargetType="Button">
            ...
          </ControlTemplate>
        </Setter.Value>
      </Setter>
    </Style>
  </Button.Style>
</Button>
```

Some controls may require more than one template. For example, `CheckBox` controls use one template for a check box (`CheckBox.Template`) and one template to output text next to the check box (`CheckBox.ContentTemplate`).

Templates that allow you to change the content of the control can do so by including a `ContentPresenter` at the location where you want to output content.

Earlier in the chapter you developed three dialogs with a similar look and feel. One of the common elements of the dialogs is the header where you changed the text of the label in each dialog. You can define that header as a label, and in the next Try It Out you will develop a new `Label` style and use it to replace the headers in all of the dialogs.

TRY IT OUT Creating the Main Window: BensCards.WPF\GameClientWindow.xaml

1. Create a new Resource Dictionary by right-clicking the project and selecting Add ⇨ Resource Dictionary (WPF). Name it `ControlResources.xaml`.

2. Create a new Control Template for a label like this:

```
<ControlTemplate x:Key="HeaderTemplate" TargetType="{x:Type Label}">
    <Canvas Background="#C40D42" >
        <Image Height="56" Canvas.Left="0" Canvas.Top="0"
            Stretch="UniformToFill" Source=".\Images\Banner.png"/>
        <ContentPresenter Canvas.Right="10" Canvas.Top="25"
            Content="{TemplateBinding Content}" />
    </Canvas>
</ControlTemplate>
```

3. Add a style that includes the Control Template:

```
<Style x:Key="HeaderLabelStyle" TargetType="Label">
    <Setter Property="Template" Value="{StaticResource HeaderTemplate}" />
    <Setter Property="FontFamily" Value="Times New Roman" />
    <Setter Property="FontSize" Value="24" />
    <Setter Property="FontWeight" Value="Bold" />
    <Setter Property="Foreground" Value="#FFF7EFEF" />
</Style>
```

4. Create a new window called `GameClientWindow.xaml`.

5. Change the title to "Ben's Cards Game Client" and remove the `Height` and `Width` properties.

6. Set the `WindowState` property to `Maximized`.

7. At the top of the window, just before the `Grid`, import the Resource Dictionary like this:

```
<Window.Resources>
    <ResourceDictionary>
        <ResourceDictionary.MergedDictionaries>
            <ResourceDictionary Source="ControlResources.xaml" />
        </ResourceDictionary.MergedDictionaries>
    </ResourceDictionary>
</Window.Resources>
```

8. Insert the grid's row definitions inside the `Grid` control like this:

```
<Grid.RowDefinitions>
    <RowDefinition Height="58"/>
    <RowDefinition Height="20"/>
    <RowDefinition />
    <RowDefinition Height="42"/>
</Grid.RowDefinitions>
```

9. Insert a new `Label` control like this:

```
<Label Grid.Row="0" Style="{StaticResource HeaderLabelStyle}">Ben's Cards</Label>
```

How It Works

When you look at the Control Template, you will see that it is almost exactly the same as the controls in the windows you developed earlier in the chapter; the only differences are the `ControlTemplate` declaration and a `ContentPresenter` that has replaced the `Label` control.

The `ControlTemplate TargetType` declaration is very important as it specifies which control this template will target. This allows you to bind properties from the parent control to controls within the template. Examine the `ContentPresenter`:

```
<ContentPresenter Content="{TemplateBinding Content}" />
```

The `ContentPresenter` control allows you to specify where the content of the control type is going to go. In the `GameClientWindow` you specify that the content of the `Label` should be Ben's Cards, which causes the text to be displayed. That is what you would normally do, but the control presenter allows you to specify any content, just like you would expect from the content property.

The `Style` control sets the properties that we want to set on the label, but notice that the `Template` property is set to a reference to the new `HeaderTemplate`:

```
<Setter Property="Template" Value="{StaticResource HeaderTemplate}" />
```

Triggers

Events in WPF can include all manner of things, including button clicks, application startup and shutdown events, and so on. WPF makes use of several types of triggers to provide functionality like events, all of which inherit from a base `TriggerBase` class. One such trigger is the `EventTrigger` class, which contains a collection of actions, each of which is an object that derives from the base `TriggerAction` class. These actions are executed when the trigger is activated.

You can use `EventTrigger` to trigger animations using the `BeginStoryboard` action, manipulate storyboards using `ControllableStoryboardAction`, and trigger sound effects with `Sound-PlayerAction`.

Every control has a `Triggers` property that you can use to define triggers directly on that control. You can also define triggers further up the hierarchy—for example, on a `Window` object. The type of trigger you will use most often when you are styling controls is `Trigger` (although you will still use `EventTrigger` to trigger control animations). The `Trigger` class is used to set properties in response to changes to other properties and is particularly useful when used in `Style` objects.

Trigger objects are configured as follows:

➤ To define what property a `Trigger` object monitors, you use the `Trigger.Property` property.

➤ To define when the `Trigger` object activates, you set the `Trigger.Value` property.

➤ To define the actions taken by a `Trigger`, you set the `Trigger.Setters` property to a collection of `Setter` objects.

The `Setter` objects referred to here are exactly the same objects that you saw in the "Styles" section earlier.

The following code shows a `Trigger` as you would use it in a `Style` object:

```
<Style TargetType="Button">
  <Style.Triggers>
    <Trigger Property="IsMouseOver" Value="true">
      <Setter Property="Foreground" Value="Yellow" />
    </Trigger>
  </Style.Triggers>
</Style>
```

This code changes the `Foreground` property of a `Button` control to `Yellow` when the `Button.IsMouseOver` property is `true`. `IsMouseOver` is one of several extremely useful properties that you can use as a shortcut to find out information about controls and control state. As its name suggests, it is `true` if the mouse is over the control. This enables you to code for mouse rollovers. Other properties like this include `IsFocused`, to determine whether a control has focus; `IsHit-TestVisible`, which indicates whether it is possible to click a control (that is, it is not obscured by controls further up the stacking order); and `IsPressed`, which indicates whether a button is pressed. The last of these only applies to buttons that inherit from `ButtonBase` whereas the others are available on all controls.

You can also achieve a great deal by using the `ControlTemplate.Triggers` property, which enables you to create templates for controls that include triggers. This is how the default `Button` template is able to respond to mouse rollovers, clicks, and focus changes with its template. This is also what you must modify to implement this functionality for yourself.

Animations

Animations are created by using storyboards. The best way to define complex animations is to use a designer such as Expression Blend. However, you can also define them by editing XAML code directly and through C# code.

> **NOTE** *Detailed graphical animations are well beyond the scope of this book. The information in this section will give you an idea of what you can do with animations.*

Animations in WPF are defined using an object called a `Storyboard`. Using storyboards, you can animate the value of a property—for example, the background color of a button. It is very important to realize that you can animate just about any property in this way, not just properties that affect how a control is displayed.

A storyboard can be defined on its own in a Resource Dictionary or inside controls using the `Begin-Storyboard` property of an event trigger. Inside the storyboard you define one or more animations, or timelines.

In the previous section, you used a trigger to set the foreground value of a `Button` control when the mouse rolls over the control. Examine the following code, which uses storyboards instead:

```
<Button Content="Animation" HorizontalAlignment="Left" Margin="197,63,0,0"
                                       VerticalAlignment="Top" Width="75">
    <Button.Triggers>
        <EventTrigger RoutedEvent="Button.MouseEnter">
            <BeginStoryboard>
                <Storyboard>
                    <ColorAnimation To="Yellow"
                            Storyboard.TargetProperty="(Button.Foreground)
                                            .(SolidColorBrush.Color)"
                            FillBehavior="HoldEnd"
                            Duration="0:0:1" AutoReverse="False" />
                </Storyboard>
            </BeginStoryboard>
        </EventTrigger>
        <EventTrigger RoutedEvent="Button.MouseLeave">
            <BeginStoryboard>
                <Storyboard>
                    <ColorAnimation To="Black"
                            Storyboard.TargetProperty="(Button.Foreground)
                                            .(SolidColorBrush.Color)"
                            FillBehavior="HoldEnd"
                            Duration="0:0:1"/>
                </Storyboard>
            </BeginStoryboard>
        </EventTrigger>
    </Button.Triggers>
</Button>
```

The `Button` contains two triggers, one for `MouseEnter` and one for `MouseLeave`. Each of these contains a `ColorAnimation` that changes the foreground color of the text to yellow and black, respectively. The difference between using the `Trigger` to set the `Foreground` property directly and using a storyboard is in the details: With the storyboard you get a flowing transition over 1 second, but when you set the property directly, it happens instantaneously. Both are valuable tools to have and they should be used when appropriate—too many animations may annoy your users, but a few well-placed ones can make an application look spectacular.

WPF USER CONTROLS

One key feature of a graphical card game is. . .the cards. Obviously, you are not going to find a "Playing Card" control in the standard controls that ship with WPF, so you have to create it yourself.

WPF provides a set of controls that are useful in many situations. However, as with all the .NET development frameworks, it also enables you to extend this functionality. Specifically, you can create your own controls by deriving your classes from classes in the WPF class hierarchy.

One of the most useful controls you can derive from is `UserControl`. This class gives you all the basic functionality that you are likely to require from a WPF control and it enables your control to snap in beside the existing WPF control suite seamlessly. Everything you might hope to achieve with a WPF control—such as animation, styling, and templating—can be achieved with user controls.

You can add user controls to your project by using the Project ➪ Add User Control menu item. This gives you a blank canvas (well, actually a blank `Grid`) to work from. User controls are defined using the top-level `UserControl` element in XAML, and the class in the code-behind derives from the `System.Windows.Controls.UserControl` class.

Once you have added a user control to your project, you can add controls to lay out the visual appearance and code-behind to configure the control. When you have finished doing that, you can use it throughout your application, and even reuse it in other applications.

One of the crucial things you need to know when creating user controls is how to implement dependency properties. We briefly discussed this kind of property earlier in the chapter, and now that you are getting closer to writing your own controls, it is time to take a look at them.

Implementing Dependency Properties

You can add dependency properties to any class that inherits from `System.Windows.DependencyObject`. This class is in the inheritance hierarchy for many classes in WPF, including all the controls and `UserControl`.

To implement a dependency property in a class, you add a public, static member to your class definition of type `System.Windows.DependencyProperty`. The name of this member is up to you, but best practice is to follow the naming convention `<PropertyName>Property`:

```
public static DependencyProperty MyStringProperty;
```

It might seem odd that this property is defined as static, as you end up with a property that can be uniquely defined for each instance of your class. The WPF property framework keeps track of things for you, so you don't have to worry about this for the moment.

The member you add must be configured by using the static `DependencyProperty.Register()` method:

```
public static DependencyProperty MyStringProperty =
    DependencyProperty.Register(...);
```

This method takes between three and five parameters, as shown in the Table 21-11 (these are shown in order, with the first three parameters being the mandatory ones).

TABLE 21-11: The Register( ) Method's Parameters

PARAMETER	USAGE
`string name`	The name of the property
`Type propertyType`	The type of the property
`Type ownerType`	The type of the class containing the property
`PropertyMetadata typeMetadata`	Additional property settings: the default value of the property and callback methods to use for property change notifications and coercion
`ValidateValueCallback validateValueCallback`	The callback method to use to validate property values

> **NOTE** *There are other methods that you can use to register dependency properties, such as* `RegisterAttached()`, *which you can use to implement an attached property. You won't look at these other methods in this chapter, but it's worth reading up on them.*

For example, you could register the `MyStringProperty` dependency property using three parameters as follows:

```
public class MyClass : DependencyObject
{
    public static DependencyProperty MyStringProperty = DependencyProperty.Register(
        "MyString",
        typeof(string),
        typeof(MyClass));
}
```

You can also include a .NET property that can be used to access dependency properties directly (although this isn't mandatory, as you will see shortly). However, because dependency properties are defined as static members, you cannot use the same syntax you would use with ordinary properties. To access the value of a dependency property, you have to use methods that are inherited from `DependencyObject`, as follows:

```
public string MyString
{
    get { return (string)GetValue(MyStringProperty); }
    set { SetValue(MyStringProperty, value); }
}
```

Here, the `GetValue()` and `SetValue()` methods get and set, respectively, the value of the `MyString-Property` dependency property for the current instance. These two methods are public, so client code can use them directly to manipulate dependency property values. This is why adding a .NET property to access a dependency property is not mandatory.

If you want to set metadata for a property, then you must use an object that derives from `PropertyMetadata`, such as `FrameworkPropertyMetadata`, and pass this instance as the fourth parameter to `Register()`. There are 11 overloads of the `FrameworkPropertyMetadata` constructor, and they take one or more of the parameters shown in Table 21-12.

TABLE 21-12: Overloads for the FrameworkPropertyMetadata Constructor

PARAMETER TYPE	USAGE
`object defaultValue`	The default value for the property.
`FrameworkPropertyMetadataOptions flags`	A combination of the flags (from the `FrameworkPropertyMetadataOptions` enum) that you can use to specify additional metadata for a property. For example, you might use `AffectsArrange` to declare that changes to the property might affect control layout. This would cause the layout engine for a window to recalculate control layout if the property changed. See the MSDN documentation for a full list of the options available here.
`PropertyChangedCallback propertyChangedCallback`	The callback method to use when the property value changes.
`CoerceValueCallback coerceValueCallback`	The callback method to use if the property value is coerced.
`bool isAnimationProhibited`	Specifies whether this property can be changed by an animation.
`UpdateSourceTrigger defaultUpdateSourceTrigger`	When property values are data-bound, this property determines when the data source is updated, according to values in the `UpdateSourceTrigger` enum. The default value is `PropertyChanged`, which means that the binding source is updated as soon as the property changes. This is not always appropriate—for example, the `TextBox.Text` property uses a value of `LostFocus` for this property. This ensures that the binding source is not updated prematurely. You can also use the value `Explicit` to specify that the binding source should be updated only when requested (by calling the `UpdateSource()` method of a class derived from `DependencyObject`).

A simple example of using `FrameworkPropertyMetadata` is to use it to set the default value of a property:

```
public static DependencyProperty MyStringProperty =
      DependencyProperty.Register(
            "MyString",
            typeof(string),
            typeof(MyClass),
            new FrameworkPropertyMetadata("Default value"));
```

You have so far learned about three callback methods that you can specify, for property change notification, property coercion, and property value validation. These callbacks, like the dependency property itself, must all be implemented as public, static methods. Each callback has a specific return type and parameter list that you must use on your callback method.

Now it is time to get back on track and continue with the game client for Ben's Cards. In the following Try It Out, you create a user control that can represent a playing card in the application.

> **NOTE** *You can add dependency properties by typing* `propdp` *in the C# editor and pressing the Tab key.*

TRY IT OUT User Controls: BensCards.WPF\CardControl.xaml

Return to the BensCards.WPF project from the previous Try It Out.

1. This example uses the CardLib project that you created in Chapter 13, so you have to add this to the solution. Begin by right-clicking the solution name in the Solution Explorer and choosing Add ➪ Existing Project. Browse to and select the `Ch13CardLib.csproj` file from the Chapter 13 code examples.

2. In the BensCards.WPF project, add a reference to the Ch13CardLib project by right-clicking References and choosing Add Reference in the BensCards.WPF project. Click Projects ➪ Solution from the tree on the left and select Ch13CardLib. Click OK.

3. Add a new value converter by adding a new class to the project. Name it `RankNameConverter.cs` and add this code:

```
using System;
using System.Windows;
using System.Windows.Data;
namespace BensCards.WPF
{
  [ValueConversion(typeof(Ch13CardLib.Rank), typeof(string))]
  public class RankNameConverter : IValueConverter
  {
    public object Convert(object value, Type targetType,
          object parameter, System.Globalization.CultureInfo culture)
    {
      int source = (int)value;
      if (source == 1 || source > 10)
      {
```

```
                switch (source)
                {
                  case 1:
                    return "Ace";
                  case 11:
                    return "Jack";
                  case 12:
                    return "Queen";
                  case 13:
                    return "King";
                  default:
                    return DependencyProperty.UnsetValue;
                }
              }
              else
                return source.ToString();
            }
            public object ConvertBack(object value, Type targetType,
                    object parameter, System.Globalization.CultureInfo culture)
            {
                return DependencyProperty.UnsetValue;
            }
          }
        }
```

4. Add a new user control called CardControl to the BensCards.WPF project.

5. Remove the line from the XAML setting d:DesignHeight="300" d:DesignWidth="300" then set
   the Height, Width, and Name properties of the UserControl like this:

   ```
   Height="154" Width="100" Name="UserControl"
   ```

6. Before the Grid control, add the resources that will be used in the definition of the control. Make
   sure to add the image files to your project with Build Action set to Resource.

   ```
   <UserControl.Resources>
     <local:RankNameConverter x:Key="rankConverter"/>
     <DataTemplate x:Key="SuitTemplate">
       <TextBlock Text="{Binding}"/>
     </DataTemplate>
     <Style TargetType="Image" x:Key="SuitImage">
       <Style.Triggers>
         <DataTrigger Binding="{Binding ElementName=UserControl, Path=Suit}"
             Value="Club">
           <Setter Property="Source" Value="Images\Clubs.png" />
         </DataTrigger>
         <DataTrigger Binding="{Binding ElementName=UserControl, Path=Suit}"
             Value="Heart">
           <Setter Property="Source" Value="Images\Hearts.png" />
         </DataTrigger>
         <DataTrigger Binding="{Binding ElementName=UserControl, Path=Suit}"
             Value="Diamond">
           <Setter Property="Source" Value="Images\Diamonds.png" />
         </DataTrigger>
         <DataTrigger Binding="{Binding ElementName=UserControl, Path=Suit}"
             Value="Spade">
   ```

```
                    <Setter Property="Source" Value="Images\Spades.png" />
                </DataTrigger>
            </Style.Triggers>
        </Style>
    </UserControl.Resources>
```

7. Inside the `Grid` control, add a `Rectangle` control like this:

```
<Rectangle RadiusX="12.5" RadiusY="12.5">
  <Rectangle.Fill>
    <LinearGradientBrush EndPoint="0.47,-0.167" StartPoint="0.86,0.92">
      <GradientStop Color="#FFD1C78F" Offset="0"/>
      <GradientStop Color="#FFFFFFFF" Offset="1"/>
    </LinearGradientBrush>
  </Rectangle.Fill>
  <Rectangle.Effect>
    <DropShadowEffect Direction="145" BlurRadius="10" ShadowDepth="0" />
  </Rectangle.Effect>
</Rectangle>
```

8. Next, add a `Path` control. Once this is done, you should have a control that looks like Figure 21-14.

FIGURE 21-14

```
<Path Fill="#FFFFFFFF" Stretch="Fill" Stroke="{x:Null}"
  Margin=" 0,0,35,0" Data="M12,0
                          L47,0
                          C18,25 17,81 23,98
                          35,131 54,144 63,149
                          L12,149
                          C3,149 0,143 0,136
                          L0,12
                          C0,5 3,0 12,0
                          z">
  <Path.OpacityMask>
    <LinearGradientBrush EndPoint="0.957,1.127" StartPoint="0,-0.06">
      <GradientStop Color="#FF000000" Offset="0"/>
      <GradientStop Color="#00FFFFFF" Offset="1"/>
```

```
    </LinearGradientBrush>
  </Path.OpacityMask>
</Path>
```

9. You now have something that looks kind of like the back of a playing card, but we want this control to display the front as well, so we continue with some labels to display the suit and rank of the card. After the Path code, add the following to `CardControl.xaml`.

```xml
<Label x:Name="SuitLabel"
  Content="{Binding Path=Suit, ElementName=UserControl, Mode=Default}"
  ContentTemplate="{DynamicResource SuitTemplate}"
  HorizontalAlignment="Center" VerticalAlignment="Center"
  Margin="8,51,8,60" />
<Label x:Name="RankLabel"  Grid.ZIndex="1"
  Content="{Binding Path=Rank, ElementName=UserControl, Mode=Default,
      Converter={StaticResource ResourceKey=rankConverter}}"
  ContentTemplate="{DynamicResource SuitTemplate}"
  HorizontalAlignment="Left" VerticalAlignment="Top"
  Margin="8,8,0,0" />
<Label x:Name="RankLabelInverted"
  Content="{Binding Path=Rank, ElementName=UserControl, Mode=Default,
      Converter={StaticResource ResourceKey=rankConverter}}"
  ContentTemplate="{DynamicResource SuitTemplate}"
  HorizontalAlignment="Right" VerticalAlignment="Bottom"
  Margin="0,0,8,8" RenderTransformOrigin="0.5,0.5">
  <Label.RenderTransform>
    <RotateTransform Angle="180"/>
  </Label.RenderTransform>
</Label>
```

10. Finally, at the end of `CardControl.xaml`, add images to display the suit of the card in order to give a nice visual representation of the suit:

```xml
<Image Name="TopRightImage" Style="{StaticResource ResourceKey=SuitImage}"
        Margin="12,12,8,0" HorizontalAlignment="Right" VerticalAlignment="Top"
        Width="18.5" Height="18.5" Stretch="UniformToFill" />
<Image Name="BottomLeftImage" Style="{StaticResource ResourceKey=SuitImage}"
        Margin="12,0,8,12" HorizontalAlignment="Left" VerticalAlignment="Bottom"
        Width="18.5" Height="18.5" Stretch="UniformToFill"
        RenderTransformOrigin="0.5,0.5">
  <Image.RenderTransform>
    <RotateTransform Angle="180" />
  </Image.RenderTransform>
</Image>
```

11. Go to the code-behind for the `CardControl` and add three dependency properties to the class (you can type `propdp` and press the Tab key twice to make Visual Studio create the template for the properties):

```csharp
public static DependencyProperty SuitProperty = DependencyProp-
erty.Register(
    "Suit",
    typeof(Ch13CardLib.Suit),
    typeof(CardControl),
    new PropertyMetadata(Ch13CardLib.Suit.Club,
```

```
new PropertyChangedCallback(OnSuitChanged)));
  public static DependencyProperty RankProperty = DependencyProperty.Register(
    "Rank",
    typeof(Ch13CardLib.Rank),
    typeof(CardControl),
    new PropertyMetadata(Ch13CardLib.Rank.Ace));
  public static DependencyProperty IsFaceUpProperty = DependencyProperty.Register(
"IsFaceUp",
typeof(bool),
typeof(CardControl),
new PropertyMetadata(true, new PropertyChangedCallback(OnIsFaceUpChanged)));
  public bool IsFaceUp
  {
    get { return (bool)GetValue(IsFaceUpProperty); }
    set { SetValue(IsFaceUpProperty, value); }
  }
  public Ch13CardLib.Suit Suit
  {
    get { return (Ch13CardLib.Suit)GetValue(SuitProperty); }
    set { SetValue(SuitProperty, value); }
  }
  public Ch13CardLib.Rank Rank
  {
    get { return (Ch13CardLib.Rank)GetValue(RankProperty); }
    set { SetValue(RankProperty, value); }
  }
```

12. Add the change event handlers to the class:

```
public static void OnSuitChanged(DependencyObject source,
  DependencyPropertyChangedEventArgs args)
{
  var control = source as CardControl;
  control.SetTextColor();
}
private static void OnIsFaceUpChanged(DependencyObject source,
           DependencyPropertyChangedEventArgs args)
{
  var control = source as CardControl;
  control.RankLabel.Visibility = control.SuitLabel.Visibility =
           control.RankLabelInverted.Visibility =
  control.TopRightImage.Visibility =
  control.BottomLeftImage.Visibility = control.IsFaceUp ?
           Visibility.Visible : Visibility.Hidden;
}
```

13. Add a property to the class:

```
private Ch13CardLib.Card card;
public Ch13CardLib.Card Card
{
    get { return card; }
    private set { card = value; Suit = card.suit; Rank = card.rank; }
} }
```

14. Add a helper method to set the text colors and overload the constructor to take a card:

```
public CardControl(Ch13CardLib.Card card)
    {
        InitializeComponent();
        Card = card;
    }
    private void SetTextColor()
    {
        var color = (Suit == Ch13CardLib.Suit.Club || Suit == Ch13CardLib.Suit.
Spade) ?
            new SolidColorBrush(Color.FromRgb(0, 0, 0)) :
            new SolidColorBrush(Color.FromRgb(255, 0, 0));
        RankLabel.Foreground = SuitLabel.Foreground = RankLabelInverted.Foreground =
                            color;
    }
```

15. Go to the GameClientWindow and add a new grid to the window below the label:

```
<Grid x:Name="contentGrid" Grid.Row="2" />
```

16. Set the main grid's `Background` color to green:

```
<Grid Background="Green">
```

17. Go to the code-behind file and change the constructor like this:

```
public GameClientWindow()
    {
        InitializeComponent();
        var position = new Point(15, 15);
        for (var i = 0; i < 4; i++)
        {
            var suit = (Ch13CardLib.Suit)i;
            position.Y = 15;
            for (int rank = 1; rank < 14; rank++)
            {
                position.Y += 30;
                var card = new CardControl(new Ch13CardLib.Card((Ch13CardLib.Suit)suit,
                                                    (Ch13CardLib.Rank)rank));
                card.VerticalAlignment = VerticalAlignment.Top;
                card.HorizontalAlignment = HorizontalAlignment.Left;
                card.Margin = new Thickness(position.X, position.Y, 0, 0);
                contentGrid.Children.Add(card);
            }
            position.X += 112;
        }
    }
```

18. Change the `StartupUri` in the `App.xaml` file to `GameClientWindow.xaml` and run the application. The result is shown in Figure 21-15.

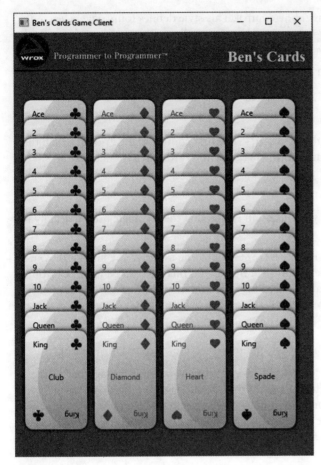

FIGURE 21-15

How It Works

This example creates a user control with two dependent properties and includes client code to use the control. This example covers plenty of ground, and the place to start looking at the code is with the Card control.

The Card control consists mostly of code that will be familiar to you from code you've seen earlier in this chapter. The first section defines a number of resources for the control. First, it defines an instance of the RankConverter class, ensuring that this can be used in the XAML.

```
<local:RankNameConverter x:Key="rankConverter"/>
```

Next, a DataTemplate is defined. A DataTemplate is similar to a ControlTemplate in that it can be used to change the visual appearance of a control. However, where a ControlTemplate is typically used only to modify the look and feel of the control, a DataTemplate is used to present the underlying data of a control, so, for example, it can be used to display properties from the control's DataContext.

The final resource that is defined is a style for an `Image` control. This style defines four triggers, each of which are bound to the `Suit` property of the `UserControl` class. Depending on the value of the control, the trigger will set the `Source` property of the `Image` control to the appropriate picture:

```
<DataTrigger Binding="{Binding ElementName=UserControl, Path=Suit}"
             Value="Club">
  <Setter Property="Source" Value="Images\Clubs.png" />
</DataTrigger>
```

Once the resources are in place, the drawing of the card starts. The first control in the grid on which the card is drawn is a `Rectangle`, which may be a little surprising since the cards have rounded corners. This is achieved by setting the `RadiusX` and `RadiusY` properties of the control:

```
<Rectangle RadiusX="12.5" RadiusY="12.5">
```

These two properties actually control the x and y radius of an ellipse that the rectangle uses internally to display rounded corners.

The rectangle is then filled with color using a `LiniarGradientBrush`. The `StartPoint` and `EndPoint` properties dictate the line along which the gradient is drawn. By default, this line will be from 0,0 (top-left corner) to 1,1 (bottom-right corner). The gradient used here specifies that the line starts close to the bottom-right corner and ends close to the middle of the x-axis, above the top of the control:

```
<LinearGradientBrush EndPoint="0.47,-0.167" StartPoint="0.86,0.92">
```

Finally, a `DropShadow` effect is added to the rectangle, which draws a shadow around the control.

Next a `Path` control is placed in the `Grid`. This control allows you to draw polygons using lines and curves. You can use C# code to program the path that the control should describe, or you can use markup syntax as you did in this example. As the `Path` is defined for the control, it can be difficult to see the polygon that is drawn. This is because the `Stroke` property is set to `null`, so for the purpose of this explanation, try changing it to `Red` instead. You should then see the card with the polygon outlined in red as shown in Figure 21-16.

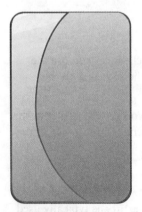

FIGURE 21-16

The stretch property is also important. When this is set to Fill, and the control in which the Path is defined is resized, the polygon will resize gracefully with the parent control. Finally, the Margin causes the Path control to move its right edge 35 pixels to the left of the parent's right edge.

Now, take a look at the Data Property:

```
Data="M12,0
      L47,0
      C18,25 17,81 23,98
      35,131 54,144 63,149
      L12,149
      C3,149 0,143 0,136
      L0,12
      C0,5 3,0 12,0
      z"
```

You use the Data property to set the path. This property takes a string in a very specific format. Some of the numbers in the string are prefixed with letters; others are not, so let's dig into it.

The path starts with M12,0. The M before the coordinate instructs the path that this is a start point for the path. The fact that it is an uppercase M is important, because that means that this coordinate is an absolute position; if it had been lowercase instead, it would mean that the coordinate is an offset to the previous point. If no such point exists, 0,0 is used as a previous point. This positions the start of the polygon 12 pixels to the left of the top-left corner.

The next instruction is L47,0. This creates a straight line from the current point to the specified point. In this case, it draws a horizontal line from 12,0 to 47,0. Another way to achieve the same effect would be to write h35 or H47. The H, either upper- or lowercase, instructs the path to draw a horizontal line. Once again, an uppercase letter means an absolute position; lowercase means a distance from the previous point.

The third instruction is a little longer:

```
C18,25 17,81 23,98
```

The C means that this is a cubic Bezier curve. To draw such a curve, you need four points: the starting point, two points to specify the starting and ending tangents, and the endpoint. The starting point is given by the endpoint of the preceding line. The first two points in the set are the control points that define the starting and ending tangents of the curve, respectively. The third point is the ending point.

The next set of points isn't prefixed with a letter. When this happens, the instructions are treated as the same type as the previous instruction, so this is another curve.

The remainder of the instructions are just more lines and curves, until you reach the very end, where a lowercase z is specified. This means that the polygon must be closed, so a straight line is drawn from the current position to the starting point. In this case, it could have been omitted, since the final curve meets up with the start of the polygon, but it is included for the sake of completeness. Closing the curve is important if you want the closure to use the join cap. If you just make the curve start and end at the same point, then the start and end use the end cap.

The code in `CardControl` exposes three dependency properties, `Suit`, `Rank`, and `IsFaceUp`, to client code, and binds these properties to visual elements in the control layout. As a result, when you set `Suit` to `Club`, the word `Club` is displayed in the center of the card and the Club image is displayed in the top-right and bottom-left corners of the card. Similarly, the value of `Rank` is displayed in the other two corners of the card.

You'll look at the implementation of these properties in a moment. For now, it is enough to know that they are enumerations originating from the CardLib project that you started in Chapter 10.

The three labels display the rank and suit of the card. Even though they are bound to different properties, they have a few things in common. They must display some text in red or black depending on the values of the bound properties. In this example, the color is set using the events raised when the `Rank` changes, but you can use triggers for this:

```
<Label x:Name="SuitLabel"
    Content="{Binding Path=Suit, ElementName=UserControl, Mode=Default}"
    ContentTemplate="{DynamicResource SuitTemplate}" HorizontalAlignment="Center"
    VerticalAlignment="Center" Margin="8,51,8,60" />
```

When you bind property values, you can also specify how to render the bound content, by using a data template. In this example, the *data template* is `SuitTemplate`, referenced as a dynamic resource (although in this case a static resource binding would also work fine). This template is defined in the user control resources section as follows:

```
<UserControl.Resources>
  <DataTemplate x:Key="SuitTemplate">
    <TextBlock Text="{Binding}"/>
  </DataTemplate>
</UserControl.Resources>
```

The string value of `Suit` is therefore used as the `Text` property of a `TextBlock` control. This same `Data-Template` definition is reused for the two rank labels. `Suit` is an enumeration, and the name of the value in the enumeration is automatically converted to a string to be displayed in the `Text` property.

The two `Rank` labels include a value converter in the binding:

```
<Label x:Name="RankLabel" Grid.ZIndex="1"
        Content="{Binding Path=Rank, ElementName=UserControl, Mode=Default,
                Converter={StaticResource ResourceKey=rankConverter}}"
        ContentTemplate="{DynamicResource SuitTemplate}"
        HorizontalAlignment="Left" VerticalAlignment="Top"
        Margin="8,8,0,0" />
```

The converter is included in the `UserControl` resources through this declaration:

```
<local:RankNameConverter x:Key="rankConverter"/>
```

You will not break the control if you remove the value converter. Instead, you will see Ace, 2, 3, 4, and so on. You will also see the names of the enumeration values converted to string—Ace, Deuce, Three, Four, and so on. Although this is technically correct, it doesn't look quite right, so you convert the values to a combination of numbers and strings.

The final point to notice is the `Grid.ZIndex="1"` property assignment on the `RankLabel`. The `ZIndex` of a control on a `Grid` or `Canvas` determines the visual layer that holds the control. If two or more controls occupy the same space, then you can use the `ZIndex` to force one of them to go to the front. Normally, all controls have a `ZIndex` of zero, so setting a single control to 1 means that it is moved to the front. This is necessary because the blur of the path would otherwise obscure the text.

For this data binding to work, you must define three dependency properties using techniques you learned previously. These are defined in the code-behind for the user control as follows (they have simple .NET property wrappers, which there is no need to show here because of the simplicity of the code):

```
public static DependencyProperty SuitProperty = DependencyProperty.
Register(
        "Suit",
        typeof(CardLib.Suit),
        typeof(CardControl),
        new PropertyMetadata(CardLib.Suit.Club,
        new PropertyChangedCallback(OnSuitChanged)));
        public static DependencyProperty RankProperty = DependencyProperty.
Register(
        "Rank",
        typeof(CardLib.Rank),
        typeof(CardControl),
        new PropertyMetadata(CardLib.Rank.Ace));
        public static DependencyProperty IsFaceUpProperty = DependencyProperty.
Register(
        "IsFaceUp",typeof(bool),
        typeof(CardControl),
        new PropertyMetadata(true, new PropertyChangedCallback(OnIsFaceUpChanged)));
```

The dependency properties use a callback method to validate their values, and the `Suit` and `IsFaceUp` properties also have a callback method for when their values change.

When the value of `Suit` changes, the `OnSuitChanged()` callback method is called. This method is responsible for setting the text color to red (for hearts and diamonds) or black (for clubs and spades). It does this by calling a utility method on the source of the method call. This is necessary because the callback method is implemented as a static method, but it is passed the instance of the user control that raised the event as a parameter so that it can interact with it. The method called is `SetTextColor()`:

```
public static void OnSuitChanged(DependencyObject source,
    DependencyPropertyChangedEventArgs args)
{
    var control = source as CardControl;
    control.SetTextColor();
}
```

The `SetTextColor()` method is private but is obviously still accessible from `OnSuitChanged()`, as they are both members of the same class, despite being instance and static methods, respectively. `SetTextColor()` simply sets the `Foreground` property of the various labels of the control to a solid color brush that is either black or red, depending on the `Suit` value.

When `IsFaceUp` changes, the control displays or hides the images and labels that are used to display the current value of the control.

The code in the `GameClientWindow.xaml.cs` code-behind file is included to display the cards and is only temporary. It generates one card for each of the 13 possible values and displays each suit in a column.

THE MAIN WINDOW

The main window of the application is where the game is played, and it therefore has only a few controls on it. You'll construct the game in this section, but before you start, there are a couple of things that you need to do. You need to add menus to the game client window and bind the windows you already constructed to the menu items.

The Menu Control

Most applications include menus and toolbars of some kind. Both are a means to the same end: to provide easy navigation of the application's content. Toolbars generally contain a subset of the same entries that the menus provide and can be thought of as shortcuts to the menu items.

Visual Studio ships with both a `Menu` and a `Toolbar` control. The example here shows the use of the `Menu` control, but using the `Toolbar` is very similar.

By default, the menu item appears as a horizontal bar from which you can drop down lists of items. The control is an Items control, so it is possible to change the default items contained in the content; however, you would normally use `MenuItem` controls in some form, as shown in the following example. Each `MenuItem` can contain other menu items, and you can build complex menus by nesting `MenuItem` controls within each other, but you should try to keep the menu structure as simple as possible.

You can control how the `MenuItem` displays using a number of properties (see Table 21-13).

TABLE 21-13: Displaying MenuItem Properties

PROPERTY	DESCRIPTION
Icon	Displays an icon by the left edge of the control
IsCheckable	Displays a CheckBox by the left edge of the control
IsChecked	Gets or sets the value of a CheckBox on a MenuItem

Routed Commands with Menus

Routed commands were briefly discussed earlier in this chapter, but now you are going to see them in action for the first time. Recall that these commands are akin to events in that they execute code when a user performs an action, and they can return a state indicating whether they can be executed at any given time.

There are at least three reasons why you would want to use routed commands instead of events:

1. The action that will cause an event to occur can be triggered from multiple locations in your application.

2. The UI element should be accessible only under certain conditions, such as a Save button being disabled if there's nothing to save.

3. You want to disconnect the code that handles the event from the code-behind file.

If any of these scenarios matches yours, consider using routed commands. In the case of the game, some of the items in the menu should also potentially be available from a toolbar. In addition, the Save action should be available only when a game is in progress and it should potentially be available from both a menu and the toolbar.

> **NOTE** *It is important to have the correct default namespace set in the Bens-Cards.WPF project in order to make the examples work. If you get compiler errors stating that a class or resource isn't a member of a namespace, you probably used a different namespace than the one being used in the book. The BensCards solution uses two root namespaces:* Ch13CardLib *for the Ch13CardLib project and* BensCards.WPF *for the BensCards.WPF project. If you experience problems, try changing the namespaces throughout the projects to match those used in the book.*

TRY IT OUT   Creating the Main Window: BensCards.WPF\GameClientWindow.xaml

In this example you continue to work on the GameClientWindow you created earlier in this chapter.

1. Open the ControlResource.xaml file and add these styles for use by the Menu control:

```
<Style x:Key="MainMenuStyle" TargetType="Menu">
    <Setter Property="Background" Value="Black" />
    <Setter Property="Foreground" Value="White" />
    <Setter Property="FontWeight" Value="Bold" />
</Style>
<Style x:Key="MainMenuItemStyle" TargetType="MenuItem">
    <Setter Property="Foreground" Value="White" />
</Style>
<Style x:Key="MainMenuSubMenuItemStyle" TargetType="MenuItem">
    <Setter Property="Foreground" Value="Black" />
    <Setter Property="Width" Value="200" />
    <Setter Property="Height" Value="22" />
</Style>
<Style x:Key="MenuItemSeperatorStyle" TargetType="Separator">
    <Setter Property="Foreground" Value="Black"/>
</Style>
```

2. Open the `GameClientWindow` and drag a `Menu` control into the grid. Set its properties like this:

```
<Menu Grid.Row="1" Margin="0" Style="{StaticResource MainMenuStyle}">
</Menu>
```

3. Right-click the menu in the Design View and choose Add MenuItem.

4. Change the `Header` property to `_File`. Note the leading underscore. Remove `Height` and `Width` properties (if set) and set the `Style` to `MainMenuStyle`:

```
<MenuItem Header="_File" Style="{StaticResource MainMenuItemStyle}"/>
```

5. Add another `MenuItem` inside the `_File` item by right-clicking the `_File` item and selecting Add MenuItem. Set the `Header` and `Style` properties like this:

```
<MenuItem Header="_File" Style="{StaticResource MainMenuItemStyle}">
    <MenuItem Header="_New Game" Style="{StaticResource
                            MainMenuSubMenuItemStyle}"/>
</MenuItem>
```

6. Add the following `MenuItems` to the File menu:

```
<MenuItem Header="_Open" Style="{StaticResource
                    MainMenuSubMenuItemStyle}"/>
<MenuItem Header="_Save" Style="{StaticResource
        MainMenuSubMenuItemStyle}" Command="Save">
    <MenuItem.Icon>
        <Image Source="Images\base_floppydisk_32.png" Width="20" />
    </MenuItem.Icon>
</MenuItem>
<Separator  Style="{StaticResource MenuItemSeperatorStyle}"/>
<MenuItem Header="_Close"
    Style="{StaticResource MainMenuSubMenuItemStyle}" Command="Close"/>
```

7. Add these `MenuItems` to the menu on the same level as the File `MenuItem`:

```
<MenuItem Header="_Game" Style="{StaticResource MainMenuItemStyle}">
    <MenuItem Header="_Undo" Style="{StaticResource
                        MainMenuSubMenuItemStyle}"/>
</MenuItem>
<MenuItem Header="_Tools" Style="{StaticResource MainMenuItemStyle}">
    <MenuItem Header="_Options" Style="{StaticResource
                            MainMenuSubMenuItemStyle}"/>
</MenuItem>
<MenuItem Header="Help" Style="{StaticResource MainMenuItemStyle}">
    <MenuItem Header="_About" Style="{StaticResource
                            MainMenuSubMenuItemStyle}"/>
</MenuItem>
```

8. Above the main grid control, below the `</Window.Resources>` tag, add this command binding to the window:

```
<Window.CommandBindings>
  <CommandBinding Command="ApplicationCommands.Close"
      CanExecute="CommandCanExecute" Executed="CommandExecuted" />
  <CommandBinding Command="ApplicationCommands.Save"
      CanExecute="CommandCanExecute" Executed="CommandExecuted" />
</Window.CommandBindings>
```

Your window should now look like Figure 21-17.

FIGURE 21-17

9. Go to the `GameClientWindow.xaml.cs` code-behind file and add the following two methods. You must include the `System.Windows.Input` namespace:

```
private void CommandCanExecute(object sender, CanExecuteRoutedEventArgs e)
{
    if (e.Command == ApplicationCommands.Close)
        e.CanExecute = true;
    if (e.Command == ApplicationCommands.Save)
        e.CanExecute = false;
    e.Handled = true;
}
private void CommandExecuted(object sender, ExecutedRoutedEventArgs e)
{
    if (e.Command == ApplicationCommands.Close)
        this.Close();
    e.Handled = true;
}
```

10. Change the constructor of the `GameClientWindow` so it only calls `InitializeComponent()`:

```
public GameClientWindow()
{
    InitializeComponent();
}
```

11. Run the application.

How It Works

When you run the application, you will notice that the Game Client window is initially displayed as maximized, but you can resize the window as you like. When you hold down the Alt key, the File menu gets focus and the F in File is underlined, indicating that you can expand the menu by pressing F.

When you expand the menu, you can see that the Save menu is disabled, but it displays a disk icon as well as the text "Ctrl+S" to the right of the element title. This means that you can access it by pressing Ctrl+S (when it is enabled). You might wonder why this is displayed, as you haven't set any shortcut keys anywhere. However, you did set a command for the menu item:

```
<MenuItem Header="_Save" Style="{StaticResource MainMenuSubMenuItemStyle}"
                                                        Command="Save">
```

The Save command is defined by WPF. Save and Close, which are used in the File menu, are defined in the `ApplicationCommands` class, which also defines Cut, Copy, Paste, and Print. When you specify the Save command for a `MenuItem`, the shortcut key Ctrl+S is assigned to the menu item because it's the standard key combination used to access that function in most Windows applications.

In the code-behind file, you added two methods used to determine the state and action taken by the commands. In the XAML, you created two command bindings that used the methods like this:

```
<Window.CommandBindings>
    <CommandBinding Command="ApplicationCommands.Close"
        CanExecute="CommandCanExecute" Executed="CommandExecuted" />
    <CommandBinding Command="ApplicationCommands.Save"
        CanExecute="CommandCanExecute" Executed="CommandExecuted" />
</Window.CommandBindings>
    private void CommandCanExecute(object sender, CanExecuteRoutedEventArgs e)
    {
        if (e.Command == ApplicationCommands.Close)
            e.CanExecute = true;
        if (e.Command == ApplicationCommands.Save)
            e.CanExecute = false;
        e.Handled = true;
    }
    private void CommandExecuted(object sender, ExecutedRoutedEventArgs e)
    {
        if (e.Command == ApplicationCommands.Close)
            this.Close();
        e.Handled = true;
    }
```

The CanExecute part of the command binding specifies a method that is called to determine whether the command should be available to the user at the moment. The Executed part specifies a method that should be called when the user activates the command. Note that it doesn't matter from where the command is activated. If a menu item and a button both include the Save command, the binding works for both.

The current implementation of CommandCanExecute is too simple for real life, where you would do some calculation to determine whether the application is ready to save anything. Since you don't have a game to save yet, just returning false for the Save command is appropriate. You do this by setting the e.CanExecute property on the CanExecuteRoutedEventArgs class. The Close command, on the other hand, can be executed just fine, so you return true for that one.

CommandExecuted performs the same test as CommandCanExecute. If it determines that the command to execute is the Close command, then it closes the current window.

PUTTING IT ALL TOGETHER

At this point in the development of the game, you have two independent dialog boxes, a card library, and a main window that provides a blank space for the game to be displayed on. That still leaves quite a lot of work, but with the foundation built, it's time to start on the game itself. The classes in the CardLib library describe the game "domain model," that is, the objects that a game can be broken down into. These need to be refactored a bit to make the game work better with a Windows application. Next you are going to write the game's "View Model," which is a class that is able to control the display of the game. Then you will create two additional user controls that use the Card user control to display the game visually. Finally, you will bind it all together in the game client.

> **NOTE** *The term "View Model" comes from a much used design pattern in WPF: Model - View - ViewModel (MVVM). This design pattern describes how to separate code from the view and link it together. Although this book doesn't attempt to conform to this pattern, this example uses a lot of the elements from it, such as separating the ViewModel from the views. In this context, the domain model described next is the "model" part of the MVVM name, and the windows you have been creating are the views.*

Refactoring the Domain Model

As stated, the domain model is the code that describes the objects of the game. At the moment, you have these classes in the CardLib project that describe objects of the game:

➤ Card

➤ Deck

➤ Rank

➤ Suit

In addition to these classes, the game needs a `Player` and a `ComputerPlayer` class, so you are going to add those. You also need to modify the `Card` and `Deck` classes a bit to make them work better in a Windows application.

There is a lot of work to do, so let's get started.

> **NOTE** *This example does not use the* `CardClient` *class from the earlier chapters because the differences between console and Windows applications are so great that very little code can be reused.*

TRY IT OUT   Finishing the Domain Model: BensCards.WPF

This example continues where the previous example left off.

1. Each player in the game can be in a number of "states" during the game. You can model this in a `PlayerState` enumeration. Go to the Ch13CardLib project and create a new `PlayerState` enumeration for the project. You can simply create a new class and replace its code like this:

    ```
    [Serializable]
    public enum PlayerState
    {
        Inactive,
        Active,
        MustDiscard,
        Winner,
        Loser
    }
    ```

2. Next, you raise a few events when something happens on a player. For that, you need some custom event arguments, so add another class named `PlayerEventArgs`. For now, don't worry that the `Player` class is missing:

    ```
    public class PlayerEventArgs : EventArgs
    {
      public Player Player { get; set; }
      public PlayerState State { get; set; }
    }
    ```

3. You also need to raise events when something happens to a card, so go ahead and create another class called `CardEventArgs`:

    ```
    public class CardEventArgs : EventArgs
    {
      public Card Card { get; set; }
    }
    ```

4. The enumeration `ComputerSkillLevel` currently exists in the `GameOptions.cs` class (in the BensCards.WPF project). Go ahead and cut it from there and move it to its own file in the Ch13CardLib project. This changes its namespace to `Ch13CardLib`, so you have to add the `Ch13CardLib` namespace to the `GameOptions.cs` and `OptionsWindow.Xaml.cs` files:

    ```
    using Ch13CardLib;
    ```

5. The `Deck` class should be changed. Rather than going back to this class multiple times over the course of this chapter, the following listing is the complete class:

```csharp
using System;
using System.Collections.Generic;
using System.Linq;
namespace Ch13CardLib
{
  public delegate void LastCardDrawnHandler(Deck currentDeck);
  public class Deck : ICloneable
  {
    public event LastCardDrawnHandler LastCardDrawn;
    private Cards cards = new Cards();
    public Deck()
    {
      InsertAllCards();
    }
    protected Deck(Cards newCards)
    {
      cards = newCards;
    }
    public int CardsInDeck
    {
      get { return cards.Count; }
    }
    public Card GetCard(int cardNum)
    {
      if (cardNum >= 0  && cardNum <= 51)
      {
        if ((cardNum == 51)  && (LastCardDrawn != null)) LastCardDrawn(this);
        return cards[cardNum];
      }
      else
        throw new CardOutOfRangeException(cards.Clone() as Cards);
    }
    public void Shuffle()
    {
      Cards newDeck = new Cards();
      bool[] assigned = new bool[cards.Count];
      Random sourceGen = new Random();
      for (int i = 0; i < cards.Count; i++)
      {
        int sourceCard = 0;
        bool foundCard = false;
        while (foundCard == false)
        {
          sourceCard = sourceGen.Next(cards.Count);
          if (assigned[sourceCard] == false)
            foundCard = true;
        }
        assigned[sourceCard] = true;
        newDeck.Add(cards[sourceCard]);
      }
      newDeck.CopyTo(cards);
    }
```

```
        public void ReshuffleDiscarded(List<Card> cardsInPlay)
        {
          InsertAllCards(cardsInPlay);
          Shuffle();
        }
        public Card Draw()
        {
          if (cards.Count == 0) return null;
          var card = cards[0];
          cards.RemoveAt(0);
          return card;
        }
        public Card SelectCardOfSpecificSuit(Suit suit)
        {
          Card selectedCard = cards.FirstOrDefault(card => card?.suit == suit);
          if (selectedCard == null) return Draw();
          cards.Remove(selectedCard);
          return selectedCard;
        }
        public object Clone()
        {
          Deck newDeck = new Deck(cards.Clone() as Cards);
          return newDeck;
        }
        private void InsertAllCards()
        {
          for (int suitVal = 0; suitVal < 4; suitVal++)
          {
            for (int rankVal = 1; rankVal < 14; rankVal++)
            {
              cards.Add(new Card((Suit)suitVal, (Rank)rankVal));
            }
          }
        }
        private void InsertAllCards(List<Card> except)
        {
          for (int suitVal = 0; suitVal < 4; suitVal++)
          {
            for (int rankVal = 1; rankVal < 14; rankVal++)
            {
              var card = new Card((Suit)suitVal, (Rank)rankVal);
              if (except?.Contains(card) ?? false)              continue;
              cards.Add(card);
            }
          }
        }
      }
    }
```

6. There will be two types of players in the game: a Player, which is controlled by a real person; and a ComputerPlayer, which is controlled by the game. Add the Player class to the Ch13CardLib project like this:

```
        using System;
        using System.ComponentModel;
```

```csharp
using System.Linq;

namespace Ch13CardLib
{
    [Serializable]
  public class Player : INotifyPropertyChanged
  {
    public int Index { get; set; }
    protected Cards Hand { get; set; }
    private string name;
    private PlayerState state;

    public event EventHandler<CardEventArgs> OnCardDiscarded;
    public event EventHandler<PlayerEventArgs> OnPlayerHasWon;

    public PlayerState State
    {
      get { return state; }
      set
      {
        state = value;
        OnPropertyChanged(nameof(State));
      }
    }

    public virtual string PlayerName
    {
      get { return name; }
      set
      {
        name = value;
        OnPropertyChanged(nameof(PlayerName));
      }
    }

    public void AddCard(Card card)
    {
      Hand.Add(card);
      if (Hand.Count > 7)
        State = PlayerState.MustDiscard;
    }

    public void DrawCard(Deck deck)
    {
      AddCard(deck.Draw());
    }

    public void DiscardCard(Card card)
    {
      Hand.Remove(card);
      if (HasWon)
        OnPlayerHasWon?.Invoke(this, new PlayerEventArgs { Player = this, State =
                                                           PlayerState.Winner });
      OnCardDiscarded?.Invoke(this, new CardEventArgs { Card = card });
    }
```

```csharp
    public void DrawNewHand(Deck deck)
    {
      Hand = new Cards();
      for (int i = 0; i < 7; i++)
        Hand.Add(deck.Draw());
    }

        public bool HasWon => Hand.Count == 7  && Hand.Select(x => x.suit)
                                                  .Distinct().Count() == 1;

        public Cards GetCards() => Hand.Clone() as Cards;

    public event PropertyChangedEventHandler PropertyChanged;
    private void OnPropertyChanged(string propertyName) => PropertyChanged?
                .Invoke(this, new PropertyChangedEventArgs(propertyName));
  }
}
```

7. Add the `ComputerPlayer` class to the Ch13CardLib project like this:

```csharp
using System;
using System.Collections.Generic;
using System.Linq;
using System.Text;

namespace Ch13CardLib
{
    [Serializable]
    public class ComputerPlayer : Player
    {
        private Random random = new Random();
        public ComputerSkillLevel Skill { get; set; }
        public override string PlayerName => $"Computer {Index}";

        public void PerformDraw(Deck deck, Card availableCard)
        {
            if (Skill == ComputerSkillLevel.Dumb)
                DrawCard(deck);
            else
                DrawBestCard(deck, availableCard, (Skill ==
                            ComputerSkillLevel.Cheats));
        }

        public void PerformDiscard(Deck deck)
        {
            if (Skill == ComputerSkillLevel.Dumb)
                DiscardCard(Hand[random.Next(Hand.Count)]);
            else
                DiscardWorstCard();
        }

        private void DrawBestCard(Deck deck, Card availableCard, bool cheat = false)
        {
            var bestSuit = CalculateBestSuit();
            if (availableCard.suit == bestSuit)
```

```
                AddCard(availableCard);
            else if (cheat == false)
                DrawCard(deck);
            else
                AddCard(deck.SelectCardOfSpecificSuit(bestSuit));
        }

        private void DiscardWorstCard()
        {
            DiscardCard(Hand.First(x => x.suit == CalculateWorstSuit()));
        }

        private Suit CalculateBestSuit() => OrderSuitsInHand().Last();

        private Suit CalculateWorstSuit() => OrderSuitsInHand().First();

        private List<Suit> OrderSuitsInHand()
        {
            var cardSuits = new Dictionary<Suit, int>
            {
                { Suit.Club, 0 },
                { Suit.Diamond, 0 },
                { Suit.Heart, 0 },
                { Suit.Spade, 0 }
            };
            foreach (var card in Hand)
                cardSuits[card.suit]++;
            return cardSuits.OrderBy(x => x.Value).Select(y => y.Key).ToList();
        }
    }
}
```

How It Works

That was a lot of code and a lot of changes! However, when you run the application, nothing seems to have changed, but a lot of plumbing has been put in to make the game work.

The `Deck` class has been extended with a few new methods. Whenever the deck is emptied, the discarded cards should be put back in play. In order to do this, an overload of the `InsertAllCards` method that takes a list of the cards that are in play has been added. The property `CardsInDeck` will be used to tell how many cards are left in the deck. If the players draw every card in the deck, you want to shuffle all the discarded cards back into the deck, and so the `Shuffle` method now allows the deck to contain fewer than 52 cards and the `ReshuffleDiscarded` method allows you to perform the reshuffle. `Draw` and `SelectCardOfSpecificSuit` are both used to draw a card. Most of the code in the `Player` and `ComputerPlayer` classes that you added to the project from the downloaded code is pretty easy to understand. The `Player` class can draw and discard cards. This is shared with the `ComputerPlayer`, but the computer is also equipped with the ability to decide which cards to draw and discard without user interaction. The `ComputerPlayer` class can also cheat:

```
public void PerformDraw(Deck deck, Card availableCard)
{
    if (Skill == ComputerSkillLevel.Dumb)
        DrawCard(deck);
    else
```

```
                DrawBestCard(deck, availableCard, (Skill == ComputerSkillLevel
                                                        .Cheats));
        }

        public void PerformDiscard(Deck deck)
        {
            if (Skill == ComputerSkillLevel.Dumb)
                DiscardCard(Hand[random.Next(Hand.Count)]);
            else
                DiscardWorstCard();
        }

        private void DrawBestCard(Deck deck, Card availableCard, bool cheat = false)
        {
            var bestSuit = CalculateBestSuit();
            if (availableCard.suit == bestSuit)
                AddCard(availableCard);
            else if (cheat == false)
                DrawCard(deck);
            else
                AddCard(deck.SelectCardOfSpecificSuit(bestSuit));
        }
```

Cheating is assisted by a deck that allows the computer to select a card of a specific suit. If you allow the computer to cheat, you are going to have a hard time winning any games!

You will also notice that the `Player` class implements the `INotifyPropertyChanged` interface and the properties `PlayerName` and `State` use this to notify any observers of changes. Particularly, the `State` property is important later as changes to this property will drive the game forward.

The View Model

The purpose of a view model is to hold the state of the view that displays it. In the case of Ben's Cards, this means that you already have a view model class: the `GameOptions` class. This class holds the state of the `Options` and `StartGame` windows. At the moment, you can't get the selected players from the options, so you have to add that ability. The view model of the game client window is missing, so that is the next task to do.

The view model for the execution of the game must reflect all the parts of the game as it is running. The parts of the game are:

➤   The deck from which the current player draws a card

➤   A card that can be taken by the current player instead of drawing a card

➤   A current player

➤   A number of participating players

The view model should also be able to notify observers of changes, and that means implementing `INotifyPropertyChanged` again.

In addition to these abilities, the view model should also provide a way of starting a new game. You will do this by creating a new routed command for the menu. The command is created in the view model, but is called from the view.

TRY IT OUT The View Model: BensCards.WPF

This example continues with the BensCards.WPF project.

1. Add the following namespaces to the `GameOptions` class using statements:

```
using System.Windows.Input;
using System.IO;
using System.Xml.Serialization;
```

2. Add a new command to the `GameOptions` class:

```
public static RoutedCommand OptionsCommand = new RoutedCommand("Show Options",
typeof(GameOptions), new InputGestureCollection(new List<InputGesture>
{ new KeyGesture(Key.O, ModifierKeys.Control) }));
```

3. Add two new methods to the class:

```
public void Save()
{
  using (var stream = File.Open("GameOptions.xml", FileMode.Create))
  {
    var serializer = new XmlSerializer(typeof(GameOptions));
    serializer.Serialize(stream, this);
  }
}
public static GameOptions Create()
{
  if (File.Exists("GameOptions.xml"))
  {
    using (var stream = File.OpenRead("GameOptions.xml"))
    {
      var serializer = new XmlSerializer(typeof(GameOptions));
      return serializer.Deserialize(stream) as GameOptions;
    }
  }
  else
    return new GameOptions();
}
```

4. Change the OK click event handler of the `OptionsWindow.xaml.cs` code-behind file like this:

```
private void okButton_Click(object sender, RoutedEventArgs e)
{
    DialogResult = true;
    gameOptions.Save();
    Close();
}
```

5. Delete everything except the `InitializeComponent` call from the constructor and hook up the `DataContextChanged` event like this:

```
public OptionsWindow()
{
    gameOptions = GameOptions.Create();
    DataContext = gameOptions;
    InitializeComponent();
}
```

6. Open the `StartGameWindow.xaml.cs` code-behind file and select the last four lines of the code in the constructor. Extract a new method called `ChangeListBoxOptions` by right-clicking the selected code and selecting Quick Actions and Refactorings ⇨ ExtractMethod:

```
private void ChangeListBoxOptions()
{
    if (gameOptions.PlayAgainstComputer)
        playerNamesListBox.SelectionMode = SelectionMode.Single;
    else
        playerNamesListBox.SelectionMode = SelectionMode.Extended;
}
```

7. Add the `StartGame_DataContextChanged` event handler:

```
void StartGame_DataContextChanged(object sender,
DependencyPropertyChangedEventArgs e)
{
    gameOptions = DataContext as GameOptions;
    ChangeListBoxOptions();
}
```

8. Delete everything except the `InitializeComponent` call from the `StartGameWindow` constructor and hook up the `DataContextChanged` event like this:

```
public StartGameWindow()
{
    InitializeComponent();
    DataContextChanged += StartGame_DataContextChanged;
}
```

9. Change the OK click event handler like this:

```
private void okButton_Click(object sender, RoutedEventArgs e)
{
    var gameOptions = DataContext as GameOptions;
    gameOptions.SelectedPlayers = new List<string>();
    foreach (string item in playerNamesListBox.SelectedItems)
    {
        gameOptions.SelectedPlayers.Add(item);
    }
    this.DialogResult = true;
    this.Close();
}
```

10. Create a new class and name it `GameViewModel`. Start by implementing the `INotifyProperty-tyChanged` interface:

```
using Ch13CardLib;
using System.Collections.Generic;
using System.ComponentModel;
using System.Linq;
using System.Windows.Input;
namespace BensCards.WPF
{
  public class GameViewModel : INotifyPropertyChanged
  {
    public event PropertyChangedEventHandler PropertyChanged;
    private void OnPropertyChanged(string propertyName) =>
PropertyChanged?.Invoke(this, new PropertyChangedEventArgs(propertyName));
  }
}
```

11. Add a property to hold the current player. This property should use the `OnPropertyChanged` event:

```
private Player currentPlayer;
public Player CurrentPlayer
{
    get { return currentPlayer; }
    set
    {
        currentPlayer = value;
        OnPropertyChanged(nameof(CurrentPlayer));
    }
}
```

12. Add four more properties and their related fields to the class, just as you did with the `Current-Player` property. The property names and field names are shown in Table 21-14.

TABLE 21-14: Property and Field Names

TYPE	PROPERTY NAME	FIELD NAME
List<Player>	Players	players
Card	CurrentAvailableCard	availableCard
Deck	GameDeck	deck
Bool	GameStarted	gameStarted

13. Add this private field to hold the game options:

```
private GameOptions gameOptions;
```

14. Add two Routed commands:

```
public static RoutedCommand StartGameCommand =
new RoutedCommand("Start New Game", typeof(GameViewModel),
```

```
new InputGestureCollection(new List<InputGesture>
{ new KeyGesture(Key.N, ModifierKeys.Control) }));
    public static RoutedCommand ShowAboutCommand =
new RoutedCommand("Show About Dialog", typeof(GameViewModel));
```

15. Add a new default constructor:

```
public GameViewModel()
    {
        Players = new List<Player>();
        gameOptions = GameOptions.Create();
    }
```

16. When a game is started, the players and deck must be initialized. Add this code to the class:

```
public void StartNewGame()
    {
    if (gameOptions.SelectedPlayers.Count < 1 ||
(gameOptions.SelectedPlayers.Count == 1
  && !gameOptions.PlayAgainstComputer))
            return;
        CreateGameDeck();
        CreatePlayers();
        InitializeGame();
        GameStarted = true;
}
private void InitializeGame()
{
    AssignCurrentPlayer(0);
    CurrentAvailableCard = GameDeck.Draw();
}
private void AssignCurrentPlayer(int index)
{
    CurrentPlayer = Players[index];
    if (!Players.Any(x => x.State == PlayerState.Winner))
        Players.ForEach(x => x.State = (x == Players[index] ?
                                        PlayerState.Active :
PlayerState.Inactive));
}
private void InitializePlayer(Player player)
{
    player.DrawNewHand(GameDeck);
    player.OnCardDiscarded += player_OnCardDiscarded;
    player.OnPlayerHasWon += player_OnPlayerHasWon;
    Players.Add(player);
}
private void CreateGameDeck()
{
    GameDeck = new Deck();
    GameDeck.Shuffle();
}
private void CreatePlayers()
{
    Players.Clear();
    for (var i = 0; i < gameOptions.NumberOfPlayers; i++)
    {
```

```
                    if (i < gameOptions.SelectedPlayers.Count)
                        InitializePlayer(new Player
                        {
                            Index = i,
                            PlayerName =
                    gameOptions.SelectedPlayers[i]
                        });
                    else
                        InitializePlayer(new ComputerPlayer
                        {
                            Index = i,
                            Skill =
                    gameOptions.ComputerSkill
                        });
                }
            }
```

17. Finally, add the two event handlers for the events generated by the players:

```
void player_OnPlayerHasWon(object sender, PlayerEventArgs e)
{
    Players.ForEach(x => x.State = (x == e.Player ? PlayerState.Winner :
                                    PlayerState.Loser));
}
void player_OnCardDiscarded(object sender, CardEventArgs e)
{
    CurrentAvailableCard = e.Card;
    var nextIndex = CurrentPlayer.Index + 1 >= gameOptions.NumberOfPlayers ? 0 :
                                    CurrentPlayer.Index + 1;
    if (GameDeck.CardsInDeck == 0)
    {
        var cardsInPlay = new List<Card>();
        foreach (var player in Players)
            cardsInPlay.AddRange(player.GetCards());
        cardsInPlay.Add(CurrentAvailableCard);
        GameDeck.ReshuffleDiscarded(cardsInPlay);
    }
    AssignCurrentPlayer(nextIndex);
}
```

18. Go to the GameClientWindow.xaml. Below the Window declaration, add a DataContext declaration:

```
<Window.DataContext >
  <local:GameViewModel />
</Window.DataContext>
```

19. Add three command bindings to the CommandBindings declarations:

```
    <CommandBinding Command="local:GameViewModel.StartGameCommand"
CanExecute="CommandCanExecute" Executed="CommandExecuted" />
    <CommandBinding Command="local:GameViewModel.ShowAboutCommand"
CanExecute="CommandCanExecute" Executed="CommandExecuted" />
        <CommandBinding Command="local:GameOptions.OptionsCommand"
CanExecute="CommandCanExecute" Executed="CommandExecuted" />
```

20. Add a command to the New Game menu item:

```
<MenuItem Header="_New Game" Style="{StaticResource MainMenuSubMenuItemStyle}"
                             Command="local:GameViewModel.StartGameCommand"/>
```

21. Add a command to the Options menu item:

```
Command="local:GameOptions.OptionsCommand"
```

22. Add a command to the About menu item:

```
Command="local:GameViewModel.ShowAboutCommand"
```

23. Go to the code-behind file and change the `CommandCanExecute` and `CommandExecuted` methods:

```
private void CommandCanExecute(object sender, CanExecuteRoutedEventArgs e)
{
    if (e.Command == ApplicationCommands.Close)
        e.CanExecute = true;
    if (e.Command == ApplicationCommands.Save)
        e.CanExecute = false;
    if (e.Command == GameViewModel.StartGameCommand)
        e.CanExecute = true;
    if (e.Command == GameOptions.OptionsCommand)
        e.CanExecute = true;
    if (e.Command == GameViewModel.ShowAboutCommand)
        e.CanExecute = true;
    e.Handled = true;
}
private void CommandExecuted(object sender, ExecutedRoutedEventArgs e)
{
    if (e.Command == ApplicationCommands.Close)
        this.Close();
    if (e.Command == GameViewModel.StartGameCommand)
    {
        var model = new GameViewModel();
        var startGameDialog = new StartGameWindow();
        var options = GameOptions.Create();
        startGameDialog.DataContext = options;
        var result = startGameDialog.ShowDialog();
        if (result.HasValue  && result.Value == true)
        {
            options.Save();
            model.StartNewGame();
            DataContext = model;
        }
    }
    if (e.Command == GameOptions.OptionsCommand)
    {
        var dialog = new OptionsWindow();
        var result = dialog.ShowDialog();
        if (result.HasValue  && result.Value == true)
            DataContext = new GameViewModel(); // Clear current game
    }
```

```
if (e.Command == GameViewModel.ShowAboutCommand)
{
    var dialog = new AboutWindow();
    dialog.ShowDialog();
}
e.Handled = true;
}
```

How It Works

Once again you have done a lot of work with very little to show for it when you run the application. The Options and New Game menu items have been given shortcut keys and can now be accessed using Ctrl+O and Ctrl+N. This is displayed when you drop down the menus. This has happened because you created two new commands for the menu. You did this in `GameOptions.cs` and `GameViewModel.cs`, respectively:

```
public static RoutedCommand OptionsCommand = new RoutedCommand("Show
Options",
    typeof(GameOptions), new InputGestureCollection(new List<InputGesture>
{ new KeyGesture(Key.O, ModifierKeys.Control) }));
    public static RoutedCommand StartGameCommand =
new RoutedCommand("Start New Game", typeof(GameViewModel),
new InputGestureCollection(new List<InputGesture>
{ new KeyGesture(Key.N, ModifierKeys.Control) }));
```

When you assign a list of `InputGestures` to the command, the shortcuts are automatically associated with the menus.

In the code-behind for the game client, you also added code to display the two windows as dialog boxes:

```
if (e.Command == GameViewModel.StartGameCommand)
{
    var model = new GameViewModel();
    var startGameDialog = new StartGameWindow();
    startGameDialog.DataContext = model.GameOptions;
    var result = startGameDialog.ShowDialog();
    if (result.HasValue  & & result.Value == true)
    {
        model.GameOptions.Save();
        model.StartNewGame();
        DataContext = model;
    }
}
```

By showing the windows as dialog boxes, you can return a value that indicates whether the result of the dialog box should be used. You can't return a value directly from the window; instead, you set the window's `DialogResult` property to either `true` or `false` to indicate success or failure:

```
private void okButton_Click(object sender, RoutedEventArgs e)
{
    this.DialogResult = true;
    this.Close();
}
```

Earlier in the chapter you were told that if you want to set the DataContext to an existing object instance, you had to do so from code. This happens in the previous code, but the XAML in GameClientWindow.xaml also instantiates a new instance when the application starts:

```
<Window.DataContext >
  <local:GameViewModel />
</Window.DataContext>
```

This instance ensures that there is a DataContext for the view, but it isn't used for much before it is exchanged for a new instance in the StartGame command.

The GameViewModel contains a lot of code but much of it is just properties and instantiation of the players and the Deck instances.

Once the game has started, the state of the players and GameViewModel drive the game forward as the computer or the players make choices. The PlayerHasWon event is handled in GameViewModel and ensures that the states of the other players change to Loser:

```
void player_OnPlayerHasWon(object sender, PlayerEventArgs e)
{
    Players.ForEach(x => x.State = (x == e.Player ? PlayerState.Winner :
PlayerState.Loser));
}
```

The other event you created for the player is also handled here: CardDiscarded is used to indicate that a player has completed her turn. This causes the CurrentPlayer to be set to the next available player:

```
void player_OnCardDiscarded(object sender, CardEventArgs e)
{
    CurrentAvailableCard = e.Card;
  var nextIndex = CurrentPlayer.Index + 1 >= gameOptions.NumberOfPlayers ? 0 :
                    CurrentPlayer.Index + 1;
  if (GameDeck.CardsInDeck == 0)
  {
    var cardsInPlay = new List<Card>();
    foreach (var player in Players)
      cardsInPlay.AddRange(player.GetCards());
    cardsInPlay.Add(CurrentAvailableCard);
    GameDeck.ReshuffleDiscarded(cardsInPlay);
  }
  AssignCurrentPlayer(nextIndex);
}
```

This event handler also checks whether there are any more cards in the deck. If there are no more cards, the event handler collects a list of cards that are currently used in the game and makes the deck generate a new, shuffled deck containing only cards that have been discarded.

The StartGame method is called from the CommandExecuted method in the GameClient.xaml.cs code-behind file. This method uses three methods to create a new deck, create and deal cards to the players, and finally set the CurrentPlayer to start the game.

Completing the Game

You now have a complete game that you can't play because nothing is being displayed in the game client. For the game to run, you need two additional user controls that will be positioned on the game client using a dock panel.

The two user controls are called `CardsInHand`, which displays a player's hand, and `GameDecks`, which displays the main deck and the available card.

TRY IT OUT Completing the Game: BensCards.WPF

Once again, this example continues with the BensCards.WPF project you have been working on.

1. Create a new user control in the BensCards.WPF project by right-clicking the project and selecting Add ⇨ User Control (WPF). Name it `CardsInHandControl`.

2. Add a `Label` and a `Canvas` control to the `Grid` like this:

```
<Grid>
    <Label Name="PlayerNameLabel" Foreground="White" FontWeight="Bold"
FontSize="14" >
        <Label.Effect>
          <DropShadowEffect ShadowDepth="5" Opacity="0.5" Direction="145" />
        </Label.Effect>
    </Label>
    <Canvas Name="CardSurface">
    </Canvas>
</Grid>
```

3. Go to the code-behind file and use these `using` directives:

```
using Ch13CardLib;
using System;
using System.Threading;
using System.Windows;
using System.Windows.Controls;
using System.Windows.Input;
using System.Windows.Media;
using System.Windows.Threading;
```

4. There are four dependency properties. Type `propdp` and press the Tab key twice to insert the property template. Insert the `Type`, `Name`, `OwnerClass`, and default value. Use Tab to switch from one value to the next. Set the values as shown in Table 21-15. Press the Return key after you finish editing the values to complete the template.

TABLE 21-15: Cards in Hand Dependency Properties

TYPE	NAME	OWNERCLASS	DEFAULT VALUE
Player	Owner	CardsInHandControl	null
GameViewModel	Game	CardsInHandControl	null
PlayerState	PlayerState	CardsInHandControl	PlayerState.Inactive
Orientation	PlayerOrientation	CardsInHandControl	Orientation.Horizontal

5. Add callback methods that will be used when the properties of the `Owner`, `PlayerState`, and `PlayerOrientation` change:

```
        private static void OnOwnerChanged(DependencyObject source,
DependencyPropertyChangedEventArgs e)
        {
          var control = source as CardsInHandControl;
          control.RedrawCards();
        }
        private static void OnPlayerStateChanged(DependencyObject source,
DependencyPropertyChangedEventArgs e)
        {
          var control = source as CardsInHandControl;
          var computerPlayer = control.Owner as ComputerPlayer;
          if (computerPlayer != null)
          {
            if (computerPlayer.State == PlayerState.MustDiscard)
            {
              Thread delayedWorker = new Thread(control.DelayDiscard);
              delayedWorker.Start(new Payload { Deck = control.Game.GameDeck,
AvailableCard = control.Game.CurrentAvailableCard, Player = computerPlayer });
            }
            else if (computerPlayer.State == PlayerState.Active)
            {
              Thread delayedWorker = new Thread(control.DelayDraw);
              delayedWorker.Start(new Payload { Deck = control.Game.GameDeck,
AvailableCard = control.Game.CurrentAvailableCard, Player = computerPlayer });
            }
          }
          control.RedrawCards();
        }
        private static void OnPlayerOrientationChanged(DependencyObject source,
DependencyPropertyChangedEventArgs args)
        {
          var control = source as CardsInHandControl;
          control.RedrawCards();
        }
```

6. The callbacks require a number of helper methods. Start by adding the private class and two methods that are used by the `delayedWorker` threads in the `OnPlayerStateChanged` method:

```
        private class Payload
        {
          public Deck Deck { get; set; }
          public Card AvailableCard { get; set; }
          public ComputerPlayer Player { get; set; }
        }
        private void DelayDraw(object payload)
        {
          Thread.Sleep(1250);
          var data = payload as Payload;
          Dispatcher.Invoke(DispatcherPriority.Normal,
new Action<Deck, Card>(data.Player.PerformDraw), data.Deck, data.AvailableCard);
        }
        private void DelayDiscard(object payload)
```

```
            {
                Thread.Sleep(1250);
                var data = payload as Payload;
                Dispatcher.Invoke(DispatcherPriority.Normal,
        new Action<Deck>(data.Player.PerformDiscard), data.Deck);
            }
```

7. The `Owner` property requires a callback that should be called whenever the property changes. You can specify this as the second parameter of the constructor of the `PropertyMetadata` class that is used as the fourth parameter of the `register()` method. Change the registration like this:

```
        public static readonly DependencyProperty OwnerProperty =
            DependencyProperty.Register(
            "Owner",
            typeof(Player),
            typeof(CardsInHandControl),
            new PropertyMetadata(null, new PropertyChangedCallback(OnOwnerChanged)));
```

8. Like the `Owner` property, the `PlayerState` and `PlayerOrientation` properties should also register a callback. Repeat step 7 for these two properties using the names `OnPlayerStateChanged` and `OnPlayerOrientationChanged` for the callback methods.

9. Add the methods used to draw the control:

```
            private void RedrawCards()
            {
                CardSurface.Children.Clear();
                if (Owner == null)
                {
                    PlayerNameLabel.Content = string.Empty;
                    return;
                }
                DrawPlayerName();
                DrawCards();
            }
            private void DrawCards()
            {
                bool isFaceup = (Owner.State != PlayerState.Inactive);
                if (Owner is ComputerPlayer)
                    isFaceup = (Owner.State == PlayerState.Loser ||
            Owner.State == PlayerState.Winner);
                var cards = Owner.GetCards();
                if (cards == null || cards.Count == 0)
                    return;
                for (var i = 0; i < cards.Count; i++)
                {
                    var cardControl = new CardControl(cards[i]);
                    if (PlayerOrientation == Orientation.Horizontal)
                        cardControl.Margin = new Thickness(i * 35, 35, 0, 0);
                    else
                        cardControl.Margin = new Thickness(5, 35 + i * 30, 0, 0);
                    cardControl.MouseDoubleClick += cardControl_MouseDoubleClick;
                    cardControl.IsFaceUp = isFaceup;
                    CardSurface.Children.Add(cardControl);
                }
```

```
        }
        private void DrawPlayerName()
        {
            if (Owner.State == PlayerState.Winner || Owner.State ==
                                          PlayerState.Loser)
                PlayerNameLabel.Content = Owner.PlayerName +
        (Owner.State == PlayerState.Winner ?
        " is the WINNER" : " has LOST");
            else
                PlayerNameLabel.Content = Owner.PlayerName;
            var isActivePlayer = (Owner.State == PlayerState.Active ||
        Owner.State == PlayerState.MustDiscard);
            PlayerNameLabel.FontSize = isActivePlayer ? 18 : 14;
            PlayerNameLabel.Foreground = isActivePlayer ?
        new SolidColorBrush(Colors.Gold) :
        new SolidColorBrush(Colors.White);
        }
```

10. Finally, add the double-click handler that is called when the player double-clicks a card:

```
        private void cardControl_MouseDoubleClick(object sender,
                                          MouseButtonEventArgs e)
        {
            var selectedCard = sender as CardControl;
            if (Owner == null)
                return;
            if (Owner.State == PlayerState.MustDiscard)
                Owner.DiscardCard(selectedCard.Card);
            RedrawCards();
        }
```

11. Create another user control like you did in step 1 and name it GameDecksControl.

12. Remove the Grid and insert a Canvas control instead:

```
    <Canvas Name="controlCanvas" Width="250" />
```

13. Go to the code-behind file and use these namespaces:

```
    using Ch13CardLib;
    using System.Collections.Generic;
    using System.Linq;
    using System.Windows;
    using System.Windows.Controls;
    using System.Windows.Documents;
    using System.Windows.Input;
```

14. As you did in step 4, add four dependency properties with these values (see Table 21-16).

TABLE 21-16: Game Decks Dependency Properties

TYPE	NAME	OWNERCLASS	DEFAULT VALUE
bool	GameStarted	GameDecksControl	false
Player	CurrentPlayer	GameDecksControl	null
Deck	Deck	GameDecksControl	null
Card	AvailableCard	GameDecksControl	null

15. Add the `DrawDecks` method:

```
private void DrawDecks()
{
  controlCanvas.Children.Clear();
  if (CurrentPlayer == null || Deck == null || !GameStarted)
    return;
  List<CardControl> stackedCards = new List<CardControl>();
  for (int i = 0; i < Deck.CardsInDeck; i++)
    stackedCards.Add(new CardControl(Deck.GetCard(i)) { Margin =
new Thickness(150 + (i * 1.25), 25 - (i * 1.25), 0, 0), IsFaceUp = false });
  if (stackedCards.Count > 0)
    stackedCards.Last().MouseDoubleClick += Deck_MouseDoubleClick;
  if (AvailableCard != null)
  {
    var availableCard = new CardControl(AvailableCard) { Margin =
new Thickness(0, 25, 0, 0) };
    availableCard.MouseDoubleClick += AvailalbeCard_MouseDoubleClick;
    controlCanvas.Children.Add(availableCard);
  }
  stackedCards.ForEach(x => controlCanvas.Children.Add(x));
}
```

16. All four dependency properties you added in step 14 require a callback method for when the property changes. Add these as you did in step 5 with the names `OnGameStarted`, `OnPlayerChanged`, `OnDeckChanged`, and `OnAvailableCardChanged`.

17. Add the callback methods:

```
private static void OnGameStarted(DependencyObject source,
    DependencyPropertyChangedEventArgs e) => (source as GameDecksControl)?
                                                          .DrawDecks();

private static void OnDeckChanged(DependencyObject source,
DependencyPropertyChangedEventArgs e) => (source as GameDecksControl)?.DrawDecks();

private static void OnAvailableCardChanged(DependencyObject source,
```

```
            DependencyPropertyChangedEventArgs e) => (source as GameDecksControl)?
                                                    .DrawDecks();

        private static void OnPlayerChanged(DependencyObject source,
            DependencyPropertyChangedEventArgs e)
        {
            var control = source as GameDecksControl;
            if (control.CurrentPlayer == null)
                return;
            control.CurrentPlayer.OnCardDiscarded +=
                        control.CurrentPlayer_OnCardDiscarded;
            control.DrawDecks();
        }
        private void CurrentPlayer_OnCardDiscarded(object sender, CardEventArgs e)
        {
            AvailableCard = e.Card;
            DrawDecks();
        }
```

18. Finally, add the event handlers for the cards:

```
        void AvailalbleCard_MouseDoubleClick(object sender, MouseButtonEventArgs e)
        {
          if (CurrentPlayer.State != PlayerState.Active)
            return;
          var control = sender as CardControl;
          CurrentPlayer.AddCard(control.Card);
          AvailableCard = null;
          DrawDecks();
        }
        void Deck_MouseDoubleClick(object sender, MouseButtonEventArgs e)
        {
          if (CurrentPlayer.State != PlayerState.Active)
            return;
          CurrentPlayer.DrawCard(Deck);
          DrawDecks();
        }
```

19. Return to the GameClientWindow.xaml file and remove the Grid that is currently in Row 2.
    Instead, insert a new dock panel like this:

```
        <DockPanel Grid.Row="2">
            <local:CardsInHandControl x:Name="Player2Hand" DockPanel.Dock="Right"
    Height="380" Game="{Binding}"
                VerticalAlignment="Center" Width="180" PlayerOrientation="Vertical"
                Owner="{Binding Players[1]}" PlayerState="{Binding Players[1].State}" />
            <local:CardsInHandControl x:Name="Player4Hand" DockPanel.Dock="Left"
                HorizontalAlignment="Left" Height="380" VerticalAlignment="Center"
                PlayerOrientation="Vertical" Owner="{Binding Players[3]}" Width="180"
                PlayerState="{Binding Players[3].State}" Game="{Binding}"/>
            <local:CardsInHandControl x:Name="Player1Hand" DockPanel.Dock="Top"
                HorizontalAlignment="Center" Height="154" VerticalAlignment="Top"
                PlayerOrientation="Horizontal" Owner="{Binding Players[0]}" Width="380"
                PlayerState="{Binding Players[0].State}" Game="{Binding}"/>
            <local:CardsInHandControl x:Name="Player3Hand" DockPanel.Dock="Bottom"
                HorizontalAlignment="Center" Height="154" VerticalAlignment="Top"
                PlayerOrientation="Horizontal" Owner="{Binding Players[2]}" Width="380"
```

```
                  PlayerState="{Binding Players[2].State}" Game="{Binding}"/>
            <local:GameDecksControl Height="180" x:Name="GameDecks"
                                        Deck="{Binding GameDeck}"
            AvailableCard="{Binding CurrentAvailableCard}"
            CurrentPlayer="{Binding CurrentPlayer}"
            GameStarted="{Binding GameStarted}"/>
        </DockPanel>
```

20. Run the application. By default, the `ComputerPlayer` class is enabled and the number of players is set to two. This means you select a single name in the Start Game dialog box. After that, you should be able to see something like Figure 21-18.

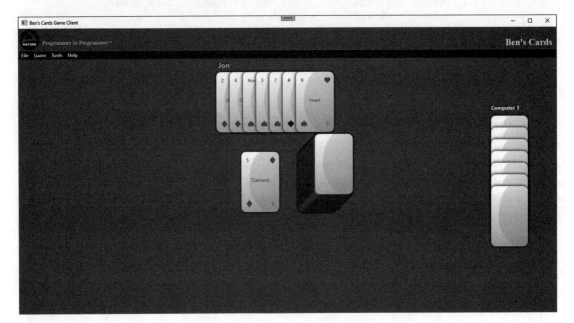

FIGURE 21-18

Double-click the deck or available card to draw and then click a card from your hand to discard it.

How It Works

Even though there is quite a bit of code in this example, most of it is the dependency properties, and the XAML is all about data binding these properties. The `CardsInHandControl` creates three properties that it uses to display itself and react to changes: `Game`, `Owner`, and `PlayerState`. `Game` and `Owner` are mostly used to draw, but the `PlayerState` is also used to control the `ComputerPlayer` actions:

```
private static void OnPlayerStateChanged(DependencyObject source,
                        DependencyPropertyChangedEventArgs e)
{
  var control = source as CardsInHandControl;
  var computerPlayer = control.Owner as ComputerPlayer;
  if (computerPlayer != null)
  {
    if (computerPlayer.State == PlayerState.MustDiscard)
```

```
        {
          Thread delayedWorker = new Thread(control.DelayDiscard);
          delayedWorker.Start(new Payload
          {
            Deck = control.Game.GameDeck,
            AvailableCard = control.Game.CurrentAvailableCard,
            Player = computerPlayer
          });
        }
        else if (computerPlayer.State == PlayerState.Active)
        {
          Thread delayedWorker = new Thread(control.DelayDraw);
          delayedWorker.Start(new Payload
          {
            Deck = control.Game.GameDeck,
            AvailableCard = control.Game.CurrentAvailableCard,
            Player = computerPlayer
          });
        }
      }
      control.RedrawCards();
    }
```

The OnPlayerStateChanged method, which is used to react to changes in the state of the player, determines if the current player is a ComputerPlayer. If it is, it checks to make sure that the computer player draws or discards a card. If this is the case, it creates a worker thread for this to happen and executes the methods on this thread. This allows the application to continue working while the computer is waiting:

```
      private void DelayDraw(object payload)
      {
        Thread.Sleep(1250);
        var data = payload as Payload;
        Dispatcher.Invoke(DispatcherPriority.Normal,
    new Action<Deck, Card>(data.Player.PerformDraw), data.Deck, data.AvailableCard);
      }
```

The Dispatcher is used to invoke the call. This ensures that the calls are made on the GUI thread.

Drawing the cards is pretty straightforward. The program simply stacks them vertically or horizontally depending on the settings in PlayerOrientation.

The GameDecksControl uses the CurrentPlayer class to be notified that the CurrentPlayer has changed. When this happens, it hooks the CardDiscarded event on the player and uses this event to be notified that the card was discarded.

Finally, you added a dock panel to the game client with a CardsInHandControl on each side and with a GameDecksControl in the middle:

```
        <local:CardsInHandControl x:Name="Player1Hand" DockPanel.Dock="Top"
          HorizontalAlignment="Center" Height="154" VerticalAlignment="Top"
          PlayerOrientation="Horizontal" Owner="{Binding Players[0]}" Width="380"
          PlayerState="{Binding Players[0].State}" Game="{Binding}" />
```

The binding for Game binds the DataContext of the game client directly to the Game property of the CardsInHandControl. The PlayerState is bound to the State property of a player. In this case, the player at index 0 is used to access the state.

21.1 A TextBlock control can be used to display large amounts of text, but the control does not provide any way to scroll the text itself if the text extends beyond the viewport. By combining the TextBlock with another control, create a window that contains a TextBlock with a lot of text that can be scrolled and where the scrollbar appears only if the text extends beyond the viewport.

21.2 The Slider and Progress controls have a few things in common, such as a minimum, maximum, and current value. Using only data binding on the ProgressBar, create a window with a slider and a progress bar, where the Slider control controls the minimum, maximum, and current value of the progress bar.

21.3 Change the ProgressBar in the previous question to display itself diagonally from the bottom-left corner to the top-right corner of the window.

21.4 Create a new class with the name PersistentSlider and three properties: MinValue, MaxValue, and CurrentValue. The class must be able to participate in data binding, and all the properties must be able to notify bound controls of changes.

    a. In the code-behind of the window you created in the two previous exercises, create a new field of type PersistentSlider and initialize it with some default values.

    b. In the constructor, bind the instance to the window's data source.

    c. Bind the slider's Minimum, Maximum, and Value properties to the data source.

21.5 The current game client has a problem. From the Options dialog box, you can set the skill level of the computer. The problem is that the radio buttons are not updated to reflect the choice the next time you open the Options dialog box. This is partly because there is nothing that tries to update them and partly because there is no value converter from ComputerSkillLevel. Fix this problem by creating a new value converter and setting the IsChecked binding instead of using the Checked event that is currently being used.

Hint: You must use the ConverterParameter part of the Converter binding.

21.6 The computer cheats, so you might want to allow the players to cheat as well. On the Options dialog box, create an option for the computer to play with open cards.

21.7 Create a status bar at the bottom of the game client that displays the current state of the game.

Answers to the exercises can be found in the Appendix.

▶ WHAT YOU LEARNED IN THIS CHAPTER

TOPIC	KEY CONCEPTS
XAML	XAML is a language that uses XML syntax and enables controls to be added to a user interface in a declarative, hierarchical way.
Data binding	You can use data binding to connect properties of controls to the values of other controls. You can also define resources and use code defined in classes outside your views as a data source for both values of properties and as content for controls. `DataContexts` can be used to specify the binding source of existing object instances and thereby allow you to bind to instances that are created in other parts of your application.
Routed events	Routed events are special events used in WPF. They come in two flavors: bubbling and tunneling. Bubbling events are first called on the control on which they are activated and then bubble up through the view tree to the root element. Tunneling events move the other way, from the root element to the control that was activated by the user. Both bubbling and tunneling can be stopped by setting the `Handled` property of the event arguments to `true`.
`INotifyPropertyChanged`	The `INotifyPropertyChanged` interface is implemented by a class that will be used from a WPF view. When property setters of the class are called, they raise the event `PropertyChanged` with the name of the property that changed its value. Any control property that is bound to the property that raised the event will be notified of the change and can update itself accordingly.
`ObservableCollection`	An `ObservableCollection` is a collection that, among other things, implements the `INotifyPropertyChanged` interface. You use this specialized collection when you want to provide properties or values that are lists to a WPF view for data binding.
Content controls	Content controls can contain a single control in their content. An example of such a control is `Button`. The contained control can be `Grid` or `StackPanel`; they allow you to create complex customizations.

TOPIC	KEY CONCEPTS
Items controls	Items controls can contain a list of controls in their content. An example of such a control is the `ListBox`. Each control in the list can be customized.
Layout controls	You learned to use a number of controls that are used to help you create the view: 1. `Canvas` allows for explicit positioning of controls but little else. 2. `StackPanel` stacks controls horizontally or vertically. 3. `WrapPanel` stacks controls and wraps them to the next line or column depending on the orientation of the panel. 4. `DockPanel` allows you to dock controls to the edges of the control or fill the entire content. 5. `Grid` allows you to define rows and columns and use these to position the controls.
UI controls	UI controls display themselves on the view, often using the layout controls to guide their positions. These controls were used: 1. `Label` controls display short text. 2. `TextBlock` controls display text that can need multiple lines to display. 3. `TextBox` controls allow the users to provide text input. 4. `Button` controls allow the users to perform a single action. 5. `Image` controls are used to display an image. 6. `CheckBoxes` let the users answer yes/no questions such as "Play Against Computer?" 7. `RadioButton` controls let the users select exactly one from multiple options. 8. `ComboBox` controls display a drop-down list of items from which the user can select a single item. The control can also display a `TextBox`, letting the user enter new options. 9. `ListBox` controls display a list of items. Unlike the `ComboBox` the list is always expanded. The control allows for multiple items being selected. 10. `TabControl` allows you to group controls on pages.

TOPIC	KEY CONCEPTS
Styles	You can use styles to create styles for XAML elements that can be reused on many elements. Styles allow you to set the properties of an element. When you set the `Style` property of an element to point to a style you have defined, the properties of the element will use the values you specified in the `Style` property.
Templates	Templates are used to define the content of a control. Using templates, you can change how standard controls are displayed. You can also build complex custom controls with them.
User controls	User controls are used to create code and XAML that can be reused easily in your own project. This code and XAML can also be exported for use in other projects.

APPENDIX

Exercise Solutions

There are no exercises in Chapters 1, 2, and 18.

CHAPTER 3 SOLUTIONS

Exercise 1

```
super.smashing.great
```

Exercise 2

The second bulleted item because it starts with a number and the last bulleted item because it contains a period.

Exercise 3

No, the value is not too big. The limit is 2 GB, which is about 1 billion characters.

Exercise 4

The * operator has the highest precedence here. The % and / are evaluated from left to right, then + and then +=. The precedence in the exercise can be illustrated using parentheses as follows:

```
resultVar += (var1 * var2) + ((var3 % var4) / var5);
```

Exercise 5

```
using static System.Console;
using static System.Convert;
static void Main(string[] args)
{
    int firstNumber, secondNumber, thirdNumber, fourthNumber;
    WriteLine("Give me a number:");
    firstNumber = ToInt32(ReadLine());
    WriteLine("Give me another number:");
```

```
      secondNumber = ToInt32(Console.ReadLine());
      WriteLine("Give me another number:");
      thirdNumber = ToInt32(ReadLine());
      WriteLine("Give me another number:");
      fourthNumber = ToInt32(ReadLine());
      WriteLine($"The product of {firstNumber}, {secondNumber}, " +
            $"{thirdNumber}, and {fourthNumber} is " +
            $"{firstNumber * secondNumber * thirdNumber * fourthNumber}.");
   }
```

Note that `Convert.ToInt32()` is used here, which isn't covered in the chapter.

CHAPTER 4 SOLUTIONS

Exercise 1

```
(var1 > 10) ^ (var2 > 10)
```

Exercise 2

Note that at least one number must be >10 for the messages to be consistent with the entered scenario. Also, consider checking whether a value has been entered before attempting to convert it using `ToDouble()`.

```
using static System.Console;
using static System.Convert;
static void Main(string[] args)
{
  bool numbersOK = false;
  double var1, var2;
  var1 = 0;
  var2 = 0;
  while (!numbersOK)
  {
    WriteLine("Enter 2 numbers, both numbers cannot be greater than 10.");
    WriteLine("Please enter the first number:");
    var1 = ToDouble(ReadLine());
    WriteLine("Please enter the second number:");
    var2 = ToDouble(ReadLine());

    WriteLine($"The first number entered is {var1} " +
            $"and the second is {var2}");

    if ((var1 > 10) ^ (var2 > 10))
    {
      numbersOK = true;
    }

    else
    {
      WriteLine("Only one number may be greater than 10, " +
            "please try again.");
    }
```

```
    }
    WriteLine("Press the <ENTER> key to exit.");
    ReadLine();
}
```

Exercise 3

The code should read:

```
int i;
for (i = 1; i <= 10; i++)
{
    if ((i % 2) == 0)
        continue;
    WriteLine(i);
}
```

Using the = assignment operator instead of the Boolean == operator is a very common mistake.

CHAPTER 5 SOLUTIONS

Exercise 1

Conversions a and c can't be performed implicitly.

Exercise 2

```
enum color : short
{
    Red, Orange, Yellow, Green, Blue, Indigo, Violet, Black, White
}
```

Yes. The byte type can hold numbers between 0 and 255, so byte-based enumerations can hold 256 entries with individual values or more if duplicate values are used for entries.

Exercise 3

The code will not compile, for the following reasons:

➤ End of statement semicolons are missing.

➤ Second line attempts to access a nonexistent sixth element of blab, which would result in a runtime exception.

➤ Second line attempts to assign a string that is not enclosed in double quotes.

Exercise 4

```
using static System.Console;
static void Main(string[] args)
{
    WriteLine("Enter a string:");
    string myString = ReadLine();
```

```
        string reversedString = "";
        for (int index = myString.Length - 1; index >= 0; index--)
        {
            reversedString += myString[index];
        }
        WriteLine($"Reversed: {reversedString}");
    }
```

Exercise 5

```
using static System.Console;
static void Main(string[] args)
{
    WriteLine("Enter a string:");
    string myString = ReadLine();
    myString = myString.Replace("no", "yes");
    WriteLine($"Replaced \"no\" with \"yes\": {myString}");
}
```

Exercise 6

```
using static System.Console;
static void Main(string[] args)
 {
    WriteLine("Enter a string:");
    string myString = ReadLine();
    myString = "\"" + myString.Replace(" ", "\" \"") + "\"";
    WriteLine($"Added double quotes around words: {myString}");
 }
```

Or using `String.Split()`:

```
using static System.Console;
static void Main(string[] args)
 {
    WriteLine("Enter a string:");
    string myString = ReadLine();
    string[] myWords = myString.Split(' ');
    WriteLine("Adding double quotes around words:");
    foreach (string myWord in myWords)
    {
      Write($"\"{myWord}\" ");
    }
 }
```

CHAPTER 6 SOLUTIONS

Exercise 1

The first function has a return type of bool but does not return a bool value.

The second function has a params argument, but this argument is not at the end of the argument list.

Exercise 2

```
using static System.Console;
using static System.Convert;

static void Main(string[] args)
{
    if (args.Length != 2)
    {
        WriteLine("Two arguments required.");
        return;
    }
    string param1 = args[0];
    int param2 = ToInt32(args[1]);
    WriteLine($"String parameter: {param1}");
    WriteLine($"Integer parameter: {param2}");
}
```

Note that this answer contains code that checks that two arguments have been supplied, which was not part of the question but seems logical in this situation.

Exercise 3

```
using static System.Console;
class Program
{

    delegate string ReadLineDelegate();
    static void Main(string[] args)
    {
        ReadLineDelegate readLine = new ReadLineDelegate(ReadLine);
        WriteLine("Type a string:");
        string userInput = readLine();
        WriteLine($"You typed: {userInput}");
    }
}
```

Exercise 4

```
struct order
{
    public string itemName;
    public int    unitCount;
    public double unitCost;
    public double TotalCost() => unitCount * unitCost;
}
```

Exercise 5

```
struct order
{
    public string itemName;
    public int    unitCount;
    public double unitCost;
    public double TotalCost() => unitCount * unitCost;
```

```
        public string Info() => "Order information: " + unitCount.ToString() +
            " " + itemName + " items at $" + unitCost.ToString() +
            " each, total cost $" + TotalCost().ToString();
    }
```

CHAPTER 7 SOLUTIONS

Exercise 1

This statement is true only for information that you want to make available in all builds. More often, you will want debugging information to be written out only when debug builds are used. In this situation, the Debug.WriteLine() version is preferable.

Using the Debug.WriteLine() version also has the advantage that it will not be compiled into release builds, thus reducing the size of the resultant code.

Exercise 2

```
static void Main(string[] args)
{
    for (int i = 1; i < 10000; i++)
    {
        WriteLine($"Loop cycle {i}");
        if (i == 5000)
        {
            WriteLine(args[999]);
        }
    }
}
```

In VS, you can place a breakpoint on the following line:

```
            WriteLine("Loop cycle {0}", i);
```

The properties of the breakpoint should be modified such that the hit count criterion is "break when hit count is equal to 5000."

Exercise 3

False. finally blocks always execute. This may occur after a catch block has been processed.

Exercise 4

```
static void Main(string[] args)
{
    Orientation myDirection;
    for (byte myByte = 2; myByte < 10; myByte++)
    {
        try
        {
            myDirection = checked((Orientation)myByte);
            if ((myDirection < Orientation.North) ||
                (myDirection > Orientation.West))
```

```
        {
            throw new ArgumentOutOfRangeException("myByte", myByte,
                "Value must be between 1 and 4");
        }
    }
    catch (ArgumentOutOfRangeException e)
    {
        // If this section is reached then myByte < 1 or myByte > 4.
        WriteLine(e.Message);
        WriteLine("Assigning default value, Orientation.North.");
        myDirection = Orientation.North;
    }
    WriteLine($"myDirection = {myDirection}");
}
}
```

Note that this is a bit of a trick question. Because the enumeration is based on the `byte` type, any `byte` value may be assigned to it, even if that value isn't assigned a name in the enumeration. In the previous code, you can generate your own exception if necessary.

CHAPTER 8 SOLUTIONS

Exercise 1

b, d, and e. Public, private, and protected are all real levels of accessibility.

Exercise 2

False. You should never call the destructor of an object manually; the .NET runtime environment will do this for you during garbage collection.

Exercise 3

No, you can call static methods without any class instances.

Exercise 4

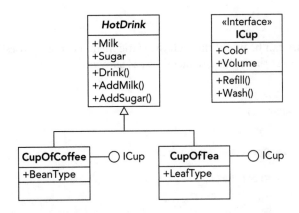

Exercise 5

```
static void ManipulateDrink(HotDrink drink)
{
    drink.AddMilk();
    drink.Drink();
    ICup cupInterface = (ICup)drink;
    cupInterface.Wash();
}
```

Note the explicit cast to `ICup`. This is necessary as `HotDrink` does not support the `ICup` interface, but you know that the two cup objects that might be passed to this function do. However, this is dangerous, as other classes deriving from `HotDrink` are possible, which might not support `ICup`, but could be passed to this function. To correct this, you should check to see if the interface is supported:

```
static void ManipulateDrink(HotDrink drink)
{
    drink.AddMilk();
    drink.Drink();
    if (drink is ICup)
    {
        ICup cupInterface = drink as ICup;
        cupInterface.Wash();
    }
}
```

The `is` and `as` operators used here are covered in Chapter 11.

CHAPTER 9 SOLUTIONS

Exercise 1

`myDerivedClass` derives from `MyClass`, but `MyClass` is sealed and cannot be derived from.

Exercise 2

You can define a non-creatable class by defining it as a static or abstract class or by defining all its constructors as private.

Exercise 3

Non-creatable classes can be useful through the static members they possess. In fact, you can even get instances of these classes through these members, as shown here:

```
class CreateMe
{
    private CreateMe()
    {
    }
    static public CreateMe GetCreateMe()
    {
        return new CreateMe();
    }
}
```

Here, the public constructor has access to the private constructor, as it is part of the same class definition. Non-creatable classes can also be useful as base classes.

Exercise 4

For simplicity, the following class definitions are shown as part of a single code file, rather than listing a separate code file for each:

```
namespace Vehicles
{
    public abstract class Vehicle
    {
    }
    public abstract class Car : Vehicle
    {
    }
    public abstract class Train : Vehicle
    {
    }
    public interface IPassengerCarrier
    {
    }
    public interface IHeavyLoadCarrier
    {
    }
    public class SUV : Car, IPassengerCarrier
    {
    }
    public class Pickup : Car, IPassengerCarrier, IHeavyLoadCarrier
    {
    }
    public class Compact : Car, IPassengerCarrier
    {
    }
    public class PassengerTrain : Train, IPassengerCarrier
    {
    }
    public class FreightTrain : Train, IHeavyLoadCarrier
    {
    }
    public class T424DoubleBogey : Train, IHeavyLoadCarrier
    {
    }
}
```

Exercise 5

```
using System;
using static System.Console;
using Vehicles;
namespace Traffic
{
    class Program
    {
        static void Main(string[] args)
        {
```

```
        AddPassenger(new Compact());
        AddPassenger(new SUV());
        AddPassenger(new Pickup());
        AddPassenger(new PassengerTrain());
        ReadKey();
    }
    static void AddPassenger(IPassengerCarrier Vehicle)
    {
        WriteLine(Vehicle.ToString());
    }
  }
}
```

CHAPTER 10 SOLUTIONS

Exercise 1

```
class MyClass
{
   protected string myString;
   public string ContainedString
   {
      set
      {
         myString = value;
      }
   }
   public virtual string GetString() => myString;
}
```

Exercise 2

```
class MyDerivedClass : MyClass
{
   public override string GetString() => base.GetString() +
         " (output from derived class)";
}
```

Exercise 3

If no implementation is provided for a partial method, then it will be removed by the compiler along with all places where it is used. In the preceding code, this would leave the result of x unclear because no replacement for the Manipulate() method is available. It might be the case that without this method you would simply want to ignore the entire line of code, but the compiler cannot decide whether this is what you want.

Methods with no return types are not called as part of expressions, so it is safe for the compiler to remove all references to the partial method calls.

Similarly, out parameters are forbidden since variables used as an out parameter are undefined before the method call and will be defined after the method call. Removing the method call would break this behavior.

Exercise 4

```
class MyCopyableClass
{
    protected int myInt;
    public int ContainedInt
    {
        get
        {
            return myInt;
        }
        set
        {
            myInt = value;
        }
    }
    public MyCopyableClass GetCopy() => (MyCopyableClass)MemberwiseClone();
}
```

The client code:

```
class Program
{
    using static System.Console;
    static void Main(string[] args)
    {
        MyCopyableClass obj1 = new MyCopyableClass();
        obj1.ContainedInt = 5;
        MyCopyableClass obj2 = obj1.GetCopy();
        obj1.ContainedInt = 9;
        WriteLine(obj1.ContainedInt);
        WriteLine(obj2.ContainedInt);
    }
}
```

This code displays 5, showing that the copied object has its own version of the myInt field.

Exercise 5

```
using System;
using static System.Console;
using Ch10CardLib;
namespace Exercise_Answers
{
    class Class1
    {
        static void Main(string[] args)
        {
            while(true)
            {
                Deck playDeck = new Deck();
                playDeck.Shuffle();
                bool isFlush = false;
                int flushHandIndex = 0;
                for (int hand = 0; hand < 10; hand++)
```

```
            {
                isFlush = true;
                Suit flushSuit = playDeck.GetCard(hand * 5).suit;
                for (int card = 1; card < 5; card++)
                {
                    if (playDeck.GetCard(hand * 5 + card).suit != flushSuit)
                    {
                        isFlush = false;
                        break;
                    }
                }
                if (isFlush)
                {
                    flushHandIndex = hand * 5;
                    break;
                }
            }
            if (isFlush)
            {
                WriteLine("Flush!");
                for (int card = 0; card < 5; card++)
                {
                    WriteLine(playDeck.GetCard(flushHandIndex + card));
                }
            }
            else
            {
                WriteLine("No flush.");
            }
            ReadLine();
        }
    }
}
```

This code is looped as flushes are uncommon. You might need to press Return several times before a flush is found in a shuffled deck. To verify that everything is working as it should, try commenting out the line that shuffles the deck.

CHAPTER 11 SOLUTIONS

Exercise 1

```
using System;
using System.Collections;
namespace Exercise_Answers
{
    public class People : DictionaryBase
    {
        public void Add(Person newPerson) =>
                Dictionary.Add(newPerson.Name, newPerson);

        public void Remove(string name) => Dictionary.Remove(name);
```

```
        public Person this[string name]
        {
            get
            {
                return (Person)Dictionary[name];
            }
            set
            {
                Dictionary[name] = value;
            }
        }
    }
}
```

Exercise 2

```
public class Person
{
    private string name;
    private int age;
    public string Name
    {
        get
        {
            return name;
        }
        set
        {
            name = value;
        }
    }
    public int Age
    {
        get
        {
            return age;
        }
        set
        {
            age = value;
        }
    }
    public static bool operator >(Person p1, Person p2) =>
            p1.Age > p2.Age;
    public static bool operator <(Person p1, Person p2) =>
            p1.Age < p2.Age;
    public static bool operator >=(Person p1, Person p2) =>
            !(p1 < p2);
    public static bool operator <=(Person p1, Person p2) =>
            !(p1 > p2);
}
```

Exercise 3

```
public Person[] GetOldest()
{
    Person oldestPerson = null;
    People oldestPeople = new People();
    Person currentPerson;
    foreach (DictionaryEntry p in Dictionary)
    {
        currentPerson = p.Value as Person;
        if (oldestPerson == null)
        {
            oldestPerson = currentPerson;
            oldestPeople.Add(oldestPerson);
        }
        else
        {
            if (currentPerson > oldestPerson)
            {
                oldestPeople.Clear();
                oldestPeople.Add(currentPerson);
                oldestPerson = currentPerson;
            }
            else
            {
                if (currentPerson >= oldestPerson)
                    {
                        oldestPeople.Add(currentPerson);
                    }
            }
        }
    }
    Person[] oldestPeopleArray = new Person[oldestPeople.Count];
    int copyIndex = 0;
    foreach (DictionaryEntry p in oldestPeople)
    {
        oldestPeopleArray[copyIndex] = p.Value as Person;
        copyIndex++;
    }
        return oldestPeopleArray;
}
```

This function is made more complex by the fact that no == operator has been defined for Person, but the logic can still be constructed without this. In addition, returning a People instance would be simpler, as it is easier to manipulate this class during processing. As a compromise, a People instance is used throughout the function, and then converted into an array of Person instances at the end.

Exercise 4

```
public class People : DictionaryBase, ICloneable
{
    public object Clone()
    {
        People clonedPeople = new People();
```

```
            Person currentPerson, newPerson;
            foreach (DictionaryEntry p in Dictionary)
            {
                currentPerson = p.Value as Person;
                newPerson = new Person();
                newPerson.Name = currentPerson.Name;
                newPerson.Age = currentPerson.Age;
                clonedPeople.Add(newPerson);
            }
            return clonedPeople;
        }
        ...
    }
```

You could simplify this by implementing ICloneable on the Person class.

Exercise 5

```
public IEnumerable Ages
{
    get
    {
        foreach (object person in Dictionary.Values)
            yield return (person as Person).Age;
    }
}
```

CHAPTER 12 SOLUTIONS

Exercise 1

a, b, and e: Yes.

c and d: No, although they can use generic type parameters supplied by the class containing them.

f: No.

Exercise 2

```
public static double? operator *(Vector op1, Vector op2)
{
    try
    {
        double angleDiff = (double)(op2.ThetaRadians.Value -
            op1.ThetaRadians.Value);
        return op1.R.Value * op2.R.Value * Math.Cos(angleDiff);
    }
    catch
    {
        return null;
    }
}
```

Exercise 3

You cannot instantiate T without enforcing the `new()` constraint on it, which ensures that a public default constructor is available:

```
public class Instantiator<T>
   where T : new()
{
   public T instance;
   public Instantiator()
   {
      instance = new T();
   }
}
```

Exercise 4

The same generic type parameter, T, is used on both the generic class and the generic method. You need to rename one or both. For example:

```
public class StringGetter<T>
{
   public string GetString(T item) => item.ToString();
}
```

Exercise 5

One way of doing this is as follows:

```
public class ShortList<T> : IList<T>
{
   protected IList<T> innerCollection;
   protected int maxSize = 10;
   public ShortList()
      : this(10)
   {
   }
   public ShortList(int size)
   {
      maxSize = size;
      innerCollection = new List<T>();
   }
   public ShortList(IEnumerable<T> list)
      : this(10, list)
   {
   }
   public ShortList(int size, IEnumerable<T> list)
   {
      maxSize = size;
      innerCollection = new List<T>(list);
      if (Count > maxSize)
      {
         ThrowTooManyItemsException();
      }
   }
```

```
protected void ThrowTooManyItemsException()
{
    throw new IndexOutOfRangeException(
        "Unable to add any more items, maximum size is " + maxSize.ToString()
        + " items.");
}
#region IList<T> Members
public int IndexOf(T item) => innerCollection.IndexOf(item);
public void Insert(int index, T item)
{
    if (Count < maxSize)
    {
        innerCollection.Insert(index, item);
    }
    else
    {
        ThrowTooManyItemsException();
    }
}
public void RemoveAt(int index)
{
    innerCollection.RemoveAt(index);
}
public T this[int index]
{
    get
    {
        return innerCollection[index];
    }
    set
    {
        innerCollection[index] = value;
    }
}
#endregion
#region ICollection<T> Members
public void Add(T item)
{
    if (Count < maxSize)
    {
        innerCollection.Add(item);
    }
    else
    {
        ThrowTooManyItemsException();
    }
}
public void Clear()
{
    innerCollection.Clear();
}
public bool Contains(T item) => innerCollection.Contains(item);
public void CopyTo(T[] array, int arrayIndex)
{
    innerCollection.CopyTo(array, arrayIndex);
```

```
   }
   public int Count
   {
      get
      {
         return innerCollection.Count;
      }
   }
   public bool IsReadOnly
   {
      get
      {
         return innerCollection.IsReadOnly;
      }
   }
   public bool Remove(T item) => innerCollection.Remove(item);
   #endregion
   #region IEnumerable<T> Members
   public IEnumerator<T> GetEnumerator() =>
            innerCollection.GetEnumerator();
   #endregion
   #region IEnumerable Members
   IEnumerator IEnumerable.GetEnumerator() => GetEnumerator();
   #endregion
}
```

Exercise 6

No, it will not. The type parameter T is defined as being covariant. However, covariant type parameters can be used only as return values of methods, not as method arguments. If you try this out, you will get the following compiler error (assuming you use the namespace VarianceDemo):

```
Invalid variance: The type parameter 'T' must be contravariantly valid on
'VarianceDemo.IMethaneProducer<T>.BelchAt(T)'. 'T' is covariant.
```

CHAPTER 13 SOLUTIONS

Exercise 1

```
using static System.Console;
public void ProcessEvent(object source, EventArgs e)
{
   if (e is MessageArrivedEventArgs)
   {
      WriteLine("Connection.MessageArrived event received.");
      WriteLine($"Message: {(e as MessageArrivedEventArgs).Message }");
   }
   if (e is ElapsedEventArgs)
   {
      WriteLine("Timer.Elapsed event received.");
      WriteLine($"SignalTime: {(e as ElapsedEventArgs ).SignalTime }");
   }
}
```

Exercise 2

Modify `Player.cs` as follows (one modified method, two new ones—comments in the code explain the changes):

```
public bool HasWon()
{
    // get temporary copy of hand, which may get modified.
    Cards tempHand = (Cards)PlayHand.Clone();
    // find three and four of a kind sets
    bool fourOfAKind = false;
    bool threeOfAKind = false;
    int fourRank = -1;
    int threeRank = -1;
    int cardsOfRank;
    for (int matchRank = 0; matchRank < 13; matchRank++)
    {
        cardsOfRank = 0;
        foreach (Card c in tempHand)
        {
            if (c.rank == (Rank)matchRank)
            {
                cardsOfRank++;
            }
        }
        if (cardsOfRank == 4)
        {
            // mark set of four
            fourRank = matchRank;
            fourOfAKind = true;
        }
        if (cardsOfRank == 3)
        {
            // two threes means no win possible
            // (threeOfAKind will be true only if this code
            // has already executed)
            if (threeOfAKind == true)
            {
                return false;
            }
            // mark set of three
            threeRank = matchRank;
            threeOfAKind = true;
        }
    }
    // check simple win condition
    if (threeOfAKind && fourOfAKind)
    {
        return true;
    }
    // simplify hand if three or four of a kind is found,
    // by removing used cards
    if (fourOfAKind || threeOfAKind)
    {
        for (int cardIndex = tempHand.Count - 1; cardIndex >= 0; cardIndex--)
```

```
        {
            if ((tempHand[cardIndex].rank == (Rank)fourRank)
                || (tempHand[cardIndex].rank == (Rank)threeRank))
            {
                tempHand.RemoveAt(cardIndex);
            }
        }
    }
}
// at this point the method may have returned, because:
// - a set of four and a set of three have been found, winning.
// - two sets of three have been found, losing.
// if the method hasn't returned then:
// - no sets have been found, and tempHand contains 7 cards.
// - a set of three has been found, and tempHand contains 4 cards.
// - a set of four has been found, and tempHand contains 3 cards.
// find run of four sets, start by looking for cards of same suit
// in the same way as before
bool fourOfASuit = false;
bool threeOfASuit = false;
int fourSuit = -1;
int threeSuit = -1;
int cardsOfSuit;
for (int matchSuit = 0; matchSuit < 4; matchSuit++)
{
    cardsOfSuit = 0;
    foreach (Card c in tempHand)
    {
        if (c.suit == (Suit)matchSuit)
        {
            cardsOfSuit++;
        }
    }
    if (cardsOfSuit == 7)
    {
        // if all cards are the same suit then two runs
        // are possible, but not definite.
        threeOfASuit = true;
        threeSuit = matchSuit;
        fourOfASuit = true;
        fourSuit = matchSuit;
    }
    if (cardsOfSuit == 4)
    {
        // mark four card suit.
        fourOfASuit = true;
        fourSuit = matchSuit;
    }
    if (cardsOfSuit == 3)
    {
        // mark three card suit.
        threeOfASuit = true;
        threeSuit = matchSuit;
    }
}
if (!(threeOfASuit || fourOfASuit))
```

```
{
    // need at least one run possibility to continue.
    return false;
}
if (tempHand.Count == 7)
{
    if (!(threeOfASuit && fourOfASuit))
    {
        // need a three and a four card suit.
        return false;
    }
    // create two temporary sets for checking.
    Cards set1 = new Cards();
    Cards set2 = new Cards();
    // if all 7 cards are the same suit...
    if (threeSuit == fourSuit)
    {
        // get min and max cards
        int maxVal, minVal;
        GetLimits(tempHand, out maxVal, out minVal);
        for (int cardIndex = tempHand.Count - 1; cardIndex >= 0; cardIndex--)
        {
            if (((int)tempHand[cardIndex].rank < (minVal + 3))
                || ((int)tempHand[cardIndex].rank > (maxVal - 3)))
            {
                // remove all cards in a three card set that
                // starts at minVal or ends at maxVal.
                tempHand.RemoveAt(cardIndex);
            }
        }
        if (tempHand.Count != 1)
        {
            // if more then one card is left then there aren't two runs.
            return false;
        }
        if ((tempHand[0].rank == (Rank)(minVal + 3))
            || (tempHand[0].rank == (Rank)(maxVal - 3)))
        {
            // if spare card can make one of the three card sets into a
            // four card set then there are two sets.
            return true;
        }
        else
        {
            // if spare card doesn't fit then there are two sets of three
            // cards but no set of four cards.
            return false;
        }
    }
    // if three card and four card suits are different...
    foreach (Card card in tempHand)
    {
        // split cards into sets.
        if (card.suit == (Suit)threeSuit)
        {
```

```
                set1.Add(card);
            }
            else
            {
                set2.Add(card);
            }
        }
        // check if sets are sequential.
        if (isSequential(set1) && isSequential(set2))
        {
            return true;
        }
        else
        {
            return false;
        }
    }
    // if four cards remain (three of a kind found)
    if (tempHand.Count == 4)
    {
        // if four cards remain then they must be the same suit.
        if (!fourOfASuit)
        {
            return false;
        }
        // won if cards are sequential.
        if (isSequential(tempHand))
        {
            return true;
        }
    }
    // if three cards remain (four of a kind found)
    if (tempHand.Count == 3)
    {
        // if three cards remain then they must be the same suit.
        if (!threeOfASuit)
        {
            return false;
        }
        // won if cards are sequential.
        if (isSequential(tempHand))
        {
            return true;
        }
    }
    // return false if two valid sets don't exist.
    return false;
}
// utility method to get max and min ranks of cards
// (same suit assumed)
private void GetLimits(Cards cards, out int maxVal, out int minVal)
{
    maxVal = 0;
    minVal = 14;
    foreach (Card card in cards)
```

```
        {
            if ((int)card.rank > maxVal)
            {
                maxVal = (int)card.rank;
            }
            if ((int)card.rank < minVal)
            {
                minVal = (int)card.rank;
            }
        }
    }
    // utility method to see if cards are in a run
    // (same suit assumed)
    private bool isSequential(Cards cards)
    {
        int maxVal, minVal;
        GetLimits(cards, out maxVal, out minVal);
        if ((maxVal - minVal) == (cards.Count - 1))
        {
            return true;
        }
        else
        {
            return false;
        }
    }
```

Exercise 3

To use an object initializer with a class, you must include a default, parameter less constructor. You could either add one to this class or remove the nondefault constructor that is there already. Once you have done this, you can use the following code to instantiate and initialize this class in one step:

```
Giraffe myPetGiraffe = new Giraffe
{
    NeckLength = 3.14,
    Name = "Gerald"
};
```

Exercise 4

False. When you use the var keyword to declare a variable, the variable is still strongly typed; the compiler determines the type of the variable.

Exercise 5

You can use the Equals() method that is implemented for you. Note that you cannot use the == operator to do this, as this compares variables to determine if they both refer to the same object.

Exercise 6

The extension method must be static:

```
public static string ToAcronym(this string inputString)
```

Exercise 7

You must include the extension method in a static class that is accessible from the namespace that contains your client code. You could do this either by including the code in the same namespace or by importing the namespace containing the class.

Exercise 8

One way to do this is as follows:

```
public static string ToAcronym(this string inputString) =>
    inputString.Trim().Split(' ').Aggregate<string, string>("",
        (a, b) => a + (b.Length > 0 ?
        b.ToUpper()[0].ToString() : ""));
```

Here the tertiary operator prevents multiple spaces from causing errors. Note also that the version of `Aggregate()` with two generic type parameters is required, as a seed value is necessary.

CHAPTER 14 SOLUTIONS

Exercise 1

`System.IO`

Exercise 2

You use a `FileStream` object to write to a file when you need random access to files, or when you are not dealing with string data.

Exercise 3

➤ `Peek()`: Gets the value of the next character in the file but does not advance the file position

➤ `Read()`: Gets the value of the next character in the file and advances the file position

➤ `Read(char[] buffer, int index, int count)`: Reads `count` characters into `buffer`, starting at `buffer[index]`

➤ `ReadLine()`: Gets a line of text

➤ `ReadToEnd()`: Gets all remaining text in a file

Exercise 4

`DeflateStream`

Exercise 5

➤ `Changed`: Occurs when a file is modified

➤ `Created`: Occurs when a file is created

➤ `Deleted`: Occurs when a file is deleted

➤ `Renamed`: Occurs when a file is renamed

➤ `Error`: Occurs when an error is raised

Exercise 6

Add a button that toggles the value of the `FileSystemWatcher.EnableRaisingEvents` property.

CHAPTER 15 SOLUTIONS

Exercise 1

1. Double-click the Create Node button to go to the event handler doing the work.

2. Below the creation of the `XmlComment`, insert the following three lines:

```
XmlAttribute newPages = document.CreateAttribute("pages");
newPages.Value = "1001";
newBook.Attributes.Append(newPages);
```

Exercise 2

1. `//elements`—Returns all nodes in the document.

2. `element`—Returns every element node in the document but leaves the element root node out.

3. `element[@Type='Noble Gas']`—Returns every element that includes an attribute with the name `Type`, which has a value of `Noble Gas`.

4. `//mass`—Returns all nodes with the name `mass`.

5. `//mass/..`—The `..` causes the XPath to move one up from the selected node, which means that this query selects all the nodes that include a mass node.

6. `element/specification[mass='20.1797']`—Selects the specification element that contains a mass node with the value `20.1797`.

7. `element/name[text()='Neon']`—To select the node whose contents you are testing, you can use the `text()` function. This selects the `name` node with the text `Neon`.

Exercise 3

Recall that XML can be valid, well-formed, or invalid. Whenever you select part of an XML document, you are left with a fragment of the whole. This means that there is a good chance that the XML you have selected is in fact invalid XML on its own. Most XML viewers will refuse to display XML that is not well-formed, so it is not possible to display the results of many queries directly in a standard XML viewer.

CHAPTER 16 SOLUTIONS

Exercise 1

```
static void Main(string[] args)
{
    string[] names = { "Alonso", "Zheng", "Smith", "Jones", "Smythe",
    "Small", "Ruiz", "Hsieh", "Jorgenson", "Ilyich", "Singh", "Samba", "Fatimah"};
```

```
                var queryResults =
                    from n in names
                    where n.StartsWith("S")
                    orderby n descending
                    select n;

            Console.WriteLine("Names beginning with S:");

            foreach (var item in queryResults) {
                Console.WriteLine(item);
            }

            Console.Write("Program finished, press Enter/Return to continue:");
            Console.ReadLine();
    }
```

Exercise 2

Sets smaller than 5,000,000 have no numbers < 1000:

```
    static void Main(string[] args)
    {
        int[] arraySizes = {     100,     1000,    10000,   100000,
                           1000000, 5000000, 10000000, 50000000 };

        foreach (int i in arraySizes) {
            int[] numbers = generateLotsOfNumbers(i);
            var queryResults = from n in numbers
                               where n < 1000
                               select n;
            Console.WriteLine("number array size = {0}: Count(n < 1000) = {1}",
                    numbers.Length, queryResults.Count()
            );
        }

        Console.Write("Program finished, press Enter/Return to continue:");
        Console.ReadLine();
    }
```

Exercise 3

This does not affect performance noticeably for n < 1000:

```
    static void Main(string[] args)
    {

        int[] numbers = generateLotsOfNumbers(12345678);

        var queryResults =
            from n in numbers
            where n < 1000
            orderby n
            select n
        ;
```

```
        Console.WriteLine("Numbers less than 1000:");
        foreach (var item in queryResults)
        {
            Console.WriteLine(item);
        }

        Console.Write("Program finished, press Enter/Return to continue:");
        Console.ReadLine();
    }
```

Exercise 4

Very large subsets such as n > 1000 instead of n < 1000 are very slow:

```
static void Main(string[] args)
{

    int[] numbers = generateLotsOfNumbers(12345678);

    var queryResults =
        from n in numbers
        where n > 1000
        select n
        ;

    Console.WriteLine("Numbers less than 1000:");
    foreach (var item in queryResults)
    {
        Console.WriteLine(item);
    }

    Console.Write("Program finished, press Enter/Return to continue:");
    Console.ReadLine();
}
```

Exercise 5

All the names are output because there is no query.

```
static void Main(string[] args)
{
        string[] names = { "Alonso", "Zheng", "Smith", "Jones", "Smythe",
        "Small", "Ruiz", "Hsieh", "Jorgenson", "Ilyich", "Singh", "Samba", "Fatimah" };

        var queryResults = names;


        foreach (var item in queryResults) {
            Console.WriteLine(item);
        }

        Console.Write("Program finished, press Enter/Return to continue:");
        Console.ReadLine();
}
```

Exercise 6

Only `Min()` and `Max()` are available for a result set like this consisting only of `string` data (if no lambda is used).

```
static void Main(string[] args)
{
    string[] names = { "Alonso", "Zheng", "Smith", "Jones", "Smythe",
    "Small", "Ruiz", "Hsieh", "Jorgenson", "Ilyich", "Singh", "Samba", "Fatimah"};
    // only Min() and Max() are available (if no lambda is used)
    // for a result set like this consisting only of strings
    Console.WriteLine("Min(names) = " + names.Min());
    Console.WriteLine("Max(names) = " + names.Max());
    var queryResults =
            from n in names
            where n.StartsWith("S")
            select n;

    Console.WriteLine("Query result: names starting with S");
    foreach (var item in queryResults)
    {
        Console.WriteLine(item);
    }

    Console.WriteLine("Min(queryResults) = " + queryResults.Min());
    Console.WriteLine("Max(queryResults) = " + queryResults.Max());

    Console.Write("Program finished, press Enter/Return to continue:");
    Console.ReadLine();
}
```

CHAPTER 17 SOLUTIONS

Exercise 1

Comment out the explicit creation of the two books and replace with code to prompt for a new title and author such as shown in this code:

```
//Book book = new Book { Title = "Beginning C# and .NET",
//                       Author = "Perkins and Reid" };
//db.Books.Add(book);
//book = new Book { Title = "Beginning XML",
//Author = "Fawcett, Quin, and Ayers"};

    string title;
    string author;
    Book book;

    do
    {
        Console.Write("Title: "); title = Console.ReadLine();
        Console.Write("Author: "); author = Console.ReadLine();
```

```
        if (!string.IsNullOrEmpty(author))
        {
            book = new Book { Title = title, Author = author };

            db.Books.Add(book);

            db.SaveChanges();
        }
    } while (!string.IsNullOrEmpty(author));
```

Exercise 2

Add a test LINQ query to see if a book with the same title and author already exists before adding it to the database. Use code like this:

```
Book book = new Book { Title = "Beginning C# and .NET",
                       Author = "Perkins and Reid"};

var testQuery = from b in db.Books
                where b.Title == book.Title && b.Author == book.Author
                select b;

if (testQuery.Count() < 1)
{
    db.Books.Add(book);
    db.SaveChanges();
}
```

Exercise 3

Modify the generated classes `Stock.cs`, `Store.cs`, and `BookContext.cs` to use the `Inventory` and `Book` names, then change the references to these in `Program.cs`:

```
public partial class Stock
{
    ...
    public virtual Book Book { get; set; }
}
public partial class Store
{
    ...
    public Store()
    {
        Inventory = new HashSet<Stock>();
    }

    ...

    public virtual ICollection<Stock> Inventory { get; set; }
}

public partial class BookContext : DbContext
{
    ...
```

```
        protected override void OnModelCreating(ModelBuilder modelBuilder)
        {
            ...

            modelBuilder.Entity<Stock>(entity =>
            {
                ...

                entity.HasOne(d => d.Book)
                    .WithMany(p => p.Inventory)
                    .HasForeignKey(d => d.ItemCode);

                entity.HasOne(d => d.Store)
                    .WithMany(p => p.Inventory)
                    .HasForeignKey(d => d.StoreId);
            });

            OnModelCreatingPartial(modelBuilder);
        }
    }

    class Program
    {
        static void Main(string[] args)
        {
            using (var db = new BookContext())
            {
                var query = from store in db.Stores
                            orderby store.Name
                            select store;
                foreach (var s in query)
                {
                    XElement storeElement = new XElement("store",
                        new XAttribute("name", s.Name),
                        new XAttribute("address", s.Address),
                        from stock in s.Inventory
                        select new XElement("stock",
                                new XAttribute("StockID", stock.StockId),
                                new XAttribute("onHand",
                                 stock.OnHand),
                                new XAttribute("onOrder",
                                 stock.OnOrder),
                        new XElement("book",
                        new XAttribute("title",
                            stock.Book.Title),
                        new XAttribute("author",
                            stock.Book.Author)
                        )// end book
                      ) // end stock
                    ); // end store
                    Console.WriteLine(storeElement);
                }
            }
        }
    }
}
```

Exercise 4

Use the following code as shown here. Note that you will need to add the `Microsoft.EntityFrame-workCore` and related packages to your solution with the NuGet Package Manager, and then use the Package Manager Console to run the commands `Add-Migration Initial` followed by `Update-Database` to create the `GhostStories` database.

```
using Microsoft.EntityFrameworkCore;
using System;
using System.Linq;
using System.ComponentModel.DataAnnotations;
using static System.Console;

namespace BeginningCSharpAndDotNET_17_Exercise4_GhostStories
{
    public class Story
    {
        [Key]
        public int StoryID { get; set; }
        public string Title { get; set; }
        public Author Author { get; set; }
        public string Rating { get; set; }
    }

    public class Author
    {
        [Key]
        public int AuthorId { get; set; }
        public string Name { get; set; }
        public string Nationality { get; set; }
    }

    public class StoryContext : DbContext
    {
        public DbSet<Author> Authors { get; set; }
        public DbSet<Story> Stories { get; set; }

        protected override void
            OnConfiguring(DbContextOptionsBuilder optionsBuilder)
        {
            optionsBuilder.UseSqlServer(
@"Server=(LocalDB)\MSSQLLocalDB;Database=GhostStories;Integrated Security=True");
        }
    }

    class Program
    {
        static void Main(string[] args)
        {
            using (var db = new StoryContext())
            {
                Author author1 = new Author
                {
```

```
        Name = "Henry James",
        Nationality = "American"
    };
    Story story1 = new Story
    {
        Title = "The Turn of the Screw",
        Author = author1,
        Rating = "a bit dull"
    };
    db.Stories.Add(story1);
    db.SaveChanges();

    var query = from story in db.Stories
                orderby story.Title
                select story;

    WriteLine("Ghost Stories:");
    WriteLine();
    foreach (var story in query)
    {
        WriteLine(story.Title);
        WriteLine();
    }

    WriteLine("Program finished. Press a key to exit...");
        }
      }
    }
}
```

CHAPTER 19 SOLUTIONS

Exercise 1

To find the answer to this question, you should have a look at the PlayGame() method in the Game .cs file. Have a look through the method and list the variables it references while within the main do...while loop. This information would need to be sent back and forth between the client and server for the game to work via a website:

➤ How many people are playing and what are their names?

➤ Who is the current player?

➤ The player's hand of cards.

➤ The current card in play.

➤ The player's action, for example taking, drawing or discarding.

➤ A list of discarded cards.

➤ The status of the game, such as whether somebody won.

Exercise 2

You can store the information in a database and then retrieve the required data with each call, and you can pass the required information back and forth between the client and server using the ASP.NET Session Object or VIEWSTATE.

For information about the ASP.NET Session Object, read this article:

docs.microsoft.com/en-us/previous-versions/ms178581(v=vs.140)

For information about VIEWSTATE, read this article: docs.microsoft.com/en-us/previous-versions/dotnet/articles/ms972976(v=msdn.10)

Exercise 3

```
...
using System.Net;
using System.IO;
using Newtonsoft.Json;
using static System.Console;
namespace handofcards
{
 class Program
 {
  static void Main(string[] args)
  {
   List<string> cards = new List<string>();
   var playerName = "Benjamin";
   string GetURL =
    "http://handofcards.azurewebsites.net/api/HandOfCards/" +
     playerName;
   WebClient client = new WebClient();
   Stream dataStream = client.OpenRead(GetURL);
   StreamReader reader = new StreamReader(dataStream);
   var results =
    JsonConvert.DeserializeObject<dynamic>(reader.ReadLine());
   reader.Close();
   foreach (var item in results)
   {
    WriteLine((string)item.imageLink);
   }
   ReadLine();
  }
 }
}
```

CHAPTER 20 SOLUTIONS

Exercise 1

All of the above.

Exercise 2

You would implement a data contract, with the `DataContractAttribute` and `DataMemberAttribute` attributes.

Exercise 3

Use the `.svc` extension.

Exercise 4

That is one way of doing things, but it is usually easier to put all your WCF configuration in a separate configuration file, either `web.config` or `app.config`.

Exercise 5

```
[ServiceContract]
public interface IMusicPlayer
{
    [OperationContract(IsOneWay=true)]
    void Play();
    [OperationContract(IsOneWay=true)]
    void Stop();
    [OperationContract]
    TrackInformation GetCurrentTrackInformation();
}
```

You would also want a data contract to encapsulate track information; `TrackInformation` in the preceding code.

CHAPTER 21 SOLUTIONS

Exercise 1

Wrap the `TextBlock` control in a `ScrollViewer` panel. Set the `VerticalScrollBarVisibility` property to `Auto` to make the scrollbar appear when the text extends beyond the bottom edge of the control.

```
<Window x:Class="Answers.MainWindow"
        xmlns="http://schemas.microsoft.com/winfx/2006/xaml/presentation"
        xmlns:x="http://schemas.microsoft.com/winfx/2006/xaml"
        Title="21.1 Solution" Height="350" Width="525">
    <Grid>
    <Grid.RowDefinitions>
      <RowDefinition Height="75"/>
      <RowDefinition />
    </Grid.RowDefinitions>
    <Label Content="Enter text" HorizontalAlignment="Left" Margin="10,10,0,0"
            VerticalAlignment="Top"/>
    <TextBox HorizontalAlignment="Left" Margin="76,12,0,0" TextWrapping="Wrap"
            VerticalAlignment="Top" Height="53" Width="423" AcceptsReturn="True"
            Name="textTextBox">
```

```
        </TextBox>
        <ScrollViewer HorizontalAlignment="Left" Height="217" Margin="10,10,0,0"
                Grid.Row="1" VerticalAlignment="Top" Width="489"
                VerticalScrollBarVisibility="Auto">
            <TextBlock TextWrapping="Wrap" Text="{Binding ElementName=textTextBox,
                Path=Text}"/>
        </ScrollViewer>
    </Grid>
</Window>
```

Exercise 2

After dragging a `Slider` and `ProgressBar` control into the view, set the minimum and maximum values of the slider to 1 and 100 and the `Value` property to 1. Bind the same values of the `Progress-Bar` to the `Slider`.

```
<Window x:Class="Answers. Ch14Solution2"
        xmlns="http://schemas.microsoft.com/winfx/2006/xaml/presentation"
        xmlns:x="http://schemas.microsoft.com/winfx/2006/xaml"
        Title="21.2 Solution" Height="300" Width="300">
    <Grid>
        <Slider HorizontalAlignment="Left" Margin="10,10,0,0" VerticalAlignment="Top"
            Width="264" Minimum="1" Maximum="100" Name="valueSlider"/>
        <ProgressBar HorizontalAlignment="Left" Height="24" Margin="10,77,0,0"
            VerticalAlignment="Top" Width="264"
            Minimum="{Binding ElementName=valueSlider, Path=Minimum}"
            Maximum="{Binding ElementName=valueSlider, Path=Maximum}"
            Value="{Binding ElementName=valueSlider, Path=Value}"/>
    </Grid>
</Window>
```

Exercise 3

You can use a `RenderTransform` to do this. In Design View, you can position the cursor over the edge of the control and when you see a quarter circle icon for the mouse pointer, click and drag the control to the desired position.

```
<Window x:Class="Answers. Ch14Solution3"
        xmlns="http://schemas.microsoft.com/winfx/2006/xaml/presentation"
        xmlns:x="http://schemas.microsoft.com/winfx/2006/xaml"
        Title="21.3 Solution" Height="300" Width="300">
    <Grid>
        <Slider HorizontalAlignment="Left" Margin="10,10,0,0" VerticalAlignment="Top"
            Width="264" Minimum="1" Maximum="100" Name="valueSlider"/>
        <ProgressBar HorizontalAlignment="Left" Height="24" Margin="-17,125,-10,0"
            VerticalAlignment="Top" Width="311"
            Minimum="{Binding ElementName=valueSlider, Path=Minimum}" Maximum="{Binding
    ElementName=valueSlider, Path=Maximum}"
            Value="{Binding ElementName=valueSlider, Path=Value}"
            RenderTransformOrigin="0.5,0.5">
            <ProgressBar.RenderTransform>
                <TransformGroup>
                    <ScaleTransform/>
                    <SkewTransform/>
```

```
        <RotateTransform Angle="-36.973"/>
        <TranslateTransform/>
      </TransformGroup>
    </ProgressBar.RenderTransform>
  </ProgressBar>
  </Grid>
</Window>
```

Exercise 4

The `PersistentSlider` class must implement the `INotifyPropertyChanged` interface.

Create fields to hold the value of each of the three properties.

In each of the setters of the properties, implement a call to any subscribers of the `PropertyChanged` event. You are advised to create a helper method, called `OnPropertyChanged`, for this purpose.

PersistentSlider.cs:

```csharp
using System.ComponentModel;
namespace Answers
{
  public class PersistentSlider : INotifyPropertyChanged
  {
    private int _minValue;
    private int _maxValue;
    private int _currentValue;
    public int MinValue
    {
      get { return _minValue; }
      set { _minValue = value; OnPropertyChanged(nameof(MinValue)); }
    }
    public int MaxValue
    {
      get { return _maxValue; }
      set { _maxValue = value; OnPropertyChanged(nameof(MaxValue)); }
    }
    public int CurrentValue
    {
      get { return _currentValue; }
      set { _currentValue = value; OnPropertyChanged(nameof(CurrentValue)); }
    }
    public event PropertyChangedEventHandler PropertyChanged;
    protected void OnPropertyChanged(string propertyName) =>
        PropertyChanged?.Invoke(this, new PropertyChangedEventArgs(propertyName));
  }
}
```

a. In the code-behind file, add a field like this:

```csharp
private PersistentSlider _sliderData = new PersistentSlider
{ MinValue = 1, MaxValue = 200, CurrentValue = 100 };
```

b. In the constructor, set the `DataContext` property of the current instance to the field you just created:

```
this.DataContext = _sliderData;
InitializeComponent();
```

c. In the XAML, change the `Slider` control to use the data context. Only the `Path` needs to be set:

```xml
<Window x:Class="Answers. Ch21Solution4"
        xmlns="http://schemas.microsoft.com/winfx/2006/xaml/presentation"
        xmlns:x="http://schemas.microsoft.com/winfx/2006/xaml"
        Title="14.4 Solution" Height="300" Width="300">
  <Grid>
    <Slider HorizontalAlignment="Left" Margin="10,10,0,0"
            VerticalAlignment="Top"
            Width="264" Minimum="{Binding Path=MinValue}"
            Maximum="{Binding Path=MaxValue}"
            Value="{Binding Path=CurrentValue}"
            Name="valueSlider"/>
    <ProgressBar HorizontalAlignment="Left" Height="24"
            Margin="-17,125,-10,0"
            VerticalAlignment="Top" Width="311"
            Minimum="{Binding ElementName=valueSlider, Path=Minimum}"
            Maximum="{Binding ElementName=valueSlider, Path=Maximum}"
            Value="{Binding ElementName=valueSlider, Path=Value}"
            RenderTransformOrigin="0.5,0.5">
      <ProgressBar.RenderTransform>
        <TransformGroup>
          <ScaleTransform/>
          <SkewTransform/>
          <RotateTransform Angle="-36.973"/>
          <TranslateTransform/>
        </TransformGroup>
      </ProgressBar.RenderTransform>
    </ProgressBar>
  </Grid>
</Window>
```

Exercise 5

1. Create a new class with the name `ComputerSkillValueConverter` like this:

```csharp
using Ch13CardLib;
using System;
using System.Windows.Data;

namespace KarliCards_Gui
{
  [ValueConversion(typeof(ComputerSkillLevel), typeof(bool))]
  public class ComputerSkillValueConverter : IValueConverter
  {
    public object Convert(object value, Type targetType, object parameter,
System.Globalization.CultureInfo culture)
```

```
    {
      string helper = parameter as string;
      if (string.IsNullOrWhiteSpace(helper))
        return false;

      ComputerSkillLevel skillLevel = (ComputerSkillLevel)value;
      return (skillLevel.ToString() == helper);
    }

    public object ConvertBack(object value, Type targetType, object parameter,
System.Globalization.CultureInfo culture)
    {
      string parameterString = parameter as string;
      if (parameterString == null)
        return ComputerSkillLevel.Dumb;

      return Enum.Parse(targetType, parameterString);
    }
  }
}
```

2. Add a static resource declaration to the Options.xaml:

```xml
<Window.Resources>
      <src:ComputerSkillValueConverter x:Key="skillConverter" />
</Window.Resources>
```

3. Change the radio buttons like this:

```xml
<RadioButton Content="Dumb" HorizontalAlignment="Left"
        Margin="37,41,0,0" VerticalAlignment="Top" Name="dumbAIRadioButton"
        IsChecked="{Binding ComputerSkill,
        Converter={StaticResource skillConverter},
        ConverterParameter=Dumb}" />
<RadioButton Content="Good" HorizontalAlignment="Left"
        Margin="37,62,0,0" VerticalAlignment="Top" Name="goodAIRadioButton"
        IsChecked="{Binding ComputerSkill,
        Converter={StaticResource skillConverter},
        ConverterParameter=Good}" />
<RadioButton Content="Cheats" HorizontalAlignment="Left"
        Margin="37,83,0,0" VerticalAlignment="Top"
        Name="cheatingAIRadioButton"
        IsChecked="{Binding ComputerSkill,
        Converter={StaticResource skillConverter},
        ConverterParameter=Cheats}" />
```

4. Delete the events from the code-behind file.

Exercise 6

1. Add a new check box to the `Options.xaml` dialog box:

```
<CheckBox Content="Plays with open cards" HorizontalAlignment="Left"
        Margin="10,100, 0,0" VerticalAlignment="Top"
    IsChecked="{Binding ComputerPlaysWithOpenHand}" />
```

2. Add a new property to the `GameOptions.cs` class:

```
private bool _computerPlaysWithOpenHand;
public bool ComputerPlaysWithOpenHand
{
 get { return _computerPlaysWithOpenHand; }
 set
 {
   _computerPlaysWithOpenHand = value;
   OnPropertyChanged(nameof(ComputerPlaysWithOpenHand));
 }
}
```

3. Add a new dependency property to the `CardsInHandControl`:

```
public bool ComputerPlaysWithOpenHand
{
 get { return (bool)GetValue(ComputerPlaysWithOpenHandProperty); }
 set { SetValue(ComputerPlaysWithOpenHandProperty, value); }
}

public static readonly DependencyProperty ComputerPlaysWithOpenHandProperty =
    DependencyProperty.Register("ComputerPlaysWithOpenHand", typeof(bool),
    typeof(CardsInHandControl), new PropertyMetadata(false));
```

4. In the `DrawCards` method of the `CardsInHandControl`, change the test for `isFaceUp`:

```
if (Owner is ComputerPlayer)
    isFaceup = (Owner.State == CardLib.PlayerState.Loser ||
    Owner.State == CardLib.PlayerState.Winner || ComputerPlaysWithOpenHand);
```

5. Add a new property to the `GameViewModel` class:

```
public bool ComputerPlaysWithOpenHand
{
 get { return _gameOptions.ComputerPlaysWithOpenHand; }
}
```

6. Bind the new property to the `CardsInHandControls` on the game client to all four players:

```
ComputerPlaysWithOpenHand="{Binding GameOptions.ComputerPlaysWithOpenHand}"
```

Exercise 7

1. Add a new property to the `GameViewModel` like this:

```
private string _currentStatusText = "Game is not started";
public string CurrentStatusText
{
  get { return _currentStatusText; }
  set
  {
    _currentStatusText = value;
    OnPropertyChanged(nameof(CurrentStatusText));
  }
}
```

2. Change the `CurrentPlayer` property like this:

```
public Player CurrentPlayer
{
  get { return _currentPlayer; }
  set
  {
    _currentPlayer = value;
    OnPropertyChanged("CurrentPlayer");
    if (!Players.Any(x => x.State == PlayerState.Winner))
    {
      Players.ForEach(x => x.State =
          (x == value ? PlayerState.Active : PlayerState.Inactive));
      CurrentStatusText = $"Player {CurrentPlayer.PlayerName} ready";
    }
    else
    {
      var winner = Players.Where(x => x.HasWon).FirstOrDefault();
      if (winner != null)
        CurrentStatusText = $"Player {winner.PlayerName} has WON!";
    }
  }
}
```

3. Add this line at the end of the `StartNewGame` method:

```
CurrentStatusText = string.Format("New game stated. Player {0} to start",
CurrentPlayer.PlayerName);
```

4. Add a status bar to the game client XAML and set the binding to the new property:

```
<StatusBar Grid.Row="3" HorizontalAlignment="Center" Margin="0,0,0,15"
      VerticalAlignment="Center" Background="Green" Foreground="White"
FontWeight="Bold">
    <StatusBarItem VerticalAlignment="Center">
    <TextBlock Text="{Binding CurrentStatusText}" />
  </StatusBarItem>
</StatusBar>
```

INDEX

E

F

X

Y